# IN HARMONY

## Reading and Writing

### Annotated Instructor's Edition

## KATHLEEN T. McWHORTER
Niagara County Community College

Boston Columbus Indianapolis New York San Francisco Upper Saddle River
Amsterdam Cape Town Dubai London Madrid Milan Munich Paris Montreal Toronto
Delhi Mexico City São Paulo Sydney Hong Kong Seoul Singapore Taipei Tokyo

**Senior Acquisitions Editor:** Nancy Blaine
**Editorial Assistant:** Jamie Fortner
**Senior Development Editor:** Gill Cook
**Executive Market Development Manager:** Dona Kenly
**Marketing Manager:** Kurt Massey
**Senior Supplements Editor:** Donna Campion
**Executive Digital Producer:** Stefanie A. Snajder
**Digital Project Manager:** Janell Lantana
**Digital Editor:** Robert St. Laurent

**Production Manager:** Ellen MacElree
**Project Coordination, Text Design, and Electronic Page Makeup:** PreMediaGlobal
**Cover Design Manager:** John Callahan
**Cover Designer:** Laura Shaw
**Cover Photo:** Exactostock/SuperStock
**Senior Manufacturing Buyer:** Dennis J. Para
**Printer/Binder:** Courier/Kendallville
**Cover Printer:** Lehigh-Phoenix Color/Hagerstown

This title is restricted to sales and distribution in North America only.

Credits and acknowledgments borrowed from other sources, and reproduced, with permission, in this textbook, appear on pages 689–693.

**Library of Congress Cataloging-in-Publication Data**

McWhorter, Kathleen T., author.
 In harmony : reading and writing / Kathleen T. McWhorter, Niagara County Community College.
    pages cm
 ISBN 978-0-321-87185-5
 1. Reading (Higher education) 2. English language—Rhetoric—Study and teaching (Higher) I. Title.
 LB2395.3.M393 2014
 428.40711—dc23

                                                                                        2012038029

10 9 8 7 6 5 4 3 2 1—CRK—15 14 13 12

www.pearsonhighered.com

Student ISBN-13: 978-0-321-87185-5
Student ISBN-10:  0-321-87185-5
AIE ISBN-13: 978-0-321-87196-1
AIE ISBN-10:  0-321-87196-0

# Brief Contents

# Detailed Contents

Chapter 13   Patterns of Organization: Example, Cause and Effect, and Comparison and Contrast   408

Chapter 14   Revision and Proofreading   450

## PART SIX    REVIEWING THE BASICS: A BRIEF GRAMMAR HANDBOOK  583

# Preface to the Instructor

There are two student comments many of us have heard in our classrooms over and over. In reading classes we hear, "I read it, but I cannot remember most of it." In writing classes we hear, "I just don't know what to write about." Teaching reading and writing together can overcome these common problems, as well as many others. In a combined class students learn that writing can often strengthen and improve both their understanding and their recall of what they read; they also learn that what they read can provide ample and diverse ideas to react and respond to in writing.

Reading and writing have much in common and are commonly performed together, so it makes sense that they be taught together. Readers must develop skills to comprehend and analyze the message put forth by the writer. The writer must express ideas clearly, concisely, and correctly while using various writing conventions to guide the reader and to assure that the message is understood. Consequently, I am pleased to have created a book that integrates these skills—a book that demonstrates that reading and writing do work together—in harmony.

## Purpose

*In Harmony* is the first text in a two-part series that features a comprehensive, integrated approach to reading and writing that is developed through structured, sequential instruction and guided practice. *In Harmony* focuses on sentence- and paragraph-level reading and writing skills, while the second text, *In Concert,* focuses on paragraph- and essay-writing skills.

*In Harmony* emphasizes the complementary nature of the reading and writing processes, demonstrating to students that reading and writing are best learned together. The text also features critical thinking and explores and reinforces its relationship to the reading and writing processes. Visual literacy is discussed in Chapter 1 to enable students to learn to read and respond to images and photographs.

## Emphases

*In Harmony* has three primary emphases:

- **The Reading–Writing Connection** The book provides an overview of the reading and writing processes, and it presents skills and strategies for reading and writing sentences and paragraphs as well as an introduction to essay writing. Many chapters offer complementary instruction, first examining how readers approach a skill and then moving to how writers use the same skill. For example, in Chapter 10 students learn how to identify main ideas and topic sentences in paragraphs and then move immediately to learning how to choose manageable topics and write effective topic sentences for paragraphs. Models of student and professional writing are included in most chapters. Students read the models, examine their features and characteristics, and demonstrate their comprehension of the content by completing related exercises and writing in response to what they have read.

■ **Critical Thinking** The text emphasizes the role and benefits of critical thinking in reading and writing. Students learn skills and strategies for thinking critically while reading. They also learn to write critical responses to what they read. The apparatus for each full-length reading contains a section titled "Thinking and Writing Critically."

■ **Visual Literacy** Print and electronic sources, including textbooks, are becoming increasingly visual. This book includes instructional material on thinking critically about visuals. Students read and write about visuals and analyze how they contribute meaning to text. Visuals with related writing prompts also accompany each professional reading.

# Approach to the Integration of Reading and Writing

The following features distinguish this text from other developmental books and make its approach unique:

■ **Reading and Writing Process Instruction Part One** provides an introduction to both reading and writing skills and offers important vocabulary instruction and practice for readers and writers. Reading and writing sentences is the focus of the five chapters in **Part Two**. **Part Three** guides students in reading, writing, organizing, and revising paragraphs. Techniques for outlining, mapping and writing paraphrases and summaries are included in **Part Four**, as are critical thinking strategies for recognizing audience and purpose, fact and opinion, and inference and conclusion; reading and writing are integrated throughout this part. **Part Five** provides an introduction to essay writing—planning, drafting, and revising—and presents information on how to read and use sources.

Most chapters focus on both reading and writing using a particular skill. Students begin by learning how the skill applies to both reading and writing and then move to applying the skill to materials they read and using the skill as they write. End-of-chapter student essays and professional essays enable students to integrate and practice skills they have learned in the chapter. Chapters in each of these parts open with the section "Focus on Reading and Writing," in which students learn what the skill involves for both readers and writers, setting the stage for them to develop specific, but complementary, reading and writing skills.

■ **Emphasis on Student Success** The book begins with an introduction, "Reading and Writing Success Starts Here!," that focuses on the skills first semester students need to be successful not only in their reading and writing classes but in other college courses, as well. Topics include setting goals, getting organized, managing time effectively, using college textbooks, and taking class notes. This section also includes specific strategies and suggestions for succeeding in a reading–writing class and for using MySkillsLab.

- **Metacognitive Approach to Reading and Writing** Both reading and writing are approached as thinking processes, and students are encouraged to be aware of, control, assess, and adjust how they are reading and writing. Chapters 1 and 2 provide an overview of the reading and writing processes and guide students in thinking about and applying them.

- **Coverage of Critical Thinking** To handle college-level work and to be well prepared for freshman composition classes, students need to be able to think critically about what they read as well as respond in writing to what they have read. Critical thinking skills are introduced in Chapter 1. Chapter 16 addresses specific critical thinking skills for both reading and writing. The apparatus for each professional reading contains a section titled "Thinking and Writing Critically."

- **Visual Literacy** Reading and interpreting visuals is introduced in Chapter 1, where students learn to read and interpret a variety of visuals and to think critically about them. Each chapter opens with a visual that demonstrates the purpose of the chapter; within chapters, the feature "Visualize It!" identifies useful maps and diagrams; and the apparatus of each professional reading contains a question about interpreting visuals.

- **Vocabulary Coverage** Because a strong vocabulary is important to both readers and writers, vocabulary-building skills are emphasized throughout the book. Chapter 3 presents an introduction to vocabulary; it discusses dictionary usage, selection of appropriate meanings, denotative and connotative meanings, and synonyms and antonyms. Chapter 4 features strategies for identifying and figuring out unknown words: pronunciation, context clues, and word parts, as well as strategies for learning and remembering unfamiliar words. The apparatus following each professional reading includes a Strengthening Your Vocabulary section that focuses on learning words used in the reading.

- **Grammar Coverage/Sentence Coverage** Part Two focuses on sentence reading and writing skills. Essential sentence skills and major sentence error identification and correction topics are included, while more specific aspects of correctness and clarity are treated in Part Six, "Reviewing the Basics: A Brief Grammar Handbook." Both the chapters and the handbook contain ample exercises for practice and application and more are available online at MySkillsLab.com.

- **Reviewing the Basics: A Brief Grammar Handbook** For students who need a review of basic principles and rules of grammar, a handbook is provided at the end of the book. Topics include a review of the parts of speech and parts of sentences, writing effective sentences, using punctuation effectively, and managing mechanics and spelling.

- **Coverage of Organizational Patterns** Chapters 12 and 13 cover six patterns of organization—chronological order, process, narration, description, example, cause and effect, and comparison and contrast—showing students how to identify each pattern to improve their comprehension and demonstrating how to use these patterns to organize and explain their ideas in writing.

- **Introductory Material on Reading and Writing Using Sources** As preparation for college courses that require the use of sources in writing academic papers, Chapter 18 offers a brief overview of identifying appropriate sources, taking notes, using quotations, and avoiding plagiarism.

- **MySkillsLab Instructional Support** Because a book can never offer enough practice exercises to meet the diverse needs of all students within a classroom, MySkillsLab is available to students. It provides a wealth of exercises and mastery tests on most of the topics covered in the book.

# Chapter Features

Every chapter includes the following features:

- **Visual and Engaging Chapter Openers** Each chapter opens with a photograph or other image that is intended to capture students' attention, generate interest, and connect the topic of the chapter to their experience. This feature gets students writing immediately about chapter-related content.

- **Learning Objectives Tied to Interactive Summaries** Learning objectives at the beginning of each chapter (and repeated next to relevant section heads) identify what students can expect to learn and correspond directly to the end-of-chapter interactive summaries that students can use to check their recall of chapter content.

- **Visualize It!** Many chapters contain idea maps that show how paragraphs and essays are organized from both a reading and a writing perspective. The professional readings also contain partially completed maps for students to finish.

- **Need to Know Boxes** These boxes summarize key concepts and strategies in an easy reference format.

- **Linked Writing Exercises** Writing in Progress exercises guide students step by step through the writing process.

- **Collaborative Activities** Many chapters contain collaborative activities designed to help students apply skills and learn from their peers.

- **Read and Revise** Every chapter in Parts II and III contains a Read and Revise activity in which students are asked to read, analyze, and revise sample student writing that contains errors that pertain to the topics taught in the chapter.

- **Read and Respond: A Student Essay** Most chapters contain an annotated student essay for students to read and respond to. These student samples provide realistic models of the writing process and set realistic, attainable expectations for students. Students read and respond to each model.

- **Read and Respond: A Professional Essay** This feature presents a short professional essay. The apparatus following each reading guides students in assessing their comprehension, building their vocabulary, examining the structure of the essay, thinking critically about the essay, and writing about the essay.

MySkillsLab®

Complete
this
Exercise

- **Writing About the Reading at MySkillsLab** The paragraph and essay writing options that follow each of the professional readings can now be completed online. Students are directed to MySkillsLab in the print text and can click on a direct link to the site in the e-book.

- **Self-Test Summary** A Self-Test Summary included at the end of each chapter corresponds to the learning goals stated at the beginning of the chapter. This summary allows students to test their recall of chapter content and mastery of each learning goal. The summary also provides a means by which students can review immediately upon completion of their first reading of the chapter.

- ■ **A Lexile® Measure** This measure—the most widely used reading metric in U.S. schools—provides valuable information about a student's reading ability and the complexity of text. It helps match students with reading resources and activities that are targeted to their ability level. Lexile measures indicate the reading levels of content in MySkillsLab and the longer selections in the Annotated Instructor's Editions of all of Pearson's reading books. See the Annotated Instructor's Edition of *In Harmony* and the *Instructor's Manual* for more details.

# Book-Specific Ancillary Materials

**Annotated Instructor's Edition for *In Harmony: Reading and Writing*** (ISBN 0321871960/9780321871961). Identical to the student text, but with answers printed directly on the pages where questions and exercises appear.

**Instructor's Manual/Test Bank for *In Harmony: Reading and Writing*** (ISBN 0321871979/9780321871978). The instructor's manual features lecture hints, in-class activities, handouts, and quizzes to accompany each chapter, as well as sample course outlines and a primer on teaching an integrated reading and writing course. Available both in print and for download from the Instructor Resource Center.

**PowerPoint Presentation** (ISBN 0321872002/9780321872005). PowerPoint presentations to accompany each chapter consist of classroom-ready lecture outline slides, lecture tips and classroom activities, and review questions. Available for download from the Instructor Resource Center.

**Answer Key** (ISBN 0321848489/9780321848482). The Answer Key contains the solutions to the exercises in the student edition of the text. Available for download from the Instructor Resource Center.

**MySkillsLab®**   Where better practice makes better writers!

## What makes the practice in MySkillsLab better?

- ■ **Diagnostic Testing:** MySkillsLab's diagnostic Path Builder test comprehensively assesses proficiency in reading skills as well as basic grammar, sentence grammar, punctuation and mechanics, and usage and style. Students are provided an individualized learning path based on the diagnostic's results, identifying the areas where they most need help.

- ■ **Progressive Learning:** MySkillsLab's learning path offers Open sequence or Preset sequence. The Open sequence allows students to freely access all resources and assessment at any point. The Preset sequence prompts students to build knowledge by first reading, viewing, and listening to instructional material before they can move forward to a series of activities and then a post test. This progressive path from preparation (Overview, Animation) to literal comprehension (Recall) to critical understanding (Apply) to written knowledge (Write) to mastery (Posttest) is not available in any other online resource. MySkillsLab enables students to truly master the skills and concepts they need to become successful writers.

■ **eText.** The *In Harmony* eText is accessed through MySkillsLab. Students now have the eText at their fingertips while completing the various exercises and activities within MyWritingLab, including those specific to this text.

# Acknowledgements

I would like to express my gratitude to my reviewers for their excellent ideas, suggestions, and advice on the preparation of this text:

Craig Barto, Charleston Southern University

Frank Lammer, Northeast Iowa Community College

Lisa Barnes, Delaware County Community College

Michalle Barnett, Gulf Coast State College

Cindy Beck, Pulaski Technical College

Gail Bradstreet, Cincinnati State Technical and Community College

Shiela Bunker, State Fair Community College

Teresa Carrillo, Joliet Junior College

Sharon M. Cellemme, South Piedmont Community College

Dorothy Chase, College of Southern Nevada

Marlys Cordoba, College of the Siskiyous

Barbara, Doyle Arkansas State University

Margot A.Edlin, Ed.D., Queensborough Community College - CUNY

Kim Edwards, Tidewater Community College

Adam Floridia, Middlesex Community College

Marianne Friedell, College of the Mainland

Teresa Fugate, Lindsey Wilson College

Laura Girtman, Tallahassee Community College

M. Elizabeth Grooms, Cameron University

Barbara Hampton, Rend Lake College

Jessie M. Harding, LCNE Southington, CT

Curtis Harrell, NorthWest Arkansas Community College

Annaliese Hausler-Akpovi, Modesto Junior College

Sharon Moran, Hayes Community College of Baltimore County

Beverly J. Heam, University of Tennessee at Martin

Eric Hibbison, J. Sargeant Reynolds Community College

Carlotta W. Hill, Oklahoma City Community College

lizabeth Huergo, Montgomery College

Pamela Hunt, Paris Junior College

Julie Jackson-Coe, Genesee Community College

Magdalena Jacobo, San Bernardino Valley College

Kim Jameson, Oklahoma City Community College

Courtney R. Johnson, Montgomery College

Stanley Johnson, Southside Virginia Community College

Janice Johnson, Missouri State University

Suzanne Jones, Ed.D. Collin College

Sally Kloepfer, Tiffin University

Teresa Kozek, Housatonic Community College

Vicky M. Krug, Westmoreland County Community College

Terri LaRocco, University of Findlay

Debra F. Lee, Nash Community College

Glenda Lowery, Rappahannock Community College

Agnes Malicka Northern Virginia Community College

Patricia A. Malinowski, Finger Lakes Community College

Barbara Marshall, Rockingham Community College

Jennifer McCann, Bay de Noc
Community College
Nancy McKenzie, Tarrant County
College South Campus
Laura Meyers, Hawkeye Community
College
Linda Miniger, Harrisburg Area
Community College
Carol Miyake, Laramie County
Community College
Julie Monroe, Madison Area Technical
College
Debbie Naquin, NVCC
Gayle Norman, South Arkansas
Community College
Carl Olds, University of Central
Arkansas
Debbie Lamb, Ousey Penn State
Brandywine
Catherine G. Parra, Northern Virginia
Community College
Lisa Parra, Johnson County
Community College
Herman Pena, UT brownsville and
Texas Southmost College

Dr. Elizabeth Price, Ranger College
Sue Rauch, Germanna Community
College
Regia J. Ray, Dalton State College
Joan Reeves, Northeast Alabama
Community College
Adalia Reyna, South Texas College
Vanessa Ruccolo, Virginia Tech
Rebecca Samberg, Housatonic
Community College
Emmie D. Stokes, Augusta Technical
College
Dr. Catherine Swift, University of
Central Arkansas
Kathy Tyndall, Wake Technical
Community College
Jeanine Williams, The Community
College Baltimore County
Lisa Williams, Kirkwood Community
College
Michelle Zollars, Patrick Henry
Community College
Lark Zunich, Long Beach
City College

I would also like to thank the students who wrote and revised the essays included in this book:

Alphea Bartley
Alex Boyd
Bryan Dube
Santiago Quintana Garcia
Giovanny Guzman
Elaina Mayer
Dave Myers

Elena Pineda
Lekisha Roberson
Roan Rodriguez
Loretta Scott
Yuliya Seitkulova
Bogyeong Son

Nancy Blaine, Senior Acquisitions Editor, deserves special thanks for her enthusiastic support of the project and for providing advice and resources for the book's development. I also wish to thank Jeanne Jones for her assistance in drafting and preparing the manuscript and Gillian Cook, Senior Development Editor, for helping me carry out the vision of this book through essential day-to-day collaboration.

Kathleen T. McWhorter

# Reading and Writing Success Starts Here!

Regardless of your curriculum or major, reading and writing are an important part of your everyday life, your college career, and your workplace. Knowing how to read effectively and being comfortable expressing yourself in writing in each of these areas can add a whole new dimension to your life and increase your potential for success. In this introduction you will learn numerous success strategies for becoming a better reader and writer.

Success in any college course involves accepting responsibility for your own learning. Your reading and writing instructor is your guide, but you are in charge. It is not enough to attend class and do what you are asked. You have to decide what to learn and how to learn it.

# Use the Help Features in This Book

## LEARNING GOALS

Learn how to ...

■ GOAL 1
Read actively

■ GOAL 2
Preview before reading

■ GOAL 3
Highlight and annotate as you read

■ GOAL 4
Strengthen your comprehension and recall

■ GOAL 5
Read and think about visuals

■ GOAL 6
Think critically

Although your instructor and your classmates are your most important sources for learning, this book also contains numerous features to help you become a successful reader and writer.

### Learning Goals

These lists of topics tell you what you should expect to learn in each chapter and correspond to the major headings in each chapter. The Self-Test Summary at the end of each chapter provides a brief overview of the main points you have learned about each of the learning goals.

### Think About It!

Each chapter opens with a photograph or other visual image that is intended to capture your attention, generate interest, and connect the topic of the chapter to your experience. This "Think About It!" feature encourages you to start writing immediately about chapter-related content using a relevant topic. It also makes clear the close connection between reading and writing.

Using Sources When You Write

THINK About It!

Write a sentence identifying the issue the photograph confronts. Suppose you were asked to write a paper about this issue. How would you begin? Unless you are very familiar with it, you would need to do research on the topic. You would need to locate print and Internet sources that provide further information, and use that information

1

## Idea Maps

Idea maps, labeled "Visualize It!" are diagrams that show the content and organization of a piece of writing. You can use these maps in several ways:

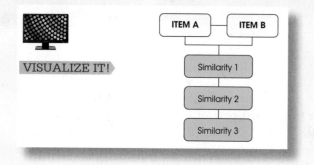

- **To organize and guide your own writing.** Think of them as models you can follow.

- **To help you analyze a paragraph or essay you have written.** Drawing a map of your writing will help you identify problems in organization or spot ideas that do not belong in a paragraph or essay.

- **As an aid to understanding a professional reading that you have been assigned.** By filling in an idea map, you can assure yourself that you have understood the reading, and the process of drawing the map will help you to remember what you read.

## Need to Know Boxes

In many chapters you will find boxes titled "Need to Know." Pay particular attention to these boxes because they present or summarize important information. They are a quick way to review information, so refer to them often. You may want to mark boxes that you find particularly valuable.

## NEED TO KNOW

### Comprehension Signals

| POSITIVE SIGNALS | NEGATIVE SIGNALS |
|---|---|
| Everything seems to fit and make sense; ideas flow logically from one to another. | Some pieces do not seem to belong; the material seems disjointed. |
| You understand what is important. | Nothing or everything seems important. |
| You are able to see where the author is leading. | You feel as if you are struggling to stay with the author and are unable to predict what will follow. |
| You are able to make connections among ideas. | You are unable to detect relationships; the organization is not apparent. |
| You read at a regular, comfortable pace. | You often slow down or reread. |
| You understand why the material was assigned. | You do not know why the material was assigned and cannot explain why it is important. |
| You can express the main ideas in your own words. | You must reread often and find it hard to paraphrase the author's ideas. |
| You recognize most words or can figure them out from the context. | Many words are unfamiliar. |
| You feel comfortable and have some knowledge about the topic. | The topic is unfamiliar, yet the author assumes you understand it. |

## Student Writing Samples

Sentences, paragraphs, and essays written by students appear throughout this book. These pieces of student writing are included to illustrate particular writing techniques. Chapter 11, for example, includes a sample student paragraph that lacks details followed by its revision showing the addition of details to make the paragraph more lively and informative. Study each of these samples to see how each writing technique works.

*What does brainstorming look like?* Imagine that you have been asked to write an essay about "identity" and how you see yourself. Here is the brainstorming list that one student, Santiago Quintana Garcia, wrote about his identity.

Identity—Mexican? White? Very arbitrary and flimsy

Easily deconstructed when seen from the edges

Not wrong to subscribe to a certain identity

Everyone has their in-betweens, not all race and nationality

Mexican stereotype: I don't look Mexican. I'm foreign in my own country/race

White: Not quite. I am Mexican after all.

Creates a struggle between the ideal and the reality, from this comes synthesis, movement

Feelings of not belonging as a teenager. No comfort objects. No cushion to fall back to easily, BUT

growth and awareness.

I am Mexican. I still subscribe but with a lot more awareness of how that label is not

representative and exhaustive. It is necessary; practical.

Living in between = energy, movement, growth.

**Tip for Writers**

The simple present tense is used for repeated action. "Allison *walks* across campus after lunch" means she does this regularly. On the other hand, "Allison is walking" (present continuous tense) means right now or at some stated future time (perhaps tomorrow) she is or will be walking.

## Tips for Writers

"Tips for Writers" boxes appear throughout the book. They are intended to help you learn and apply chapter content by pointing out special concerns, explaining typical grammatical errors, and defining the meaning of specific words and phrases.

## Read and Revise

Many chapters include an excerpt from a student essay that demonstrates errors or writing problems addressed in the chapter. This feature allows you to practice identifying weaknesses or errors in the writing of others. It also gives you the opportunity to practice your revision skills. As you work through these exercises, apply the skills taught in each chapter as you examine and revise the excerpt.

### READ AND REVISE

The following excerpt is from a student essay called "Coming to America." This excerpt contains sentence fragments that were subsequently corrected in a later draft. Read the excerpt, and underline the sentence fragments caused by missing subjects, verbs, or dependent clauses. Then write out a revised version of the paragraph, correcting the errors using the techniques discussed in this chapter.

frag   There are many events that happened during my lifetime, but the main one that echoes in my mind. Coming to America. I'm originally from Port-au-Prince, Haiti. I moved to the United States at the age of 10. Which changed my life in many ways. Coming to America took away all the pain and suffering I went through growing up as a child. I didn't have an education, and now it's possible. The hardest thing to learn is a new language.

frag   Imagine living in a place where there is severe violence, hunger, and poverty. Where there are no jobs. Kids and adults are crying from hunger, waiting for a miracle. Most of the time they have to steal or make a kill to have

### READ AND RESPOND: A Student Essay

*Bogyeong Son is a student at Bunker Hill Community College where she is studying for an associate's degree. She plans to transfer to a four-year college to obtain a bachelor's degree in business. She submitted this essay to the Writing Rewards Essay Contest sponsored by Pearson Education. The assignment she responded to directed her to write an essay about cultural differences.*

Title gives the subject

## A Korean Girl in Boston

Background details

A common saying is "Do in Rome as the Romans do." There are countries in the world that have their own laws, so we must observe the laws. I am a Korean who lived in Korea for 21 years, but I am living in the United States now. Last year, my older sister and I arrived in Boston after enduring a 16-hour flight. At that time, I did not have any basic knowledge about the United States. The dollar as currency and English as the spoken language were the only things that I knew about. Not knowing English and the U.S. culture was the same as if I went to a field of battle without a gun. My new life started in a place which was alien to me because of a language barrier and culture shock.

Topic sentence

Topic sentence

The language barrier was the most difficult part of living in another country. Here were the only sentences I could speak: "Hi. My name is Bogyeong Son. I am Korean. Thanks. Sorry. Bye." If I met a real native speaker, my tongue set hard, and my eyes blinked five times a second. The first episode started when my sister and I arrived in Boston's Logan Airport. We finished the long flight and just followed most passengers after we got off the airplane. Because of going through immigration, most people disappeared very quickly, and eventually we lost the way to the exit. If I were in Korea, I would be able to ask someone or read the directory. In order to find the exit, we looked around many times, and one staff member who wore a uniform thought we were strange. So he asked us something, but we could not understand him. We just looked at each other, wondering what to do. We typed the word "exit" by using a dictionary and showed him; finally, we were shown how to go out from the airport.

Example illustrates language barrier

Example follows, showing her lack of knowledge about American culture

The next problem was in getting a cab. Fortunately, there were many cabs in front of the airport, so we put the luggage in the trunk, and we could get in the cab easily with a basic "Hi." We did not know how to give the driver our destination, so we just showed him a paper with our hotel address. The problem happened when we got in front of our hotel. After I saw twenty dollars come up on the taxi meter, I opened my wallet and gave the driver twenty dollars, saying, "Thank you." Suddenly his facial emotion changed, and he said something; of course, we did not understand. He repeated "blah blah blah" many times, and eventually I could hear a word: "Tip." He wanted to get a tip. I was unfamiliar with this because in my country,

## Read and Respond: A Student Essay

Many chapters include a sample student essay. These essays were written by real college students who were writing in response to classroom writing assignments. The essays are realistic models of good writing, but they are not perfect. They show you how the writer applied the techniques taught in the chapter to produce a good essay. Before each essay, the writer and his or her writing task are described. The essays are annotated to call your attention to particular writing features or techniques. Questions follow each essay to help you further examine the writer's techniques, and academic writing assignments are suggested.

Here are some suggestions for reading and learning from student writing:

■ **Read the piece of writing more than once.** Read it once to understand the writer's message. Read it again to examine the writing technique it illustrates.

■ **Read the piece to answer this question:** What does this writer do that I can use in my own writing?

■ **Highlight as you read.** Mark words, sentences, or paragraphs that you want to study further or that you feel work particularly well.

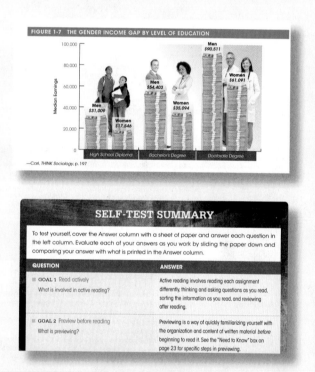

### READ AND RESPOND: A Professional Essay

**Thinking Before Reading**

The following selection originally appeared in "Earth Island Journal," an environmental magazine. In the selection, the author discusses the health risks of radiation from cell phone towers and other media technology.

1. Preview the reading, using the steps discussed in Chapter 1 on page 25.
2. Connect the reading to your own experience by answering the following questions:
   a. What health effects have you heard of regarding cell phones, cell phone towers, and other types of technology?
   b. What type of technology do you think carries the most risk?
3. Highlight and annotate as you read.

1270L/1212 words

### Wireless Interference: The Health Risks

**Christopher Ketcham**

*We now live in a wireless-saturated normality that has never existed in the history of the human race, and the effects of EMFs on human beings are largely untested.*

—Dan McCarthy/DANMCCARTHY.ORG

1    In January 1990, a cell tower goes up 800 feet from Alison Rall's dairy farm in Mansfield, Ohio. By fall, the cattle herd that pastures near the tower is sick, and Rall's three young children begin suffering bizarre skin rashes, raised red "hot spots." The kids are hit with waves of hyperactivity. The girls lose hair. Rall, when she becomes pregnant with a fourth child, can't gain weight.

## Read and Respond: A Professional Essay

The professional essays in this book were written by expert writers and have been published in books, textbooks, news magazines, and journals. A professional essay appears at the end of most chapters. By studying the writing of professional writers, you can improve your own writing. As with the student writing, plan on reading each essay several times. Be sure to look for techniques that the writer uses that you can use in your own writing. Both before and after each reading, you will find questions and activities intended to guide you in reading, examining, and writing about the reading. You should complete these, even if they are not assigned by your instructor, because doing so will help you be better prepared to discuss and write about the reading.

## Photographs and Graphics

Many of the professional readings include graphs, charts, or photographs that illustrate concepts and ideas presented in the reading. At least one question is included in the exercises following each reading that asks you to respond to the visual. These visuals are included to enhance your ability to read, interpret, and react to graphics and images. As you examine them, always consider why the writer included them and what they add to the reading.

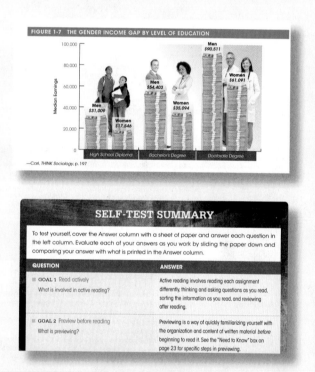

**FIGURE 1-7   THE GENDER INCOME GAP BY LEVEL OF EDUCATION**

Men $31,009 / Women $17,546 (High School Diploma)
Men $54,403 / Women $35,094 (Bachelor's Degree)
Men $90,511 / Women $61,091 (Doctorate Degree)

—Carl, *THINK Sociology*, p. 197

## Self-Test Summary

The Self-Test Summary at the end of each chapter provides you with an opportunity to test your recall of chapter content and mastery of each learning goal. Use this as a review, both immediately upon finishing the chapter and later, as needed.

### SELF-TEST SUMMARY

To test yourself, cover the Answer column with a sheet of paper and answer each question in the left column. Evaluate each of your answers as you work by sliding the paper down and comparing your answer with what is printed in the Answer column.

| QUESTION | ANSWER |
|---|---|
| **GOAL 1**  Read actively<br>What is involved in active reading? | Active reading involves reading each assignment differently, thinking and asking questions as you read, sorting the information as you read, and reviewing after reading. |
| **GOAL 2**  Preview before reading<br>What is previewing? | Previewing is a way of quickly familiarizing yourself with the organization and content of written material *before* beginning to read it. See the "Need to Know" box on page 23 for specific steps in previewing. |

## MySkillsLab

A MySkillsLab box at the end of each chapter directs you to the lab for additional practice with the chapter topic. The MSL logo and the **Complete** this **Exercise** at **myskillslab.com** icon appear in the margin beside exercises that can be completed online.

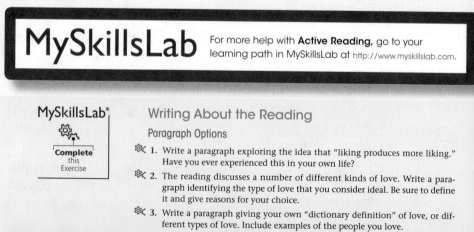

# MySkillsLab

For more help with **Active Reading,** go to your learning path in MySkillsLab at http://www.myskillslab.com.

MySkillsLab®

Complete this Exercise

## Writing About the Reading

### Paragraph Options

1. Write a paragraph exploring the idea that "liking produces more liking." Have you ever experienced this in your own life?
2. The reading discusses a number of different kinds of love. Write a paragraph identifying the type of love that you consider ideal. Be sure to define it and give reasons for your choice.
3. Write a paragraph giving your own "dictionary definition" of love, or different types of love. Include examples of the people you love.

# Keys to College Success

College is a different world from the one you know. For younger students, college is very different from high school because college students are responsible for their own learning. For older or returning students, college is different from the world of work and raising a family.

This section offers 10 keys for overall college success, including specific strategies to help you succeed in your reading and writing course.

The following keys will help you become a more successful student. Be sure to try out each strategy and adapt it to make it fit how best you learn.

1. Set Goals and Monitor Them
2. Get Organized
3. Manage Your Time: Balance School, Work, and Family
4. Take Charge of Your Learning
5. Get the Most Out of Your Textbooks

6. Focus Your Attention and Avoid Distractions
7. Take Effective Class Notes
8. Learn to Take Tests
9. Be Successful in Your Reading–Writing Course
10. Work Successfully with Classmates

## KEY 1 Set Goals and Monitor Them

Anyone who's ever watched or played hockey or soccer knows what every team wants to achieve: goals. In the larger sense, a **goal** is any result you are aiming for. In terms of your college courses, you can think of three categories of goals.

- **Short-term goals:** What you need to accomplish today or this week

- **Medium-term goals:** What you need to accomplish this month or this term

- **Long-term goals:** What you want to accomplish in terms of your education, life, and career

Goals are essential because they keep you on track. They provide you with a road map for your life, a set of tasks you must accomplish to move forward. People without goals often feel like they are accomplishing nothing.

To be achievable, goals must be

- **Positive.** Think about what you want out of life and set goals to help you stay focused.
- **Specific and clearly defined.** Don't say, "I want a good job." Say, "I want to become a computer technician, working with and repairing computer hardware and networks."
- **Achievable.** Focus on what you can realistically achieve in a certain time frame. Trying to accomplish too much, too soon is a recipe for frustration. (For example, you may have the admirable goal of finishing school in two years, but realistically it may take three.)

Monitoring your progress is essential. Keep a notebook with you, and make a list of tasks you need to accomplish each day, week, or month. When you've accomplished the task, cross it off your list—you'll be amazed at the sense of satisfaction you feel.

For maximum success in college, you should set *reading goals*. Most of your courses will require sizable amounts of reading. Make a schedule outlining what you need to read each day, and stick to it. If you feel yourself slipping behind, take action to get back on track. Rearrange your priorities and put off nonessentials until you've accomplished what you need to do.

## Use This Textbook!

*In Harmony* is structured to help you practice setting and achieving goals. At the start of each chapter you will find a set of learning goals. These goals are revisited throughout the chapter. The end of the chapter then provides a summary of the goals in an interactive Self-Test Summary.

**Try It Out!**

### Setting Goals

Take a look at your life right now and list your goals and your time frame for accomplishing them. Make sure your goals are specific, positive, and achievable. Write additional goals on a separate sheet of paper if you wish.

**Short-Term Goals (to do today or this week)**

#1 _____ Due date: _____

#2 _____ Due date: _____

**Medium-Term Goals (to accomplish this month or term)**

#1 _____ Due date: _____

#2 _____ Due date: _____

**Long-Term Goals (to accomplish within the next few years)**

#1 _____ Due date: _____

#2 _____ Due date: _____

# Get Organized

Becoming a successful student requires planning and organization. Here are a few suggestions for ensuring your success.

1. **Organize a place to study.** Select a quiet, comfortable location and study in the same place each day. Be sure to have all your materials (paper, pens, etc.) at hand.

2. **Use a pocket or online calendar and a small notebook.** Record exams and due dates for papers on the calendar; record daily assignments in the notebook.

3. **Get to know someone in each class.** You might enjoy having someone to talk to. Also, in case you miss a class, you will have someone from whom you can get the assignment and borrow notes.

4. **Attend all classes, whether or not it is required.** Studies show that successful students attend class regularly, whereas students who do not are unsuccessful.

5. **Get to know your instructors.** Use your instructors' office hours to talk about exams or assignments, ask questions, and discuss ideas for papers.

6. **Control electronic time wasters.** Avoid getting caught up in social media by turning off your electronic devices and setting aside specific times for checking them.

7. **Create lists of new terminology for each of your courses.** You can group similar terms, organize them by chapter, or sort them into "know" and "don't know" files.

8. **Choose a study partner or create online study groups.** Instant messaging (IM) allows you to talk back and forth with a classmate, as long as you are both online at the same time. Members can share notes, quiz each other, and discuss course content.

**Try It Out!**

## *Getting Organized*

Take a few moments to think about where the best place is for you to study and what you will need on hand when you go there to study. Write your study location below, then use the list that follows to equip the area with items you will need. Check off each item after you have placed it in your chosen study location.

Study location: _____

Materials I will need:

_____ pencils

_____ erasers

_____ pens

_____ highlighters

_____ stapler

_____ tape

_____ pencil sharpener

_____ paper clips/fasteners

_____ note paper/note pads

_____ sticky notes

_____ dictionary

_____ thesaurus

# Manage Your Time: Balance School, Work, and Family

Many students find they must juggle school responsibilities with their part-time job commitments. Still others must make time for household and/or family responsibilities, as well. Use the following suggestions to help you keep your life running smoothly and efficiently:

1. **Understand how much you can handle.** It is good to be ambitious, but don't take on too much. For example, you may feel much less stress if you think about taking an extra year to complete your degree. You will have more time for work and family.

2. **Have a family conversation.** Your family benefits from your college degree. Discuss all family members' responsibilities and the roles they play in your college success. It is important for everyone to understand that some sacrifices must be made for the family's benefit.

3. **Take study breaks at your job.** On most jobs, employees have coffee breaks and lunch breaks. Find a quiet place to read or review your notes while you eat a light lunch or dinner. You will have less to do at home.

4. **Build a compact class schedule.** In future semesters, select a class schedule that is compact and convenient, without too many hours between classes. This will free up larger blocks of time for work and study. (If you have time between classes, find a quiet place in the library to study.)

5. **Make a schedule to reflect your priorities.** Don't try to fit college into your old weekly schedule from before you started college; succeeding in college takes too much time for this to work well. You will need to reserve plenty of time for reading, writing, and studying.

6. **Make a household schedule.** Just as you have planned a weekly study schedule, develop a weekly household schedule. Instead of hoping that all jobs will get done, plan when you or a family member will tackle each. Designate specific times for laundry, shopping, errands, and so forth.

7. **Increase your efficiency by doing things at off-peak times.** Don't go to the grocery store or laundromat on a busy Saturday morning; instead, choose a weekday, early in the morning or later in the evening.

8. **Use weekends for study.** Try to take care of work and household responsibilities during the week by "sandwiching" them between each other. For instance, you could run a load of laundry while washing your car. This will free up larger blocks of time on the weekend for study.

9. **Use weekends wisely.** Some students think of weekdays as the time to concentrate on school and work, and weekends as the time to have fun. This approach can lead to very stressful weeks. Make your weekdays less stressful by scheduling study or reading time each weekend.

10. **Take care of yourself.** Eat a healthy diet, get some exercise, and take some time for yourself occasionally. "Reward" yourself with small things when you accomplish important tasks—for example, a new song for your iPod when you have finished writing your paper, or a cup of coffee at the local coffeehouse after you have taken your exam.

**Try It Out!** *Setting Priorities*

Practice balancing school, work, and family by completing the following activity.

On Sunday evening, you sit down and make a list of everything you need or want to get done during the coming week. In the space provided, indicate:

**1:** for top priority—you must get this done early in the week

**2:** for medium priority—you need this done by the end of the week

**3:** for low priority—this can be put off until next week if necessary

____ See that new movie that is a sequel to one of my favorite films.

____ Turn in psychology assignment/worksheet to my professor on Tuesday, when it's due—I haven't even started it yet!

____ Sign the permission slip allowing my daughter to go on her field trip. Her teacher said she needs it by Friday.

____ Prepare for the presentation I need to give at work on Tuesday.

____ Meet up with my three old high school friends at a local diner.

____ Study for my sociology exam, which will be given on Thursday.

____ Start the research for my English paper, which is due a month from tomorrow.

____ Take Mom to her doctor's appointment on Monday.

____ Read that new vampire novel that I have been looking forward to.

____ Make child care arrangements so that I can attend the biology exam review session on Thursday.

**KEY 4**

# Take Charge of Your Learning

Students who make plans and decisions are more successful than those who do not. Students without definite plans and goals drift through life passively, letting things happen and allowing others to control their lives. Active decision makers, on the other hand, know what they want and plan strategies to obtain it. Here's how to take charge.

## Accept Responsibility for Grades

Certainly you have heard comments such as, "Dr. Smith only gave me a B on my last paper" or "I got a C on my first lab report." Students often think of grades as rewards that teachers give to students. Thinking this way is avoiding responsibility, blaming the instructor instead of owning up to the fact that a paper or exam failed to meet the standards set by the instructor.

Be honest; you will not always earn the grades you want and you will not always score as well as you expect to on every exam. Analyze what you could have done to improve a disappointing grade, and put this to work in preparing for the next exam.

## Don't Make Excuses

Studying is not easy; it requires time and conscious effort. Try not to make it more difficult than it really is by avoiding it. Some students avoid studying by following a variety of escape routes. Here are a few common ones:

- I can't study tonight because I promised to drive my sister to the mall.
- I can't study for my physics test because the dorm is too noisy.
- I can't finish reading my psychology assignment because the chapter is boring.
- I didn't finish writing my essay because I fell asleep.

If you find yourself making excuses to avoid studying, step back and analyze the problem. Consider possible causes and solutions. For example, if the dorm really is too noisy to study, could you study at a different time or find a new place to study? More likely, the problem is that you were just not in the mood to study. Be honest! Before you quit and go on to something else, make a definite commitment to finish the assignment later; be specific about when and where. Postponing study may be better than avoiding it completely, but bear in mind that it probably will not be much easier after it has been postponed.

**Try It Out!**  *Analyzing Study Situations*

Analyze your past study performance by answering the following two questions honestly.

1. What excuses have you used to avoid study?

   _____

   _____

   _____

2. Whom have you blamed when you did not study or did not earn the grade you expected?

   _____

   _____

   _____

# Get the Most Out of Your Textbooks

Other than your instructor, your single greatest source of information will be your textbook. Textbook authors are not only experts in their field but also are experienced teachers who understand students' needs.

Understanding how to access information in a textbook is as important as reading the textbook itself. Most textbooks contain the following features that are designed to help you learn:

| FEATURE | HOW TO USE IT |
|---|---|
| Preface or "To the Student" | • Read it to find out how the book is organized, what topics it covers, and what learning features it contains. |
| Chapter Opener (may include chapter objectives, photographs, and introductory text) | • Read it to find out what the chapter is about.<br>• Use it to test yourself later to see if you can recall the main points. |
| Marginal Vocabulary Definitions | • Learn the definition of each term.<br>• Create a vocabulary log (in a notebook or computer file) and enter words you need to learn. |
| Photographs and Other Visual Elements | • Determine their purpose: what important information do they illustrate?<br>• For diagrams, charts, and tables, note the process or trend they illustrate. Make marginal notes.<br>• Practice redrawing diagrams without referring to the originals. |
| Test Yourself Questions (after sections within the chapter) | • Always check to see if you can answer them before going on to the next section.<br>• Use them to check your recall of chapter content when studying for an exam. |
| Special Interest Inserts (can include profiles of people, coverage of related issues, critical thinking topics, etc.) | • Discover how the inserts are related to the chapter content: what key concepts do they illustrate? |
| Review Questions/Problems/Discussion Questions | • Read them once *before* you read the chapter to discover what you are expected to learn.<br>• Use them after you have read the chapter to test your recall. |
| Chapter Summary | • Test yourself by converting summary statements into questions using the words *Who? Why? When? How?* and *So What?* |
| Chapter Review Quiz | • Use this to prepare for an exam. Pay extra attention to items you get wrong. |

**Try It Out!**     *Getting the Most Out of Your Textbooks*

Choose one of your textbooks and identify the five most useful features in it. Explain how you will use each feature to get the most out of your textbook.

1. _____

_____

2. _____

_____

3. _____

_____

4. _____

_____

5. _____

_____

# KEY 6  Focus Your Attention and Avoid Distractions

We are a society bombarded by information—millions of Web sites, hundreds of cable TV channels, the constant ringing of the cell phone or beeping of incoming text messages.

As a result of all the interruptions we face, our attention spans have decreased significantly. Some experts now estimate that the average attention span is just seven minutes. How much do you think you can read, write, or research in just seven minutes? The answer is probably "Not much." If you are constantly interrupted, the chances of accomplishing your tasks and meeting your goals are quite slim.

Thus it is essential that you find ways to focus your attention and eliminate distractions. Here are some specific tips for achieving these goals:

1. **Set up a study space.** If possible, always use the same area of your home in which to study. Make it conducive to study by keeping it clutter-free.

2. **Turn off the TV and the iPod.** It is difficult to understand complicated materials when the TV or iPod is competing for your attention.

3. **Turn off the cell phone.** Don't turn it on again until you have completed your assignment.

4. **Monitor your attention span.** It is normal to lose focus occasionally, to feel tired or hungry. It is perfectly fine to take study breaks, to have a healthy snack, or to get some exercise. But a break should be just a brief "time out," not an extended vacation from study.

5. **Work in places conducive to study.** A quiet library is usually a much better place to read than a busy student center or a bustling cafeteria.

6. **Avoid social networking sites during study time.** Facebook and the Internet are massive time wasters. Students report losing hours at a time simply checking e-mail and updates.

**Try It Out!**

## Examining Distractions

Many electronic advances—such as e-mail and the Internet—have become primarily forms of entertainment. Answer the following questions to get a sense of the type and number of distractions in your life and how they affect your ability to focus.

1. How many text messages do you send and receive per day? _____ How many of these are "important"? _____ Do you stop what you are doing to check your cell phone the second a text message arrives? _____ Have you ever "texted" while driving? _____

2. How many e-mails do you send and receive per day? _____ How many of these are valuable in terms of communicating important information? _____ How many are purely for entertainment or socializing? _____ How much time do you spend each day on e-mail unrelated to your college work or your job? _____

3. How many calls do you receive on your cell phone each day? _____ Do you leave your cell phone on all the time? _____ Do you answer it every time it rings, even when you're in class or studying? _____ Do you ever use your cell phone as a way to procrastinate? _____

4. How many hours a day do you spend surfing the Internet or posting on social networking sites like Facebook? _____ Does this socializing affect your studying, concentration, and grades? _____

# KEY 7 Take Effective Class Notes

In many courses, your instructor will lecture, and you will need to take accurate notes for study and review. Use the following suggestions to take effective notes.

1. **Read the textbook material on which the lecture will be based before attending the lecture.**

2. **Listen carefully to the lecturer's opening comments;** they often reveal the purpose, focus, or organization of the lecture.

3. **Focus on ideas, not facts.** Do not try to record everything the lecturer says.

4. **Record the main ideas and enough details and examples so that the ideas will make sense later.** Use an abbreviation system for commonly used words (psy = *psychology*, w/ = *with*, etc.) to save time.

5. **Record the organization of the lecture.** Use an indentation system to show the relative importance of ideas. Be sure to leave plenty of space as you take notes so you have room to fill in missed information later.

6. **Review and edit your notes as soon as possible after the lecture.** Fill in missing or additional information. This review will also help you remember the lecture.

7. **Test yourself using the Recall Clue System** (also known as the **Cornell System**). Simply rereading your notes is not an effective study strategy.

Instead, you need to be active and test yourself. Here is how the Recall Clue System works:

■ **Leave a 2-inch margin at the left side of each page of notes.** Keep the margin blank while you are taking notes.

■ **After you have edited your notes, write words or phrases in the left margin that briefly summarize each section.** You can also write questions that are answered by the information in your notes. These recall clues will help trigger your recall of the details of your lecture notes.

■ **To study for tests or exams, cover up your notes, exposing only the left margin.** Read each recall clue and try to remember the information in the corresponding portion of your notes. After you have completed a section, check your notes to see if you were accurate and remembered all of the important points.

Figure A shows an excerpt from a set of notes using the Recall Clue System.

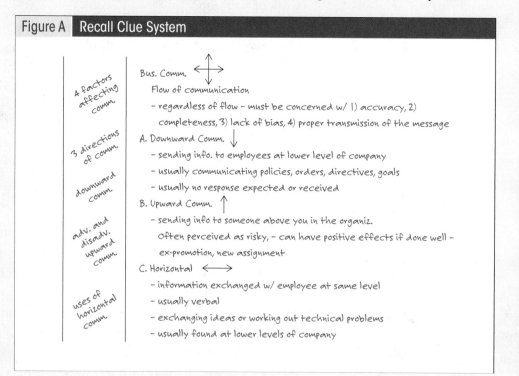

**Figure A     Recall Clue System**

---

**Try It Out!** ▶ *Taking Notes*

Use the morning or evening television news to practice taking notes using the Recall Clue System. First, review the suggestions for taking effective notes and the steps in the Recall Clue System. Then listen to a segment of the news while taking notes and keeping the margin of your paper blank. Apply the Recall Clue System to your notes, and complete the exercise by reading your recall clues and trying to remember the corresponding information in your notes. Check your notes to see if you remembered the important points from the news segment.

# Learn to Take Tests

Quizzes, midterms, and final exams are often the basis on which grades are awarded. But they are also valuable thinking and learning experiences. Quizzes force you to keep up with reading assignments, while longer exams require you to consolidate and integrate concepts and information. Exam questions fall into two general categories: objective (multiple-choice or true/false) and essay exams.

## Multiple-Choice and True/False Questions

Here are some tips for answering multiple-choice and true/false questions on exams.

- **Read the directions thoroughly.** The directions may contain crucial information you need to answer the questions correctly.

- **Leave nothing blank.** Even if you guess at the answer, you have nothing to lose.

- **Watch for absolute words such as *all, none, always,* and *never.*** Absolute statements tend to be false or incorrect.

- **Read two-part statements carefully in true/false questions.** If both parts are not correct, then the answer must be "false."

- **Read all choices before choosing your answer,** even if you think you have found the correct one. In multiple-choice tests, remember that your job is to choose the *best* answer.

- **Avoid selecting answers that are unfamiliar or that you do not understand.**

- **When you have to guess at an answer, pick the one that seems complete and contains the most information.** Instructors are usually careful to make the best answer completely correct and recognizable. Such a choice often becomes long or detailed.

- **Play the odds.** In a multiple-choice test, if you can eliminate a couple of choices that are absolutely incorrect, you greatly increase your chances of getting the answer right.

- **If two of the answer choices are opposites, it is likely that one of them is the correct answer.**

- **If two similar answer choices are presented, one is likely to be correct.**

- **Don't change answers without a good reason.** When reviewing your answers before you turn in your exam, don't make a change unless you have a good reason for doing so. Very often your first impressions are correct.

- **Mark any item that contains unfamiliar terminology as false.** If you have studied the material thoroughly, trust that you would recognize as true anything that was part of the course content.

- **When all else fails, it is usually better to guess true rather than false.** It is more difficult for instructors to write plausible false statements than true statements. As a result, many exams have more true items than false.

- **Choose a midrange number.** When a question asks you to select a number, such as a percentage or other statistic, choose a midrange number. Test writers often include choices that are both higher and lower than the correct answer.

## Essay Exams

Here are some tips for preparing for and taking essay exams.

- **Determine the likely questions on the exam.** You can do this by reviewing your lecture notes, thinking about the topics your instructor emphasized in class, rereading parts of your textbook, or talking with your classmates about possible questions. Write up the possible questions and practice answering them.

- **Remember that an essay exam requires an essay with a good topic sentence and adequate support.** Before you start writing, quickly outline your answer so that your essay has form and structure.

- **Keep your eye on the time.** Bring a watch to class, and plan how much time you will spend on each question. You must answer each question to get a good grade.

- **Read the directions carefully before you start the exam,** looking for clues that will tell you what the instructor is looking for.

- **If you have a choice of questions, select carefully.** Read all the questions first, and then choose the questions on which you will be able to score the most points.

- **If you don't know the answer, do not leave the page blank; write something.** In attempting to answer the question, you may hit upon some partially correct information. However, the main reason for writing something is to give the instructor an opportunity to give you at least a few points for trying. If you leave a blank page, your instructor has no choice but to give you zero points.

Be sure to begin studying for each major exam at least a week before the test. Research has shown that early preparation leads to higher grades than an all-night cram session the day before the test. Show up for the exam a few minutes early, sit at the front of the room (to minimize distractions and be one of the first to get the exam), and bring the necessary materials (including pens, pencils, and erasers).

**Try It Out!**

## Analyzing Test Questions

The following multiple-choice items appeared on a psychology exam. Study each item and use your reasoning skills to eliminate items that seem incorrect. Then, making an educated guess, select the best answer.

_c_ 1. If a psychologist were personally to witness the effects of a tornado on the residents of a small town, what technique would she be using?
   a. experimentation            c. observation
   b. correlational research      d. none of the above

_d_ 2. A case study is a(n)
   a. synonym for a longitudinal study.
   b. comparison of similar events.
   c. study of changes and their effects.
   d. intense investigation of a particular occurrence.

_b_    **3.** Approximately what percentage of men are color blind?
      a.  1 percent            c.  99 percent
      b.  10 percent          d.  100 percent

_d_    **4.** Jane Goodall has studied the behavior of chimpanzees in their own habitat. She exemplifies a school of psychology that is concerned with
      a.  theories.            c.  human behavior.
      b.  mental processes.      d.  naturalistic behavior.

# KEY 9 Be Successful in Your Reading-Writing Course

Because reading and writing skills are essential in all of your other college courses, it is especially important to learn as much as you can from your reading–writing class. Use the suggestions below to succeed in this course.

## Success with Reading Assignments

The following suggestions will help you to be successful with the reading assignments and reading skills taught in this book.

1. **Complete all your reading assignments.** Be sure to read your assignments in full to master the reading skills being taught. The more you read and the more you practice, the more quickly your skills will improve. Simply attending class is not enough; you have to apply what you learn in class to your reading assignments.

2. **Pay close attention to the vocabulary chapters and exercises.** Vocabulary is essential to both reading and writing, and words are the vehicles for thought. You will find that as your vocabulary expands, both reading and writing will become easier tasks. A strong vocabulary is important for all your college classes, as well as for communicating effectively in your chosen career.

3. **Use the reading selections to explore areas of interest.** As you read the selections, you'll encounter a wide range of materials including essays, textbooks, magazine articles, and online sources. These will broaden your knowledge, expand your areas of interest, and may even suggest possible new fields of study or areas of career interest.

4. **Apply the skills you are learning to everything you read.** Go beyond assigned readings and use the skills you are developing when you read textbooks for other courses, as well as everyday and on-the-job materials— online sources, newspapers, magazines, and workplace communications.

5. **Get through the "boring" parts.** It would be unrealistic for you to find every reading selection or exercise interesting or fascinating. Do your best to keep an open mind. If you have trouble concentrating, try working with a classmate, discussing the reading and working together on completing assignments.

**Try It Out!**    *Making College Reading Assignments Relevant to Your Life*

One of the ways to make the most of college reading assignments is to connect the material to your own life. For this activity, read the following four paragraphs found in Chapter 11. For each paragraph, identify your level of interest (high, medium, or low) and suggest ways it is relevant to your life, your studies, your family, or your community.

| READING | INTEREST LEVEL (HIGH, MEDIUM, OR LOW) | APPLICATION OR RELEVANCE TO YOUR LIFE |
|---|---|---|
| Ex 11-3 Paragraph A (p. 334) | | |
| Ex. 11-6 item 2 (p. 342) | | |
| Ex. 11-7 Paragraph B (p. 344) | | |
| Ex. 11-10 Paragraph B (p. 347) | | |

## Success with Writing Assignments

College writing strikes fear into the hearts of some students. They mistakenly think that writing is all about grammar, punctuation, and spelling. While it's true that good writing follows grammatical rules, it's much more about clear communication, about developing ideas and providing examples to support them. Here are some tips for doing well in your writing course.

1. **Understand that writing skills are at the core of not only college success but also workplace success.** When asked what they are seeking in job applicants, employers put "good writing skills" at the top of the list. The writing and editing techniques you learn in your college writing course will not only help you do well on term papers and essay exams; they will also help you in the job market and in advancing in your chosen career.

2. **Make use of electronic learning and editing aids.** All computerized word processing programs come with tools designed to check spelling, grammar, and punctuation; they do not catch all errors, but they will identify some. The Internet provides free online dictionaries, handbooks, and thesauruses.

3. **Understand the differences between formal and informal writing.** All the writing you do in college and in the workplace should follow the rules of formal English. Abbreviations commonly used in e-mail and text messages (for example, *u* instead of *you,* and *2* instead of *too*) are not acceptable in college writing. Emoticons, such as ☺, are also informal and not used in college writing.

4. **Read and learn from your instructor's feedback.** Most instructors spend a huge amount of time commenting on your writing, offering tips to make it more effective. Aim for major improvements from draft to draft, and from paper to paper. Be sure to attend any instructor conferences, and use your instructor's office hours to get help and ask questions.

5. **Write, write, write.** The only way to learn how to write well is to write often. Do not let writing assignments become a source of anxiety. See them as a way of exploring a topic, learning more about an area of interest, and developing your communication skills.

6. **Understand your instructor's expectations.** Most instructors are very specific about their assignments. They clearly spell out what you are to write—how long it should be, what it should contain, and so forth. Following instructions and providing what is requested increase your chances of a good grade.

7. **Make use of the writing center.** Many campuses offer additional help or tutoring in their writing center. Don't be shy about making an appointment or dropping in for help when you need it.

8. **Consider getting extra help if English is not your first language.** Students who are not native speakers of English may benefit from reviewing Part Seven: "The ELL Guide for Nonnative Speakers" on page 661.

**Try It Out!**

## *Focusing on Success in College Writing*

A good way to gain confidence as a writer is to complete an exercise that demonstrates how much you already know about effective writing. A key strategy for writing well is to make a specific point and then provide support for it or explain it. For each point below, provide three supporting statements.

1. Life is easier when you have money.

   a. _____

   b. _____

   c. _____

2. There are three key elements to maintaining a healthy lifestyle.

   a. _____

   b. _____

   c. _____

## Success Using MySkillsLab: Practice, Practice, Practice

MySkillsLab is an extensive set of electronic materials designed to assess your skills and offer you practice where you need it most and at a level appropriate for you, individually.

■ **Why Practice?** Practice is one of the best ways to improve your reading and writing skills. The more you practice, the more you improve, and the more likely it will be that you will remember and be able to apply the skills you are learning to your other college courses and, later, to workplace tasks.

■ **When to Practice?** Practice often and frequently. Several spaced-out practice sessions are more effective than one long, marathon session.

■ **How to Practice?** Schedule sessions to work through your individualized learning path on MySkillsLab close in time to your reading–writing class. The more closely in time you are able to practice and apply skills taught in class, the more likely it is that you will learn and remember them. If you designate several specific times each week to work in MySkillsLab, you will make sure you won't procrastinate or forget to use it.

■ **What to Practice?** As well as practicing your skills using your individualized learning path on MySkillsLab, you can also complete the Writing About Reading assignments at the end of each chapter online. Look for the MySkillsLab logo and the following icon at the end of each professional reading.

**MySkillsLab®**

Complete
this
Exercise

### Writing About the Reading

**Paragraph Options**

1. Write a paragraph exploring the idea that "liking produces more liking." Have you ever experienced this in your own life?

2. The reading discusses a number of different kinds of love. Write a paragraph identifying the type of love that you consider ideal. Be sure to define it and give reasons for your choice.

3. Write a paragraph giving your own "dictionary definition" of love, or different types of love. Include examples of the people you love.

**MySkillsLab**  For more help with **Active Reading,** go to your learning path in MySkillsLab at http://www.myskillslab.com.

## KEY 10 Work Successfully with Classmates

While *you* are responsible for your writing success, you'll need the help of others along the way. Instructors will offer feedback on your work, and you'll sometimes work closely with classmates as well.

### Learning from Peer Review

In writing classes, you'll often participate in *peer review*, in which you comment on your classmates' writing and they comment on yours. How can you make peer reviewing as valuable as possible? Here are some suggestions:

### When You Are the Writer . . .

1. **Prepare your draft in readable form.** Double-space your work and print it on standard 8.5" × 11" paper.

2. **When you receive your peers' comments, weigh them carefully.** Keep an open mind, but do not feel that you must accept every suggestion that is made.

3. **If you have questions or are uncertain about your peers' advice, talk with your instructor.**

## When You Are the Reviewer . . .

1. **Read the draft through at least once before making any suggestions.**

2. **As you read, keep the writer's intended audience in mind** (see Chapter 2). The draft should be appropriate for that audience.

3. **Offer positive comments first.** Say what the writer did well.

4. **Use the Revision Checklists and "Need to Know" boxes in this book to guide your reading and comments.** Be specific in your review and offer suggestions for improvement.

5. **Be supportive;** put yourself in the place of the person whose work you are reviewing. Phrase your feedback in the way you would want to hear it!

**Try It Out!**

### Practicing Peer Review

Exchange writing samples with a classmate. Then do the following:

1. List two things the writer did well.

    a. _____

    b. _____

2. List two areas for improvement.

    a. _____

    b. _____

## A Final Word

You will be successful in each of your college courses if you work hard and read, write, learn, and study the right way. The remainder of this book will give you the skills you need. Be sure to apply everything you learn in this book to each of your other courses.

# The Reading Process: An Overview

## THINK About It!

Study this photograph that shows members of Greenpeace protesting the hunting and killing of whales. Notice that the protesters are *actively* involved. (This is why they are sometimes referred to as activists.) They are approaching and confronting the whaling ship. They feel as if it is their cause and the killing of whales is their problem. These activists are engaged, involved, and taking specific steps to interfere with a whale hunt. In a similar way, active readers get involved with the material they are reading. They think, question, challenge, criticize, and take specific steps to understand, remember, and evaluate what they read. This chapter will give you some tips on how to become an active reader. The skills you will learn will also help you to write in response to what you read.

## FOCUSING ON READING AND WRITING

# What Are Active Reading and Writing?

Reading involves much more than moving your eyes across a line of print. It is more than recognizing words, and it is more than reading sentences. Reading requires thinking. It is an active process of identifying important ideas written by others and interpreting, comparing, and evaluating them.

Writing, too, involves much more than typing words on your computer or moving your pen across a page. Writing requires thinking. It is an active process of deciding what you want to say, organizing it, and expressing it clearly and effectively so your readers understand your ideas.

In this chapter, and in many other chapters in the book, you will learn strategies for becoming an active, involved reader. In the next chapter, and in many others throughout the book, you will learn strategies for becoming an active, thoughtful, expressive writer.

## READING

# Active Reading: How to Get Started

■ **GOAL 1**
Read actively

Many readers open a book, read, and then close the book. They think of it as a one-step process—reading words. To become a solid, strong reader who understands, remembers, and evaluates what you read, think of reading as a set of skills that involves activities before, during, and after reading. To get the most out of college textbooks and reading assignments and to remember what you read for tests and writing assignments, use the suggestions in the following "Need to Know" box.

**EXERCISE 1-1**     Analyzing How You Read

**Directions:** Using the "Need to Know" box, analyze how you read and place a check mark beside items in the box that you already do. Place an asterisk (*) next to items you'd like to learn to do.

## ! NEED TO KNOW

### Active Reading: An Overview

| ACTIVE READING INVOLVES . . . | CHECK |
|---|---|
| **Reading each assignment differently.** For each assignment, determine <br> • Why it was assigned | |
| • What you need and want to learn | |
| • What you need to do with the information (pass a test, write an essay, apply the information) | |
| • How the material is organized | |

*(continues)*

| ACTIVE READING INVOLVES … | CHECK |
|---|---|
| • How difficult the material is | |
| • What you already know | |
| **Thinking and asking questions as you read.** Do this by<br>• Identifying what is important | |
| • Recognizing when something is confusing or not understandable | |
| • Determining how the key ideas are organized | |
| • Drawing connections between ideas | |
| • Anticipating what is to come next | |
| • Relating ideas to what you already know | |
| **Sorting the information as you read.** Identify what you need to learn and remember by using<br>• Highlighting | |
| • Outlining | |
| • Mapping (drawing diagrams that show how ideas are organized) | |
| • Summarizing | |
| **Reviewing after reading.** To build retention and recall, be sure to<br>• Do a quick one- to three-minute review immediately after reading | |
| • Review your highlighting, outlining, notes, and maps periodically to keep information fresh in your mind. | |
| • Test yourself. Find out what you know and don't know before attending class or taking an exam. | |

Throughout the chapters in this book, you will learn many strategies to help you use the suggestions above.

---

### EXERCISE 1-2    Analyzing Assignments

WORKING TOGETHER

**Directions:** Working in small groups, consider each of the following reading assignments. Discuss ways to get actively involved in each assignment.

1. Reading two poems by Maya Angelou for an American literature class

   Find some background information on Angelou; read the poems several times, once for an
   overview, and then in-depth; highlight key words/phrases/lines

2. Reading the procedures for your next biology lab

   Identify the purpose of the lab; highlight important steps; review the steps after
   reading

3. Reading an article in *Time* magazine assigned by your political science instructor in preparation for a class discussion

   Discover how the article relates to course content; highlight key ideas; write marginal
   notes about how the article relates to course content

4. Reading an online article about leadership styles as part of your research for a management paper

*Read quickly to determine if the article is useful for your paper; if so, highlight each*

*leadership style; note how they are similar or different*

# Preview Before Reading

■ GOAL 2
Preview before reading

You would not cross a city street without checking for traffic first. You would not pay to see a movie you had never heard of and knew nothing about. You would not buy a car without test-driving it or checking its mechanical condition.

Nor should you read an article or a textbook chapter without knowing what it is about or how it is organized. **Previewing** is a way of quickly familiarizing yourself with the organization and content of written material *before* beginning to read it. It is an easy method to use and will make a dramatic difference in how effectively you read.

## How to Preview

When you preview, try to

■ find only the most important ideas in the material

■ note how the text is organized

To do this, look only at the parts that state these important ideas and skip the rest. Previewing is a fairly rapid technique; it should take only a minute or two to preview any reading selection in this book. In fact, previewing is so fast that you should *not* take time to highlight or make notes. To preview an article or textbook chapter, follow the steps in the following "Need to Know" box.

---

## ! NEED TO KNOW

### How to Preview

1. **Read the title and subtitle.** The title is a label that explains what the chapter is about. The subtitle, if there is one, suggests additional perspectives on the subject. For example, an article titled "Brazil" might be subtitled "The World's Next Superpower." In this instance, the subtitle tells which aspects of Brazil the article discusses.

2. **Read the first paragraph.** The first paragraph or introduction of a reading may provide an overview and offer clues about how a chapter or article is organized. If it is lengthy, read just the first few sentences.

3. **Read section headings.** Section headings, like titles, identify and separate important topics and ideas.

4. **Read the first sentence under each heading.** The first sentence following a heading often further explains the heading. It may also state the central thought of the section it introduces.

5. **If the reading lacks headings, read the first sentence of each of a few paragraphs on each page.** You will discover many of the main ideas of the reading.

6. **Notice typographical aids.** Typographical aids are those features of a page that help to highlight and organize information. These include *italics*, **boldfaced type**, marginal notes, colored ink, underlining, and numbering.

7. **Read the final paragraph or summary.** The final paragraph may review the main points of the reading or bring it to a close.

### *Demonstration of Previewing*

The following excerpt, from a chapter of a psychology textbook, discusses several practical suggestions for managing anger. It has been included to help you understand previewing. Everything that you should look at or read has been highlighted. Preview this selection now, reading *only* the highlighted portions.

# The Dilemma of Anger:
## "Let It Out" or "Bottle It Up"?

1      What do you do when you feel angry? Do you tend to brood and sulk, collecting your righteous complaints like acorns for the winter, or do you erupt, hurling your wrath upon anyone or anything at hand? Do you discuss your feelings when you have calmed down? Does "letting anger out" get rid of it for you, or does it only make it more intense? The answers are crucial for how you get along with your family, neighbors, employers, and strangers.

2      Critical thinkers can learn to think carefully about how and when to express anger, and make a calm decision on how to proceed. Chronic feelings of anger and an inability to control anger can be as emotionally devastating and unhealthy as chronic problems with depression or anxiety. Yet in contrast to much pop-psych advice, research shows that expressing anger does not always get it "out of your system"; often people feel worse, physically and mentally, after an angry confrontation. When people brood and ruminate about their anger, talk to others incessantly about how angry they are, or ventilate their feelings in hostile acts, their blood pressure shoots up, they often feel angrier, and they behave even *more* aggressively later than if they had just let their feelings of anger subside. Conversely, when people learn to control their tempers and express anger constructively, they usually feel better, not worse; calmer, not angrier.

3      When people are feeling angry, they have a choice of doing any number of things, some of which will be more beneficial than others. Some people sulk, expecting everyone else to read their minds, which is hardly a way to communicate clearly. Many post impulsive comments on blogs that have annoyed them or send nasty texts on the spur of the moment. Some scream abuses at their friends or family, or strike out physically. If a particular action soothes their feelings or gets the desired response from others, they are likely to acquire a habit. Soon that habit feels "natural," as if it could never be changed. Some habits are better than others, though! Baking bread or going for a jog is fine, whereas many people justify their violent tempers by saying, "I couldn't help myself." But they can. If you have acquired an abusive or aggressive habit, the research in this chapter offers practical suggestions for learning constructive ways of managing anger:

### *Don't sound off in the heat of anger; let bodily arousal cool down.*

4      Whether your arousal comes from background stresses such as heat, crowds, or loud noise or from conflict with another person, take time to relax. Time allows

you to decide whether you are really angry or just tired and tense. This is the reason for the sage old advice to count to 10, count to 100, or sleep on it. Other cooling-off strategies include taking a time-out in the middle of an argument, meditating or relaxing, and calming yourself with a distracting activity.

### Don't take it personally.

5      If you feel that you have been insulted, check your perception for its accuracy. Could there be another reason for the behavior you find offensive? People who are quick to feel anger tend to interpret other people's actions as intentional offenses. People who are slow to anger tend to give others the benefit of the doubt, and they are not as focused on their own injured pride. Empathy ("Poor guy, he's feeling rotten") is usually incompatible with anger, so practice seeing the situation from the other person's perspective.

### Beware of road rage—yours and the other person's.

6      Driving increases everyone's level of physiological arousal, but not everyone becomes a hotheaded driver. Some drivers make themselves angry by having vengeful and retaliatory thoughts about other drivers (who have the nerve to change lanes or want to park! Who dare to drive at the speed limit in a school zone!). Hotheaded drivers take more risks while driving (rapidly switching lanes in their impatience), behave more aggressively (swearing, giving other drivers the finger or cursing them), and have more accidents.

### If you decide that expressing anger is appropriate, be sure you use the right verbal and nonverbal language to make yourself understood.

7      Because cultures (and families) have different display rules, be sure the recipient of your anger understands what you are feeling and what complaint you are trying to convey—and whether or not the person thinks your anger is *appropriate*. For example, a study compared the use of anger by Asian-American and Anglo-American negotiators. Expressing anger was effective for the Anglo teams—it got more concessions from the other side—but was much less effective for the Asian negotiators.

### Think carefully about how to express anger so that you will get the results you want.

8      What do you want your anger to accomplish? Do you just want to make the other person feel bad, or do you want the other person to understand your concerns and make amends? Shouting "You moron! How *could* you be so stupid!" might accomplish the former goal, but it's not likely to get the person to apologize, let alone to change his or her behavior. If your goal is to improve a bad situation or achieve justice, learning how to express anger so the other person will listen is essential.

9      Of course, if you just want to blow off steam, go right ahead; but you risk becoming a hothead.

—Wade and Tavris, *Invitation to Psychology*, p. 461

Bizarro by Dan Piraro

Would anyone in the group like to respond to the way Frank is dealing with his anger?

Bizarro copyright © 1999 Dan Piraro. Distributed by King Features Syndicate

# Evaluating Your Previewing

**Directions:** Read the following statements and mark each one true (T) or false (F) based on what you learned by previewing the selection above. Answers to this exercize can be found at the bottom of page 30.

__T__ **1.** It is important to let bodily arousal cool down before expressing anger.

__F__ **2.** You should take it personally if you feel that you have been insulted.

__T__ **3.** Driving increases everyone's level of physiological arousal.

__F__ **4.** All cultures share the same verbal and nonverbal language.

__T__ **5.** Consider the results you want when you think about how to express anger.

This exercise tested your recall of some of the most important ideas in the selection. Check your answers using the answer key on page 30. Did you get most or all of the items correct? You can see, then, that previewing helps you learn the major ideas in a section before you read it.

### Why Previewing Is Effective

Previewing is effective for several reasons:

■ **Previewing helps you to make decisions about how you will approach the material.** On the basis of what you discover about the assignment's organization and content, you can select the reading and study strategies that will be most effective.

■ **Previewing puts your mind in gear.** It helps you start thinking about the subject.

■ **Previewing gives you a mental outline of the chapter's content.** It enables you to see how ideas are connected, and since you know where the author is headed, your reading will be easier than if you had not previewed. Previewing, however, is never a substitute for careful, thorough reading.

## Make Predictions

We make predictions about many tasks before we undertake them. We predict how long it will take to drive to a shopping mall, how much dinner will cost at a new restaurant, how long a party will last, or how difficult an exam will be. Prediction helps us organize our time and cope with new situations.

Prediction is an important part of active reading as well. It enables you to approach the material systematically. Also, it helps you to read actively because you continually accept or reject your predictions. As you preview, you can predict the development of ideas, the organization of the material, and the author's conclusions. For example, for her philosophy class, a student began to preview an essay titled "Do Computers Have a Right to Life?" From the title, she predicted that the essay would discuss the topic of artificial intelligence: whether computers can "think." Then, as she read the essay, she discovered that this prediction was correct.

In textbook chapters, the boldfaced headings serve as section "titles" and also are helpful in predicting content and organization. Considered together, chapter headings often suggest the development of ideas through the chapter.

For instance, the following headings appeared in a sociology text chapter titled "Energy and the Environment":

The Limits of Fossil Fuels

Nuclear Power: High Promises, Serious Risks

Conservation: The Hidden "Energy Source"

Solar Power: An Emerging Role

These headings reveal the author's approach to energy resources. We can predict that the chapter will describe the supply of fossil fuels as finite and nuclear power as risky; conservation and solar energy will be offered as viable alternatives.

## EXERCISE 1-4    Making Predictions

**Directions:** Predict the subject and/or point of view of each of the following essays or articles.

1. "The Nuclear Test-Ban Treaty: It's Time to Sign"

   *opposed to nuclear testing*

2. "Flunking Lunch: The Search for Nutrition in School Cafeterias"

   *cafeteria food lacks nutritional value*

3. "Professional Sports: Necessary Violence"

   *violence is an acceptable part of sports*

## EXERCISE 1-5    Making Predictions

**Directions:** Based on your previewing of "The Dilemma of Anger" on page 26, list at least three topics about which you expect to learn more. Also predict the author's purpose for writing. *Answers will vary. Possible answers include whether it is better to express anger or hold it in, strategies for anger management, ways to appropriately express anger.*

## Form Guide Questions

Did you ever read an entire page or more and not remember anything you read? Have you found yourself going from paragraph to paragraph without really thinking about what the writer is saying? Guide questions can help you overcome these problems. **Guide questions** are questions you expect to be able to answer while or after you read. Most students form them mentally, but you can jot them in the margin if you prefer.

The following tips can help you form questions and use them to guide your reading. It is best to develop guide questions *after* you preview but *before* you read.

1. **Turn each major heading into a series of questions.** The questions should ask something that you feel is important to know.

2. **As you read a section, look for the answers to your questions.** Highlight the answers as you find them.

3. **When you finish reading a section, stop and check to see whether you can recall the answers.** Place check marks by those you cannot recall. Then reread.

4. **Avoid asking questions that have one-word answers, like *yes* or *no*.** Questions that begin with *what, why,* or *how* are more useful.

Here are a few textbook headings and some examples of questions you might ask:

| HEADING | QUESTIONS |
|---|---|
| **Managing Interpersonal Conflict** | What is interpersonal conflict? What are strategies for managing conflict? |
| **Paralegals at Work** | What is a paralegal? What do paralegals do? |
| **Kohlberg's Theory of Moral Development** | Who was Kohlberg? How did Kohlberg explain moral development? |

## EXERCISE 1-6 Forming Guide Questions

**Directions:** Select the guide question that would be most helpful in improving your understanding of the textbook chapter sections that begin with the following headings:

___b___ 1. Defining Loneliness
    **a.** Is loneliness unusual?
    **b.** What does loneliness mean?
    **c.** Are adults lonelier than children?
    **d.** Can loneliness ever be positive?

___c___ 2. The Four Basic Functions of Management
    **a.** How important is management?
    **b.** Are there other functions of management?
    **c.** What are management's four basic functions?
    **d.** Do poor managers cause serious problems?

___c___ 3. Surface Versus Depth Listening
    **a.** Is surface listening difficult?
    **b.** What is listening?
    **c.** How do surface and depth listening differ?
    **d.** Is depth listening important?

___a___ 4. The Origins of the Cold War
    **a.** How did the Cold War start?
    **b.** Is the Cold War still going on?
    **c.** How did the United States deal with the Cold War?
    **d.** Did the Cold War end through compromise?

___b___ 5. Some People Are More Powerful than Others
    **a.** Does power affect relationships?
    **b.** Why are some people more powerful than others?
    **c.** What is power?
    **d.** Can people learn to become more powerful?

<table>
<tr><td>**EXERCISE 1-7**</td><td></td></tr>
</table>

# Writing Guide Questions

**Directions:** Use the headings in "The Dilemma of Anger" on page 26 to write guide questions that would help improve your understanding of the selection. *Possible answers are shown.*

1. Why should you let bodily arousal cool down before expressing anger?

2. Why is it important not to take a possible insult personally?

3. What is road rage? Why should you beware of road rage in yourself and others?

4. How can you use the right verbal and nonverbal language?

5. What results do you want from expressing your anger?

## Connect the Reading to Your Own Experience

Once you have previewed a reading, try to connect the topic to your own experience. Take a moment to recall what you already know or have read about the topic. This activity will make the reading more interesting and easier to write about. Here are a few suggestions to help you make connections:

- **Ask questions and answer them.** Suppose you have just previewed a reading titled "Advertising: Institutionalized Lying." Ask questions such as: *Do ads always lie? If not, why not? What do I already know about deceptive advertising?*

- **Brainstorm.** Jot down everything that comes to mind about the topic on a sheet of paper or in a computer file. For example, if the topic of a reading is "The Generation Gap," write down ideas as they occur to you. You might list reasons for such a gap, try to define it, or mention names of families in which you have observed it. For more about brainstorming, see Chapter 2, page 63.

- **Think of examples.** Try to think of situations, people, or events that relate to the topic. For instance, suppose you have previewed a reading titled "Fashions, Fads, and Crazes." You might think of recent examples of each: *pajamas as casual attire, iPods, or tattoos.*

Each of these techniques will help you identify ideas or experiences that you may share with the writer and that will help you focus your attention on the reading. In this book, the section titled "Thinking Before Reading," which comes before each selection, lists several questions that will help you make connections between the reading and your own experience.

<table>
<tr><td>**EXERCISE 1-8**</td><td></td></tr>
</table>

# Connecting the Reading to Your Own Experience

**Directions:** Based on your preview of "The Dilemma of Anger" on page 26, use one or more of the above techniques to connect the reading to your own experience. You might consider how you typically manage feelings of anger—whether you "let it out" or "bottle it up"—or think of situations in which you wish you had managed your anger differently.

# Highlight and Annotate As You Read

■ **GOAL 3**
Highlight and annotate as you read

Reading is time-consuming. To avoid having to reread an entire essay or chapter in order to review it or locate important ideas, be sure to highlight and annotate as you read.

- ■ Highlighting is a process of sorting ideas, identifying those that you need to learn, remember, or review.
- ■ Annotating, or making marginal notes, is a way of recording your thinking as you read.

## Highlight to Identify What Is Important

In some cases, the easiest and fastest way to mark important facts and ideas is to **highlight** them with a pen or highlighter. (Many students prefer highlighters because they come in different colors, such as bright yellow or pink, which draw the eye to important material.) When highlighting, you mark the portions of a reading that you need to study, remember, or locate quickly.

Here are a few suggestions for highlighting effectively.

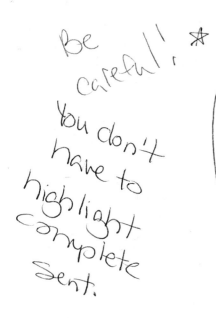

- ■ **Read a paragraph or section first,** then go back and highlight what is important.
- ■ **Highlight the topic sentence and any important details you want to remember.**
- ■ **Be accurate.** Make sure your highlighting reflects the content of the reading. Incomplete highlighting may cause you to miss the main point.
- ■ **Use a system for highlighting.** For instance, use two different highlighter colors to distinguish between topic sentences and supporting details.
- ■ **Highlight the right amount.** By highlighting too little, you miss valuable information. By highlighting too much, you are not identifying the most important ideas. As a general rule, the only complete sentences that should be highlighted are topic sentences. In all other sentences, highlight only key phrases or words.

Here is an example of effective highlighting:

> Money (or actually the lack of it) is a major source of stress for many people. In a sense, this is one of the most "valid" stressors because so many of our basic survival needs require money. Anyone struggling to survive on a small income is likely to feel plenty of stress. But money has significance beyond its obvious value as a medium of exchange. Even some of the wealthiest people become stressed over money-related issues. To some people, wealth is a measurement of human value, and their self-esteem is based on their material assets. Stress management for such people requires taking an objective look at the role money plays for them.

—Byer and Shainberg, *Living Well*, pp. 78–79

## Annotate to Record Your Thinking

**Annotation** is a way of jotting down your ideas, reactions, and opinions as you read. Think of annotation as recording your ideas while you read. It is a way to "talk back" to the author—to question, agree, disagree, or comment.

Annotations are particularly useful when you will be writing about what you have read.

Two different types of annotations are useful: *symbols and abbreviations*, and *statements and questions*. Depending on your preferences, you may choose to use one or both of these methods.

### Symbols and Abbreviations

Marking key parts of an essay with symbols or abbreviations can help you clarify meaning and remember key information. Table 1-1 provides a list of useful symbols and abbreviations. You should feel free to add to this list in any way that suits your reading and learning styles.

| TABLE 1-1   ANNOTATION SYMBOLS AND ABBREVIATIONS | | |
|---|---|---|
| **Type of Annotation** | | **Symbol and Example** |
| **Underlining key ideas** | | The <u>most prominent unions in the United States are among public-sector employees</u> such as teachers and police. |
| **Circling unknown words** | | One goal of labor unions is to address the apparent (asymmetry) of power in the employer–worker relationship. |
| **Marking definitions** | def. | To say that the balance of power favors one party over another is to introduce a disequilibrium. |
| **Marking examples** | ex. | Concessions may include additional benefits, increased vacation time, or higher wages. |
| **Numbering lists of ideas, causes, reasons, or events** | | The components of power include ① self-range, ② population, ③ natural resources, and ④ geography. |
| **Placing asterisks (stars) next to important passages** | * | Once a dominant force in the United States economy, labor unions have been shrinking over the last few decades. |
| **Putting question marks next to confusing passages** | ? | Strikes can be averted through the institutionalization of mediated bargaining. |
| **Marking possible test items** | T | A *closed shop* is a form of union agreement in which the employer agrees to hire only union workers. |
| **Drawing arrows to show relationships** | | Standing between managers and employees is the (shop steward), who is both a union employee and a rank-and-file worker within the company that employs union members. |
| **Marking summary statements** | sum. | The greater the degree of conflict between labor and management, the more sensitive the negotiations need to be. |
| **Marking essential information that you must remember** | | The largest and most important trade union in the United States, and the one that has had the most influence on labor-union relations, is the AFL-CIO. ! |
| **Noting author's opinion of or attitude toward the topic** | opinion | In a world where the gap between rich and poor is increasing, labor unions are essential to ensuring that workers are paid and treated fairly. |
| **Indicating material to reread later** | RR | At the apex of union density in the 1940s, only about 9.8 percent of public employees were represented by unions, while 33.9 percent of private, nonagricultural workers had such representation. In this decade, those proportions have essentially reversed, with 36 percent of public workers being represented by unions while private sector union density has plummeted to around 7 percent. |

Here is an example of an annotated reading:

> Sitting on the top rung of the class ladder is a powerful elite that consists of just 1 percent of the U.S. population. This <u>capitalist</u> class is so wealthy that it owns one-third of all the nation's assets. This tiny 1 percent is worth more than the entire bottom 90 percent of the country. <u>Power and influence</u> cling to this small elite. They have direct access to politicians, own major media and entertainment outlets (newspapers, magazines, TV stations, sports franchises), and control the boards of directors of our most influential colleges and universities.
>
> The capitalist class can be divided into "old money" and "new money." <u>The longer that wealth has been in a family, the more it adds to the family's prestige.</u> The children of old money (sometimes called <u>blue-bloods</u>) seldom mingle with "common" folk. Instead, they attend exclusive private schools where they learn ways of life that support their <u>privileged positions.</u> They don't work for wages; instead, many study business or become lawyers so that they can manage the family fortune. The people with "new money" are also known as the <u>nouveau riche.</u> Although they have made fortunes in business, entertainment, or sports, they are <u>outsiders to the upper class.</u> They have not attended the "right" schools, and they don't share the social networks that come with old money. Children of the new-moneyed can ascend into the top part of the capitalist class—if they go to the right schools *and* marry old money.

—Henslin, *Sociology*, p. 272

### Statements and Questions

In many of your writing assignments, you'll be asked to respond to an author's presentation, opinion, or suggestions. By recording your responses in the margin as you read, you take the first step toward writing about your own ideas.

Table 1-2 lists some types of statements and questions you might write in the margins of a reading. Note that it is perfectly acceptable to use abbreviations in your statements and questions. You should feel free to expand this list in any way that helps you "talk" with the reading.

| TABLE 1-2    RESPONDING TO A READING IN THE MARGIN | |
|---|---|
| Based on "The Dilemma of Anger," page 26 | |
| **Ways of Responding** | **Example of Marginal Annotation** |
| **Ask questions.** | What are the "right" verbal/nonverbal ways to express anger? |
| **Challenge the author's ideas.** | Not sounding off in the heat of anger is easier said than done! |
| **Look for inconsistencies.** | Plenty of examples of bad behavior here—need more examples of people showing anger appropriately. |
| **Add examples.** | Mom's cool-off strategies always mean exercise: take the dog for a run, swim laps, go for a long bike ride. |
| **Note exceptions.** | The problem is, sometimes your perception is accurate. How *do* you respond to an insult? |
| **Disagree with the author.** | Counting to 10 or 100 never really worked for me. |
| **Make associations with other sources.** | What does my physiology book say about the physical effects of anger/stress? |
| **Make judgments.** | This reading has some good ideas, but not all of them apply to me. |
| **Make notes to yourself.** | Try to find that online article from last year on tips for coping with road rage. |
| **Ask instructor to clarify.** | Ask prof: What do the authors mean by the "display rules" in other cultures? |

EXERCISE 1-9 | Highlighting and Annotating

**Directions:** Preview the following selection, "Is Bottled Water Safer Than Tap Water?" and then read, highlight, and annotate the selection using the techniques described above.

# Is Bottled Water Safer Than Tap Water?

1    Bottled water has become increasingly popular during the past 20 years. It is estimated that Americans drink almost 9 billion gallons of bottled water each year. Many people prefer the taste of bottled water to that of tap water. They also feel that bottled water is safer than tap water. Is this true?

2    The water we drink in the United States generally comes from two sources: surface water and groundwater.

- *Surface water* comes from lakes, rivers, and reservoirs. Common contaminants of surface water include runoff from highways, pesticides, animal wastes, and industrial wastes. Many of the cities across the United States get their water from surface-water sources.

- *Groundwater* comes from spaces between underground rock formations called *aquifers*. Many people who live in rural areas consume groundwater pumped from a well as their main water source. Hazardous substances leaking from waste sites, dumps, landfills, and oil and gas pipelines can contaminate groundwater. Groundwater can also be contaminated by naturally occurring substances, such as arsenic or high levels of iron in soil.

3    The most common chemical used to treat and purify our water is *chlorine*, which is effective in killing many dangerous microbes. Water treatment plants also routinely check water supplies for hazardous chemicals, minerals, and other contaminants. Because of these efforts, the United States has one of the safest water systems in the world.

4    The Environmental Protection Agency (EPA) sets and monitors the standards for our municipal water systems. The EPA does not monitor water from private wells, but it publishes recommendations for well owners to help them maintain a safe water supply. Local water regulatory agencies, such as cities and counties, must provide an annual report on specific water contaminants to all households served by that agency.

5    In contrast, the Food and Drug Administration (FDA) regulates bottled water. It does not require that bottled water meet higher quality standards than public water. Despite many people's assumptions, bottled water is taken from either surface-water or groundwater sources, the same as tap water. However, bottled water is often treated and filtered differently than tap water, which changes its taste and appearance.

6    Although bottled water may taste better to some than tap water, there is actually no evidence that it is safer to drink. Look closely at the label of your favorite bottled water. If the label states "From a public water source," it has come directly from the tap! Some types of bottled water may contain more minerals than tap water, but there are no other additional nutritional benefits of drinking bottled water. *Micron filtration* and *reverse osmosis* are two treatments that are very effective against the most common

waterborne disease–causing microorganisms. Purification of bottled water by filtration, carbon-filtration, particle-filtration, or treatment with ultraviolet light or ozone may be less effective, since these methods have not been proven to be effective against the most common disease-producing microbes.

7    Should you spend money on bottled water? The answer depends on personal preference and your source of drinking water. If you live in an area where you don't have reliable access to safe drinking water, bottled water may be your only safe water source. Whenever you choose to drink bottled water, look for brands that carry the trademark of the International Bottled Water Association (IBWA). This association follows the regulations of the FDA.

8    Be wary of vending machines dispensing filtered water where you can fill your own bottles. These machines may not be cleaned, and the filters may not be changed on a regular basis, so before using them, contact the vendor to determine how often and how they are serviced. If you get your water from a water cooler, make sure the cooler is cleaned once per month according to the manufacturer's instructions.

9    If you use a special or additional filtration system at home, be familiar with the specific contaminants it removes from your water, and make sure you change the filters regularly as recommended by the manufacturer. Be cautious of companies making claims about impurities in your tap water. If a private company tests your water and reports contamination, confirm those results with your local water agency. It could save you hundreds or thousands of dollars on an unnecessary or ineffective home water-purifying system.

10   For more information on drinking water safety, go to the EPA website at www .epa.gov. For information on bottled water, search the FDA website at www.fda.gov.

—Thompson and Manore, *Nutrition for Life*, p. 233

# Strengthen Your Comprehension and Recall

■ **GOAL 4**
Strengthen your comprehension and recall

For many daily activities, you maintain an awareness of how well you are performing them. In sports such as racquetball, tennis, or bowling, you know if you are playing a poor game; you actually keep score and deliberately try to correct errors and improve your performance. When preparing a favorite food, you often taste it as you cook to be sure it will turn out as you want. When washing your car, you check to be sure that you have not missed any spots.

A similar type of monitoring or checking should occur as you read. You need to keep score of how well you understand. Comprehension, however, is difficult to assess, because it is not always either good or poor. You may understand certain ideas you read and be confused by others. At times, comprehension may be incomplete—you may miss certain key ideas and not know you missed them.

## Pay Attention to Comprehension Signals

Think for a moment about what occurs when you read material you can understand easily, and then compare this with what happens when you read complicated material that is difficult to understand. When you read certain material, does it seem that everything clicks—that is, do ideas seem to fit together and make sense? Is that click noticeably absent at other times? The "Need to Know" box on p. 37 lists and compares common signals that may help you assess your comprehension. Not all signals appear at the same time, and not all signals work for everyone.

## ! NEED TO KNOW

### Comprehension Signals

| POSITIVE SIGNALS | NEGATIVE SIGNALS |
|---|---|
| Everything seems to fit and make sense; ideas flow logically from one to another. | Some pieces do not seem to belong; the material seems disjointed. |
| You understand what is important. | Nothing or everything seems important. |
| You are able to see where the author is leading. | You feel as if you are struggling to stay with the author and are unable to predict what will follow. |
| You are able to make connections among ideas. | You are unable to detect relationships; the organization is not apparent. |
| You read at a regular, comfortable pace. | You often slow down or reread. |
| You understand why the material was assigned. | You do not know why the material was assigned and cannot explain why it is important. |
| You can express the main ideas in your own words. | You must reread often and find it hard to paraphrase the author's ideas. |
| You recognize most words or can figure them out from the context. | Many words are unfamiliar. |
| You feel comfortable and have some knowledge about the topic. | The topic is unfamiliar, yet the author assumes you understand it. |

---

## EXERCISE 1-10     Assessing Your Comprehension

**Directions:** Answer the following questions based on your reading of the selection "Is Bottled Water Safer Than Tap Water?" on page 35. Answers will vary.

1. How would you rate your overall comprehension? What positive signals did you sense? Did you feel any negative signals? Did you encounter unfamiliar vocabulary?

2. Did you feel at any time that you had lost, or were about to lose, comprehension? If so, go back to that section now. What made that section difficult to read?

3. Do you think previewing, highlighting, and annotating strengthened your comprehension? If so, how?

## EXERCISE 1-11     Assessing Your Comprehension

**Directions:** Select a three- to four-page section of a chapter in one of your textbooks. Read the section, and then answer questions 1 and 3 in Exercise 1-10.
Answers will vary.

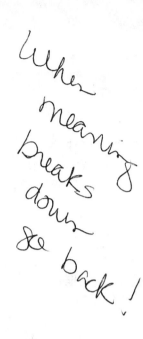

When meaning breaks down go back !

## Strengthen Your Comprehension

Whenever you sense your comprehension is weak or insufficient, take immediate action. Rereading is often *not* the best solution. Instead, try to figure out what is going wrong and change what you are doing. Ask yourself the following questions:

- **Could the time, place, or distractions be interfering with my reading?** If so, make changes.
- **Is vocabulary the problem?** If so, slow down, mark words you do not know, and look them up.
- **Is background knowledge the problem?** Often if you lack background information that a writer assumes you have, you will have comprehension difficulties. For example, if you are reading about global climate change, and the author assumes you know what greenhouse gases are but you don't, you would be unable to understand the greenhouse effect. You may have to Google a topic and read a bit about it before returning to the material you are reading.
- **Are you reading too fast?** Difficult, complex, or technical material requires very slow reading; adjust your rate.
- **Will reading aloud help?** Often hearing as well as seeing ideas helps to make them clearer.
- **Will writing help?** Outlining, drawing maps, and highlighting may help you examine each idea separately and then see how they fit together.

---

**EXERCISE 1-12**

*WORKING TOGETHER*

## Strengthening Your Comprehension

**Directions:** Find a difficult section in one of your textbooks; then work with a classmate to read each other's textbook sections and identify which strategies above would be most useful.

---

## Draw Idea Maps

An **idea map** is a visual picture of the organization and content of an essay. It is a drawing that enables you to see what is included in an essay in a brief outline form. Idea maps are used throughout this book for both reading and writing. For reading, you can use them to help you understand a reading by discovering how it is organized and studying how ideas relate to one another. For writing, an idea map can help you organize your own ideas and check to be sure that all the ideas you have included belong in the essay.

By filling in an idea map for a reading, you are reviewing the reading and analyzing its structure. Both of these activities will help you remember what you read. Though it takes time to draw, an idea map will save you time in the long run. You can avoid rereading, and the content of the essay will stick in your mind, preparing you for class discussions and writing about the reading. Use the model that follows to draw idea maps. You may need to add extra boxes or you may not need all the boxes included, depending on the number of ideas and details in the essay. The following model shows only the essay's main point (thesis) and the key ideas. You can draw idea maps that include details as well, if it suits your purpose.

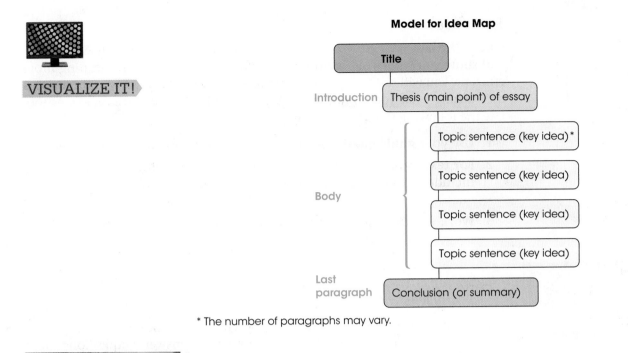

**Model for Idea Map**

* The number of paragraphs may vary.

---

**EXERCISE 1-13**

# Drawing Idea Maps

**Directions:** Read the professional essay "Liking and Loving: Interpersonal Attraction" on page 50. Draw an idea map of the essay using the model shown above as a guide.

---

## Review to Strengthen Recall

After finishing reading any essay or chapter once, you probably cannot recall everything you read. After reading, be sure to review and test yourself.

### Review Immediately After Reading

**Immediate review** is done right after you have finished reading an assignment or writing an outline or summary. When you finish any of these, you may feel like breathing a sigh of relief and taking a break. However, it is worth the time and effort to spend another five minutes reviewing what you just read and refreshing your memory. The best way to do this is to go back through the chapter and reread the headings, graphic material, introduction, summary, and any underlining or marginal notes.

Immediate review works because it consolidates, or draws together, the material just read. It also gives a final, lasting impression of the content. Considerable research has been done on the effectiveness of immediate review. Results indicate that review done immediately rather than delayed until a later time makes a large difference in the amount remembered.

### Review Periodically

Although immediate review will increase your recall of information, it will not help you retain information for long periods of time. To remember information over time, periodically refresh your memory. This is known as **periodic review**. Go back over the material on a regular basis. Do this by looking again at those sections that carry the basic meaning and reviewing your underlining, outlining, and/or summaries.

### Test Yourself

One of the best ways to remember what you read is to test yourself. Self-testing will show you what you do and do not know, thereby making learning more efficient. You will not waste time learning what you already know and can focus on learning what you do not know. Self-testing is good practice for exams too. Use the following steps to test yourself:

1. **Use your guide questions** (see p. 29). Check your ability to answer each.
2. **For textbooks, use all in- and end-of-chapter review materials.** These include self-checks, vocabulary lists, review questions, and discussion questions.
3. **Work with a classmate.** Practice asking and answering questions.

---

**EXERCISE 1-14**

*WORKING TOGETHER*

## Reviewing to Strengthen Your Recall

**Directions:** Working with a classmate, test each other on the selection "Is Bottled Water Safer Than Tap Water?" Take turns asking and answering questions about the reading.

---

# Read and Think About Visuals

■ GOAL 5
Read and think
about visuals

All **visual aids** share one goal: to illustrate concepts and help you understand them better. Visual aids work best when you read them *in addition to* the text, not *instead of* the text. Keep in mind that the author chose the visual aid, or **graphic**, for a specific purpose. To fully understand the reading, you should be able to explain that purpose.

## A General Approach to Reading Graphics

You will encounter many types of graphics in your reading materials. These include:

- ■ Photos
- ■ Charts
- ■ Infographics
- ■ Graphs
- ■ Diagrams

Here is a step-by-step approach to reading any type of graphic effectively. As you read, apply each step to Figure 1-1.

1. **Look for the reference in the text.** When you see a reference, finish reading the sentence, then look at the specific graphic. In some cases, you will need to go back and forth between the text and the graphic, especially if the graphic has multiple parts. Here is the reference in which Figure 1-1 originally appeared:

   > I'm going to reveal how you can make an extra $1,356 per month between the ages of 25 and 65. Is this hard to do? Actually, it is simple for some, and impossible for others. As Figure 1-1 shows, all you have to do is be born a male.

2. **Read the title and caption.** The **title** will identify the subject, and the **caption** will provide important information. In some cases, the caption

**FIGURE 1-1    THE GENDER PAY GAP, BY EDUCATION[1]**

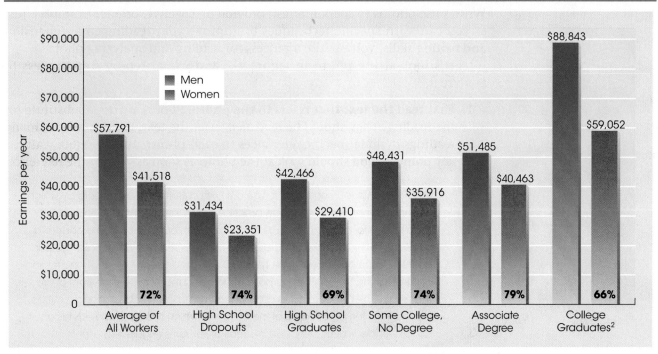

[1]Full-time workers in all fields. The percentage at the bottom of each red bar indicates the women's average percentage of the men's income.
[2]Bachelor's and all higher degrees, including professional degrees.

—Henslin, *Sociology: A Down-to-Earth Approach*, p. 317. By the author. Based on *Statistical Abstract of the United States 2009*: Table 681.

will specify the graphic's key take-away point. The title of Figure 1-1 makes the graph's subject clear: *the differences between men's and women's salaries.*

3. **Examine how the graphic is organized and labeled.** Read all headings and labels. **Labels** tell you what topics or categories are being discussed. Sometimes a label is turned sideways, like the words "Earnings per year" in Figure 1-1. Note that the title has a note (found at the bottom of the graphic) that provides information on how to read the graphic. The category "College Graduates" (at the bottom right of the figure) also has a note providing more specific information.

4. **Look at the legend.** The **legend** is the guide to the graphic's colors, terms, and other important information. In Figure 1-1, the legend appears toward the upper left and shows blue for men and red for women.

5. **Analyze the graphic.** Based on what you see, determine the graphic's key purpose. For example, is its purpose to show change over time, describe a process, present statistics? The purpose of Figure 1-1 is clear: it compares men's and women's salaries for a number of categories based on education level.

6. **Study the data to identify trends or patterns.** If the graphic includes numbers, look for unusual statistics or unexplained variations. What conclusions can you draw from the data?

7. **Make a brief summary note.** In the margin, jot a brief note summarizing the graphic's trend, pattern, or key point. Writing will help cement the idea in your mind. A summary note of Figure 1-1 might read, "Both male and female college graduates earn higher salaries than anyone else, but regardless of education level, men have historically earned more than women."

## Read and Analyze Photographs

Writers use photos to spark interest, provide perspective, or offer examples. Just as you can learn specific techniques to improve your reading comprehension and writing skills, you can use a process for reading and analyzing photos.

Let's look at the photo in Figure 1-2 and use a step-by-step process to analyze it.

1. **First read the text that refers to the photo.** Photos are not a substitute for the reading. They should be read *along with* the text. For this reason, many readings include specific references to each photo, usually directly after a key point, so you should look at the photo as soon as you see the reference.

> To counter our tendency to use our own culture as the standard by which we judge other cultures, we can practice cultural relativism; that is, we can try to understand a culture on its own terms. With our own culture embedded so deeply within us, however, practicing cultural relativism can challenge our orientations to life. For example, most U.S. citizens appear to have strong feelings against raising bulls for the purpose of stabbing them to death in front of crowds that shout "Olé!" According to cultural relativism, however, bullfighting must be viewed from the perspective of the culture in which it takes place—*its* history, *its* folklore, *its* ideas of bravery, and *its* ideas of sex roles (Figure 1-2).

—Henslin, *Sociology*, p. 39

**FIGURE 1-2    THE BULLFIGHT: CULTURAL EXPERIENCE OR ANIMAL CRUELTY?**

The photo will help you visualize the concept under discussion, making it easier to remember.

2. **Read the photo's title and/or caption.** The caption is usually placed above, below, or to the side of the photo and explains how the photo fits into the discussion.

3. **Ask: What is my first overall impression? Why has the author included this photo?** Because photos can be so powerful, they are often chosen

to elicit a strong reaction. For example, Figure 1-2 is quite violent; note the blood running down the side of the bull. What purpose is the author trying to achieve by including this photo?

4. **Examine the details.** Look closely at the picture, examining both the foreground and the background. Details can provide clues regarding the date and location of the photograph. For example, people's hairstyles and clothing often give hints to the year or decade. Landmarks help point to location. In Figure 1-2, you can see that bullfighting takes place in front of an audience. What point is the author making about the audience's cultural experiences and beliefs regarding bullfighting?

5. **Look for connections to society or your life.** Ask yourself how the photo relates to what you are reading or to your own experiences. For example, what are your own thoughts about bullfighting? Do you know anyone who feels differently? What are the sources of your disagreement?

## EXERCISE 1-15    Analyzing a Photograph

**Directions:** Flip through this book and choose a photo of interest to you. Analyze it according to the five-step process just outlined.

## Read and Analyze Bar and Line Graphs

A **graph** shows the relationship between two ideas, sometimes called *variables* because they can change depending on the circumstances. Graphs fall into two general categories:

- Bar graphs
- Line graphs

To read and understand a graph, do the following:

1. Read all the labels, which identify the variables.
2. Read the legend, which explains how the information is presented.
3. Summarize the graph's key points in a few sentences.

**Bar graphs** illustrate relationships with thick bars. Sometimes the bars are horizontal (left to right); sometimes they are vertical (up and down); and sometimes multiple sets of bars appear on one graph. Regardless of their format, bar graphs are often used to compare amounts. They are particularly useful for showing changes over time.

Figure 1-3 (p. 44) is a simple vertical bar graph showing the importance of small business in the United States. Part (a) of the graph shows that almost 86 percent of all U.S. companies have fewer than 20 employees. Part (b) shows that 25.6 percent of U.S. workers work at a company with fewer than 20 employees. Note a special feature of this graph: the author has included a built-in note summarizing the key point.

## FIGURE 1-3   THE IMPORTANCE OF SMALL BUSINESS IN THE UNITED STATES

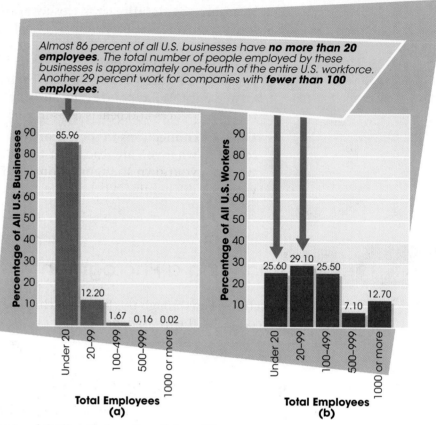

—Ebert and Griffin, *Business Essentials*, p. 38

**Line graphs** connect data points along a line. Connecting points in this manner often gives a sense of trends or changes over time. Sometimes only one variable is shown in a line graph, but it is common to see line graphs with multiple variables, as in Figure 1-4, which shows how Americans answer the question "How much of the time do you think you can trust the government?" changed over the period 1958–2006.

## FIGURE 1-4   THE DECLINE OF TRUST IN GOVERNMENT, 1958-2006

*This graph shows how people have responded over time to the following question: How much of the time do you think you can trust the government in Washington to do what is right—just about always, most of the time, or only some of the time?*

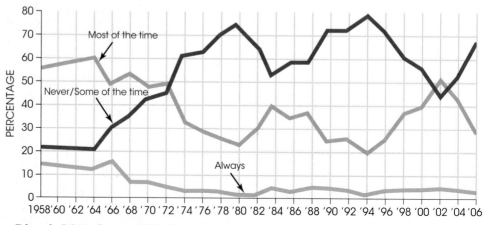

—Edwards, Wattenberg, and Lineberry, *Government in America: People, Politics, and Policy*, p. 201

| EXERCISE 1-16 | Reading and Analyzing Graphics |

**Directions:** Use Figures 1-3 and 1-4 to answer the following questions.

1. Write a brief summary statement for Figure 1-3.

   *Only about 2 percent of U.S. companies employ 100 workers or more.*

2. Use Figure 1-4 to complete this statement: The number of people saying they trust government *most of the time* reached its peak in  1964 , while the number of people saying that they trust the government *never/some of the time* reached its peak in  1994 . Trust in government was the highest in  1966 ; that was the year that the most people said they *always* trust the government to do what is right.

## Read and Analyze Charts and Diagrams

Unlike graphs, which illustrate two or more variables, a **chart** often focuses on just one variable or concept.

   **Pie charts**, also called *circle graphs*, show whole/part relationships. The pie or circle represents the whole (or 100 percent), and each "slice" of the pie represents a smaller part. Figure 1-5, a pie chart illustrating bias-motivated crimes (sometimes called *hate crimes*), indicates that racial bias is the most common cause of hate crimes.

| FIGURE 1-5  BIAS-MOTIVATED CRIMES |

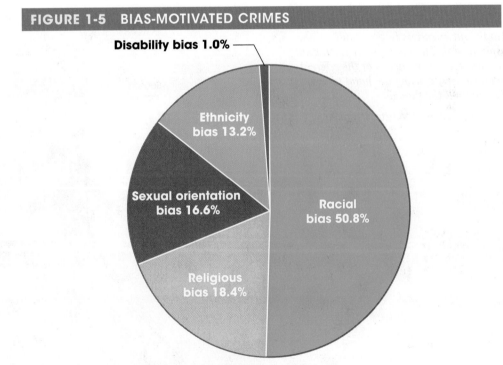

Disability bias 1.0%
Ethnicity bias 13.2%
Sexual orientation bias 16.6%
Racial bias 50.8%
Religious bias 18.4%

—Donatelle, *Health: The Basics, Green Edition*, p. 104

   A **diagram** is a simplified drawing showing the appearance, structure, or workings of something. Diagrams are common in technical and scientific readings and are used to introduce key vocabulary, show the parts of a system, and illustrate relationships. They often correspond to fairly large segments of text, requiring you to switch back and forth frequently between the text and the diagram. Consider the following excerpt from a psychology textbook:

The inside section of the spinal cord, which is made up of cell bodies separated by glial cells, is actually a primitive sort of "brain." This part of the spinal cord is responsible for certain reflexes—very fast, lifesaving reflexes. To understand how the spinal cord reflexes work, it is important to know there are three basic types of neurons: **afferent (sensory) neurons** that carry messages from the senses to the spinal cord, **efferent (motor) neurons** that carry messages from the spinal cord to the muscles and glands, and **interneurons** that connect the afferent neurons to the motor neurons and make up the inside of the spinal cord and much of the brain itself. [See Figure 1-6.] Touch a flame or a hot stove with your finger, for example, and an afferent neuron will send the pain message up to the spinal column where it enters into the central area of the spinal cord. The interneuron in that central area will then receive the message and send out a response along an efferent neuron, causing your finger to pull back. This all happens very quickly. If the pain message had to go all the way up to the brain before a response could be made, the response time would be greatly increased and more damage would be done to your finger.

## FIGURE 1-6   THE SPINAL CORD REFLEX

*The pain from the burning heat of the candle flame stimulates the afferent nerve fibers, which carry the message up to the interneurons in the middle of the spinal cord. The interneurons then send a message out by means of the efferent nerve fibers, causing the hand to jerk away from the flame.*

—Ciccarelli and White, *Psychology*, p. 56

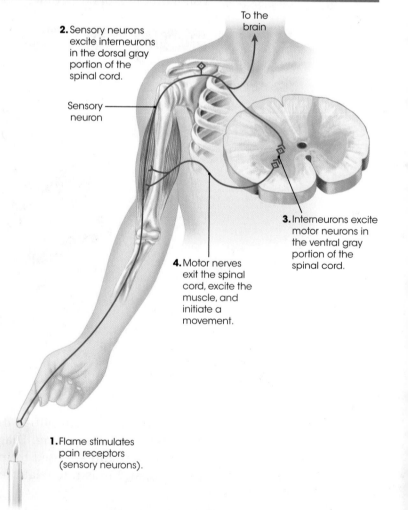

**2.** Sensory neurons excite interneurons in the dorsal gray portion of the spinal cord.

Sensory neuron

To the brain

**3.** Interneurons excite motor neurons in the ventral gray portion of the spinal cord.

**4.** Motor nerves exit the spinal cord, excite the muscle, and initiate a movement.

**1.** Flame stimulates pain receptors (sensory neurons).

## Read and Analyze Infographics

In recent years, a new type of visual aid called an *infographic* has become popular (see Figure 1-7 below). While the definition is not precise, **infographics** usually combine several types of visual aids into one, often merging photos with text, diagrams, or tables. Unlike other graphics, infographics are sometimes designed to stand on their own; they do not necessarily repeat or summarize what is in the text. Use these steps to read infographics:

1. **Identify the subject.** What is the purpose of the infographic?

2. **Identify how you should follow the "flow" of the infographic.** Should you read it from top to bottom, left to right, clockwise or counterclockwise? Look for visual clues, such as arrows or headings, to determine where you should start.

3. **Examine how the artist has chosen to present the information.** That is, how is the infographic organized? Does it fit into any particular pattern?

4. **How do the words and pictures work together?** How close is the correspondence between the words and the visual elements?

5. **When you've finished, describe the infographic and its information in your own words.** Try to draw it from memory. Compare your drawing with the infographic and take note of anything you forgot or misplaced.

**FIGURE 1-7   THE GENDER INCOME GAP BY LEVEL OF EDUCATION**

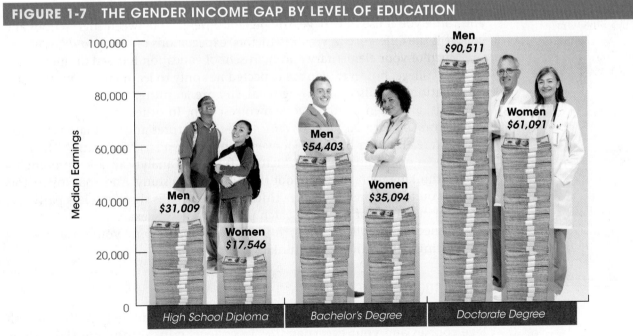

—Carl, *THINK Sociology*, p. 197

---

| EXERCISE 1-17 | Reading and Analyzing Charts, Diagrams, and Infographics |
|---|---|

**Directions:** Use Figures 1-5, 1-6 and 1-7 to answer the following questions.

1. Write a brief statement summarizing the two most common bias-based crimes (Figure 1-5). *The two most common bias-based crimes are based on racial bias (50.8 percent) or religious bias (18.4 percent).*

2. True or false? Hate crimes against gay people would fall into the "ethnicity bias" category of the pie chart (Figure 1-5). *False*

3. What types of neurons are stimulated by pain, such as a flame burning the finger (Figure 1-6)? *sensory or afferent neurons*

4. Which type of neuron acts as a "communicator" to and from the spinal cord (Figure 1-6)? *interneurons*

5. Without reading a word of the infographic (Figure 1-7), what do you think this visual is about? *Answers will vary. Difference in salaries for men and women*

6. What is the main point of the infographic? *Whatever level of education men have, they earn more than women with the same level of education.*

# *In College*
# Think Critically *Deep!*

■ GOAL 6
Think critically

While there will be some overlap between the skills you developed in high school and those you'll use in college, the biggest difference between high school and college is the difference in your instructors' expectations of how you *think*.

Much of your elementary and high school education focused on memorization. In college, however, you are expected not only to learn and memorize new information, but also to analyze what you are learning, formulate your own opinions, and even conduct your own research. In other words, your college instructors expect you to *think critically*—to interpret and evaluate what you hear and read, rather than accept everything you read as "the truth." The term *critical* does not mean "negative." Rather, it means "analytical" and "probing"—that is, thinking more deeply about the subjects you study. And your instructors expect you to demonstrate your critical thinking skills through class participation and in writing of essays, research papers, and essay exams.

To succeed in college, then, you will need to combine your basic reading and writing skills with critical thinking skills.

## The Value of Critical Thinking

The benefits of developing your critical thinking skills apply to both your college courses and your everyday life. In college, critical thinking skills allow you to

■ do well on essay exams

■ write effective essays and research papers

■ evaluate whether print and online sources are reliable

■ distinguish good information from bad, incomplete, inaccurate, or misleading information

In your everyday life, critical thinking skills will help you

- become a savvy consumer and make good financial choices
- understand when companies are trying to manipulate you with their advertising or public-relations efforts
- resolve conflicts or come to acceptable compromises
- solve problems using a logical, step-by-step process

College is about opening your mind to new ways of thinking and expressing those thoughts in writing. These new ways of thinking may challenge some of your attitudes, opinions, or beliefs. Be sure to recognize and analyze these different attitudes, opinions, and beliefs. Avoid the temptation to reject them only because they are different from yours.

This book will help you develop your critical thinking skills in several ways. Chapter 16 is devoted to more specific critical reading skills such as distinguishing between fact and opinion, making inferences, and writing for a specific audience and purpose. The questions that follow each end-of-chapter professional reading contain a section titled "Thinking Critically: Discussion and Journal Writing" that offers you practice in applying critical thinking skills.

| EXERCISE 1-18 | Thinking Critically |

**Directions:** Answer the following critical thinking questions for the reading "Is Bottled Water Safer Than Tap Water?" on page 35.

1. What is the authors' purpose for writing?

2. Do you think the authors are trying to influence your opinions?

3. Based on the reading, what do you think the authors see as valid reasons for drinking bottled water?

# INTEGRATING READING AND WRITING

# READ AND RESPOND: A Professional Essay

## Thinking Before Reading

This selection, taken from a psychology textbook, explores the factors surrounding attraction and love. This selection is a good example of the type of professional essay you will be asked to read in this book.

1. Preview the reading, using the steps discussed on page 25.

2. Connect the reading to your own experience by answering the following questions:

    a. What factors influence your choices in the people you want to know better?

    b. How would you define *love*?

3. Highlight and annotate as you read.

1200**L**/1398 words

# Liking and Loving:
## Interpersonal Attraction
### Saundra K. Ciccarelli and J. Noland White

1   Prejudice pretty much explains why people don't like each other. What does psychology say about why people like someone else? There are some "rules" for those whom people like and find attractive. Liking or having the desire for a relationship with someone else is called interpersonal attraction, and there's a great deal of research on the subject. (Who wouldn't want to know the rules?)

## The Rules of Attraction

**WHAT FACTORS GOVERN ATTRACTION AND LOVE, AND WHAT ARE SOME DIFFERENT KINDS OF LOVE?**

2   Several factors are involved in the attraction of one person to another, including both superficial physical characteristics, such as physical beauty and proximity, as well as elements of personality.

**PHYSICAL ATTRACTIVENESS**

3   When people think about what attracts them to other people, one of the topics that usually arises is the physical attractiveness of the other person. Some research suggests that physical beauty is one of the main factors that influence people's choices for selecting people they want to know better, although other factors may become more important in the later stages of relationships.

**PROXIMITY—CLOSE TO YOU**

4   The closer together people are physically, such as working in the same office building or living in the same dorm, the more likely they are to form a relationship. Proximity refers to being physically near someone else. People choose friends and lovers from the pool of people available to them, and availability depends heavily on proximity.

5   One theory about why proximity is so important involves the idea of repeated exposure to new stimuli. The more people experience something, whether it is a song, a picture, or a person, the more they tend to like it. The phrase "it grew on me" refers to this reaction. When people are in physical proximity to each other, repeated exposure may increase their attraction to each other.

**BIRDS OF A FEATHER—SIMILARITY**

6   Proximity does not guarantee attraction, just as physical attractiveness does not guarantee a long-term relationship. People tend to like being around others who are *similar* to them in some way. The more people find they have in common with others—such as attitudes, beliefs, and interests—the more they tend to be attracted to those others. Similarity as a factor in relationships makes sense when seen in terms of validation of a person's beliefs and attitudes. When other people

**interpersonal attraction**
liking or having the desire for a relationship with another person

**proximity**
physical or geographical nearness

hold the same attitudes and beliefs and do the same kinds of actions, it makes a person's own concepts seem more correct or valid.

### WHEN OPPOSITES ATTRACT

Isn't there a saying that "opposites attract"? Aren't people sometimes attracted to people who are different instead of similar?

*Isn't there a saying that "opposites attract"? Aren't people sometimes attracted to people who are different instead of similar?*

7    There is often a grain of truth in many old sayings, and "opposites attract" is no exception. Some people find that forming a relationship with another person who has *complementary* qualities (characteristics in the one person that fill a need in the other) can be very rewarding. Research does not support this view of attraction, however. It is similarity, not complementarity, that draws people together and helps them stay together.

### RECIPROCITY OF LIKING

8    Finally, people have a very strong tendency to like people who like them, a simple but powerful concept referred to as reciprocity of liking. In one experiment, researchers paired college students with other students. Neither student in any of the pairs knew the other member. One member of each pair was randomly chosen to receive some information from the experimenters about how the *other* student in the pair felt about the first member. In some cases, target students were led to believe that the other students liked them and, in other cases, that the targets disliked them.

**reciprocity of liking**
tendency of people to like other people who like them in return

*Famed athlete Joe DiMaggio and actress Marilyn Monroe are seen driving away after their 1954 marriage ceremony. While they had in common the fact that they were two of the most famous people in the United States at that time, many people viewed the marriage of the very modest and somewhat shy Joe to the outgoing, vivacious sex symbol that was Marilyn as an example of "opposites attract."*

9    When the pairs of students were allowed to meet and talk with each other again, they were friendlier, disclosed more information about themselves, agreed with the other person more, and behaved in a warmer manner *if they had been told* that the other student liked them. The other students came to like these students better as well, so liking produced more liking.

10    The only time that liking someone does not seem to make that person like the other in return is if a person suffers from feelings of low self-worth. In that case, finding out that someone likes you when you don't even like yourself makes you question his or her motives. This mistrust can cause you to act unfriendly to that person, which makes the person more likely to become unfriendly to you in a kind of self-fulfilling prophecy.

## Love Is a Triangle—Robert Sternberg's Triangular Theory of Love

11    Dictionary definitions of love refer to a strong affection for another person due to kinship, personal ties, sexual attraction, admiration, or common interests.

But those aren't all the same kind of relationships. I love my family and I love my friends, but in different ways.

*But those aren't all the same kind of relationships. I love my family and I love my friends, but in different ways.*

12    Psychologists generally agree that there are different kinds of love. One psychologist, Robert Sternberg, outlined a theory of what he determined were the three main components of love and the different types of love that combinations of these three components can produce.

### THE THREE COMPONENTS OF LOVE

13     According to Sternberg, love consists of three basic components: intimacy, passion, and commitment.

14     *Intimacy*, in Sternberg's view, refers to the feelings of closeness that one has for another person or the sense of having close emotional ties to another. Intimacy in this sense is not physical but psychological. Friends have an intimate relationship because they disclose things to each other that most people might not know, they feel strong emotional ties to each other, and they enjoy the presence of the other person.

15     *Passion* is the physical aspect of love. Passion refers to the emotional and sexual arousal a person feels toward the other person. Passion is not simply sex; holding hands, loving looks, and hugs can all be forms of passion.

16     *Commitment* involves the decisions one makes about a relationship. A short-term decision might be, "I think I'm in love." An example of a more long-term decision is, "I want to be with this person for the rest of my life."

### THE LOVE TRIANGLES

17     A love relationship between two people can involve one, two, or all three of these components in various combinations. The combinations can produce seven different forms of love, as seen in Figure A.

**romantic love**
type of love consisting of intimacy and passion

18     Two of the more familiar and more heavily researched forms of love from Sternberg's theory are romantic love and companionate love. When intimacy and passion are combined, the result is the more familiar romantic love, which is sometimes called passionate love by other researchers. Romantic love is often the basis for a more lasting relationship. In many Western cultures, the ideal relationship begins with liking, then becomes romantic

### FIGURE A   STERNBERG'S TRIANGULAR THEORY OF LOVE

*This diagram represents the seven different kinds of love that can result from combining the three components of love: intimacy, passion, and commitment. Notice that some of these types of love sound less desirable or positive than others. What is the one key element missing from the less positive types of love?*

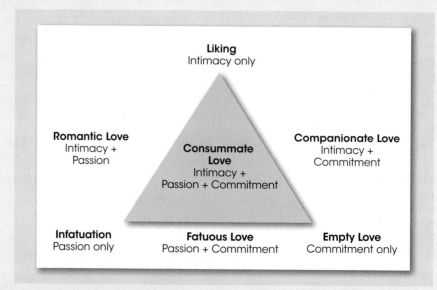

*Source:* Adapted from Sternberg (1986b).

love as passion is added to the mix, and finally becomes a more enduring form of love as a commitment is made.

19    When intimacy and commitment are the main components of a relationship, it is called companionate love. In companionate love, people who like each other, feel emotionally close to each other, and understand one another's motives have made a commitment to live together, usually in a marriage relationship. Companionate love is often the binding tie that holds a marriage together through the years of parenting, paying bills, and lessening physical passion. In many non-Western cultures, companionate love is seen as more sensible. Choices for a mate on the basis of compatibility are often made by parents or matchmakers rather than the couple themselves.

**companionate love**
type of love consisting of intimacy and commitment

20    Finally, when all three components of love are present, the couple has achieved *consummate love*, the ideal form of love that many people see as the ultimate goal. This is also the kind of love that may evolve into companionate love when the passion lessens during the middle years of a relationship's commitment.

—Ciccarelli and White, *Psychology*, pp. 365–367

# Getting Ready to Write

## Checking Your Comprehension

Answer each of the following questions using complete sentences.

1. What does interpersonal attraction mean?
2. According to the reading, what factors are involved in the attraction of one person to another?
3. Explain the concept of reciprocity of liking.
4. What are the three components of Robert Sternberg's theory of love? Define each component.
5. Describe the components of *romantic love*, *companionate love*, and *consummate love*.

## Strengthening Your Vocabulary

Using the word's context, word parts, or a dictionary, write a brief definition of each of the following words as it is used in the reading.

1. interpersonal (paragraph 1) between people
2. superficial (paragraph 2) surface; external
3. validation (paragraph 6) confirmation
4. disclosed (paragraph 9) told, shared
5. prophecy (paragraph 10) prediction
6. binding (paragraph 19) uniting
7. evolve (paragraph 20) develop; turn into

## Examining the Reading: Using Idea Maps

Review the reading by completing the missing parts of the following idea map.

**VISUALIZE IT!**

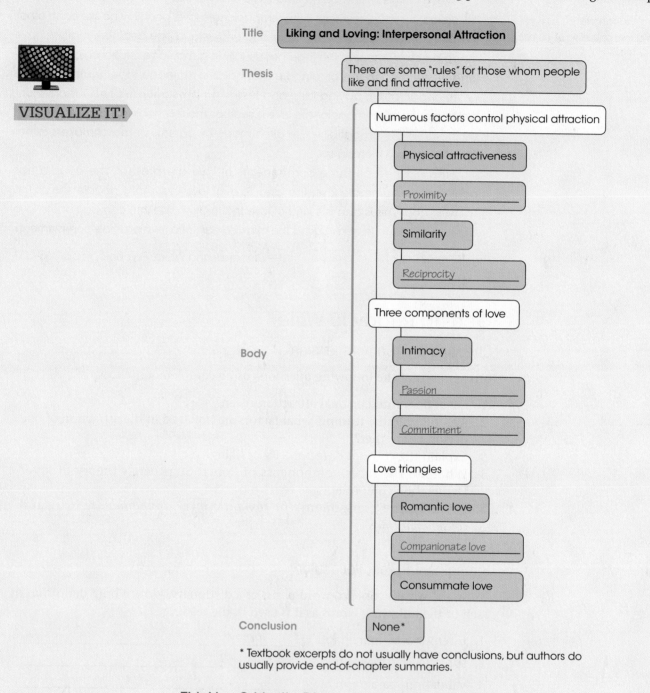

Title: **Liking and Loving: Interpersonal Attraction**

Thesis: There are some "rules" for those whom people like and find attractive.

Body:

Numerous factors control physical attraction
- Physical attractiveness
- Proximity
- Similarity
- Reciprocity

Three components of love
- Intimacy
- Passion
- Commitment

Love triangles
- Romantic love
- Companionate love
- Consummate love

Conclusion: None*

\* Textbook excerpts do not usually have conclusions, but authors do usually provide end-of-chapter summaries.

## Thinking Critically: Discussion and Journal Writing

React and respond to the reading by discussing the following:

1. Discuss the idea that opposites attract. Do you find it more rewarding to form a relationship with someone who has similar qualities or complementary qualities?

2. What are the factors that make you want to know someone better? What are the qualities you look for in a friend or romantic interest?

3. Write a journal entry giving examples from your own experience that illustrate the concepts of proximity, similarity, complementarity, and reciprocity of liking.

## Thinking and Writing Critically

**THINKING VISUALLY**

1. What is the authors' purpose for writing this? How well do they achieve their purpose?

2. For what audience is this selection written?

3. Why did the authors include the photo of Joe DiMaggio and Marilyn Monroe?

4. Consider the seven different kinds of love shown in Figure A. Which types of love sound least desirable or positive? What element is missing from the less positive types of love?

5. What types of evidence do the authors use to support their ideas? How convincing or believable is the evidence?

## MySkillsLab®

**Complete** this Exercise

## Writing About the Reading

### Paragraph Options

1. Write a paragraph exploring the idea that "liking produces more liking." Have you ever experienced this in your own life?

2. The reading discusses a number of different kinds of love. Write a paragraph identifying the type of love that you consider ideal. Be sure to define it and give reasons for your choice.

3. Write a paragraph giving your own "dictionary definition" of love, or different types of love. Include examples of the people you love.

### Essay Options

4. Do the "rules of attraction" described in the selection reflect your own experiences? Write an essay exploring the different factors in interpersonal attraction. What qualities make you want to know someone better? How important to you are each of the factors described in the selection?

5. Consider the author's reference to non-Western cultures in which choices for a mate are often made by parents or matchmakers (paragraph 19). How would you respond to someone else's choosing your mate? What advantages and disadvantages can you imagine in this situation? Write an essay exploring the answers.

6. The authors state that one form of love may evolve into another. Do some forms of love remain the same? Have you observed an evolution in any of your relationships or in those of others around you? Consider friendships and family relationships as well as romantic relationships, and write an essay exploring these questions.

# SELF-TEST SUMMARY

To test yourself, cover the Answer column with a sheet of paper and answer each question in the left column. Evaluate each of your answers as you work by sliding the paper down and comparing your answer with what is printed in the Answer column.

| QUESTION | ANSWER |
|---|---|
| ■ **GOAL 1** Read actively<br><br>What is involved in active reading? | Active reading involves reading each assignment differently, thinking and asking questions as you read, sorting the information as you read, and reviewing after reading. |
| ■ **GOAL 2** Preview before reading<br><br>What is previewing? | Previewing is a way of quickly familiarizing yourself with the organization and content of written material *before* beginning to read it. See the "Need to Know" box on page 23 for specific steps in previewing. |
| ■ **GOAL 3** Highlight and annotate as you read<br><br>What are highlighting and annotating? | Highlighting is a process of sorting ideas, identifying those that you need to learn, remember, or review. Annotating, or making marginal notes, is a way of recording your thinking as you read. |
| ■ **GOAL 4** Strengthen your comprehension and recall<br><br>What strategies can I use to strengthen my comprehension and recall? | Pay attention to comprehension signals, draw idea maps, use immediate and periodic review after reading, and test yourself. |
| ■ **GOAL 5** Read and think about visuals<br><br>Why is it important to read and think about visuals? | Visuals allow you to understand main ideas, implied main ideas, and details very quickly and retrieve the information more easily. |
| ■ **GOAL 6** Think critically<br><br>What is critical thinking? | Critical thinking means interpreting and evaluating what you hear and read, rather than accepting everything as "the truth." Critical thinking skills are important in college and in everyday life. |

# MySkillsLab

For more help with **Active Reading,** go to your learning path in MySkillsLab at http://www.myskillslab.com.

# The Writing Process:
# An Overview

## THINK About It!

## The Writing Process

In the photo above, the students are completing an assignment for their reading–writing class. They are reading an assignment and writing an essay in response to it. Write a few sentences describing what the students might be feeling, using your own experiences with reading and writing as a guide. What problems might they be facing? What things can they do well? What are possible trouble spots?

Did you identify problems and trouble spots such as not understanding the reading assignment, not knowing what to write about, not knowing what to say, or not knowing how to produce a clear, correct paper? This chapter will give you an overview of the writing process and begin to address some of the writing problems you may have identified.

## FOCUSING ON READING AND WRITING

# What Is the Writing Process?

Writing is a skill that you can learn with the help of this book, your instructor, and your classmates. Like any other skill, such as basketball, accounting, or cooking, writing requires both instruction and practice. Be sure to focus your attention on new techniques suggested by your instructor as well as the ones given in each chapter of this book. To improve, you often need to be open to doing things differently. Expect success; don't hesitate to experiment.

In this chapter you will see that there is much more to writing than sitting down at your computer and starting to type. It involves reading the ideas of others, generating and organizing your own ideas, and expressing your ideas in sentence, paragraph, and essay form. Writing is a process that involves working through and going back and forth among several steps. Once a draft is written, it also involves reading, rereading, and revising your work. Following the sample student writing in this chapter will give you a good sense of what writing involves.

## WRITING

# Understand What Writing Is and Is Not

The following list explains some correct and incorrect notions about writing:

*Writing is . . .*

- following a step-by-step process of planning, drafting, and revising
- thinking through and organizing ideas
- explaining *your* ideas or experiences clearly and correctly
- using precise, descriptive, and accurate vocabulary
- constructing clear, understandable sentences
- a skill that can be learned

*Writing is not . . .*

- being able to pick up a pen (or sit at a computer) and write something wonderful on your first try
- developing new, earthshaking ideas no one has ever thought of before
- being primarily concerned with grammatical correctness
- showing off a large vocabulary
- constructing long, complicated sentences

### EXERCISE 2-1 | Describing the Writing Process

**Directions:** Suppose you are writing a letter to a toy manufacturer about a defective toy you purchased for your niece or nephew. You feel the toy is unsafe for toddlers. Describe, step by step, how you would go about writing this letter.

(What is the first thing you would do? What would you do after that? And so forth.) You are not actually writing the letter in this exercise or listing what you would say. You are describing your writing *process*.

# Practical Advice About Writing

■ **GOAL 1**
Get the most out of your writing class

Use the following suggestions for becoming a successful writer.

## Get the Most Out of Your Writing Class

Attend all classes. Do not miss any classes, and be sure to come prepared to class with readings and writing assignments complete. Take notes during class, and ask questions about things you do not understand. Be sure to participate in class discussions and attend all writing conferences offered by your instructor.

## Take a Positive Approach to Writing

Use the following tips to achieve success:

### Think First, Then Write

Writing is a thinking process: it is an expression of your thoughts. Don't expect to be able to pick up a pen or sit down at a computer and immediately produce a well-written paragraph or essay. Plan to spend time generating ideas and deciding how to organize them before you write your first draft.

### Plan on Making Changes

Most writers revise (rethink, rewrite, change, add, and delete) numerous times before they are pleased with their work. For example, I revised this chapter of *In Harmony* five times before I was satisfied with it.

### Give Yourself Enough Time to Write

For most of us, writing does not come easily. It takes time to think, select a topic, generate ideas, organize them, draft a piece of writing, revise it, and proofread it. Reserve a block of time each day for writing. Use the time to read this book and to work on its writing exercises and assignments. Begin by reserving an hour per day. This may seem like a lot of time. However, most instructors expect you to spend at least two hours outside of class for every hour you spend in class. If your writing class meets for a total of three hours per week, then you should spend at least six hours per week working on writing.

### Develop a Routine

Try to work at the same time each day. You will develop a routine that will be easy to follow. Be sure to work at peak periods of concentration. Don't write when you are tired, hungry, or likely to be interrupted.

### Take Breaks

If you get stuck and cannot think or write, take a break. Clear your mind by going for a walk, talking to a friend, or having a snack. Set a time limit for your break, though, so you return to work in a reasonable time. When you begin again, start by rereading what you have already written. If you still cannot make progress, use freewriting, brainstorming, and branching techniques (see pp. 62–64) to generate more ideas about your topic.

## Keep a Journal

A **writing journal** is a collection of your writing and reflections. Keeping a writing journal is an excellent way to <u>improve your writing and keep track of your thoughts and ideas.</u>

### How to Keep a Writing Journal

1. Buy an 8.5-by-11-inch spiral-bound notebook. Use it exclusively for journal writing. Alternatively, you can use a computer file.

2. Reserve ten to fifteen minutes a day to write in your journal. Write every day, not just on days when a good idea strikes.

3. Write about whatever comes to mind. You might write about events that happened and your reactions to them, or describe feelings, impressions, or worries.

If you have trouble getting started, ask yourself some questions:

- What happened at school, work, or home?

- What world, national, or local events occurred?

- What am I worried about?

- What is a positive experience I have had lately? Maybe it was eating a good meal, making a new friend, or finding time to wash your car.

- What did I see today? Practice writing descriptions of beautiful, funny, interesting, or disturbing things you've noticed.

- What is the best or worst thing that happened today?

- Who did I talk to? What did I talk about? Record conversations as fully as you can.

### Sample Journal Entries

The following student journal entries will give you a better picture of journal writing. They have been edited for easy reading. However, as you write, do not be concerned with neatness or correctness.

> *Jeffrey*  The best thing that happened today happened as soon as I got home from work. My cell phone rang. At first, I wasn't going to answer it because I was tired and in one of those moods when I wanted to be by myself. It rang so many times I decided to answer it. Am I glad I did! It was MaryAnn, a long-lost girlfriend whom I'd always regretted losing touch with. She said she had just moved back into the neighborhood, and . . . I took it from there.

*Acacia*   This morning while walking across campus to my math class, I stopped for a few minutes under a chestnut tree. Perfect timing! I've always loved collecting chestnuts, and they were just beginning to fall. When I was a kid, I used to pick up lunch bags full of them. I never knew what to do with them once I had them. I just liked picking them up, I guess. I remember liking their cold, sleek, shiny smoothness and how good they felt in my hand. So I picked up a few, rubbed them together in my hand, and went off to class, happy that some things never change.

### Benefits of Journal Writing

When you write in your journal, you are practicing writing and becoming better at expressing your thoughts in writing. You can practice without pressure or fear of criticism. Besides practice, journal writing has other benefits:

■ Your journals will become a good source of ideas. When you have a paper assigned and must select your own topic, review your journal for ideas.

■ You may find that journal writing becomes a way to think through problems, release pent-up feelings, or keep an enjoyable record of life experiences. Journal writing is writing *for yourself.*

## Use Peer Review

Not everything you write in a college writing class needs to be graded by your instructor. Instead, you can get valuable "peer review," or feedback, from other members of your class. Peers (classmates) can tell you what they like and what they think you need to do to improve your writing. You can also learn a lot from reading and commenting on the work of other students. To learn more about peer review, see page 73 later in this chapter.

# Five Steps in the Writing Process

■ GOAL 2
Use the writing process

Writing, like many other skills, is not a single-step process. Think of the game of football, for instance. Football players spend a great deal of time planning and developing offensive and defensive strategies, trying out new plays, improving existing plays, and practicing. Writing involves similar planning and preparation. It also involves testing ideas and working out the best way to express them. Writers often explore how their ideas might "play out" in several ways before settling upon one plan of action.

People have many individual techniques for writing, but all writing involves five basic steps, as shown in Table 2-1.

### Tip for Writers

A *draft* is a piece of writing that is not finished.

*Revising* is the process of rethinking your ideas. It involves adding ideas, deleting ideas, rearranging ideas, and changing the way you have expressed your thoughts.

| **TABLE 2-1** | |
| --- | --- |
| **Steps in the Writing Process** | **Description of Steps** |
| 1. Generating ideas | Finding ideas to write about. |
| 2. Organizing your ideas | Discovering ways to arrange your ideas logically. |
| 3. Writing a first draft | Expressing your ideas in sentence and paragraph form without worrying about spelling, punctuation, capitalization, and grammar. |
| 4. Revising | Rethinking your ideas and finding ways to make your writing clearer, more complete, and more interesting. Revising involves changing, adding, deleting, and rearranging your ideas and words to make your writing better. |
| 5. Proofreading | Checking for errors in grammar, spelling, punctuation, and capitalization. |

> ## ❗ NEED TO KNOW
>
> ### The Writing Process
> - Writing is a step-by-step process of explaining your ideas and experiences.
> - Writing involves five basic steps: generating ideas, organizing your ideas, writing a first draft, revising, and proofreading.

# Generate Ideas

■ **GOAL 3**
Generate ideas

Before you can write about a topic, you have to collect ideas to write about. Because many students need help with this right away, three helpful techniques are described here: (1) freewriting, (2) brainstorming, and (3) branching. Here is a brief introduction to each.

## Freewriting

*What is freewriting?*   Freewriting is writing nonstop about a topic for a specified period of time.

*How does freewriting work?*   You write whatever comes into your mind, and you do not stop to be concerned about correctness. After you have finished, you go back through your writing and pick out ideas that you might be able to use.

*What does it look like?*   Here is a sample of freewriting done on the topic of owning a dog.

### Sample Freewriting

I really wish I had a dog. I need some what's it called . . . oh, yeah, unconditional love. Something that never gets mad at me, no matter what I do. Jumping up and happy whenever it sees me. Definitely loves me best. I could teach it tricks, like roll over and speak or dance with me. Maybe I could get on TV, like Letterman's Stupid Pet Tricks or Those Amazing Animals. What breeds are the smartest? I don't want one that's so big I can't lift it by myself. But I hate those yappy little ones that shiver all the time. I saw a woman walking one once in the winter. It had a little coat on that matched the woman's coat. I wouldn't do something that lame. How do you get them to be good guard dogs? Guess I'd have to pay for training. Ow. What else would I have to pay for; shots, neutering, bed, collar, vet bills? I can't afford that stuff, even if I get a mutt from the shelter. Can I take it to work? Ha! I can just see my boss's face when I walk in with a giant, slobbering Newfoundland! There goes that job. And how could I get home to walk it in between work and class? I only have half an hour. Guess I'd better wait.

# Brainstorming

*What is brainstorming?* Brainstorming is making a list of everything you can think of that has to do with your topic.

*How does brainstorming work?* Try to stretch your imagination and think of everything related to your topic. Include facts, ideas, examples, questions, and feelings. When you have finished, read through what you have written and highlight usable ideas.

*What does brainstorming look like?* Imagine that you have been asked to write an essay about "identity" and how you see yourself. Here is the brainstorming list that one student, Santiago Quintana Garcia, wrote about his identity.

---

Identity—Mexican? White? Very arbitrary and flimsy

Easily deconstructed when seen from the edges

Not wrong to subscribe to a certain identity

Everyone has their in-betweens, not all race and nationality

Mexican stereotype: I don't look Mexican. I'm foreign in my own country/race

White: Not quite. I *am* Mexican after all.

Creates a struggle between the ideal and the reality, from this comes synthesis, movement

Feelings of not belonging as a teenager. No comfort objects. No cushion to fall back to easily, BUT growth and awareness.

I am Mexican. I still subscribe but with a lot more awareness of how that label is not representative and exhaustive. It is necessary; practical.

Living in between = energy, movement, growth.

---

This chapter will follow Santiago through the writing process, from brainstorming through drafting (see p. 70) and revising (see p. 72).

# Branching

*What is branching?* Branching is a way of using diagrams or drawings to generate ideas.

*How does branching work?* Begin by drawing a 2-inch oval in the middle of a page. Write your topic in that oval. Think of the oval as a tree trunk. Next, draw lines radiating out from the trunk, as branches would. Write an idea related to your topic at the end of each branch. When you have finished, highlight the ideas you find most useful.

*What does branching look like?*   Here is a sample of branching done on the topic of religious holidays:

## Practicing Generating Ideas

**Directions:** Choose one of the following topics. Then try out two of the techniques described for generating ideas.

1. Identity theft
2. Internet communication
3. Telemarketing
4. Advertising ploys and gimmicks
5. Airport security

# Organize Ideas

■ GOAL 4
Organize ideas

Two common methods of organizing ideas are outlining and idea mapping. Understanding each of them will help you decide how to arrange the ideas that you have identified as useful.

## Outlining

*What is outlining?*   Outlining is a method of listing the main points you will cover and their subpoints (details) in the order in which you will present them.

*How does outlining work?*   To make an outline of a paragraph or essay, you list the most important ideas on separate lines at the left margin of a sheet of paper, leaving space underneath each idea. In the space under each main idea, list the details that you will include to explain that main idea. Indent the list of details that fits under each of your most important ideas.

*What does outlining look like?*   As a sample, here is an outline Santiago wrote for paragraph 4 of the first draft of his essay on page 70.

### Sample Paragraph Outline for Santiago's Essay

I.  Living in two worlds
    A.  Never completely part of either world
        1.  Complicated
        2.  Interesting
    B.  Living in between encourages growth and maturity
        1.  Nothing to hold onto
        2.  Effects of culture
    C.  Living in between offers a vantage point
        1.  Analyze opinions and habits
        2.  See virtues and faults through different eyes
    D.  Live where outsider meets insider

## Idea Mapping

*What is idea mapping?*   An idea map is a drawing that shows the content and organization of a piece of writing.

*How does idea mapping work?*   An idea map shows you how ideas are connected and can help you see which ideas are not relevant to the topic of your paragraph or essay.

*What does an idea map look like?*   Here is a sample idea map drawn for a paragraph on the topic of choosing an Internet password:

**VISUALIZE IT!**

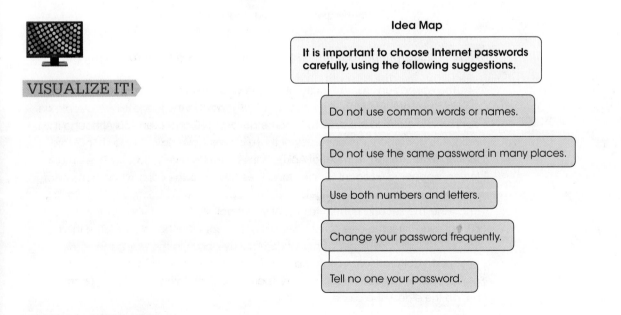

**Idea Map**

It is important to choose Internet passwords carefully, using the following suggestions.

Do not use common words or names.

Do not use the same password in many places.

Use both numbers and letters.

Change your password frequently.

Tell no one your password.

---

**EXERCISE 2-3**

**WRITING IN PROGRESS**

## Using Outlining or Mapping

**Directions:** For the topic you chose in Exercise 2-2, use outlining or idea mapping to organize your ideas for a paragraph.

# Write Paragraphs

A **paragraph** is a group of sentences, usually at least three or four, that expresses one main idea. Paragraphs may stand alone to express one thought, or they may be combined into essays. Paragraphs are one of the basic building blocks of writing, so it is important to learn to write them effectively.

A paragraph's one main idea is expressed in a single sentence called the **topic sentence**. The other sentences in the paragraph, called **supporting details**, explain or support the main idea. You can visualize a paragraph as follows:

VISUALIZE IT!

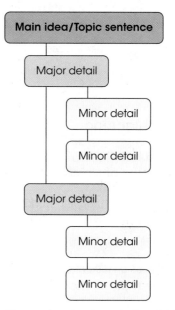

*The number of major and minor details may vary.

Here is a sample paragraph; its idea map appears on the following page.

The Abkhasians (an agricultural people who live in a mountainous region of Georgia, a republic of the former Soviet Union) may be the longest-lived people on earth. Many claim to live past 100—some beyond 120 and even 130. Although it is difficult to document the accuracy of these claims, government records indicate that an extraordinary number of Abkhasians do live to a very old age. Three main factors appear to account for their long lives. The first is their diet, which consists of little meat, much fresh fruit, vegetables, garlic, goat cheese, cornmeal, buttermilk and wine. The second is their lifelong physical activity. They do slow down after age 80, but even after the age of 100 they still work about four hours a day. The third factor—a highly developed sense of community—goes to the very heart of the Abkhasian culture. From childhood, each individual is integrated into a primary group, and remains so throughout life. There is no such thing as a nursing home, nor do the elderly live alone.

—adapted from Henslin, *Sociology*, pp. 380–381

**VISUALIZE IT!**

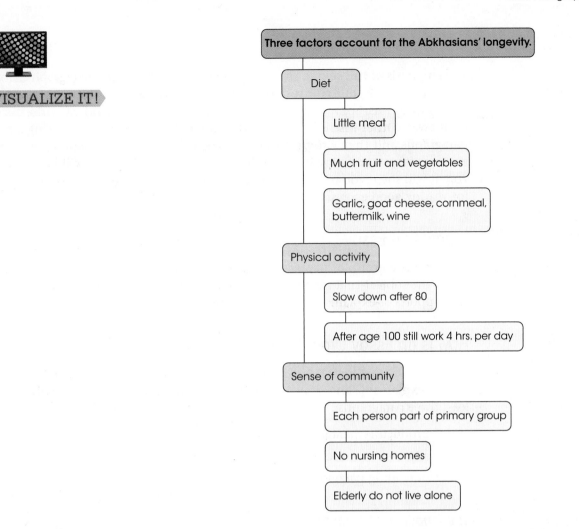

Three factors account for the Abkhasians' longevity.

Diet
- Little meat
- Much fruit and vegetables
- Garlic, goat cheese, cornmeal, buttermilk, wine

Physical activity
- Slow down after 80
- After age 100 still work 4 hrs. per day

Sense of community
- Each person part of primary group
- No nursing homes
- Elderly do not live alone

---

## EXERCISE 2-4

**WRITING IN PROGRESS**

## Writing a Paragraph

**Directions:** Using one or more of the ideas you generated and organized in Exercises 2-2 and 2-3, write a paragraph about the topic you chose.

---

## EXERCISE 2-5

*WORKING TOGETHER*

## Writing a Paragraph

**Directions:** Write a paragraph on one of the following topics. Be sure to begin with a sentence that states the one idea your paragraph is about.

TOPIC 1.  Describe a space alien's fear or surprise when stepping out of a spaceship onto Earth. Explain what the alien sees or hears and how it reacts to what it sees.

TOPIC 2.  Describe your reaction to your first day of college classes. Include specific examples to support your description.

Working with a classmate, compare and evaluate each other's paragraphs. Is the opening sentence clear? Is that idea explained in the remainder of the paragraph?

# Write Essays

■ GOAL 6
Write essays

The emphasis of this text is on writing effective sentences and paragraphs. However, in some of your courses your instructors may ask you to write essays or take essay exams. Some writing instructors prefer that their students write essays right away. Other instructors prefer that their students begin by writing single paragraphs and then progress to essay writing. Regardless of when you begin writing essays, the following introduction to essay techniques will be useful to you. It will show you why good paragraph-writing skills are absolutely necessary for writing good essays.

## What Is an Essay?

An **essay** is a group of paragraphs about one subject. It contains one key idea about the subject that is called the **thesis statement**. Each paragraph in the essay supports or explains some aspect of the thesis statement.

## How Is an Essay Organized?

An essay follows a logical and direct plan: it introduces an idea (the thesis statement), explains it, and draws a conclusion. Therefore, an essay usually has at least three paragraphs:

1. Introductory paragraph
2. Body (one or more paragraphs)
3. Concluding paragraph

### The Introductory Paragraph

Your **introductory paragraph** should accomplish three things:

- It should establish the topic of the essay.
- It should present the thesis statement of your essay in an appropriate way for your intended audience.
- It should interest your audience in your essay.

### The Body

The **body** of your essay should accomplish three things:

- It should provide information that supports and explains your thesis statement.
- It should present each main supporting point in a separate paragraph.
- It should contain enough detailed information to make the main point of each paragraph understandable and believable.

### The Concluding Paragraph

Your **concluding paragraph** should accomplish two things:

- It should reemphasize but not restate your thesis statement.
- It should draw your essay to a close.

You can visualize the organization of an essay using the following idea map:

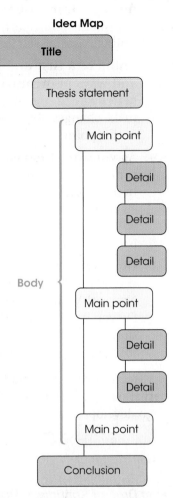

**Idea Map**

Title

Thesis statement

Main point

Detail

Detail

Detail

Body

Main point

Detail

Detail

Main point

Conclusion

*The number of main points and details may vary.

# Write a First Draft

■ **GOAL 7**
Write a first draft

Suppose you need to buy a car. You have decided that you can afford a used car and you have in mind the basic features you need. You visit a used car lot and look at various cars that fit your requirements. After narrowing down your choices, you test drive several cars, then go home to think about how each one might suit you. You revisit the used car lot, go for another test drive, and finally decide which one to buy.

Writing a draft of a paragraph or essay is similar to buying a car. You have to try out different ideas, see how they work together, express them in different ways, and, after several versions, settle upon what your paper will include. Drafting is a way of trying out ideas to see if and how they work.

A first draft expresses your ideas in sentence form. Work from your list of ideas, and don't be concerned with grammar, spelling, or punctuation at this point. Instead, focus on expressing and developing each idea fully. The following suggestions will help you write effective first drafts:

1. **After you have thought carefully about the ideas on your list, write one sentence that expresses the main point of your paragraph (working topic sentence) or essay (thesis statement).**

2. **Concentrate on explaining your topic sentence or thesis statement, using ideas from your list.** Focus first on those ideas that you think express your main point particularly well. Later in the writing process, you may find you need to add other ideas from your list.

3. **Think of a first draft as a chance to experiment with different ideas and ways of organizing them.** While you are working, if you think of a better way to organize or express your ideas, or if you think of new ideas, make changes. Be flexible. Do not worry about getting your wording exact at this point.

4. **As your draft develops, feel free to change your focus or even your topic, if it has not been assigned.** If your draft is not working out, don't hesitate to start over completely. Go back to generating ideas. It is always all right to go back and forth among the steps in the writing process. Most writers make a number of "false starts" before they produce a draft that satisfies them.

5. **Don't expect immediate success.** When you finish your first draft, you should feel that you have the *beginnings* of a paper you will be happy with. Now, ask yourself if you have a sense of the direction your paper will take. Do you have a main idea? Do you have supporting details? Is the organization logical? If you can answer "yes" to these questions, you have something on paper to work with and revise.

The following first draft evolved from the brainstorming list on page 63 and partial outline on page 65. The highlighting indicates the main points that Santiago developed as he wrote.

### First Draft of Santiago's Essay

1    There are around twenty million people living in Mexico City, and this number is constantly increasing. Mexico is where I was born and grew up, before I moved to Beloit, Wisconsin to attend Beloit College. The town of Beloit has roughly thirty thousand people. This means that about seven hundred towns the size of Beloit would fit inside Mexico City. In Mexico City, I was no more than a speck of dust in a dirty room. In Beloit, if I go have breakfast in one of three downtown cafés, I can be sure that there will be at least one person I know, probably around five or more. Beloit and Mexico City are two completely different worlds that I have come to call home.

2    I am Mexican. I probably have beautiful cinnamon skin, hair black as night and falling straight like a waterfall to frame two glowing brown eyes. Many people think this is what a 'true Mexican' looks like. Drawing a line between what is a true Mexican and what isn't based on looks is not a simple task. I myself think it is impossible. This stereotype has played a role in my life both in Mexico and Beloit. I have white skin, the only blue eyes in my family of brown eyes, and curly light brown hair. When I go to the market to buy vegetables for the week, people don't bother to ask my name. They call me güerito, blond. I get asked if I am from the United States or from another country. I was never completely a part of the nation I was born and grew up in. In Beloit though, people are fascinated by my cultural background and ask about my customs

and daily life back home. Inevitably, at some point in the conversation they tell me that I don't look Mexican. I live between two worlds; being racially 'foreign' in Mexico, and being culturally 'foreign' in Beloit.

3    Living a life in-between two worlds, never completely a part of any, is a very complicated and extremely interesting place to be. Living in-between encourages growth and maturity. On one hand, in my teenage years, when I desperately wanted to feel I was a part of something, there wasn't anything to take refuge in and feel strongly about. On the other, though, this made me see the effects of the culture I grow up in my way of thinking. Standing in this middle grown was a vantage point where I could analyze the opinions I held and the habits I developed and see the virtues and faults through different eyes. The hardiest weeds live where the pavement meets the prairie. I live where outsider meets insider.

4    I became used to being in the middle. I discovered that most questions can have more than one answer, or no answer at all. I realized that people are a lot more complex that I thought, and you really can't stick a label to them that won't become old and fall off. I had thought that people who fit snugly into the stereotype would never experience being an outsider. But I soon found out otherwise. Some had to choose between going to the cinema with their friends and going to church with their family. Some loved playing soccer in the mornings, and then go ballroom dancing in the afternoon. Everyone had their own experience of being in-between two places they sometimes love and sometimes hate.

5    It is the places in-between where the most potential for growth lives. Everyone has their own place where they feel like outsiders, or not completely insiders. Realizing that this is where you are standing, and that it is perfectly fine to have one foot inside and one foot outside, will let the unique reveal itself through you. Being in-between can be difficult, but it is there that the most unexpected and wonderful things happen.

---

## EXERCISE 2-6

## Writing a First Draft of Your Essay

**WRITING IN PROGRESS**

**Directions:** Using one of the topics you did not use in Exercise 2-2, generate ideas about it using freewriting, brainstorming, or branching. Then create an outline or idea map to organize the ideas that best support your topic, and write a short essay.

---

# Revise Drafts

■ GOAL 8
Revise a draft

Let's think again about the process of buying a car. At first you may think you have considered everything you need and are ready to make a decision. Then, a while later, you think of other features that would be good to have in your car; in fact, these features are at least as important as the ones you have already thought of. Now you have to rethink your requirements and perhaps reorganize your thoughts about what features are most important to you. You might eliminate some features, add others, and reconsider the importance of still others.

A similar thing often happens as you revise your first draft. When you finish a first draft, you are more or less satisfied with it. Then you reread it later and see you have more work to do. When you revise, you have to rethink your entire paper, reexamining every part and idea. Revising is more than changing a word or rearranging a few sentences, and it is not concerned with correcting punctuation, spelling errors, or grammar. Make these editing changes later when you are satisfied that you have presented your ideas in the optimal way. Revision is your chance to make significant improvements to your draft. It might mean changing, adding, deleting, or rearranging whole sections.

Here is an excerpt from a later draft of the essay shown on page 78. In this draft, you will see how Santiago expands his ideas, adding words and details (underlined), and deletes others in paragraphs 3 and 4 of his first draft. After you have read the essay once, study the annotations. They will help you see the changes Santiago made.

### Santiago's Revision of Paragraphs 3 and 4

**Santiago adds details to explain living in between**

3　Living a life in-between two worlds, never completely a part of any, is a very complicated and extremely interesting place to be. Living in-between encourages growth and maturity. As a teenager, I struggled with feelings of belonging and wanting to be a part of a group. I did not play soccer, or the guitar, and suffered from bullying. The impact this had in my life was emotionally wrecking. Often when people find themselves in similar situations, they turn to familiar things for comfort. Things like a group you belong to, like a culture, or a race, or a religious group. This was not accessible to me in the same way as it was to others. ~~On one hand, in my teenage years, when I desperately wanted to feel I was part of something, there wasn't anything to take refuge in and feel strongly about.~~ On the other hand, though, standing on no man's land let ~~this made~~ me observe ~~see~~ the effects

**Santiago adds mentions of college**

of the culture I grew up with on my way of thinking, and has greatly influenced my area of focus in my college studies. Standing in this middle ground was a vantage point from which I could analyze the opinions I held and the habits I developed and see my virtues and faults through different eyes. The hardiest weeds live where the pavement meets the prairie. I live where outsider meets insider.

**Santiago revises to add specifics about his conflict**

4　~~I became used to being in the middle. I discovered that most questions can have more than one answer, or no answer at all. I realized that people are a lot more complex that I thought, and you really can't stick a label to them that won't become old and fall off.~~ What happens in this middle ground is that concepts such as gender, race, nationality and other identities seem held up by pins. They are extremely volatile and impermanent; constantly changing and molding. This knowledge is present with me every time I say "I am Mexican" or "I am white." I had thought that people who fit snugly into a stereotype would never experience being an outsider. But I soon found out otherwise.

## How to Know What to Revise

✓ **Peer review** means asking one or more of your classmates to read and comment on your writing. It is an excellent way to find out what is good in your draft and what needs to be improved. While *you* are responsible for your writing success, instructors will offer feedback on your work, and you'll sometimes work closely with classmates as well.

### Learning from Peer Review

How can you make peer review as valuable as possible? Here are some suggestions:

**When You Are the Writer . . .**

1. Prepare your draft in readable form. Double-space your work and print it on standard 8.5" × 11" paper.

2. When you receive your peers' comments, weigh them carefully. Keep an open mind, but do not feel that you must accept every suggestion that is made.

3. If you have questions or are uncertain about your peers' advice, talk with your instructor.

**When You Are the Reviewer . . .**

1. Read the draft through at least once before making any suggestions.

2. As you read, keep the writer's intended audience in mind. The draft should be appropriate for that audience.

3. Offer positive comments first. Say what the writer did well.

4. Use the Revision Checklists and "Need to Know" boxes in this book to guide your reading and comments. Be specific in your review and offer suggestions for improvement.

5. Be supportive; put yourself in the place of the person whose work you are reviewing. Phrase your feedback in the way you would want to hear it!

| EXERCISE 2-7 | Revising a Draft |
|---|---|
| **WRITING IN PROGRESS** | **Directions:** Revise the first draft you wrote for Exercise 2-6, following steps 1 through 6 in the "Tips for Revising" box. |

| EXERCISE 2-8 | Using Peer Review |
|---|---|
| *WORKING TOGETHER* | **Directions:** Pair with a classmate for this exercise. Read and evaluate each other's drafts written for Exercise 2-6, page 71, using peer review guidelines and the "Tips for Revising" box. |

## Tips for Revising

Use these suggestions to revise effectively:

1. **Reread the sentence that expresses your main point.** It must be clear, direct, and complete. Experiment with ways to improve it.

2. **Reread each of your other sentences.** Does each relate directly to your main point? If not, cross it out or rewrite it to clarify its connection to the main point. If all your sentences suggest a main point that is different from the one you've written, rewrite the topic sentence or thesis statement.

3. **Make sure your writing has a beginning and an end.** A paragraph should have a clear topic sentence and concluding statement. An essay should have introductory and concluding portions, their length depending on the length of your essay.

4. **Replace words that are vague or unclear with more specific or descriptive words.**

5. **Seek advice.** If you are unsure about how to revise, visit your writing instructor during office hours and ask for advice, or try peer review. Ask a classmate or friend to read your paper and mark ideas that are unclear or need further explanation.

6. **When you have finished revising, you should feel satisfied with what you have said and with the way you have said it.** You will learn additional strategies for revising in Chapter 14.

# Proofread

■ GOAL 9
Proofread for correctness

**Proofreading** is a final reading of your paper to check for errors. In this final polishing of your work, the focus is on correctness, so don't proofread until you have done all your rethinking of ideas and revision. When you are ready to proofread your writing you should check for errors in:

- sentences (run-ons or fragments)
- grammar
- spelling
- punctuation
- capitalization

The following tips will ensure that you don't miss any errors:

1. **Review your paper once for each type of error.** First, read it for run-on sentences and fragments. Take a short break, and then read it four more times, each time paying attention to one of the following: *grammar, spelling, punctuation,* and *capitalization.*

2. **To find spelling errors, read your paper from last sentence to first sentence and from last word to first word.** Reading in this way, you will not

get distracted by the flow of ideas, so you can focus on finding errors. Also use the spell-checker on your computer, but be sure to proofread for the kinds of errors it cannot catch: missing words, errors that are themselves words (such as *of* for *or*), and homonyms (for example, using *it's* for *its*).

3. **Read each sentence aloud, slowly and deliberately.** This technique will help you catch endings that you have left off verbs or missing plurals.

4. **Check for errors one final time after you print out your paper.** Don't do this when you are tired; you might introduce new mistakes. Ask a classmate or friend to read your paper to catch any mistakes you missed.

Here is a paragraph that shows the errors in grammar, punctuation, and spelling that a student corrected during proofreading.

> The Robert Burns said that the dog is man's best friend. To a large extent, this statement may be more true than we thinks. What makes dogs so special to human is they're unending loyalty and their unconditional love. Dogs have been known to cross the entire United States to return home. Never make fun of you or criticize you, Or throw fits, and they are alsways happey to see you. Dogs never lye to you, never betray your confidences, and never stays angry with you for more than five minutes. World would be a better place if only people could be more like dogs.

Chapter 14, page 469, shows you how to keep a proofreading error log and includes a proofreading checklist.

---

| EXERCISE 2-9 | ## Proofreading |
| --- | --- |

**WRITING IN PROGRESS**

**Directions:** Revise your essay using suggestions from peer review (Exercise 2-8). Then prepare and proofread the final version of the essay.

---

# Consider Your Audience and Purpose

■ **GOAL 10**
Consider your audience and purpose

Good writing is directed toward an audience and achieves a purpose.

## Consider Your Audience

When you write, ask yourself, Who will be reading what I write? How should I express myself so that my readers will understand what I write? Considering your audience is essential to good writing.

What is appropriate for one audience may be inappropriate for another. For example, if you were writing about a storm that knocked out the power at your dorm, you would write one way to a close friend and another way to your professor. Because your friend knows you well, she would be interested in all of the details. Conversely, because you and your professor don't know each other well, she would want to know less about your feelings and more about how the storm would affect your course work. Study the following excerpts. What differences do you notice?

## E-mail to a Friend

| From: | Magellan, Marcie [marcie123@noodle.com] |
|---|---|
| Sent: | Thursday, November 15, 2012 9:33 AM |
| To: | Janice@network.com |
| Subject: | Weather!!!! |

Hi Janice,

We were in the dorm when the sirens went off. Pretty scary! We knew there was a thunderstorm warning but we weren't expecting the hail. There were hailstones the size of golf balls!! The wind was slamming the rain and hail against our window and Megan had just said she thought the power would go off when the lights flickered and everything went dark. Luckily, we had flashlights and were able to get downstairs with everyone else. It would have been kind of fun if I didn't have that Econ paper due and no way to print it out or e-mail it. Not as bad as you though, because we got power back this morning and Mike says you're still in the dark.

Marcie :)

## E-mail to a Professor

| From: | Magellan, Marcie [marcie123@noodle.com] |
|---|---|
| Sent: | Thursday, November 15, 2012 9:45 AM |
| To: | Luis.T.Fernandez@school.edu |
| Subject: | Missing Due Date for Second History Paper |
| Attachment: | Economics of Small Business in Rural United States |

Dear Professor Fernandez,

I apologize for submitting my paper late. You may know that the storm caused a power outage last night in the dorms on the west side of campus. The power has just been restored, so I am attaching my paper to this e-mail. I will also bring a printed copy of my paper to your office after my 11:00 class.

Marcie Magellan

While the e-mail to the friend is casual and personal, the note to the professor is businesslike and direct. The writer included details and described her feelings when telling her friend about the storm but focused on missing the deadline in her note to her professor.

Writers make many decisions based on the audience they have in mind. As you write, consider the following:

- How many and what kinds of details are appropriate?
- What format is appropriate (paragraph, essay, letter, e-mail, etc.)?
- What kinds of words should you use (simple, technical, emotional, etc.)?
- What tone should you use (friendly, knowledgeable, formal, etc.)?

Here are four key questions you can ask to assess and write for your audience:

- Who is your audience and what is your relationship with your audience?
- How is your audience likely to respond to your message?
- What does your audience already know about your topic?
- What does your audience need to know to understand your point?

## Write for a Purpose

When you call a friend on the phone, you have a reason for calling, even if it is just to stay in touch. When you ask a question in class, you have a purpose for asking. When you describe to a friend an incident you were involved in, you are relating the story to make a point or share an experience. These examples demonstrate that you use spoken communication to achieve specific purposes.

Good writing must also achieve your *intended purpose*. If you write a paragraph on how to change a flat tire, your reader should be able to change a flat tire after reading the paragraph. Likewise, if your purpose is to describe the sun rising over a misty mountaintop, your reader should be able to visualize the scene. If your purpose is to argue that the legal age for drinking alcohol should be 25, your reader should be able to follow your reasoning, even if he or she is not won over to your view.

In later chapters, you will learn more about writing to achieve your purpose. The chapter readings will also show you how other writers accomplish their purposes.

---

**EXERCISE 2-10**    ## Writing a Paragraph

**Directions:** Think of a public event you have attended recently, such as a concert or film showing. Complete two of the following activities:

1. Write a paragraph describing the event to a friend.

2. Write a paragraph describing the event to your English instructor.

3. Write a paragraph describing the event as the movie or music critic for your local newspaper.

---

# INTEGRATING READING AND WRITING

## READ AND RESPOND: A Student Essay

*Santiago Quintana Garcia is a sophomore at Beloit College in Wisconsin. He is majoring in literature and is the author of the essay that we have been following in this chapter. As you read, notice the revisions Santiago made from his first draft (shown on p. 70) to the final draft that follows.*

# The Space In-Between

Title suggests thesis

Background information on Mexico City and Beloit

Santiago provides the physical description of himself that people expect because he is Mexican

Thesis statement

Topic sentence

Explanation of meaning of living in between

Topic sentence

Details about how being "in-between" changes how one views certain concepts

1   There are around twenty million people living in Mexico City, and this number is constantly increasing. Mexico is where I was born and grew up, before I moved to Beloit, Wisconsin to attend Beloit College. The town of Beloit has roughly thirty thousand people. This means that about seven hundred towns the size of Beloit would fit inside Mexico City. In Mexico City, I was no more than a speck of dust in a dirty room. In Beloit, if I go have breakfast in one of three downtown cafés, I can be sure that there will be at least one person I know, probably around five or more. Beloit and Mexico City are two completely different worlds that I have come to call home.

2   I am Mexican. I probably have beautiful cinnamon skin, hair black as night and falling straight like a waterfall to frame two glowing brown eyes. Many people think this is what a "true Mexican" looks like. Drawing a line between what is a true Mexican and what isn't based on looks is not a simple task. I myself think it is impossible. This stereotype has played a role in my life both in Mexico and Beloit. I have white skin, the only blue eyes in my family of brown eyes and curly light brown hair. When I go to the market to buy vegetables for the week, people don't bother to ask my name. They call me *güerito*, blond. I get asked if I am from the United States or from another country. I was never completely a part of the nation I was born and grew up in. In Beloit though, people are fascinated by my cultural background and ask about my customs and daily life back home. Inevitably, at some point in the conversation they tell me that I don't look Mexican. I live between two worlds; being racially "foreign" in Mexico, and being culturally "foreign" in Beloit.

3   Living a life in-between two worlds, never completely a part of any, is a very complicated and extremely interesting place to be. Living in-between encourages growth and maturity. As a teenager, I struggled with feelings of not belonging and wanting to be a part of a group. I did not play soccer, or the guitar, and suffered from bullying. The impact this had on my life was emotionally wrecking. Often when people find themselves in similar situations, they turn to familiar things for comfort. Things like a group they belong to, like a culture, or a race, or a religious group. This was not accessible to me in the same way as it was to others. On the other hand, though, standing on no man's land let me observe the effects of the culture I grew up with on my way of thinking and has greatly influenced my area of focus in my college studies. Standing in this middle ground was a vantage point from which I could analyze the opinions I held and the habits I developed and see my virtues and faults through different eyes. The hardiest weeds live where the pavement meets the prairie. I live where outsider meets insider.

4   What happens in this middle ground is that concepts such as gender, race, nationality and other identities seem held up by pins. They are extremely volatile and impermanent, constantly changing and molding. This knowledge is present with me every time I say "I am Mexican" or "I am white." I had thought that people who fit snugly into a stereotype would never experience being an outsider. But I soon found out otherwise.

5    The first time I touched on this subject with a friend of mine, he said that he saw what I meant. I was convinced he didn't. He was the perfect example of the "Mexican" racial stereotype. He explained that he couldn't know about my situation, but that he was having a similar problem with his family. His mom had recently mentioned that he should be going to church more, instead of hanging out with his friends on Sunday mornings. That was his middle place. He identified with these two seemingly separate identities that he had created: his Catholic self and his social self. He was having trouble negotiating between the two. He stood in a place in the middle, where his church community was not understanding about his absences, and his friends made fun of his religious background. At the edges of these groups, he had thought about these two in much greater depth than I ever had, and he shared some incredible insights about the baggage associated with both identities, and how they weren't as solid as he thought; they had blurry edges and a lot of holes subject to interpretation.

6    It is the places in-between where the most potential for growth lives. Everyone has their own place where they feel like outsiders, or not completely insiders. Realizing that this is where you are standing, and that it is perfectly fine to have one foot inside and one foot outside, will let the unique reveal itself through you. Being in-between can be difficult, but it is there that the most unexpected and wonderful things happen.

## Examining Writing

1. Compare Santiago's first draft on page 70 with his final draft. What content did he delete? What did he add? Why do you think he made these decisions?

2. How would you describe Santiago's audience for this essay? What was his purpose in writing it?

3. What does the title refer to in the essay? Evaluate the effectiveness of the title, introduction, and conclusion.

4. What other changes would you recommend to improve this essay?

## Writing Assignments

1. The author writes about living between two worlds. Have you ever experienced "living in-between"? Do you agree with the author that unexpected and wonderful things can happen in such a place? Write a paragraph describing an experience or aspect of your life in which you felt like an outsider.

2. Brainstorm some ideas about your own identity. How would you describe yourself? How would others describe you? Write a paragraph about who you are.

3. Write a paragraph explaining what the author means by his statement, "The hardiest weeds live where the pavement meets the prairie."

## READ AND RESPOND: A Professional Essay

### Thinking Before Reading

In the following selection, the author explores the elements that make a movie scary. As you read, identify the thesis statement and the major details the author uses to support it.

1. Preview the reading, using the steps discussed in Chapter 1 on page 25.
2. Connect the reading to your own experience by answering the following questions:
   a. What is the scariest movie you have ever seen? How did you feel about it?
   b. What do you think makes a movie scary?
3. Highlight and annotate as you read.

1250**L**/1014 words

# What Makes a Scary Movie Scary
## Dorothy Hoffman

1    On the surface, the water looks serene and harmless as the carefree young woman takes a midnight swim. Just yards away her young companion is passed out, drunk, on the beach. The music starts low and persistent like a beating heart— DA duh, DA duh, DA duh, DAduhDAduhDAduh—faster and faster till the girl jerks and gasps as something below the ocean's surface attacks. She struggles, cries for help, but is pulled into the cold, dark waters.

2    *Jaws* wasted no time creating an atmosphere of terror and sustained the tension and fear with brilliant use of all the filmmakers' techniques for building an atmosphere of danger and menace. The movie changed the way millions of people viewed a summer vacation at the shore for years after, and it did it with a minimum of blood and gore.

3    So, if it's not blood and gore and gut-wrenching deaths and dismemberment, what does make scary movies scary? A skillful filmmaker doesn't need a big budget, A-list actors, or cutting-edge special effects. Sometimes the less you put up on the screen, the more terrifying the effect. In movies like *The Blair Witch Project* and the first *Paranormal Activity* movie, for example, a shaky handheld camera and "frightened" narrator supposedly documenting real events can be extremely effective for next to nothing. George Romero's classic *Night of the Living Dead* manages to create a terrifying scenario with a bunch of amateur zombies in minimal gory makeup.

4    Whatever the budget, scary movies rely on a variety of elements to keep the audience on the edge of their seats.

### Music that Chills Your Spine

5    Music is always important in creating a mood in movies. The shark theme in *Jaws* has an almost **visceral** effect on the audience, like a pounding heartbeat. In Hitchcock's classic *Psycho*, Bernard Herrmann's brilliant score punctuates shocking surprises on screen with "screaming" violins. Other movies take a different approach: *The Exorcist* and *Halloween* use hypnotically repetitive, eerie musical themes to underscore the supernatural evil of villains. And many ghost stories and horror flicks create a surprisingly creepy effect with sweet nursery rhyme songs.

### Dark and Gloomy Atmosphere

6    Bad things always happen on dark and stormy nights. Cars break down on creepy deserted roads; travelers seek refuge in vampire-infested castles; when the electricity and phone lines go down in haunted houses, the residents become easy prey for lurking psycho killers or evil spirits.

7    Fear of the dark is deeply rooted in the human **psyche**, and when you add a dash of unearthly mist, menacing shadows, and strange things going bump in the night, you have the perfect setting for terror.

8    On the other hand, there's something a little creepy about a much too "normal" suburban setting filled with "perfect," unnaturally cheerful **Stepford-type** residents. Evil sometimes stands out more starkly in the midst of our ordinary, everyday world.

### The Unknown/Unseen Terror

9    Today's horror movies seem to be outdoing each other with ever more gruesome violence and nauseating scenes of torture and dismemberment. But the classic horror filmmakers understood that the human imagination can conjure up more terrifying primal fears than any special effects department could create. From scene to scene in *Alien*, we didn't even know what the creature was going to look like—or what it was capable of. Until the end, we saw the fully developed creature only in quick, shadowy glimpses or as a blip on a monitoring screen. By the time the first sequel was released, everyone knew exactly what the creature looked like

**visceral**
related to physical instinct rather than intellect

**psyche**
consciousness

**Stepford-type**
Refers to the science-fiction novel *The Stepford Wives*, in which women are replaced with unnaturally docile robots

and familiarity made it less fearsome. Fortunately, James Cameron had another sure-fire horror trick up his sleeve—an innocent child in peril.

### Innocents in Peril

10    We instinctively feel protective toward the innocent and vulnerable, and the terror is always greater when there's a sympathetic character we can identify with in peril. What could be more frightening than a helpless child being menaced by an evil creature?

11    A seemingly innocent child who IS evil, of course. It's a surprisingly common theme (*Village of the Damned, The Omen, Children of the Corn, Rosemary's Baby*), and never fails to creep us out. It must tap into some primal fear of harboring, in our wombs and in our homes, an evil little monster or spawn of the devil.

### The Uncanny and Unnatural

12    Long before we reach adulthood, we know how the world works, and have a visceral response to the paranormal. Even animals respond to the uncanny with goose bumps and a sense of horror. We all know, for instance, that human heads don't naturally spin around 360 degrees, as the possessed girl's in *The Exorcist* did.

13    But the uncanny isn't always so obvious. In *Bringing Out the Dead*, Martin Scorsese created a creepy, eerie effect in one scene by filming his actors walking backwards, then running the film in reverse and slightly slowed down. The scene has kind of dreamlike feel—you sense something's "not right," but you're not sure what.

**archetypal**

related to an original model or type that others are patterned after

### Archetypal Fears and Hideous Beasts

14    The classic horror films tap into our deepest unconscious fears. From deep in our collective unconscious come our darkest nightmare demons—the undead; monsters; demons and witches; sadistic, deranged murderers; evil that never dies.

15    Ugly, repulsive, deformed and unnatural creatures are innately scary. The original Nosferatu was a hideous vampire with claw-like hands and a face even an un-dead mother couldn't love. Today's vampires have undergone a major makeover; the pouty, eternally young and beautiful teenage sex symbols are only scary to their swooning teenybopper fans' parents.

**phobias**

fears

16    Many people have profound phobias of snakes, spiders, wolves—even cats are often associated with the supernatural and witchcraft. Even in their natural form these animals can make convincing horror film villains. But when they're mutated by radioactivity or deranged and seeking vengeance on humanity, they're even scarier.

17    Possibly the dumbest idea any filmmaker ever came up with was a "horror" movie about giant flesh-eating bunny rabbits. In *Night of the Lepus*, a mad scientist for reasons even the screenwriter couldn't explain transformed harmless hares into carnivorous marauding armies of hoppers, trampling over the countryside in what may be the unscariest horror movie ever conceived. All the scary movie tricks in the world aren't going to make a bunch of cute, cuddly critters look menacing.

## Getting Ready to Write

### Checking Your Comprehension

Answer each of the following questions using complete sentences.

1. According to the author, what are the elements that make a movie scary?
2. Describe three examples from the selection showing how music is used to create a scary effect.
3. What does the author say is more frightening than a helpless child being menaced by an evil creature?
4. Describe what Martin Scorsese did to create a scary effect in *Bringing Out the Dead*.
5. What movie is cited by the author as the dumbest idea for a horror movie?
6. Describe the photo that accompanies the selection and explain why it was included.

**THINKING VISUALLY**

### Strengthening Your Vocabulary

Using the word's context, word parts, or a dictionary, write a brief definition of each of the following words as it is used in the reading.

1. minimal (paragraph 3) *the least amount*
2. underscore (paragraph 5) *emphasize*
3. conjure (paragraph 9) *imagine*
4. peril (paragraph 9) *danger*
5. primal (paragraph 11) *deepest, most basic*
6. innately (paragraph 15) *by nature*
7. profound (paragraph 16) *deep, intense*

### Examining the Reading: Using an Idea Map

Review the reading by completing the missing parts of the following idea map.

**VISUALIZE IT!**

Title — **What Makes a Scary Movie Scary**

Thesis — Scary movies use several elements to frighten the audience.

Music

- Pounding heartbeat in *Jaws*
- Screaming violins in *Psycho*
- Repetitive, eerie music in *The Exorcist* and *Halloween*
- Sweet nursery rhyme songs

Atmosphere

- Stormy nights
- Too "normal" or ordinary setting

Unknown/Unseen Terror

- Human imagination

Innocents in Peril

- Helpless or vulnerable child/sympathetic character
- Seemingly innocent but evil child

The Uncanny and Unnatural

- The paranormal
- Dreamlike/creepy effect

Archetypal Fears and Hideous Beasts

- Deepest unconscious fears
- Monsters
- Phobias

Conclusion — Movie tricks aren't enough to make a bad idea scary.

## Thinking Critically: Discussion and Journal Writing

React and respond to the reading by discussing the following:

1. Discuss the elements that the author has identified. Do you agree with each element identified? What would you add to the list of what makes a movie scary?

2. Discuss the movies that were mentioned in the selection. Which ones were familiar to you? Which ones had you never heard of? Are there others that should have been mentioned? Are there any you are interested in seeing (or seeing again) as a result of reading the selection?

3. What is the author's attitude toward scary movies? Do you think she enjoys them? Why or why not?

MySkillsLab®

**Complete** this Exercise

## Writing About the Reading

### Paragraph Options

1. Write a paragraph evaluating the effectiveness of the title and introduction of this selection. What other titles can you think of for this subject? Was *Jaws* an appropriate example for the introduction?

2. Consider the archetypal fears, creatures, and phobias that are mentioned in the selection and write a paragraph describing which ones are most frightening to you.

3. Write a paragraph agreeing or disagreeing with the author's statement that "Sometimes the less you put up on the screen, the more terrifying the effect."

### Essay Options

4. Write an essay describing the scariest movie you have ever seen. Describe your response to the movie both at the time you saw it and looking back at it now. What made it scary? Is it still scary to you today? Why or why not?

5. Think about a recent movie or theater production you have seen, and write an essay in the form of a review. Use the elements discussed in the selection as a basis for evaluating the movie or performance. For example, how did music enhance or detract from your experience?

6. What makes a fictional character sympathetic? Consider movies, books, music, or other sources and write an essay describing a character whom you found especially sympathetic. What qualities made you identify with him or her?

# SELF-TEST SUMMARY

To test yourself, cover the Answer column with a sheet of paper and answer each question in the left column. Evaluate each of your answers as you work by sliding the paper down and comparing your answer with what is printed in the Answer column.

| QUESTION | ANSWER |
| --- | --- |
| ■ **GOAL 1** Get the most out of your writing class<br><br>How can you get the most out of your writing class? | To be successful in your writing class, attend all classes, come prepared, take notes, ask questions, participate in class discussions, and attend writing conferences. You should also think before you write, plan on revising, schedule writing time, develop a routine, keep a journal, and use peer review. |
| ■ **GOAL 2** Use the writing process<br><br>What are the steps in the writing process? | The writing process has five basic steps: *generating ideas, organizing ideas, writing a first draft, revising,* and *proofreading.* |
| ■ **GOAL 3** Generate ideas<br><br>What are some ways to generate ideas? | Three techniques for generating ideas are *freewriting, brainstorming,* and *branching.* |
| ■ **GOAL 4** Organize ideas<br><br>What methods can you use to organize ideas? | Two common methods of organizing ideas are *outlining* (listing main points and details in the order in which you will present them) and *mapping* (creating a drawing that shows the content and organization of your writing). |
| ■ **GOAL 5** Write paragraphs<br><br>What is a paragraph? | A paragraph is a group of sentences that expresses one main idea. |
| ■ **GOAL 6** Write essays<br><br>What is an essay? | An essay is a group of paragraphs about one subject. (See the idea map for paragraphs on page 66 and for essays on page 69.) |
| ■ **GOAL 7** Write a first draft<br><br>What is drafting and how can you write an effective first draft? | Drafting is a way of trying out ideas to see if and how they work. Begin by writing one sentence expressing your main point, then focus on explaining that sentence. Experiment with different ideas and ways of organizing them. |

*(Continued)*

| QUESTION | ANSWER |
|---|---|
| ■ **GOAL 8** Revise a draft<br><br>Why is revision important? | Revision is your chance to make significant improvements to your draft by changing, adding, deleting, or rearranging parts and ideas. (See the "Tips for Revising" box on p. 74.) |
| ■ **GOAL 9** Proofread for correctness<br><br>How do you proofread for correctness? | Proofread by checking for errors in sentences, grammar, spelling, punctuation, and capitalization. Read your paper once for each type of error, read your paper from the end to the beginning, read aloud, and check for errors again after you print your paper. |
| ■ **GOAL 10** Consider your audience and purpose<br><br>How do you consider your audience and purpose? | To consider your audience, ask yourself who will be reading what you write. To consider your purpose, think about what you are trying to achieve through your writing. |

# MySkillsLab

For more help with **The Writing Process**, go to your learning path in MySkillsLab at http://www.myskillslab.com.

# 3

# Vocabulary: Working with Words

## THINK About It!

### Vocabulary

Study the photograph. Did it catch your eye and start you thinking about the person? It is interesting and engaging because it reveals a great deal of information about the person. It shows a young dark-haired man, sitting on a dock beside peaceful water playing a guitar. The tattoo on his shoulder suggests a deep interest in music. Is he a folk singer, a rock musician or maybe a classical guitarist? Your vocabulary is like a photograph—it can be lively, interesting, and descriptive, conveying a great deal of information, or it can be dull and uninteresting and convey very little information.

Your vocabulary can be one of your strongest assets in college and in your career. A strong vocabulary allows you to understand what you read and express yourself clearly and effectively, both in speech and in writing. In this chapter you will learn a variety of strategies for strengthening your vocabulary.

# Why Is Vocabulary Important?

Your vocabulary is one of your most valuable assets. Because words are the basic building blocks of language, you need a strong vocabulary to express yourself clearly in both speech and writing. A strong vocabulary identifies you as an effective communicator—an important skill both in college and in the workplace. Further, a solid vocabulary is the mark of an educated person—someone who is able to think, write and read critically, and speak effectively. Vocabulary building is well worth your while and will pay off hundreds of times both in college and on the job.

## READING

# Use a Dictionary Effectively

■ GOAL 1
Use a dictionary
effectively

Every writer needs to use a dictionary, not only to check spellings, but also to check meanings and the appropriate usage of words.

## Types of Dictionaries

There are several types of dictionaries, useful for a variety of situations.

### Print Dictionaries

You should have a desk or collegiate dictionary plus a pocket dictionary that you can carry with you to classes. Widely used dictionaries include:

- *The American Heritage Dictionary of the English Language*
- *Merriam-Webster's Collegiate Dictionary*
- *Webster's New World Dictionary of the American Language*

If you have difficulty with spelling, a misspeller's dictionary is another valuable reference tool. It can help you locate correct spellings easily. Two commonly used sources are *Webster's New World Misspeller's Dictionary* and *How to Spell It: A Handbook of Commonly Misspelled Words.*

### Online Dict ionaries

Several dictionaries are available online. Two of the most widely used are *Merriam-Webster Online* (http://www.Merriam-Webster.com) and *The American Heritage Dictionary* (http://yourdictionary.com/index.shtml).

Online dictionaries have several important advantages over print dictionaries.

- **Audio component.** Some online dictionaries such as *Merriam-Webster* and *American Heritage* feature an audio component that allows you to hear how a word is pronounced.
- **Multiple dictionary entries.** Some sites, such as Dictionary.com, display entries from several dictionaries at once for a particular word.
- **Misspellings.** If you aren't sure of how a word is spelled or you mistype it, several suggested words will be returned.

### ESL Dictionaries

If you are an ESL student, be sure to purchase an ESL dictionary. Numerous ones are available in paperback editions, including *The Longman Advanced American Dictionary.*

—By permission. *Merriam-Webster's Collegiate Dictionary,*
11th Edition © 2012 by Merriam-Webster, Incorporated
(www.Merriam_Webster.com)

## Using a Dictionary

The first step in using your dictionary is to become familiar with the kinds of
information it provides.

Here is a brief review of the information a dictionary entry contains. As you
read, refer to the sample dictionary entry below.

Pronunciation

Parts of speech
Verb forms

Restrictive meanings

Word history

◆ drink (drĭngk) *v.* drank (drăngk), drunk (drŭngk), drink·ing, drinks
—*tr.* 1. To take into the mouth and swallow (a liquid). 2. To swallow
the liquid contents of (a vessel): *drank a cup of tea.* 3. To take in or soak
up; absorb: *drank the fresh air; spongy earth that drank up the rain.* 4.
To take in eagerly through the senses or intellect: *drank in the beauty of
the day.* 5a. To give or make (a toast). b. To toast (a person or an
occasion, for example): *We'll drink to your health.* 6. To bring to a
specific state by drinking alcoholic liquors: *drank our sorrows away.*
—*intr.* 1. To swallow liquid: *drank noisily; drink from a goblet.* 2. To
imbibe alcoholic liquors: *They only drink socially.* 3. To salute a person
or an occasion with a toast: *We will drink to your continued success.*
❖*n.* 1. A liquid that is fit for drinking; a beverage. 2. An amount of
liquid swallowed: *took a long drink from the fountain.* 3. An alcoholic
beverage, such as a cocktail or highball. 4. Excessive or habitual
indulgence in alcoholic liquor. 5. *Chiefly Southern U.S.* See soft drink.
See Regional Note at tonic. 6. *Slang* A body of water; the sea: *The hatch
cover slid off the boat and into the drink.* [Middle English, *drinken,*
from Old English *drincan.* See dhreg- in Appendix I.]

—Copyright © 2011 by Houghton Mifflin Harcourt Publishing Company. Adapted
and reproduced by permission from *The American Heritage Dictionary of the
English Language,* Fifth Edition

1. **Pronunciation.** The pronunciation of the word is given in parentheses. Symbols are used to indicate the sounds letters make within specific words. Refer to the pronunciation key printed on each page or on alternate pages of your print dictionary.

2. **Grammatical information.** The part of speech is indicated, as well as information about different forms the word may take. Most dictionaries include
   - spellings of word variations
   - principal forms of verbs (both regular and irregular)
   - plural forms of irregular nouns
   - comparative and superlative forms of adjectives and adverbs

3. **Meanings.** Meanings are numbered and are usually grouped by the part of speech they represent.

4. **Restrictive meanings.** Meanings that are limited to special situations are labeled. Some examples are:
   - *Slang*—casual language used only in conversation
   - *Biol.*—words used in specialized fields, in this case biology
   - *Regional*—words used only in certain parts of the United States

5. **Synonyms.** Words with similar meanings may be listed.

6. **Word history.** The origin of the word (its etymology) is described. (Not all dictionaries include this feature.)

Beyond definitions, a dictionary contains a wealth of other information as well. For example, in the *American Heritage Dictionary,* Fifth Edition, you can find the history of the word *vampire,* or an explanation of the New England expression "Vum!" Consider your dictionary a helpful and valuable resource that can assist you in expressing your ideas more clearly and correctly.

7. **Usage notes.** Some collegiate dictionaries contain a usage note or synonym section of the entry for words that are close in meaning to others. For example, a usage note for the word *indifferent* may explain how it differs in meaning from *unconcerned, detached,* and *uninterested.*

8. **Idioms.** An idiom is a phrase that has a meaning other than what the common definitions of the words in the phrase indicate. For example, the phrase *wipe the slate clean* is not about slates. It means "to start over." Most idiomatic expressions are not used in academic writing because they are considered trite or overused.

## EXERCISE 3-1    Using a Dictionary

**Directions:** Use a dictionary to answer the following questions.

1. How many meanings are listed for the word *fall?*

   Answers will vary. (Encarta Dictionary lists 38.)

2. How is the word *phylloxera* pronounced? (Record its phonetic spelling.)

   fĭl′ ŏk-sî r̂-a

3. Can the word *protest* be used other than as a verb? If so, how?

   Yes, it can be used as a noun, meaning strong objection or complaint.

4. The word *prime* can mean first or original. List some of its other meanings.

   *earliest, distinguishing mark, to prepare for painting, to prepare a pump to start*

5. What does the French expression *savoir faire* mean?

   *ability to act appropriately in a situation*

6. List three synonyms for the word *fault*.

   *mistake, penalty, shortcoming*

7. List several words that are formed using the word *dream*.

   *dreamy, daydream, dreamful, dreamed*

8. What is the plural spelling of *addendum*?

   *addenda*

9. Explain the meaning of the idiom *turn over a new leaf*.

   *to make a fresh start*

10. Define the word *reconstitute* and write a sentence using the word.

    *to add water to rehydrate food. Reconstituted orange juice does not taste fresh.*

## Selecting Appropriate Meanings

Because most words have more than one meaning, you must choose the meaning that fits the way the word is used in the context of the sentence. For example, one dictionary entry for the word *run* lists 74 meanings. For the word *green*, 19 meanings are given.

The meanings are often grouped by part of speech and are numbered consecutively in each group. Generally, the most common meanings of the word are listed first, with more specialized, less common meanings appearing toward the end of the entry.

Here are a few suggestions for choosing the correct meaning from among those listed in an entry:

1. **If you are familiar with the parts of speech, try to use these to locate the correct meaning.** For instance, if you are looking up the meaning of a word that names a person, place, or thing, you can save time by reading only those entries given after *n.* (noun).

2. **For most types of college reading, you can skip definitions that give slang and colloquial (abbreviated *colloq.*) meanings.** Colloquial meanings refer to informal or spoken language.

3. **If you are not sure of the part of speech, read each meaning until you find a definition that seems correct.** Skip over restrictive meanings that are inappropriate.

4. **Test your choice by substituting the meaning in the sentence with which you are working.** Substitute the definition for the word and see whether it makes sense in context.

Suppose you are looking up the word *oblique* to find its meaning in the following sentence:

My sister's **oblique** answers to my questions made me suspicious.

*Oblique* is used in the preceding sentence as an adjective. Looking at the entries listed after *adj.* (adjective), you can skip over the definition under the heading *Mathematics,* as it wouldn't apply here: Definition 4a (*indirect or evasive*) best fits the way *oblique* is used in the sentence.

> **oblique** (ō-blēk´, ō-blīk´) *adj.* **1a.** Having a slanting or sloping direction, course, or position; inclined. **b.** *Mathematics* Designating geometric lines or planes that are neither parallel nor perpendicular. **2.** *Botany* Having sides of unequal length or form: *an oblique leaf.* **3.** *Anatomy* Situated in a slanting position; not transverse or longitudinal: *oblique muscles or ligaments.* **4a.** Indirect or evasive: *oblique political maneuvers.* **b.** Devious, misleading, or dishonest: *gave oblique answers to the questions.* **5.** Not direct in descent; collateral. **6.** *Grammar* Designating any noun case except the nominative or the vocative. N. **1.** An oblique thing, such as a line, direction, or muscle. **2.** *Nautical* The act of changing course by less than 90°. *adv.* (ō-blēk´, ō-blīk´) At an angle of 45°. [Middle English, from Old French, from Latin *obliquis*] —o·**blique´-ly** *adv.* o·**blique´ness** *n.*

> —Copyright © 2011 by Houghton Mifflin Harcourt Publishing Company. Reproduced by permission from *The American Heritage Dictionary of the English Language,* Fifth Edition

## EXERCISE 3-2    Finding Multiple Meanings

**Directions:** The following words have two or more meanings. Look them up in your dictionary and write two sentences with different meanings for each word.    Answers will vary.

1. culture  She is a woman of culture who values music, literature, and art.

   My uncle is very involved with the culture of roses.

2. perch  The parrot spent most of its day on its perch.

   The small cabin was perched high in the mountains.

3. surge  The small boat was capsized by the sudden surge.

   The music surged through the auditorium.

4. apron  The blacksmith wore a leather apron.

   Park your car on the apron beside the garage.

5. irregular  Your behavior is highly irregular.

   New England's coastline is irregular.

## EXERCISE 3-3    Finding the Right Meaning

**Directions:** Use a dictionary to help you find an appropriate meaning for the boldfaced word in each of the following sentences.

1. The last contestant did not have a **ghost** of a chance.

   slightest trace

**2.** The race1 car driver won the first **heat**.

*a round in a race*

**3.** The police took all possible **measures** to protect the witness.

*courses of action; procedures*

**4.** The orchestra played the first **movement** of the symphony.

*principal division within a musical symphony*

**5.** The plane stalled on the **apron**.

*hard-surfaced area in front of an airplane hangar*

# Synonyms and Antonyms

**GOAL 2**
Use synonyms and antonyms

**Synonyms** are words with similar meanings; **antonyms** are words with opposite meanings. Both categories of words are useful to expand and diversify your vocabulary.

When writing or speaking, you may want to find a *synonym*, a word with a more exact, descriptive, or specific meaning than the one that comes to mind. For example, you might want to describe how a person walks. There are many words that mean *walk*, although each may have a different connotation: *strut, meander, stroll, hike, saunter,* and *march*.

*Antonyms* are useful when making a contrast or explaining differences. You might be describing two different communication styles of friends. One style is decisive. Finding antonyms for the word *decisive* may suggest a way to describe the opposite style of the other person such as *faltering, hesitant,* or *wavering*.

**EXERCISE 3-4**    Refining Synonyms

**Directions:** For each of the pairs or sets of synonyms listed, explain the difference in meaning between the words. Use a dictionary if necessary.

**EXAMPLE**   subject, topic: *both denote the principal idea or point of a speech, a piece of writing, or an artistic work; subject is the more general term, whereas topic is a subject of discussion, argument, or conversation*

**1.** form, figure, shape: *All refer to the external outline of a thing, but form is its outline and structure as opposed to its substance; figure refers to form as established by bounding or enclosing lines; shape implies three-dimensional definition indicating both outline and bulk or mass.*

**2.** bright, brilliant, radiant: *All refer to what emits or reflects light, but bright is the most general; brilliant implies intense brightness and sparkling, glittering, or gleaming light; radiant radiates or seems to radiate light.*

**3.** offend, insult: *Both mean to cause resentment, humiliation, or hurt, but offend is to cause displeasure, hurt feelings, or repugnance in another; insult implies gross insensitivity, insolence, or contemptuous rudeness resulting in shame or embarrassment.*

4. perform, accomplish, achieve: _All mean to carry through to completion, but perform is to carry out an action, observing due form or exercising skill or care; accomplish connotes the successful completion of something requiring tenacity or talent; achieve is to accomplish something through effort or despite difficulty, implying a significant result._

5. complex, complicated: _Both mean having parts so interconnected as to make the whole perplexing, but complex implies a combination of many associated parts, whereas complicated stresses elaborate relationship of parts._

---

**EXERCISE 3-5**    ## Using Antonyms

**Directions:** Find an antonym for each of the following words and then write a sentence using the antonym. Consult a dictionary or thesaurus, if necessary.    _Answers will vary._

1. prohibit _allow_

2. obtuse _sharp, alert_

3. tedious _challenging_

4. compliant _disagreeable_

5. rebuke _accept_

---

## Using a Thesaurus

A **thesaurus** is a dictionary of synonyms that also includes antonyms. It groups words with similar meanings together. A thesaurus is particularly useful when you want to

- locate the precise term to fit a particular situation
- find an appropriate descriptive word
- replace an overused or unclear word
- convey a different or more specific shade of meaning
- find a word that means the opposite of another word

Suppose you are looking for a more precise word for the expression _look into_ in the following sentence:

The marketing manager will **look into** the decline of recent sales in the Midwest.

The thesaurus lists the following synonyms for "look into":

**look into** [v.] check, research

audit, check out, delve into, dig, examine, explore, follow up, go into, inquire, inspect, investigate, look over, make inquiry, probe, prospect, scrutinize, sift, study

—From _Roget's 21st Century Thesaurus_. Copyright © 1992, 1993, 1999, 2005 by The Philip Lief Group. Published by Dell Publishing. Reprinted by permission of The Philip Lief Group.

Read the dictionary entry on page 95 and underline words or phrases that you think would be more descriptive than *look into.* You might underline words and phrases such as *examine, investigate,* and *scrutinize.*

The most widely used thesaurus is *Roget's Thesaurus.* Inexpensive paperback editions are available in most bookstores. *Merriam-Webster's Collegiate Thesaurus* is available free online (http://www.merriam-webster.com/thesaurus.htm). You can also access a thesaurus at http://www.dictionary.com.

When you first consult a thesaurus, you will need to familiarize yourself with its format and learn how to use it. The following is a step-by-step approach:

1. **Begin by locating the word you are trying to replace.** Many thesauruses are organized alphabetically, much like a dictionary. Following the word, you will find numerous entries that list the synonyms of that word. Select words that seem like possible substitutes. (The hardback edition of *Roget's* is organized by subject with an index in the back.)

2. **Test each of the words you selected in the sentence in which you will use it.** The word should fit the context of the sentence.

3. **Select the word that best expresses what you are trying to say.**

4. **Choose only words whose shades of meaning you know.** Check unfamiliar words in a dictionary before using them. Remember, misusing a word is often a more serious error than choosing an overused, vague, or general one.

| EXERCISE 3-6 | Using a Thesaurus |
|---|---|

**Directions:** Using a thesaurus, replace the boldfaced word or phrase in each sentence with a more precise or descriptive word. Write the word in the space provided. Rephrase the sentence, if necessary.   *Answers will vary.*

  **EXAMPLE**   The union appointed Corinne Miller to act as the **go-between** in its negotiations with management. _liaison_

1. The two interviewers **went back and forth** asking questions of the candidate. _alternated_

2. On the night of the inauguration, the ballroom looked **very nice.**
   _festive_

3. More than anything, he **wanted** a new minivan. _desired_

4. The town had gone through an economic decline, but now it appeared to be on the verge of an **increase.** _boom_

5. The two brothers were opposites: Chester **liked to talk a lot,** whereas John was content to sit quietly and listen. _was talkative_

6. Freshwater lakes that are in the process of accelerated eutrophication are often **cloudy-looking.** _milky_

7. Daylilies range in color from **dark red** to yellow to almost white.
   _burgundy, ruby_

8. Today's trend toward casual clothing in the workplace has made the demand for high-quality custom suits **fall.** _decrease, plummet_

9. The children were **so sad** over the loss of their old dog, Chumley.
*sorrowful, doleful, desolate*

10. The first speaker was interesting, but the second one was so **dull** I almost fell asleep. *colorless, pedestrian, uninspiring, stodgy*

# Understand Denotative and Connotative Language

■ GOAL 3
Understand denotative and connotative language

■ Would you rather be part of a *crowd* or *mob*?

■ If you were wearing a leather-looking jacket that was made out of man-made fibers, would you prefer that it be called *fake* or *synthetic*?

■ Would you rather be called a *college student* or a *college kid*?

Each of the above pairs of words has basically the same meaning. A *crowd* and a *mob* are both groups of people. Both *college student* and *college kid* refer to someone who attends college. If the words have similar meanings, why did you choose *crowd* rather than *mob* and *college student* rather than *college kid*? Although the pairs of words have similar primary meanings, they carry different shades of meaning; each creates a different image or association in your mind. This section will explore these shades of meaning, called connotative meanings.

All words have one or more standard meanings; these meanings are called **denotative meanings**. Think of them as those meanings listed in the dictionary. They tell us what the word names. Many words also have connotative meanings. **Connotative meanings** include the feelings and associations that may accompany a word. For example, the denotative meaning of *mother* is female parent. However, the word carries many connotations. For many, *mother* suggests a warm, loving, caring person. Let's take another example, the word *home*. Its denotative meaning is "a place where one lives," but to many its connotative meaning suggests comfort, privacy, and coziness. Figure 3-1 shows some connotative meanings of the word *mother*.

**FIGURE 3-1 ONE PERSON'S CONNOTATIONS FOR THE WORD *MOTHER***

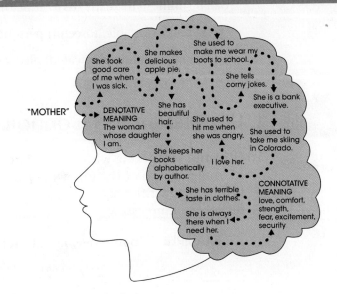

Writers and speakers use connotative meanings to stir emotions or to bring to mind positive or negative associations. Suppose a writer is describing how someone walks. The writer could choose words such as *strut, stroll, swagger,* or *amble.* Do you see how each creates a different image of the person? Connotative meanings, then, are powerful tools of language. When you read, be alert for meanings suggested by the author's word choice. When writing or speaking, be sure to choose words with appropriate connotations.

Connotations can vary from individual to individual. The denotative meaning for the word *flag* is a piece of cloth used as a national emblem. To many, the American flag is a symbol of patriotism and love of one's country. To some people, though, it may mean an interesting decoration to place on their clothing. The word *cat* to cat lovers suggests a fluffy, furry, cuddly animal. To those who are allergic to cats, however, the word *cat* connotes discomfort and avoidance—itchy eyes and a runny nose.

---

**EXERCISE 3-7** | ## Using Connotation to Make a Point

**Directions:** For each of the following sentences, underline the word in parentheses that best completes the sentence. Consult a dictionary, if necessary.

1. The price of the dinner was (<u>exorbitant</u>, extravagant).

2. The discipline policy at the boarding school was (stiff, <u>rigid</u>).

3. Using coupons at the grocery store is one way of being (<u>frugal</u>, stingy).

4. Jay had several friends with tattoos, but he never felt (influenced, <u>pressured</u>) to get one himself.

5. The neighbors were embroiled in a (<u>dispute</u>, debate) over property lines.

6. The restaurant manager (<u>warned</u>, threatened) us that it could be well over an hour before we were seated.

7. The couple (hesitated, <u>wavered</u>) several times before finally deciding to put their house on the market.

8. The millionaire made his fortune through several (<u>bold</u>, brash) investments.

9. He had a (forcible, <u>forceful</u>) personality that was difficult to ignore.

10. The physician is (<u>dedicated</u>, pledged) to the well-being of her patients.

---

**EXERCISE 3-8** | ## Understanding Connotative Meanings

*WORKING TOGETHER*

**Directions:** Working with a classmate, discuss the differences in connotative meaning of each of the following pairs or sets of words. Write the definitions below. Then write a sentence using one word from each of the sets. Consult a dictionary, if necessary.   Answers will vary.

**EXAMPLE**   To improve: **mend—reform**

*Mend* implies repairing something that is broken; means changing something, often a document or law, to improve it or eliminate its faults.

1. To find fault: **admonish—reprimand**

   *Admonish* implies giving advice or warning so that a fault can be rectified or a danger avoided (more positive), whereas *reprimand* refers to sharp, often angry, criticism (more negative).

2. A competitor: **rival—opponent**

   A *rival* is one who seeks to equal or surpass another, and an *opponent* is one who opposes, resists, or combats opposition.

3. Working together: **accomplice—colleague**

   An *accomplice* is one who aids a lawbreaker in a criminal activity (negative), whereas a *colleague* is an associate, a peer, a fellow member of a profession (positive).

4. Stated briefly: **pithy—concise**

   *Pithy* is forceful and brief, precisely meaningful (more negative); *concise* is clear and succinct, expressing much in few words (more positive).

5. Long lasting: **perpetual—interminable—eternal**

   *Perpetual* means lasting for eternity or continuing indefinitely (as in perpetual friendship); *interminable* is more negative, as something endless, tiresomely long, wearisome (an interminable wait); and *eternal* is without beginning or end, seemingly endless, with a spiritual connotation.

6. Inactive: **idle—lethargic—languid**

   *Idle* is not employed or busy, avoiding work (negative connotation of laziness); *lethargic* is a sluggish, drowsy dullness possibly caused by illness, fatigue or overwork; and *languid* implies a lack of energy or spirit in one who is satiated by a life of luxury or pleasure.

7. Ability: **proficiency—aptitude—dexterity**

   *Proficiency* implies a learned competence; *aptitude* implies an inherent ability or talent; and *dexterity* can mean skill or grace, especially in the use of hands, or mental skill and cleverness.

8. Old: **antique—old-fashioned—obsolete—dated**

   *Antique* is typical of an earlier period, belonging to ancient times (implies value); *old-fashioned* is of a style or method formerly in vogue, now outdated; *obsolete* is no longer in use, outmoded in design, style, or construction; and *dated* is outmoded.

9. Cautious: **wary—vigilant—careful**

   *Wary* is on guard, watchful, characterized by caution; *vigilant* is also watchful, alert, aware (may imply more aggressive watchfulness); and *careful* is attentive to potential danger, error, or harm.

10. Trip: **excursion—pilgrimage—vacation—tour**

    An *excursion* is a pleasure trip or outing; *pilgrimage* implies a spiritual aspect, as in a journey to a sacred place; *vacation* is a holiday from work; and *tour* is a trip to various places for business, pleasure, or instruction.

# Use Words with Multiple or Unusual Meanings

■ GOAL 4

Use words with multiple or unusual meanings

Many words have more than one meaning or meanings that change depending on the situation in which they are used. If you learn to use words in new, creative, and interesting ways, your vocabulary will expand quickly and you will be able to express yourself more clearly.

## Figurative Language

Here are three sentences that make sense in one way but not in another:

- The cake tasted like sawdust.
- Her answer was as unexpected as a white tiger appearing in my yard.
- Today, my boss, Martha Yarfield, is as nervous as an expectant father.

You know that a cake cannot really be made of sawdust, that answers are not white tigers, and that the boss is not an expectant father. Instead, you know that the writer means that the cake was dry and tasteless, that the answer was totally unexpected, and that the boss is full of anxious anticipation.

Each of these statements is an example of **figurative language**—a way of describing something that makes sense on an imaginative or creative level but not on a factual or literal level. None of the above statements is literally true, but each is meaningful. In many figurative expressions, one thing is compared to another for some quality they have in common. Two unlike objects, the cake and sawdust, share the characteristic of dryness.

The purpose of figurative language is to paint a word picture that will help the reader or listener visualize how something looks, feels, or smells. Figurative language allows the writer or speaker the opportunity to be creative and to express attitudes and opinions without directly stating them. Figurative language is used widely in literature, as well as many forms of expressive writing. Here are a few examples:

> I will speak daggers to her, but use none. (Shakespeare, *Hamlet*)
>
> An aged man is but a paltry thing, / a tattered coat upon a stick . . . (W. B. Yeats, *Sailing to Byzantium*)
>
> Time is but the stream I go a-fishing in. (Henry David Thoreau, *Walden*)
>
> Announced by all the trumpets of the sky, / arrives the snow . . . (Ralph Waldo Emerson, *The Snowstorm*)

The two most common types of figurative language are similes and metaphors. A **simile** uses the word *like* or *as* to make a comparison. A **metaphor** states or implies that one thing *is* another thing. If you say, "Mary's dress looks *like* a whirlwind of color," you have created a simile. If you say, "Mary's dress *is* a whirlwind of color," you have created a metaphor. Notice that each compares two unlike things, the dress and the whirlwind.

**EXERCISE 3-9**  Understanding Figurative Expressions

**Directions:** For the figurative expression indicated in each sentence, select the choice that best explains its meaning.

_b_    **1.** It was **an uphill battle** to get the insurance claim approved.
  a. dangerous
  b. extremely difficult
  c. physically tiring
  d. complicated

_a_    **2.** His face **clouded over** as soon as she said no.
  a. looked unhappy
  b. cleared up
  c. cooled off
  d. was shaded

_b_    **3.** She asked for the favor in a voice **dripping with honey.**
  a. sentimental
  b. overly sweet
  c. unpleasant
  d. sticky

_b_    **4.** At sunset, the surface of the lake was **like a piece of glass.**
  a. sharp
  b. smooth
  c. wavy
  d. hard

_d_    **5.** After dining at the all-you-can-eat buffet, he was **as full as a tick.**
  a. still hungry
  b. like a parasite
  c. rude
  d. stuffed with food

_c_    **6.** She politely asked her visitors to leave, but **icicles were hanging on every word.**
  a. it was winter
  b. she had a sparkling voice
  c. she spoke in a cold, unwelcoming manner
  d. she used fancy words

_a_    **7.** As he dozed in the hammock, the sun slowly moved across the yard and dropped **a soft, golden blanket** on him.
  a. warmth
  b. yellow leaves
  c. rain
  d. pollen

_c_    **8.** The sound of the chainsaw outside her window was **like a dentist drilling on her nerves.**
  a. a pleasant humming
  b. a sound she could ignore
  c. an extremely unpleasant sound
  d. an important and necessary sound

_d_    **9.** His birthday money was **burning a hole in his pocket!**
  a. on fire
  b. too heavy for his pocket to hold
  c. causing people to look at him
  d. making him anxious to spend it

_d_    **10.** Our computer is **a dinosaur.**
  a. huge
  b. awkward
  c. heavy
  d. outdated

## Idioms

Each of the following italicized expressions is an idiom:

- Does a *flea market* sell fleas?
- Does the *graveyard shift* mean you work in a graveyard?
- Does *"Close, but no cigar"* involve tobacco?

**Idioms** are phrases that have a meaning other than what the common definitions of the words in the phrase indicate. In the examples above, a *flea market* refers to an outdoor market where used goods and antiques are sold, the *graveyard shift* refers to a work shift beginning late at night, and *"Close, but no cigar"* is another way of saying "that's almost correct but not quite." There are thousands of idioms in use in the English language, and they are often particularly puzzling to nonnative speakers. To find the meaning of an idiom, look in a dictionary under one of the key words. For instance, look under *crow* to find the meaning of the idiom *as the crow flies*. In a dictionary, idioms are often labeled "idiom" and followed by the complete phrase and its meaning.

## EXERCISE 3-10 | Defining Idioms

**Directions:** Write a definition of each of the following idioms.    Answers will vary.

1. to keep tabs on  to observe carefully

2. to learn the ropes  to learn something new

3. like a chicken with its head cut off  in a crazed or frenzied manner

4. peeping tom  a man who enjoys observing naked or sexually active people

5. to steal someone's thunder  to use someone else's ideas without his or her consent

6. rule of thumb  a practical rule or guideline, often based on estimation rather than exact science

7. straight from the horse's mouth  from the highest authority or original source

8. in the dark  uninformed

9. under the weather  slightly ill

10. let the cat out of the bag  to reveal a secret

## Euphemisms

What do each of the following sentences have in common?

- Where is the ladies' room?
- My aunt passed away.
- I work for the sanitation department.

Each uses an expression called a **euphemism**—a word or phrase that is used in place of a word that is unpleasant, embarrassing, or otherwise objectionable. The expression *passed away* replaces the word *died, ladies' room* is a substitute for *toilet*, and *sanitation* is a more pleasing term than *garbage*.

The word *euphemism* comes from the Greek roots *eu*, meaning "sounding good," and *pheme*, meaning "speech." Euphemisms have a long history going back to ancient languages and cultures. Ancient people thought of names as extensions of the things themselves. To know and say the name of a person or object gave the speaker power over that person or object. Thus, calling something by its name was avoided, even forbidden. God, Satan, deceased relatives, and hunted animals would often be referred to indirectly. For example, in one culture God was called the Kindly One; the bear was called the Grandfather.

Today, many euphemisms are widely used in both spoken and written language. Here are a few more examples:

> The objective of the air strike was to **neutralize** the enemy. (kill the enemy)
>
> Some **collateral damage** occurred as a result of the air strike. (death to civilians)
>
> When it is hot, women **glow**. (sweat)

Euphemisms tend to minimize or downplay the importance or seriousness of something. They are often used in politics and advertising. They can be used to camouflage actions or events that may be unacceptable to readers or listeners if bluntly explained. For example, the word *casualties of war* may be used instead of the phrase *dead soldiers* to lessen the impact of an attack. To say that a politician's statement was *at variance with the truth* is less forceful than to say that the politician *lied*.

When you speak or write, be sure to avoid euphemisms that obscure or interfere with your intended meaning. Euphemisms can lead your listeners or readers to believe that you have something to hide or that you are not being completely truthful with them.

## EXERCISE 3-11    Understanding Euphemisms

**Directions:** For each of the boldfaced euphemisms, determine the meaning of the term, and then write a new sentence that does not minimize or avoid the term's real meaning.   Answers will vary.

**EXAMPLE**    The theater had only one **ladies' room**.

*The theater had only one toilet for several hundred women.*

1. The search continued for the **remains** of the victims of the air crash.
   bodies

2. The advertising campaign was an **incomplete success**.
   failure

3. The presidential aide was accused of spreading **disinformation**.
   deliberately misleading information (lies)

4. We took our broken refrigerator to the **sanitary landfill**.
   garbage dump

5. The company announced that it would be **downsizing** several hundred employees over the next few months. firing

6. The business recorded a **negative cash flow** last month.
   loss of money

7. We noticed that she **was carrying a little extra weight**.
   was overweight, heavy

8. The car dealership sold both new and **previously owned** automobiles.
   used

9. Witnesses reported that the two men **exchanged words** before the gun was fired. argued

10. The veterinarian recommended that the elderly cat be **put to sleep**.
    killed

## Commonly Confused Words

Which sentence in each of the following pairs is correct?

The stationary bike is broken.

The stationary is on my desk.

Lay the package on the table.

Lie the package on the table.

The couple will divide the settlement between them.

The couple will divide the settlement among them.

Answers: The first sentence in each pair is correct.

There are many word pairs or groups, such as those above, that are commonly confused and misused.

---

**EXERCISE 3-12**   ## Identifying Commonly Confused Words

**Directions:** Underline the correct word in parentheses to complete each of the following sentences.

1. It is my pleasure to (<u>accept</u>, except) your offer.

2. Please (<u>wait for</u>, wait on) me to move those books before you (sit, <u>set</u>) your laptop on the desk.

3. They had hoped to meet us for dinner before the play, but (<u>their</u>, they're, there) babysitter was late, so (their, <u>they're</u>, there) going to meet us (their, they're, <u>there</u>).

4. Baked apples make a delicious (<u>complement</u>, compliment) to roast pork.

5. My husband is (to, too, <u>two</u>) years younger (<u>than</u>, then) his brother.

6. When the (<u>principal</u>, principle) retired after 20 years, she offered excellent (<u>advice</u>, advise) to her successor.

7. The announcement had such an (affect, <u>effect</u>) on her that she gave (<u>explicit</u>, implicit) instructions not to be disturbed for the rest of the day.

8. I know (its, <u>it's</u>) still early, but what are (<u>your</u>, you're) thoughts about where (your, <u>you're</u>) going to work next summer?

9. She made several (<u>allusions</u>, illusions) to his mysterious past, but we were unable to (imply, <u>infer</u>) what she was trying to (<u>imply</u>, infer).

10. I need to (<u>elicit</u>, illicit) more information about what happened before I decide (who's, <u>whose</u>) side I am on.

---

**EXERCISE 3-13**   ## Using Commonly Confused Words Correctly

**Directions:** For the following pairs of words, write a sentence using each word correctly.   Answers will vary.

1. bring: *Please bring a dessert.*

   take: *Take the leftovers home with you.*

2. conscience: *Peter's conscience bothered him because he failed to report the crime.*

   conscious: *Jose was conscious of the error.*

3. real: *The gemstone was real.*

   really: *Peter said he was really sorry for his rudeness.*

4. good: *I really need a good hamburger.*

   well: *The performance went well.*

5. loose: *There was a loose stone in the ring.*

   lose: *I lose my glasses frequently.*

# Understand Vocabulary in College Courses

■ GOAL 5
Understand vocabulary in college courses

For each course you take, you encounter an extensive set of words and terms that are used in a particular way in that subject area. One of the most important tasks you face in college is to learn the vocabulary of each course. This task is especially important in introductory courses in which the subject is new and unfamiliar.

## College Textbooks

Because textbooks are written by professors, the authors know which words you know and which you need to learn. They include various features in their textbooks to help you learn the vocabulary needed to master the course.

■ **Context clues.** Because textbook authors know much of the terminology they use is unfamiliar, they often provide obvious context clues. *Definition, synonym,* and *example clues* are the most common. (Context clues will be discussed in detail in Chapter 4.)

*synonym*

Actus reus or "guilty deed" occurs when an individual (whether as a principal, accessory, or accomplice) engages in a behavior prohibited by the criminal law. This can involve either doing something wrong (commission) or failing to do something that is legally obligated (omission).

—Fuller, *Criminal Justice*, p. 135

When a case is scheduled to be heard, the attorneys file written arguments, as well as briefs on behalf of other parties that are called

*synonym*

amicus curiae ("friend of the court") briefs. For instance, an organization such as the American Civil Liberties Union or Amnesty International may file an *amicus curiae* brief in a case involving the death penalty for someone who is mentally retarded.

— Fuller, *Criminal Justice*, p. 280

■ **Marginal definitions.** Many textbooks include the meaning of unfamiliar terms in the margin next to where the word is first used.

**Magna Carta**
"Great Charter"; a guarantee of liberties signed by King John of England in 1215.

The English **Magna Carta,** a major document that contributed to U.S. law, limited the king's power and provided for the rights of citizens. King John signed the Magna Carta at Runnymede, England, on June 15, 1215, conceding a number of legal rights to the barons and the people. To finance his foreign wars, King John had taxed abusively. His barons threatened rebellion and coerced the king into committing to rudimentary judicial guarantees, such as freedom of the church, fair taxation,

*habeas corpus*
A writ issued to bring a party before the court.

controls over imprisonment (*habeas corpus*), and the rights of all merchants to come and go freely, except in times of war.

—Fuller, *Criminal Justice*, p. 120

Highlight these definitions as you read. Be sure to check them again as you review and study for exams. If there is a lot of terminology to learn, use the index card system described below.

■ **Chapter vocabulary review.** This list identifies key terms introduced during the chapter, often followed by page numbers indicating where the terms were first used. This list may appear either at the beginning or at the end of the chapter. Check this list before you read the chapter so you will know what key words to look for.

---

## Key Terms

| | |
|---|---|
| bedding plane (p. 154) | cross-bedding (p. 154) |
| beds (strata) (p. 154) | crystalline texture (p. 151) |
| biochemical origin (p. 144) | detrital sedimentary rock (p. 139) |
| cap rock (p. 158) | diagenesis (p. 149) |
| cementation (p. 149) | environment of deposition (p. 151) |
| chemical sedimentary rock (p. 139) | evaporite (p. 148) |
| clastic (p. 150) | fossil (p. 156) |
| compaction (p. 149) | fossil fuel (p. 157) |

---

—Lutgens et al., *Essentials of Geology*, p. 160

As you read, highlight each term and its definition. Use the list as a study aid later: test yourself to be sure you can define each term. You might place each term on an index card, writing the word on the front and its meaning on the back. Shuffle the pack frequently, define each term, and then check the accuracy of your definition by turning the card over.

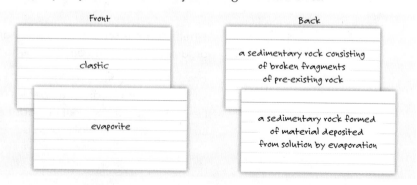

Front

clastic

evaporite

Back

a sedimentary rock consisting of broken fragments of pre-existing rock

a sedimentary rock formed of material deposited from solution by evaporation

■ **Glossaries**. Appearing at the end of a text, a glossary is an alphabetical list of new terms introduced in the text. Use it to check the meanings of words not defined in the text or those you may have forgotten. If all the chapters in a text have been assigned, you can use the glossary to review for final exams. Scan the glossary; look for words that are unfamiliar or that you are unable to give a complete definition for and learn their meanings.

---

**Berm**   The dry, gently sloping zone on the backshore of a beach at the foot of the coastal cliffs or dunes.

**Biochemical**   Describing a type of chemical sediment that forms when material dissolved in water is precipitated by water-dwelling organisms. Shells are common examples.

**Biogenous sediment**   Seafloor sediments consisting of material of marine-organic origin.

**Bituminous coal**   The most common form of coal, often called soft, black coal.

**Block lava**   Lava having a surface of angular blocks associated with material having andesitic and rhyolitic compositions.

---

—Lutgens et al., *Essentials of Geology*, p. 484

## EXERCISE 3-14

## Using Vocabulary in Textbooks

**Directions:** Choose a textbook chapter that you have been assigned to read for one of your other courses. Identify ten new words that you are able to determine the meaning of using context clues, marginal definitions, the chapter vocabulary review, or the glossary.

## EXERCISE 3-15

*WORKING TOGETHER*

## Using Vocabulary in Textbooks

**Directions:** Working with a classmate, each choose a textbook from one of your courses and then exchange textbooks. Identify five words or terms in your classmate's textbook and write each one on the front of an index card, then return the cards and the textbook to your classmate. Each of you should then look for the terms in your textbook, and write each definition on the back of the corresponding card.

### Classes and Lectures

Often, the first few class lectures in a course are devoted to acquainting students with the nature and scope of the field and introducing them to its specialized language.

You can see, then, that many disciplines devote considerable time to presenting the language of the course carefully and explicitly. Be sure to record accurately each new term for later review and study. Good lecturers give students clues to what terms and definitions are important to record. They may

- write new words on the board, as a means of emphasis
- highlight new terms using PowerPoint
- slow down, almost dictating so that you can record definitions
- repeat a word and its definition several times or offer several variations of meaning

As a part of your note-taking system (see Tip #7 on p. 13), develop a consistent way of easily identifying new terms and definitions recorded in your notes. You might circle or draw a box around each new term; or, as you edit your notes, highlight each new term; or write "def." in the margin each time a definition is included. The particular mark or symbol you use is a matter of preference; the important thing is to find some way to mark definitions for further study.

## EXERCISE 3-16  Identifying New Terms

**Directions:** Estimate the number of new terms that each of your instructors introduced during the first several weeks for each of your courses. Now, check the accuracy of your estimates by reviewing the first two weeks of your class notes for each course you are taking. How many new terms and definitions were included for each course?

# INTEGRATING READING AND WRITING

## READ AND RESPOND: A Professional Essay

### Thinking Before Reading

In the following selection from an interpersonal communication textbook, the authors explore the idea that words have power. As you read, look for examples of connotative language, figurative language, and idioms.

1. Preview the reading, using the steps discussed in Chapter 1 on page 25.
2. Connect the reading to your own experience by answering the following questions:
   a. Have you ever been hurt by someone else's use of words?
   b. When have you been persuaded or influenced by words? (Hint: Think of the words used in recent commercial or political advertisements.)
3. Highlight and annotate as you read.

1080*L*/916 words

# The Power of Words

## Beebe, Beebe, and Redmond

Sticks and stones may break my bones,
But words can never hurt me.

1    This old schoolyard chant may provide a ready retort for the desperate victim of name-calling, but it is hardly convincing. With more insight, the poet Robert Browning wrote, "Words break no bones; hearts though sometimes." And in his book *Science and Sanity,* mathematician and engineer Alfred Korzybski argued that the words we use (and misuse) have tremendous effects on our thoughts and actions. Browning and Korzybski were right. Words have power.

### Words Create Perceptions

2    "To name is to call into existence—to call out of nothingness," wrote French philosopher Georges Gusdorff. Words give you a tool to create how you perceive the world by naming and labeling what you experience. You undoubtedly learned in your elementary science class that Sir Isaac Newton discovered gravity. It would be more accurate to say that he *labeled* rather than discovered it. His use of the word *gravity* gave us a cognitive category; we now converse about the pull of the earth's forces that keeps us from flying into space. Words give us the symbolic vehicles to communicate our creations and discoveries to others.

3    When you label something as "good" or "bad," you are using language to create your own vision of how you experience the world. If you tell a friend that the movie you saw last night was vulgar and obscene, you are not only providing your friend with a critique of the movie; you are also communicating your sense of what is appropriate and inappropriate.

### Words Influence Thoughts

4    If someone says, "Don't think about a pink elephant," it's hard *not* to think about a pink elephant, because just thinking the words *pink elephant* more than likely triggers an image of a pink pachyderm. Words and thoughts are inextricably linked. Words influence our thoughts

5    Is it possible to think without using words or numbers? Yes, we can certainly experience emotions without describing them in words and enjoy music without lyrics. Artists paint, dancers dance, and architects dream new structures, all without words. Yet words are what transmit our dreams and our emotions to others when we verbalize what we feel. Words have tremendous power to influence what we think about, just as our thinking influences the words we use.

6    There is scientific evidence that words influence our thoughts. As Figure A illustrates, the process of hearing, seeing, or saying words influences different parts of the brain. How we use words literally changes our brain activity.

7    Because words have the power to influence our thoughts, the meaning of a word resides within us, rather than in the word itself. Words *symbolize* meaning, but the precise meaning of a word originates in the mind of the sender and the receiver. The meaning of a word is not static; it evolves as a conversation evolves. Your

## FIGURE A    WORDS INFLUENCE BRAIN ACTIVITY

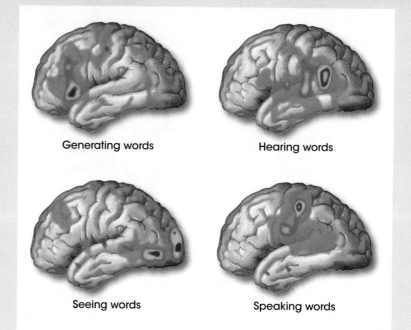

Generating words                    Hearing words

Seeing words                    Speaking words

meanings for words and phrases change as you gain additional experiences and have new thoughts about the words you use.

### Words Influence Actions

8    A paraphrase of a well-known verse from the book of Proverbs in the Bible tells us, "As a person thinks, so is he or she." Words not only have the power to create and influence your thoughts, they also influence your actions—because your thoughts, which are influenced by words, affect how you behave. Advertisers have long known that slogans and catch phrases sell products. Political candidates also know that the words they use influence whether they will get your vote.

9    Words are powerful in influencing behaviors. Bumper stickers about gay marriage and abortion refer to contemporary issues that pack an emotional wallop and generate intense reactions. What other words that appear on bumper stickers today might elicit strong reactions?

10    Research suggests that the very way we use language can communicate the amount of power we have in a conversation with others. We use language in ways that are both powerful and powerless. When we use powerless speech, we are less persuasive and have less influence on others. Powerless speech is characterized by more frequent use of pauses, which may be filled with "umm," "ahhh," and "ehh." We also express our lack of power by using more hesitation and unnecessary verbal fillers like "you know," and "I mean." We communicate our low power when we hedge our conclusions by saying "I guess" and "sort of." Another way of communicating a lack of power is by tacking on a question at the end of a statement, such as "I'm right, aren't I?" or "This is what I think, OK?" So, the very way in which you speak can influence the thoughts and actions of others.

### Words Make and Break Relationships

11    What you say and how you say it have a strong impact on how you relate to others. Relationships are the connections we make with others. To relate to another person is like dancing with the person. When you dance with a partner, your moves and countermoves respond to the rhythm of the music and the moves your partner makes. In our interpersonal relationships with others, we "dance" as we relate to our communication partners with both language and nonverbal cues. A good conversation has a rhythm, created by both communicators as they listen and respond to each other. Even our "small talk," which is our everyday, sometimes brief, responses and exchanges with others ("Nice weather we're having" or, simply, "Oh, that's nice"), is important in establishing how we feel about others. The words we use, especially in our daily conversations, are directly related to the quality of the relationships we have with others.

—Beebe, Beebe, and Redmond, *Interpersonal Communication*, pp. 157–161

# Getting Ready to Write

## Checking Your Comprehension

Answer each of the following questions using complete sentences.

1.  Who is Alfred Korzybski and what does he say about words?
2.  What happens when we label something as "good" or "bad"?
3.  What four processes involving words change our brain activity?
4.  Describe four characteristics of powerless speech.
5.  What activity do the authors compare to how we communicate in interpersonal relationships?
6.  Define the idiom "small talk."

## Strengthening Your Vocabulary

Using the word's context, word parts, or a dictionary, write a brief definition of each of the following words as it is used in the reading.

1.  converse (paragraph 2) _talk_
2.  inextricably (paragraph 4) _so closely tied as to be difficult to separate_
3.  transmit (paragraph 5) _communicate_
4.  resides (paragraph 7) _is located in, lives_
5.  static (paragraph 7) _unchanging_
6.  elicit (paragraph 9) _draw out_
7.  hedge (paragraph 10) _are cautious about_

## Examining the Reading: Using Idea Maps

Review the reading by completing the missing parts of the following idea map.

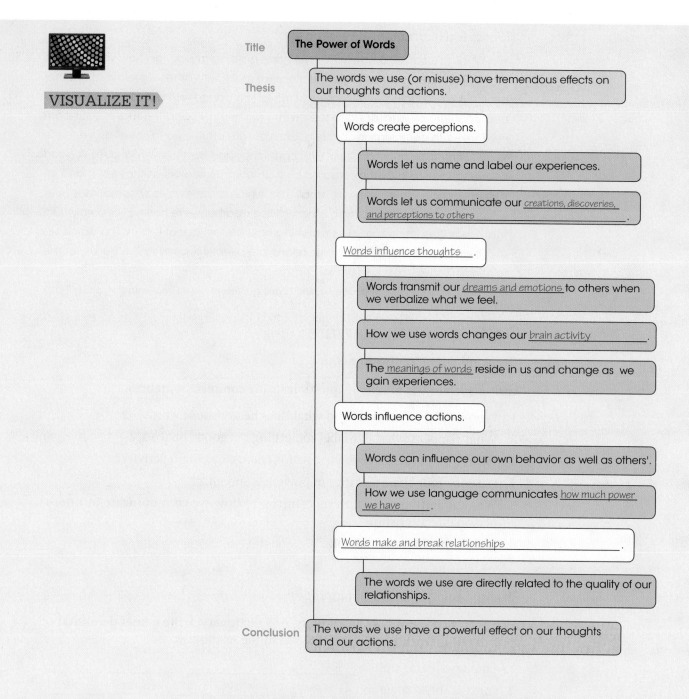

**VISUALIZE IT!**

Title — **The Power of Words**

Thesis — The words we use (or misuse) have tremendous effects on our thoughts and actions.

Words create perceptions.

Words let us name and label our experiences.

Words let us communicate our <u>creations, discoveries, and perceptions to others</u>.

<u>Words influence thoughts</u>.

Words transmit our <u>dreams and emotions</u> to others when we verbalize what we feel.

How we use words changes our <u>brain activity</u>.

The <u>meanings of words</u> reside in us and change as we gain experiences.

Words influence actions.

Words can influence our own behavior as well as others'.

How we use language communicates <u>how much power we have</u>.

<u>Words make and break relationships</u>.

The words we use are directly related to the quality of our relationships.

Conclusion — The words we use have a powerful effect on our thoughts and our actions.

## Thinking Critically: Discussion and Journal Writing

React and respond to the reading by discussing the following:

1.  Does the schoolyard chant ("Sticks and stones . . .") at the beginning of the reading capture your attention? Discuss why this rhyme is relevant to the subject of the reading.

2.  Why is it important to be able to name or label our experiences? Write a journal entry answering this question and discussing the idea of words as symbolic vehicles.

3. Discuss the idea that the meanings of words and phrases change. Can you think of an example of a word that has evolved as you have gained life experiences?

4. Discuss current advertisements for products or politicians. What are examples of words used to influence your actions?

5. Why did the authors include Figure A? What concept in the reading does it illustrate?

**MySkillsLab®**

Complete this Exercise

## Writing About the Reading

### Paragraph Options

1. In addition to the schoolyard chant, the authors quote the poet Robert Browning (paragraph 1), the French philosopher Georges Gusdorff (paragraph 2), and the Book of Proverbs in the Bible (paragraph 8). Choose one of these quotations and write a paragraph explaining its meaning.

2. Choose an advertising slogan or catch phrase that has made an impression on you and write a paragraph explaining what makes the slogan or phrase effective, persuasive, or memorable.

3. Identify five words in the reading that have positive or negative connotations and write a paragraph describing the denotative and connotative meanings of these words.

### Essay Options

4. What does the phrase "'packs an emotional wallop" mean? Write an essay that first explains the meaning of that phrase, and then describes and explains an issue that packs an emotional wallop for you.

5. Consider how power is communicated through language. Who do you know who communicates power (or lack of power) in conversation? In what situations do you typically use powerful language? Are there situations or relationships in which you use powerless speech? Write an essay exploring these questions and using examples from your own experience.

6. The authors say that "to relate to another person is like dancing with the person." How effectively does this comparison express the authors' point? Write an essay exploring the idea that we "dance" in our interpersonal relationships with others, and see if you can come up with your own comparison describing what happens as we relate to our communication partners.

# SELF-TEST SUMMARY

To test yourself, cover the Answer column with a sheet of paper and answer each question in the left column. Evaluate each of your answers as you work by sliding the paper down and comparing your answer with what is printed in the Answer column.

| QUESTION | ANSWER |
|---|---|
| **GOAL 1** Use a dictionary effectively<br><br>What is involved in using a dictionary effectively? | Using a dictionary effectively involves selecting the right type of dictionary for the situation, understanding the kinds of information provided in a dictionary, and choosing the appropriate meaning of a word. |
| **GOAL 2** Use synonyms and antonyms<br><br>What are synonyms and antonyms? What is a thesaurus? | *Synonyms* are words with similar meanings; *antonyms* are words with opposite meanings.<br>A *thesaurus* is a dictionary of synonyms and can be used to find a precise term, to replace overused words, and to provide antonyms for words. |
| **GOAL 3** Understand denotative and connotative language<br><br>What are denotative and connotative language? | The *denotative* meaning of a word is its standard, dictionary meaning. The *connotative* meaning of a word includes the feelings and associations that may accompany it. |
| **GOAL 4** Use words with multiple or unusual meanings<br><br>What is figurative language and what are some types of figurative language?<br><br>What is an idiom? | *Figurative language* is a way of describing something that makes sense on an imaginative or creative level but not on a factual or literal level. Two common types of figurative language are *similes* (comparisons using the word *like* or *as*) and *metaphors* (comparisons stating or implying that one thing is another thing). An *idiom* is a phrase that has a meaning other than what the common definitions of the words in the phrase indicate. |
| **GOAL 5** Understand vocabulary in college courses<br><br>What features are included in college textbooks to help you learn vocabulary? | Textbooks include context clues, marginal definitions, chapter vocabulary reviews, and glossaries. |

# MySkillsLab

For more help with **Vocabulary**, go to your learning path in MySkillsLab at http://www.myskillslab.com.

# Vocabulary: Approaching Unknown Words

# 4

## LEARNING GOALS

Learn how to . . .

- **GOAL 1**
  Figure out unknown words

- **GOAL 2**
  Pronounce unknown words

- **GOAL 3**
  Use context clues

- **GOAL 4**
  Use word parts

- **GOAL 5**
  Learn new words

## THINK About It!

### Building Your Vocabulary

The photograph shows a sign using the word *illegal*. If you did not know the meaning of *illegal*, how would you figure it out? One option is to check a dictionary. Another is to analyze word parts—the beginnings, middles, and endings of words. If you knew that the prefix *il-* means "not," you could work out that *illegal* means "not legal." Another option is to use the situation (or context) to help you figure out its meaning. In the photo, the other signs give you a clue to the meaning of *illegal*; in writing, other words in the same or surrounding sentences may provide clues to the meanings of unfamiliar words. Once you figured out the meaning of the word, how would you use it in your reading and writing? The purpose of this chapter is to show you how to expand your vocabulary by figuring out unfamiliar words and learning them so that you can read more effectively and write more clearly and precisely.

115

## FOCUSING ON READING AND WRITING

# Why Is Learning New Words Important?

Both in college and in the workplace, as well as in everyday life, you will constantly encounter and be expected to learn new words. In college, each course has its own language and your success in each course depends, in part, on your ability to read, speak, and write in the language of the discipline. In psychology, you are expected to learn and use words such as *conditioned stimulus, endorphins,* and *habituation.* In the workplace, you need to learn and use the terms that refer to products, procedures, policies, and business strategies. As a nurse, you would need to know terms such as *agglutinins, dehiscence,* and *hordeolum.* In everyday life, new words are constantly introduced into the language. New phrases introduced recently include *cloud computing, flash mob, gastropub,* and *helicopter parents.*

## READING

# Figure Out Unknown Words: A Strategy

■ **GOAL 1**
Figure out unknown words

What should you do when you are reading a passage and you come to a word you don't know?

Despite what you might expect, looking up a word in a dictionary is not the first thing to do when you encounter a word you don't know. In fact, a dictionary is your last resort—somewhere to turn when all else fails. Instead, first try pronouncing the word aloud. Hearing the word may help you recall its meaning. If pronouncing the word does not help, try to figure out the meaning of the word from the words around it in the sentence, paragraph, or passage that you are reading. Very often, these surrounding words include various clues that enable you to reason out the meaning of the unknown word. The words around an unknown word that contain clues to its meaning are referred to as the context. The clues themselves are called *context clues.* You can use five basic types of context clues in determining word meanings in textbook material: *definition, synonym, example, contrast,* and *inference.*

If a word's context does not provide clues to its meaning, you might try breaking the word into parts. Analyzing a word's parts, which may include its prefix, root, and suffix, also provides clues to its meaning. Finally, if word parts do not help, look up the word in a dictionary. Regardless of the method you use to find a word's meaning, be sure to record its meaning in the margin of the page. Later, transfer its meaning to your vocabulary log (see p. 142).

# Pronounce Unknown Words

■ **GOAL 2**
Pronounce unknown words

At one time or another, each of us comes across words that we are unable to pronounce. To pronounce an unfamiliar word, sound it out syllable by syllable. Here are a few simple rules for dividing words into syllables:

■ **Divide compound words between the individual words that form the compound word.**

| | | |
|---|---|---|
| house/broken | house/hold | space/craft |
| green/house | news/paper | sword/fish |

■ **Divide words between prefixes (word beginnings) and roots (base words) and/or between roots and suffixes (word endings).**

**Prefix + Root**

pre/read                post/pone               anti/war

**Root + Suffix**

sex/ist                 agree/ment              list/ing

For a more complete discussion of prefixes, roots, and suffixes, see "Use Word Parts" on page 128.

■ **Each syllable is a separate, distinct speech sound.** Pronounce the following words and try to hear the number of syllables in each:

| | |
|---|---|
| expensive | ex/pen/sive = 3 syllables |
| recognize | rec/og/nize = 3 syllables |
| punctuate | punc/tu/ate = 3 syllables |
| complicated | com/pli/cat/ed = 4 syllables |

■ **Each syllable has at least one vowel and usually one or more consonants.** The letters *a, e, i, o, u,* and sometimes *y* are vowels. All other letters are consonants.

as/sign         re/act          cou/pon         gen/er/al

■ **Divide words before a single consonant, unless the consonant is the letter *r*.**

hu/mid          re/tail         fa/vor          mor/on

■ **Divide words between two consonants appearing together.**

pen/cil         lit/ter         lum/ber         sur/vive

■ **Divide words between two vowel sounds that appear together.**

te/di/ous       ex/tra/ne/ous

These rules will prove helpful but, as you no doubt already know, there will often be exceptions.

---

**EXERCISE 4-1**  ## Dividing Words into Syllables

**Directions:** Use slash marks (/) to divide each of the following words into syllables.

1. political
   po/lit/i/cal
2. irregular
   ir/reg/u/lar
3. ordinal
   or/di/nal
4. hallow
   hal/low
5. judicature
   ju/di/ca/ture

6. innovative
   in/no/va/tive
7. obtuse
   ob/tuse
8. germicide
   ger/mi/cide
9. futile
   fu/tile
10. extoll
    ex/toll

11. tangelo
    tan/ge/lo
12. symmetry
    sym/me/try
13. telepathy
    te/lep/a/thy
14. librarian
    li/brar/i/an
15. hideous
    hid/e/ous

16. tenacity
    te/nac/i/ty
17. mesmerize
    mes/mer/ize
18. intrusive
    in/tru/sive
19. infallible
    in/fal/li/ble
20. fanaticism
    fa/nat/i/cism

# Use Context Clues

Closely studying the words in a sentence can help you figure out the meaning of a particular word within the sentence. Read the following brief paragraph. Several words are missing. Try to figure out the missing words and write them in the blanks.

> Jayla has never been to Mexico, but she loves _____ food. Her favorite dish is _____, those delicious tortilla chips covered with cheese, beef, and beans. Just thinking about them makes Sally _____.

Did you insert the word *Mexican* in the first blank, *nachos* in the second blank, and *hungry* in the third blank? You were probably able to correctly identify all three missing words. You could tell from each sentence which word to put in. The words around each word—the sentence **context**—gave you clues as to which word would fit and make sense. Such clues are called **context clues.**

Even though you won't find missing words on a printed page, you will often find words that you do not know. Context clues can help you figure out the meanings of unfamiliar words.

> Tony noticed that the **wallabies** at the zoo looked like kangaroos.

From the sentence, you can tell that *wallabies* are "animals that look like kangaroos."

> Many people have **phobias**, such as a fear of heights, a fear of water, or a fear of confined spaces.

You can figure out that *phobia* means "a fear of specific objects or situations."

## Types of Context Clues

When you have trouble with a word, look for five types of context clues: (1) definition, (2) synonym, (3) example, (4) contrast, and (5) inference.

### Definition Clues

Writers often define a word right after they use it. They may use words and phrases such as *means, is, refers to,* and *are called* to signal that a definition is to follow.

> Broad, flat noodles that are served covered with sauce or butter *are called* **fettuccine.**
>
> **Corona** *refers to* the outermost part of the sun's atmosphere.

At other times, rather than formally define a word, a writer may provide a clue to its meaning.

> During the Christmas season, many people use decorative lights to **illuminate** their homes.

Here the word *lights* is a clue to the meaning of *illuminate*, which means to "light up."

Sometimes a definition is only part of a sentence. In this kind of sentence, a writer may use three kinds of punctuation (commas, dashes, or parentheses) to separate the definition from the rest of the sentence.

My Aunt Martha often serves **glögg**, *a Swedish hot punch,* at her holiday parties.

The judge's **candor**—*his sharp, open frankness*—shocked the jury.

A leading cause of heart disease is a diet with too much **cholesterol** (*a fatty substance made of carbon, hydrogen, and oxygen*).

Textbook writers often use definition clues. As you read your texts, look for important words in **boldfaced type** or *italics*. These terms are usually right before or after a definition. Based on what you have just learned, what is the definition of **context** on page 118? What clues did you use to identify it?

## EXERCISE 4-2    Using Definition Clues

**Directions:** Using the definition clues in each sentence, select the choice that best defines each boldfaced word.

_a_   **1.** After taking a course in **genealogy**, Xavier was able to create a record of his family's history dating back to the eighteenth century.
  **a.** the study of ancestry
  **b.** creative writing
  **c.** the study of plants
  **d.** personal finance

_b_   **2.** Participants in a **triathlon** compete in long-distance swimming, bicycling, and running.
  **a.** hiking trail
  **b.** three-part race
  **c.** large group
  **d.** written test

_d_   **3.** Louie's **dossier** is a record of his credentials, including college transcripts and letters of recommendation.
  **a.** briefcase or valise
  **b.** checking account statement
  **c.** diploma
  **d.** file of documents

_b_   **4. Audition**, the process of hearing, begins when a sound wave reaches the outer ear.
  **a.** loud sound
  **b.** process of hearing
  **c.** deafness
  **d.** the inner ear

_a_   **5.** A person who becomes an **entrepreneur** must be willing to take on both the risks and opportunities of his or her new business.
  **a.** business owner
  **b.** stockbroker
  **c.** employee
  **d.** designer

### Synonym Clues

At other times, rather than formally define a word, a writer may provide a **synonym**—a word or brief phrase that is close in meaning. The synonym may appear in the same sentence as the unknown word.

> The main character in the novel was an **amalgam**, or *combination,* of several people the author met during the war.

Other times, it may appear anywhere in the passage, in an earlier or later sentence.

> Isabella took a *break* from teaching in order to serve in the Peace Corps. Despite the **hiatus**, Isabella's school was delighted to rehire her when she returned.

**EXERCISE 4-3**

## Using Synonym Clues

**Directions:** Using the synonym clues in each sentence, select the choice that best defines each boldfaced word.

_d_ **1.** The noise in the nursery school was **incessant**; the crying, yelling, and laughing never stopped.
   **a.** careless        **c.** bold
   **b.** harmful        **d.** continuous

_d_ **2.** There was a **consensus**—or unified opinion—among the students that the exam was difficult.
   **a.** requirement        **c.** disagreement
   **b.** consequence        **d.** agreement

_c_ **3.** The family's decision to donate their land to the park system was **altruistic**; they were unselfish in their desire to do what was best for the community.
   **a.** shrewd        **c.** selfless
   **b.** thoughtless        **d.** greedy

_b_ **4.** After each course heading there was a **synopsis**, or summary, of the content and requirements for the course.
   **a.** correction        **c.** illustration
   **b.** brief description        **d.** continuation

_b_ **5.** When preparing job application letters, Serena develops one standard letter or **template**. Then she changes that letter to fit the specific jobs she is applying for.
   **a.** variation        **c.** detail
   **b.** model        **d.** introduction

_b_ **6.** The mayor worried that the town council was trying to **usurp** her power, but how could she prevent the council members from taking over?
   **a.** support        **c.** improve
   **b.** take away        **d.** allow

_b_ **7.** Joe was **hesitant** about asking Katy for a date because he was unsure if she liked him.
   **a.** definite        **c.** casual
   **b.** uncertain        **d.** heroic

_c_ **8.** The old man avoided his family; in fact, he **eschewed** the company of anyone who knew about his past.
  **a.** sought out          **c.** shunned
  **b.** enjoyed             **d.** welcomed

_d_ **9.** Rico approves of the new drunk driving laws, but he does not **endorse** taking away drunk drivers' cars.
  **a.** stop                **c.** start
  **b.** regret              **d.** support

_c_ **10.** The teenager died from drinking a **lethal** amount of alcohol during a party.
  **a.** harmless            **c.** deadly
  **b.** moderate            **d.** excessive

### Example Clues

Writers, especially textbook writers, often include examples to help explain or clarify a word. Suppose you do not know the meaning of the word *toxic,* and you find it used in a science text:

> **Toxic** materials, such as arsenic, asbestos, pesticides, and lead, can cause bodily damage.

This sentence gives four examples of toxic materials, all of which are poisonous substances. You could conclude, then, that *toxic* means "poisonous." When writers put examples in a sentence, they often introduce them with the words *like, such as, for example,* or *including.*

> In the past month, we have had almost every type of **precipitation,** including rain, snow, sleet, and hail.
>
> **Newsmagazines,** like *Time* or *Newsweek,* are more detailed than newspapers.
>
> Lena doesn't mind planting her favorite **annuals**—marigolds and zinnias—even though she has to do it every year.

By using the example clues, can you figure out that *precipitation* means "the forms in which water returns to earth" and that *newsmagazines* are "magazines that give in-depth coverage of news events"? Can you also tell that *annuals* are "plants that can't survive the winter"?

| EXERCISE 4-4 | Using Example Clues |

**Directions:** Using the example clues in each sentence, select the choice that best defines each boldfaced word.

_c_ **1.** Many **pharmaceuticals,** including morphine and penicillin, are not readily available in some countries.
  **a.** aspirin tablets      **c.** drugs
  **b.** pharmacists          **d.** substances

___a___ 2. Diego's child was **reticent** in every respect; she would not speak, refused to answer questions, and avoided looking at anyone.
a. reserved        c. undisciplined
b. noisy           d. rigorous

___b___ 3. Most **condiments**, such as pepper, mustard, and catsup, are used to improve the flavor of foods.
a. ingredients     c. sauces
b. seasonings      d. appetizers

___b___ 4. Dogs, cats, parakeets, and other **sociable** pets can provide senior citizens with companionship.
a. weak            c. dangerous
b. friendly        d. unattractive

___b___ 5. Paul's grandmother is a **sagacious** businesswoman; once she turned a small ice cream shop into a popular restaurant and sold it for a huge profit.
a. old fashioned   c. dishonest
b. shrewd          d. foolish

___b___ 6. Rosie's dog was **submissive**—crouching, flattening its ears, and avoiding eye contact.
a. friendly and excitable    c. aggressive
b. yielding to the control    d. active
   of another

___c___ 7. Many things about the library make it **conducive** to study, including good lighting and many reference books.
a. unattractive    c. helpful
b. uncomfortable   d. sociable

___c___ 8. Clothing is available in a variety of **fabrics**, including cotton, wool, polyester, and linen.
a. types of leather  c. materials
b. styles            d. fashions

___c___ 9. The raccoons were a **menace** to our backyard. They ate all of our tomato plants and dug holes in the grass.
a. help            c. threat
b. barrier         d. force

___c___ 10. Murder, rape, and armed robbery are **reprehensible** crimes.
a. reasonable      c. blameworthy
b. unusual         d. rural

### Contrast Clues

Sometimes you can determine the meaning of an unknown word from an **antonym**—a word or phrase that has an opposite meaning. Notice how the antonym *resisted* in the following sentence provides a clue to the meaning of the boldfaced term:

> One of the dinner guests **succumbed** to the temptation to have a second piece of cake, but the others resisted.

Since the others resisted a second dessert, you can tell that one guest gave in and had a piece. Thus, *succumbed* means the opposite of *resisted*; that is, "gave in to."

When writers use contrasting words or phrases, they often introduce them with words such as *but, though,* and *whereas.*

> The professor **advocates** testing on animals, but many of her students are opposed to it.
>
> Though Sofia felt sad and depressed, most of the graduates were **elated.**
>
> My Uncle Saul is quite **portly,** whereas his wife is very thin.

Can you tell from the contrast clues that *advocates* means "favors," *elated* means "happy," and *portly* means "heavy"?

## EXERCISE 4-5     Using Contrast Clues

**Directions:** Using the contrast clues or antonyms in each sentence, select the choice that best defines each boldfaced word or phrase.

_a_  1. Freshmen are often **naive** about college at first, but by their second semester they are usually quite sophisticated in the ways of their new school.
    **a.** innocent        **c.** annoyed
    **b.** sociable        **d.** elated

_d_  2. Although most members of the class agreed with the instructor's evaluation of the film, several strongly **objected.**
    **a.** agreed        **c.** obliterated
    **b.** debated        **d.** disagreed

_b_  3. Little Lola hid shyly behind her mother when she met new people, yet her brother Matthew was very **gregarious.**
    **a.** insulting        **c.** concerned
    **b.** sociable        **d.** embarrassed

_a_  4. The child remained **demure** while the teacher scolded but became violently angry afterward.
    **a.** quiet and reserved        **c.** cowardly
    **b.** boisterous        **d.** upset and distraught

_c_  5. Some city dwellers are **affluent;** others live in or near poverty.
    **a.** poor        **c.** wealthy
    **b.** arrogant        **d.** agreeable

_b_  6. I am certain that the hotel will hold our reservation; however, if you are **dubious,** call to make sure.
    **a.** confused        **c.** sure
    **b.** doubtful        **d.** energetic

_c_  7. The speaker **denounced** certain legal changes while praising other reforms.
    **a.** laughed at        **c.** spoke out against
    **b.** cherished        **d.** denied

_a_  8. The woman's parents **thwarted** her marriage plans, though they liked her fiancé.
    **a.** prevented        **c.** idolized
    **b.** encouraged        **d.** organized

_a_ **9.** Extroverted people tend to be outgoing and talkative, while introverted people are more **reticent**.
- **a.** reserved
- **b.** showy
- **c.** overbearing
- **d.** helpless

_c_ **10.** Unlike other male-dominated species, Indian elephants live in a **matriarchal** society.
- **a.** aggressive
- **b.** nonthreatening
- **c.** led by females
- **d.** passive

### Inference Clues

When you read, you often figure out the meaning of an unknown word through **inference**—a process that uses logic and reasoning skills. For instance, look at the following sentence:

> Bob is quite versatile: he is a good student, a top athlete, an excellent car mechanic, and a gourmet cook.

Since Bob is successful at many different types of activities, you could infer that *versatile* means "capable of doing many things well."

> When my friend tried to pay with Mexican **pesos**, the clerk explained that the store accepted only U.S. dollars.

> On hot, humid summer afternoons, I often feel **languid**.

> The vase must have been **jostled** in shipment because it arrived with several chips in it.

By using logic and your reasoning skills, can you figure out that *pesos* are a kind of "Mexican money"? Can you also tell that *languid* means "lacking energy" and *jostled* means "bumped"?

### EXERCISE 4-6 — Using Inference Clues

**Directions:** Using logic and your reasoning skills, select the choice that best defines each boldfaced word.

_c_ **1.** To **compel** Clare to hand over her wallet, the mugger said he had a gun.
- **a.** discourage
- **b.** entice
- **c.** force
- **d.** imagine

_b_ **2.** Student journalists are taught how to be **concise** when writing in a limited space.
- **a.** peaceful
- **b.** clear and brief
- **c.** proper
- **d.** wordy

_c_ **3.** There should be more **drastic** penalties to stop people from littering.
- **a.** dirty
- **b.** suitable
- **c.** extreme
- **d.** dangerous

_d_ **4.** To **fortify** his diet while weightlifting, Monty took 12 vitamins a day.
- **a.** suggest
- **b.** approve of
- **c.** avoid
- **d.** strengthen

_b_  **5.** On our wedding anniversary, my husband and I **reminisced** about how we first met.
    **a.** sang     **c.** argued
    **b.** remembered     **d.** forgot

_a_  **6.** For their own safety, household pets should be **confined** to their own yards.
    **a.** restricted     **c.** shown
    **b.** led     **d.** used

_d_  **7.** The quarterback **sustained** numerous injuries: a fractured wrist, two broken ribs, and a hip injury.
    **a.** caused     **c.** displayed
    **b.** noticed     **d.** experienced

_a_  **8.** Sam's brother advised him to be **wary** of strangers he meets on the street.
    **a.** suspicious     **c.** congenial with
    **b.** trusting     **d.** generous toward

_c_  **9.** The lawyer tried to confuse the jury by bringing in many facts that weren't **pertinent** to the case.
    **a.** obvious     **c.** relevant
    **b.** continuous     **d.** harmful

_a_  **10.** We keep candles in the house to **avert** being left in the dark during power failures.
    **a.** prevent     **c.** accommodate
    **b.** ensure     **d.** begin

## EXERCISE 4-7    Using Context Clues

**Directions:** Using context clues, select the choice that best defines each bold-faced word.

_c_  **1.** The cat and her newborn kittens had to be **isolated** from the family dog after he tried to attack them.
    **a.** combined     **c.** separated
    **b.** heated up     **d.** rejected

_d_  **2.** All of the movies I wanted to rent were taken, so as an **alternative** I went home and watched television.
    **a.** command     **c.** assignment
    **b.** design     **d.** another option

_a_  **3.** The baby birds needed a place of **refuge** from the summer storm.
    **a.** shelter     **c.** building
    **b.** rejection     **d.** separation

_b_  **4.** Mike's efforts to buy a car were **futile**, so he continued to ride his bike to work.
    **a.** helpful     **c.** necessary
    **b.** useless     **d.** careless

_a_    5. Janice **persistently** asked her mother to buy a new car, so her mother finally gave in and bought one.
   a. constantly            c. briefly
   b. lazily                 d. unenthusiasticly

_c_    6. The meal was prepared perfectly, but the young woman found it **repugnant.**
   a. overpriced            c. distasteful
   b. lovely                d. delicious

_d_    7. Getting our car fixed after the accident was an **ordeal.**
   a. good time             c. unexpected event
   b. relaxing opportunity   d. painful experience

_d_    8. Candace wore a red, low-cut dress to the party, but her sister was dressed more **decorously.**
   a. fashionably           c. attractively
   b. warmly                d. modestly

_b_    9. Kayla let a few weeks **elapse** before returning her ex-boyfriend's phone call.
   a. separate              c. slow down
   b. pass                  d. speed up

_c_   10. Gorillas can **convey** messages to humans through gestures and sounds.
   a. invent                c. communicate
   b. allow                 d. approve of

---

## EXERCISE 4-8    Using Context Clues

**Directions:** Write the meaning of the boldfaced word in each of the following sentences.    Answers will vary.

1. The economy was in a state of continual **flux;** inflation increased one month and decreased the next. _____ *change* _____

2. Art is always talkative, but Ed is usually **taciturn.** _____ *silent* _____

3. Many **debilities** of old age, including poor eyesight and loss of hearing, can be treated medically. _____ *disabilities* _____

4. The soap opera contained numerous **morbid** events: the death of a young child, the suicide of her father, and the murder of his older brother. _____ *gruesome* _____

5. After long hours of practice, Antonio finally learned to type; Sam's efforts, however, were **futile.** _____ *useless* _____

6. The newspaper's error was **inadvertent;** the editor did not intend to include the victim's name. _____ *not intended* _____

7. To save money, we have decided to **curtail** the number of CDs we buy each month. _____ *limit* _____

**8.** Steam from the hot radiator **scalded** the mechanic's hand.

*burned*

**9.** Sonia's **itinerary** outlined her trip and listed Cleveland as her next stop.

*travel plan*

**10.** Chang had very good **rapport** with his father, but he was unable to get along with his mother. _____ *good (harmonious) connection*

**EXERCISE 4-9**

## Using Context Clues

**Directions:** Write the meaning of each boldfaced word from the passage below.

**COLLEGE FOOTBALL AS SOCIAL STRUCTURE**   *Answers will vary.*

To gain a better idea of what *social structure* is, think of college football. You probably know the various positions on the team: center, guards, tackles, ends, quarterback, running backs, and the like. Each is a **status;** that is, each is a social position. For each of the statuses, there is a *role;* that is, each of these positions has certain expectations attached to it. The center is expected to snap the ball, the quarterback to pass it, the guards to block, the tackles to tackle or block, the ends to receive passes, and so on. Those role expectations guide each player's actions; that is, the players try to do what their particular role requires.

Let's suppose that football is your favorite sport and you never miss a home game at your college. Let's also suppose that you graduate, get a great job, and move across the country. Five years later, you return to your campus for a nostalgic visit. The **climax** of your visit is the biggest football game of the season. When you get to the game, you might be surprised to see a different coach, but you are not surprised that each playing position is occupied by people you don't know, for all the players you knew have graduated, and their places have been filled by others.

This **scenario** mirrors *social structure,* the framework around which a group exists. In football, that framework consists of the coaching staff and the eleven playing positions. The game does not depend on any particular individual, but, rather, on *social statuses,* the positions that the individuals **occupy.** When someone leaves a position, the game can go on because someone else takes over that position or status and plays the role. The game will continue even though not a single individual remains from one period of time to the next. Notre Dame's football team **endures** today even though Knute Rockne, the Gipper, and his teammates are long dead.

—Henslin, *Sociology: A Down-to-Earth Approach,* p. 99

**1.** status *social position*

**2.** climax *highlight*

**3.** scenario *situation*

**4.** occupy *hold*

**5.** endures *lasts*

# Use Word Parts

■ GOAL 4
Use Word Parts

Many students build their vocabulary word by word: if they study ten new words, then they have learned ten new words. If they study 30 words, they can recall 30 meanings. Would you like a better and faster way to build your vocabulary?

By learning the meanings of the parts that make up a word, you will be able to figure out the meanings of many more words. For example, if you learn that *pre-* means "before," then you can begin to figure out hundreds of words that begin with *pre-* (*premarital, premix, preemployment*). In this section you will learn about the beginnings, middles, and endings of words called *prefixes*, *roots*, and *suffixes*.

Suppose that you came across the following sentence in a human anatomy textbook:

> Trichromatic plates are used frequently in the text to illustrate the position of body organs.

If you did not know the meaning of *trichromatic,* how could you determine it? There are no clues in the sentence context. One solution is to look up the word in a dictionary. An easier and faster way is to break the word into parts and analyze the meaning of each part. Many words in the English language are made up of word parts called prefixes, roots, and suffixes. These word parts have specific meanings that, when added together, can help you determine the meaning of the word as a whole.

The word *trichromatic* can be divided into three parts: its *prefix*, *root*, and *suffix*.

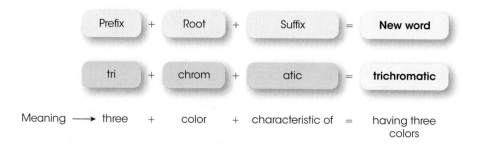

You can see from this analysis that *trichromatic* means "having three colors."

Here are a few other examples of words that you can figure out by using prefixes, roots, and suffixes:

The parents thought the child was **unteachable.**

*un-* = not

*teach* = help someone learn

*-able* = able to do something

*unteachable* = not able to be taught

The student was a **nonconformist.**

*non-* = not

*conform* = go along with others

*-ist* = one who does something

*nonconformist* = someone who does not go along with others

The first step in using the prefix-root-suffix method is to become familiar with the most commonly used word parts, which will give you a good start in determining the meanings of thousands of words without looking them up in the dictionary. For instance, more than ten thousand words can begin with the prefix *non-*. Not all these words are listed in a collegiate dictionary, but they would appear in an unabridged dictionary. Another common prefix, *pseudo-*, is used in more than four hundred words. A small amount of time spent learning word parts can yield a large payoff in new words learned.

Before you begin to use word parts to figure out new words, there are a few things you need to know:

- **In most cases, a word is built upon at least one root.**
- **Words can have more than one prefix, root, or suffix.**
  - Words can be made up of two or more roots (*geo/logy*).
  - Some words have two prefixes (*in/sub/ordination*).
  - Some words have two suffixes (*beauti/ful/ly*).
- **Words do not always have a prefix and a suffix.**
  - Some words have neither a prefix nor a suffix (*read*).
  - Others have a suffix but no prefix (*read/ing*).
  - Others have a prefix but no suffix (*pre/read*).
- **The spelling of roots may change as they are combined with suffixes.** Some common variations are included in Table 4-2 (p. 133).
- **Different prefixes, roots, or suffixes may have the same meaning.** For example, the prefixes *bi-*, *di-*, and *duo-* all mean "two."
- **Sometimes you may identify a group of letters as a prefix or root but find that it does not carry the meaning of that prefix or root.** For example, the letters *mis* in the word *missile* are part of the root and are not the prefix *mis-*, which means "wrong, bad."

## Prefixes

**Prefixes** appear at the beginning of many English words: they alter the meaning of the root to which they are connected. For example, if you add the prefix *re-* to the word *read*, the word *reread* is formed, meaning "to read again." If *pre-* is added to the word *reading*, the word *prereading* is formed, meaning "before reading." If the prefix *post-* is added, the word *postreading* is formed, meaning "after reading." Table 4-1 includes more than 40 common prefixes grouped according to meaning and shows how they affect the meaning of words they are affixed to.

| TABLE 4-1 | COMMON PREFIXES | | |
|---|---|---|---|
| **Prefix** | **Meaning** | **Sample Words** | **Definitions** |
| *Prefixes referring to amount or number* | | | |
| mono-/uni- | one | monocle/unicycle | eyeglass for one eye/one wheel vehicle |
| bi-/di-/duo- | two | bimonthly/diandrous/duet | twice a month/flower with two stamens/two singers |
| tri- | three | triangle | a figure with three sides and three angles |
| quad- | four | quadrant | any of four parts into which something is divided |
| quint-/pent- | five | quintet/pentagon | a group of five/five-sided figure |
| deci- | ten | decimal | based on the number ten |

*(Continued)*

**TABLE 4-1 COMMON PREFIXES** *(Continued)*

| Prefix | Meaning | Sample Words | Definitions |
|--------|---------|--------------|-------------|
| *Prefixes referring to amount or number (cont.)* | | | |
| centi- | hundred | centigrade | divided into 100 degrees, as a thermometer scale |
| milli- | thousand | milligram | one thousandth of a gram |
| micro- | small | microscope | an instrument used to see a magnified image of a small object |
| multi-/poly- | many | multipurpose/polygon | having several purposes/figure with three or more sides |
| semi- | half | semicircle | half of a circle |
| equi- | equal | equidistant | at equal distances |
| *Prefixes meaning "not" (negative)* | | | |
| a- | not | asymmetrical | not identical on both sides of a central line |
| anti- | against | antiwar | against war |
| contra- | against, opposite | contradict | deny by stating the opposite |
| dis- | apart, away, not | disagree | have a different opinion |
| in-/il-/ir-/im- | not | incorrect/illogical/ irreversible/impossible | wrong/not having sound reasoning/cannot be changed back/ not possible |
| mis- | wrongly | misunderstand | fail to understand correctly |
| non- | not | nonfiction | writing that is factual, not fiction |
| pseudo- | false | pseudoscientific | a system of theories or methods mistakenly regarded as scientific |
| un- | not | unpopular | not popular |
| *Prefixes giving direction, location, or placement* | | *not popular* | |
| ab- | away | absent | away or missing from a place |
| ad- | toward | adhesive | able to stick to a surface |
| ante-/pre- | before | antecedent/premarital | something that came before/before marriage |
| circum-/peri- | around | circumference/perimeter | the distance around something/border of an area |
| com-/col-/con- | with, together | compile/collide/convene | put together/come into violent contact/come together |
| de- | away, from | depart | leave, go away from |
| dia- | through | diameter | a straight line passing through the center of a circle |
| ex-/extra- | from, out of, former | ex-wife/extramarital | former wife/occurring outside marriage |
| hyper- | over, excessive | hyperactive | unusually or abnormally active |
| inter- | between | interpersonal | existing or occurring between people |
| intro-/intra- | within, into, in | introvert/intramural | turn or direct inwards/involving only students within the same school |
| post- | after | posttest | a test given after completion of a program or course |
| re- | back, again | review | go over or inspect again |
| retro- | backward | retrospect | a survey or review of the past |
| sub- | under, below | submarine | a ship designed to operate under water |
| super- | above, extra | supercharge | increase or boost the power of something |
| tele- | far | telescope | an instrument for making distant objects appear nearer |
| trans- | across, over | transcontinental | extending across a continent |

## EXERCISE 4-10   Using Prefixes

**Directions:** Use the list of common prefixes in Table 4-1 to determine the meaning of each of the following words. Write a brief definition or synonym for each. If you are unfamiliar with the root, you may need to check a dictionary.   *Answers will vary.*

**1.** interoffice: _____ *between offices* _____

**2.** supernatural: _____ *above natural; unusual; exceeding normal bounds* _____

**3.** nonsense: _____ *not making sense* _____

**4.** introspection: _____ *looking within oneself* _____

**5.** prearrange: _____ *arrange ahead of time* _____

**6.** reset: _____ *set again* _____

**7.** subtopic: _____ *a topic below or of less importance than a main topic* _____

**8.** transmit: _____ *to send from one place to another* _____

**9.** multidimensional: _____ *having many dimensions* _____

**10.** imperfect: _____ *not perfect; flawed* _____

## EXERCISE 4-11   Using Prefixes

**Directions:** Read each of the following sentences. Use your knowledge of prefixes to fill in the blank to complete the word.

**1.** A person who speaks two languages is _____*bi*_____**lingual.**

**2.** A letter or number written beneath a line of print is called a _____*sub*_____**script.**

**3.** The new sweater had a snag, and I returned it to the store because it was _____*im*_____ **perfect.**

**4.** The flood damage was permanent and _____*ir*_____**reversible.**

**5.** I was not given the correct date and time; I was _____*mis*_____**informed.**

**6.** People who speak several different languages are _____*multi*_____**lingual.**

**7.** A musical _____*inter*_____**lude** was played between the events in the ceremony.

**8.** I decided the magazine was uninteresting, so I _____*dis*_____**continued** my subscription.

**9.** Merchandise that does not pass factory inspection is considered _____*sub*_____ **standard** and sold at a discount.

**10.** The tuition refund policy approved this week will apply to last year's tuition as well; the policy will be _____*retro*_____**active** to January 1 of last year.

**11.** The elements were _____*re*_____**acting** with each other when they began to bubble and their temperature rose.

**12.** _____*Contra*_____**ceptives** are widely used to prevent unwanted pregnancies.

13. All of the waitresses were required to wear the restaurant's _____ uni _____ **form.**

14. The _____ inter _____ **viewer** asked the presidential candidates unexpected questions about important issues.

15. The draperies were _____ dis _____ **colored** from long exposure to the sun.

---

**EXERCISE 4-12**

*WORKING TOGETHER*

## Using Prefixes

**Directions:** Working in teams of two, choose two of the following prefixes and list as many words as you can think of that begin with them: *multi-, mis-, trans-, com-, inter-.* Then share your lists with the class. Answers will vary.

---

**EXERCISE 4-13**

## Using Prefixes to Figure Out Words

**Directions:** Read the following paragraphs and use your knowledge of prefixes to identify the meaning of each of the words in boldfaced type. Use a dictionary if necessary. Answers will vary.

A.  How can we **reconcile** such **contradictory** conclusions about heroin addiction? Certainly William Burroughs' description of his own addiction to heroin (and similar reports by others) is accurate. He did not make it up. At the same time, Johnson and his associates are also accurate. They did not make up their findings either. And other researchers have noted that some people use heroin on an **irregular** basis, such as at weekend parties, without becoming addicted. Where does this leave us? From the mixed reports, it seems reasonable to conclude that heroin is addicting to some people, but not to others. Some people do become addicts and match the **stereotypical** profile. Others use heroin on a recreational basis. Both, then, may be right. With the evidence we have at this point, it would be **inappropriate** to side with either extreme.

—adapted from Henslin, *Social Problems*, p. 118

1. reconcile _to make compatible or consistent_

2. contradictory _situation in which two or more ideas are opposite or inconsistent_

3. irregular _not regular_

4. stereotypical _following a set image or type_

5. inappropriate _not suitable_

B.  Why are there such **unaccounted** for differences in promiscuity and commitment between male and female **homosexuals**? Some would argue that the chief reason can be traced to differences in their socialization. Girls are more likely to associate sex with emotional relationships, and, like their **heterosexual** counterparts, lesbians tend to conform to this basic expectation. Similarly, boys tend to learn to separate sex from affection, to validate their **self-images** by how much sex they have, and to see fidelity as a restriction on their **independence**.

—adapted from Henslin, *Social Problems*, p. 72

6. unaccounted  *not explained*

7. homosexuals  *individuals attracted to those of the same sex*

8. heterosexual  *individuals attracted to those of the opposite sex*

9. self-images  *concepts of ones' selves*

10. independence  *freedom, not dependent*

C.    An especially **unstable** class of molecules are oxygen free radicals, sometimes just called free radicals. Some free radicals are accidentally produced in small amounts during the normal process of energy transfer within living cells. Exposure to chemicals, radiation, **ultraviolet** light, cigarette smoke, and air pollution may also create free radicals. We now know that certain enzymes and nutrients called **antioxidants** are the body's natural defense against oxygen free radicals. Antioxidants may prevent oxidation by **inactivating** them quickly before they can damage other molecules. Many health experts believe that antioxidant vitamins reduce the chance of certain cancers and the risk of **cardiovascular** death.

—adapted from Johnson, *Human Biology,* p. 27

11. unstable  *not steady, easily changed*

12. ultraviolet  *rays beyond violet in the visible spectrum*

13. antioxidants  *substances that prevent or inhibit oxidation*

14. inactivating  *stopping the activity of*

15. cardiovascular  *pertaining to the heart and blood vessels*

## Roots

**Roots** carry the basic or core meaning of a word. Hundreds of root words are used to build words in the English language. More than thirty of the most common and most useful are listed in Table 4-2. Knowledge of the meanings of these roots will enable you to unlock the meanings of many words. For example, if you know that the root *dic/dict* means "tell or say," then you would have a clue to the meanings of such words as *dictate* (to speak for someone to write down), *diction* (wording or manner of speaking), or *dictionary* (book that tells what words mean).

### TABLE 4-2  COMMON ROOTS

| Common Root | Meaning | Sample Word | Definition |
| --- | --- | --- | --- |
| aster/astro | star | astronaut | a person trained to travel in space |
| aud/audit | hear | audible | able to be heard |
| bene | good, well | benefit | an advantage gained from something |
| bio | life | biology | the scientific study of living organisms |
| cap | take, seize | captive | a person who has been taken prisoner |
| chron/chrono | time | chronology | the order in which events occur |
| cog | to learn | cognitive | relating to mental processes |

*(Continued)*

**TABLE 4-2   COMMON ROOTS** (*Continued*)

| Common Root | Meaning | Sample Word | Definition |
|---|---|---|---|
| corp | body | corpse | dead body |
| cred | believe | incredible | difficult/impossible to believe |
| dict/dic | tell, say | predict | declare something will happen in the future |
| duc/duct | lead | introduce | bring in or present for the first time |
| fact/fac | make, do | factory | a building where goods are manufactured |
| geo | earth | geophysics | the physics of the earth |
| graph | write | telegraph | a system for sending messages to a distant place |
| log/logo/logy | study, thought | psychology | the scientific study of the human mind |
| mit/miss | send | permit/dismiss | allow or make possible |
| mort/mor | die, death | immortal | everlasting, not subject to death |
| path | feeling | sympathy | sharing the feelings of another |
| phon | sound, voice | telephone | a device used to transmit voices |
| photo | light | photosensitive | responding to light |
| port | carry | transport | carry from one place to another |
| scop | seeing | microscope | an instrument that magnifies small objects |
| scrib/script | write | inscription | a written note |
| sen/sent | feel | insensitive | lacking concern for others' feelings |
| spec/spic/spect | look, see | retrospect | a survey or review of the past |
| tend/tens/tent | stretch or strain | tension | mental or emotional strain |
| terr/terre | land, earth | territory | a geographic area, a tract of land |
| theo | god | theology | the study of the nature of God and religious belief |
| ven/vent | come | convention | a meeting or formal assembly |
| vert/vers | turn | invert | put upside down or in the opposite position |
| vis/vid | see | invisible/video | not able to be seen |
| voc | call | vocation | a person's occupation or calling |

**EXERCISE 4-14**   Completing Sentences

**Directions:** Complete each of the following sentences with one of the words listed below.

| | | | | |
|---|---|---|---|---|
| apathetic | extensive | phonics | spectators | verdict |
| captivated | extraterrestrial | prescribed | synchronized | visualize |

1. The jury brought in its _____verdict_____ after one hour of deliberation.

2. She closed her eyes and tried to _____visualize_____ the license plate number.

3. The _____spectators_____ watching the football game were tense.

4. The doctor _____prescribed_____ two types of medication.

5. The list of toys the child wanted for his birthday was _____extensive_____.

6. The criminal appeared _____apathetic_____ when the judge pronounced the sentence.

7. The runners _____synchronized_____ their watches before beginning the race.

8. The study of the way different parts of words sound is called _____phonics_____.

9. The movie was about a(n) _____extraterrestrial_____, a creature not from Earth.

10. Through his attention-grabbing performance, he _____captivated_____ the audience.

---

**EXERCISE 4-15**

## Using Roots

**Directions:** Use the list of common roots in Table 4-2 to determine the meanings of the following words. Write a brief definition or synonym for each, checking a dictionary if necessary.   Answers will vary.

1. porter: _____one who carries or transports something_____

2. credentials: _____written evidence of one's qualifications_____

3. speculate: _____to guess, reflect, take a risk_____

4. terrain: _____a tract of land; the character or quality of land_____

5. audition: _____sense of hearing; tryout by actor or singer for potential role_____

6. astrophysics: _____a branch of physics dealing with the stars_____

7. capacity: _____ability to hold or absorb_____

8. chronicle: _____a record of events in time order or sequence_____

9. autograph: _____a person's signature_____

10. sociology: _____a study of human social behavior_____

---

**EXERCISE 4-16**

## Using Roots to Determine Meaning

**Directions:** Read each of the following paragraphs and use your knowledge of roots as well as a dictionary to determine the meaning of each of the boldfaced words.   Answers will vary.

**A.**   Is it possible that humankind is now, at last, at the end of its ability to increase food supplies? The answer to this question is a cautious "probably not." If demographers are correct in their **projections** of Earth's future **population**, the population can be fed. **Humankind** has scarcely begun to maximize **productivity** with the best contemporary technology, and that leading technology has been applied to only a small portion of Earth. Spreading **urbanization** is replacing agriculture in many places, but more lands can still be farmed.

—Bergman and Renwick, *Introduction to Geography*, p. 323

1. projections <u>estimates into the future</u>

2. population <u>total number of inhabitants</u>

3. humankind <u>the human race</u>

4. productivity <u>ability to produce or create</u>

5. urbanization <u>creation of a city-like environment</u>

**B.** Many of the problems found in Mexico's **agricultural** economy can also be found in Africa. Landholding is often **communal**, so successful farmers cannot expand their productivity. Many African governments themselves hold owner-ship of agricultural land and lease it to farmers. In Zimbabwe, for example, the government **nationalized** numerous large white-owned private farms that were **exporting** food. The government **relocated** black settlers onto the properties but retained ownership, so the farmers cannot borrow to invest in increasing productivity.

—Bergmann and Renwick, *Introduction to Geography*, p. 332

6. agricultural <u>related to the science of farming</u>

7. communal <u>shared by the community</u>

8. nationalized <u>converted from private to government ownership</u>

9. exporting <u>shipping goods out of the country</u>

10. relocated <u>moved to a new place</u>

**C.** No country is completely self-sufficient in food. Most countries both im-port and export food despite the fact that portions of their own populations are **undernourished**. This may be due to **injustice** or civil strife. Political **instability** contributes to hunger. Several African countries, for example, are environmentally richly endowed, yet a great many of their people go hungry. Peter Rosset, director of the Institute for Food and Development Policy, wrote, "There is no relationship between the **prevalence** of hunger in a given country and its population. The world today produces more food per **inhabitant** than ever before."

—Bergman and Renwick, *Introduction to Geography*, p. 329

11. undernourished <u>not given a sufficient amount of food</u>

12. injustice <u>a wrong, a violation of rights</u>

13. instability <u>not constant, not reliable or dependable</u>

14. prevalence <u>widely or commonly occurring</u>

15. inhabitant <u>one who occupies an area</u>

## Suffixes

**Suffixes** are word endings that often change the part of speech of a word. For example, adding the suffix *-y* to the noun *cloud* forms the adjective *cloudy*. Ac-companying the change in part of speech is a shift in meaning (*cloudy* means "resembling clouds; overcast with clouds; dimmed or dulled as if by clouds").

Often, several different words can be formed from a single root word by adding different suffixes. The chart below shows how adding a suffix changes the meaning and often the part of speech of a word.

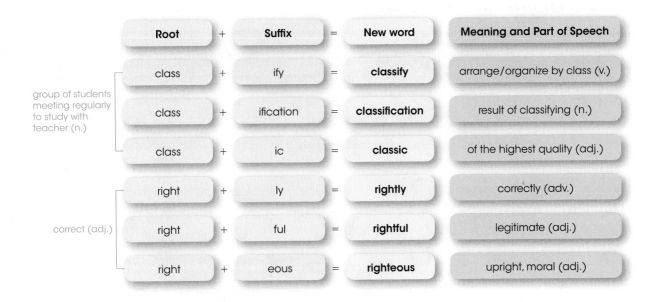

| Root | + | Suffix | = | New word | Meaning and Part of Speech |
|------|---|--------|---|----------|----------------------------|
| class | + | ify | = | classify | arrange/organize by class (v.) |
| class | + | ification | = | classification | result of classifying (n.) |
| class | + | ic | = | classic | of the highest quality (adj.) |
| right | + | ly | = | rightly | correctly (adv.) |
| right | + | ful | = | rightful | legitimate (adj.) |
| right | + | eous | = | righteous | upright, moral (adj.) |

*group of students meeting regularly to study with teacher (n.)* — class

*correct (adj.)* — right

If you know the meaning of the root word and the ways in which different suffixes affect the meaning of the root word, you will be able to figure out a word's meaning when a suffix is added. A list of common suffixes and their meanings appears in Table 4-3 on page 138.

You can expand your vocabulary by learning the variations in meaning that occur when suffixes are added to words you already know. When you find a word that you do not know, look for the root. Then, using the sentence the word is in (its context), figure out what the word means with the suffix added. Occasionally you may find that the spelling of the root word has been changed. For instance, a final *e* may be dropped, a final consonant may be doubled, or a final *y* may be changed to *i*. Consider the possibility of such changes when trying to identify the root word.

The article was a **compilation** of facts.

root + suffix

compil(e) + -ation = something that has been compiled, or put together into an orderly form

We were concerned with the **legality** of our decision to change addresses.

root + suffix

legal + -ity = lawfullness

Our college is one of the most **prestigious** in the state.

root + suffix

prestig(e) + -ious = having prestige or distinction

## TABLE 4-3    COMMON SUFFIXES

| Suffix | | Sample Words | Meaning |
|---|---|---|---|
| **Suffixes that refer to a state, condition, or quality** | | | |
| -able | capable of | touchable | capable of being touched |
| -ance | characterized by | assistance | the action of helping |
| -ation | action or process | confrontation | an act of confronting or meeting face to face |
| -ence | state or condition | reference | an act or instance of referring or mentioning |
| -ible | capable of | tangible | capable of being felt, having substance |
| -ion | action or process | discussion | |
| -ity | state or quality | superiority | the quality or condition of being higher in rank or status |
| -ive | performing action | permissive | characterized by freedom of behavior |
| -ment | action or process | amazement | a state of overwhelming surprise or astonishment |
| -ness | state, quality, condition | kindness | the quality of being kind |
| -ous | possessing, full of | jealous | envious or resentful of another |
| -ty | characterized by | loyalty | the state of being loyal or faithful |
| -y | condition, quality | creamy | resembling or containing cream |
| **Suffixes that mean "one who"** | | | |
| -an | | Italian | one who is from Italy |
| -ant | | participant | one who participates |
| -ee | | referee | one who enforces the rules of a game or sport |
| -eer | | engineer | one who is trained in engineering |
| -ent | | resident | one who lives in a place |
| -er | | teacher | one who teaches |
| -ist | | activist | one who takes action to promote or advocate a cause |
| -or | | advisor | one who advises |
| **Suffixes that mean "pertaining to or referring to"** | | | |
| -al | | autumnal | occurring in or pertaining to autumn |
| -ship | | friendship | the state of being friends |
| -hood | | brotherhood | the relationship between brothers |
| -ward | | homeward | leading towards home |

## EXERCISE 4-17    Using Suffixes

**Directions:** For each suffix shown in Table 4-3, write another example of a word you know that has that suffix and its meaning.   Answers will vary.

## EXERCISE 4-18    Adding Suffixes

WORKING TOGETHER

**Directions:** Working with a classmate, for each word listed below, write as many new words as you can create by adding suffixes, and note their meanings and parts of speech. Share your findings with the class.   Answers will vary.

1. compare: _____ comparison, comparable, comparative _____

2. adapt: _____ adaptation, adaptable, adaptability _____

3. direct: _____ direction, directness, director _____

4. identify: _____ identification, identity, identical _____

5. will: _____ willful, willing, willfulness _____

6. prefer: _____ preferable, preferred, preferring _____

7. notice: _____ noticeable, noticed, noticing _____

8. like: _____ likeable, likeness, likely _____

9. pay: _____ payable, payee, payment _____

10. promote: _____ promotion, promotable, promoter _____

**EXERCISE 4-19**    ## Using Suffixes

**Directions:** For each of the words listed below, add a suffix so that the word will complete the sentence. Write the new word in the space provided. Check a dictionary if you are unsure of the spelling.

    **EXAMPLE**   sex: _____ Sexist _____ language should be avoided in both speech and writing.

1. **eat:** We did not realize that the plant was _____ edible _____ until we tasted its delicious fruit.

2. **compete:** The gymnastics _____ competition _____ was our favorite part of the Olympics.

3. **decide:** It was difficult to be _____ decisive _____ in such a stressful situation.

4. **Portugal:** Our favorite restaurant specializes in _____ Portuguese _____ food.

5. **active:** She gained fame as a civil rights _____ activist _____ in the 1960s.

6. **parent:** _____ Parenthood _____ is one of the most rewarding experiences in life.

7. **vaccine:** You must receive several different _____ vaccinations _____ before your trip to Africa.

8. **member:** We inadvertently allowed our _____ membership _____ to the botanical garden to lapse.

9. **drive:** The abandoned car did not appear _____ drivable _____ so a tow truck was summoned.

10. **celebrate:** The girls waited at the airport for hours to catch a glimpse of their favorite _____ celebrity _____ .

## How to Use Word Parts

Think of roots as being at the root or core of a word's meaning. There are many more roots than are listed in Table 4-2. You already know many of these because they are used in everyday speech. Think of prefixes as word parts that are added before the root to qualify or change its meaning. Think of suffixes as add-ons that make the word fit grammatically into the sentence in which it is used.

When you come upon a word you do not know, keep the following pointers in mind:

---

## ❗ NEED TO KNOW

### How to Use Word Parts

1. **First, look for the root.** Think of this as looking for a word inside a larger word. Often a letter or two will be missing.

   | | |
   |---|---|
   | un/**utter**/able | **defens**/ible |
   | inter/**colleg**/iate | re/**popular**/ize |
   | post/**operat**/ive | non/**adapt**/able |
   | im/**measur**/ability | non/**commit**/tal |

2. **If you do not recognize the root, then you will probably not be able to figure out the word.** The next step is to check its meaning in a dictionary. For tips on locating words in a dictionary rapidly and easily, see "Using a Dictionary," page 90.

3. **If you did recognize the root word, look for a prefix.** If there is one, determine how it changes the meaning of the word.

   | | |
   |---|---|
   | **un**/utterable | un- = not |
   | **post**/operative | post- = after |

4. **Locate the suffix.** Determine how it further adds to or changes the meaning of the root word.

   | | |
   |---|---|
   | unutter/**able** | -able = able to |
   | postoperat/**ive** | -ive = state or condition |

5. **Next, try out the meaning in the sentence in which the word was used.** Substitute your meaning for the word, and see whether the sentence makes sense.

   Some of the victim's thoughts were **unutterable** at the time of the crime.
   unutterable = cannot be spoken

   My sister was worried about the cost of **postoperative** care.
   postoperative = describing state or condition after an operation

---

**EXERCISE 4-20**

## Using Prefixes, Roots and Suffixes to Determine Meaning

**Directions:** Read the following paragraphs and use your knowledge of prefixes, roots, and suffixes to determine the meaning of the boldfaced words.  Answers will vary.

A.    **Professional** criminals make their **livelihood** from crime. They include not only the highly **romanticized** jewel thieves, **safecrackers**, and **counterfeiters**, but also professional shoplifters, pickpockets, and fences—those who buy stolen goods for resale. Their activities, although illegal, are a form of work, and they pride themselves on their skills and successes.

—Henslin, *Social Problems*, p. 187

1. professional _engaged in a profession_

2. livelihood _means of support, subsistence_

3. romanticized _invested with romance (adventure, chivalry, idealism, etc.)_

4. safecrackers _people who break into safes_

5. counterfeiters _people who produce fake currency_

B.    Certain types of crime are easier to get away with than others. Running less risk are **political** criminals who attempt to maintain the status quo and white-collar criminals who commit crimes in the name of a **corporation**, and those who comprise the top levels of organized crime. **Respectability**, wealth, power, and underlings insulate them. Those in the second group are insulated by the corporation's desire to avoid negative **publicity**. Those who run the highest risk of arrest are "soldiers" at the lowest levels of organized crime, who are considered **expendable**.

—adapted from Henslin, *Social Problems*, p. 192

6. political _related to the affairs of government_

7. corporation _body legally recognized to conduct business_

8. respectability _quality of being respected; regarded as worthy and proper_

9. publicity _coverage by the media_

10. expendable _not worth saving; open to sacrifice_

C.    The proponents of capital punishment argue that it is an appropriate **retribution** for **heinous** crimes, that it deters, and, of course, that it is an effective **incapacitator**. Its critics argue that killing is never justified. Opponents also argue that the death penalty is **capricious**: Jurors deliberate in secrecy and indulge their prejudices in recommending death, and judges are **irrational**—merciful to some but not to others.

—adapted from Henslin, *Social Problems*, p. 205

11. retribution _punishment; something justly deserved_

12. heinous _abominable, very wicked and hateful_

13. incapacitator _something that stops people acting in a certain way_

14. capricious _unpredictable, subject to whim_

15. irrational _not logical_

# Learn New Words

■ GOAL 5
Learn new words

While learning new words is important, it is also important to make sure you remember what you learn. In this section, you will learn two effective systems for learning and remembering new words.

## Write to Learn: Keeping a Vocabulary Log

A **vocabulary log** is a list of words you want to learn. They may be words that you find in textbooks, articles and essays, or magazines, newspapers, or books. You might also record words you heard in class lectures. Be sure to record only useful words—those you want to learn. You can use a variety of formats. You can create a vocabulary log for each course you are taking, reserving a section in each of your notebooks in which you record lecture notes. You can keep a separate notebook and designate it as your vocabulary log. You can create a computer file or files.

In addition to recording words and their meanings, be sure to record each word's pronunciation if it is not familiar. Some students also record a sentence using the word. Others include a text reference page number so they can locate where they first found the word. Experiment with different formats and different organizations until you find one that works for you. An excerpt from one student's vocabulary log for psychology is shown in Figure 4-1.

**FIGURE 4-1 SAMPLE VOCABULARY LOG FOR A PSYCHOLOGY COURSE**

| Word | Meaning | Page |
|------|---------|------|
| intraspecific aggression | attack by one animal upon another member of its species | 310 |
| orbitofrontal cortex | region of the brain that aids in recognition of situations that produce emotional responses | 312 |
| modulation | an attempt to minimize or exaggerate the expression of emotion | 317 |
| simulation | an attempt to display an emotion that one does not really feel | 319 |
|  |  |  |

**EXERCISE 4-21**    ## Creating an Index Card/Vocabulary Log

**Directions:** Create an index card file or vocabulary log for one of your other courses. Update it weekly.

## Use Spare Moments: The Index Card System

As you read textbook assignments and reference sources, and while listening to your instructors' class presentations, you are constantly exposed to new words. Unless you make a deliberate effort to remember and use these words, many of them will probably fade from your memory. One of the most practical and easy-to-use systems for expanding your vocabulary is the index card system. It works like this:

1. **Write down new words.** Whenever you hear or read a new word that you intend to learn, jot it down in the margin of your notes or mark it in some way in the material you are reading.

2. **Later, write the word on the front of an index card.** Then look it up in a dictionary, and underneath the word, record the word's pronunciation and write in its part of speech. On the back of the card, write other forms the word may take and a sample sentence or example of how the word is used. If you are a visual learner, draw a diagram or picture to depict the word as well. Your cards should look like the one in Figure 4-2.

3. **Once a day, take a few minutes to go through your pack of index cards.** For each card, look at the word on the front and try to recall its meaning on the back. Then check the back of the card to see whether you were correct. If you are unable to recall the meaning or if you confuse the word with another word, retest yourself. Shuffle the cards after each use.

4. **After you have gone through your pack of cards several times, sort the cards into two piles—words you know and words you have not learned.** Then, putting the known words aside, concentrate on the words still to be learned.

5. **Once you have learned the entire pack of words, review them often to refresh your memory.**

This index card system is effective for several reasons. First, you can review your cards in the spare time that is often wasted waiting for a class to begin, riding a bus, and so on. Second, the system enables you to spend time learning what you do *not* know rather than wasting time studying what you already know. Finally, the system overcomes a major problem that exists in learning information that appears in list form. If the material to be learned is presented in a fixed order, you tend to learn it in that order and may be unable to recall individual items when they appear alone or out of order. By shuffling the cards, you scramble the order of the words and thus avoid this problem.

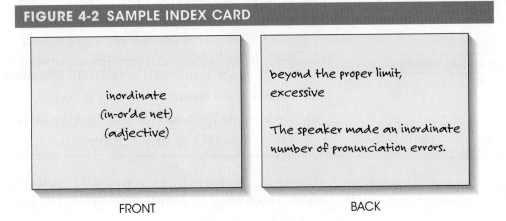

**FIGURE 4-2 SAMPLE INDEX CARD**

inordinate
(in-or'de net)
(adjective)

beyond the proper limit, excessive

The speaker made an inordinate number of pronunciation errors.

FRONT                    BACK

## Tips for Using the Words You Learn

Here are some suggestions for learning and retaining words. Depending on your learning style, some of the suggestions will work better than others.

- **Write the word immediately.** If you find the word in a textbook, you will have a better chance of remembering it if you write it rather than just high-light it. In fact, write it several times, once in the margin of the text, then again on an index card or in your vocabulary log. Write it again as you test yourself.

- **Write a sentence using the word.** Make the sentence personal, about you or your family or friends. The more meaningful the sentence is, the more likely you are to remember the word.

- **Try to visualize a situation involving the word.** For instance, for the word *restore* (to bring back to its original condition), visualize an antique car restored to its original condition.

- **Draw a picture or diagram that involves the word.** For example, for the word *squander* (to waste), draw a picture of yourself squandering money by throwing dollar bills out of an open car window.

- **Talk about the word.** With a classmate, try to hold a conversation in which each of you uses at least ten new words you have learned. Your conversation may become comical, but you will get practice using new words.

- **Try to use the word in your own academic speech or writing as soon as you have learned it.**

- **Give yourself vocabulary tests or, working with a friend, make up tests for each other.**

---

**EXERCISE 4-22**   ## Learning and Remembering New Words

**Directions:** For words in your index card file or vocabulary log, experiment with the above suggestions. List two suggestions that seem to work well for you.

1. _____

2. _____

---

Once you have learned a new word, make sure you can spell it correctly. To learn the spelling of a word, use these four steps:

1. **Look for familiar or similar parts in a word.** For example, when you see the word *budgetary*, you can see the word *budget*. See if a word is spelled in a similar way to another word you already know. *Perceive* is spelled in a similar way to *receive*, for example. The more meaningful you can make the word's spelling, the easier it will be to remember it.

2. **Say the word aloud and copy it as you speak.** Copy it several more times.

3. **Try to write the word without looking at the original word.**

4. **Check to see if you spelled it correctly.** If not, repeat the above steps until you can spell it correctly.

Keep a list or log of words you have misspelled on papers or exams. Work on learning each word on the list. Periodically, test yourself to see if you can still spell each one correctly.

# INTEGRATING READING AND WRITING

## READ AND RESPOND: A Professional Essay

### Thinking Before Reading

In the following selection, the author tells about Koko and his experience interacting with this unusual animal. As you read, keep a vocabulary log of unfamiliar words that you come across in the selection.

1. Preview the reading, using the steps discussed in Chapter 1 on page 25.

2. Connect the reading to your own experience by answering the following questions:

    a. Have you ever tried to learn a new language? How difficult was it?

    b. If you have pets, how do they communicate with you (and you with them)?

3. Highlight and annotate as you read.

1170**L**/1816 words

# Talking to Koko the Gorilla

## Alex Hannaford

*This 40-year-old lowland gorilla, says Alex Hannaford, understands English and longs for a baby.*

1    My location is a closely guarded secret: a ranch somewhere in the Santa Cruz Mountains, several miles outside the small California town of Woodside. Its resident is something of a celebrity. She lives here with a male friend and both value their privacy, so much so that I'm asked to keep absolutely silent as I walk through a grove of towering redwoods up to a little Portakabin. Inside, I'm asked to put on a thin medical mask to cover my nose and mouth, and a pair of latex gloves. Then my guide, Lorraine, tells me to follow another dirt trail to a different outbuilding. It's here that I sit on a plastic chair and look up at an open door, separated from the outside world by a wire fence that stretches the length and width of the frame. And there she is: Koko. A 300-pound lowland gorilla, sitting staring back at me and pointing to an impressive set of teeth.

2    I was told beforehand not to make eye contact initially, as it can be perceived as threatening, and so I glare at the ground. But I can't help stealing brief glances at this beautiful creature. Koko, in case you're not familiar with her story, was taught

American sign language when she was about a year old. Now 40, she apparently has a working vocabulary of more than 1,000 signs, and understands around 2,000 words of spoken English. Forty years on, the Gorilla Foundation's Koko project has become the longest continuous interspecies communications program of its kind anywhere.

3    I sign "hello," which looks like a sailor's salute, and she emits a long, throaty growl. "Don't worry, that means she likes you," comes the disembodied voice of Dr. Penny Patterson, the foundation's president and scientific director, from somewhere inside the enclosure. "It's the gorilla equivalent of a purr." Koko grins at me, then turns and signs to Dr. Patterson. "She wants to see your mouth . . . wait, she particularly wants to see your tongue," Dr. Patterson says, and I happily oblige, pulling my mask down, poking my tongue out, and returning the grin. Another soft, deep roar. Dr. Patterson emerges from a side door, closing it behind her, and joins me on the porch. Koko makes a sign. Dr. Patterson translates: "'Visit. Do you . . . , Oh, sweetheart," she says to Koko, then turns to me: "She'd like you to go inside."

4    Over the years Koko has inadvertently become a poster child for the gorilla conservation movement. There are several subspecies of gorillas, all in sub-Saharan Africa, and today, according to the International Union for Conservation of Nature, all are either endangered or critically endangered. They are threatened by disease, the illegal trade in bush meat, and loss of habitat due to logging and agricultural expansion. Attempts to educate communities where poaching is rife have largely failed; statistics about dwindling numbers of great apes don't resonate with people who can make good money from gorilla meat or body parts, or for whom the logging industry puts dinner on the table.

5    But some conservationists believe stories such as Koko's—of how an "inculturated" gorilla (the word researchers use for primates that have essentially had their own culture suppressed and have adopted a more human-like culture) has actually communicated with us—could be the answer. We should attempt, in other words, to win hearts rather than minds. At 40, Koko could possibly be more relevant than ever. But she's advanced in years, and the Gorilla Foundation is determined to ensure her legacy. That means allowing her to pass on her knowledge of sign language to her offspring, but despite repeated attempts to get her to mate—first with the silverback Michael and more recently with another, Ndume, her current partner—Koko's keepers' efforts have been in vain.

6    It's rare that anyone gets to meet Koko up close. Most of the staff at the Gorilla Foundation have only ever been outside her enclosure. A handful of celebrities, Leonardo DiCaprio and Robin Williams included, have had the pleasure, but this was to secure publicity for the foundation. I'm told no journalist has spent as long as I will—an hour and a half—in her company. Looming above is a huge three-story enclosure that Koko can access via a hatch. Inside it is Ndume, the male silverback. We can't see each other, but I'm told he is well aware I'm here and I have to keep my voice down, as he's protective of Koko. Inside the kitchen area, I'm still separated from Koko by bars. Watched by Koko's official photographer, Gorilla Foundation co-founder Ron Cohn, I open up the bag of goodies I bought at Toys R Us and flick through a picture book on zoo animals, touching each page and holding it up to her eyes. She then points to the padlock on the door and signs for Dr. Patterson to open it. I sit cross-legged, and Koko shuffles her 300-pound frame toward me.

7    I'm sweating now and still trying desperately not to make eye contact. Suddenly, I feel her leathery hand softly touch mine. She pulls me gently toward her chest, wrapping her arms around me. I can smell her breath—sweet and warm, not unlike a horse's. After she releases me from her embrace, she makes another sign—fists together. "She wants you to follow—to chase her," Dr. Patterson says. Koko lightly takes my hand and places it in the bend in her arm before leading me around the small room, cluttered with soft toys and clothes. I shuffle along the floor so as not to seem threatening, but it's amazing how gentle she is.

8    My wife and I had a baby daughter just three weeks before my visit, and I pull a photo out of my pocket to show her. I've learned the sign—pointing to myself and then making a rocking motion with my arms—to indicate "my baby." Incredibly, Koko takes the photo, looks at it, and kisses it. She then turns, picks up a doll from the mound of toys beside her, and holds it up to me. At one point she tugs lightly on my arm to indicate I'm to lie down beside her. Dr. Patterson says she can sense I'm nervous and does this to make people feel at ease. Another time she turns her back to me and indicates I'm to scratch it for her. She swings herself up onto a large plastic chair and Dr. Patterson turns on a video for her. It's Mary Poppins, and Koko signals that I'm to sit next to her. If my day wasn't surreal enough, it dawns on me that I'm watching Dick Van Dyke while sitting next to a gorilla. After two more hugs, Koko is coaxed away by Dr. Patterson, wielding a nut. And it's over. I stand outside on the porch again and wave good-bye, and she blows me a kiss, then puts her head up to the cage and puckers her lips. I reach out and touch them and then disappear back up the path.

9    The Gorilla Foundation was born in the late 1970s when Dr. Patterson was studying for a Ph.D. in developmental psychology at Stanford University. After discovering a small, undernourished baby gorilla at the San Francisco Zoo, Dr. Patterson persuaded the institution to lend her the animal and started her dissertation on the linguistic capabilities of a lowland gorilla. Two weeks into her studies, Dr. Patterson noted that Koko was able to make the signs to indicate food and drink. Project Koko, Dr. Patterson's life's work, was born. She makes it clear to me how she feels about gorillas in captivity—40 percent of males die of heart problems before the age of 30, she tells me, something that doesn't happen in the wild—but while it was never her decision for Koko to be born in a zoo, she says, the gorilla's contribution to our understanding of her species has been immeasurable.

10    Dr. Patterson says Koko is extremely sophisticated in her thought processes, using not just sign language but communication cards, books, and multimedia to express herself. Some skeptics have argued that Koko does not understand the meaning behind what she is doing and simply learns to sign because she'll be rewarded. Dr. Patterson admits that in the beginning she, too, thought Koko was simply doing it to "get stuff," but the gorilla began stringing words together to describe objects she didn't know the signs for. A hairbrush, for example, became a "scratch comb"; a mask was an "eye hat"; and a ring was a "finger bracelet." From my own limited time with Koko, I could see reward wasn't her motivation. Yes, she signed to achieve goals, but these goals weren't treats: They were to get me to follow her around the room, to get me to lie down, to get me to play with her—to interact.

11    The idea that Koko might teach sign language to any future offspring is fascinating to researchers. Dr. Patterson says Koko's desire for a baby has evolved over

the years. From the age of about 6 she was caring for dolls, and her maternal instincts progressed to living things: a rabbit "wandering around Stanford—obviously a lab escapee"—and then a kitten that Koko named All Ball, eventually the subject of a children's book by Dr. Patterson.

12    "She was very gentle and careful with All Ball," says Dr. Patterson. "She wanted to nurture it." But a few months after All Ball came into Koko's life, the cat escaped from her enclosure and was run over by a car. Dr. Patterson says that when Koko found out, she signed "bad, sad, bad" and "frown, cry, frown." Recently, Dr. Patterson says, Koko has shown no interest in visiting kittens—an indication, she believes, that she is now after the real thing. Through pictures and signs, Koko has indicated that she'd like to raise a child in a group situation. "A mother gorilla and baby in isolation aren't healthy. Zoos have discovered this," Dr. Patterson says. "It takes a village to raise a baby gorilla—just like humans." The ideal scenario is that a zoo or wildlife park loans the Gorilla Foundation a couple of females. Ndume would then impregnate one of them and the three mothers, Koko included, would raise the baby in a group.

13    The book *Koko's Kitten* was published 24 years ago, but now Patterson aims to distribute it in areas in Africa where gorillas are threatened—to teach children there how a great ape can love and care for an animal of another species. We've also learned that great apes, like humans, have the capacity for empathy, says Dr. Patterson. "Their politics work like our politics," she says. "If you're not nice, you're out of the group."

—*The London Telegraph*, September 17, 2011

## Getting Ready to Write

### Checking Your Comprehension

Answer each of the following questions using complete sentences.

1. Who is Koko and how does she communicate?

2. Why is the author told not to make eye contact with Koko?

3. According to the selection, what are the three primary threats endangering gorillas in sub-Saharan Africa?

4. What is the Gorilla Foundation and how did it begin?

5. What does *inculturated* mean?

6. Who was All Ball and why was she important to Koko?

## Strengthening Your Vocabulary

Using the word's context, word parts, or a dictionary, write a brief definition of each of the following words as it is used in the reading.

1. perceived (paragraph 2) _viewed_
2. emits (paragraph 3) _produces; puts forth_
3. rife (paragraph 4) _widespread; rampant_
4. resonate (paragraph 4) _have meaning or significance_
5. suppressed (paragraph 5) _subdued; put down_
6. surreal (paragraph 8) _strange, unreal_
7. wielding (paragraph 8) _carrying_

## Examining the Reading: Using Idea Maps

Review the reading by completing the missing parts of the following idea map.

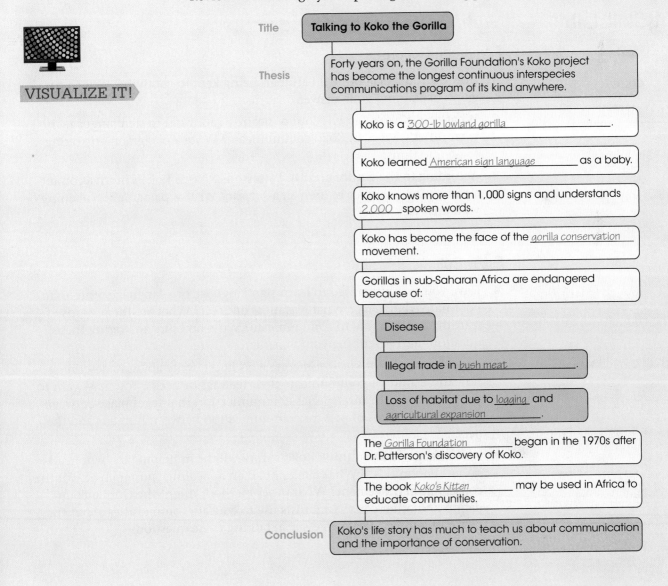

**VISUALIZE IT!**

Title — **Talking to Koko the Gorilla**

Thesis — Forty years on, the Gorilla Foundation's Koko project has become the longest continuous interspecies communications program of its kind anywhere.

Koko is a _300-lb lowland gorilla_ .

Koko learned _American sign language_ as a baby.

Koko knows more than 1,000 signs and understands _2,000_ spoken words.

Koko has become the face of the _gorilla conservation_ movement.

Gorillas in sub-Saharan Africa are endangered because of:

Disease

Illegal trade in _bush meat_ .

Loss of habitat due to _logging_ and _agricultural expansion_ .

The _Gorilla Foundation_ began in the 1970s after Dr. Patterson's discovery of Koko.

The book _Koko's Kitten_ may be used in Africa to educate communities.

Conclusion — Koko's life story has much to teach us about communication and the importance of conservation.

## Thinking Critically: Discussion and Journal Writing

React and respond to the reading by discussing the following:

1. Evaluate the title and introduction of this selection. What other titles can you think of that would be appropriate? How effectively does the introduction capture your attention?

2. Discuss Koko's reaction to the photo of the author's new baby. What does her reaction tell you about her and about the author?

3. What is most interesting or compelling to you about Koko's story? Discuss the different aspects of her story, including her knowledge and use of sign language as well as her desire for motherhood and her role in the conservation movement.

4. Describe the photograph that accompanies this reading. What does it tell you about Koko? What details correspond to what you have learned about her?

**THINKING VISUALLY**

**MySkillsLab®**

**Complete** this Exercise

## Writing About the Reading

### Paragraph Options

1. How do you feel about wild animals being kept in captivity? Write a paragraph explaining your answer.

2. What does Koko's "growl" sound mean? In addition to sign language, in what other ways does Koko communicate? Write a paragraph answering these questions.

3. According to the author and Dr. Patterson, what is Koko's motivation for signing? Do you agree or are you a skeptic? Write a paragraph explaining your answer.

### Essay Options

4. Have you ever attempted to learn sign language or a language other than your native language? What was most difficult? What are the rewards of learning another way to communicate? Write an essay answering these questions and describing your experience.

5. If you have pets (or know someone who does), write an essay describing how these animals communicate their feelings or needs. You may want to consider either the interspecies communication that takes place between two different kinds of pets, or communication between humans and their pets.

6. How effective do you think Koko's story will be in helping to "win hearts rather than minds"? What makes Koko an appealing "poster child" for the conservation movement? What other methods might the Gorilla Foundation and other conservationists use to educate communities about the plight of gorillas? Write an essay exploring these questions.

# SELF-TEST SUMMARY

To test yourself, cover the Answer column with a sheet of paper and answer each question in the left column. Evaluate each of your answers as you work by sliding the paper down and comparing your answer with what is printed in the Answer column.

| QUESTION | ANSWER |
|---|---|
| ■ GOAL 1 Figure out unknown words<br><br>What are strategies for figuring out words you don't know? | To figure out the meaning of an unknown word, try pronouncing it aloud, use context clues, and use word parts. |
| ■ GOAL 2 Pronounce unknown words<br><br>How do you pronounce unknown words? | To pronounce an unfamiliar word, sound it out syllable by syllable. (See helpful rules for dividing words into syllables on pp. 116–117.) |
| ■ GOAL 3 Use context clues<br><br>What is context? What are the five types of context clues? | Context refers to the words surrounding an unfamiliar word; context often provides clues to a word's meaning. Types of context clues include *definition, synonym, example, contrast*, and *inference*. |
| ■ GOAL 4 Use word parts<br><br>What are word parts and how do they help you learn words? | The beginnings, middles, and endings of words are called *prefixes, roots*, and *suffixes*. By learning the meanings of the parts that make up a word, you can figure out the meaning of the word. (See tips for how to use word parts on pp. 128–141.) |
| ■ GOAL 5 Learn new words<br><br>What are two systems for learning and remembering new words? | A vocabulary log and the index card system will help you learn and remember new words. |

**MySkillsLab** For more help with **Vocabulary,** go to your learning path in MySkillsLab at http://www.myskillslab.com.

# 5

# Complete Sentences Versus Sentence Fragments

## LEARNING GOALS

Learn how to …

**GOAL 1**
Identify subjects and predicates

**GOAL 2**
Identify sentence fragments

**GOAL 3**
Recognize and correct fragments caused by missing subjects

**GOAL 4**
Recognize and correct fragments caused by missing verbs

**GOAL 5**
Recognize and correct fragments caused by dependent clauses

**GOAL 6**
Understand sentences

Protecting the Future of Nature

Ten million people in sub-Saharan Africa make a living fishing. In the past three decades the number of fish in their waters has declined by 50 percent. Around the world, oceans and the life they support are at risk. WWF is at work in more than 40 countries, developing responsible fishing practices and collaborating with governments and coastal communities on managing their fisheries while safeguarding livelihoods. We can protect marine populations from overfishing and still ensure a catch big enough to feed fishermen, their families and you.

**Be Part of Our Work**          worldwildlife.org

## THINK About It!

When you read the caption under the picture in the advertisement—"Protecting the Future of Nature"—does it make sense? No doubt your answer is yes. Write a sentence stating the message it communicates about the World Wildlife Federation (WWF). From the caption, the photo, and the accompanying text, you know that the WWF is working toward the development of responsible fishing practices.

Now suppose you saw the caption alone, without the accompanying photograph and text. Would it make sense? Would you understand the message of the advertisement? Probably not. You do not know who is protecting the future of nature. The caption is a sentence fragment. A fragment is an incomplete sentence. It lacks a subject.

Fragments are problems for both readers and writers. For readers, the meaning is incomplete, which results in confusion. For writers, fragments are a problem because the intended message is not being conveyed clearly and in an understandable way. When meaning is not clear, misunderstandings are possible, leading to a breakdown in communication.

How can the fragment in the above advertisement be corrected? It does have a verb—*protecting*. To make the caption into a complete sentence, you must add a subject:

|  | Subject | Verb |
|---|---|---|
| COMPLETE SENTENCE | The World Wildlife Federation | is protecting the future of nature. |

The new version now makes sense even without the photograph. This version has a subject and a verb and expresses a complete thought.

In this chapter you will learn to write effective, complete sentences and to identify and correct fragments. You will also learn how to read sentences effectively by identifying the parts that all complete sentences contain to convey meaning.

# FOCUSING ON READING AND WRITING

# What Is a Complete Sentence?

A **complete sentence** is a statement that contains both a subject and a **predicate**—a verb or verbs and the words that govern or modify them—and expresses a complete thought. Being able to identify subjects and predicates will help you avoid errors in writing and will help you read sentences more effectively.

# WRITING

# Identify Subjects and Predicates

■ GOAL 1
Identify subjects and
predicates

Writing effective sentences involves being able to identify the subject and predicate of a sentence.

## Subjects

The **subject** of a sentence is whom or what the sentence is about. It is who or what performs or receives the action expressed in the predicate.

### Nouns as Subjects

The **subject** of a sentence is usually a **noun**. (For a review of nouns, see Part VI, "Handbook: Reviewing the Basics," p. 585.)

The Babylonians wrote the first advertisements.

The advertisements were inscribed on bricks.

The kings conducted advertising campaigns for themselves.

### Pronouns as Subjects

The subject of a sentence can also be a **pronoun**, a word that refers to, or substitutes for, a noun. For example, *I, you, he, she, it, they,* and *we* are all familiar pronouns. (For a review of pronouns, see Part VI, p. 586.)

Early <u>advertisements</u> were straightforward. <u>They</u> carried the names of temples.

The <u>wall</u> was built. <u>It</u> was seen by thousands of people.

### Groups of Words as Subjects

The subject of a sentence can also be a group of words:

<u>Inscribing the bricks</u> was a difficult task.

<u>Uncovering the bricks</u> was a surprise.

<u>To build the brick wall</u> was a time-consuming task.

| EXERCISE 5-1 | Identifying Subjects |
|---|---|

**Directions:** Underline the subject in each of the following sentences.

> **EXAMPLE**   The <u>Babylonians</u> wrote the first advertisements.

1. The <u>thrush</u> was singing.

2. <u>Digging the hole</u> was a strenuous task.

3. After the lecture, <u>we</u> are going to the movies.

4. <u>Vanessa</u> organized the performance.

5. <u>It</u> was only a raccoon outside.

6. Do <u>you</u> want to eat the last cookie?

7. The <u>weeds</u> spread quickly.

8. <u>To swim the English Channel</u> is my goal.

9. <u>Antoan</u> went running.

10. <u>They</u> circumnavigated the globe.

### Compound Subjects

Some sentences contain two or more subjects joined with a coordinating conjunction (*and, but, for, nor, or, so, yet*). Those subjects together form a **compound subject**.

Compound subject

<u>Maria</u> and <u>I</u> completed the marathon.

Compound subject

The <u>computer</u>, the <u>printer</u>, and the <u>DVD player</u> were unusable during the blackout.

## Predicates

The **predicate** indicates what the subject does, what happened to the subject, or what is being said about the subject. The predicate must include a **verb**, a word or group of words that expresses an action or a state of being (for example, *run, invent, build, know, will decide, become*). The predicate can consist of a single word or several words, including other verbs and words that modify or govern them.

> Joy <u>swam</u> sixty laps.
>
> The thunderstorm <u>replenished</u> the reservoir.

Sometimes the predicate consists of only one verb, as in the previous examples. Often, however, the main verb is accompanied by a **helping verb**. A helping verb is used with another verb to express time, obligation, possibility, and so forth.

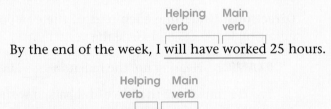

By the end of the week, I <u>will have worked</u> 25 hours.

The training session <u>had begun</u>.

The professor <u>did return</u> the journal assignments.

---

**EXERCISE 5-2**     ## Identifying Verbs

**Directions:** Underline the verb in each of the following sentences. Circle any helping verbs.

> **EXAMPLE**   The next blue moon (will occur) in April.

1. (May) I <u>sit</u> here?

2. Jay <u>practiced</u> the saxophone every day.

3. The divers <u>found</u> the wreckage of an eighteenth-century schooner.

4. Camila (had) <u>written</u> several articles for the school newspaper.

5. Some whale vocalizations (can be) <u>heard</u> for many miles.

6. You (must) <u>wear</u> your seatbelt in my car.

7. She <u>lost</u> her keys down the storm drain.

8. The flood <u>damaged</u> several homes on River Road.

9. A cracking whip (does) <u>break</u> the sound barrier.

10. Mr. Park <u>hired</u> three new employees.

### Compound Predicates

Some sentences have two or more predicates, each of which contains one or more verbs, joined by a coordinating conjunction (*and, but, nor*). These predicates together form a **compound predicate.**

Subject | Compound predicate

Marcia unlocked her bicycle and rode away.

Subject | Compound predicate

The supermarket owner will survey his customers and order the specialized foods they desire.

---

**EXERCISE 5-3** | ## Identifying Compound Predicates

**Directions:** Underline each part of the compound predicate in each of the following sentences and circle the verbs in it.

> **EXAMPLE**  Heating up, the radiator (hissed) and (clanked).

1. The dog (ran) along the fence and (barked) with excitement.

2. The toddler (slipped) and (fell) down the last few stairs but (was) unhurt.

3. I (can) neither (snap) my fingers nor (raise) one eyebrow.

4. In the meantime, Diego (finished) his homework and (made) himself a snack.

5. The final step is to (add) the wet ingredients and (mix) until smooth.

---

# Identify Sentence Fragments

◼ GOAL 2
Identify sentence
fragments

A **fragment** is a sentence that lacks a subject, a verb, or both, or does not express a complete thought. Following are a few more statements taken from magazine ads. Each one is a sentence fragment because each one lacks a subject or a verb or does not express a complete thought. As you read the fragments that follow, they may be difficult to understand. Try to guess what product each sentence fragment describes. Correct answers appear at the bottom of page 158.

| FRAGMENT | PRODUCT |
| --- | --- |
| 1. "Where dreams come true." | 1. *Disney* |
| 2. "All the news that's fit to print." | 2. *New York Times* |
| 3. "Zoom zoom." | 3. *Mazda* |
| 4. "Made from the best stuff on Earth." | 4. *Snapple* |

Because advertisers use visuals to complete their messages, they do not have to worry about the confusing nature of sentence fragments. Also, no one requires writers of ads to use complete sentences. Your instructors, however, expect you to write sentences that are complete and correct. You will, therefore, need to know how to spot and correct sentence fragments. To do so, you need to understand three sentence elements:

- subjects
- verbs
- dependent clauses (also called subordinate clauses)

> ## ❗ NEED TO KNOW
>
> ### Subjects, Verbs, and Sentence Fragments
>
> The **subject** of a sentence tells you whom or what the sentence is about—who or what does or receives the action of the verb. (Note: The direct object can also receive the action of the verb.)
>
> A **verb** expresses action or state of being. Sometimes a verb consists of only one word. (The doorbell *rang*.) Often, however, the main verb has a helping verb. (The guest *had arrived*.)
>
> | SUBJECT | VERB |
> | --- | --- |
> | Heat | rises. |
> | Joyce | laughed. |
> | Weeds | are growing. |
>
> **Dependent, or subordinate, clauses** do not express a complete thought.
>
> A **sentence fragment** is not a complete idea because it lacks a subject and/or a verb or does not express a complete thought. It needs either to be expanded into a complete sentence through the addition of a subject and/or a verb, or it needs to be connected to a preceding or following sentence.

# Recognize and Correct Fragments Caused by Missing Subjects

■ GOAL 3
Recognize and correct fragments caused by missing subjects

A common sentence-writing error is to write a sentence *without a subject*. The result is a sentence fragment. Writers often make this mistake when they think the subject of a previous sentence or a noun in a previous sentence also applies to the next sentence.

| Complete sentence | Fragment |
| --- | --- |
| Marge lost her keys on Tuesday. | And found them on Wednesday. |

[The missing subject is *Marge*.]

| Complete sentence | Fragment |
| --- | --- |
| The instructor canceled class. | But did not postpone the quiz. |

[The missing subject is *instructor*.]

Complete sentence

Relieved that it had stopped raining, Teresa rushed into the mall.

Fragment

Then remembered her car window was open.

[The missing subject is *Teresa*.]

You can revise a fragment that lacks a subject in two ways:

1. **Add a subject, often a pronoun referring to the subject of the preceding sentence.**

| FRAGMENT | And found them on Wednesday. |
|---|---|
| REVISED | She found them on Wednesday. |
| FRAGMENT | Then remembered her car window was open. |
| REVISED | Then she remembered her car window was open. |

2. **Connect the fragment to the preceding sentence.**

| FRAGMENT | And found them on Wednesday. |
|---|---|
| REVISED | Marge lost her keys on Tuesday and found them on Wednesday. |
| FRAGMENT | But did not postpone the quiz. |
| REVISED | The instructor canceled class but did not postpone the quiz. |

Each of these sentences now has a subject and a compound verb.

## EXERCISE 5-4 Revising Fragments by Adding Subjects

**Directions:** Each of the following items consists of a complete sentence followed by a sentence fragment that lacks a subject. Make each fragment into a complete sentence by adding a subject. You may need to take out words, add new ones, capitalize words, or make them lowercase as you revise.

**EXAMPLE** Bert threw the basketball. ^He^ And cheered when it went in the hoop.

1. The president waved as he left the building. Then ^he^ got in the car and drove away.

2. The novel was complex. ^It w^ Was also long and poorly written.

3. The scissors were not very sharp. ^They w^ Were old and rusty, you see.

4. Hundreds of students waited to get into the bookstore. ^They m^ Milled around until the manager unlocked the door.

5. My roommate, whose name is Speed, is an excellent skater. ^She g^ Gets teased sometimes about her name.

6. The computer printed out the list of names. Then ^it^ beeped loudly.

7. Fans crowded the stadium. ^They^ And cheered after each touchdown.

Answers to sentence fragments: 1. Disney; 2. *New York Times*; 3. Mazda; 4. Snapple.

8. Many guests arrived early for the wedding. Unfortunately, ^they^ were not seated until ten o'clock.

9. The delivery person put the large package down. Then ^he^ rang the doorbell.

10. The big black dog sat obediently. ~~But~~ ^It^ growled nonetheless.

| EXERCISE 5-5 | Writing About an Advertisement |
|---|---|

**WRITING IN PROGRESS**

**Directions:** Write a paragraph describing an advertisement you have seen or heard recently. Explain to whom the advertisement appeals and why. After you have finished revising and proofreading your paragraph, underline the subject of each sentence. Exchange papers with a peer reviewer and see if you agree on the identification of subjects. Discuss any differences of opinion with another peer reviewer or with your instructor. Save your paper. You will need it for another exercise in this chapter.

# Recognize and Correct Fragments Caused by Missing Verbs

■ **GOAL 4**
Recognize and correct fragments caused by missing verbs

A **verb** is a word or word group that indicates what the subject does or what happens to the subject. Most verbs express action or a state of being, for example, *run, invent, build, know, be.* (For a review of verbs, see Part VI, p. 590.)

Advertising is bland without a slogan.
Slogans promote a specific product.

Sometimes a verb consists of only one word.

The announcer speaks.

Often, however, the main verb is accompanied by one or more helping (auxiliary) verbs such as *will, can,* and forms of *be, have,* or *do.* (For a review of helping verbs, see Part VI, p. 590.)

Helping verb   Main verb
The announcer will speak.

Helping verb       Main verb
The announcer will be speaking.

Helping verb   Main verb
The first trademark was registered in 1870.

Helping verb     Main verb
Do any companies use animals as trademarks?

Helping verb   Main verb
The lion has been MGM's trademark for a long time.

<table>
<tr><td>EXERCISE 5-6</td><td># Identifying Verbs</td></tr>
</table>

**Directions:** Underline the verb(s), including any helping verb(s), in each of the following sentences.

**EXAMPLE** The lectures in psychology <u>have been focusing</u> on instinctive behavior lately.

1. Preschools <u>teach</u> children social and academic skills.

2. Exercise clubs <u>offer</u> instruction and <u>provide</u> companionship.

3. Millions of people <u>have watched</u> soap operas.

4. Essay exams <u>are given</u> in many college classes.

5. The audience <u>will be surprised</u> by the play's ending.

---

## How to Revise Fragments Without Complete Verbs

> ### Tip for Writers
>
> The simple present tense is used for repeated action. "Allison *walks* across campus after lunch" means she does this regularly. On the other hand, "Allison is walking" (present continuous tense) means right now or at some stated future time (perhaps tomorrow) she is or will be walking.

Fragments often occur when word groups begin with words ending in -*ing* or with phrases beginning with the word *to*. These words and phrases are verb forms and may look like verbs, but they cannot function as verbs in sentences.

### How to Revise Fragments with -ing Verbs

Note the -*ing* word in the fragment below:

FRAGMENT <u>Walking</u> across campus after lunch.

In this word group, *walking* has no subject. Who is walking? Now let's add a subject and see what happens:

*Allison* <u>walking</u> across campus after lunch.

The word group still is not a complete sentence; the verb form *walking* cannot be used alone as a sentence verb. You can make the word group a complete sentence by adding a helping verb (for example, *is, was, has been*) or by using a different verb form (*walked* or *walks*).

Helping verb added

REVISED Allison <u>was walking</u> across campus after lunch.

Verb form changed to present tense

REVISED Allison <u>walks</u> across campus after lunch.

Now the word group is a complete sentence.

You can correct fragments beginning with -*ing* words in four ways:

1. **Add a subject and change the -*ing* verb form to a verb that completes the sentence.**

Fragment

FRAGMENT Morris was patient. Waiting in line at the bank.

Subject   Verb changed to past tense

REVISED Morris was patient. <u>He</u> <u>waited</u> in line at the bank.

2. **Add a subject and a form of *be* (such as *am, are, will be, has been, is, was, were*) as a helping verb.**

Fragment

FRAGMENT    Juan was bored. Listening to his sister complain about her

boyfriend.

Subject   Form of *be*   Main verb

REVISED    Juan was bored. He was listening to his sister complain about her

boyfriend.

3. **Connect the fragment to the sentence that comes before or after it.**

Fragment

FRAGMENT    Mark finished lunch. Picking up his tray. Then he left the cafeteria.

Modifies *he*

REVISED    Mark finished lunch. Picking up his tray, he left the cafeteria.

4. **If the *-ing* word is *being*, change its form to another form of *be (am, are, is, was, were).***

Fragment

FRAGMENT    Jayla failed the math quiz. Her mistakes being careless errors.

Verb form changed

REVISED    Jayla failed the math quiz. Her mistakes were careless errors.

### How to Revise Fragments with To Phrases

A phrase beginning with *to* cannot be the verb of the sentence. When it stands alone, it is a sentence fragment.

FRAGMENT    To review for the psychology test.

This word group lacks a subject and a verb that completes the sentence. To make a complete sentence, you need to add a subject and a verb.

Subject   Verb

REVISED    Deon plans to review for the psychology test.

You can revise fragments that begin with *to* in two ways:

1. **Add a subject and a verb that complete the sentence.**

FRAGMENT    To reach my goal.

Subject   Verb

REVISED    I hope to reach my goal.

**2. Connect the *to* phrase to a nearby sentence.**

FRAGMENT    To earn the highest grade. Antonio studied for eight hours.

REVISED     To earn the highest grade, Antonio studied for eight hours.

---

EXERCISE 5-7

*WORKING TOGETHER*

# Correcting Fragments by Adding Verbs

**Directions:** Each of the following word groups is a fragment. Revise each one to form a complete sentence, and then compare your revisions with those of a classmate.    Answers will vary.

**EXAMPLE**

FRAGMENT              Walking along the waterfront.

COMPLETE SENTENCE    Andrea was walking along the waterfront.

1. Photographing the wedding.

   Lourdes was photographing the wedding all day.

2. To have a family.

   Sarah and Joe hope to have a family after they graduate.

3. Hanging up the suit in the closet.

   Anthony hung up the suit in the closet.

4. Deciding what to have for dinner.

   Lucas decided what to have for dinner.

5. To attend the awards ceremony.

   We wanted to attend the awards ceremony.

6. Writing the speech.

   Alfredo was writing the speech in the library.

7. To sketch a diagram.

   The student attempted to sketch a diagram.

8. To quit her job.

   Maria unexpectedly decided to quit her job.

9. Making the paper less repetitious.

   Anne will be making the paper less repetitious in her next draft.

10. Being old and in disrepair.

    The car is old and in disrepair.

**EXERCISE 5-8**

## Revising Your Paragraph

**WRITING IN PROGRESS**

**Directions:** Go back to the paragraph you wrote in Exercise 5-5 and circle the verb(s) in each sentence. Exchange papers with a peer reviewer and check each other's work.

# Recognize and Correct Fragments Caused by Dependent Clauses

■ GOAL 5
Recognize and correct fragments caused by dependent clauses

A sentence not only must contain a subject and a verb but also *must express a complete thought.* That is, a sentence should not leave a question in your mind as to its meaning or leave an idea unfinished. To spot and avoid sentence fragments in your writing, you must be able to recognize the difference between independent and dependent (or subordinate) clauses.

A **clause** is a group of related words that contains a subject and its verb. There are two types of clauses, independent and dependent. An **independent clause** expresses a complete thought and can stand alone as a complete sentence. A **dependent** (or **subordinate**) **clause** does not express a complete thought. When a dependent clause stands alone, it is a fragment.

## Recognize Independent Clauses

An **independent clause** has a subject and a verb and can stand alone as a complete and correct sentence. It expresses a complete thought.

COMPLETE THOUGHT

Independent clause

Subject        Verb

Advertising was not halted during World War II.

COMPLETE THOUGHT

Independent clause

Subject             Verb

Advertisers prominently displayed brand names.

COMPLETE THOUGHT

Independent clause

Subject     Verb

Produce will be in short supply this year.

## Recognize Dependent (or Subordinate) Clauses

A **dependent clause** has a subject and a verb but cannot stand alone as a complete and correct sentence. It does not express a complete thought. A dependent clause makes sense only when it is joined to an independent clause. When a dependent clause stands alone, it is a **dependent clause fragment**. A dependent clause fragment leaves an unanswered question in your mind.

INCOMPLETE THOUGHT

Dependent clause fragment

Subject      Verb

After World War II ended. [What happened after World War II ended?]

INCOMPLETE THOUGHT

Dependent clause fragment

Subject      Verb

If new products are developed. [What happens if new products are developed?]

INCOMPLETE THOUGHT

Dependent clause fragment

Subject      Verb

When magazine circulation increased. [What happened when circulation increased?]

How can you spot dependent clauses? A dependent clause often begins with a word or group of words called a subordinating conjunction.

A **subordinating conjunction** explains the relationship between the dependent clause and the independent clause to which it is joined. Subordinating conjunctions signal dependent clauses. When you see a clause beginning with one of these words (shown in the "Need to Know" box on page 165), make sure the clause is attached to an independent clause.

Dependent clause          Independent clause

After World War II ended, advertising became more glamorous.

Subordinating
conjunction

Independent clause          Dependent clause

There will be new advertising campaigns if new products are developed.

Subordinating
conjunction

Dependent clause          Independent clause

When magazine circulation increased, magazines became a popular new

advertising medium.

Subordinating
conjunction

## ! NEED TO KNOW

### Subordinating Conjunctions

A clause beginning with a subordinate conjunction is a **dependent clause**. It cannot stand alone. It must be connected to an independent clause. Here is a list of common subordinating conjunctions:

| | | |
|---|---|---|
| after | even though | than |
| although | if | that |
| as | inasmuch as | though |
| as far as | in case | unless |
| as if | in order that | until |
| as long as | in order to | when |
| as soon as | now that | whenever |
| as though | once | where |
| because | provided that | whereas |
| before | rather than | wherever |
| during | since | whether |
| even if | so that | while |

## EXERCISE 5-9 — Identifying Clauses

**Directions:** Decide whether the following clauses are independent or dependent. Write "I" for independent or "D" for dependent before each clause.

   D   **1.** While Arturo was driving to school.

   I   **2.** *Sesame Street* is a children's educational television program.

   I   **3.** Samantha keeps a diary of her family's holiday celebrations.

   D   **4.** Because Aretha had a craving for chocolate.

   I   **5.** Exercise can help to relieve stress.

   D   **6.** When Peter realized he would be able to meet the deadline.

   I   **7.** A snowstorm crippled the Eastern Seaboard states on New Year's Eve.

   D   **8.** Unless my uncle decides to visit us during spring break.

   I   **9.** Long-distance telephone rates are less expensive during the evening than during the day.

   D  **10.** As long as Jacqueline is living at home.

## Correct Dependent Clause Fragments

You can correct a dependent clause fragment in two ways:

**1. Join the dependent clause to an independent clause to make the dependent clause fragment part of a complete sentence.**

| | |
|---|---|
| FRAGMENT | Although competition increased. |
| COMPLETE SENTENCE | Although competition increased, the sales staff was still getting new customers. |
| | |
| FRAGMENT | Because market research expanded. |
| COMPLETE SENTENCE | The company added new accounts because market research expanded. |
| | |
| FRAGMENT | Although statistics and market research have become part of advertising. |
| COMPLETE SENTENCE | Although statistics and market research have become part of advertising, consumers' tastes remain somewhat unpredictable. |

**2. Take away the subordinating conjunction, and the dependent clause fragment becomes an independent clause that can stand alone as a complete sentence.**

| | |
|---|---|
| FRAGMENT | Although competition increased. |
| COMPLETE SENTENCE | Competition increased. |
| | |
| FRAGMENT | Because market research expanded. |
| COMPLETE SENTENCE | Market research expanded. |
| | |
| FRAGMENT | Although statistics and market research have become part of advertising. |
| COMPLETE SENTENCE | Statistics and market research have become part of advertising. |

Keep in mind that, when you join a dependent clause to an independent clause, you need to think about punctuation:

■ **If the *dependent* clause comes first, follow it with a comma.** The comma separates the dependent clause from the independent clause and helps you know where the independent clause begins.

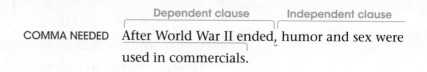

Dependent clause      Independent clause

COMMA NEEDED   After World War II ended, humor and sex were used in commercials.

■ **If the *independent* clause comes first, do *not* use a comma between the two clauses.**

Independent clause

NO COMMA NEEDED   Humor and sex were used in commercials

Dependent clause

after World War II ended.

## Revising Fragments by Adding Independent Clauses

**Directions:** Make each of these dependent clause fragments into a sentence by adding an independent clause before or after the fragment. Add or remove punctuation if necessary.    Answers will vary.

**EXAMPLE**    After we got to the beach/, we put on sunscreen.

1. Since the surgery was ~~expensive.~~ *to be expensive/,*  I questioned the doctor carefully.

2. As long as my boss allows me/, I plan to walk during my lunch break.

3. Because I want to be a journalist/, I am doing an internship with my local newspaper.

4. ∪ntil ~~the roof~~ is repaired. *The roof will be covered with a tarp*  *it*

5. Once I returned the library books/, I took out three more.

6. So that I do not miss class. *I arrive on campus early*

7. Provided that Marietta gets the loan/, she will purchase a used car.

8. ∪nless you would rather go to the movies. *Let's go bowling,*

9. If the thunderstorm comes during the barbecue/, we will move indoors.

10. Although we visited Disney last summer/, we hope to return next year.

## Recognize Dependent Clauses Beginning with Relative Pronouns

Dependent clauses also may begin with relative pronouns. A **relative pronoun** relates groups of words to nouns or other pronouns and often introduces other clauses. (For more information on relative pronouns, see Part VI, p. 588.)

> ### NEED TO KNOW
>
> #### Relative Pronouns
>
> | RELATIVE PRONOUNS THAT REFER TO PEOPLE | | RELATIVE PRONOUNS THAT REFER TO THINGS | |
> |---|---|---|---|
> | who | whom | that | whichever |
> | whoever | whomever | which | whatever |
> | whose | | | |

The relative pronoun that begins a dependent clause connects the dependent clause to a noun or pronoun in the independent clause. However, the verb in the dependent clause is *never* the main verb of the sentence. The independent clause has its own verb, which is the main verb of the sentence and expresses a complete thought.

The following sentence fragments each consist of a noun followed by a dependent clause beginning with a relative pronoun. They are not complete sentences because the noun does not have a verb and the fragment does not express a complete thought.

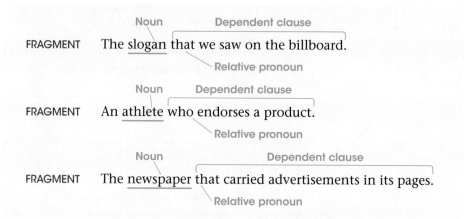

You can correct this type of fragment by adding a verb to make the noun the subject of an independent clause. Often the independent clause will be split, and the dependent clause will appear between its parts.

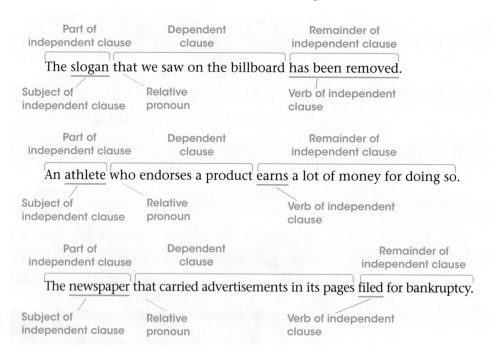

EXERCISE 5-11   Revising Fragments

**Directions:** Make each of these fragments into a complete sentence. Add words, phrases, or clauses, and punctuation as needed.   *Answers will vary.*

**EXAMPLE**   The usher who was available, led us to our seats.

1. The radio that Trevor had purchased last night, was defective.

   _____

2. The official who had signed the peace treaty, was honored upon his return to the U.S.

   _____

3. The athlete who won the tennis tournament, had practiced extensively.

   _____

4. Mark, whose nose had been broken in a fight, , wore a bandage.

   _____

5. The advice that his lawyer gave him, was sound.

   _____

6. The student who needed the scholarship the most, did not win one.

   _____

7. The answering machine that is in the kitchen, needs to be removed.

   _____

8. Sarah, whom I knew in high school, , is my daughter's teacher.

   _____

9. The problems that the professor assigned, were difficult.

   _____

10. The men who signed the Declaration of Independence, are famous.

    _____

## Review How to Spot and Revise Fragments

Now that you have learned to identify subjects, verbs, and dependent clauses, you will be able to spot and correct fragments. The following "Need to Know" boxes provide a brief review of the questions to ask and the actions to take to do so.

## NEED TO KNOW

### How to Spot Fragments

Use the following questions to check for fragments:

1. **Does the word group have a subject?** The subject is a noun or pronoun that performs or receives the action of the sentence. To find the subject, ask *who* or *what* performs or receives the action of the verb.
2. **Does the word group have a verb?** Be sure that the verb is complete and correct. Watch out for sentences that begin with an *-ing* word or a *to* phrase.
3. **Does the word group begin with a subordinating conjunction (*since, after, because, as, while, although,* and so forth) introducing a dependent clause?** Unless the dependent clause is attached to an independent clause, it is a fragment.
4. **Does the word group begin with a relative pronoun (*who, whom, whose, whoever, whomever, that, which, whatever*) introducing a dependent clause?** Unless the dependent clause forms a question, is part of an independent clause, or is attached to an independent clause, it is a fragment.

## NEED TO KNOW

### How to Revise Fragments

Once you spot a fragment in your writing, correct it in one of the following ways:

**1. Add a subject if one is missing.**

| FRAGMENT | Appeared on television ten times during the game. |
| REVISED | The advertisement for Pepsi appeared on television ten times during the game. |

**2. Add a verb if one is missing.** Add a helping verb if one is needed, or change the verb form.

| FRAGMENT | An action-packed commercial with rap music. |
| REVISED | An action-packed commercial with rap music advertised a new soft drink. |

**3. Combine the dependent-clause fragment with an independent clause to make a complete sentence.**

| FRAGMENT | Because advertising is expensive. |
| REVISED | Because advertising is expensive, companies are making shorter commercials. |

**4. Remove the subordinating conjunction or relative pronoun so the group of words can stand alone as a sentence.**

| FRAGMENT | Since viewers can "zap" out commercials on video-recorders. |
| REVISED | Viewers can "zap" out commercials on video-recorders. |

---

## EXERCISE 5-12   Revising Fragments

**Directions:** Make each of the following sentence fragments a complete sentence by adding the missing subject or verb, combining it with an independent clause, or removing the subordinating conjunction or relative pronoun.   Answers will vary.

**EXAMPLE**

| FRAGMENT | Many environmentalists are concerned about the spotted owl. Which is almost extinct. |
| COMPLETE SENTENCE | Many environmentalists are concerned about the spotted owl, which is almost extinct. |

*We    ed*

1. Renting a DVD of the movie *The Hunger Games*.

   _____

   _____

2. Spices that have been imported from India/ *can be expensive.*

   _____

   _____

3. The police officer walked to Jerome's van. *t* To give him a ticket.

_____

_____

4. My English professor, with the cup of tea he brought to each class, *greeted us as we arrived.*

_____

_____

5. After the table is refinished, *it will look much better.*

_____

_____

6. Roberto memorized his lines, *f* For the performance tomorrow night.

_____

_____

7. A tricycle with big wheels, *was* painted red.

_____

_____

8. On the shelf, an antique crock used for storing lard. *was priced at thirty dollars.*

_____

_____

9. Because I always wanted to learn to speak Spanish, *I enrolled in a conversational Spanish course.*

_____

_____

10. *Because I was* Looking for the lost keys, I was late for class.

_____

_____

**EXERCISE 5-13**   Revising a Paragraph

**Directions:** The following paragraph is correct except that it contains sentence fragments. Underline each fragment. Then revise the paragraph by rewriting or combining sentences to eliminate fragments.   Answers will vary.

Social networks such as Facebook and MySpace appeal to college students for a variety of reasons. Social networks are a way of having conversations. <u>Staying in touch with friends without the inconvenience of getting dressed and meeting them somewhere.</u> Friends can join or drop out of a conversation whenever they want. Social networks also allow college students to meet new people and make new friends. Members can track who is friends with whom. Students may choose to share only portions of their profiles. To protect their privacy. Some students use social networks to form groups. Such as clubs, study groups, or special interest groups. Other students use networks to screen dates. And discover who is interested in dating or who is already taken.

---

| EXERCISE 5-14 | ## Revising Sentence Fragments |
|---|---|

**WRITING IN PROGRESS**

**Directions:** Review the paragraph you wrote for Exercise 5-5, checking for sentence fragments. If you find a fragment, revise it.

---

| EXERCISE 5-15 | ## Revising Sentence Fragments |
|---|---|

**Directions:** The following paragraph contains numerous fragments. Underline each fragment and then revise each to eliminate the fragment.   *Sample answers provided in Instructor's Manual.*

> More than 300 million cubic miles. That's how much water covers our planet. However, 97 percent being salty. Which leaves 3 percent fresh water. Three-quarters of that fresh water is in icecaps. And in glaciers. Sixteen thousand gallons. That's how much water the average person drinks in a lifetime. Each family of four, using more than 300 gallons per day. Although the world's demand for water has more than doubled since 1960. There is still a sufficient supply to take care of humanity's needs. However, regular water shortages in certain parts of the world. Because the pattern of rainfall throughout the world is uneven. For instance, 400 inches of rain per year in some parts of India, but no rain for several years in other parts of the world.

---

# READING

# Understand Sentences

■ GOAL 6
Understand sentences

Suppose you read the following sentence in a U.S. government textbook:

> The president is the party's leader, not by any authority of the Constitution, whose authors abhorred parties, but by strong tradition and practical necessity.

Try to explain what this sentence means. The real test of whether you understand an idea is whether you can express it in your own words.

Basically, the sentence explains why the president is the leader of his or her political party. Although less important, the sentence also explains that this is not a rule stated in the Constitution. Finally, the sentence contains the additional information that the authors of the Constitution abhorred, or hated, political parties.

Now let us look at how you might have arrived at this meaning. Answer each of the following questions:

1. Did you search for the most important information in the sentence?
2. Did you try to discover how various parts of the sentence were connected?
3. Did you check the meaning of any unfamiliar words such as *abhorred?*
4. Did you put the meaning of the sentence in your own words?

If you answered "yes" to each of these questions, you are well on your way to reading sentences effectively. Together, these questions suggest a four-step approach to sentence reading:

1: Locate the key ideas

2: Study the modifiers

3: Check unknown words

4: Paraphrase, or use your own words to express ideas

This section of the chapter will show you how to find important information in sentences, sort or sift out less important ideas, see how ideas are connected, and paraphrase sentences.

## Locate Key Ideas

Every sentence expresses at least one key idea, or main point. This main idea is a statement about someone or something. You can identify the main point by finding the subject and the predicate.

### *Find the Subject and Predicate*

Every sentence is made up of at least two parts, a subject and a predicate. The subject, often a noun, identifies the person or object the sentence is about. The main part of the predicate—the verb—tells what the person or object is doing or has done. Usually a sentence contains additional information about the subject and/or the predicate.

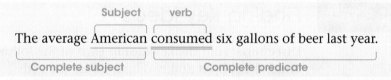

The key idea of this sentence is "American consumed." It is expressed by the subject and verb. The simple subject of this sentence is *American;* it explains who the sentence is about. The words *the* and *average* give more information about the subject, American, by explaining which one. The main part of the predicate is the verb *consumed;* this tells what the average American did. The rest of the sentence gives more information about the verb by telling what (beer) and how much (six gallons last year) was consumed. Here are a few more examples:

The ship entered the harbor early this morning.

Lilacs bloom in the spring.

Jeff cooks dinner for the family every night.

In many long and complicated sentences, the key idea is not as obvious as in the previous examples. To find the key idea, ask these questions:

■ Whom or what is the sentence about?

■ What is happening in the sentence?

Here is an example of a complicated sentence that might be found in a psychology textbook:

Intelligence, as measured by IQ, depends on the kind of test given, the skill of the examiner, and the cooperation of the subject.

In this sentence, the answer to the question, "Whom or what is the sentence about?" is *intelligence.* The verb is *depends,* and the remainder of the sentence explains the factors upon which intelligence depends. Let us look at a few more examples:

William James, often thought of as the father of American psychology, tested whether memory could be improved by exercising it.

Violence in sports, both at amateur and professional levels, has increased dramatically over the past ten years.

Some sentences may have more than one subject and/or more than one verb in the predicate.

    Subject        Subject       Verb
Poor diet and lack of exercise can cause weight gain.

    Subject        Verb       Verb
My brother always worries and complains about his job.

    Subject        Subject       Verb       Verb
Many homes and businesses are burglarized or vandalized each year.

    Subject        Verb       Verb       Verb
The angry customer was screaming, cursing, and shouting.

## EXERCISE 5-16    Finding Key Ideas

**Directions:** Find the key idea in each of the following sentences. Draw one line under the subject and two lines under the verb.

    **EXAMPLE**   The instructor assigned a fifteen-page article to read.

1. Every summer my parents travel to the eastern seacoast.

2. Children learn how to behave by imitating adults.

3. William Faulkner, a popular American author, wrote about life in the South.

4. Psychologists are interested in studying human behavior in many different situations.

5. Terminally ill patients may refuse to take their prescribed medication.

6. The use of cocaine, although illegal, is apparently increasing.

7. The most accurate method we have of estimating the age of the Earth is based on our knowledge of radioactivity.

8. Elements exist either as compounds or as free elements.

9. <u>Attention</u> <u>may be defined</u> as a focusing of perception.

10. The specific <u>instructions</u> in a computer program <u>are written</u> in a computer language.

## Study Modifiers

After you have identified the key ideas, the next step in understanding a sentence is to see how the modifiers affect its meaning. **Modifiers** are words that change, describe, qualify, or limit the meaning of another word or sentence part. Most modifiers either add to or change the meaning of the key idea. Usually they answer such questions about the subject or predicate as *what, where, which, when, how,* or *why.* For example:

Where    When

<u>Sam</u> <u>drove</u> his car to Toronto last week.

When    How

Last night <u>I</u> <u>read</u> with interest a magazine article on sailing.

As you read a sentence, be sure to notice how the details change, limit, or add to the meaning of the key idea. Decide, for each of the following examples, how the underlined portion affects the meaning of the key idea.

Maria took her dog to the pond <u>yesterday.</u>

Recently, I selected <u>with great care</u> a wedding gift for my sister.

The older Cadillac <u>with the convertible top</u> belongs to my husband.

In the first example, the underlined detail explains *when* Maria took her dog to the pond. In the second example, the underlined words tell *how* the gift was selected. In the last example, the underlined phrase indicates *which* Cadillac.

---

**EXERCISE 5-17**

## Identifying Modifiers

**Directions:** Read each of the following sentences. Circle the subject and verb, and decide what the underlined part of the sentence tells about the key idea. Write *which, when, where, how,* or *why* in the space provided.

*how*    1. (You) (can relieve) tension <u>through exercise.</u>

*which*    2. Many (students) <u>in computer science courses</u> (can spend) 12-hour days using computers.

*why*    3. Many (shoppers) (clip) coupons <u>to reduce their grocery bills.</u>

*when*    4. <u>After class</u> (I) (am going) to talk to my instructor.

*where*    5. The world's oil (supply) (is concentrated) <u>in only a few places around the globe.</u>

---

## Check Unfamiliar Vocabulary

If a word (or words) interferes with your comprehension of the sentence, you will need to figure out its meaning. Try the following steps until you have figured out the word's meaning.

1. **Pronounce it.** Often hearing the word will help you recognize it and recall its meaning.
2. **Use context.** Try to figure out the meaning of the word from the way it is used in a sentence (see Chapter 4 for specific techniques).
3. **Analyze word parts.** Look for prefixes, roots, and suffixes that you are familiar with (refer to Chapter 4).
4. **Check the glossary.** Many textbooks include glossaries to define words used in that particular subject matter.
5. **Check a dictionary.** Some words do have several meanings. Be sure to find the meaning that fits the way the word is used in the sentence you are working with.

## Paraphrase

**Paraphrasing** means putting an author's thoughts in your own words. Paraphrasing is the true test of whether you have understood an author's ideas. It provides a useful way to figure out what difficult and confusing sentences mean and it helps you remember what you read. By taking time with and thinking through an idea in order to paraphrase it, you'll find you'll be able to remember it.

Refer to Chapter 18 for more information on how to paraphrase.

---

**EXERCISE 5-18**

# Expressing the Meaning of a Sentence in Your Own Words

**Directions:** Use the four-step approach described in this section to express the meaning of each of the following sentences in your own words.   *Answers will vary.*

1. The chef explained that the odd appearance of chocolate truffles—misshapen, lumpy, and covered in a dirt-like cocoa powder—was intended to mimic the wild mushrooms known as truffles.

   _____

   _____

2. Despite the long and arduous day of travel, the children were amenable to stopping at the grocery store on our way back into town.

   _____

   _____

3. The harsh and inhospitable conditions of Australia dissuaded early explorers from attempting to settle there.

   _____

   _____

4. In addition to lights and sounds, certain foods have been identified as triggers for migraine headaches; these triggers include coffee, chocolate, aged cheeses, and foods containing excessive salt or artificial sweeteners.

   _____

   _____

5.  Although it originated in California in the 1920s, beach volleyball made huge gains in popularity during the 2008 Summer Olympics in Beijing, and in 2012, teams from 15 colleges participated in the inaugural season of collegiate sand volleyball.

_____

_____

# INTEGRATING READING AND WRITING

## READ AND REVISE

The following excerpt is from a student essay called "Coming to America." This excerpt contains sentence fragments that were subsequently corrected in a later draft. Read the excerpt, and underline the sentence fragments caused by missing subjects, verbs, or dependent clauses. Then write out a revised version of the paragraph, correcting the errors using the techniques discussed in this chapter.

frag    There are many events that happened during my lifetime, but the main one
that echoes in my mind, Coming to America. I'm originally from Port-au-Prince,
frag    Haiti. I moved to the United States at the age of 10. Which changed my life in
many ways. Coming to America took away all the pain and suffering I went
through growing up as a child. I didn't have an education, and now it's possible.
frag    The hardest thing to learn a new language.

frag    Imagine living in a place where there is severe violence, hunger, and poverty. Where there are no jobs. Kids and adults are crying from hunger, waiting for a miracle. Most of the time they have to steal or make a kill to have
frag    something on their plate. Losing friends and family members day by day from
sickness or disease. Because there was no hospital to go to. People were killing
themselves because they were suffering too much and could not take the pain
frag    anymore. That's something I had to see every day. For the 10 years that I lived
in Haiti. My father was in America, and I prayed every day that he would come
frag    and get me and my brother. Until one day my prayers were answered. We were
coming to a better place. Haiti is not the best place to live, but I respect and cher-
ish where I am from, for who I am today.

## READ AND RESPOND: A Professional Essay

### Thinking Before Reading

In the following reading, the author describes a recent experience on the subway in New York. As you read, notice Doloff's effective use of adjectives and adverbs. Before you read:

1. Preview the reading, using the steps discussed in Chapter 1, p. 25.
2. Connect the reading to your own experience by answering the following questions:
   a. Have you ever heard a norteño group or a mariachi band perform? Where did the performance take place and what was your reaction?
   b. When you ride a bus or subway, what (if any) interactions do you typically have with other passengers?
3. Highlight and annotate as you read.

1340*L*/576 words

# Norteño en Manhattan

## Steven Doloff

1    At 14th Street on an "N" train heading uptown one recent Friday morning, a three-man norteño band boarded the half-empty subway car I was riding in. Norteño performers are not mariachi (who wear Mexican-style "charro" outfits and use more instruments, like horns), but rather stylistically different "northern" Mexico musicians. And this was an impressive group: short stocky guys in identical black ten gallon hats, fiery red cowboy shirts, black jeans and polished black cowboy boots. Two had acoustic guitars slung over their backs and the third toted a stubby accordion strapped across his stomach.

2    Maybe 30 seconds after they entered the train and without saying a word, they suddenly launched into a driving rendition of "Cielito Lindo" (you know—"ai, ai, aiai"). They were loud, and really good, and did I mention loud? After about two minutes they stopped dead and just stood there silently while one of them changed the position of the capo on the neck of his guitar.

**capo**
a movable device attached to the fingerboard of a guitar to uniformly raise the pitch of all the strings

3    At the opposite end of the car, sprawled across the "Priority seating for persons with disabilities" bench, a clearly inebriated member of the train's captive audience voiced his even clearer indignation at the intrusive performance by provocatively croaking into the palpable quiet after the band stopped, "Wetbacks!"

**inebriated**
drunk

4    Given the offensive nature of the term, his timing, and the raspiness of his voice, its effect felt almost as thunderous as the previous song. Everyone (maybe 25 people) stared down the car at the drunk and then more indirectly at the performers, who seemed completely oblivious to the epithet. But the dissatisfied audience member was not finished. He proceeded to rant incoherently, half to the other riders and half to the air, about illegal aliens, unemployment, and the current stock market crisis.

**epithet**
a disparaging or abusive word or phrase

5    The accordion player swiveled on his polished heels to look blankly at the drunk. He then hit a single note on his keyboard and the band again slammed into a pounding version of another Mexican standard. At the 28th Street stop, the irate audience member gave up, got up, and lurched off the train.

6    The band finished their second number as the train pulled out of the station. The accordion player then took off his cowboy hat and, with a broad grin, walked down the car holding it out upside down for contributions. Almost everyone started coughing up money—and lots of it. The accordionist just kept smiling and saying "gracias" for each donation, while the other two musicians impassively reslung their guitars over their shoulders. The last person to drop a bill in the hat, who was sitting next to me, mumbled quietly, "Sorry about that guy …"

7    At 34th Street, my stop, they got off the car right in front of me, and as they did, they actually spoke, though not very much. My Spanish is minimal, but I made out two sentences. The accordionist said without the slightest inflection of irony, "América es un país muy bueno" ("America's a very good country"), to which one of the guitar players responded, "La segunda canción fue muy rápida" ("The second song was too fast").

**irony**
sarcasm or mockery

8    I know things are going to be economically rough for a while in this country and in this city too. But if the immigrants who pour into the United States every day have this kind of implacable confidence, so can the rest of us, whose parents or grandparents no doubt came here with much the same resolution.

9    I think we'll be okay.

—*The Epoch Times*, January 9, 2009

## Getting Ready to Write

### Checking Your Comprehension

Answer each of the following questions using complete sentences.

1. What is a norteño band? Describe how it is different from a mariachi band.

2. What did the norteño band do after it boarded the subway car?

3. What did the drunken passenger call the norteño band? Describe how the band and the other passengers reacted to the outburst.

4. What happened when the norteño band finished playing and asked for contributions?

5. What two comments did the norteño band members make when they got off the train?

## Strengthening Your Vocabulary

Using the word's context, word parts, or a dictionary, write a brief definition of each of the following words as it is used in the reading.

1. rendition (paragraph 2) _version, performance_

2. provocatively (paragraph 3) _with the intent to provoke, incite, or irritate_

3. palpable (paragraph 3) _plainly seen, heard, or felt_

4. incoherently (paragraph 4) _without making sense_

5. impassively (paragraph 6) _calmly, unemotionally_

6. inflection (paragraph 7) _tone_

7. implacable (paragraph 8) _not capable of being changed or compromised_

## Examining the Reading: Using Idea Maps

Review the reading by completing the missing parts of the following idea map.

**VISUALIZE IT!**

Title — **Norteño en Manhattan**

Thesis — If immigrants have confidence in America, so can the rest of us.

A norteño band boards the subway and begins to perform.

A passenger insults the band and begins a drunken rant.

The band begins to play another song.

The drunk gets off the train.

A band member passes a hat for contributions from passengers.

Passengers donate generously and one apologizes about the drunk.

The writer overhears a band member say America is a good country.

Conclusion — Despite our economic troubles, we can be optimistic about our country.

## Thinking Critically: Discussion and Journal Writing

Analyze and evaluate by discussing the following:

1. Consider how the musicians responded to the drunk. Do you think it was the first time they had experienced negative or offensive behavior during a performance? In what ways was the band's response effective?

2. How do you know the other passengers on the subway were more sympathetic to the norteño musicians than to the drunk? Why do you think they were?

3. What was the author's purpose in writing this essay?

4. What effect do you think the setting—a half-empty subway train in Manhattan—has on this story? Discuss how the events might have played out differently in another setting.

5. Consider how the author describes the members of the norteño band. How does that description compare with what he tells the reader about the drunk passenger?

6. What aspect of the reading is illustrated by the accompanying photograph? What details do you notice about the photograph that correspond to the reading?

**THINKING VISUALLY**

---

**MySkillsLab®**

Complete
this
Exercise

## Writing About the Reading

### Paragraph Options

1. Imagine that you were on the same subway car as the author that day. How would you have reacted to what happened? Write a paragraph describing your response.

2. How would you characterize your interactions with others who behave poorly or inappropriately? Write a paragraph describing how you respond.

3. The drunk's use of the derogatory term *wetbacks* made the other passengers uncomfortable. Think of a time when you heard someone use a disparaging or abusive term and write a paragraph describing your response.

### Essay Options

4. What can you tell from this reading about the author's attitudes toward the norteño group and toward the drunk? Write an essay examining the ways in which the author reveals his feelings toward each. Identify specific examples of connotative language that reveal the author's tone, and explain how his tone affects you as the reader.

5. Write an essay describing the same events from the point of view of one of the members of the norteño band.

6. The author uses his experience on the train as a basis for feeling optimistic about the United States. Write an essay explaining whether you agree or disagree with the author's conclusion based on your experiences.

# SELF-TEST SUMMARY

To test yourself, cover the Answer column with a sheet of paper and answer each question in the left column. Evaluate each of your answers as you work by sliding the paper down and comparing your answer with what is printed in the Answer column.

| QUESTION | ANSWER |
|---|---|
| ■ **GOAL 1** Identify subjects and predicates<br><br>What are subjects and predicates? | The **subject** of a sentence is whom or what the sentence is about. The subject is often a noun or a pronoun. The **predicate** indicates what the subject does, what happened to the subject, or what is being said about the subject. The predicate must include a **verb**, a word or group of words that expresses an action or a state of being. |
| ■ **GOAL 2** Identify sentence fragments<br><br>What is a fragment? | A fragment is an incomplete sentence that lacks a subject, a verb, or both, or does not express a complete thought. |
| ■ **GOAL 3** Recognize and correct fragments caused by missing subjects<br><br>What are two ways to revise a fragment that lacks a subject? | 1. Add a subject, often a pronoun referring to the subject of the preceding sentence.<br>2. Connect the fragment to the preceding sentence. |
| ■ **GOAL 4** Recognize and correct fragments caused by missing verbs<br><br>What are two common ways that fragments without complete verbs occur, and how can you correct them? | Fragments without complete verbs often occur when word groups begin with -*ing* words or with *to* phrases. Correct -*ing* fragments by (1) adding a subject and changing the -*ing* verb to one that will complete the sentence; (2) adding a subject and a form of *be* as a helping verb; (3) connecting the fragment to a sentence that comes before or after it; and (4) if the -*ing* word is being, changing it to another form of *be*. Correct fragments caused by to phrases by adding a subject and verb that complete the sentence or connecting the fragment to a nearby sentence. |
| ■ **GOAL 5** How can you recognize and correct fragments cause by dependent clauses<br><br>What are two ways to correct dependent clause fragments? | A dependent clause does not express a complete thought and often begins with a subordinating conjunction. It can be corrected in two ways:<br>1. Join the dependent clause to an independent clause.<br>2. Take away the subordinating conjunction. |
| ■ **GOAL 6** Understand sentences<br><br>What are four steps to reading sentences effectively? | 1. Locate the key ideas.<br>2. Study the modifiers.<br>3. Check unknown words.<br>4. Paraphrase, or use your own words to express ideas. |

# MySkillsLab

For more help with **Sentence Fragments**, go to your learning path in MySkillsLab at http://www.myskillslab.com.

# Run-on Sentences and Comma Splices

## LEARNING GOALS

Learn how to . . .

**GOAL 1**
Use punctuation correctly within and between sentences

**GOAL 2**
Recognize and correct run-on sentences

**GOAL 3**
Recognize and correct comma splices

**GOAL 4**
Use punctuation as a guide to reading

## THINK About It!

Read the passage below.

> Food trucks mobile kitchens that sell food are popular in many cities some trucks have fixed locations others move about daily customers can track a truck's location and menu changes on Facebook often operated by laid off chefs from expensive restaurants some trucks offer gourmet food choices long lines of hungry customers eager to buy tacos lobster rolls or specialty burgers for example can be seen at lunch and dinner hours food trucks are successful because they are convenient accessible and inexpensive some traditional restaurant owners feel they are losing business to food trucks and some cities have passed laws prohibiting food trucks from parking within a specified distance of restaurants

Did you have trouble reading this paragraph? Why? Write a sentence explaining your difficulty. Most likely you said that the paragraph lacked punctuation. You could not see where one idea ended and another began. It is important to pay attention to punctuation to avoid confusion when you are writing. If you run your sentences together, you run the risk of confusing your readers. When reading, it is important to pay attention to punctuation, since it provides helpful clues about the relationships among and relative importance of ideas.

# What Is Punctuation and Why Is It Important to Use It Correctly?

**■ GOAL 1**
Use punctuation correctly within and between sentences

Punctuation is a useful tool as it helps writers communicate their thoughts clearly and helps readers follow and understand those thoughts. **Punctuation** serves one primary purpose—to separate. Periods, question marks, and exclamation points separate complete sentences from one another. Think of these punctuation marks as *between*-sentence separators. All other punctuation marks—*commas, colons, semicolons, hyphens, dashes, quotation marks*, and *parentheses*—separate parts *within* a sentence. To avoid or correct run-on sentences and comma splices that can cause a reader confusion, the focus of this chapter, you need a good grasp of both between-sentence and within-sentence punctuation.

## Between-Sentence Punctuation

The period, question mark, and exclamation point all mark the end of a sentence. Each has a different function.

### ! NEED TO KNOW

**Between-Sentence Punctuation**

| PUNCTUATION | FUNCTION | EXAMPLE |
|---|---|---|
| Period (.) | Marks the end of a complete statement or command | *The lecture is about to begin. Please be seated.* |
| Question mark (?) | Marks the end of a direct question | *Are you ready?* |
| Exclamation point (!) | Marks the end of statements of excitement or strong emotion | *We are late! I won an award!* |

## Within-Sentence Punctuation

Commas, colons, semicolons, hyphens, dashes, quotation marks, and parentheses all separate parts of a sentence from one another. For a complete review of how and when to use each, refer to Part VI, pages 639–649.

The comma is the most commonly used within-sentence punctuation mark and is the most commonly misused. The **comma** separates parts of a sentence from one another. In this chapter, we will be concerned with just one type of separation: the separation of two complete thoughts, or independent clauses. An **independent clause** has a subject and a verb and can stand alone as a sentence.

The comma can be used to separate two complete thoughts within a sentence *if and only if* it is used along with one of the coordinating conjunctions (*for, and, nor, but, or, yet, so*). **Coordinating conjunctions** are words that link and relate equally important parts of a sentence. The comma is not a strong enough separator to be used between complete thoughts without one of the coordinating conjunctions.

Complete thought    Coordinating conjunction    Complete thought

I work now for a big company, <u>but</u> I am hoping someday to take over my father's business.

Complete though    Coordinating conjunction    Complete thought

I am undecided about a career, <u>so</u> I am majoring in liberal arts.

## WRITING

# Recognize and Correct Run-on Sentences

■ **GOAL 2**
Recognize and correct run-on sentences

When you do not separate two complete thoughts (two independent clauses) with the necessary punctuation, the two clauses run together and form a **run-on sentence**.

## How to Recognize Run-on Sentences

1. **Read each sentence aloud.** Listen for a break or change in your voice mid-way through the sentence. Your voice automatically pauses or slows down at the end of a complete thought. If you hear a break but have no punctuation at that break, you may have a run-on sentence. Try reading the following run-on sentences aloud. Place a slash mark (/) where you hear a pause.

> RUN-ON    The library has a copy machine it is very conveniently located.
>
> RUN-ON    The Career Planning Center on campus is helpful one of the counselors suggested I take a career-planning course.
>
> RUN-ON    My major is nursing I do enjoy working with people.

Did you mark the sentences as follows?

> The library has a copy machine / it is very conveniently located.
>
> The Career Planning Center on campus is helpful / one of the counselors suggested I take a career-planning course.
>
> My major is nursing / I do enjoy working with people.

The pause in each indicates the need for punctuation.

## Tip for Writers

*Then* cannot be used to connect two independent clauses even if it is preceded by a comma. When using *then* as a connector, write the sentence one of these ways:

- We adopted a dog, **and then** we adopted four cats.
- We adopted a dog: **then** we adopted four cats.
- We adopted a dog **and then** four cats.

2. **Look for sentences that contain two complete thoughts (independent clauses) without punctuation to separate them.**

Complete thought (independent clause)

RUN-ON  Houseplants are pleasant additions to a home or office

Complete thought (independent clause)

they add color and variety.

Complete thought (independent clause)  Complete thought (independent clause)

RUN-ON  My sister decided to wear black I chose red.

Complete thought (independent clause)  Complete thought (independent clause)

RUN-ON  Having a garage sale is a good way to make money it unclutters

the house, too.

Complete thought (independent clause)  Complete thought (independent clause)

RUN-ON  We bought a portable phone then we had to connect the

base unit into our phone line.

3. **Look for long sentences. Not every long sentence is a run-on, but run-ons do tend to occur more frequently in longer sentences than in shorter ones.**

RUN-ON  Choosing a mate is one of the most important decisions you will ever make unless you make the right choice, you may be unhappy.

RUN-ON  I plan to work in a day-care center some days taking care of my own kids is enough to make me question my career choice.

## EXERCISE 6-1 | Identifying Run-on Sentences

**Directions:** Read each sentence aloud. Place a check mark before each sentence that is a run-on. Use a slash mark to show where punctuation is needed. Not all of these sentences are run-ons.

  ✓   1. Parking spaces on campus are limited/often I must park far away and walk.

      2. Before exercising, you should always stretch and warm up to prevent injury.

  ✓   3. Theodore's car wouldn't start/fortunately Phil was able to use jumper cables to help him get it started.

  ✓   4. The skydiver jumped from the plane/when she had fallen far enough she released her parachute.

_____ **5.** Radio stations usually have a morning disc jockey whose job is to wake people and cheer them up on their way to work.

__✓__ **6.** It continued to rain until the river overflowed/many people had to be evacuated from their homes.

__✓__ **7.** Calla bought a bathrobe for her brother as a birthday gift/it was gray with burgundy stripes.

__✓__ **8.** The rooms in the maternity section of the hospital have colorful flowered wallpaper/they are cheerful and pleasant.

_____ **9.** Because my cousin went to nursing school and then to law school, she is going to practice medical malpractice law.

__✓__ **10.** We rented *The Fighter* to watch on the DVD player/later we practiced boxing moves.

## How to Correct Run-on Sentences

There are four possible ways to correct run-on sentences:

1. Create two separate sentences.
2. Use a semicolon.
3. Use a comma and a coordinating conjunction.
4. Make one thought dependent.

### Create Two Separate Sentences

Split the two complete thoughts into two separate sentences. End the first thought with a *period* (or a *question mark* or an *exclamation point* if one is needed). Begin the second thought with a capital letter.

|  | Complete thought.            Complete thought. |
|---|---|
| **RUN-ON** | Many students do not have a specific career goal they do have some general career directions in mind. |
| CORRECT | Many students do not have a specific career goal. They do have some general career directions in mind. |
| **RUN-ON** | Are there really students who choose courses without studying degree requirements these students may make unwise choices. |
| CORRECT | Are there really students who choose courses without studying degree requirements? These students may make unwise choices. |
| **RUN-ON** | Some people love their jobs they are delighted that someone is willing to pay them to do what they enjoy. |
| CORRECT | Some people love their jobs. They are delighted that someone is willing to pay them to do what they enjoy. |
| **RUN-ON** | Some people hate their jobs going back to school may be a good idea in these cases. |
| CORRECT | Some people hate their jobs! Going back to school may be a good idea in these cases. |

The separation method is a good choice if the two thoughts are not closely related or if joining the two thoughts correctly (by one of the methods described next) creates an extremely long sentence.

| | |
|---|---|
| **EXERCISE 6-2** | ## Correcting Run-on Sentences by Making Separate Sentences |
| **WRITING IN PROGRESS** | |

**Directions:** Revise the run-on sentences you identified in Exercise 6-1 by creating two separate sentences in each case.   Answers will appear in the Instructor's Manual.

### Use a Semicolon

Use a **semicolon** (;) to connect two complete thoughts that will remain parts of the same sentence.

<u>Complete thought</u>   ;   <u>complete thought.</u>

| RUN-ON | Our psychology instructor is demanding he expects the best from all his students. |
|---|---|
| CORRECT | Our psychology instructor is demanding; he expects the best from all his students. |
| RUN-ON | Sunshine is enjoyable it puts people in a good mood. |
| CORRECT | Sunshine is enjoyable; it puts people in a good mood. |
| RUN-ON | A course in nutrition may be useful it may help you make wise food choices. |
| CORRECT | A course in nutrition may be useful; it may help you make wise food choices. |

Use this method when your two complete thoughts are closely related and the relationship between them is clear and obvious.

| | |
|---|---|
| **EXERCISE 6-3** | ## Correcting Run-on Sentences Using Semicolons |

**Directions:** Place a check mark before each sentence that is a run-on. Correct each run-on by using a semicolon. Not all of these sentences are run-ons.

___✓___ 1. The economic summit meeting was held in Britain; many diplomats attended.

___✓___ 2. I especially enjoy poetry by Emily Dickinson; her poems are intense, concise, and revealing.

_____ 3. The Use and Abuse of Drugs is a popular course because the material is geared for non-science majors.

___✓___ 4. The food festival offered a wide selection of food; everything from hot dogs to elegant desserts was available.

_____ 5. Since the flight was turbulent, the flight attendant suggested that we remain in our seats.

____✓____ 6. The bowling alley was not crowded; most of the lanes were open.

____✓____ 7. Swimming is an excellent form of exercise; it gives you a good aerobic workout.

_____ 8. When the disabled aircraft landed safely, the onlookers cheered.

____✓____ 9. The two-lane highway is being expanded to four lanes; even that improvement is not expected to solve the traffic congestion problems.

____✓____ 10. Before visiting Israel, Carolyn read several guidebooks; they helped her plan her trip.

---

### Use a Comma and a Coordinating Conjunction

Use a **comma** *and* a **coordinating conjunction** to separate two complete thoughts placed within one sentence. The "Need to Know" below box lists the seven coordinating conjunctions along with a handy trick to help you remember them. *Note that* whenever you separate two complete thoughts by using a coordinating conjunction, you must also use a comma.

Complete thought, **Coordinating Conjunction** complete thought.

When you use a coordinating conjunction to separate two complete thoughts, be sure to use the right one. Since each coordinating conjunction has a particular meaning, you should choose the one that shows the right relationship between the two thoughts. For example, the conjunction *and* indicates that the ideas are equally important and similar. The words *but* and *yet* indicate that one idea is contrary to or in opposition to the other. *For* and *so* emphasize cause and effect connections. *Or* and *nor* indicate choice.

## ! NEED TO KNOW

### How to Use Coordinating Conjunctions

There are seven coordinating conjunctions. An easy way to remember them is the acronym FANBOYS (*for, and, nor, but, or, yet,* and *so*). Choose the one that shows the right relationship between the two complete thoughts in a sentence.

| COORDINATING CONJUNCTION | MEANING | EXAMPLE |
|---|---|---|
| **for** | since, because | Sarah is taking math, *for* she is a chemistry major. |
| **and** | added to, in addition, along with | Budgeting is important, *and* it is time well spent. |
| **nor** | and not, or not, not either | Sam cannot choose a career, *nor* can he decide on a major. |
| **but** | just the opposite, on the other hand, however | I had planned to visit Chicago, *but* I changed my mind. |
| **or** | either | I will major in liberal arts, *or* I will declare myself "undecided." |
| **yet** | but, despite, nevertheless | I plan to become a computer programmer, *yet* a change is still possible. |
| **so** | as a result, consequently | Yolanda enjoys mathematics, *so* she is considering it as a career. |

The following examples show how to use a comma and an appropriate coordinating conjunction to correct a run-on sentence:

RUN-ON  Interests change and develop throughout life_you may have a different set of interests 20 years from now.

*Comma and conjunction so used to show cause-and-effect relationship*

CORRECT  Interests change and develop throughout lif<u>e, so </u>you may have a different set of interests 20 years from now.

RUN-ON  Take courses in a variety of disciplines_you may discover new interests.

*Comma and conjunction for used to show cause and effect relationship*

CORRECT  Take courses in a variety of disciplines<u>, for </u>you may discover new interests.

RUN-ON  Alexis thought she was not interested in biology_by taking a biology course, she discovered it was her favorite subject.

*Comma and conjunction but used to show contrast*

CORRECT  Alexis thought she was not interested in biology<u>, but,</u> by taking a biology course, she discovered it was her favorite subject.

RUN-ON  The weather forecast threatened severe thunderstorms_just as the day ended, the sky began to cloud over.

*Comma and conjunction and used to show addition*

CORRECT  The weather forecast threatened severe thunderstorms<u>, and</u> just as the day ended, the sky began to cloud over.

This method of correcting run-ons allows you to indicate to your reader how your two ideas are connected. Use this method for correcting run-on sentences when you want to explain the relationship between the two thoughts.

## Correcting Run-on Sentences Using Commas and Conjunctions

**EXERCISE 6-4**

*WORKING TOGETHER*

**Directions:** Working with a classmate, correct each of the following run-on sentences by using a comma and a coordinating conjunction. Think about the relationship between the two thoughts, and then choose the best coordinating conjunction. (These are the coordinating conjunctions you should use: *for, and, nor, but, or, yet, so.*)

**EXAMPLE**  I thought I had left for class in plenty of time ^*, but* I was two minutes late.

1. Jameel got up half an hour late ^*, so* he missed the bus.

2. My creative-writing teacher wrote a book ^*, but* our library did not have a copy.

3. *Ford* is an interesting first name ^ , *but* we did not choose it for our son.

4. Smoking cigarettes is not healthy ^ , *for* it can cause lung cancer.

5. My paycheck was ready to be picked up ^ , *yet* I forgot to get it.

6. The window faces north ^ , *so* the room gets little sun.

7. I may order Chinese food for dinner ^ , *or* I may bake a chicken.

8. Miranda had planned to write her term paper about World War I ^ , *but* she switched her topic to the Roaring Twenties.

9. The journalist arrived at the fire ^ , *and* she began to take notes.

10. The table is wobbly ^ , *so* we keep a matchbook under one leg to stabilize it.

### *Make One Thought Dependent*

Make one thought dependent by making it a dependent clause. A **dependent clause** depends on an independent clause for its meaning. It cannot stand alone because it does not express a complete thought. In a sentence, a dependent clause must always be linked to an independent clause, which expresses a complete thought. By itself, a dependent clause always leaves a question in your mind; the question is answered by the independent clause to which it is joined.

Dependent clause raises a question

Because I missed the bus          [What happened?]

Independent clause answers the question

Because I missed the bus, I was late for class.

Dependent clause raises a question

When I got my exam back          [What did you do?]

Independent clause answers the question

When I got my exam back, I celebrated.

Did you notice that each dependent clause began with a word that made it dependent? In the above sentences, the words that make the clauses dependent are *because* and *when*. These words are called subordinating conjunctions. **Subordinating conjunctions** let you know that the sense of the clause that follows them depends on another idea, an idea you will find in the independent clause of the sentence. Some common subordinating conjunctions are *after, although, before, if, since,* and *unless*. (For a more complete list of subordinating conjunctions, see Chapter 5, p. 166.)

You can correct a run-on sentence by changing one of the complete thoughts into a dependent clause and joining the ideas in the two clauses with a subordinating conjunction. This method places more emphasis on the idea expressed in the complete thought (independent clause) and less emphasis on the idea in the dependent clause.

RUN-ON   Aptitudes are built-in strengths‿they are important in career planning.

|   | Dependent clause | | |
|---|---|---|---|
| | Subordinating conjunction | Comma | Complete thought (independent clause) |

CORRECT   <u>Because</u> aptitudes are built-in strengths, they are important in

career planning.

RUN-ON   Emotional involvement can interfere with job performance‿be sure to keep work and friends and family separate.

|   | Dependent clause | |
|---|---|---|
| | Subordinating conjunction | Comma |

CORRECT   <u>Since</u> emotional involvement can interfere with job performance,

Complete thought (independent clause)

be sure to keep work and family and friends separate.

*Note:* A dependent clause can appear before or after an independent clause. If the dependent clause appears first, it must be followed by a comma, as in the examples above. If the complete thought comes first, then no comma is needed.

**dependent clause** comma **complete thought**

**independent clause** no comma **dependent clause**

RUN-ON   Personal relationships are enjoyable‿they should be minimized in the workplace.

|   | Dependent clause | |
|---|---|---|
| | Subordinating conjunction | Comma |

CORRECT   <u>Even though</u> personal relationships are enjoyable,

Complete thought (independent clause)

they should be minimized in the workplace.

Complete thought (independent clause)

No comma

CORRECT   Personal relationships should be minimized in the workplace‿

Dependent clause

Subordinating conjunction

<u>even though</u> they are enjoyable.

<table>
<tr><td colspan="2">! **NEED TO KNOW**</td></tr>
</table>

### How to Correct Run-on Sentences

You can correct run-on sentences in four ways:

| Method 1 | Separate the two complete thoughts into two sentences. |
|----------|--------------------------------------------------------|
| Method 2 | Separate the two complete thoughts with a semicolon. |
| Method 3 | Join the two complete thoughts with a comma and a coordinating conjunction (*and, but, for, nor, or, so, yet*). |
| Method 4 | Make one thought dependent on the other by using a subordinating conjunction (see the list on p. 166). |

**EXERCISE 6-5**

## Revising Run-on Sentences Using Subordinating Conjunctions

**Directions:** In each of the following run-on sentences, make one thought dependent on the other by using the subordinating conjunction in boldface. Don't forget to use a comma if the dependent clause comes first.   Answers will vary.

**EXAMPLE**

**until**
            Until w
            ~~We~~ called the plumber¸ we were without water.

**even though**
                                        even though
    1. David wants a leather jacket¸ it is very expensive.

**so that**
                                        so that
    2. Margery runs ten miles every day¸ she can try out for the cross-country squad in the spring.

**when**
            When t
    3. ~~The~~ television program ended¸ Gail read a book to her son.

**because**
                                        because
    4. The pool was crowded¸ it was 95 degrees that day.

**although**
            Although i
    5. ~~Industry~~ is curbing pollution¸ our water supply still is not safe.

**because**
                                        because
    6. I always obey the speed limit¸ speeding carries a severe penalty in my state.

**while**
                                        while
    7. The crowd fell silent¸ the trapeze artist attempted a quadruple flip.

**since**
            Since t
    8. ~~The~~ school year ended¸ I have had more time for my hobbies.

**as**
            As t
    9. ~~The~~ storm approached¸ I stocked up on batteries.

**whenever**
            Whenever t
    10. ~~The~~ moon is full¸ our dog is restless.

**EXERCISE 6-6**    # Revising Sentences

**Directions:** Write five sentences, each of which has two complete thoughts. Then revise each sentence so that it has one dependent clause and one complete thought (independent clause). Use a comma, if needed, to separate the two clauses. You may want to refer to the list of subordinating conjunctions on page 166.

# Recognize and Correct Comma Splices

■ **GOAL 3**
Recognize and correct comma splices

Like run-ons, comma splices are serious sentence errors that can confuse and annoy your readers. Also, like run-ons, they are easy to correct once you know what to look for. In fact, they are corrected in the same way that run-ons are. A **comma splice** occurs when you use *only* a comma to separate two complete thoughts. A comma alone is not sufficient to divide the two thoughts. A stronger, clearer separation is necessary. You can visualize a comma splice this way:

Complete thought    ,    complete thought.

| COMMA SPLICE | Spatial aptitude is the ability to understand and visualize objects in physical space, it is an important skill for engineers and designers. |
| COMMA SPLICE | Some people have strong mechanical ability, they often prefer hands-on tasks. |
| COMMA SPLICE | Verbal reasoning is important to many careers, it is the ability to think through problems. |

## How to Recognize Comma Splices

To avoid comma splices, you have to make sure that you do not place *only a comma* between two complete thoughts. To test a sentence to see if you have written a comma splice, take the sentence apart at the comma. If the part before the comma is a complete thought and the part after the comma is a complete thought, then you need to check whether the second clause starts with a coordinating conjunction (*for, and, nor, but, or, yet, so*). If you do not have a coordinating conjunction to separate the two complete thoughts, then you have a comma splice.

## How to Correct Comma Splices

To correct comma splices, use any one of the four methods you used to correct run-ons:

1. **Separate the thoughts into two complete sentences, deleting the comma.**

Complete thought. Complete thought.

2. **Separate the two thoughts with a semicolon, deleting the comma.**

> Complete thought; complete thought.

3. **Separate the two thoughts by adding a coordinating conjunction after the comma.**

> Complete thought, **coordinating conjunction** complete thought.

4. **Make one thought dependent on the other by using a subordinating conjunction to separate the two thoughts.** (For a complete list of subordinating conjunctions, see Chapter 5, p. 166.)

> **Subordinating conjunction** dependent clause, independent clause.
>
> Independent clause **subordinating conjunction** dependent clause.

## ! NEED TO KNOW

### How to Correct Comma Splices

Correct comma splices the same way you correct run-on sentences:

| | |
|---|---|
| **Method 1** | Separate the two complete thoughts into two sentences. |
| **Method 2** | Separate the two complete thoughts with a semicolon. |
| **Method 3** | Join the two complete thoughts with a comma and a coordinating conjunction (*for, and, nor, but, or, yet, so*). |
| **Method 4** | Make one thought dependent upon the other by using a subordinating conjunction. (See the list on p. 166.) |

## EXERCISE 6-7    Correcting Comma Splices

**Directions:** Some of the following sentences have comma splices. Correct each comma splice by using one of the four methods described in this chapter. Write "OK" before each sentence that is correct.    Answers will vary.

_____ 1. The stained glass window is beautiful; it has been in the church since 1880.

_____ 2. Replacing the spark plugs was simple, but replacing the radiator was not.

_____ 3. School buses lined up in front of the school because three o'clock was dismissal time.

_____ **4.** The gymnast practiced her balance-beam routine; she did not make a single mistake.

_____ **5.** A huge branch fell on the driveway, it just missed my car.

_____ **6.** The receptionist answered the phone, and she put the caller on hold.

__OK__ **7.** The couple dressed up as zombies for Halloween, but their bandages kept falling off.

_____ **8.** Bill left his notebook in the cafeteria, he was confused later when he was unable to find it.

_____ **9.** The strawberries are red and sweet, but the blueberries are not ripe yet.

__OK__ **10.** There had been a severe drought, so the waterfall dried up.

---

**EXERCISE 6-8**

# Identifying and Correcting Run-on Sentences and Comma Splices

**Directions:** Identify each sentence as a run-on sentence (RO), a comma splice (CS), or a correct sentence (C). Then correct the faulty sentences using one of the four methods discussed.   Answers will vary.

|  | EXAMPLE | __CS__ | When the children chased the ball into the street, cars screeched to a halt. |

__RO__ **1.** When Inez packed for the camping trip, she remembered everything except insect repellant.

__CS__ **2.** A limousine drove through our neighborhood, and everybody wondered who was in it.

__RO__ **3.** The defendant pleaded not guilty, but the judge ordered him to pay the parking fine.

__RO__ **4.** Before a big game, Louis, who is a quarterback, eats a lot of pasta and bread. he says it gives him energy.

__CS__ **5.** Four of my best friends from high school have decided to go to law school, but I have decided to become a legal secretary.

__RO__ **6.** Felicia did not know what to buy her parents for their anniversary, so she went to a lot of stores, and she finally decided to buy them a camera.

__RO__ **7.** After living in a dorm room for three years, Jason found an apartment. The rent was very high, so he had to get a job to pay for it.

__CS__ **8.** The cherry tree had to be cut down, because it stood right where the new addition was going to be built.

__C__ **9.** Amanda worked every night for a month on the needlepoint pillow that she was making for her grandmother.

__CS__ **10.** Driving around in the dark, we finally realized we were lost; Dwight went into a convenience store to ask for directions.

| EXERCISE 6-9 | # Identifying and Correcting Run-on Sentences and Comma Splices |

**Directions:** Find and correct the run-on sentence and comma splices in the following paragraph. You should find one run-on sentence and three comma splices.

*comma splice*
*run-on*

*comma splice*

*comma splice*

If you work in an office with cubicles—small partitioned workspaces—make sure to observe cubicle etiquette. Most cubicles are composed of three chest-high partitions; the fourth side is an open entryway. Cubicle etiquette is designed to minimize invasions of personal space for example as you walk past a cubicle, resist the temptation to peer down at the person. If you need to talk to a cubicle occupant, do not startle the person by entering abruptly or speaking loudly. Similarly, do not silently lurk in the entryway if the person's back is turned, speak quietly to announce your presence. Try to keep cubicle conversations or phone calls brief, in deference to your co-workers in adjacent cubicles. Finally, remember that odors as well as noise can "pollute" the cubicle environment, don't even think about eating leftover garlic pasta at your desk!

| EXERCISE 6-10 | # Revising a Paragraph |

**Directions:** Revise the following paragraphs, correcting the run-on sentences and comma splices. *Answers will vary. Possible answers provided.*

1. The oldest map we have dates back to ancient Babylonia, it shows an estate surrounded by mountains. As in so many other undertakings, the Greeks were ahead of their time in mapmaking their maps showed the world as round rather than flat, the Greeks also developed a system of longitude and latitude for identifying locations. The Romans were excellent administrators and military strategists therefore, it was no surprise that they made reliable road maps and military maps. The most famous mapmaker of ancient times was Claudius Ptolemy of Alexandria, Egypt, he created a comprehensive map of the world.

   *The oldest map we have dates back to ancient Babylonia. It shows an estate surrounded by mountains. As in so many other undertakings, the Greeks were ahead of their time in mapmaking. Their maps showed the world as round rather than flat. The Greeks also developed a system of longitude and latitude for identifying locations. The Romans were excellent administrators and military strategists; therefore, it was no surprise that they made reliable road maps and military maps. The most famous mapmaker of ancient times was Claudius Ptolemy of Alexandria, Egypt; he created a comprehensive map of the world.*

2. It seems there is a problem on the Internet with certain types of messages that people post. There are people who argue that anyone has the right to say anything on the Internet people do have the right of free speech, but the line should be drawn when it comes to hate messages. It is immoral—and should be illegal—to make remarks that are racist, sexist, and anti-Semitic. After all, these verbal attacks are no longer tolerated in the classroom or in the workplace, why should the Internet be different? The problem with the Internet is that there seem to be no established rules of etiquette among users, maybe there should be some guidelines about what people should and should not say on the Internet. Why should people be subjected to hate-filled speech in order to preserve the right of free speech?

*It seems there is a problem on the Internet with certain types of messages that people post. There are people who argue that anyone has the right to say anything on the Internet because people do have the right to freedom of speech. However, the line should be drawn when it comes to hate messages. It is immoral—and should be illegal—to make remarks that are racist, sexist, and anti-Semitic. After all, these verbal actions are no longer tolerated in the classroom or in the workplace. Why should the Internet be different? The problem with the Internet is that there seem to be no established rules of etiquette among users. Maybe there should be some guidelines about what people should and should not say on the Internet. Why should people be subjected to hate-filled speech in order to preserve the right of free speech?*

## READING

# Punctuation as a Guide to Reading

■ **GOAL 4**
Use punctuation as a guide to reading

Paying attention to punctuation can make reading easier. It helps comprehension in several ways:

- It separates different pieces of a sentence from one another.
- It suggests thought or idea groupings.
- It provides clues to the relative importance of ideas within a sentence.

Each type of punctuation mark has specific functions. Those punctuation marks most useful to sentence comprehension are described below.

## The Comma

The comma has a number of different uses, but in each case it separates some type of information from other parts of the sentence. Several uses of the comma are explained below; others are discussed in Chapter 8.

### The Introductory Use

The comma can be used to separate introductory, beginning, or opening parts of a sentence from the main part of the sentence. These parts may connect what will be said in one sentence with what has already been said in a previous sentence, provide some background information, set the scene or time frame, or offer some qualifying information or considerations. These introductory comments are less important, and tend to explain or modify the sentence's main thought.

<u>Not surprisingly</u>, it is not only the size of America's corporations that is at issue.

### The Parenthetical Use

The comma can be used to separate additional information from the main part of the sentence. Writers occasionally interrupt the core sentence to add some extra (parenthetical) information that is important but not crucial to the sentence meaning. They use a comma before and after this parenthetical information. This use of a comma helps you tell important from less important information.

Dolphins, as a matter of fact, are very friendly creatures that frequently come to the rescue of people.

Drugs and alcohol, experts warn, are an unsafe and dangerous combination.

The Coal Mine Safety Act, one of the first federal efforts to enforce safety standards, reduced worker productivity.

### The Serial Use

Whenever several items are presented in a list, or series, in a sentence, they are separated by commas. In all cases, the items in a series are consistent and equally important.

Each state maintained its sovereignty, freedom, and independence.

Social adjustment requires that an individual maintain himself independently, be gainfully employed, and conform to the social standards set by the community.

## Using Commas to Identify Less Important Information

**EXERCISE 6-11**

**Directions:** In each sentence that follows, underline the parts that you identify as less important based on the use and placement of commas.

1. Undeniably, industrialization made a strong impact on society.

2. That is, no member of the Congress should serve more than three years in any six.

3. How is it, then, that we perceive depth as a third dimension?

4. Perhaps even more important, when humans think, they know they are thinking.

5. Graphite, on the other hand, is made of carbon layers stacked one on top of the other, like sheets of paper.

## The Semicolon

The primary use of the semicolon is to separate two very closely related ideas that have been combined into one sentence.

When you are reading a sentence that contains a semicolon, be alert for two separate ideas. When a semicolon is used, you know that the two ideas have equal weight or importance. Each of the following sentences contains two ideas separated by a semicolon. The key ideas of each sentence are underlined.

The fishermen caught fifteen trout; they cooked them over an open fire.

All objects radiate some form of electromagnetic radiation; the amount depends on their temperature and physical state.

Occasionally, a semicolon is used to separate sentence parts that, if divided by commas, would be confusing or difficult to read. To illustrate this use of the semicolon, the following example has been written in two versions.

Speakers at the conference included Dr. Frank, a biologist, Dr. Flock, a philosopher, and Professor Smich, a geneticist.

Speakers at the conference included Dr. Frank, a biologist; Dr. Flock, a philosopher; and Professor Smich, a geneticist.

As you read the first version of the sentence, you are not sure whether the speakers include Dr. Frank and a biologist or whether it was Dr. Frank who was being described as a biologist. The use of the semicolon in the second version makes it clear that Dr. Frank is the biologist.

## The Colon

The **colon** is most often used to introduce a list, statement, or quotation. The colon tells you, the reader, that some type of additional information, which further explains the main idea of a sentence, is to follow. The colon also tells you that the sentence's key idea comes before the colon.

The causes of the war can be divided into three categories: social, economic, and political. (Here the colon indicates that a list of categories will follow.)

Chomsky described two levels of language: One underlying or deep structure involved with meaning, and a surface level used in ordinary conversation. (The colon in this example signals that an explanation of the two levels of language is to follow.)

## The Dash

The **dash** is most commonly used in a sentence to separate unessential or parenthetical elements from the core sentence, when using a comma would be confusing.

At least three sports—basketball, football, and tennis—are continually gaining television fans.

## Using Punctuation to Identify Less Important Information

**EXERCISE 6-12**

**Directions:** In each sentence that follows, underline the parts that you identify as less important based on the use and placement of colons, semicolons, or dashes.

1. Local restaurateurs have begun to use social media—<u>Facebook, Twitter, LinkedIn, and Yelp</u>—to garner publicity and gain new customers.

2. While Gabe is in town, we plan to explore a mix of old and new attractions: <u>the Liberty Memorial, the Sea Life Aquarium, Legoland Discovery Center, and the Kansas City Zoo.</u>

3. The poodle has been a popular choice for cross-breeding with other dogs, resulting in new mixed-breeds such as the Labradoodle, a <u>Labrador/poodle combination</u>; the Schnoodle, a <u>Schnauzer/poodle combination</u>; and the Whoodle, a <u>Wheaten terrier/poodle combination</u>.

4. Many types of plants will grow well in dry shade: <u>hosta, Lenten rose, wild ginger, epimedium, lily of the valley, and Japanese painted fern</u>.

5. The variety of foreign languages spoken by students—<u>Spanish, Vietnamese, Swahili, Mai-Mai, Kurdish, and Arabic</u>—is proof of the school's growing diversity.

# INTEGRATING READING AND WRITING

## READ AND REVISE

The following excerpt is from a student essay called "Little Miracles." Read the excerpt, and underline the run-on sentences and comma splices. Then write out a revised version of the paragraph, correcting the errors using the techniques discussed in this chapter.   *Answers will vary.*

**Run-on**

Everyone in their lives faces a life changing experience. February 9, 2008 was the day I became a mother ~~on~~ *. On* this very day my daughter Kamber was born, and my life from that point on has been different in every aspect. The responsibilities and obstacles I face, who I am, and the joy that comes along with being a mother are just the few things that have changed. There are no words that sum up the feeling I had when she was placed in my arms on that

**Comma splice**

day, ~~all~~ *. All* that mattered was that she was the greatest gift I have ever been blessed with. The impact that a child has on a parent is tremendous*;* it molds you into a

**Comma splice**

whole new human being.

**Run-on**

Life is a revolving cycle. We grow into adults, have children, and raise them *,and* then they follow our steps and have a family of their own, and it just repeats itself. Maybe I wasn't ready financially for having a child, but I believe things

**Comma splice**

happen for a reason. I use a lot of the same techniques my mother did with me*;* I also develop my own. There are sad times as a mother such as when your child is sick or gets hurt. The feeling of your child only wanting her mommy at those

**Run-on**

times is overwhelming. We all fall in love in our lives *, but* the love of a child is such a different but amazing emotion.

## READ AND RESPOND: A Professional Essay

### Thinking Before Reading

The following selection is taken from an introductory sociology textbook by John J. Macionis. Much of college reading examines different perspectives on a topic. This reading provides an example of multiple viewpoints on the topic of sports.

1. Preview the reading, using the steps discussed in Chapter 1 on page 25.
2. Connect the reading to your own experience by answering the following questions:
   a. Which sport(s) do you play or follow? Do you have a favorite team?
   b. What are the pros and cons of professional sports?
3. Highlight and annotate as you read.

1290**L**/820 words

# The Role of Sports in Our Lives

1    Who doesn't enjoy sports? Children as young as six or seven take part in organized sports, and many teens become skilled at three or more. Weekend television is filled with sporting events for viewers of all ages, and whole sections of our newspapers are devoted to teams, players, and scores. In the United States, top players such as Alex Rodriguez (baseball), Tiger Woods (golf), and Serena Williams (tennis) are among our most famous celebrities. Sports in the United States are also a multibillion-dollar industry.

### The Functions of Sports

2    The functions of sports include providing recreation as well as offering a means of getting in physical shape and, a relatively harmless way to let off steam. Sports have important latent functions as well, which include building social relationships and also creating tens of thousands of jobs across the country. Participating in sports encourages competition and the pursuit of success, both of which are values that are central to our society's way of life.

3    Sports also have dysfunctional consequences. For example, colleges and universities try to field winning teams to build a school's reputation and also to raise money from alumni and corporate sponsors. In the process, however, these schools sometimes recruit students for their athletic skill rather than their academic ability. This practice not only lowers the academic standards of the college or university but also shortchanges athletes, who spend little time doing the academic work that will prepare them for later careers.

### Sports and Conflict

4    The games people play reflect their social standing. Some sports—including tennis, swimming, golf, sailing, and skiing—are expensive, so taking part is largely limited to the well-to-do. Football, baseball, and basketball, however, are accessible to people at almost all income levels. Thus the games people play are not simply a matter of individual choice but also a reflection of their social standing.

*Serena Williams*

5    Throughout history, men have dominated the world of sports. For example, the first modern Olympic Games, held in 1896, barred women from competition. Throughout most of the twentieth century, Little League teams barred girls based on the traditional ideas that girls and women lack the strength to play sports and risk losing their femininity if they do. Both the Olympics and the Little League are now open to females as well as males, but even today, our society still encourages men to become athletes while expecting women to be attentive observers and cheerleaders. At the college level, men's athletics attracts a greater amount of attention and resources compared to women's athletics, and men greatly outnumber women as coaches, even in women's sports. At the professional level, women also take a back seat to men, particularly in the sports with the most earning power and social prestige.

6    For decades, big league sports excluded people of color, who were forced to form leagues of their own. Only in 1947 did Major League Baseball admit the first African American player when Jackie Robinson joined the Brooklyn Dodgers. More than fifty years later, professional baseball honored Robinson's amazing career by retiring his number 42 on *all* of the teams in the league. In 2009, African Americans (13 percent of the U.S. population) accounted for 9 percent of Major League Baseball players, 67 percent of National Football League (NFL) players, and 77 percent of National Basketball Association (NBA) players.

7    One reason for the high number of African Americans in many professional sports is that athletic performance—in terms of batting average or number of points scored per game—can be precisely measured and is not influenced by racial prejudice. It is also true that some people of color make a particular effort to excel in athletics, where they see greater opportunity than in other careers. In recent years, in fact, African American athletes have earned higher salaries, on average, than white players.

8    But racial discrimination still exists in professional sports. For one thing, race is linked to the *positions* athletes play on the field, in a pattern called "stacking." Figure A (p. 204) shows the results of a study of race in professional baseball. Notice that white athletes are more concentrated in the central "thinking" positions of pitcher (68 percent) and catcher (64 percent). By contrast, African Americans represent only 4 percent of pitchers and 1 percent of catchers. At the same time, 9 percent of infielders are African Americans, as are 28 percent of outfielders, positions characterized as requiring "speed and reactive ability."

9    More broadly, African Americans have a large share of players in only five sports: baseball, basketball, football, boxing, and track. And across all professional sports, the vast majority of managers, head coaches, and team owners are white.

10    Who benefits most from professional sports? Although many individual players get sky-high salaries and millions of fans enjoy following their teams, the vast profits sports generate are controlled by small number of people—predominantly white men. In sum, sports in the United States are bound up with inequalities based on gender, race, and wealth.

### FIGURE A "STACKING" IN PROFESSIONAL BASEBALL

*Does race play a part in professional sports? Looking at rhe various positions in professional baseball, we see that white players are more likely to play the central positions in the infield, while people of color are more likely to play in the outfield. What do you make of this pattern?*

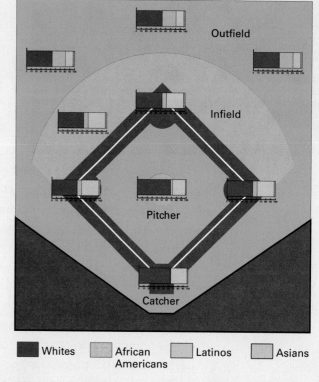

Outfield

Infield

Pitcher

Catcher

| Whites | African Americans | Latinos | Asians |

*Source:* Lapchick (2010).

## Getting Ready to Write

### Checking Your Comprehension

Answer each of the following questions using complete sentences.

1. Describe five functions of sports and two consequences of schools recruiting students based on athletic skill rather than academic ability.

2. Which sports are limited to wealthy participants, and which are accessible to people at almost all income levels?

3. Why were girls barred from participating in Little League throughout most of the twentieth century?

4. What does "stacking" mean?

5. According to the author, who benefits most from professional sports?

### Strengthening Your Vocabulary

Using the word's context, word parts, or a dictionary, write a brief definition of each of the following words as it is used in the reading.

1. latent (paragraph 2) _____ *underlying*

2. dysfunctional (paragraph 3) _____ *not functioning normally*

3. accessible (paragraph 4) _____ *available* _____

4. attentive (paragraph 5) _____ *paying special attention* _____

5. excel (paragraph 7) _____ *be the best at* _____

6. predominantly (paragraph 10) _____ *mainly* _____

## Examining the Reading: Using Idea Maps

Review the reading by completing the missing parts of the following idea map.

**VISUALIZE IT!**

Title — **The Role of Sports in Our Lives**

Thesis — Sports are an important element of our society.

The Functions of Sports

- *Provide recreation*
- Offer a way to get in shape
- *Build social relationships*
- Create jobs
- *Encourage competition and the pursuit of success*

Dysfunctional Consequences of Sports

- Recruiting based on athletic ability rather than academics
- *Lowers academic standards*
- Shortchanges athletes

Sports and Conflict

- Sports reflect *social standing*
- *Men* dominate sports
- *Racial* discrimination exists

Conclusion — Sports in the United States include inequalities based on *gender*, *race*, and *wealth*.

### Thinking Critically: Discussion and Journal Writing

Analyze and evaluate by discussing the following:

**THINKING VISUALLY**

1. What do you think is the most important or valuable function of sports? What aspects of sports should change?

2. In what ways does society encourage men to become athletes and women to be observers? Do you think college and/or professional sports are improving in this regard? Discuss why or why not.

3. Write a journal entry describing the purpose of Figure A ("'Stacking' in Professional Baseball"), summarizing the information presented in the figure, and evaluating its effectiveness.

---

**MySkillsLab®**

**Complete** this Exercise

## Writing About the Reading

### Paragraph Options

1. What are other functions and consequences of sports in addition to the ones described in paragraphs 2 and 3? Write a paragraph explaining your answer.

2. Have you ever been prevented or discouraged from participating in a sport (or other activity) because of your gender, race, or social standing, or do you know someone who has? Write a paragraph describing the experience.

3. Write a paragraph making predictions about the future of college or professional sports. For example, what sport will be the most popular in 30 years? Or will student-athletes be paid for competing in college sports?

### Essay Options

4. Do you think the benefits outweigh any of the negative aspects of sports? Why or why not? Write an essay explaining your answer.

5. Write an essay answering the questions posed in the caption of Figure A. In your opinion, does race play a part in professional sports? Can you apply the concept of stacking to other sports?

6. Consider the phenomenon of celebrity-athletes. Why do so many athletes become celebrities? What qualities make a professional athlete most (and least) appealing? Should professional athletes be viewed as role models? Why or why not? Write an essay exploring these questions.

# SELF-TEST SUMMARY

To test yourself, cover the Answer column with a sheet of paper and answer each question in the left column. Evaluate each of your answers as you work by sliding the paper down and comparing your answer with what is printed in the Answer column.

| QUESTION | ANSWER |
|---|---|
| **GOAL 1** Use punctuation correctly within and between sentences<br><br>Can a comma be used to separate two complete thoughts? | A comma can be used to separate two complete thoughts within a sentence only if it is accompanied by a coordinating conjunction. |
| **GOAL 2** Recognize and correct run-on sentences<br><br>What is a run-on sentence?<br>What are four ways to correct run-on sentences? | A run-on sentence occurs when two complete thoughts are joined without punctuation or a connecting word.<br>1. Create two separate sentences.<br>2. Use a semicolon.<br>3. Use a comma and a coordinating conjunction.<br>4. Make one thought dependent on the other by using a subordinating conjunction. |
| **GOAL 3** Recognize and correct comma splices<br><br>What is a comma splice?<br>How can a comma splice be corrected? | A comma splice is a sentence error that occurs when only a comma separates two complete thoughts.<br>It can be corrected using one of the four techniques listed above for correcting run-on sentences. |
| **GOAL 4** Use punctuation as a guide to reading<br><br>How does paying attention to punctuation help your comprehension? What four punctuation marks are most useful to sentence comprehension? | Punctuation separates different pieces of a sentence from one another, suggests thought or idea groupings, and provides clues to the relative importance of ideas within a sentence. Useful punctuation marks for sentence comprehension are the *comma*, the *semicolon*, the *colon*, and the *dash*. |

# MySkillsLab

For more help with **Run-on Sentences and Comma Splices,** go to your learning path in MySkillsLab at http://www.myskillslab.com.

# 7

# Using Verbs Correctly

*"Then she goes, 'I gotta go," and I go, 'Okay," and she goes, 'Later," and I go, 'Go already!"*

## THINK About It!

Have you ever stopped to listen to the way people misuse verbs? Write a sentence evaluating this teenager's use of language.

Did you notice that in this teenager's sentence, she used *go* instead of more interesting and descriptive verbs like *yelled*, *retorted*, *said*, *replied*, *snorted*, or *exclaimed*? Verbs are words that express action. Using them correctly is essential to good writing and can make the difference between something that is dull or difficult to read and something that is interesting or fun to read. In this chapter you will focus on using verb tenses correctly as you write and will learn how to avoid some common verb errors. You will also learn to pay attention to the information verbs give to readers and examine how they affect meaning.

# FOCUSING ON READING AND WRITING

# What Is a Verb?

A **verb** is a part of speech that expresses action or state of being. Verbs are important to writers because they allow them to explain what action occurred or is occurring or in what state of being something is.

| ACTION | The dog leaped over the fence. |
|---|---|
| STATE OF BEING | Facebook is popular among college students. |

Verbs are important to readers because they carry a great deal of information. They give a sense of time, telling when something *is* happening, *has* happened, or *will* happen. They also can be very descriptive, allowing you to create a mental picture of an action. A grammatically correct sentence has at least one verb in it.

# WRITING

# Recognize Forms of the Verb

**■ GOAL 1**
Identify verb forms

The primary function of verbs is to express action or a condition. However, verbs also indicate time. **Verb tenses** tell us whether an action takes place in the present, past, or future. The three basic verb tenses are the *simple present, simple past,* and *simple future.* There are also nine other verb tenses in English.

There are two types of verbs: *regular* and *irregular.* The forms of **regular verbs** follow a standard pattern of endings; the forms of **irregular verbs** do not. The English language contains many more regular verbs than irregular verbs.

All verbs except *be* have five forms: the **base form** (or dictionary form), the *past tense,* the *past participle,* the *present participle,* and the *-s form* (see Table 7-1). The first three forms are called the verb's **principal parts.** For regular verbs, the past tense and past participle are formed by adding *-d* or *-ed* to the base form. Irregular verbs follow no set pattern to form their past tense and past participle.

Verbs change form to agree with their subjects in person and number (see p. 220); to express the time of their action (**tense**); to express whether the action is a fact, command, or wish (**mood**); and to indicate whether the subject is the doer or the receiver of the action (**voice**).

| TABLE 7-1 | THE FIVE VERB FORMS | |
|---|---|---|
| **Tense** | **Regular** | **Irregular** |
| Base form | work | eat |
| Past tense | worked | ate |
| Past participle | worked | eaten |
| Present participle | working | eating |
| *-s* form | works | eats |

# Understand Verb Tense: An Overview

■ GOAL 2
Identify verb tenses

The tenses of a verb express time. They convey whether an action, process, or event takes place in the present, past, or future.

The three simple tenses are *present*, *past*, and *future*. The **simple present tense** is the base form of the verb (and the *-s* form of third-person singular subjects); the **simple past tense** is the past-tense form; and the **simple future tense** consists of the helping verb *will* plus the base form.

The **perfect tenses**, which indicate completed action, are *present perfect*, *past perfect*, and *future perfect*. They are formed by adding the helping verbs *have* (or *has*), *had*, or *will have* to the past participle. These are discussed in the Handbook: Reviewing the Basics, p. 621.

# Use the Simple Tenses

■ GOAL 3
Use simple verb tenses correctly

The simple present, simple past, and simple future are the most basic of the verb tenses. You will need to make frequent use of them in your writing, so it is important to become adept in these tenses.

## The Simple Present Tense

The **present tense** indicates action that is occurring at the time of speaking or describes regular, habitual action.

| | |
|---|---|
| HABITUAL ACTION | Maria works hard. |
| ACTION AT TIME OF SPEAKING | I see a rabbit on the lawn. |

In the simple present tense, the verb for first person (*I* or *we*), second person (*you*), or third-person plural (*they*) is the same as the base form; no ending is added. The verb for third-person singular subjects (noun or pronoun) must end in *-s*. (See Table 7-2.)

| TABLE 7-2 SIMPLE PRESENT TENSE FORMS OF *LIKE* | | | |
|---|---|---|---|
| **Singular** | | **Plural** | |
| *Subject* | *Verb* | *Subject* | *Verb* |
| I | like | we | like |
| you | like | you | like |
| he, she, it | likes | they | like |
| Sam | likes | Sara and Marisa | like |

To most third-person singular base verbs, just add *-s* (*I run, she runs*). If the verb ends in *s, sh, ch, x,* or *z,* add *-es* to make the third-person singular form (*I crunch, she crunches*). If the verb ends in a consonant plus *y,* change the *y* to *i,* and then add *-es* (*I hurry, he hurries*). If the verb ends in a vowel plus *y,* just add *-s.* (*I stay, he stays*).

Third-person singular subjects include the pronouns *he, she,* and *it* and all singular nouns (*a desk, the tall man*). In addition, uncountable nouns (*money, music, homework,* abstractions such as *beauty* and *happiness,* liquids, and so on) are followed by third-person singular verbs. (*Water is essential for life.*) Singular collective nouns, such as *family, orchestra, team,* and *class,* also usually take a third-person singular verb since they refer to one group.

In speech we often use nonstandard verb forms, and these forms are perfectly acceptable in informal conversation. However, these nonstandard forms are *not* used in college writing or in career writing. In the examples in Table 7-3, note the nonstandard forms of the verb *lift* and the way these forms differ from the correct, standard forms that you should use in your writing.

**TABLE 7-3   NONSTANDARD AND STANDARD FORMS OF *LIFT***

| Nonstandard Present | Standard Present | Nonstandard Present | Standard Present |
|---|---|---|---|
| *Singular* | *Singular* | *Plural* | *Plural* |
| I lifts | I lift | we lifts | we lift |
| you lifts | you lift | you lifts | you lift |
| she (he) lift | she (he) lifts | they lifts | they lift |

**EXERCISE 7-1**

## Identifying Verb Forms

**Directions:** The sentences below are in the simple present tense. First, underline the subject or subjects in each sentence. Then circle the correct verb form.

    **EXAMPLE**   <u>Sal</u> (pick, (picks)) apples.

1. <u>Planes</u> ((take,) takes) off from the runway every five minutes.
2. <u>I</u> ((enjoy,) enjoys) sailing.
3. <u>She</u> (own, (owns)) a pet bird.
4. <u>We</u> ((climb,) climbs) the ladder to paint the house.
5. <u>Engines</u> ((roar,) roars) as the race begins.
6. <u>They</u> always ((answer,) answers) the phone on the first ring.
7. That <u>elephant</u> (walk, (walks)) very slowly.
8. <u>You</u> ((speak,) speaks) Spanish fluently.
9. <u>He</u> (say, (says)) his name is Luis.
10. Dinosaur <u>movies</u> ((scare,) scares) me.

**EXERCISE 7-2**

## Using the Present Tense

**Directions:** For each of the following verbs, write a sentence using the simple present tense. Use a noun or *he, she, it,* or *they* as the subject of the sentence.   Answers will vary. Possible answers are shown.

    **EXAMPLE**  prefer   *Priya prefers to sit in the front of the bus.*

1. call    *Mark calls his grandmother weekly.*

2. request    *Sam requests an answer by tomorrow.*

3. laugh   They laugh together, and they cry together.

4. grow   Yolanda grows a vegetable garden each summer.

5. hide   My son hides under the table.

---

### Tip for Writers

**Subject Pronouns**

Remember, in English you must include the subject pronoun with the verb. In some languages you do not need to do this because the verb ending indicates the person (first, second, or third) and number (singular or plural) of the sentence's subject.

**EXAMPLE**

He goes to the store.

### Tip for Writers

Occasionally, *shall* (rather than *will*) is used as the first-person helping verb in the *simple future* and *future continuous* tenses. It may be used in these situations:

**TALKING ABOUT A SERIOUS MATTER**

Our country shall win this war no matter how long it takes!

**MAKING A SUGGESTION OR AN OFFER**

Shall we go now? Shall I get you some tea?

## The Simple Past Tense

The **past tense** refers to action that was completed in the past. To form the simple past tense of regular verbs, add -*d* or -*ed* to the verb (see Table 7-4). Note that with the simple past tense, the verb form does not change with person or number.

In nonstandard English, the -*d* or -*ed* is often dropped. You may hear "Last night I work all night" instead of "Last night I work*ed* all night." In written English, be sure to include the -*d* or -*ed* ending.

| TABLE 7-4 | SIMPLE PAST TENSE FORMS OF *WORK* | | |
|-----------|------|------|------|
| **Singular** | | **Plural** | |
| *Subject* | *Verb* | *Subject* | *Verb* |
| I | worked | we | worked |
| you | worked | you | worked |
| he, she, it | worked | they | worked |
| Sam | worked | Sara and Marisa | worked |

## The Simple Future Tense

The **future tense** refers to action that *will* happen in the future. Form the simple future tense by adding the helping verb *will* before the verb (see Table 7-5). Note that the verb form does not change with person or number.

| TABLE 7-5 | SIMPLE FUTURE TENSE FORMS OF *WORK* | | |
|-----------|------|------|------|
| **Singular** | | **Plural** | |
| *Subject* | *Verb* | *Subject* | *Verb* |
| I | will work | we | will work |
| you | will work | you | will work |
| he, she, it | will work | they | will work |
| Sam | will work | Sara and Marisa | will work |

---

## ❗ NEED TO KNOW

### Verb Tense

- **Verb tense** indicates whether an action takes place in the present, past, or future.
- There are three basic verb tenses: **simple present**, **simple past**, and **simple future**.

- The **simple present tense** is used to describe regular, habitual action or can be used for nonaction verbs. It can also indicate action that is occurring at the time of speaking. The ending of a simple present tense verb must agree with the subject of the verb.
- The **simple past tense** refers to action that was completed in the past. For regular verbs, the simple past tense is formed by adding *-d* or *-ed*.
- The **simple future tense** refers to action that will happen in the future. The simple future tense is formed by adding the helping verb *will* before the verb.

## EXERCISE 7-3 Using the Simple Past and Simple Future Tenses

**Directions:** For each of the following verbs, write a sentence using the simple past tense and one using the simple future tense.   Answers will vary. Possible answers are shown.

**EXAMPLE**   overcook   The chef overcooked my steak.

I know he will overcook my steak.

1. dance   I danced until midnight.

We will dance until midnight.

2. hunt   My uncle hunted elk in Canada.

My uncle will hunt elk in Canada.

3. joke   The professor joked with the class.

The professor will joke with the class.

4. watch   We watched the sunset.

We will watch the sunset.

5. photograph   We photographed the sunset.

We will photograph the sunset.

## EXERCISE 7-4 Writing a Paragraph

**WRITING IN PROGRESS**

**Directions:** Write a paragraph on one of the following topics, using either the simple past tense or the simple future tense.

1. Selecting a movie to download
2. Cleaning your apartment after a party
3. Selecting an internship program
4. Buying new clothes for school
5. Caring for a three-year-old child

# Use Irregular Verbs Correctly

■ GOAL 4
Use irregular verbs
correctly

Errors in verb tense can occur easily with irregular verbs. Irregular verbs do not form the simple past tense according to the pattern we have studied. A regular verb forms the simple past tense by adding -*d* or -*ed*. An **irregular verb** forms the simple past tense by changing its spelling internally (for example, *I feed* becomes *I fed*) or by not changing at all (for example, *I cut* in present form remains *I cut* in past form).

## Tip for Writers

### Helping Verbs

A helping verb is used before the main verb to form certain tenses.

helping verb   main verb

Ericka will sit in front of the television for hours.

Common helping verbs include:

| have | has | had |
| be | am | is |
| do | does | did |
| are | was | were |
| being | been | |

The following verbs can be used only as helping verbs:

| can | could |
| will | would |
| shall | should |
| may | might |
| must | ought to |

## Tip for Writers

The pronoun *you* is always grammatically plural in English. Use plural verbs (*are*, *have*, or *were*) with *you*, not singular forms such as *is*, *has*, or *was*. Use a plural verb with *you* even when you are speaking or writing to one person.

## Three Troublesome Irregular Verbs

The verbs *be*, *do*, and *have* can be especially troublesome. You should master the correct forms of these verbs in both the present tenses and the past tenses since they are used so often.

1. **Irregular Verb:** *Be*

| TABLE 7-6 | FORMS OF THE IRREGULAR VERB *BE* | | |
|---|---|---|---|
| **Present** | | **Past** | |
| *Singular* | *Plural* | *Singular* | *Plural* |
| I am | we are | I was | we were |
| you are | you are | you were | you were |
| he, she, it is | they are | he, she, it was | were they |

■ It is nonstandard to use *be* for all present tense forms.

| INCORRECT | I be finished. |
| CORRECT | I am finished. |

| INCORRECT | They be surprised. |
| CORRECT | They are surprised. |

■ Another error is to use *was* instead of *were* for plural past tenses or with *you*.

| INCORRECT | We was late. |
| CORRECT | We were late. |

| INCORRECT | You was wrong. |
| CORRECT | You were wrong. |

■ Note that the verb *to be* never takes an object.

2. **Irregular Verb:** *Do*

| TABLE 7-7 | FORMS OF THE IRREGULAR VERB *DO* | | |
|---|---|---|---|
| **Present** | | **Past** | |
| *Singular* | *Plural* | *Singular* | *Plural* |
| I do | we do | I did | we did |
| you do | you do | you did | you did |
| he, she, it does | they do | he, she, it did | they did |

■ A common error is to use *does* instead of *do* for present plural forms.

| INCORRECT | We does our best. |
| CORRECT | We do our best. |

| INCORRECT | They doesn't know the answer. |
| CORRECT | They don't know the answer. |

■ Another error is to use *done* instead of *did* for past plural forms.

| INCORRECT | We done everything. You done finish. |
| CORRECT | We did everything. You did finish. |

## Tip for Writers

*Does,* as a main verb or a helping verb, is used only with third-person singular such as *he, Maria, the book* or with uncountable subjects such as *homework, music,* or *an idea.* Use *do,* not *does,* after *I, you,* or *they.*

**3. Irregular Verb:** *Have*

**TABLE 7-8   FORMS OF THE IRREGULAR VERB *HAVE***

| Present | | Past | |
|---|---|---|---|
| *Singular* | *Plural* | *Singular* | *Plural* |
| I have | we have | I had | we had |
| you have | you have | you had | you had |
| he, she, it has | they have | he, she, it had | they had |

■ A common nonstandard form uses *has* instead of *have* for the present plural.

| INCORRECT | We has enough. They has a good reason. |
| CORRECT | We have enough. They have a good reason. |

■ Another error occurs in the past singular.

| INCORRECT | I has nothing to give you. You has a bad day. |
| CORRECT | I had nothing to give you. You had a bad day. |

## EXERCISE 7-5    Using Standard Verb Forms

**Directions:** Circle the correct, standard form of the verb in each of the following sentences.

**EXAMPLE**    Last April, Anne (was, were) in Nevada.

1. After I watched the news, I (does, did) my homework.

2. You (be, were) lucky to win the raffle.

3. The electrician (have, has) enough time to complete the job.

4. When I am reading about the Civil War, I (am, be) captivated.

5. All the waitresses I know (have, has) sore feet.

6. We (was, (were)) at the grocery store yesterday.

7. He (do, (does)) his studying at the library.

8. We ((did,) done) the jigsaw puzzle while it rained.

9. Alice Walker (be, (is)) a favorite author of mine.

10. You (was, (were)) in the audience when the trophy was awarded.

---

**EXERCISE 7-6**  ## Using Irregular Verbs

**Directions:** Write sentences for each pair of irregular verbs shown below. Try to write several sentences that ask questions.   *Answers will vary. Possible answers are shown.*

|  | **EXAMPLE** | am | I am going to the Bulls game tonight. |
|  |  | be | Will you be at home tonight? |

1. do — Do you know the answer?

   does — Tammy does know the answer.

2. was — Ellen was late for class.

   were — Were you late for class?

3. is — Is class cancelled?

   be — When will you be out of class?

4. do — Do you know where I live?

   did — Did you lose your parking spot?

5. am — I am going bowling.

   was — Was the exam difficult?

---

**EXERCISE 7-7**  ## Using Irregular Verbs

**Directions:** Write sentences for each pair of irregular verbs shown below. Use a plural pronoun (*we, you, they*) or a plural noun.   *Answers will vary. Possible answers are shown.*

|  | **EXAMPLE** | be | We will be at my dad's house. |
|  |  | were | They were happy to see us. |

1. do — We do not want to be overcharged.

   did — We did not attend the lecture.

2. are — We are leaving at two o'clock.

   be — Dion and Taye will be late for dinner.

3. have — Students often have specific career goals.

   had — Maria and John had planned to leave campus at noon.

**4.** are     The leaves are falling.

     were     The leaves were falling yesterday.

**5.** be     We will be late for the movie.

     were     Sal and Anthony were planning to be home for dinner, but their plans changed.

---

**EXERCISE 7-8**

*WORKING TOGETHER*

## Correcting Verb Errors

**Directions:** Working with a classmate, read the following student paragraph and correct all verb errors.

Sometimes first impressions of people ~~is~~ *are* very inaccurate and can lead to problems. My brother, Larry, ~~learn~~ *learned* this the hard way. When he was 17, Larry and I ~~was~~ *were* driving to the mall. Larry decided to pick up a hitchhiker because he ~~looks~~ *looked* safe and trustworthy. After the man got in the car, we ~~notice~~ *noticed* that he was wearing a knife. A few miles later, the man suddenly ~~fell~~ *told* us to take him to Canada. So my brother said we'd have to stop for gas and explained that he did not have any money. The man ~~get~~ *got* out of the car to pump the gas. When he ~~goes~~ *went* up to the attendant to pay for the gas, we took off. We ~~do~~ *did* not stop until we ~~reach~~ *reached* the police station, where we ~~tell~~ *told* the officer in charge what ~~happens~~ *had happened*. The police caught the man several miles from the gas station. He ~~be~~ *had been* serving time in prison for burglary and had escaped over the weekend. Later, Larry said, "I was lucky that my first impression ~~were~~ *was* not my last!"

---

## Other Irregular Verbs

Among the other verbs that form the past tense in irregular ways are *become* (*became*), *drive* (*drove*), *hide* (*hid*), *stand* (*stood*), and *wear* (*wore*). For a list of the past-tense forms of other common irregular verbs, see Part Six, page 591. If you have a question about the form of a verb, consult this list or your dictionary.

## Confusing Pairs of Irregular Verbs

Two particularly confusing pairs of irregular verbs are *lie/lay* and *sit/set*.

### Lie/Lay

*Lie* means to recline. *Lay* means to put something down. The past tense of *lie* is *lay*. The past tense of *lay* is *laid*.

| TABLE 7-9   VERB FORMS OF *LIE* AND *LAY* | |
|---|---|
| **Simple Present** | **Simple Past** |
| Command the dog to lie down. | The dog lay down. |
| Lay the boards over here. | The carpenter laid the boards over there. |

### Sit/Set

*Sit* means to be seated. *Set* means to put something down. The past tense of *sit* is *sat*. The past tense of *set* is *set*.

| TABLE 7-10 VERB FORMS OF *SIT* AND *SET* | |
| --- | --- |
| **Simple Present** | **Simple Past** |
| Please sit over here. | We sat over here. |
| Set the books on the table. | He set the books on the table. |

> ## ! NEED TO KNOW
>
> ### Irregular Verbs
>
> - An **irregular verb** does not form the simple past tense with *-d* or *-ed*.
> - Three particularly troublesome irregular verbs are *be, do,* and *have*.
> - Two confusing pairs of verbs are *lie/lay* and *sit/set*. Each has a distinct meaning.

---

**EXERCISE 7-9** ## Using Correct Verbs

**Directions:** Circle the correct verb in each of the following sentences.

**EXAMPLE** Eric plans to (lay, **lie**) in bed all day.

1. The chef (sat, **set**) the mixer on "high" to beat the eggs.
2. I prefer to (**lie**, lay) on the hammock rather than on a chaise.
3. The students (**sit**, set) in rows to take the exam.
4. After putting up the wallboard, Santiago (lay, **laid**) the hammer on the floor.
5. Bags of grain (set, **sat**) on the truck.
6. I'm going to (**lie**, lay) down and take a short nap.
7. Because we came late, we (**sat**, set) in the last row.
8. The kitten (**lay**, laid) asleep in the laundry basket.
9. Bob (sat, **set**) the groceries on the counter.
10. Completely exhausted, Shawna (**lay**, laid) on the sofa.

---

# Understanding Voice: Using Active Instead of Passive Voice

■ **GOAL 5**
Use active instead of passive voice in most situations

**Transitive verbs** (those that take objects) may be in either the active voice or the passive voice. In an **active-voice** sentence, the subject performs the action described by the verb; that is, the subject is the actor. In a **passive-voice** sentence, the subject is the receiver of the action. The passive voice of a verb is formed by using an appropriate form of the helping verb *be* and the past participle of the main verb.

|  | Subject is actor | Active voice |  |
|---|---|---|---|
| **ACTIVE VOICE** | Dr. Hillel | delivered | the report on global warming. |

|  | Subject is receiver |  | Passive voice |
|---|---|---|---|
| **PASSIVE VOICE** | The report on global warming | | was delivered by Dr. Hillel. |

The following passive-voice sentences do not name the person who wiped away the fingerprints or broke the vase. Passive-voice sentences seem indirect, as if the writer were purposefully avoiding giving information the reader might need or want.

| **PASSIVE VOICE** | The fingerprints had been carefully wiped away. |
|---|---|
| **PASSIVE VOICE** | The vase had been broken. |

Both active and passive voices are grammatically correct. However, the active voice is usually more effective because it is simpler, more informative, and more direct. Use the active rather than the passive voice unless

■ **you do not know who or what performs the action of the verb.**

| PASSIVE | The broken window had been wiped clean of fingerprints. |
|---|---|

■ **you want to emphasize the object of the action rather than who or what performs the action.**

| PASSIVE | The poem "The Chicago Defender Sends a Man to Little Rock" by Gwendolyn Brooks was discussed in class. [Here, exactly who discussed the poem is less important than what poem was discussed.] |
|---|---|

As a general rule, try to avoid writing passive-voice sentences. Get in the habit of putting the subject—the person or thing performing the action—at the beginning of each sentence. If you do this, you will usually avoid the passive voice.

---

**! NEED TO KNOW**

### Active and Passive Voices

■ When a verb is in the **active voice**, the *subject performs* the action.

■ When a verb is in the **passive voice**, the *subject receives* the action.

■ Because the active voice is straightforward and direct, use it unless you do not know who or what performed the action or unless you want to emphasize the object of the action rather than who or what performed it.

| EXERCISE 7-10 | Using Active Voice |

**Directions:** Revise each of the following sentences by changing the verb from passive to active voice.

**EXAMPLE** The china cups and saucers were painted carefully by Lois and her friends.

**REVISED** *Lois and her friends carefully painted the china cups and saucers.*

1. *Goodnight Moon* was read by the mother to her daughter.

   *The mother read Goodnight Moon to her daughter.*

2. The maple tree was trimmed by the telephone company.

   *The telephone company trimmed the maple tree.*

3. The vacuum cleaner was repaired by Mr. Fernandez.

   *Mr. Fernandez repaired the vacuum cleaner.*

4. Many bags of flour were donated by the fraternity.

   *The fraternity donated many bags of flour.*

5. Six quarts of strawberries were made into jam by Alice.

   *Alice made six quarts of strawberries into jam.*

# Avoid Errors in Subject–Verb Agreement

■ GOAL 6
Avoid errors in subject–verb agreement

A subject and its verb must agree (be consistent) in person (first, second, third) and in number (singular, plural). (For more on pronoun forms, see Chapter 9.

The most common problems with subject–verb agreement occur with third-person present-tense verbs, which are formed for most verbs by adding *-s* or *-es.* (For the present-tense and past-tense forms of certain irregular verbs, see p. 214.)

## Agreement Rules

■ **If a verb's subject is third-person singular, use the present tense ending *-s* or *-es*.** For first and second person, no ending is added. (See Table 7-11.)

| TABLE 7-11 THIRD PERSON SINGULAR PRESENT TENSE ENDINGS | | | |
|---|---|---|---|
| **Singular Subject** | **Verb** | **Singular Subject** | **Verb** |
| I | talk | it | talks |
| you | talk | Santiago | talks |
| he | talks | a boy | talks |
| she | talks | | |

■ **For a plural subject (more than one person, place, thing, or idea), use a plural form of the verb.** (See Table 7-12.)

| TABLE 7-12 VERB FORMS FOR PLURAL SUBJECTS | | | |
| --- | --- | --- | --- |
| **Plural Subject** | **Verb** | **Plural Subject** | **Verb** |
| we | talk | Santiago and Nina | talk |
| you | talk | boys | talk |
| they | talk | | |

## Common Errors

The following circumstances often lead to errors in subject–verb agreement:

■ **Third-person singular** A common error is to omit the -s or -es in a third-person singular verb in the present tense. The subjects *he, she,* and *it,* or a noun that could be replaced with *he, she,* or *it,* all take a third-person singular verb.

| INCORRECT | She act like a professional. |
| --- | --- |
| CORRECT | She acts like a professional. |

| INCORRECT | Professor Simmons pace while he lectures. |
| --- | --- |
| CORRECT | Professor Simmons paces while he lectures. |

■ **Verbs before their subjects** When a verb comes before its subject, as in sentences beginning with *Here* or *There,* it is easy to make an agreement error. Because *here* and *there* are adverbs, they are never subjects of a sentence and do not determine the correct form of the verb. Look for the subject *after* the verb and, depending on its number, choose a singular or plural verb.

Singular verb    Singular subject

There is a pebble in my shoe.

Plural verb    Plural subject

There are two pebbles in my shoe.

*Note:* Using contractions such as *here's* and *there's* leads to mistakes because you cannot "hear" the mistake. "Here's two pens" may not sound incorrect, but "Here is two pens" does.

■ **Words between the subject and its verb** Words, phrases, and clauses coming between the subject and its verb do not change the fact that the verb must agree with the subject. To check that the verb is correct, mentally remove everything between the subject and its verb and make sure that the verb agrees in number with its subject.

Singular subject    Singular verb

A list of course offerings is posted on the bulletin board.

Plural subject    Plural verb

Details of the accident were not released.

*Note:* Phrases beginning with prepositions such as *along with, together with, as well as,* and *in addition to* are not part of the subject and should not be considered in determining the number of the verb.

Singular subject                                                    Singular verb

The stereo, together with the radios, televisions, and lights, goes dead during electrical storms.

■ **Compound subjects** Two or more subjects joined by the coordinating conjunction *and* require a plural verb, even if one or both of the subjects are singular.

| INCORRECT | Anita and Mark plays cards. |
| CORRECT | Anita and Mark play cards. |

When both of the subjects refer to the same person or thing, however, use a singular verb.

The president and chairman of the board is in favor of more aggressive marketing.

When a compound subject is joined by the conjunction *or* or *nor* or the correlative conjunctions *either/or, neither/nor, both/and, not/but,* or *not only/but also,* the verb should agree in number with the subject nearer to it.

Neither the books nor the article was helpful to my research.

Yesenia or the boys are coming tomorrow.

■ **Indefinite pronouns as subjects** Some indefinite pronouns (such as *everyone, neither, anybody, nobody, one, something,* and *each*) take a singular verb.

Everyone appreciates the hospital's volunteers.

Of the two applicants, neither seems well qualified.

The indefinite pronouns *both, many, several,* and *few* always take a plural verb. Some indefinite pronouns, such as *all, any, most, none,* and *some,* may take either a singular or plural verb. Treat the indefinite pronoun as singular if it refers to something that cannot be counted and as plural if it refers to more than one of something that can be counted.

Some of the ice is still on the road.

Some of the ice cubes are still in the tray.

All of the spaghetti tastes overcooked.

All of the spaghetti dishes taste too spicy.

■ **Collective nouns** A collective noun refers to a group of people or things (*audience, class, flock, jury, team, family*). When the noun refers to the group as one unit, use a singular verb.

The herd stampedes toward us.

When the noun refers to the group members as separate individuals, use a plural verb.

> The <u>herd</u> <u>scatter</u> in all directions.

■ **Nouns with plural forms but singular meaning** Some words appear plural (that is, they end in *-s* or *-es*) but have a singular meaning. *Measles, hysterics, news,* and *mathematics* are examples. Use a singular verb with them.

> <u>Mathematics</u> <u>is</u> a required course.

*Note:* Other nouns look plural and have singular meanings, but take a plural verb: *braces, glasses, trousers, slacks, jeans, jodhpurs,* and *pajamas*. Even though they refer to a single thing (to one pair of jeans, for example), these words take a plural verb.

> His <u>pajamas</u> <u>were covered</u> with pictures of tumbling dice.

■ **Relative pronouns in adjective clauses** The relative pronouns *who, which,* and *that* sometimes function as the subject of an adjective clause. When the relative pronoun refers to a singular noun, use a singular verb. When the pronoun refers to a plural noun, use a plural verb.

> Anita is a person <u>who</u> never <u>forgets</u> faces. [*Who* refers to *person,* which is singular.]
>
> The students <u>who</u> lost their keys <u>are</u> here. [*Who* refers to *students,* which is plural.]

---

## ! NEED TO KNOW

### Subject–Verb Agreement

- ■ A **subject** of a sentence must agree (be consistent) with the **verb** in person (first, second, or third) and in number (singular or plural).
- ■ Watch for errors when using the third-person singular, placing verbs before their subjects, using compound subjects, and adding words, phrases, or clauses between the subject and the verb.

---

**EXERCISE 7-11**   ## Choosing Correct Verbs

**Directions:** Circle the verb that correctly completes each sentence.

> **EXAMPLE**   The newspapers (is, (are)) on the desk.

1. The hubcaps that fell off the car (was, (were)) expensive to replace.

2. The conductor and orchestra members ((ride), rides) a bus to their concerts.

3. A Little League team (practice, practices) across the street each Tuesday.

4. Here (is, are) the computer disk I borrowed.

5. Not only the news reporters but also the weather forecaster (are broadcasting, is broadcasting) live from the circus tonight.

6. Nobody older than 12 (ride, rides) the merry-go-round.

7. The discussion panel (offer, offers) its separate opinions after the debate.

8. Terry's green shorts (hang, hangs) in his gym locker.

9. Several of the cookies (taste, tastes) stale.

10. A mime usually (wear, wears) all-black or all-white clothing.

---

**EXERCISE 7-12** | ## Choosing Correct Verbs

**Directions:** Circle the verb that correctly completes each sentence.

> **EXAMPLE**  Everybody (like, likes) doughnuts for breakfast.

1. Physics (is, are) a required course for an engineering degree.

2. Most of my courses last semester (was, were) in the morning.

3. The orchestra members who (is, are) carrying their instruments will be able to board the plane first.

4. Suzanne (sing, sings) a touching version of "America the Beautiful."

5. Here (is, are) the performers who juggle plates.

6. Kin Lee and his parents (travel, travels) to Ohio tomorrow.

7. A box of old and valuable stamps (is, are) in the safe-deposit box at the bank.

8. The family (sit, sits) together in church each week.

9. Judith and Erin (arrive, arrives) at the train station at eleven o'clock.

10. Directions for the recipe (is, are) on the box.

---

**EXERCISE 7-13** | ## Correcting Subject–Verb Agreement Errors

**Directions:** Revise any sentences that contain errors in subject–verb agreement.

>     Los Angeles ~~have~~ [has] some very interesting and unusual buildings. There ~~is~~ [are] the Victorian houses on Carroll Avenue, for example. The gingerbread-style trim and other ornate architectural features ~~makes~~ [make] those houses attractive to tourists and photographers. The Bradbury Building and the Oviatt Building ~~was~~ [were] both part of the nineteenth-century skyline. They ~~was~~ [were] restored as office buildings that now houses twentieth-century businesses. Some of the architecture in Los Angeles ~~seem~~ [seems] to disguise a building's function. One of the most startling sights ~~are~~ [is] a building that ~~look~~ [looks] like a huge ship.

## EXERCISE 7-14 | Revising a Paragraph

**Directions:** The following student paragraph has been revised to correct all errors except for those in subject–verb agreement and shifts in person and number. Complete the revision by correcting all such problems. Answers will vary. Possible revision is shown.

Now that the fascination with exercise has been in full swing for a decade, the public are starting to get tired of our nation's overemphasis on fitness. It seems as though every time you turn on the TV or pick up a newspaper or talk with a friend, all we hear about is how we don't exercise enough. The benefits of exercise is clear, but do we really need to have them repeated to us in sermonlike fashion every time we turn around? Each of us are at a point now where we are made to feel almost guilty if we haven't joined a health club or, at the very least, participated in some heavy-duty exercise every day. It may be time you realized that there's better ways to get exercise than these. Americans might be better off just exercising in a more natural way. Taking a walk or playing a sport usually fit in better with our daily routines and isn't so strenuous. It could even be that our obsession with extreme forms of exercise may be less healthy than not exercising at all.

Now that the fascination with exercise has been in full swing for a decade, the public is starting to get tired of our nation's overemphasis on fitness. It seems as though every time we turn on the TV or pick up a newspaper or talk with a friend, all we hear about is how we don't exercise enough. The benefits of exercise are clear, but do we really need to have them repeated to us in sermonlike fashion every time we turn around? Each of us is at a point now where we are made to feel almost guilty if we haven't joined a health club or, at the very least, participated in some heavy-duty exercise every day. It may be time we realized that there are better ways to get exercise than these. Americans might be better off just exercising in a more natural way. Taking a walk or playing a sport usually fits in better with our daily routines and isn't so strenuous. It could even be that our obsession with extreme forms of exercise may be less healthy than not exercising at all.

## EXERCISE 7-15 | Revising a Paragraph

**WRITING IN PROGRESS**

**Directions:** Reread the paragraph you wrote in Exercise 7-4. Check for subject–verb agreement errors and for sentences you wrote in the passive voice. Revise as necessary.

# READING

# What Verbs Tell Readers

■ **GOAL 7**
Understand what verbs tell readers

Verbs, when used properly, convey a great deal of information to a reader. They indicate time, they present descriptive information, and they may help indicate who performed an action.

## Verbs Indicate Time

Verbs in the present tense indicate that an action is occurring at the time of speaking or writing is (ongoing), is constant, or is habitual.

| | |
|---|---|
| ONGOING | I am working on math problems. |
| CONSTANT | Maria loves soccer. |
| HABITUAL | Sam lifts weights every day. |

Verbs in the past tense tell readers about past events, prior conditions, and completed processes.

| | |
|---|---|
| PAST EVENTS | I left campus at 2 p.m. |
| PRIOR CONDITIONS | People believed that the Earth was flat. |
| COMPLETED PROCESSES | The house burned to the ground yesterday. |

Verbs in the future tense explain events to happen in the future.

| | |
|---|---|
| FUTURE EVENTS | I will leave for California tomorrow. |

## Verbs Convey Descriptive Information

A reader can learn a great deal of information about an event or action by paying close attention to the writer's choice of verbs. Notice in the following sentences how, while each expresses a form of movement, each suggests an entirely different action:

Yolanda crawled. Yolanda ambled. Yolanda toddled. Yolanda shuffled. Yolanda meandered. Yolanda hiked. Yolanda traipsed. Yolanda waddled.

Each verb creates a different mental picture.

---

**EXERCISE 7-16** ## Using Verbs

**Directions:** Replace the underlined word or phrase in each sentence with a verb that creates an entirely different meaning or impression and write the complete sentence below.   *Answers will vary. Possible answers are shown.*

1. We were <u>disappointed</u> by the restaurant menu.

   *We were impressed with the restaurant menu.*

2. The children <u>like</u> Halloween.

   *The children detest Halloween.*

3. Nick <u>works</u> at the pool every weekend.

   *Nick lazes at the pool every weekend.*

4. We <u>enjoyed</u> our trip to Minnesota.

   *We delighted in our trip to Minnesota.*

5. The dog <u>ran</u> to the water's edge and then <u>went</u> into the lake.

   *The dog raced to the water's edge and then plunged into the lake.*

## Verbs Identify Who Performed the Action

Use of the active voice enables you to determine who or what performed the action. In the following sentence, the use of active voice makes it clear that it was the writer's uncle who ruined the day's plans.

My uncle ruined our plans to spend the day at the beach.

Had passive voice been used, "Our plans for the beach were ruined," you would have less information about the situation.

When reading sentences that do use the passive voice, ask yourself whether the writer is deliberately avoiding naming the actor, and if so, why. In the following sentence, the writer may prefer not to say who performed the action in order to protect the whistle-blowers.

The politician's dishonest practices were reported to authorities.

# INTEGRATING READING AND WRITING

## READ AND REVISE

The following excerpt is from a student essay titled "Alone but Not Lonely." This excerpt contains verb usage errors that were subsequently corrected in another draft. Read the excerpt, and then revise it to correct verb usage errors.

The summer I turned ten, I learned the difference between being alone and being lonely. Growing up in a large family, I never had much time to myself, but that summer I visit~ed~ my aunt for three weeks. She lived in the country, and I was the only kid for miles around. At first, I ~~had~~ felt lonely without my brothers and sisters, but then I discover~ed~ the boulders in the woods. The jumble of huge rocks ~~were~~ _was_ endlessly fascinating. Some days I was an explorer, moving from one rock to another, surveying the countryside from the tallest boulder. Some days, I retired to my secret fort, tucked in a shadowy crevice. I furnished my rocky fort with an old cushion to ~~set~~ _sit_ on and a cigar box for collecting treasures. On sunny mornings, before the air ~~has~~ _had_ lost its early chill, I ~~laid~~ _lay_ on the flattest boulder, its smooth surface warming my skinny arms and legs. The boulders were my audience when I read aloud the stories I had ~~wrote~~ _written_. I remember many things about my time alone in the woods that summer, but I don't recall ever feeling lonely.

*Lekisha Roberson is in her third year at Bunker Hill Community College where she is studying for a degree in medical imaging or radiography. As a single parent who works as a medical secretary, she wants to obtain a better job that will allow her to buy a house and provide more for her 19 year old daughter. She wrote this essay in a response to an assignment that asked her to describe an event that changed her life. She later submitted it to the Pearson Writing Rewards essay competition.*

# "My Kids' Father"

Title identifies the subject of the essay

Thesis statement

Death is a tragedy that affected my life and is often hard to overcome. Death happens when you don't expect it, and no one ever knows when it is going to happen to them. Unfortunately, it happened to me and my family. My kids' father, Trilane, was murdered in my apartment on April 6, 1999, by a gunshot wound to his head. Although it has been twelve years, it seems as if it just happened. We shared an apartment with our two children who were six and one year old at the time.

Background information

Topic sentence

Details describing the sequence of events

The morning of the accident, I felt something like emptiness in my stomach, although not knowing at that moment what had happened. I constantly called him while I was at work, but did not receive any response. An hour went by and I knew something was wrong, so I asked my boss if I could leave early, lying that I didn't feel too well. I rushed home by taxi, which was something unusual. When I approached the front of my house, there were police and yellow tape surrounding the apartment. At that moment, I knew that pain in my stomach was a sign. Trilane had been killed.

Details describing the effects on the family

Topic sentence

Later that evening after school was over, I was approached by my six-year-old daughter, asking why her father didn't pick her up from her bus stop that day. I did not know what to say other than, "Do you want to go to the park?" I was accompanied by Trilane's mother who helped me break this devastating news to my child, her granddaughter. The reaction that I got from her was unexpected. She told me that she knew this was going to happen, and she told herself to keep calm. My heart dropped, not knowing what to say, so I just consoled her, but I was the one who needed it. Although Trilane was an intelligent and handsome individual, he was drawn to the streets, and my six-year-old sensed that. My son was too young at the time to even understand what was going on, but he did act out in tantrums.

Topic sentence followed by explanation

The funeral services for Trilane were considered a celebration of life. Everyone was celebrating the twenty-two years of life that God spared for him with his family and the starting of his own. I was angry, hurt, and frustrated at the same time. I was angry that he left me to be a single mother of two. I was hurt because I felt empty that my first love would never come back. I was frustrated because I told him this was going to happen if he didn't change his life. Although he was involved in the streets, Trilane was an honorable person and you could always rely on him. He always tried to aim for his best, but there were always obstacles in his way.

Topic sentence

Sometimes when you hang with the wrong crowds, you draw attention to yourself. Selling drugs, hanging out and being involved in gangs was what he endured. I tried

Details about Trilane add interest

to tell him to change his life by going to school or getting involved in something in the community. He never listened to what positive people had to say. He knew everything about the street life and was willing to die by it. One day the light shined on him for the better. He wanted to change his life. Trilane went to school to obtain his G.E.D., but it was too late. Often when you try to change, you're in so deep that others don't forget. That's what happened; someone didn't forget and murdered my kids' father.

Conclusion

Even now, many years later, it's too hard to deal with. My daughter had to get counseling and that helped a lot. <u>Death is something that you will overcome, but you'll never forget the ones you loved.</u>

## Examining Writing

1. Reread Roberson's introduction. Does it capture your attention and draw you into the essay?

2. What types of details does Roberson use to support her thesis statement? Highlight details that helped you visualize the people involved and the event that changed Roberson's life.

3. How does Roberson organize her essay?

4. Evaluate the conclusion of this essay. What could Roberson add to improve the conclusion?

# READ AND RESPOND: A Professional Essay

## Thinking Before Reading

The following essay originally appeared in April 2012 on the Red Bull Rising blog, a military-focused blog written and edited by Randy Brown (also known as "Charlie Sherpa"), a former citizen-soldier of the Iowa Army National Guard.

1. Preview the reading, using the steps discussed in Chapter 1 on page 25.

2. Connect the reading to your own experience by answering the following questions:

   a. Have you ever seen a service dog or a working dog? In what context?

   b. What do you know about dogs serving in the military or helping veterans after their military service?

3. Highlight and annotate as you read.

1120**L**/1280 words

# Scenes from a Service-Dog Graduation

1    It's a sultry spring Friday afternoon outside the Gold Star Museum on Camp Dodge, Johnston, Iowa. The sun is out, the wind feels soft, and you can smell the earth. Even the military-grade grass on the adjacent parade field is beginning to turn green. To everything, there is a season.

**"Pomp and Circumstance"**

A piece of music traditionally played during graduation ceremonies that was written by the British composer Edward Elgar (1857–1934).

2    Inside, there is happy chaos. A hundred little crises have come together in an event that seems part high-school graduation open house, part family reunion, part end-of-season sports team banquet. The mood is upbeat and bittersweet, and there's often not a dry eye or nose in the room. There are a few funny stories, an emotional music video, and plenty of puppies—Labrador Retriever puppies, both black and tan. Nobody plays "Pomp and Circumstance" (or should that be "Paws and Circumstance"?), but, later, there will be marble cake. And there will be a barbecue because nothing good happens in Iowa without grilling a sacrifice.

3    More than 50 people have turned out to celebrate the next steps forward for nine Midwestern veterans and their new canine partners. The dogs are psychiatric service and mobility animals, trained by Paws & Effect to perform physical tasks that mitigate conditions such as Post-Traumatic Stress Disorder (P. T. S. D.) and limited ranges of movement. They are trained to respond to their handlers' flashbacks or nightmares, for example, or to retrieve objects that are out of reach.

4    While the animals no doubt also provide an emotional or therapeutic benefit—in covering these kinds of stories, news reporters typically cite here the calming effects of pet ownership—they are not pets. Neither are they "companion," "emotional support," or "stress-relief" animals. They are working dogs, heading out into a working world.

5    Since 2006, the Des Moines, Iowa-based non-profit organization has trained therapy and service animals for Midwestern veterans and others, and educated and advocated regarding laws requiring service-animal access to public spaces. The organization is often augmented by trainers from Canine Craze, West Des Moines.

6    In the past two weeks, the veterans have met their service dogs for the first time. They've lived, eaten, slept, played, and worked with their partners, developing emotional bonds and basic understandings. Think of it as Boot Camp, but with paws. After graduation, everything else is on-the-job training and annual refresher courses. As with military training, classroom presentations are followed by field exercises. The veterans, now dog-handlers, learn to navigate venues such as shopping malls, movie theaters, restaurants, and airport security checkpoints. When traveling by air, the dogs are trained to lie down in the underseat luggage area. The veterans practice the maneuver on a passenger aircraft parked at the Des Moines International Airport.

7    During the placement course, Paws & Effect temporarily bases its operations out of the Dodge House, a small, single-story facility across the street from the museum—and right next to the house inhabited by Maj. Gen. Timothy Orr, the adjutant general of the Iowa National Guard. Named after the same Civil War general from which Camp Dodge takes its name, the single-story Dodge House is often rented for social and other events. It features a kitchen, a sunroom, and a expansive front porch. After classroom discussions there, the veterans train with their dogs until both are tired, then sneak an occasional cat nap. After dinner, they watch movies and play training "games." The veterans cheekily rechristen the building the "Dog House."

8    The March 30 graduation is the first and last time that many recipients will see the families who helped raise their animals as puppies. Puppy-raisers include both civilian and military foster families, who volunteer to help dog-trainers from Paws & Effect socialize, work, and train animals at home and in public. (Under Iowa law, service-dogs-in-training are afforded the same rights as other service animals.) The puppy-raiser relationship lasts approximately 18 months, during

which time the non-profit carefully monitors the health, training, and personality of each animal. Paws & Effect pays for food, medicine, equipment, and other expenses. One dog can cost the organization up to $25,000 in supplies, care, and training. At the same time, Paws & Effect identifies prospective recipients through channels such as the Iowa National Guard and the Community-Based Warrior Transition Unit (C.B.W.T.U.) at Rock Island Arsenal, Ill., an installation located on the Mississippi River along the "east coast" of Iowa.

9    While there have been other dogs placed individually, Friday marks the first formal placement course and graduation for Paws & Effect. Three more litters are already in the works for placement in late-2012 and early-2013. One is named after military land navigation terms, such as "Pace," "Ridge," and "Hilltop." The other is named after radio-friendly phonetic alphabet characters, such as "Charlie," "Oscar," and "Victor." (Nicole Shumate, director and dog-trainer-in-chief for Paws & Effect, reserves the "Alpha"-dog label for herself.)

10    The 2012 class notably includes "Ryder" and "Archer," two of the "Red Bull" litter named last year in honor of the 34th Infantry "Red Bull" Division. Others still in training include "Havoc," "Avancéz" (who goes by "Van"), and "Sabre." The 2012 graduating Paws & Effect service dogs and their human partners are: Anthem and Joe Archer and Troy; Hero and Dustin; Honor and Wade; Liberty and Casey; Merit and Mitch; Roo and the Iowa National Guard (Roo will be a "facility dog," used for hospital visits to wounded warriors, Soldier Readiness Processing, behavioral health assessments, and other missions.); Ryder and Bill; and Valor and Dean.

11    The puppy-raisers have prepared "legacy" books—collections of letters, photos, memorabilia documenting their puppies' early lives. As groups of puppy-raisers, veterans, and dogs are recognized with applause, trainers and others tell stories about each match or pairing:

- ■   "It was clear that Anthem was going to be Joe's dog from the start," says Paws & Effect director Nicole. "I just wish Tammy had told me that Anthem liked carrots for rewards. And not just any carrots, mind you: They had to be coins. And they had to have ridges."

- ■   "I felt like I was writing a dating-service ad for my dog," says puppy-raiser Travis, about starting to write a note for Hero's legacy book: "'My dog is the best-looking and smartest dog.'" He ended up writing five pages.

- ■   "My dog is just the right balance of challenge and complement," says one recipient. Another says, "I got my smile back."

A number of the veterans observe the placement course was the first they'd slept soundly in a long time. Another veteran reports that, twice in one night, his dog had woken him from a nightmare by licking his face.

12      Nicole notes that one veteran had neglected to tell her that he might have a leg amputated in coming months. She and the puppy-raiser gave the dog a 6-day crash course in mobility-assistance skills, such as how to retrieve objects. "At one point, I was getting hourly updates: 'The dog is picking up keys . . .' 'The dog is picking up frozen peas . . .'" Apparently, the training took, she says, because the veteran later wondered why "the dog will not stop handing me things!"

13      Family members also offer words of wisdom, thanks, and humor. "During class, I was the one who asked one day about what happens when my husband and I start getting a little . . . 'active,'" one spouse shares, to friendly laughter. "Would the dog think I was hurting him? The group decided I should ask you, the puppy-raisers, about that." As she makes eye contact with the couple who raised her husband's new service dog, the room breaks into giggles. Not to worry, the couple responds: The dog is fully trained.

14      After the laughter, as promised, there is cake and barbecue. "To everything, there is a season." It is springtime in Iowa. You don't need to be a dog to smell the possibilities.

# Getting Ready to Write

## Checking Your Comprehension

Answer each of the following questions using complete sentences.

1. Who are the dogs trained to help, and what conditions are they specifically trained to respond to?

2. What two groups are responsible for training the dogs?

3. Where does the training take place?

4. How long does the puppy-raiser relationship last and how much does it cost to raise one dog?

5. What are the two litters for late 2012 and early 2013 named after?

6. What are legacy books?

## Strengthening Your Vocabulary

Using the word's context, word parts, or a dictionary, write a brief definition of each of the following words as it is used in the reading.

1. adjacent (paragraph 1) _nearby_____

2. mitigate (paragraph 3) _help to treat or relieve_____

3. advocated (paragraph 5) _worked on behalf of_____

4. augmented (paragraph 5) _supported, expanded_____

5. cheekily (paragraph 7) _humorously, irreverently_____

6. monitors (paragraph 8) _observes_

7. prospective (paragraph 8) _potential, future_

8. complement (paragraph 11) _something that completes_

## Examining the Reading: Using Idea Maps

Review the reading by completing the missing parts of the following idea map.

**VISUALIZE IT!**

Title — **Scenes from a Service-Dog Graduation**

Thesis — Paws & Effects trains working dogs to assist veterans and others.

Paws & Effect has trained psychiatric service and mobility dogs since 2006

Trains dogs to help those with PTSD or _limited range of movement_

Educates and advocates for _service-animal access to public spaces_

Helped by trainers from _Canine Craze_ and volunteer puppy-raisers

Veterans work with their new service dogs for two weeks

Learn to navigate _public venues and air travel_

Train with their dogs at the Dodge House

Meet puppy-raisers at graduation

Volunteers work with Paws & Effect to raise puppies

Puppy-raiser relationship lasts _18 months_

Costs up to _$25,000_ in supplies, care, and training

Prepare legacy books documenting _dogs' early lives_

Conclusion — The graduation ceremony is a joyful celebration of possibilities for the veterans and their new canine partners.

## Thinking Critically: Discussion and Journal Writing

React and respond to the reading by discussing the following:

**THINKING VISUALLY**

1. When have you seen working dogs or service dogs? Discuss the situation, the type of dog, and the work or service you observed the dog doing.

2. What do you think makes dogs useful in helping veterans and others who need therapy or assistance? Discuss the difference between pets and working dogs.

3. Discuss the photo that accompanies the essay. What does it add to the written descriptions in the essay? What details do you notice in it that relate to the article?

---

**MySkillsLab®**

Complete
this
Exercise

## Writing About the Reading

### Paragraph Options

1. How would you describe the author's attitude toward his subject? Write a paragraph about how the author reveals his feelings through his choice of details and words.

2. What does the author mean by "a hundred little crises" (paragraph 2)? Write a paragraph describing the types of crises he might be referring to.

3. What other photographs or visuals could contribute to the article if included? Write a paragraph describing the visual and explaining its purpose.

### Essay Options

4. Serving as a puppy-raiser is a form of public service, a means of helping others. Write an essay about public service. You might explain its values or discuss the contributions you or someone you know has made, for example.

5. Have you ever created a photo album such as the legacy books described in the essay? Has someone created one for you? What is the value in documenting someone's early life? Write an essay exploring these questions.

6. What is the significance of the sentence, "To everything there is a season," in the introduction and again in the conclusion? Write an essay that explains the meaning of the sentence and relate it to your own life, either agreeing or disagreeing with the statement.

# SELF-TEST SUMMARY

To test yourself, cover the Answer column with a sheet of paper and answer each question in the left column. Evaluate each of your answers as you work by sliding the paper down and comparing your answer with what is printed in the answer column.

| QUESTION | ANSWER |
|---|---|
| ■ **GOAL 1** Identify verb forms <br><br> What is the five forms of a verb? | The five verb forms are the *base form*, the *past tense*, the *past participle*, the *present participle*, and the *-s form*. |
| ■ **GOAL 2** Identify verb tenses <br><br> What is the function of verb tenses? | Verb tenses express time. They indicate whether an action, process, or event takes place in the present, past, or future. |
| ■ **GOAL 3** Use simple verb tenses correctly <br><br> In the simple present tense, the verb form for which person ends in *-s*? | In the simple present tense, the verb for third-person singular subjects ends in *-s*. (For first-person, second-person, or third-person plural, the base form of the verb is used.) |
| ■ **GOAL 4** Use irregular verbs correctly <br><br> How does an irregular verb form the simple past tense? | An irregular verb forms the simple past tense, not by adding *-d* or *-ed*, but either by changing its spelling internally or by not changing at all. |
| ■ **GOAL 5** Use active instead of passive voice in most situations <br><br> What is the difference between the active and passive voices, and why is active voice usually preferred? | In an active-voice sentence, the subject performs the action. In a passive-voice sentence, the subject receives the action. Active voice is usually more effective than passive voice because it is simpler and more direct. |
| ■ **GOAL 6** Avoid errors in subject-verb agreement <br><br> How must a subject and its verb agree? | A subject of a sentence must agree with its verb in person and in number. |
| ■ **GOAL 7** Understand what verbs tell readers <br><br> What do verbs tell readers? | Verbs indicate time, present descriptive information, and help indicate who performed an action. |

# MySkillsLab

For more help with **Verbs**, go to your learning path in MySkillsLab at http://www.myskillslab.com.

# 8

# Combining and Expanding Your Ideas

## THINK About It!

Study the six photographs shown above one at a time (cover the others with your hands as you look at them). What is happening in each one? It is probably difficult to tell because there is so little information in each one. Then look at the six photographs all together. Now it is clear what is happening. Write a sentence that states the main point of the combined photograph.

The six photographs seen separately are difficult to understand because each one contains so little information, and it is unclear if and how each is related to the others. A similar uncertainty can occur in writing when a writer uses too many very short sentences in a paragraph and the relationship between them is unclear: the reader has difficulty piecing together the meaning and grasping the larger, more important ideas.

In this chapter, as a writer, you will learn to combine your ideas to make your sentences more effective and more interesting. You will also learn how to use sentence arrangement to show the relationships and the logical connections between and among your ideas. As a reader you will learn to use sentence structure to determine how ideas are related and connected.

## FOCUSING ON READING AND WRITING

# What Are Independent and Dependent Clauses?

**GOAL 1**
Recognize independent and dependent clauses

A **clause** is a group of words that contains a subject and a verb. There are two types of clauses—independent and dependent. An **independent clause** can stand by itself and express a complete thought. A **dependent clause** hinges on another clause to complete its meaning. You can think of these two types of clauses in the following way. If you are financially independent, you alone accept full responsibility for your finances. If you are financially dependent, you depend on someone else to pay your living expenses. Similarly, clauses either stand alone and accept responsibility for their own meaning or they depend on another clause to complete their meaning. Independent clauses can stand alone as sentences. Dependent clauses can never stand alone because they are not complete sentences.

When writing, the key to combining and expanding your ideas is to recognize this difference between independent and dependent clauses. The various combinations of independent and dependent clauses shown in the "Need to Know" box below allow you to link your ideas to one another, to expand and explain ideas, and to show relationships.

When reading, it is useful to pay attention to how a writer combines clauses because relationships and connections are often suggested by how independent and dependent clauses are combined into sentences. The relative importance of ideas is also suggested.

## ! NEED TO KNOW

### Independent and Dependent Clauses

Sentences are made up of various combinations of independent and dependent clauses. Here are the possible combinations:

- **Simple sentence**   A simple sentence has one independent clause and no dependent clauses.

    Independent clause

    Richard hurried to his car.

- **Compound sentence**   A compound sentence has two or more independent clauses and no dependent clauses.

    Independent clause          Independent clause

    Richard hurried to his car, but he was already late for work.

■ **Complex sentence**   A complex sentence has one independent clause and one or more dependent clauses.

Independent clause   Dependent clause

Richard hurried to his car because he was late for work.

■ **Compound–complex sentence**   A compound–complex sentence has two or more independent clauses and one or more dependent clauses.

Dependent clause        Independent clause        Independent clause      Dependent clause

As Richard hurried to his car, he knew he would be late for work, but he hoped that he would not be docked an hour's pay.

## WRITING

# Combine Ideas of Equal Importance

■ **GOAL 2**
Combine ideas of equal importance

Many times, ideas are of equal importance. For example, in the following sentence, it is just as important to know that the writer never has enough time as it is to know that she always rushes.

I never have enough time, so I always rush from task to task.

Complete thoughts (independent clauses) of equal importance are combined by using a technique called **coordination**. *Co-* means "together." *Coordinate* means "to work together." When you want two complete thoughts to work together equally, you can combine them into a single sentence by using coordination.

There are two basic ways to join two ideas that are equally important:

METHOD 1   Join them by using a *comma* and a *coordinating conjunction (for, and, nor, but, or, yet, so)*.

Complete thought, coordinating conjunction complete thought.

METHOD 2   Join them by using a *semicolon*.

Complete thought; complete thought.

## Method 1: Use a Comma and a Coordinating Conjunction

The most common way to join ideas is by using a *comma and a coordinating conjunction*. (Use a semicolon only when the two ideas are *very* closely related and the connection between the ideas is clear and obvious.)

The following two sentences contain equally important ideas:

Samantha works 20 hours per week.

Samantha manages to find time to study.

You can combine these ideas into one sentence by using a comma and a coordinating conjunction.

|  | Idea 1 |  | Idea 2 |
|---|---|---|---|
|  | Comma | Conjunction |  |

Samantha works 20 hours per week, but she manages to find time to study.

A **coordinating conjunction** joins clauses and adds meaning to a sentence. A coordinating conjunction indicates how the ideas are related. Table 8-1 provides a brief review of the meaning of each coordinating conjunction and the relationship it expresses.

**TABLE 8-1    COORDINATING CONJUNCTIONS AND THE RELATIONSHIPS THEY EXPRESS**

| Coordinating Conjunction | Meaning | Relationship |
|---|---|---|
| **and** | in addition | The two ideas are added together. |
| **but** | in contrast | The two ideas are opposite. |
| **for** | because | The idea that follows *for* is the cause of the idea in the other clause. |
| **nor, or** | not either, either | The ideas are choices or alternatives. |
| **so** | as a result | The second idea is the result of the first. |
| **yet** | in contrast | The two ideas are opposite. |

*Note:* Do *not* use the words *also*, *plus*, and *then* to join complete thoughts. They are *not* coordinating conjunctions.

Here are a few examples of Method 1:

| SIMPLE SENTENCES | Time is valuable. I try to use it wisely. |
|---|---|
| COMBINED SENTENCE | Time is valuable, so I try to use it wisely. |
| SIMPLE SENTENCES | Many students try to set priorities for work and study. Many students see immediate results. |
| COMBINED SENTENCE | Many students try to set priorities for work and study, and they see immediate results. |
| SIMPLE SENTENCES | I tried keeping lists of things to do. My friend showed me a better system. |
| COMBINED SENTENCE | I tried keeping lists of things to do, but my friend showed me a better system. |

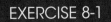 **EXERCISE 8-1**    Using Coordinating Conjunctions

**Directions:** For each of the following sentences, add the coordinating conjunction that best expresses the relationship between the two complete thoughts.

**EXAMPLE**    I never learned to manage my time, ____*so*____ I am planning to attend a time-management workshop.

1. I might study math, ___*or*___ I might review for my history exam.

2. The average person spends 56 hours a week sleeping, ___*and*___ the average person spends seven hours a week eating dinner.

3. Checking Facebook is tempting, ___*but*___ I usually log out before I start studying.

4. I do not feel like starting my research paper, ___*nor*___ do I feel like reviewing math.

5. I am never sure of what to work on first, ___*so*___ I waste a lot of time deciding.

6. A schedule for studying is easy to follow, ___*for*___ it eliminates the need to decide what to study.

7. My cousin has a study routine, ___*and*___ she never breaks it.

8. Ernesto studies his hardest subject first, ___*and*___ then he takes a break.

9. I know I should not procrastinate, ___*yet*___ I sometimes postpone an unpleasant task until the next day.

10. I had planned to study after work, ___*but*___ my exam was postponed.

## EXERCISE 8-2    Completing Sentences

**Directions:** Complete each of the following sentences by adding a second complete thought. Use the coordinating conjunction shown in bold. *Answers will vary. Possible answers are shown.*

    **EXAMPLE** I feel torn between studying and spending time with friends, **but** *I usually choose to study.*

1. My psychology class was canceled, **so** *I studied in the library.*

2. I waste time doing unimportant tasks, **and** *then I feel guilty.*

3. The phone used to be a constant source of interruption, **but** *setting up voicemail solved the problem.*

4. I had extra time to study this weekend, **for** *my three sons visited their grandfather.*

5. I had hoped to finish reading my biology chapter, **but** *I still have ten pages to go.*

6. Every Saturday I study psychology, **or** *I review for an upcoming exam.*

7. I had planned to finish work early, **yet** *my boss asked me to stay until six o'clock.*

8. I can choose a topic to write about, **or** *I can use one my instructor suggested.*

9. I had hoped to do many errands this weekend, **but** *a winter storm has changed my plans.*

10. I tried to study and watch television at the same time, **but** *I could not concentrate on my reading.*

**EXERCISE 8-3**

# Combining Sentences Using Coordinating Conjunctions

**Directions:** Combine each of the following pairs of sentences by using a comma and a coordinating conjunction (*for, and, nor, but, or, yet, so*). Change punctuation, capitalization, and words as necessary. Be sure to insert a comma before the coordinating conjunction.  Answers will vary.

**EXAMPLE**  **a.** I have a free hour between my first and second classes.

**b.** I use that free hour to review my biology notes.

I have a free hour between my first and second class, so I use that hour to review my biology notes.

1. **a.** Some tasks are more enjoyable than others.
   **b.** We tend to put off unpleasant tasks.

   Some tasks are more enjoyable than others, so we tend to put off the unpleasant ones.

2. **a.** Many people think it is impossible to do two things at once.
   **b.** Busy students soon learn to combine routine activities.

   Many people think it is impossible to do two things at once, but busy students soon learn to combine routine activities.

3. **a.** Marita prioritizes her courses.
   **b.** Marita allots specific blocks of study time for each.

   Marita prioritizes her courses, and she allots specific blocks of study time for each.

4. **a.** Marcus may try to schedule his study sessions so they are several hours apart.
   **b.** Marcus may adjust the length of his study sessions.

   Marcus may try to schedule his study sessions so they are several hours apart, or he may adjust the length of his study sessions.

5. **a.** Sherry studies late at night.
   **b.** Sherry does not accomplish as much as she expects to.

   Sherry studies late at night, so she does not accomplish as much as she expects to.

6. **a.** Marguerite studies without breaks.
   **b.** Marguerite admits she frequently loses her concentration.

   Marguerite studies without breaks, and she admits she frequently loses her concentration.

7. **a.** Alfonso studies two hours for every hour he spends in class.
   **b.** Alfonso earns high grades.

   Alfonso studies two hours for every hour he spends in class, so he earns high grades.

8. **a.** Deadlines are frustrating.
   **b.** Deadlines force you to make hasty decisions.

   Deadlines are frustrating, for they force you to make hasty decisions.

9. **a.** Juan thought he was organized.
   **b.** Juan discovered he was not.

   *Juan thought he was organized, but he discovered he was not.*

10. **a.** Monica sets goals for each course.
    **b.** Monica usually attains her goals.

    *Monica sets goals for each course, and she usually attains her goals.*

## Method 2: Use a Semicolon

*A semicolon can be used alone or with a transitional word or phrase to join independent clauses.* These transitional words and phrases are called conjunctive adverbs. **Conjunctive adverbs** are adverbs that *join.* As you can see in these examples, a semicolon comes before the conjunctive adverb, and a comma follows it.

Independent clause; therefore, independent clause.

Independent clause; however, independent clause.

Independent clause; consequently, independent clause.

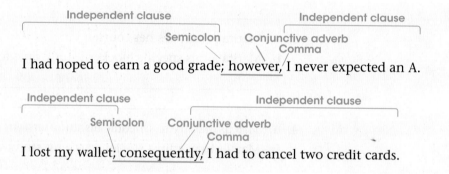

I had hoped to earn a good grade; however, I never expected an A.

I lost my wallet; consequently, I had to cancel two credit cards.

Use this method when the relationship between the two ideas is clear and requires no explanation. Be careful to choose the correct conjunctive adverb. Table 8-2 shows a list of conjunctive adverbs and their meanings.

| TABLE 8-2 CONJUNCTIVE ADVERBS AND THEIR MEANINGS | | |
|---|---|---|
| **Common Conjunctive Adverbs** | **Meaning** | **Example** |
| **as a result, therefore, consequently, thus, hence** | cause and effect | I am planning to become a nurse; *consequently,* I'm taking a lot of science courses. |
| **however, instead, nevertheless, nonetheless, otherwise, conversely** | differences or contrast | We had planned to go bowling; *however,* we went to hear music instead. |
| **further, furthermore, in addition, moreover, also** | addition; a continuation of the same idea | To save money I am packing my lunch; *also,* I am walking to school instead of taking the bus. |
| **similarly, likewise** | similarity | I left class as soon as I finished the exam; *likewise,* other students left. |
| **then, subsequently, next, finally, now, meanwhile,** | sequence in time | I walked home; *then* I massaged my aching feet. |

*Note:* If you join two independent clauses with only a comma and fail to use a coordinating conjunction or semicolon, you will produce a comma splice. If you join two independent clauses without using a punctuation mark and a coordinating conjunction, you will produce a run-on sentence. (See Chapter 6 for a review.)

## Tip for Writers

These words mean the same as **and**: *also, besides, furthermore,* and *in addition.* These mean the same as **but**: *however, nevertheless, on the other hand,* and *still.* These mean the same as **so** when it is used to introduce a result: *therefore, consequently,* and *as a result. Otherwise* and *unless* usually mean "if not."

## ! NEED TO KNOW

### How to Use Conjunctive Adverbs

Use a conjunctive adverb to join two equal ideas. Remember to put a semicolon before the conjunctive adverb and a comma after it. Here is a list of common conjunctive adverbs:

| also | in addition | otherwise |
| as a result | instead | similarly |
| besides | likewise | still |
| consequently | meanwhile | then |
| finally | nevertheless | therefore |
| further | next | thus |
| furthermore | now | undoubtedly |
| however | on the other hand | |

## EXERCISE 8-4    Completing Sentences

**Directions:** Complete each of the following sentences by adding a coordinating conjunction or a conjunctive adverb and the appropriate punctuation.    Answers will vary. Possible answers are shown.

    **EXAMPLE**    Teresa vacationed in Denver last year _____; similarly,_____ Jan will go to Denver this year.

1. Our professor did not complete the lecture _____, nor_____ did he give an assignment for the next class.

2. A first-aid kit was in her backpack ____; consequently,____ the hiker was able to treat her cut knee.

3. The opening act performed at the concert _____; next,_____ the headline band took the stage.

4. I always put a light on when I leave the house _____, and_____ I often turn on a radio to deter burglars.

5. Shania politely asked to borrow my car ____; furthermore,____ she thanked me when she returned it.

6. My roommate went to the library _____; therefore,_____ I had the apartment to myself.

7. Steve and Mario will go to a baseball game _____, or_____ they will go to a movie.

8. Mia looks like her father ____; however,____ her hair is darker and curlier than his.

9. Mi-Cha took a job at a bookstore ____; subsequently,____ she was offered a job at a museum.

10. Our neighbors bought a barbecue grill ____; likewise,____ we decided to buy one.

| EXERCISE 8-5 | Writing Compound Sentences |

**Directions:** Write five compound sentences about how you study for tests or how you spend your weekends. Each sentence should contain two complete thoughts. Join the thoughts by using a comma and a coordinating conjunction. Use a different coordinating conjunction in each sentence.

| EXERCISE 8-6 | Writing Using Compound Sentences |

**Directions:** Write a paragraph evaluating how well you manage your time. Use at least two compound sentences.

# Combine Ideas of Unequal Importance

■ GOAL 3

Combine ideas of unequal importance

Consider the following two simple sentences:

> Pete studies during his peak periods of attention.
>
> Pete accomplishes a great deal.

Reading these sentences, you may suspect that Pete accomplishes a great deal *because* he studies during peak periods of attention. With the sentences separated, however, that cause-and-effect relationship is only a guess. Combining the two sentences makes the relationship between the ideas clear.

> Because Pete studies during his peak periods of attention, he accomplishes a great deal.

Let's look at another pair of sentences:

> TaShayla analyzed her time commitments for the week.
>
> TaShayla developed a study plan for the week.

You may suspect that TaShayla developed the study plan *after* analyzing her time commitments. Combining the sentences makes the connection in time clear.

> After TaShayla analyzed her time commitments for the week, she developed a study plan.

In each of these examples, the two complete thoughts were combined so that one idea depended on the other. This process of combining ideas so that one idea is dependent on another is called **subordination.** *Sub-* means "below." Think of subordination as a way of combining an idea of lesser or lower importance with an idea of greater importance.

## Make Less Important Ideas Dependent on More Important Ones

Ideas of unequal importance can be combined by making the less important idea depend on the more important one. Notice how, in the following sentence, the part before the comma doesn't make sense without the part after the comma. If you read only the first half of the sentence, you will find yourself waiting for the idea to be completed, wondering what happened while Malcolm was

> While Malcolm was waiting for the bus, he studied psychology.

waiting. The word *while* (a subordinating conjunction) makes the meaning of the first half of the sentence incomplete by itself. Thus, the first half of the sentence is a *dependent clause*. It depends on the rest of the sentence to complete its thought. A dependent clause can never be a complete sentence. It must always be joined to an *independent clause* to make a complete thought. The dependent clause can go at the beginning, in the middle, or at the end of a sentence.

Use **subordinating conjunctions** to indicate how a less important idea—a dependent clause—relates to another, more important idea—an independent clause. (You can also use subordinating conjunctions to correct fragments.) Table 8-3 lists subordinating conjunctions that are commonly used to begin dependent clauses.

| TABLE 8-3 SUBORDINATING CONJUNCTIONS AND THEIR MEANINGS | | |
|---|---|---|
| **Subordinating Conjunction** | **Meaning** | **Example** |
| **before, after, while, during, until, when, once** | time | *When* you set time limits, you are working toward a goal. |
| **because, since, so that** | cause or effect | *Because* I felt rushed, I made careless errors. |
| **whether, if, unless, even if** | condition | *If* I finish studying before nine o'clock, I will read more of my mystery novel. |
| **as, as far as, as soon as, as long as, as if, as though, although, even though, even if, in order to** | circumstance | *Even if* I try to concentrate, I still am easily distracted. |

***Note:*** Relative pronouns (*who, whom, whose, that, which, whoever, whomever, whichever*) can also be used to show relationships and to join a dependent clause with an independent clause.

## Use Punctuation to Combine Dependent and Independent Clauses

When you combine a dependent clause with an independent clause and the dependent clause comes *first* in the sentence, use a comma to separate the clauses.

> Dependent clause    ,    Independent clause.

> Dependent clause      Comma   Independent clause
>
> When I follow a study schedule, I accomplish more.

When the dependent clause comes in the *middle* of the sentence, set it off with a *pair* of commas if the information is **not** essential to the meaning of the sentence. You can distinguish essential and nonessential clauses by using the following test. Remove the clause. If the meaning is not changed after removing it, it is not essential.

First part of independent clause , Dependent clause , Remainder of independent clause.

Subject of independent clause — Dependent clause — Remainder of independent clause
Comma — Comma

Malcolm, while he was waiting for a ride, studied psychology.

If the dependent clause is essential to the meaning of the sentence, do not use commas to set it apart.

First part of independent clause  Dependent clause  Remainder of independent clause

Subject of the independent clause — Dependent clause — Remainder of the independent clause

Those of us who did not attend the lecture on Tuesday were unprepared for the pop quiz on Thursday.

If the dependent clause comes at the *end* of the sentence, do not use a comma to separate it from the rest of the sentence.

Independent clause        Dependent clause.

Independent clause   No comma   Dependent clause

I accomplish more when I follow a study schedule.

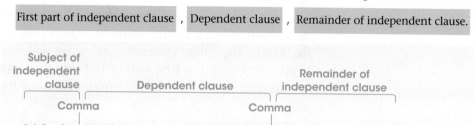

EXERCISE 8-7

# Adding Subordinating Conjunctions

**Directions:** For each of the following sentences, add a subordinating conjunction that makes the relationship between the two ideas clear. Try to use as many different subordinating conjunctions as possible.   Answers will vary.

**EXAMPLE**   _____When_____ I finish studying, I am mentally exhausted.

1. _____Because_____ math requires peak concentration, I always study it first.

2. _____When_____ Andres starts to lose concentration, he takes a short break.

3. Julia never stops in the middle of an assignment _____unless_____ she is too tired to finish.

4. _____Since_____ she likes to wake up slowly, Shannon sets her alarm for ten minutes before she needs to get up.

5. _____After_____ Sofia took a five-minute study break, she felt more energetic.

6. Alan worked on his math homework _____*while*_____ he did the laundry.

7. _____*Even if*_____ Jamille increases his study time, he may not earn the grades he hopes to receive.

8. _____*Once*_____ Marsha completes an assignment, she crosses it off her "To do" list.

9. _____*Since*_____ Robert did not know when he wasted time, he kept a log of his activities for three days.

10. _____*So that*_____ noises and conversation do not interfere with my concentration, I wear a headset with soft music playing.

---

**EXERCISE 8-8**    ## Completing Sentences

**Directions:** Make each of the following sentences complete by adding a complete thought. Be sure the meaning fits the subordinating conjunction used in the sentence.    *Answers will vary. Possible answers are shown.*

> **EXAMPLE**    *I edited my essay*_____ while the ideas were fresh in my mind.

1. *I fed my fish*_____

   **after** I finished studying.

2. **Because** my job is part-time, *I can work on my journal every day.*_____

3. **Once** I finish college, *I am going to join the Peace Corps.*_____

4. *The accident occurred*_____

   **when** I was not concentrating.

5. **If you schedule blocks of study time,** *you will accomplish more.*_____

6. *I forget my own birthday*_____

   **unless** I carry a pocket planner.

7. **Although** English is my favorite subject, *I do think 7 a.m. is too early for the class to meet.*_____

8. *There is no mystery I cannot solve,*_____

   **as far as** I can tell.

9. **Even if** I finish by eight o'clock, *there is no way I can get to the concert on time.*_____

10. **As soon as** I decide what to do, *I will tell you.*_____

**EXERCISE 8-9** Combining Sentences

**Directions:** Combine each of the following pairs of sentences by using a subordinating conjunction and a comma. Try to vary the position of the dependent clause (first or last). Change punctuation, capitalization, and words as necessary. You may wish to refer to the list of subordinating conjunctions on page 245.   *Answers will vary.*

**EXAMPLE** **a.** Yi-Min is taking voice lessons.

**b.** Yi-Min always sings scales in the shower.

*Because Yi-Min is taking voice lessons, she always sings scales in the shower.*

1. **a.** Christine has a six-month-old child.
   **b.** She must study while the baby sleeps.

   *Since Christine has a six-month-old child, she must study while the baby sleeps.*

2. **a.** Taj is often distracted by stray thoughts.
   **b.** Taj jots stray thoughts on a notepad to clear them from his mind.

   *Because Taj is often distracted by stray thoughts, he jots them down in a notepad to clear them from his mind.*

3. **a.** Gary finished a difficult biology assignment.
   **b.** He rewarded himself by ordering a pizza.

   *Gary ordered a pizza as a reward because he had just finished a difficult biology assignment.*

4. **a.** It takes Anthony 45 minutes to drive to school.
   **b.** Anthony records lectures and listens while he drives.

   *Because it takes Anthony 45 minutes to drive to school, he records lectures and listens while he drives.*

5. **a.** Ada felt disorganized.
   **b.** Ada made a priority list of assignments and due dates.

   *Ada made a list of assignments and due dates because she felt disorganized.*

6. **a.** Juanita walked from her history class to her math class.
   **b.** She observed the brilliant fall foliage.

   *As Juanita walked from her history class to her math class, she observed the brilliant fall foliage.*

7. **a.** Kevin skipped meals and ate junk food.
   **b.** Kevin signed up for a cooking class.

   *Rather than skip meals and eat junk food, Kevin signed up for a cooking class.*

8. **a.** Lian joined the soccer team.
   **b.** Lian became the first woman to do so.

   *When Lian joined the soccer team, she became the first woman to do so.*

9. **a.** John ate dinner on Saturday night.
   **b.** John reviewed his plans for the week with his less-than-fascinated date.

   *During dinner on Saturday night, John reviewed his plans for the week with his less-than-fascinated date.*

10. **a.** Frank waited for his history class to begin.
    **b.** He wondered if he was in the right room.

    *While Frank waited for his history class to begin, he wondered if he was in the right room.*

---

**EXERCISE 8-10**

*WORKING TOGETHER*

## Writing Complex Sentences

**Directions:** Working with a classmate, write ten complex sentences on a subject that interests both of you. Each must contain one dependent clause and one independent clause. Use a comma to separate the clauses when the dependent clause comes first. Use two commas to set off a dependent clause in the middle of the sentence. You do not need a comma when the dependent clause comes last.

---

**EXERCISE 8-11**

## Writing Complex Sentences

**Directions:** Write a paragraph on one of the following topics. Include at least two complex sentences.

1. Planning a summer vacation
2. Shopping online
3. Visiting a theme park
4. Advantages or disadvantages of credit cards
5. A favorite possession or a favorite piece of clothing

---

# Write Compound–Complex Sentences

■ **GOAL 4**

Write compound–complex sentences

A **compound–complex sentence** is made up of two or more independent clauses and one or more dependent clauses. This type of sentence is often used to express complicated relationships. Look at the following examples of compound–complex sentences.

■ Here, a dependent clause is followed by two independent clauses:

| Dependent clause | Independent clause |
|---|---|

Even though Marsha needed to be better organized, she avoided weekly

| Independent clause |
|---|

study plans, and she ended up wasting valuable time.

■ Here, an independent clause containing a dependent clause is followed by a second independent clause with a dependent clause:

| First part of independent clause | Dependent clause | Remainder of independent clause |
|---|---|---|

The new students, who had just arrived, wanted a tour of the town;

| Independent clause | Dependent clause |
|---|---|

Lamar told them that he had no time because of his new work schedule.

■ Here, the sentence is made up of a dependent clause, an independent clause containing a dependent clause, and another independent clause:

| | Independent clause |
|---|---|
| Dependent clause | Dependent clause |

Although Amanda changed her work schedule, she found that she

| | Independent clause |
|---|---|

still needed more time to study, and she ended up quitting her job.

Refer to page 245 to determine when to and when not to use commas to set apart a dependent clause that falls within an independent clause.

The key to writing effective and correct compound–complex sentences is to link each clause in the correct way to the one that follows it. The rules you have already learned in this chapter apply. For example, if you have two independent clauses followed by a dependent clause, link the two independent clauses as you would in a compound sentence by using a comma and a coordinating conjunction. Then link the second independent clause to the dependent clause by using a subordinating conjunction.

| Independent clause | Independent clause | Dependent clause |
|---|---|---|

I got up early, and I left the house before rush hour because I wanted to be

on time for my interview.

---

**EXERCISE 8-12**   ## Adding Conjunctions

**Directions:** Each of the following sentences is made up of at least three clauses. Read each sentence, and then make it correct by adding the necessary subordinating and/or coordinating conjunctions in the blanks.   *Answers will vary.*

**EXAMPLE** _____Because_____ they both got home from work late, Ted grilled hamburgers _____while_____ Alexa made a salad.

1. _____Because_____ Sarah's sociology class required class discussion of the readings, she scheduled time to review sociology before each class meeting _____so that_____ she would have the material fresh in her mind.

2. _____Although_____ making a "To do" list takes time, Deka found that the list actually saved her time, _____for_____ she accomplished more when she sat down to study.

3. _____When_____ Terry's history lecture was over, he reviewed his notes, _____and_____ when he discovered any gaps, he was usually able to recall the information.

4. Many students have discovered that distributing their studying over several evenings is more effective than studying in one large block of time _____because_____ it gives them several exposures to the material, _____and_____ they feel less pressured.

5. We have tickets for the concert, _____but_____ we may not go _____because_____ Jeff has a bad cold.

---

**EXERCISE 8-13**

# Writing a Compound–Complex Sentence

**Directions:** Write a compound–complex sentence, and then label its dependent and independent clauses.

---

# READING

# Identify Meaning Clues from Sentence Structure

■ **GOAL 5**

Identify meaning clues from sentence structure

The manner in which a writer structures a sentence provides clues to you as a reader about the relative importance of ideas and about how ideas are related.

## Clues from Sentence Type

Here is a summary of the meaning clues different types of sentences provide.

> ### ! NEED TO KNOW

| TYPE OF SENTENCE | MEANING CLUES |
|---|---|
| Simple Sentence | There is only one important idea. Other words and phrases may explain or provide more information. |
| Compound Sentence | There are two or more important ideas. Both or all are equally important. The ideas are also closely related; determine why the writer decided to put them together in the same sentence. |
| Complex Sentence | There is one most important idea and one or more related, but less important ideas. The less important ideas in some way explain or clarify the more important one. Try to discover how the ideas are related. |
| Compound–Complex Sentence | There are two or more important ideas and one or more less important ideas. The relationship is often complicated. Study it closely to see how all the ideas are related. |

## Clues from Connecting Words

As you learned earlier in the chapter, a coordinating conjunction, along with a comma, can join two independent clauses. A subordinating conjunction, along with a comma, joins an independent clause with a dependent one. The coordinating or subordinating conjunctions writers choose offer important clues to how two ideas are related. A coordinating conjunction can suggest addition, contrast, causes, effects, or alternatives. (See the box on p. 239.) Subordinating conjunctions can suggest time sequence, cause or effect, condition, or circumstance. (See the box on p. 245 for a review of these meaning clues.)

Conjunctive adverbs (p. 242) also can join two equally important ideas, along with a semicolon. These words are important signals to the relationship of ideas. They may suggest cause and effect, differences or contrast, continuation, or sequence. Think of all these words as signals—words that signal to the reader the relationship between the ideas.

---

| EXERCISE 8-14 | Using Clues from Sentence Structure |

**Directions:** Read each of the following sentences. In the space provided, describe how the underlined idea is related to the rest of the sentence. For example, does it *give a reason, indicate time, explain a condition or circumstance, present an opposite idea, or offer alternatives?*

1. I will probably transfer to a four-year college next year <u>unless I find a good job.</u>

    *condition*

2. <u>Although I broke my leg,</u> I am still able to drive a car.

    *opposite idea / circumstance*

3. She must find a roommate <u>or she will be forced to live at home next semester.</u>

    *alternative*

4. She always checks her e-mail <u>after she eats lunch.</u>

    *time*

5. He would have offered to pick us up at the airport, <u>but his car was in the shop.</u>

    *opposite idea*

6. <u>Since the corporation is community oriented,</u> it donates large amounts to local causes.

    *reason*

7. <u>Because of the high cost of gas,</u> many people find it too expensive to travel.

    *reason*

8. <u>As far as scientists can tell from available research,</u> some types of cancer may be caused by a virus.

    *condition*

9. <u>Because a vaccine was developed</u>, polio has practically been eliminated.

   *reason*

10. <u>Since comparison shopping is a necessary part of the buying process</u>, wise consumers look for differences in quality as well as price.

    *reason*

# INTEGRATING READING AND WRITING

## READ AND REVISE

**MySkillsLab®**

**Complete** this Exercise

The following excerpt is from a student essay called "A Victim of Circumstance." This excerpt contains errors that were subsequently corrected in another draft. Revise the excerpt by adding coordinating conjunctions, conjunctive adverbs, or subordinating conjunctions where appropriate. Change punctuation as necessary. **This exercise can be completed online at MySkillsLab.**

I was a victim, a victim of circumstance. *, and* I was introduced to this life as a small child. I was the baby out of ten children, five boys and five girls. I watched my parents work for little or nothing. *; my* ~~My~~ mom worked odd jobs as a CNA, a waitress, and a short order cook. My dad worked in a restaurant for as little as two dollars and fifty cents per hour. *, but he* ~~He~~ did earn small tips that helped a little. *Although there* ~~There~~ were many hardships. *he* ~~He~~ never complained. My mom and dad would come home, their feet would be swollen. *; they* ~~They~~ would have burns on their arms. *, but they* ~~They~~ still did not have enough money to feed the family. Often I would think, "It's going to be another long night of hunger. *or* ~~Or~~ maybe just peanut butter on a spoon.

I watched this same scene repeat itself over and over again until I was about thirteen years old. That's when my life became almost the same as theirs. I was speaking with one of my closest friends, *and* I trusted her deeply. I described to her my life and the situations I faced. I told her I faced them every day. It was at that moment she told me that her mother owned a farm. People under the age of sixteen were allowed to work there. They were paid minimum wage. *, but they* ~~They~~ were allowed to take home second-day old produce. They could also take produce that was spotted or not top quality. I thought to myself, "Yes! I can help my parents feed my brothers and sisters now."

## READ AND RESPOND: A Student Essay

*Yuliya Seitkulova submitted this essay to the Writing Rewards Essay Contest sponsored by Pearson Education. When she wrote the essay, she was a student at Pikes Peak Community College in Colorado. The assignment she responded to directed her to write an essay describing a significant childhood experience.*

Title identifies the subject of the essay

Black Friday is the day after Thanksgiving when stores offer major discounts and attract huge crowds

Topic sentence

Background information about writer and history

Topic sentence

Topic sentence

Examples add interest

Key idea

# Freedom to Buy Candy

On November twenty-sixth, when it was Black Friday, I knew it was the worst day to be shopping. When I pulled up to the store and saw a long line of people stretched along the sidewalk waiting to enter the store, I realized how lucky I am to be living in this country at this time. People have the freedom to go to the store anytime they want and buy any item they can afford. For me life was not always that easy. I looked at the long line of people, and it triggered a memory of my childhood, a time in my life when I did not have the freedoms that these people enjoy, a time when I did not have the freedom to buy candy.

I was ten-year-old girl living in a new country by the name of Kazakhstan. Kazakhstan was, in fact, an old country; however, it had been taken over by the Russians long before I was born. I was raised under the iron fist of communism. For the first ten years of my life the U.S.S.R. was my country. At that time, I knew no other form of government other than communism, and I knew of my country as Mother Russia. Yet everything changed for me that year. That was the year that the Berlin wall came down; communism was no longer our way of life, and I now lived in a country called Kazakhstan. The U.S.S.R. had split up. At the time, I didn't understand or pay attention to politics. I wasn't able to comprehend the importance of what was going on at that time. All that was important for me was that I had to stand in line for hours just to be able to buy some candy.

With the collapse of communism, also came the collapse of our economic system. All of the food and goods had to be rationed. We would receive a piece of paper in the mail from the government every month telling us what we were allowed to receive at the store for that month. The items that we could get would change from month to month. One month it might be flour, bread, chicken, and tea, and then the next month it might be corn, beef, coffee, and tomatoes. This month was a very special one because this month on the list was candy. The day after we received our voucher from the government, my mother and I woke up very early in the morning and went to the store. We had to make sure that we arrived early so that we would be guaranteed to get our items before they ran out. If the store did run out of a product, then you were simply out of luck for that month.

Descriptive details

When we turned into the street that leads to the store, we saw that there was already a long line of people waiting to get in. I wondered to myself whether some of them had slept on the streets overnight. I saw blankets wrapped around some of the people who were at the front of the line. I worried that there wouldn't be any candy left for us by the time we entered the store. My mother assured me that even though we were not at the front of the line, we had still arrived early enough to be able to get all of the items on our list, including candy. This alleviated my fears some, but I knew that I would still worry until the candy was actually in my hands.

Topic sentence

Details explain sequence of events and build interest

It was close to noon by the time we reached the front of the store. The uniformed man who was standing guard checked our papers to make sure that they were legitimate. Once he determined that the vouchers were real, we were allowed to enter the store. I ran straight for the candy section. My heart beat with excitement and trepidation. My eyes lit up as I finally reached the candy aisle and I saw that there was still plenty of candy to choose from. I snatched up three bags of my favorite candies. I knew that we were only allowed to take two of the bags, but I simply couldn't decide. With three bags of candy in my arms, I roamed the store until I found my mother. My mother made me choose which two bags of candy I wanted to keep, so with great reluctance, I finally made my choice and put two of the bags in the cart. We finished our shopping and made our way to the cashier, and then exited the store.

Descriptive details

When we emerged from the store, my mother rummaged through the bags of food and pulled out one of the bags of candy. She opened it and gave me one piece of candy. I eagerly unwrapped the sweet and popped it into my mouth. To this day, I believe that it was the best piece of candy that I have ever eaten.

Topic sentence

Her thesis connects her candy experience to larger idea of freedom

As I look back on that time of my life, I am able to put it all into perspective. At the time I didn't understand the significance of what was happening in the world. All that I knew and understood was that I didn't like being told what I could buy and when I could buy it. If I had the money to buy a piece of candy, then I felt like I should be able to go to the store and do so. All of the countries that made the former Soviet Union had to go through these hard times as they became independent. New governments, economic systems, and social structures were formed during these times. It was a painful process that took time, patience, and hard work. I hear the history of early America and realize that they also had to go through the same birth and growing pangs. Now every one of those countries is better than they were before. The key to their success was freedom: freedom from an oppressive government, freedom for the individual person to make their own choices in life, freedom to go to the store when they want to and buy a piece of candy.

## Examining Writing

1. Reread Seitkulova's introduction and conclusion. How does she capture your attention and draw you into the essay? How does she tie the introduction and conclusion together?

2. What types of details does Seitkulova use in her narrative? Highlight words and details that help you imagine and understand her description of her childhood memory.

3. Evaluate Seitkulova's sentence structure throughout this essay. Where might she have used coordinating conjunctions, conjunctive adverbs, or subordinating conjunctions to combine ideas?

4. How does Seitkulova's experience as a child compare to your own childhood? What similarities and differences can you see based on this essay?

## READ AND RESPOND: A Professional Essay

### Thinking Before Reading

In this selection from *Newsweek* magazine, Leticia Salais writes about how she changed her mind and decided to embrace her native language in "Saying 'Adios' to Spanglish." As you read, pay attention to the organization of the essay and to the reasons Salais gives for her decision.

1. Preview the reading, using the steps discussed in Chapter 1 on page 25.

2. Connect the reading to your own experience by answering the following questions:

   a. Has your ethnic background or cultural heritage played an important role in your own life?

   b. When you were younger, did you want to change anything about the circumstances in which you grew up?

   c. Mark and annotate as you read.

**adios**
Spanish for goodbye

**Spanglish**
an informal language that combines Spanish and English

950*L*/841 words

# Saying 'Adios' to Spanglish
## Leticia Salais

*Growing up, I wanted nothing to do with my heritage. My kids made me see how wrong that was.*

1    *Niños, vengan a comer.* My 18-month-old son pops out from behind the couch and runs to his high chair. My 7-year-old has no idea what I just said. He yells out from the same hiding spot: "What did you say?" My older son does not suffer from hearing loss. He is simply not bilingual like his brother, and did not understand that I was telling him to come eat.

2    Growing up in the poorest neighborhoods of El Paso, Texas, I did everything I could to escape the poverty and the color of my skin. I ran around with kids from the west side of town who came from more affluent families and usually didn't speak a word of Spanish. I spoke Spanish well enough, but I pretended not to understand it and would not speak a word of it. In school, I refused to speak Spanish even with my Hispanic friends. I wanted nothing to do with it. While they joined Chicano clubs, all I wanted to do was be in the English literacy club. Even

at home, the only person to whom I spoke Spanish was my mom, and that's only because she wouldn't have understood me otherwise.

3    After I got married and moved to Tucson, Ariz., I thought I was in heaven. Though I was actually in the minority, I felt right at home with my **Anglo** neighbors. When I got pregnant with my first son, I decided that English would be his first language and, if I could help it, his only language. I never spoke a word of Spanish around him, and when his grandparents asked why he did not understand what they were saying, I made excuses. He understands but he's very shy. He understands the language but he refuses to speak it. In reality, I didn't want him to speak it at all.

**Anglo**
a white American of non-Hispanic descent

4    In a land of opportunity, I soon realized I had made a big mistake. I was denying my son one of the greatest gifts I had to offer: the ability to be bilingual. I saw the need for interpreters on a daily basis in the health field where I worked. Even trips to the grocery store often turned into an opportunity to help someone who could not understand English or vice versa.

5    In the nursing home where I worked, I met a wonderful group of Spanish-speaking individuals, whom I bonded with right away. I longed to speak like they did, enunciating the words correctly as they rolled off their tongues. It sounded like music to me. I started watching Spanish **telenovelas** and listening to Spanish morning shows on the radio just to improve my vocabulary. I heard words that had never been uttered around me growing up in a border town where people spoke a mixture of Spanish and English. A co-worker from Peru had the most eloquent way of speaking in a language that I recognized as Spanish yet could not fully comprehend. Did I also cheat myself of being bilingual?

**telenovelas**
Spanish soap operas on television

6    Today I can take any English word and, like magic, easily find its Spanish equivalent. I now live a life that is fully bilingual. I hunger for foreign movies from Spain and the interior of Mexico just to challenge myself by trying to guess what all the words mean. I even surprise my mom when she doesn't understand what I'm saying. I know she is proud that I no longer speak Spanglish, and I am no longer embarrassed to speak Spanish in public. I see it as a secret language my husband and I share when we don't want those around us to understand what we are saying. I quickly offer the use of my gift when I see someone struggling to speak English or to understand Spanish, and I quietly say a prayer of thanks that I am not in his or her shoes. I feel empowered and blessed that I can understand a conversation in another language and quickly translate it in my head.

7    My second son has benefited from my bilingual tongue. I speak only Spanish to him while my husband speaks only English; I am proud to say that his first language was Spanish. My 7-year-old, on the other hand, still has a way to go. I'm embarrassed that I foolishly kept my beautiful native language from him. I hope I have not done irreversible damage. A couple of years ago, I began speaking to him only in Spanish, but I had not yet heard him utter a complete sentence back.

8    Then, as if my prayers were answered, from behind the couch, I heard a tiny voice exclaim, *Ven, mira esto*. It was my older son instructing his little brother to come look at what he was doing. Maybe I won't be his first bilingual teacher, but it looks like he's already learning from another expert—his bilingual brother. Maybe it's not too late after all.

## Getting Ready to Write

### Checking Your Comprehension

Answer each of the following questions using complete sentences.

1. Where did the author grow up?

   *in the poorest neighborhoods of El Paso, Texas*

2. List three examples of how the author tried to escape her heritage while she was growing up.

   *She chose friends from affluent, non-Hispanic families; she pretended not to understand*

   *Spanish and would not speak it; she joined the English literacy club rather than Chicano clubs;*

   *at home she spoke Spanish only to her mother.*

3. How did the author feel about her first son learning Spanish?

   *She wanted English to be his first and only language.*

4. How did the author improve her Spanish?

   *She started watching Spanish telenovelas and listening to Spanish radio shows.*

5. How are the author and her husband teaching their second son to be bilingual?

   *She speaks to him only in Spanish and her husband speaks to him only in English.*

### Strengthening Your Vocabulary

Using the word's context, word parts, or a dictionary, write a brief definition of each of the following words as it is used in the reading.

1. bilingual (paragraph 1) _____ *able to speak two languages fluently*
2. affluent (paragraph 2) _____ *wealthy*
3. bonded (paragraph 5) _____ *became emotionally attached; formed a friendship with*
4. enunciating (paragraph 5) _____ *pronouncing clearly or carefully*
5. eloquent (paragraph 5) _____ *expressive, well-spoken*
6. empowered (paragraph 6) _____ *enabled or permitted*
7. irreversible (paragraph 7) _____ *impossible to reverse or undo; permanent*

## Examining the Reading: Using Idea Maps

Review the reading by completing the missing parts of the following idea map.

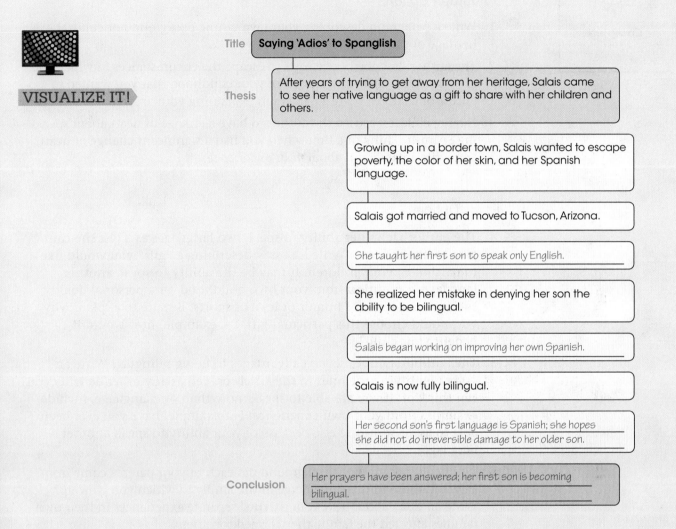

**VISUALIZE IT!**

Title — Saying 'Adios' to Spanglish

Thesis — After years of trying to get away from her heritage, Salais came to see her native language as a gift to share with her children and others.

Growing up in a border town, Salais wanted to escape poverty, the color of her skin, and her Spanish language.

Salais got married and moved to Tucson, Arizona.

She taught her first son to speak only English.

She realized her mistake in denying her son the ability to be bilingual.

Salais began working on improving her own Spanish.

Salais is now fully bilingual.

Her second son's first language is Spanish; she hopes she did not do irreversible damage to her older son.

Conclusion — Her prayers have been answered; her first son is becoming bilingual.

## Thinking Critically: Discussion and Journal Writing

React and respond to the reading by discussing the following:

1. What is the author's purpose for writing this article?

2. Why did the author think she was "in heaven" when she moved to Arizona?

3. Why did the author feel like she had to make excuses about her son not speaking Spanish?

4. Why was the author's mother proud when her daughter no longer spoke Spanglish?

5. How did the author come to view her bilingual ability as a gift? In what ways does she share her gift outside of her family?

**THINKING VISUALLY**

6. What does the photograph add to the reading? What other photographs might have been more interesting or informative?

## Writing About the Reading

### Paragraph Options

1. Write a paragraph describing your own ethnic background or cultural heritage or that of someone you know.

2. The author described her efforts to escape the circumstances in which she grew up. Were there any aspects of your childhood that you wanted to escape or change? Write a paragraph explaining your answer.

3. Having children caused the author to have a change of heart about speaking Spanish. Think of a time when you had a significant change of heart, and write a paragraph about your experience.

### Essay Options

4. The author views her ability to speak two languages as a gift she can give to her children. Write an essay describing a "gift" you would like to pass on to your children. It may be the ability to speak another language, a tradition from your own childhood, or a personal quality such as your sense of humor or love of sports. Be sure to explain why you would choose this particular gift; for example, how would it benefit your child?

5. The author describes several advantages to being bilingual. Write an essay identifying the ones in the article as well as any other benefits you can think of. If you are able to speak more than one language, include examples from your own experience. For example, have you ever been able to assist someone else because of your ability to speak another language?

6. What cultural or ethnic background did each of your parents come from? How did those influences emerge in the family in which you grew up? Write an essay about how your parents' separate experiences in their own families affected the family they formed together.

# SELF-TEST SUMMARY

To test yourself, cover the Answer column with a sheet of paper and answer each question in the left column. Evaluate each of your answers as you work by sliding the paper down and comparing your answer with what is printed in the answer column.

| QUESTION | ANSWER |
|---|---|
| ■ **GOAL 1** Recognize independent and dependent clauses<br><br>What is the difference between independent and dependent clauses? | An *independent clause* can stand alone as a sentence. A *dependent clause* does not express a complete thought. It must be joined to an independent clause to make a complete sentence. |
| ■ **GOAL 2** Combine ideas of equal importance<br><br>What are two ways to combine independent clauses? | 1. Join two independent clauses by using a comma and a coordinating conjunction.<br>2. Join two independent clauses by using a semicolon, with or without a conjunctive adverb. |
| ■ **GOAL 3** Combine ideas of unequal importance<br><br>What is subordination? | Subordination is the process of using subordinating conjunctions to combine ideas so that an idea of lesser importance is dependent on an idea of greater importance. |
| ■ **GOAL 4** Write compound–complex sentences<br><br>What is a compound–complex sentence? | A compound–complex sentence has two or more independent clauses combined with one or more dependent clauses. |
| ■ **GOAL 5** Identify meaning clues from sentence structure<br><br>How do writers provide clues about meaning? | Writers provide clues about the relative importance of ideas and how ideas are related through sentence type (*simple, compound, complex,* or *compound–complex*) and through connecting words (*coordinating conjunctions, subordinating conjunctions,* and *conjunctive adverbs*). |

# MySkillsLab

For more help with **Combining and Expanding Your Ideas**, go to your learning path in MySkillsLab at http://www.myskillslab.com.

# Revising Confusing and Inconsistent Sentences

## THINK About It!

The situation shown in the photo seems "not right." Inconsistencies in your writing can also make it seem "not right" or confusing. Here are a few examples from a book titled *Anguished English* by Richard Lederer that show how errors create confusion and sometimes unintentional humor.

■ We do not tear your clothing with machinery. We do it carefully by hand.

■ Have several very old dresses from grandmother in beautiful condition.

■ Tired of cleaning yourself? Let me do it.

Sometimes sentence errors create unintentional humor, as in Lederer's examples. Most often, though, they distract or confuse your reader. They may also convey the impression that you have not taken time to check and polish your work. In this chapter you will learn to avoid several common types of sentence errors. You will also learn how to handle difficult or confusing sentences as you read.

# What Is a Confusing or Inconsistent Sentence?

A **confusing or inconsistent sentence** is one in which the meaning is unclear. Usually, the confusion is unintentional. That is, the writer did not realize that information is missing or that several possible interpretations are possible. As a writer, you will learn to avoid common inconsistencies and confusions. As a reader, you will learn how to decipher the meaning of long and difficult sentences.

## WRITING

# Use Pronouns Clearly and Correctly

■ **GOAL 1**
Use pronouns clearly and correctly

A **pronoun** is a word that substitutes for, or refers to, a noun or another pronoun. *I, you, he, she, it, we, they, his, mine, yours, who,* and *whom* are all examples of pronouns. The noun or pronoun to which a pronoun refers is called the pronoun's **antecedent**. To use pronouns correctly, you need to make sure that the antecedent of the pronoun—the word to which the pronoun refers—is clear to your reader and that the pronoun and antecedent agree in number (singular or plural) and in gender.

## Pronoun Reference

If your pronoun reference is unclear, your sentence may be confusing and difficult to follow. Note the confusing nature of the following sentences:

> The aerobics instructor told the student that *she* made a mistake.
> [Who made the mistake?]
>
> *They* told Kevin that he was eligible for a Visa card. [Who told Kevin?]
>
> Aaron bought a bowling ball at the garage sale *that* he enjoyed.
> [Did Aaron enjoy the garage sale or the bowling ball?]

The following suggestions will help you make sure that all your pronoun references are clear:

■ **Make sure there is only one possible antecedent for each pronoun.** The antecedent (the word to which the pronoun refers) should come before the pronoun (*ante-* means "before") in the sentence. The reader should not be left wondering what the antecedent of any given pronoun is.

> UNCLEAR    The father told the child that *he* was sunburned.
>
> REVISED    The father told the child, "I am sunburned."

■ **Avoid using vague pronouns that lack an antecedent.** *They* and *it* are often mistakenly used this way.

> UNCLEAR    *They* told me my loan application needs a cosigner.
>
> REVISED    The loan officer told me my loan application needs a cosigner.

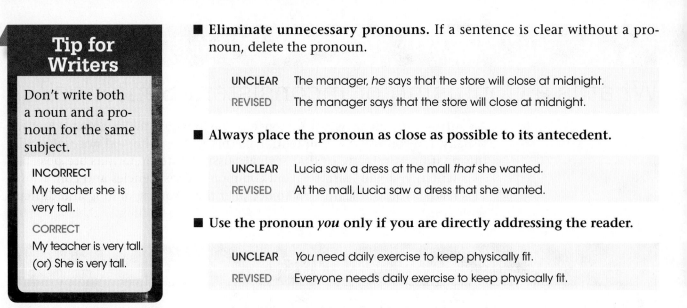

**Tip for Writers**

Don't write both a noun and a pronoun for the same subject.

INCORRECT

My teacher she is very tall.

CORRECT

My teacher is very tall. (or) She is very tall.

■ **Eliminate unnecessary pronouns.** If a sentence is clear without a pronoun, delete the pronoun.

UNCLEAR    The manager, *he* says that the store will close at midnight.

REVISED    The manager says that the store will close at midnight.

■ **Always place the pronoun as close as possible to its antecedent.**

UNCLEAR    Lucia saw a dress at the mall *that* she wanted.

REVISED    At the mall, Lucia saw a dress that she wanted.

■ **Use the pronoun *you* only if you are directly addressing the reader.**

UNCLEAR    *You* need daily exercise to keep physically fit.

REVISED    Everyone needs daily exercise to keep physically fit.

---

**EXERCISE 9-1**

## Correcting Pronoun Reference Errors

**Directions:** Revise each of the following sentences to correct problems in pronoun reference.   Answers will vary.

**EXAMPLE**   The glass, ~~it~~ ^was^ filled to the rim.

1. ~~One~~ ^You^ should try to be honest, so you do not get caught telling lies.
2. When I bought the shirt, I told ~~him~~ ^the sales clerk^ that I would pay with my credit card.
3. Jamal told Rob, ~~he had~~ ^"I^ received an A in the course.^"^
4. James ~~talked with Bill because he~~ did not know anyone else at the party. ^, so he talked with Bill^
5. The teachers told the school board members, ~~that they needed more preparation time~~. ^"We need more preparation time."^
6. The board of directors/ ~~they~~ decided that the company would have to declare bankruptcy.
7. The gallery owner hung a painting ^that was blue^ on the wall ~~that was blue~~.
8. ~~They~~ ^The registrar^ sent our grades at the end of the semester.
9. The Constitution says ~~you have~~ ^everyone has^ the right to bear arms.
10. ~~They~~ ^Antique cars^ filled the parking lot on Sunday.

---

**EXERCISE 9-2**

## Revising Sentences

**Directions:** Revise each of the following sentences to correct problems in pronoun reference. If a sentence contains no errors, write *Correct* beside it.
Answers will vary.

**EXAMPLE**   ~~It~~ ^The professor's note^ said that the grades would be posted on Tuesday.

_____ 1. ~~On~~ the bulletin board ^A notice on^ ~~it~~ says there will be a fire drill today.

_____ 2. Laverne and Louise ~~they~~ pooled their money to buy a new CD player.

_____ 3. ~~They~~ said on the news that the naval base will be shut down.
              *The reporter*

_Correct_ 4. The street that was recently widened is where I used to live.

_____ 5. Ivan sat on the couch ~~in the living room~~ that he bought yesterday.
            *in the living room*

_Correct_ 6. "Sarah," the tutor advised, "you should underline in your textbooks for better comprehension."

_____ 7. Christina handed ~~Maggie~~ the plate she had bought at the flea market.
                                *to Maggie*

_____ 8. Bridget found the cake mix ~~in the aisle with the baking supplies~~ that she needed for tonight's dessert.
                *in the aisle with the baking supplies*

_____ 9. Rick told Larry, he was right.
                     "I      "

_____ 10. ~~It said in~~ the letter ~~that~~ my payment was late.
      *According to*

---

| EXERCISE 9-3 | # Writing a Paragraph |
| --- | --- |
| **WRITING IN PROGRESS** | **Directions:** Write a paragraph on one of the following topics. After you have written your first draft, reread it to be certain your pronoun references are clear. Make corrections if needed. |

1. A recent clothing fad

2. Advice columns

3. Horoscopes

4. Remembering names

5. An extreme weather condition (heat wave, storm, blizzard, flood) that you lived through

---

## Pronoun–Antecedent Agreement

A pronoun must "agree" with its antecedent—that is, a pronoun must have the same number (singular or plural) as the noun or pronoun it refers to or replaces. Singular nouns and pronouns refer to one person, place, or thing; plural nouns and pronouns refer to more than one.

Always check your sentences for pronoun–antecedent agreement.

|  |  |
| --- | --- |
|  |     Plural    Singular |
| INCORRECT | The dogs are in its kennels. |
| CORRECT | The dogs are in their kennels. |
|  |     Plural        Singular |
| INCORRECT | Marcia and Megan called all her friends about the party. |
| CORRECT | Marcia and Megan called all their friends about the party. |

Use the following guidelines to make sure the pronouns you use agree with their antecedents:

■ **Use singular pronouns with singular nouns.**

> Singular noun   Singular pronoun
>
> Teresa sold her bicycle.

■ **Use plural pronouns with plural nouns.**

> Plural noun        Plural pronoun
>
> The neighbors always shovel their walks when it snows.

■ **Use a plural pronoun to refer to a compound antecedent joined by *and* unless both parts of the compound refer to the same person, place, or thing.**

> Plural antecedent        Plural pronoun
>
> Demond and Keith bought their concert tickets.

> Singular antecedent    Singular pronoun
>
> The pitcher and team captain broke her ankle.

■ **When antecedents are joined by *or, nor, either . . . or, neither . . . nor, not . . . but,* or *not only . . . but also,* the pronoun agrees in number with the nearer antecedent.**

> Plural noun            Plural pronoun
>
> Either the professor or the students will present their views.

*Note:* When one antecedent is singular and the other is plural, avoid awkwardness by placing the plural antecedent second in the sentence.

| | |
|---|---|
| AWKWARD | Neither the salespersons nor the manager has received his check. |
| REVISED | Neither the manager nor the salespersons have received their checks. |

■ **Avoid using *he, him,* or *his* to refer to general, singular words such as *child, person, everyone.*** These words exclude females. Use *he or she, him or her,* or *his or hers,* or rewrite your sentence to use a plural antecedent and a plural pronoun that do not indicate gender.

| | |
|---|---|
| INCORRECT | A person should not deceive his friends. |
| REVISED | A person should not deceive his or her friends. |
| BETTER | People should not deceive their friends. |

■ **With collective nouns (words that refer to a group of people such as** *army, class, congregation, audience*), **use a singular pronoun to refer to the noun when the group acts as a unit.**

> The audience showed its approval by applauding.
>
> The team chose its captain.

Use a plural pronoun to refer to the noun when each member of the group acts individually.

> The family exchanged their gifts.
>
> The team changed their uniforms.

To avoid using a plural verb or pronoun after a collective noun, write "the members of the team," which gives you a plural subject (members).

---

**EXERCISE 9-4**    ## Correcting Agreement Errors

**Directions:** Revise each of the following sentences to correct errors in pronoun-antecedent agreement.

**EXAMPLE**    Usually when a driver has been caught speeding, ~~they~~ *he or she* readily admit the mistake.

1. Each gas station in town raised ~~their~~ *its* prices in the past week.

2. Neither the waitress nor the hostess received ~~their~~ *her* paycheck from the restaurant.

3. The committee put ~~his or her~~ *their* signatures on the document.

4. An infant recognizes ~~their~~ *his or her* parents within the first few weeks of life.

5. The Harris family lives by ~~his or her~~ *its* own rules.

6. Lonnie and Jack should put ~~his~~ *their* ideas together and come up with a plan of action.

7. An employee taking an unpaid leave of absence may choose to make ~~their~~ *his or her* own health-insurance payments.

8. The amount of time a student spends researching a topic depends, in part, on ~~their~~ *his or her* familiarity with the topic.

9. Alex and Susana lost ~~her~~ *their* way while driving through the suburbs of Philadelphia.

10. Neither the attorney nor the protesters were willing to expose ~~himself~~ *themselves* to public criticism.

## Agreement with Indefinite Pronouns

**Indefinite pronouns** (such as *some, everyone, any, each*) are pronouns without specific antecedents. They refer to people, places, or things in general. When an indefinite pronoun is an antecedent for another pronoun, mistakes in pronoun agreement often result. Use the following guidelines to make your pronouns agree with indefinite pronoun antecedents:

- **Use singular pronouns to refer to indefinite pronouns that are singular in meaning.**

> ### Tip for Writers
>
> *Everybody, everyone,* and *everything* refer to a group of people or things, but these words are grammatically singular, so use a singular verb with them:
>
> When there's a snowstorm, <u>everyone gets</u> to class late.

| another | either | nobody | other |
|---------|--------|--------|-------|
| anybody | everybody | no one | somebody |
| anyone | everyone | nothing | someone |
| anything | everything | one | something |
| each | neither | | |

Singular antecedent   Singular pronoun

<u>Someone</u> left <u>his</u> dress shirt in the locker room.

Singular antecedent          Singular compound pronoun

<u>Everyone</u> in the office must pick up <u>his or her</u> paycheck.

*Note:* To avoid the awkwardness of *his or her,* use plural antecedents and pronouns.

Plural antecedent        Plural pronoun

Office <u>workers</u> must pick up <u>their</u> paychecks.

- **Use a plural pronoun to refer to indefinite pronouns that are plural in meaning.**

| both | few | many | more | several |
|------|-----|------|------|---------|

Plural antecedent                    Plural pronoun

<u>Both</u> of the police officers said that as far as <u>they</u> could tell, no traffic violations had occurred.

- **The indefinite pronouns *all, any, more, most,* and *some* can be singular or plural, depending on how they are used.** If the indefinite pronoun refers to something that cannot be counted, use a singular pronoun to refer to it. If the indefinite pronoun refers to two or more of something that can be counted, use a plural pronoun to refer to it.

> <u>Most</u> of the students feel <u>they</u> can succeed.
>
> <u>Most</u> of the air on airplanes is recycled repeatedly, so <u>it</u> becomes stale.

> !  **NEED TO KNOW**
>
> ### Pronouns
>
> - **Pronouns** substitute for, or refer to, nouns or other pronouns.
> - The noun or pronoun to which a pronoun refers is called its **antecedent**.
> - Make sure that it is always clear to which noun or pronoun a pronoun refers.
> - A pronoun must agree with its antecedent in number (singular or plural) and gender. Singular nouns and pronouns refer to one thing; plural nouns and pronouns refer to more than one thing.
> - **Indefinite pronouns** are pronouns without specific antecedents. Follow the rules given in this chapter to make indefinite pronouns agree with their antecedents.

## EXERCISE 9-5  Correcting Pronoun–Antecedent Errors

**Directions:** Revise each of the following sentences to correct errors in pronoun–antecedent agreement.    Answers will vary.

|  |  |
|---|---|
| **EXAMPLE** | No one could remember their student number. |
| **REVISED** | No one could remember his or her student number. |
| **BETTER** | The students could not remember their student numbers. |

1. Someone left ~~their~~ _his or her_ jacket in the car.

2. Everything Todd said was true, but I did not like the way he said ~~them~~ _it_.

3. In my math class, ~~everyone~~ _all students_ works at their own pace.

4. When someone exercises, ~~they~~ _he or she_ should drink plenty of liquids.

5. No one should be forced into a curriculum that ~~they do~~ _he or she does_ not want.

6. No one will receive ~~their~~ _his or her_ exam grades before Friday.

7. Many of the club members do not pay ~~his or her~~ _their_ dues on time.

8. Both of the cooks used ~~her~~ _their_ own secret recipes.

9. No one was successful on ~~their~~ _his or her_ first attempt to run the race in less than two hours.

10. Each of the workers brought ~~their~~ _his or her_ own tools.

## EXERCISE 9-6  Correcting Agreement Errors

**Directions:** Revise the sentences below that contain agreement errors. If a sentence contains no errors, write _Correct_ beside it.    Answers will vary.

**EXAMPLE**  Somebody dropped ~~their~~ _his or her_ ring down the drain.

_Correct_  1. Many of the residents of the neighborhood have had their homes tested for radon.

_____  2. Each college instructor established ~~their~~ _his or her_ own grading policies.

_____ 3. The apples fell from ~~its~~ tree.
   _their_

_____ 4. Anyone may enter ~~their~~ painting in the contest.
   _his or her_

Correct 5. All the engines manufactured at the plant have their vehicle identification numbers stamped on them.

_____ 6. No one requested that the clerk gift wrap ~~their~~ package.
   _his or her_

_____ 7. Either Professor Judith Marcos or her assistant, Maria, graded the exams, writing ~~their~~ comments in the margins.
   _her_

_____ 8. James or his parents sails the boat every weekend.

_____ 9. Most classes were not canceled because of the snowstorm; ~~it~~ met as regularly scheduled.
   _they_

_____ 10. Not only Ricky but also the Carters will take ~~his~~ children to Disneyland this summer.
   _their_

---

| EXERCISE 9-7 | Revising a Paragraph |
| --- | --- |

**WRITING IN PROGRESS**

**Directions:** Reread the paragraph you wrote for Exercise 9-3 to be certain that there are no errors in pronoun–antecedent agreement. Revise as needed.

---

# Avoid Shifts in Person, Number, and Verb Tense

■ **GOAL 2**
Avoid shifts in person, number, and verb tense

The parts of a sentence should be consistent. Shifts in person, number, or verb tense within a sentence make it confusing and difficult to read.

## Shifts in Person

**Person** is the grammatical term used to identify the speaker or writer (**first person:** *I, we*), the person spoken to (**second person:** *you*), and the person or thing spoken about (**third person:** *he, she, it, they,* or any noun, such as *Joan* or *children*). Be sure to refer to yourself, your audience (or readers), and people and things you are writing about in a consistent way throughout your sentence or paragraph.

In the following paragraph, note how the writer shifts back and forth when addressing her audience:

> A person should know how to cook. You can save a lot of money if you make your own meals instead of eating out. One can also eat more healthily at home if one cooks according to principles of good nutrition.

Here the writer shifts from sentence to sentence, first using the indefinite phrase *a person*, then the more personal *you*, then the more formal *one*.

In the next paragraph, the writer shifts when referring to himself.

> Arizona has many advantages for year-round living, so I am hoping to move there when I graduate. One reason I want to live in Arizona is that you never need to shovel snow.

In this paragraph, the writer shifts from the direct and personal *I* to the indirect and more general *you*.

To avoid making shifts in references to yourself and others, decide before you begin to write how you will refer to yourself, to your audience, and to those about whom you are writing. Base your decision on whether you want your paragraph to be direct and personal or more formal. In academic writing, most instructors prefer that you avoid using the personal pronoun *I* and try to write in a more formal style.

| PERSONAL | I want to live in Florida for a number of reasons. |
|---|---|
| MORE FORMAL | Living in Florida is attractive for a number of reasons. |

| PERSONAL | I have difficulty balancing school and a part-time job. |
|---|---|
| MORE FORMAL | Balancing school and a part-time job is difficult. |

## Shifts in Number

**Number** distinguishes between singular and plural. A pronoun must agree in number with its antecedent. Related nouns within a sentence must also agree in number.

| SHIFT | All the women wore a dress. |
|---|---|
| CONSISTENT | All the women wore dresses. |

**EXERCISE 9-8**

## Correcting Shifts in Person and Number

**Directions:** Revise each of the following sentences to correct shifts in person or number.

> **EXAMPLE**   I perform better on exams if the professor doesn't hover over ~~you~~. *me*

1. ~~Each student has~~ *Students have* to plan their schedules for the semester.

2. Eva said she doesn't want to go to the wedding because ~~you would have~~ *she would have* to bring a gift.

3. In some states, continuing education is required for doctors or lawyers; after ~~you~~ *they* pass the board or bar exam, ~~you~~ *they* are required to take a specified number of credits per year in brush-up courses.

4. Construction workers must wear ~~a hard hats~~ *hard hats*.

5. I swim with a life vest on because ~~you~~ *I* could drown without it.

6. ~~A good friend is~~ *Good friends are* always there when you need them most.

7. The first and second relay racers discussed ~~his~~ *their* strategies.

8. I always tell ~~yourself~~ *myself* to think before acting.

9. Patients often expect their doctors to have all the answers, but ~~you~~ *they* should realize doctors are not miracle workers.

10. ~~Each giraffe~~ *The giraffes* stretched their ~~neck~~ *necks* to reach the leaves in the trees.

## Shifts in Verb Tense

Use the same verb tense (past, present, future, etc.) throughout a sentence and paragraph unless meaning requires you to make a shift.

                                       Present    Future

**REQUIRED SHIFT**   After the moon rises, we will go for a moonlight swim.

Incorrect shifts in verb tense can make a sentence confusing. One of the most common incorrect shifts is between present and past tenses.

                                        Past                             Present

**INCORRECT**   After Marguerite joined the food co-op, she seems healthier.

                                        Past                             Past

**CORRECT**   After Marguerite joined the food co-op, she seemed healthier.

### ! NEED TO KNOW

#### Shifts in Person, Number, and Verb Tense

- **Person** is a term used to identify the speaker or writer (**first person**: *I, we*), the person spoken to (**second person**: *you*), and the person or thing spoken about (**third person**: *he, she, it, they,* or any noun, such as *desk* or *Robert*).
- Be sure to use first, second, and third person consistently throughout a piece of writing.
- **Number** distinguishes between singular and plural. A pronoun must agree in number with its antecedent.
- **Verb tense** is the form of a verb that indicates whether the action or state of being that the verb tells about occurs in the past, present, or future. Unless there is a specific reason to switch tenses, be sure to use a consistent tense throughout a piece of writing.

### EXERCISE 9-9   Correcting Shifts in Verb Tense

**Directions:** Revise each of the following sentences to correct shifts in verb tense.

                    *waited*

**EXAMPLE**   I ~~was waiting~~ for the hailstorm to end, and then I dashed into the restaurant.

                                                    *they do*

1. In the morning, the factory workers punch in, but ~~have~~ not punched out at night.

                                               *looked*

2. José looked muscular; then he joined a gym and ~~looks~~ even more so.

   *ran*

3. I ~~run~~ two miles, and then I rested.

                    *hung*

4. Quinne called me but ~~hangs~~ up on my answering machine.

                 *did*

5. Until I took physics, I ~~will~~ not understand the laws of aerodynamics.

                          *took*

6. While the rain fell, the campers ~~take~~ shelter in their tent.

7. Because the moon will be full, the tide ~~was~~ *will be* high.

8. Katie drives me to work, and I ~~worked~~ *work* until 9:30 p.m.

9. Richard went to the mall because he ~~need~~ *needed* to buy a suit for his job interview.

10. The speaker ~~stands~~ *stood* at the podium and cleared his throat.

---

**EXERCISE 9-10**

## Revising Sentences

**Directions:** Revise each of the following sentences to correct errors in shift of person, number, or verb tense. If a sentence contains no errors, write *Correct* beside it.

**EXAMPLE**   Boats along the river were tied to their ~~dock~~ *docks*.

_____ 1. When people receive ~~a gift, you~~ *gifts, they* should be gracious and polite.

_____ 2. When we arrived at the inn, the lights ~~are~~ *were* on and a fire ~~is~~ *was* burning in the fireplace.

_____ 3. Before Trey drove to the cabin, he ~~packs~~ *packed* a picnic lunch.

_Correct_ 4. The artist paints portraits and weaves baskets.

_____ 5. The lobsterman goes out on his boat each day and ~~will check~~ *checks* his lobster traps.

_____ 6. All the cars Honest Bob sells have ~~a new transmission~~ *new transmissions*.

_____ 7. Rosa ran the 100-meter race and ~~throws~~ *threw* the discus at the track meet.

_____ 8. Public schools in Florida have ~~an~~ air-conditioning ~~system~~ *systems*.

_____ 9. Office workers sat on the benches downtown and ~~are eating~~ *ate* their lunches outside.

_____ 10. Before ~~a scuba diver~~ *scuba divers* goes underwater, ~~you~~ *they* must check and re-check ~~your~~ *their* breathing equipment.

---

**EXERCISE 9-11**

## Writing and Revising a Paragraph

**WRITING IN PROGRESS**

**Directions:** Write a paragraph on one of the following topics. After you have written your first draft, reread it, checking for shifts in person, number, and verb tense. Revise as needed.

1. Registering to vote

2. The most beautiful place you have visited

3. A current food trend

4. The message of your favorite childhood book

5. Making polite conversation with relatives you see infrequently

# Avoid Misplaced and Dangling Modifiers

■ GOAL 3
Avoid misplaced and
dangling modifiers

A **modifier** is a word, phrase, or clause that describes, qualifies, or limits the meaning of another word. Modifiers that are not correctly placed can confuse your reader.

## Types of Modifiers

The following list will help you review the main types of modifiers:

■ **Adjectives modify nouns and pronouns.**

It is an interesting photograph.

She is very kind.

■ **Adverbs modify verbs, adjectives, or other adverbs.**

I walked quickly.

The cake tasted extremely good.

The flowers are very beautifully arranged.

■ **Prepositional phrases modify nouns, adjectives, verbs, or adverbs.**

The woman in the green dress is stunning.

They walked into the store to buy milk.

■ ***-ing* phrases modify nouns or pronouns.**

Waiting for the bus, Joe studied his history notes.

■ **Dependent clauses modify nouns, adjectives, verbs, or adverbs.** (A dependent clause has a subject and verb but is incomplete in meaning.)

After I left campus, I went shopping.

I left because classes were canceled.

The kitten that I found in the bushes was frightened.

## Misplaced Modifiers

Placement of a modifier in a sentence affects meaning:

I need only to buy Marcos a gift. (Buying the gift is the only thing I need to do.)

Only I need to buy Marcos a gift. (I'm the only one who needs to buy Marcos a gift.)

I need to buy only Marcos a gift. (Marcos is the only person for whom I need to buy a gift.)

If a modifier is placed so that it does not convey the meaning you intend, it is called a **misplaced modifier**. Misplaced modifiers can make a sentence confusing.

| MISPLACED | Anthony found a necklace at the mall that sparkled and glittered. [Which sparkled and glittered—the mall or the necklace?] |
| --- | --- |
| MISPLACED | The president announced that the club picnic would be held on August 2 at the beginning of the meeting. [Is the picnic being held at the beginning of the meeting on August 2, or did the president make the announcement at the beginning of the meeting?] |

You can avoid a misplaced modifier if you make sure that the modifier immediately precedes or follows the word it modifies.

| CORRECT | Anthony found a necklace that sparkled and glittered at the mall. |
| --- | --- |
| CORRECT | The club president announced at the beginning of the meeting that the picnic would be held on August 2. |

## Dangling Modifiers

**Dangling modifiers** are words or phrases that do not clearly describe or explain any part of the sentence. Dangling modifiers create confusion and sometimes unintentional humor. To avoid dangling modifiers, make sure that each modifying phrase or clause has a clear antecedent.

| DANGLING | Uncertain of which street to follow, the map indicated we should turn left. [The opening modifier suggests that the map was uncertain of which street to follow.] |
| --- | --- |
| CORRECT | Uncertain of which street to follow, we checked a map, which indicated we should turn left. |
| DANGLING | My shoes got wet walking across the street. [The modifier suggests that the shoes were walking across the street by themselves.] |
| CORRECT | My shoes got wet as I crossed the street. |
| DANGLING | To pass the test, careful review is essential. [Who will pass the test?] |
| CORRECT | To pass the test, I must review carefully. |

There are two common ways to revise dangling modifiers.

1. **Add a word or words that the modifier clearly describes.** Place the new material immediately after the modifier, and rearrange other parts of the sentence as necessary.

| DANGLING | While walking in the garden, gunfire sounded. [The opening modifier implies that the gunfire was walking in the garden.] |
| --- | --- |
| CORRECT | While walking in the garden, Carol heard gunfire. |

2. **Change the dangling modifier to a dependent clause.** You may need to change the verb form in the modifier.

DANGLING    While watching television, the cake burned.

CORRECT     While Pat was watching television, the cake burned.

---

## ! NEED TO KNOW

### Misplaced and Dangling Modifiers

- A **modifier** is a word, phrase, or clause that describes, qualifies, or limits the meaning of another word.
- A **misplaced modifier** is placed in a way that does not convey the sentence's intended meaning.
- To avoid misplaced modifiers, be sure that you place the modifier immediately before or after the word it modifies.
- A **dangling modifier** is a word or phrase that does not clearly describe or explain any part of the sentence.
- To revise a dangling modifier, you can add a word or words that the modifier clearly describes, or you can change the dangling modifier to a dependent clause.

---

**EXERCISE 9-12** Correcting Misplaced or Dangling Modifiers

**Directions:** Revise each of the following sentences to correct misplaced or dangling modifiers.   Answers will vary.

EXAMPLE   Jerome mailed a bill at the post office that was long overdue.
REVISED     At the post office, Jerome mailed a bill that was long overdue.

1. Running at top speed, dirt was kicked up by the horse.

   Running at top speed, the horse kicked up dirt.

2. Swimming to shore, my arms got tired.

   While I was swimming to shore, my arms got tired.

3. The helmet on the soldier's head with a red circle represented his nationality.

   On his head, the soldier wore a helmet with a red circle to represent his nationality.

4. To answer your phone, the receiver must be lifted.

   To answer your phone, you must lift the receiver.

5. Walking up the stairs, the book dropped and tumbled down.

   As I walked up the stairs, the book dropped and tumbled down.

6. Twenty-five band members picked their instruments up from chairs that were gleaming and began to play.

   *Twenty-five band members picked up their gleaming instruments from their chairs and begun to play.*

7. Laughing, the cat chased the girl.

   *The cat chased the laughing girl.*

8. When skating, skate blades must be kept sharp.

   *When you are skating, you must keep your skate blades sharp.*

9. The ball bounced off the roof that was round and red.

   *The ball that was round and red bounced off the roof.*

10. Ducking, the snowball hit Andy on the head.

    *As Andy ducked, the snowball hit him on the head.*

---

**EXERCISE 9-13**

## Correcting Misplaced or Dangling Modifiers

**Directions:** Revise each of the following sentences to correct misplaced or dangling modifiers.    *Answers will vary.*

> **EXAMPLE**  Deciding which flavor of ice cream to order, another customer cut in front of Roger.
>
> **REVISED**  While Roger was deciding which flavor of ice cream to order, another customer cut in front of him.

1. Tricia saw an animal at the zoo that had black fur and long claws.

   *At the zoo, Tricia saw an animal that had black fur and long claws.*

2. Before answering the door, the phone rang.

   *Before I answered the door, the phone rang.*

3. I could see large snowflakes falling from the bedroom window.

   *From the bedroom window, I could see large snowflakes falling.*

4. Honking, Felicia walked in front of the car.

   *Felicia walked in front of the car with the honking horn.*

5. After leaving the classroom, the door automatically locked.

*After we left the classroom, the door automatically locked.*

6. Applauding and cheering, the band returned for an encore.

*As the audience applauded and cheered, the band returned for an encore.*

7. The waiter brought a birthday cake to our table that had 24 candles.

*The waiter brought a birthday cake with 24 candles to our table.*

8. Books lined the library shelves about every imaginable subject.

*Books about every imaginable subject lined the library shelves.*

9. While sobbing, the sad movie ended and the lights came on.

*While everyone was sobbing, the sad movie ended and the lights came on.*

10. Turning the page, the book's binding cracked.

*As I turned the page, the book's binding cracked.*

---

### EXERCISE 9-14

**WRITING IN PROGRESS**

## Revising a Paragraph

**Directions:** Reread the paragraph you wrote for Exercise 9-3. Check for dangling or misplaced modifiers. Revise as needed.

---

# Use Parallelism

■ GOAL 4
Use parallelism

Study the following pairs of sentences. Which sentence in each pair reads more smoothly?

PAIR 1
1. Seth, a long-distance biker, enjoys swimming and drag races cars.
2. Seth enjoys long-distance biking, swimming, and drag racing.

PAIR 2
3. The dog was large, had a beautiful coat, and it was friendly.
4. The dog was large, beautiful, and friendly.

Do sentences 2 and 4 sound better than 1 and 3? Sentences 2 and 4 have balance. Similar words have similar grammatical form. In sentence 2, *biking, swimming,* and *drag racing* are all nouns ending in *-ing*. In sentence 4, *large, beautiful,* and *friendly* are all adjectives. The method of balancing similar elements within a sentence is called **parallelism**. Parallelism makes your writing smooth and makes your ideas easier to follow.

| EXERCISE 9-15 | Examining Parallelism |

**Directions:** In each group of words, circle the element that is not parallel.

    **EXAMPLE**   walking, running, (to jog,) dancing

1. intelligent, successful, (responsibly,) mature
2. happily, quickly, hurriedly, (hungry)
3. wrote, (answering,) worked, typed
4. to fly, (parachutes,) to skydive, to drive
5. were painting, (drew,) were carving, were coloring
6. sat in the sun, played cards, (scuba diving,) ate lobster
7. thoughtful, (honestly,) humorous, quick-tempered
8. (rewrote my résumé,) arranging interviews, buying a new suit, getting a haircut
9. buy stamps, cash check, (dry cleaning,) return library books
10. eating sensibly, (eight hours of sleep,) exercising, drinking a lot of water

## What Should Be Parallel?

When you write, be sure to keep each of the following elements parallel:

- **Nouns in a series**

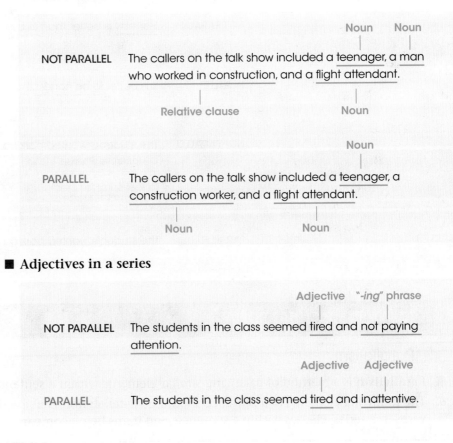

- **Adjectives in a series**

■ **Verbs in a series** (They should have the same tense.)

Simple past   Past progressive

NOT PARALLEL   The couple danced and were joking.

Simple past   Simple past

PARALLEL   The couple danced and joked.

■ **Clauses within sentences**

Prepositional phrase

NOT PARALLEL   The students were angry about the parking difficulties

Dependent clause

and that no one was concerned.

Dependent clause

PARALLEL   The students were angry that it was difficult to park

Dependent clause

and that no one was concerned.

■ **Items being compared or contrasted**

Noun   Infinitive phrase

NOT PARALLEL   Honesty is better than to be dishonest.

Infinitive phrase   Infinitive phrase

PARALLEL   It is better to be honest than to be dishonest.

Noun   Pronoun

NOT PARALLEL   The students wanted parking spaces, not someone

Infinitive Phrase

to feel sorry for them.

Noun   Noun

PARALLEL   The students wanted parking spaces, not sympathy.

---

## ❗ NEED TO KNOW

### Parallelism

■ **Parallelism** is a method of balancing similar elements within a sentence.

■ The following elements of a sentence should be parallel: nouns in a series, adjectives in a series, verbs in a series, clauses within a sentence, and items being compared or contrasted.

## EXERCISE 9-16    Correcting Parallelism Errors

**Directions:** Revise each of the following sentences to correct errors in parallel structure.

> **EXAMPLE**    The instructor ~~was demanding~~ *demanded hard work* and insisted on high standards.

1. Accuracy is more important than ~~being speedy.~~
2. The teller counted and ~~recounts~~ *recounted* the money.
3. Newspapers are blowing away and ~~scattered~~ *scattering* on the sidewalk.
4. Judith was pleased when she graduated and ~~that she~~ received an honors diploma.
5. Thrilled and ~~exhausting~~ *exhausted*, the runners crossed the finish line.
6. Our guest speakers for the semester are a radiologist, a ~~student of medicine~~ *medical student*, and a hospital administrator.
7. Students shouted and ~~were hollering~~ *hollered* at the basketball game.
8. We enjoyed seeing the Grand Canyon, riding a mule, and ~~photography.~~ *taking photographs*.
9. Laughing and ~~relaxed~~ *relaxing*, the co-workers enjoyed lunch at the Mexican restaurant.
10. Professor Higuera is well known for his humor, clear ~~lecturing~~ *lectures*, and scholarship.

## EXERCISE 9-17    Correcting Parallelism Errors

**Directions:** Revise each of the following sentences to achieve parallelism.

> **EXAMPLE**    Rosa has decided to study nursing instead of ~~going into~~ accounting.

1. The priest baptized the baby and ~~congratulates~~ *congratulated* the new parents.
2. We ordered a platter of fried clams, a platter of corn on the cob, and ‸*a platter of* fried shrimp.
3. Lucy entered the dance contest, but ~~the dance was watched by June~~ *June watched the dance* from the side.
4. Léon purchased the ratchet set at the garage sale and ~~buying~~ *bought* the drill bits there, too.
5. The exterminator told Brandon the house needed to be fumigated and ~~spraying~~ *sprayed* to eliminate the termites.
6. The bus swerved and hit the dump truck, which ~~swerves~~ *swerved* and hit the station wagon, which swerved and hit the bicycle.
7. Channel 2 covered the bank robbery, but ‸ a python that had escaped from the zoo ~~was reported by Channel 7.~~ *Channel 7 covered*

8. Sal was born when Reagan was president, and ~~Clinton was president when Rob was born.~~ *Rob was born when Clinton was president*

9. The pediatrician spent the morning ~~with~~ *looking at* sore throats, answering questions about immunizations, and treating bumps and bruises.

10. Belinda prefers to study in the library, but her brother Marcus ~~studies~~ *prefers to study* at home.

---

### EXERCISE 9-18 | Revising a Paragraph

**WRITING IN PROGRESS**

**Directions:** Reread the paragraph you wrote for Exercise 9-3. Correct any sentences that lack parallelism.

---

### EXERCISE 9-19 | Revising Sentences

**Directions:** Now that you have learned about common errors that produce confusing or inconsistent sentences, turn back to the confusing sentences used to introduce the chapter on page 262. Identify each error, and revise the sentences so they convey the intended meaning.

---

### EXERCISE 9-20 | Revising a Paragraph

**WORKING TOGETHER**

**Directions:** Working with a classmate, revise this student paragraph by correcting all instances of misplaced or dangling modifiers, shifts in verb tense, and faulty parallelism.

Robert Burns said that the dog is "man's best friend." To a large extent, this statement may be truer than you think. What makes dogs so special to humans is their unending loyalty and ~~that they love unconditionally.~~ *their unconditional love* Dogs have been known to cross the entire United States to return home. Unlike people, dogs never ~~made~~ *make* fun of you or criticize you. They never throw fits, and they ~~seem happy always~~ *always seem happy* to see you. This may not necessarily be true of your family, friends, and ~~those who live near you.~~ *neighbors* A dog never lies to you, never betrays your confidences, and never ~~stayed~~ *stays* angry with you for more than five minutes. Best of all, he *or she* never expects more ~~than the basics from you~~ *from you than the basics* of food and shelter and a simple pat on the head in return for his *or her* devotion. The world would be a better place if ~~everyone~~ *people* could only be more like their dogs.

---

### EXERCISE 9-21 | Revising a Paragraph

**Directions:** Revise the following paragraph so that all words or phrases in a series, independent clauses joined by a coordinating conjunction, and items being compared are parallel. Write your corrections above the lines.

The first practical pair of roller skates ~~was~~ made in Belgium in 1759 and ~~is~~ *was* designed like ice skates. The skates had two wheels instead of ~~being made with~~ four wheels as they ~~are~~ *have* today. The wheels were aligned down the center of the skate, but ~~were containing~~ *contained* no ball bearings. The skates had a life of their own. Without ball bearings, they resisted turning, then ~~were turning~~ *turned* abruptly, and then ~~refuse~~ *refused* to stop. Finally, they jammed to a halt on their own. Until 1884, when ball bearings were introduced, roller-skating was unpopular, difficult, and ~~it was~~ dangerous ~~for people to do~~. However, when skating technology improved, roller-skat~~es~~*ing* began to compete with ice-skating. Later, an American made roller skates with sets of wheels placed side-by-side rather than ~~by placing them~~ behind one another, and that design lasted until recently. Since 1980, however, many companies have been manufacturing skates based on the older design. In other words, in-line skates are back, and more and more people are discovering ~~Rollerblading~~ *the joys and health benefits of rollerblading* ~~joys and that it benefits their health.~~

## READING

# Understand Difficult and Complicated Sentences

■ **GOAL 5**
Understand difficult and complicated sentences

Most professional writing that you will read will not contain errors that create confusion or inconsistency. However, you are likely to find sentences that are difficult and even confusing. Sentences can be confusing for any or all of the reasons shown in the table below. Use the suggestions in the right column to help you understand difficult sentences.

### TABLE 9-1   STRATEGIES FOR HANDLING COMPLICATED SENTENCES

| Reasons Sentences May Be Difficult | Strategies for Overcoming the Problem |
| --- | --- |
| Difficult vocabulary | ■ **Try pronouncing an unfamiliar word.** You may hear a part in it that you do know. For example, you may hear the prefix *mono-*, meaning "one," in the word *monogamous*, and then be able to figure out the word from context.<br>■ **Circle unfamiliar words and figure out or look up their meanings.** Note the meanings in the margin. |
| Long sentence with numerous clauses and phrases | ■ **Read the sentence aloud.** Often, hearing it will help you grasp the relative importance of ideas.<br>■ **Divide the sentence into clauses.** Find the more important clauses. Express each in your own words. Then determine how the remaining clauses alter or add to the meaning. |
| Difficult concepts or technical material | ■ **Keep reading beyond the single difficult sentence.** The concept may be further explained later in the paragraph.<br>■ **Read the sentence several times**, and if necessary, the entire paragraph several times.<br>■ **Try expressing the sentence in your own words**, either aloud or in writing. If you cannot express it, you probably still do not understand it.<br>■ **Work with a classmate**; discuss difficult ideas. |
| Lack of background information | ■ **Look up terms the writer assumes you know but you do not.**<br>■ **Do an Internet search to fill in information that the writer assumes you have but you do not.** Try to find a source that gives you an overview or introduction to the topic. |

EXERCISE 9-22    Understanding Difficult Sentences

**Directions:** For each of the following difficult sentences, use the strategies listed in Table 9-1 to unravel its meaning. Test your understanding by writing the meaning of each in your own words.    Answers will vary.

1. Long-term consumption of fattening and sugary foods can have a negative impact on cognitive functioning.

—Krause, *Psychological Science*, p. 614

Eating fattening and sugary foods over a long period can hurt your ability to think.

2. A natural monopoly exists when the technology for producing a good or service enables one firm to meet the entire market demand at a lower average total cost than two or more firms could.

—Bade, *Essentials of Economics*, p. 306

A natural monopoly occurs when one firm can meet the entire market demand at a lower

average total cost than two or more firms could.

3. Typically, older adults have unaltered perception of light touch and superficial pain, decreased perception of deep pain, and decreased perception of temperature stimuli.

—Berman, *Nursing Basics for Clinical Practice*, p. 418

Older people usually have normal sensitivity to light touch and surface pain, but decreased

sensitivity to deep pain and heat or cold.

4. Five major seas encircle Europe; these water bodies are connected to each other through narrow straits with strategic importance for controlling waterborne trade and naval movement.

—Rowntree, *Diversity Amid Globalization*, p. 348

The five major seas that surround Europe are connected through channels that are

important for trade and military reasons.

5. Not only is the executive branch divided into departments and agencies that specialize in major areas, such as agriculture or commerce, but also within each unit of the government there are subunits that are even more specialized, each of which employs experts in various fields for which it is responsible.

—Volkomer, *American Government*, p. 248

The executive branch of government is divided into specialized units and subunits which

employ experts in each field.

# INTEGRATING READING AND WRITING

## READ AND REVISE

**MySkillsLab®**

**Complete** this Exercise

The following excerpt is from a student essay called "High Tide." This excerpt contains confusing and inconsistent sentences that were corrected in a later draft. Read the excerpt and underline pronoun reference errors, shifts in person, misplaced or dangling modifiers, and parallelism errors. Revise the excerpt to correct these errors. **You can also complete this exercise online at MySkillsLab.com.**

# High Tide

The tide rolls in. Two girls, sisters, are stuck in the water, knowing not that the water is rising all around them. The ocean not only is a picture of beauty but a picture of danger and destruction. The girls have two choices of fate: either <u>you</u> [they] will see the ocean's beauty again, or it will be their deathbed.

Shift in person

Dangling modifier
Misplaced modifier

Shift in person

Shift in person
Parallelism error

Shift in verb tense

Shift in verb tense
Parallelism error
Shift in verb tense

Shift in verb tense
Pronoun reference error
Shift in verb tense

~~Visiting their grandparents in Massachusetts, the trip~~ [The trip to visit their grandparents in Massachusetts] is very exciting and fun for them. The grandparents have ~~a lot planned to stay busy~~ [planned a lot of activities to keep the girls busy] while they are there. The one event that does not have to be scheduled is going out on <u>your</u> [their] grandfather's boat. In fact, it is their favorite part of the entire visit. They feel peaceful on the boat with the wind blowing <u>one's</u> [their] hair, seagulls crying above them, and <u>the sun</u> ~~beams~~ [the sun beaming] down on the waves. The ocean feels free and inviting.

One sunny day, the ocean beckons the sisters. The day ~~will start~~ [starts] out as usual. Their grandma is in the kitchen making sandwiches, their father and grandfather are in the living room talking, and ~~everyone else put~~ [the others are putting] on their bathing suits. The girls ~~told her~~ [tell their] parents they ~~were~~ [are] too excited to wait another minute to rush into the ocean. Little ~~did~~ [do] they know that fate ~~would~~ [will] provide a test of their courage and strength.

## READ AND RESPOND: A Student Essay

*Dave Myers graduated from high school in 1981. After a stint in the navy, a period of homelessness, and time spent working in construction and as an electrician, he became a student at Linn-Benton Community College. He plans to complete a bachelor's degree in criminal justice and hopes to use the skills he has developed as a writer to better the the lives of people who may find themselves following a difficult path in life. Myers submitted this essay to the Writing Rewards Essay Competition; the assignment he responded to asked him to write an essay describing an event that changed his life.*

# When Someday Finally Came

This story begins with a picture. It is the only picture of my family together in the world. It was taken about six months before my mom and dad divorced. After their divorce, I was raised by my mother and her side of the family only. I would forget my father's face. I would forget my short time with him. Stories about him would never be told to me. Even when I would try to start a conversation about him, the discussion would be short and bitter.

*Dave Myer's last Christmas with both his parents in 1964.*

As I grew up, my mom tried to give me as normal a life as anyone could expect. I went to school, went to Cub Scouts, joined 4-H, and learned from my mom and uncles how to play baseball. The little things a boy learns, like how to hold a bat or throw a football, were taught by my mom and her family. Every day, my dad would be in my thoughts. I would say to myself, "I wonder what he's doing right now, right at this very moment." On some days, I would think about him so hard it would hurt, and I had to come into the house and find a place to be alone. Even though it never seemed possible I would know him, he was always part of my family and I always wanted to know him.

When I was 18, I moved out to be on my own. I got in so much trouble with a fast '69 Mustang that I had to join the Navy. When I got out, I found that the life back in Grand Island, Nebraska, was way too slow a pace for a kid like me. I needed excitement in my life! So, with three hundred dollars in my pocket, I moved to Los Angeles with no place to work and nowhere to live.

I learned on my own that life can be as hard and unforgiving as you make it. My time in L.A. can be summed up as "learning life's lessons the hard way." The best thing I found in that miserable part of my existence was the love of my life, Reni. Being together didn't make our lives all that easy and carefree, though. We were homeless together. We both knew what it was like to be on the streets and sleep in parks. We were in love, but love doesn't keep you dry and secure. After living in California for twelve years, I brought Reni back to Nebraska with me.

Our lives in Nebraska were much better than when we were living on the West Coast. I worked for a guy who built mobile homes and offices. One summer, we had to move ten mobile homes from a patch of land in Broken Bow, Nebraska. Now, Broken Bow was where my dad was raised, and near the farm where my mom grew up. They were high school sweethearts and graduated together the same year. While I was working under the last home, I heard a conversation between the guy working with me and the woman who owned the home. It was the usual small talk, then through all the murmuring, I heard the woman say a name. "Stan Myers? Oh yes, I know him. He was at our class reunion last month." I hit my head on the steel frame so hard I almost knocked myself out. I came out from under that home as fast as I could to find the lady that said the name that hadn't been said for thirty-six years. "Are you referring to Stanley Spencer Myers?" I asked, while trying not to bleed on her floor from my head wound. "Why yes, do you know him?" she asked back to me. I said, "Yes ma'am, he's my father."

She told me that my dad talked about me when she saw him last. I asked if she could give me his current address or phone number. She was happy to give me both!

So, there I was, on the last day of working on that site, on the last house that was to be done that summer, holding a little piece of paper that will connect me with a man whose face I had forgotten, whose name was not spoken, and whose stories were not told. MY DAD!

After all the years of praying that someday I'll find my dad and my life will change the day I get to speak with him, I was so nervous to write him that it took two days to calm down to get started. When I finally got down to writing, I wrote this great big letter that I tried to squeeze every part of my life in. When I was done, I read it . . . and then I put it in a drawer. I wrote another letter right then, and it said, "Dear Dad, this is your son David. I just got your address a couple of days ago, and I felt that I had to write to you. I love you, and I miss you very much! I hope you're well, and if you would like to get hold of me, here's my address." And I sent it off.

A week went by, and I was beginning to wonder if I was going to get a letter back. I got a letter from my dad's wife that said my dad was so overwhelmed by my letter that he needed a little time to respond. My step-mom is a real sweetheart, and she really helped by being a cushion so that my dad and I wouldn't crash into each other so hard. She told me that he wept when he read my letter. She asked me to please be patient and know that he loved me too! My dad wrote his letter to me and came from Denver the following week to visit me. After all that time, after all the good years and bad years of my life, I was finally fulfilling my childhood dream: to be held by my father.

That happened ten years ago. I'm forty-eight now, and my dad is sixty-eight. My dad and step-mom have two sons. I'm no longer an only child because I now have two half brothers. I also have the other part of my life that I felt was missing: when I'm with my father, I look in the man's face, I listen to the stories he tells me, and I know now that my family is the same as his, and I am proud.

*Dave Myers and his father are reunited Christmas 2001.*

**Margin notes (left column):**

Topic sentence

More descriptive details revealing strong emotion

Descriptive language

Topic sentence

Conclusion echoes thesis

## Examining Writing

1. What are the most important details in Myers's narrative? Try to tell his story briefly in your own words.

2. Identify any confusing or inconsistent sentences. What strategies would help Myers improve these sentences?

3. How did Myers organize the essay?

4. Evaluate Myers's thesis statement and its placement. How could the statement be strengthened?

## READ AND RESPOND: A Professional Essay

### Thinking Before Reading

The following selection is from a sociology textbook. In the selection, the author discusses the decline in personal privacy in today's world.

1. Preview the reading, using the steps discussed in Chapter 1 on page 25.
2. Connect the reading to your own experience by answering the following questions:
   a. Where have you noticed security or surveillance cameras? What is your reaction to seeing them?
   b. Do you think your personal information is secure? How careful are you not to reveal personal information on the Internet?
3. Highlight and annotate as you read.

1350**L**/949 words

# Computer Technology, Large Organizations, and the Assault on Privacy

### John Macionis

1   *Jake completes a page on Facebook, which includes his name and college, e-mail, photo, biography, and current personal interests. It can be accessed by billions of people around the world.*

2   *Late for a meeting with a new client, Sarah drives her car through a yellow light as it turns red at a main intersection. A computer linked to a pair of cameras notes the violation and takes one picture of her license plate and another of her sitting in the driver's seat. Seven days later, she receives a summons to appear in traffic court.*

3   *Julio looks through his mail and finds a letter from a Washington, D.C., data services company telling him that he is one of about 145,000 people whose name, address, Social Security number, and credit file have recently been sold to criminals in California posing as businesspeople. With this information, other people can obtain credit cards or take out loans in his name.*

4   These are all cases showing that today's organizations—which know more about us than ever before and more than most of us realize—pose a growing threat to personal privacy. Large organizations are necessary for today's society to operate. In some cases, organizations using information about us may actually be helpful. But cases of identity theft are on the rise, and personal privacy is on the decline.

5   In the past, small-town life gave people little privacy. But at least if people knew something about you, you were just as likely to know something about them. Today, unknown people "out there" can access information about each of us all the time without our learning about it.

6    In part, the loss of privacy is a result of increasingly complex computer technology. Are you aware that every e-mail you send and every Web site you visit leaves a record in one or more computers? These records can be retrieved by people you don't know as well as by employers and other public officials.

7    Another part of today's loss of privacy reflects the number and size of formal organizations. Large organizations tend to treat people impersonally, and they have a huge appetite for information. Mix large organizations with ever more complex computer technology, and it is no wonder that most people in the United States are concerned about who knows what about them and what people are doing with this information.

8    For decades, the level of personal privacy in the United States has been declining. Early in the twentieth century, when state agencies began issuing driver's licenses, for example, they generated files for every licensed driver. Today, officials can send this information at the touch of a button not only to the police but also to all sorts of other organizations. The Internal Revenue Service and the Social Security Administration, as well as government agencies that benefit veterans, students, the unemployed, and the poor, all collect mountains of personal information.

9    Business organizations now do much the same thing, and many of the choices we make end up in a company's database. Most of us use credit—the U.S. population now has more than 1 billion credit cards, an average of five per adult—but the companies that do "credit checks" collect and distribute information about us to almost anyone who asks, including criminals planning to steal our identity.

10    Then there are the small cameras found not only at traffic intersections but also in stores, public buildings, and parking garages and across college campuses. The number of surveillance cameras that monitor our movements is rapidly increasing with each passing year. So-called security cameras may increase public safety in some ways—say, by discouraging a mugger or even a terrorist—at the cost of the little privacy we have left. In the United Kingdom, probably the world leader in the use of security cameras with 4 million of them, the typical resident of London appears on closed-circuit television about 300 times every day, and all this "tracking" is stored in computer files. Here in the United States, New York City already has 4,000 surveillance cameras in the subway system and city officials plan to have cameras installed in 1,500 city buses by 2013.

11    Government monitoring of the population in the United States has been expanding steadily in recent years. After the September 11, 2001, terrorist attacks, the federal government took steps (including the USA PATRIOT Act) to strengthen national security. Today, government officials closely monitor not only people entering the country but also the activities of all of us. These activities may increase national security, but they certainly erode personal privacy.

12    Some legal protections remain. Each of the fifty states has laws that give citizens the right to examine some records about themselves kept by employers, banks, and credit bureaus. The federal Privacy Act of 1974 also limits the exchange of personal information among government agencies and permits citizens to examine and correct most government files. In response to rising levels of identity theft, Congress is likely to pass more laws to regulate the sale of credit information. But so many organizations, private as well as public, now have information about us—experts estimate that 90 percent of U.S. households are profiled in databases somewhere—that current laws simply cannot effectively address the privacy problem.

13    The privacy issues discussed here lead us to consider others, as well. Does the use of surveillance cameras in public places enhance or significantly reduce personal privacy? Is the cost worth the gains in personal security? Does the automatic toll payment on our nation's roads, such as the E-ZPass system, which allows motorists to move quickly through toll gates, but also records information about where you go and when you got there, violate privacy?

—Macionis, *Society*, p. 123.

# Getting Ready to Write

## Checking Your Comprehension

Answer each of the following questions using complete sentences.

1.  What three aspects of modern life are used as examples of the decline in privacy?
2.  According to the author, what are two reasons for today's loss of privacy?
3.  List three examples of government organizations that collect personal information.
4.  How many credit cards does the average American adult have?
5.  How often does the typical London resident appear on closed-circuit television?
6.  What does the federal Privacy Act of 1974 do?

## Strengthening Your Vocabulary

Using the word's context, word parts, or a dictionary, write a brief definition of each of the following words as it is used in the reading.

1.  violation (paragraph 2) _____ *illegal action* _____
2.  retrieved (paragraph 6) _____ *recovered; brought back* _____
3.  impersonally (paragraph 7) _____ *in an objective or businesslike manner* _____
4.  surveillance (paragraph 10) _____ *observation* _____
5.  erode (paragraph 11) _____ *wear away; reduce* _____

## Examining the Reading: Using Idea Maps

Review the reading by completing the missing parts of the following idea map.

**VISUALIZE IT!**

| | |
|---|---|
| Title | **Computer Technology, Large Organizations, and the Assault on Privacy** |
| Thesis | Today's organizations pose a growing threat to personal privacy. |

Organizations using information about us has led to:

- Increase in public safety
- Increase in cases of _identity theft_
- Decline in _personal privacy_

Loss of privacy results from:

- Increasingly complex _computer technology_
- Number and size of _formal organizations_

Personal information is collected by:

- Government agencies
- _Business organizations_

Surveillance cameras are used increasingly:

- United Kingdom has _4 million_
- _New York City_ has 4,000 and plans for more

Government monitoring has expanded since the _September 11, 2001, attacks_  Some legal protections remain.

- State laws:
  - Let citizens examine _employee, bank, and credit records_
- Federal Privacy Act of 1974:
  - Limits the _exchange of personal information among government agencies_
  - Lets citizens examine and correct _government files_

| | |
|---|---|
| Conclusion | The privacy issues concerning computer technology and large organizations lead us to consider additional privacy issues. |

## Thinking Critically: Discussion and Journal Writing

React and respond to the reading by discussing the following:

1. Discuss the title of this selection. Why does the author use the word *assault* and what does it reveal or imply about his attitude toward the subject? What other word might he have used instead?

2. Do you consider it important to safeguard your personal information on the Internet? Why or why not?

3. Write a journal entry giving your answers to the questions posed in the final paragraph of the essay.

4. What is the purpose of the photo that accompanies the essay? Discuss the types of security or surveillance cameras you have seen in public places. How do these cameras make you feel?

**THINKING VISUALLY**

## Writing About the Reading

**MySkillsLab®**

Complete
this
Exercise

### Paragraph Options

1. How does the author capture your attention in the first three paragraphs? What do these opening paragraphs tell you about who the author's audience is? Write a paragraph answering these questions and evaluating the introduction.

2. How would you describe the author's attitude toward the subject? Write a paragraph identifying examples of language and details in the selection that reveal the author's attitude.

3. Have you ever received a ticket as the result of a traffic enforcement camera? Have you ever been notified of a breach in the security of your credit or banking information? Write a paragraph describing your experience.

### Essay Options

4. Do you think that the benefits of security cameras outweigh the costs? Are you willing to make sacrifices in your own privacy in exchange for increased public safety? Why or why not? Write an essay exploring these questions.

5. Are you careful about what personal information you reveal? What steps do you take to protect your personal information? Are you concerned about identity theft? Write an essay explaining how you guard your privacy when you are on the Internet and when you use credit to make purchases. If you do not protect your privacy, explain why.

6. What changes have you noticed in government monitoring of the population in the past decade? How have the federal government's efforts to strengthen national security affected you? If you have traveled by airplane, or crossed the borders into other countries, what have you noticed about security measures? Write an essay describing your experiences and your reaction to security measures.

# SELF-TEST SUMMARY

To test yourself, cover the Answer column with a sheet of paper and answer each question in the left column. Evaluate each of your answers as you work by sliding the paper down and comparing your answer with what is printed in the Answer column.

| QUESTION | ANSWER |
| --- | --- |
| ▪ GOAL 1 Use pronouns clearly and correctly<br><br>What is a pronoun? How do you use pronouns correctly? | A *pronoun* is a word that substitutes for, or refers to, a noun or another pronoun. To use pronouns correctly, make sure that your pronoun reference is clear to your reader and that the pronoun and antecedent agree in number and in gender. |
| ▪ GOAL 2 Avoid shifts in person, number, and verb tense<br><br>What do first, second, and third person refer to? What should you consider when choosing a person for your writing? | *First person* refers to the speaker, *second person* to the person spoken to, and *third person* to the person or thing spoken about. When choosing the person, consider whether you desire a personal or formal tone in your writing. |
| ▪ GOAL 3 Avoid misplaced and dangling modifiers<br><br>What are misplaced and dangling modifiers? What are two ways to revise dangling modifiers? | A *misplaced modifier* is placed in such a way that it does not convey the writer's intended meaning. A *dangling modifier* does not clearly describe or explain any part of the sentence it appears in.<br>1. Add a word or words that the modifier clearly describes.<br>2. Change the dangling modifier to a dependent clause. |
| ▪ GOAL 4 Use parallelism<br><br>What is parallelism? Which elements of a sentence should be parallel? | Parallelism involves using a similar grammatical form for each element of equal importance in a sentence. The following elements of a sentence should be parallel: nouns in a series, adjectives in a series, verbs in a series, clauses within sentences, and items being compared or contrasted. |
| ▪ GOAL 5 Understand difficult and complicated sentences<br><br>What makes sentences difficult, and what are strategies for handling difficult sentences? | Sentences may be difficult because of vocabulary, length, number of clauses and phrases, difficult concepts or technical material, or a lack of background knowledge. See Table 9-1 (p. 283) for strategies for handling complicated sentences. |

# MySkillsLab

For more help with **Pronouns; Avoiding Shifts in Person, Number, and Verb Tense; Avoiding Misplaced and Dangling Modifiers; and Parallelism**, go to your learning path in MySkillsLab at http://www.myskillslab.com.

# 10

# Main Ideas and Topic Sentences

## THINK About It!

Write a sentence describing the single overall feeling you get from this photograph. Do you sense the athletes' joy and elation? Many photographs convey a single impression, as this one does. Details in the photograph support that impression. Paragraphs also convey a single impression—a single important idea—and details support that impression. In this chapter you will learn how sentences in a paragraph are organized and how they work together to express a single idea.

## FOCUSING ON READING AND WRITING

# What Are Topics, Main Ideas, and Topic Sentences?

Understanding or writing a paragraph is a step-by-step process. A paragraph focuses on one subject, called the **topic**. The paragraph makes one point about that topic, called the **main idea**. That main idea is often expressed in a single sentence, called the **topic sentence**. The rest of the paragraph, called **details**, explains the main idea.

Here is a sample paragraph.

> Because students often mix energy drinks with alcohol for the sake of masking the taste or effects of alcohol, these drinks can be particularly dangerous. Students who report consuming alcohol mixed energy drinks (AMEDs) tend to drink more than students who do not drink AMEDS (8.3 drinks vs. 6.1 drinks). Students also report not noticing the signs of intoxication (dizziness, fatigue, headache, and trouble walking) when they had consumed AMEDs. Students who reported drinking AMEDs had an increased prevalence of several alcohol-related consequences of drinking. They were more likely to be taken advantage of sexually, and twice as likely to take advantage of someone sexually, ride with a drunk driver, be hurt or injured, or require medical treatment.

In this paragraph, the topic is *energy drinks and alcohol*. The main idea is that energy drinks mixed with alcohol can be dangerous. The remainder of the paragraph explains why the mix is dangerous. You can visualize the paragraph as follows:

**VISUALIZE IT!**

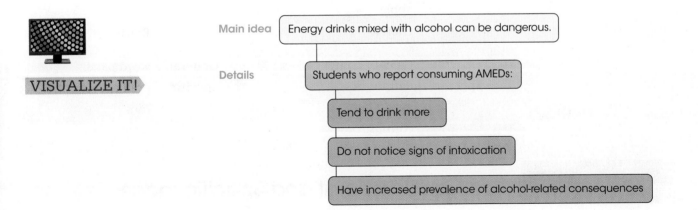

In this chapter, you will learn how to identify topics, main ideas, and topic sentences. You will also learn how to choose effective topics and write topic sentences. In the next chapter, you will learn to identify and write details that support the main idea.

> ! **NEED TO KNOW**
>
> **Important Terms**
>
> **Paragraph:** a group of sentences that focus on a single idea
>
> **Topic:** the one subject a paragraph is about
>
> **Main idea:** the point the paragraph makes about a topic
>
> **Topic sentence:** the sentence that states the paragraph's main idea
>
> **Supporting details:** those sentences that explain the topic sentence

## READING

# Understand General Versus Specific Ideas

■ GOAL 1
Understand general
versus specific ideas

To identify topics and main ideas in paragraphs, it will help you to understand the difference between general and specific. A **general** idea is a broad idea that applies to a large number of individual items. The term *clothing* is general because it refers to a large collection of individual items—pants, suits, blouses, shirts, scarves, and so on. A **specific** idea or term is more detailed or particular. It refers to an individual item. The word *scarf,* for example, is a specific term. The phrase *red plaid scarf* is even more specific.

| | | | | |
|---|---|---|---|---|
| **General:** | pies | | **General:** | countries |
| **Specific:** | chocolate cream | | **Specific:** | Great Britain |
| | apple | | | Finland |
| | cherry | | | Brazil |
| | | | | |
| **General:** | types of context clues | | **General:** | word parts |
| **Specific:** | definition | | **Specific:** | prefix |
| | example | | | root |
| | contrast | | | suffix |

**EXERCISE 10-1**  Analyzing General and Specific Ideas

**Directions:** Read each of the following items and decide what term(s) will complete the group. Write the word(s) in the spaces provided.

1. General:  college courses

   Specific:  math

   _____  Answers will vary

   _____

2. General: _____ *flowers* _____

   Specific:  roses

            tulips

            narcissus

3. General:  musical groups

   Specific: _____ *Answers will vary* _____

   _____

   _____

4. General:  art

   Specific:  sculpture

   _____ *Answers will vary* _____

   _____

5. General:  types of movies

   Specific:  comedies

   _____ *Answers will vary* _____

   _____

---

| EXERCISE 10-2 | Identifying General Ideas |

**Directions:** For each set of specifics, select the general idea that best describes it.

_c_   1. Specific ideas: Michelle Obama, Laura Bush, Nancy Reagan
      **a.** famous twentieth-century women
      **b.** famous American parents
      **c.** wives of American presidents
      **d.** famous wives

_d_   2. Specific ideas: touchdown, home run, 3-pointer, 5 under par
      **a.** types of errors in sports
      **b.** types of activities
      **c.** types of sports
      **d.** types of scoring in sports

_c_   3. Specific ideas: for companionship, to play with, because you love animals
      **a.** reasons to visit the zoo
      **b.** reasons to feed your cat
      **c.** reasons to get a pet
      **d.** ways to solve problems

_a_   4. Specific ideas: taking a hot bath, going for a walk, watching a video, listening to music
      **a.** ways to relax
      **b.** ways to help others
      **c.** ways to listen
      **d.** ways to solve problems

_b_   **5.** Specific ideas: listen, be helpful, be generous, be forgiving
   **a.** ways to get a job
   **b.** ways to keep a friend
   **c.** ways to learn
   **d.** ways to appreciate a movie

| EXERCISE 10-3 | Identifying General Terms |

**Directions:** Underline the most general term in each group of words.

**1.** pounds, ounces, kilograms, <u>weights</u>

**2.** soda, coffee, <u>beverage</u>, wine

**3.** soap operas, news, <u>TV programs</u>, sports specials

**4.** <u>home furnishings</u>, carpeting, drapes, wall hangings

**5.** sociology, <u>social sciences</u>, anthropology, psychology

## Apply General and Specific to Paragraphs

Now we will apply the idea of general and specific to paragraphs. The main idea is the most general statement the writer makes about the topic. Pick out the most general statement among the following sentences:

**1.** People differ according to height.

**2.** Hair color distinguishes some people from others.

**3.** People differ in a number of ways.

**4.** Each person has his or her own personality.

Did you choose sentence 3 as the most general statement? Now we will change this list into a paragraph by rearranging the sentences and adding a few facts.

> People differ in a number of ways. They differ according to physical characteristics, such as height, weight, and hair color. They also differ in personality. Some people are friendly and easygoing. Others are more reserved and formal.

In this brief paragraph, the main idea is expressed in the first sentence. This sentence is the most general statement expressed in the paragraph. All the other statements are specific details that explain this main idea.

| EXERCISE 10-4 | Identifying General Statements |

**Directions:** For each of the following groups of sentences, select the most general statement the writer makes about the topic.

_b_   **1. a.** Brightly colored annuals, such as pansies and petunias, are often used as seasonal accents in a garden.
   **b.** Most gardens feature a mix of perennials and annuals.

        **c.** Some perennials prefer shade, while others thrive in full sun.

        **d.** Butterfly bushes are a popular perennial.

_a_    **2. a.** Hiring a housepainter is not as simple as it sounds.

        **b.** You should try to obtain a cost estimate from at least three painters.

        **c.** Each painter should be able to provide reliable references from past painting jobs.

        **d.** The painter must be able to work within the time frame you desire.

_d_    **3. a.** Flaxseed is an herbal treatment for constipation.

        **b.** Some people use kava to treat depression.

        **c.** Gingko biloba is a popular remedy for memory loss.

        **d.** A growing number of consumers are turning to herbal remedies to treat certain ailments.

_b_    **4. a.** Many students choose to live off-campus in apartments or rental houses.

        **b.** Most colleges and universities offer a variety of student housing options.

        **c.** Sororities and fraternities typically allow members to live in their organization's house.

        **d.** On-campus dormitories provide a convenient place for students to live.

_c_    **5. a.** Try to set exercise goals that are challenging but realistic.

        **b.** Increase the difficulty of your workout gradually.

        **c.** Several techniques contribute to success when beginning an exercise program.

        **d.** Reduce soreness by gently stretching your muscles before you exercise.

# Identify the Topic

**GOAL 2**
Identify the topic

The **topic** is the subject of the entire paragraph. Every sentence in a paragraph in some way discusses or explains this topic. If you had to choose a title for a paragraph, the one or two words you would choose are the topic.

To find the topic of a paragraph, ask yourself: What is the one thing the author is discussing throughout the paragraph?

Now read the following paragraph with that question in mind:

> Asthma is caused by inflammation of the airways in the lungs, leading to wheezing, chest tightness, shortness of breath, and coughing. In most people, asthma is brought on by allergens or irritants in the air; some people also have exercise-induced asthma. People with asthma can generally control their symptoms through the use of inhaled medications, and most asthmatics keep a "rescue" inhaler of medication on hand to use in case of a flare-up.

—adapted from Donatelle, *Health: The Basics*, p. 424

In this example, the author is discussing one topic—asthma—throughout the paragraph. Notice that the word *asthma* is used several times. Often the repeated use of a word can serve as a clue to the topic.

| EXERCISE 10-5 | Identifying the Topic |

**Directions:** Read each of the following paragraphs and then select the topic of the paragraph from the choices given.

_c_ **1.** People have been making glass in roughly the same way for at least 2,000 years. The process involves melting certain Earth materials and cooling the liquid quickly before the atoms have time to form an orderly crystalline structure. This is the same way that natural glass, called obsidian, is generated from lava. It is possible to produce glass from a variety of materials, but most commercial glass is produced from quartz sand and lesser amounts of carbonate minerals.

—Lutgens et al., *Essentials of Geology*, p. 62

**a.** Earth
**b.** atoms
**c.** glass
**d.** lava

_a_ **2.** The large majority of shoplifting is not done by professional thieves or by people who genuinely need the stolen items. About 2 million Americans are charged with shoplifting each year, but analysts estimate that for every arrest, 18 unreported incidents occur. About three-quarters of those caught are middle- or high-income people who shoplift for the thrill of it or as a substitute for affection. Shoplifting is also common among adolescents. Research evidence indicates that teen shoplifting is influenced by factors such as having friends who also shoplift.

—Solomon, *Consumer Behavior*, p. 35

**a.** shoplifting
**b.** shopping
**c.** professional thieves
**d.** adolescents

_d_ **3.** Kidney transplants are performed when the kidneys fail due to kidney disease. The kidneys are a pair of bean-shaped organs located under the rib cage by the small of the back. Each kidney is a little smaller than a fist and functions as a filter to remove toxins and wastes from the blood. When kidneys fail, waste products build up in the blood, which can be toxic.

—adapted from Belk and Maier, *Biology: Science for Life with Physiology*, p. 438

**a.** organ transplants
**b.** organ disease
**c.** toxins
**d.** kidneys

_c_ **4.** In order to survive, hunting and gathering societies depend on hunting animals and gathering plants. In some groups, the men do the hunting, and the women the gathering. In others, both men and women (and children) gather plants, the men hunt large animals, and both men and women hunt small animals. Hunting and gathering societies are small, usually consisting of only 25 to 40 people. These groups are nomadic. As their food supply dwindles in one area, they move to another location. They place high value on sharing food, which is essential to their survival.

—adapted from Henslin, *Sociology: A Down-to-Earth Approach*, p. 149

  a. hunters
  b. food supplies
  c. hunting and gathering societies
  d. survival

_b_   **5.**   People who call themselves freegans are modern-day scavengers who live off discards as a political statement against corporations and consumerism. They forage through supermarket trash and eat the slightly bruised produce or just-expired canned goods that we routinely throw out, and obtain surplus food from sympathetic stores and restaurants. Freegans dress in castoff clothes and furnish their homes with items they find on the street. They get the word on locations where people are throwing out a lot of stuff by checking out postings at freecycle.org and at so-called *freemeets* (flea markets where no one exchanges money).

—adapted from Solomon, *Consumer Behavior*, pp. 392–393

  a. scavengers
  b. freegans
  c. recycling
  d. freemeets

## EXERCISE 10-6    Identifying the Topic

**Directions:** Read each of the following paragraphs and write the topic of the paragraph in the space provided.

  **1.**   The word *locavore* has been coined to describe people who eat only food grown or produced locally, usually within close proximity to their homes. Locavores rely on farmers' markets, homegrown foods, or foods grown by independent farmers. Locavores prefer these foods because they are thought to be fresher, are more environmentally friendly, and require far fewer resources to get them to market and keep them fresh for longer periods of time. Locavores believe that locally grown organic food is preferable to large corporation- or supermarket-based organic foods, as local foods have a smaller impact on the environment.

—adapted from Donatelle, *Health: The Basics*, p. 282

Topic: _____ locavores _____

  **2.**   A monopoly exists when an industry or market has only one producer (or else is so dominated by one producer that other firms cannot compete with it). A sole supplier enjoys nearly complete control over the prices of its products. Its only constraint is a decrease in consumer demand due to increased prices or government regulation. In the United States, laws forbid many monopolies and regulate prices charged by natural monopolies—industries in which one company can most efficiently supply all needed goods or services. Many electric companies are natural monopolies because they can supply all the power needed in a local area.

—adapted from Ebert and Griffin, *Business Essentials*, p. 12

Topic: _____ monopolies _____

3.    Values represent cultural standards by which we determine what is good, bad, right, or wrong. Sometimes these values are expressed as proverbs or sayings that teach us how to live. Do you recognize the phrase, "Life is like a box of chocolates—you never know what you're going to get"? This modern-day saying is popular among those who embrace life's unpredictability. Cultures are capable of growth and change, so it's possible for a culture's values to change over time.

—Carl, *Think Sociology*, p. 51

Topic: _____ values _____

4.    They go by many different names—capsule hotels, modular hotels, and pod hotels—but they all have one thing in common: very efficient use of space in a small footprint. The concept of modular hotels was pioneered by the Japanese, but the idea is sweeping across the world. Priced well below most competitors, these small, 75- to 100-square-foot rooms don't waste any space. Most modular units include the basics: private bathrooms, beds that are designed for two, flat-screen televisions, and a small work space. Weary travelers looking for nothing more than a place to sleep are finding that modular hotels "fit the bill."

—adapted from Cook et al., *Tourism: The Business of Travel*, p. 347

Topic: _____ modular hotels _____

5.    Television commercials provide a rich source of material to analyze. Begin by asking, "What reasons am I being given to lead me to want to buy this product?" Often, commercials do not overtly state the reasons; instead, they use music, staging, gestures, and visual cues to suggest the ideas they want us to have. We probably will not find a commercial that comes right out and says that buying someone a bottle of perfume or piece of jewelry will lead to a fulfilling love life, but several holiday commercials certainly imply as much.

—adapted from Facione, *Think Critically*, p. 90

Topic: _____ commercials _____

# Identify the Main Idea

■ GOAL 3
Identify the main idea

You learned on page 298 that the main idea of a paragraph is the most general statement the writer makes about the topic. Use the following suggestions for finding main ideas in paragraphs.

## Tips for Finding the Main Idea

Here are some tips that will help you find the main idea:

1. **Identify the topic.** As you did earlier, figure out the general subject of the entire paragraph. In the previous sample paragraph, "how people differ" is the topic.

2. **Locate the most general sentence (the topic sentence).** This sentence must be broad enough to include all of the other ideas in the paragraph. The topic sentence in the sample paragraph ("People differ in numerous ways.") covers all of the other details in that paragraph. The tips in the next section will help you locate topic sentences.

3. **Study the rest of the paragraph.** The main idea must make the rest of the paragraph meaningful. It is the one idea that ties all of the other details together. In the sample paragraph, sentences 2, 3, 4, and 5 all give specific details about how people differ.

# Identify the Topic Sentence

■ GOAL 4
Identify the topic sentence

The topic sentence states the main idea of a paragraph.

## Tips for Locating the Topic Sentence

Although a topic sentence can be located anywhere in a paragraph, it is usually *first* or *last*.

### Topic Sentence First

In most paragraphs, the topic sentence comes first. The author states his or her main point and then explains it.

General    Topic Sentence
               Detail
Specific       Detail
               Detail

> Good listeners follow specific steps in order to achieve accurate understanding. First, whenever possible, good listeners prepare in advance for the speech or lecture they are going to attend. They study the topic to be discussed and find out about the speaker and his or her beliefs. Second, when they arrive at the place where the speech is to be given, they choose a seat where it is easy to see, hear, and remain alert. Finally, when the speech is over, effective listeners review what was said and evaluate the ideas that were expressed.

In the first sentence, the writer states that good listeners follow specific steps. The rest of the paragraph lists those steps.

### Topic Sentence Last

The second most likely place for a topic sentence to appear is last in a paragraph. When using this arrangement, a writer leads up to the main point and then states it at the end. Here is a paragraph almost identical to the preceding one, but with the topic sentence last:

Specific    Detail
            Detail
            Detail
General     Topic Sentence

> Whenever possible, good listeners prepare in advance for the speech or lecture they plan to attend. They study the topic to be discussed and find out about the speaker and his or her beliefs. When they arrive at the place where the speech is to be given, they choose a seat where it is easy to see, hear, and remain alert. And when the speech is over, they review what was said and evaluate the ideas that were expressed. Thus, effective listeners follow specific steps in order to achieve accurate understanding.

This paragraph lists all the steps that good listeners follow. Then, at the end, the writer states the main idea.

### Topic Sentence in the Middle

If a topic sentence is placed neither first nor last, then it may appear somewhere in the middle of a paragraph. In this arrangement, the sentences before the topic sentence lead up to or introduce the main idea. Those that follow the main idea explain or describe it.

> Whenever possible, good listeners prepare in advance for the speech or lecture they plan to attend. They study the topic to be discussed and find out about the speaker and his or her beliefs. Effective listeners, then, take specific steps to achieve accurate understanding of the lecture. Furthermore, when they arrive at the place where the speech is to be given, they choose a seat where it is easy to see, hear, and remain alert. Finally, when the speech is over, effective listeners review what was said and evaluate the ideas that were expressed.

This paragraph begins with two examples of what good listeners do. Then the writer states the main idea and continues with more examples.

### Topic Sentence First and Last

Occasionally writers put the main idea at the beginning of a paragraph and again at the end. Writers may do this to emphasize the main point or to clarify it.

> Good listeners follow specific steps in order to achieve accurate understanding. First, whenever possible, good listeners prepare in advance for the speech or lecture they are going to attend. They study the topic to be discussed and find out about the speaker and his or her beliefs. Second, when they arrive at the place where the speech is to be given, they choose a seat where it is easy to see, hear, and remain alert. Finally, when the speech is over, they review what was said and evaluate the ideas that were expressed. Effective listening, then, is an active process in which listeners deliberately take certain actions to ensure that accurate communication has occurred.

The first and last sentences both state, in slightly different ways, the main idea of the paragraph—that good listeners follow certain steps.

## EXERCISE 10-7 | Identifying Topic Sentences

**Directions:** Underline the topic sentence in each of the following paragraphs. Keep in mind that topic sentences can appear at the beginning, middle, or end of a paragraph.

1. Fast foods tend to be short on fresh fruits and vegetables, and are low in calcium, although calcium can be obtained in shakes and milk. Pizza is a fast-food exception. It contains grains, meat, vegetables, and cheese, which represent four of the food groups. Pizza is often only about 25 percent fat, most of which comes from the crust. Overall, studies have shown pizza to be highly nutritious.
—Byer and Shainberg, *Living Well*, p. 289.

2. In recent years there have been many cases of college students dying from binge drinking, which involves having at least five drinks in a row for men or four drinks in a row for women. According to Dr. David Anderson, of George Mason

University in Fairfax, Virginia, at least 50 college students throughout the United States drink themselves to death every year. While endangering their own lives, binge drinkers also tend to disturb or hurt their fellow students, such as causing them to lose sleep, interrupting their studies, and assaulting them physically or sexually.

—Thio, *Sociology*, p. 141

3.   When consumers are in a store to buy an expensive product, they may feel pressured to purchase immediately. The sales staff may exert pressure, or they may create their own pressure. After all, the trip has cost time and effort, and the buyers don't want to appear indecisive. For important purchases, it is often advisable to invest a bit more time before making a final decision. In fact, consumers should go home and evaluate and weigh the purchase decision. At home consumers are free of external pressures exerted by the sales environment and the sales staff. Consumers can also ask themselves important questions such as "Can I really afford this?" and "Is this the best product I can find for the price?"

4.   Suppose you are preparing to give a speech to a group of people. Assume you are in a position where you can observe the group. What are they wearing? Are they dressed casually, formally, informally, trendily, classily, or wildly? Do they seem well-to-do or frugal? What are their hobbies? What sports are they involved with? To what age range do most of the group members belong? What are their occupations? Are they professional or blue-collar workers? Assessing the characteristics of your audience will allow you to make inferences about its values and interests and enable you to tailor your speech to those interests.

5.   In the United States, Australia, and Western Europe people are encouraged to be independent. Members of these cultures are taught to get ahead, to compete, to win, to achieve their goals, to realize their unique potential, to stand out from the crowd. In many Asian and African countries, people are taught to value an interdependent self. Members of these cultures are taught to get along, to help others, and to not disagree or stand out. Thus, there are significant cultural differences in the way people are taught to view themselves.

—adapted from DeVito, *Human Communication*, p. 78

6.   With so many people participating in social networking sites and keeping personal blogs, it's increasingly common for a single disgruntled customer to wage war online against a company for poor service or faulty products. Unhappy customers have taken to the Web to complain about broken computers or poor customer service. Individuals may post negative reviews of products on blogs, upload angry videos outlining complaints on YouTube, or join public discussion forums where they can voice their opinion about the good and the bad. In the same way that companies celebrate the viral spread of good news, they must also be on guard for online backlash that can damage a reputation.

—adapted from Ebert and Griffin, *Business Essentials*, p. 161

7.   Elections serve a critical function in American society. They make it possible for most political participation to be channeled through the electoral process rather than bubbling up through demonstrations, riots, or revolutions. Elections provide regular access to political power, so that leaders can be replaced without being overthrown. This is possible because elections are almost universally accepted as a fair and free method of selecting political leaders. Furthermore,

by choosing who is to lead the country, the people—if they make their choices carefully—can also guide the policy direction of the government.

—adapted from Edwards et al., *Government in America*, p. 306

8.     <u>Darwin hypothesized sexual selection as an explanation for differences between males and females within a species.</u> For instance, the enormous tail on a male peacock results from female peahens that choose mates with showier tails. Because large tails require so much energy to display and are more conspicuous to their predators, peacocks with the largest tails must be both physically strong and smart to survive. Peahens can use the size of the tail, therefore, as a measure of the "quality" of the male. When a peahen chooses a male with a large tail, she is making sure that her offspring will receive high-quality genes. <u>Sexual selection explains the differences between males and females in many species.</u>

—adapted from Belk and Maier, *Biology: Science for Life with Physiology*, p. 305

9.     In Japan, it's called *kuroi kiri* (black mist); in Germany, it's *schmiergeld* (grease money), whereas Mexicans refer to *la mordida* (the bite), the French say *pot-de-vin* (jug of wine), and Italians speak of the *bustarella* (little envelope). They're all talking about *baksheesh,* the Middle Eastern term for a "tip" to grease the wheels of a transaction. <u>Giving "gifts" in exchange for getting business is common and acceptable in many countries, even though this may be frowned on elsewhere.</u>

—adapted from Solomon, *Consumer Behavior*, p. 21

10.     <u>The standards of our peer groups tend to dominate our lives.</u> If your peers, for example, listen to rap, rock and roll, country, or gospel, it is almost inevitable that you also prefer that kind of music. In high school, if your friends take math courses, you probably do too. It is the same for clothing styles and dating standards. Peer influences also extend to behaviors that violate social norms. If your peers are college-bound and upwardly striving, that is most likely what you will be; but if they use drugs, cheat, and steal, you are likely to do so too.

—adapted from Henslin, *Sociology: A Down-to-Earth Approach*, p. 85

## WRITING

# Choose a Manageable Topic

■ GOAL 5
Choose a manageable topic

The topic you choose for a paragraph must not be *too broad* or *too narrow*. It must be the right size to cover in a single paragraph. If you choose a topic that is too broad, you will have too much to say. Your paragraph will wander and seem unfocused. If you choose a topic that is too narrow (too small), you will not have enough to say. Your paragraph will seem skimpy.

Suppose you want to write a paragraph about pollution. You write the following topic sentence:

Pollution is everywhere.

Clearly, the topic of global pollution is too broad to cover in a single paragraph. Pollution has numerous types, causes, effects, and potential solutions. Would you write about causes? If so, could you write about all possible causes in one paragraph? What about effects? Are you concerned with immediate effects? Long-term effects? You can see that the topic of widespread global pollution is not a manageable one for a single paragraph. You could make this topic more manageable by limiting it to a specific pollutant, an immediate source or effect, and a particular place. Your revised topic sentence might read:

> Fuel emissions from poorly maintained cars greatly increase air pollution in the United States.

This topic may still prove too broad to cover in a single paragraph. You could narrow it further by limiting the topic to a particular city in the United States, or even a particular type of fuel emission.

Shown below are a few more examples of topics that are too broad. Each one has been revised to be more specific.

| | |
|---|---|
| **TOO BROAD** | Water conservation |
| REVISED | Lawn-watering restrictions |
| | |
| **TOO BROAD** | Effects of water shortages |
| REVISED | Sinkholes caused by water shortages |
| | |
| **TOO BROAD** | Crop irrigation |
| REVISED | A system for allocating water for crop irrigation in the San Joaquin Valley |

If your topic is too narrow, you will run out of things to say in your paragraph. You also run the risk of straying from your topic as you search for ideas to include. Suppose you want to write a paragraph about environmental waste. You write the following topic sentence:

> Each year Americans discard 2 billion disposable razors.

This sentence is too specific. It could work as a detail, but it is too narrow to be a topic sentence. To turn this statement into a good topic sentence, try to make your topic more general. Your revised topic sentence could be

> Each year Americans strain their landfills with convenient but environmentally damaging products.

You then could develop a paragraph such as the following:

### Sample Paragraph

Each year Americans strain their landfills with convenient but environmentally damaging products. For example, Americans discard billions of disposable razors. Disposable diapers are another popular product. Parents use mountains of them on their children instead of washable cloth diapers. Milk, which used to come in reusable glass bottles, is now sold mainly in plastic or cardboard cartons that can only be used once. Other items, such as Styrofoam cups, aluminum cans, disposable cameras, and ballpoint pens, add to the solid-waste problem in this country. Eventually people will need to realize it's not OK to "use it once, then throw it away."

Here are a few other examples of topics that are too narrow. Each one has been revised to be less specific.

| TOO NARROW | 250 million used tires are discarded each year |
| REVISED | a solution to the problem of used tires |

| TOO NARROW | only 4 percent of plastics are recycled |
| REVISED | how consumers can take plastic recycling seriously |

| TOO NARROW | consumers receive five cents per can to recycle aluminum cans |
| REVISED | how money motivates many consumers to recycle |

## EXERCISE 10-8 — Evaluating Topics

**Directions:** For each of the following pairs of topics, place a check mark before the one that is more effective (neither too broad nor too narrow).

1. _____ **a.** team sports
   _✓_ **b.** what a child can learn by participating in team sports

2. _____ **a.** the U.S. Marshal Service
   _✓_ **b.** the role of U.S. Marshals in witness protection

3. _✓_ **a.** driving contracts between parents and teenagers
   _____ **b.** driving

4. _✓_ **a.** birthday traditions in your family
   _____ **b.** holiday celebrations

5. _____ **a.** the percentage of Americans who live on farms
   _✓_ **b.** a typical visit to your grandparents' farm

## EXERCISE 10-9 — Narrowing a Topic

**WRITING IN PROGRESS**

**Directions:** Choose three of the following topics and narrow each one to a topic manageable in a single paragraph. Use one of the techniques for generating ideas described in Chapter 2 to help you (see p. 62).

1. Packaging of products
2. The value of parks and "green spaces"
3. Rugby
4. Animal migration patterns
5. Building environmental awareness
6. Road trips
7. New electronic devices
8. Superstitions
9. Civic responsibilities
10. The importance of pets

# Write Effective Topic Sentences

**■ GOAL 6**
Write effective topic
sentences

An effective topic sentence must

■ identify what the paragraph is about (the topic).

■ make a point (an idea) about that topic.

Suppose your topic is acid rain. You could make a number of different points about acid rain. Each of the following is a possible topic sentence:

1. Acid rain has caused conflict between the United States and Canada.

2. Acid rain could be reduced by controlling factory emissions.

3. Acid rain has adversely affected the populations of fish in our lakes.

Each of the sentences identifies acid rain as the topic, but each expresses a different point about acid rain. Each would lead to a different paragraph and be supported by different details.

Think of your topic sentence as a headline; it states what your paragraph will contain. You can also think of a topic sentence as a <u>promise</u>. Your topic sentence promises your reader what you will deliver in the paragraph.

What does each of the following topic sentences promise the reader?

1. There are three basic ways to dispose of sewage sludge.

2. Each year we discard valuable raw materials into landfills.

3. Many people do not understand how easy composting is.

Sentence 1 promises to explain three ways to dispose of sewage sludge. Sentence 2 promises to tell what valuable resources we discard. Sentence 3 promises to explain how easy composting is.

Your topic sentence must be a clear and direct statement of what the paragraph will be about. Use the following suggestions to write effective topic sentences:

■ **Be sure your topic sentence is a complete thought.** If your sentence is a fragment, run-on sentence, or comma splice, your meaning will be unclear or incomplete.

| | |
|---|---|
| FRAGMENT | People who don't throw their litter in the bin. |
| REVISED | People who don't throw their litter in the bin should be fined. |
| RUN-ON SENTENCE | The audience was captivated by the speaker no one spoke or moved. |
| REVISED | The audience was captivated by the speaker; no one spoke or moved. |
| COMMA SPLICE | Many children's games copy adult behavior, playing nurse or doctor is an example |
| REVISED | Many children's games, for example playing nurse or doctor, copy adult behavior. |

Chapter 5 and Chapter 6 discuss how to spot and correct these errors.

■ **Place your topic sentence first in the paragraph.** You *may* place your topic sentence anywhere in the paragraph, but you will find it easier to develop your paragraph around the topic sentence if you put it first.

■ **Avoid direct announcements or statements of intent.** Avoid sentences that sound like formal announcements, such as the following examples:

| ANNOUNCEMENT | In this paragraph, I will show that the average American is unaware of the dangers of smog. |
| --- | --- |
| REVISED | The average American is unaware of the dangers of smog. |
| ANNOUNCEMENT | This paragraph will explain why carbon monoxide is a dangerous air pollutant. |
| REVISED | There are three primary reasons why carbon monoxide is a dangerous air pollutant. |

Not all expert or professional writers follow all of these suggestions. Sometimes, a writer may use one-sentence paragraphs or include topic sentences that are fragments to achieve a special effect. You will find these paragraphs in news and magazine articles and other sources. Although professional writers can use these variations effectively, you probably should not experiment with them too early. It is best while you are polishing your skills to use a more standard style of writing.

### EXERCISE 10-10 — Evaluating Topic Sentences

**Directions:** Evaluate each of the following topic sentences and mark them as follows:

E = effective          N = not complete thought
G = too general        S = too specific
A = announcement

___A___ **1.** I will describe what causes the hiccups and how to cure them.

___G___ **2.** Summer camps are excellent for children.

___S___ **3.** Asking a professor for a recommendation is an important part of applying for a summer internship.

___E___ **4.** Palliative care programs offer many benefits to seriously ill patients and their families.

___A___ **5.** This paper will explain why the best place to get your next dog or cat is at an animal shelter.

___N___ **6.** Learning how to drive a manual transmission car.

___S___ **7.** The number of students who participate in practical work experiences while studying abroad has increased by 35 percent.

___G___ **8.** African American soldiers played an important role during war time.

___E___ **9.** There are five factors to consider when choosing a major.

___N___ **10.** The process of chocolate-making from bean to bar.

### EXERCISE 10-11 — Revising Topic Sentences

**Directions:** Analyze the following topic sentences. If a sentence is too general or too specific, makes a direct announcement, or is not a complete thought, revise it to make it more effective. *Possible answers are shown.*

1. Short stories are fun to read.

   REVISED:    *too general*

   _Short stories often convey a message about an issue or personal concern._

2. I will explain the steps in teaching a child how to swim.

   REVISED:    *makes an announcement*

   _The steps in teaching a child to swim are easy to follow._

3. The Eastern Cougar was declared extinct in 2011.

   REVISED:    *too specific*

   _The Eastern Cougar is an example of the growing problem of species extinction._

4. Food deserts in urban areas.

   REVISED:    *incomplete thought*

   _Food deserts in urban areas make it difficult for residents to purchase healthy_
   _and reasonably priced fresh food._

5. A knowledge of world geography is important for everyone.

   REVISED:    *too general*

   _A knowledge of world geography is important when studying political conflicts._

---

| EXERCISE 10-12 | Writing a Topic Sentence |

WRITING IN PROGRESS

**Directions:** Write a topic sentence for each of the three topics that you chose in Exercise 10-9.

---

# Revise Ineffective Topic Sentences

■ GOAL 7
Revise ineffective topic
sentences

Your topic sentence is the most important sentence in the paragraph. It promises what the remainder of the paragraph will deliver. A weak topic sentence usually produces a weak paragraph. Your topic sentence will be weak if it (1) lacks a viewpoint or attitude, (2) is too broad, or (3) is too narrow.

## Topic Sentences That Lack a Point of View

A topic sentence should identify your topic *and* express an attitude or viewpoint. It must make a point about the topic.

If your topic is the old roller coaster at Starland Park, it is not enough to make a general statement of fact in your topic sentence.

LACKS POINT OF VIEW    There is an old roller coaster at Starland Park.

Your reader would rightly ask in this case, "So what?" A topic sentence needs to tell the reader what is important or interesting about your topic. It should state the point you are going to make in the rest of the paragraph. For every topic, you can find many points to make in a topic sentence. For example:

| | |
|---|---|
| EXPRESSES POINT OF VIEW | The old roller coaster at Starland Park is unsafe and should be torn down. |
| | The old roller coaster at Starland Park no longer seems as frightening as it did when I was young. |
| | Three types of people go on the old roller coaster at Starland Park: the brave, the scared, and the stupid. |

If you write a topic sentence that does not express a viewpoint, you will find you have very little or nothing to write about in the remainder of the paragraph. Look at these topic sentences:

| | |
|---|---|
| LACKS POINT OF VIEW | Pete works at the YMCA. |
| EXPRESSES POINT OF VIEW | Pete got over his shyness by working at the YMCA. |

If you used the first topic sentence, "Pete works at the YMCA," what else could you include in your paragraph? If you instead used the second topic sentence, you would have something to write about. You could describe Pete before and after he began working at the YMCA, discuss positive aspects of the job, or give examples of friends Pete has made through his work.

Notice how the following topic sentences have been revised to express a point of view.

| | |
|---|---|
| LACKS POINT OF VIEW | Mark plays soccer. |
| REVISED | Mark's true personality comes out when he plays soccer. [Details can explain Mark's personality as revealed by his soccer game.] |

| | |
|---|---|
| LACKS POINT OF VIEW | Professor Cooke teaches accounting. |
| REVISED | Professor Cooke makes accounting practical. [Details can describe how Professor Cooke makes accounting skills relevant to everyday life.] |

| | |
|---|---|
| LACKS POINT OF VIEW | I read newspapers. |
| REVISED | I recommend reading newspapers from back to front. [Details can give reasons why this method is best.] |

The following suggestions will help you revise your topic sentence if you discover that it lacks a point of view:

■ **Use brainstorming, freewriting, or branching.** Try to generate more ideas about your topic. Study your results to discover a way to approach your topic.

■ **Ask yourself questions about your topic sentence.** Specifically, ask "Why?" "How?" "So what?" or "Why is this important?" Answering your own questions will give you ideas for revising your topic sentence.

*WORKING TOGETHER*

# Revising Topic Sentences

**Directions:** The following topic sentences lack a point of view. Working with a classmate, revise each one to express an interesting view on the topic.    Answers will vary. Sample answers provided.

SENTENCE    I took a biology exam today.

REVISED    The biology exam that I took today contained a number of surprises.

1. I am taking a math course this semester.

    REVISED:    My math course this semester is more challenging than I expected it to be.

2. I purchased a video camera last week.

    REVISED:    The video camera I bought last week will be used to preserve family memories.

3. Soft rock was playing in the dentist's office.

    REVISED:    The soft rock playing in the dentist's office soothed some nervous patients but made me fish for my earplugs.

4. Sam has three televisions and four radios in his household.

    REVISED:    Because his job as a political blogger depends on his being up-to-date on current affairs, Sam has three televisions and four radios in his household.

5. There is one tree on the street where I live.

    REVISED:    The one oak tree on my street provides a canopy for children's games and play.

6. Many people wear headphones on their way to work.

    REVISED:    Many people wear headphones on their way to work to shut out surrounding noise and distractions.

7. Our sociology professor will give us three exams.

    REVISED:    The three exams our sociology professor will give us will force us to keep up with the reading assignments.

8. The first hurricane of the season is predicted to strike land tomorrow.

    REVISED:    The first hurricane of the season is predicted to strike land tomorrow, and tourists are panicking.

9. My four-year-old son has learned the alphabet.

    REVISED:    My four-year-old son has learned the alphabet, so he is eager to learn to read.

10. Juanita enrolled her son in a day-care center.

    REVISED:    Juanita enrolled her son in a day-care center to encourage him to play cooperatively with other children.

## Topic Sentences That Are Too Broad

Some topic sentences express a point of view, but they are too broad in scope.

> TOO BROAD    The death penalty is a crime against humanity.

This statement cannot be supported in a single paragraph. Lengthy essays, even entire books, have been written to argue this opinion.

A broad topic sentence promises more than you can reasonably deliver in a single paragraph. It leads to writing that is vague and rambling. With a broad topic sentence, you will end up with too many facts and ideas to cover or too many generalities (general statements) that do not sufficiently explain your topic sentence. In the following example, note the broad topic sentence and its effects on paragraph development.

### Sample Paragraph

> All kinds of violent crimes in the world today seem to be getting worse. Sometimes I wonder how people could possibly bring themselves to do such horrible things. One problem may be the violent acts shown on television programs. Some people think crime has a lot to do with horror movies and television programs. We have no heroes to identify with other than criminals. News reporting of crimes is too "real"; it shows too much. Kids watch these programs without their parents and don't know what to make of them. Parents should spend time with their children and supervise their play.

The topic sentence above promises more than a good paragraph can reasonably deliver: to discuss all violent crimes in the world today and their worsening nature. If you reread the paragraph, you will see that in the supporting sentences the author wanders from topic to topic. She first mentions violence on television, then moves to lack of heroes. Next she discusses news reporting that is too graphic, then switches to children watching programs alone. Finally, she ends with parental supervision of children. Each point about possible causes of violence or ways to prevent it seems underdeveloped.

An effective topic sentence needs to be more focused. For example, the topic sentence for a paragraph about crime might focus on one type of crime in one city and one reason for its increase.

> FOCUSED    Home burglaries are increasing in Owensville because of increased drug usage.

Another effective topic sentence for a paragraph on crime could focus on one possible cause of rising violence in the workplace.

> FOCUSED    The mass layoffs in the past few years have led to more criminal acts by desperate, unemployed workers.

The topic sentence of the following paragraph is also too broad.

### Sample Paragraph

> People often forget the spirit and value of life and concentrate on worldly goods. These people buy things for show—nice cars, nice clothes, nice houses. These people are scraping their pennies together just to live well. They do not

realize that things not from the store are just as nice. Their health, their families, and the people they care about are far more important than money. You can be rich and poor at the same time.

Because the topic was too broad, the writer continued to use general statements throughout the paragraph and to repeat the same or similar ideas. A more effective approach might be to select one worldly good and show how it affects one person.

> FOCUSED    My sister is so concerned with dressing stylishly that she ignores everyone around her.

Now the writer can explain how an emphasis on clothing detracts from her sister's relationship with others.

Another effective topic sentence might focus the paragraph on not taking good health for granted:

> FOCUSED    I used to think I could buy my way to happiness, but that was before I lost my good health.

The following suggestions will help you revise your topic sentence if you discover that it is too broad:

- **Narrow your topic.** A topic that is too broad often produces a topic sentence that is too broad. Narrow your topic by subdividing it into smaller topics. Continue subdividing until you produce a topic that is manageable in a single paragraph.

- **Rewrite your topic sentence to focus on one aspect or part of your topic.** Ask yourself, "What is the part of this topic that really interests me or that I care most about? What do I know most about the topic and have the most to say about?" Then focus on *that* aspect of the topic.

- **Apply your topic sentence to a specific time and place.** Ask yourself, "How does this broad topic that I'd like to write about relate to some particular time and place that I know about? How can I make the general topic come alive by using a well-defined example?"

- **Consider using one of your supporting sentences as a topic sentence.** Reread your paragraph; look for a detail that could be developed or expanded.

---

**EXERCISE 10-14**

*WORKING TOGETHER*

## Revising Topic Sentences

**Directions:** Turn each of the following broad topic sentences into a well-focused topic sentence that could lead to an effective paragraph. Remember that your topic sentence must also include a point of view. Then compare your answers with your classmates' answers to see the variety of effective topic sentences that can come from a broad one.    Answers will vary. Sample answers provided.

> TOO BROAD    Hunting is a worthwhile and beneficial sport.
> REVISED    Hunting deer in overpopulated areas is beneficial to the herd.

1. I would like to become more creative.

   REVISED: I would like to try writing songs as a way to express parts of

   myself that most people never see.

2. Brazil is a beautiful country.

   REVISED:   Brazil is an ideal vacation spot for people who like
   to relax and enjoy the scenery.

3. Pollution is a big problem.

   REVISED:   Asbestos in older buildings is a serious health hazard for people
   who plan to remodel these buildings.

4. The space program is amazing.

   REVISED:   The space program has enabled scientists to make technological
   advances that are useful to us in everyday life.

5. It is very important to learn Japanese.

   REVISED:   Learning Japanese will be an asset to anyone who wants to
   work in international trade.

6. We must protect the environment.

   REVISED:   To safeguard our drinking water, we must protect our lakes and
   rivers from industrial pollution.

7. Lani is a good mother.

   REVISED:   Lani feels the most important things she can teach her daughter
   are self-control and independence.

8. The book was interesting.

   REVISED:   The mystery novel *Decider*, by Dick Francis, contains many details of
   English horse racing that only a former jockey would know.

9. Lots of magazines are published.

   REVISED:   Sports fans can find a magazine to satisfy their craving
   for inside knowledge on almost any sport.

10. Honesty is important.

    REVISED:   Honesty with friends is important to maintain
    a trusting relationship.

## Topic Sentences That Are Too Narrow

If your topic sentence is too narrow, you will realize it right away because you won't have enough to write about to complete your paragraph. Topic sentences that are too narrow also frequently lack a point of view.

| TOO NARROW | My birdfeeder attracts yellow songbirds. |
| REVISED | Watching the different birds at our feeder is a pleasant diversion enjoyed by our entire family, including our cat. |
| TOO NARROW | My math instructor looks at his watch frequently. |
| REVISED | My math instructor has a number of nervous habits that detract from his lecture presentations. |

The following suggestions will help you revise your topic sentence when it is too narrow:

- **Broaden your topic to include a wider group or range of items or ideas.** For example, do not write about one nervous habit; write about several. Look for patterns and trends that could form the basis of a new, broader topic sentence.

- **Broaden your topic so that it takes in both causes and effects or makes comparisons or contrasts.** For example, do not write only about how fast an instructor lectures. Also write about the effect of his lecture speed on students trying to take notes, or contrast that instructor with others who have different lecture styles.

- **Brainstorm and research; try to develop a more general point from your narrower one.** Ask yourself, "What does this narrow point mean? What are its larger implications?" Suppose you've written the following topic sentence:

  > I wanted to buy a CD this week, but it was not in my budget.

  You could expand this idea to discuss the importance or value of making and following a weekly budget.

---

**EXERCISE 10-15**

## Broadening Topic Sentences

**Directions:** Turn each of the following narrow topic sentences into a broader, well-focused topic sentence that could lead to an effective paragraph. Remember that your topic sentence must also include a point of view. Then compare your answers with your classmates' answers to see the variety of effective topic sentences that can come from a narrow one.     Answers will vary. Sample answers provided.

**TOO NARROW**   Football players wear protective helmets.
**REVISED**   Football players wear several types of protective equipment to guard against injuries.

1. I planted a tomato plant in my garden.

   REVISED:   I planted enough vegetable plants in my garden to produce tasty salads throughout the summer.

2. The cafeteria served hot dogs and beans for lunch.

   REVISED:   The students complained that the cafeteria serves high-fat, calorie-laden foods.

3. Orlando sings in a low key.

   REVISED:   Orlando's soulful singing is intended to appeal to his audience.

4. Suzanne bought a stapler for her desk.

   REVISED:   Suzanne equipped her desk with supplies to enable her to work more efficiently.

5. Koala bears are really marsupials, not bears.

   REVISED:   Koalas, marsupials from Australia, are lovable animals that have become

   popular attractions at zoos.

6. On our vacation, we stopped at a small town called Boothbay Harbor.

   REVISED:   Boothbay Harbor is a picturesque New England coastal town that is

   ideal for a weekend vacation.

7. Homemade bread contains no preservatives.

   REVISED:   Homemade bread is healthier than most commercially made loaves.

8. At Halloween, the girl dressed as a witch.

   REVISED:   At Halloween, the girl dressed as a witch to frighten her younger brothers.

9. The comedian told a joke about dental floss.

   REVISED:   The comedian told several jokes that made fun of the dental profession.

10. We had a family portrait taken for Christmas.

    REVISED:   Each year, our family has a portrait taken for Christmas, which helps us

    trace our growth and changes in our family.

## ! NEED TO KNOW

### Topic Sentences

Ineffective paragraphs may frustrate, confuse, or bore your reader.

**A weak topic sentence may**

- lack a point of view or attitude toward the topic.
- be too broad.
- be too narrow.

**To revise a topic sentence that lacks a point of view**

- use brainstorming, freewriting, or branching.
- ask yourself questions about your topic sentence to focus on a particular viewpoint.

**To narrow a topic sentence that is too broad, consider**

- narrowing your topic.
- rewriting your topic sentence to focus on one aspect of your topic.
- applying your topic sentence to a specific time and place.
- using one of your supporting sentences as a topic sentence.

**To broaden a topic sentence that is too narrow, consider**

- broadening your topic to make it more inclusive.
- broadening your topic to consider causes and effects or to make comparisons or contrasts.
- brainstorming and researching to develop a more general point.

# INTEGRATING READING AND WRITING

## READ AND REVISE

**MySkillsLab®**

**Complete** this Exercise

The following excerpt is from an essay called "Going to the Movies." This excerpt contains topic sentences that are too broad, are too narrow, or lack a point of view. Underline each topic sentence; then revise the topic sentences to make them more effective.

Too broad [

Too specific [

There are many types of movies, and each contains unique features that make it appealing to audiences.

<u>There are many types of movies.</u> People are drawn to action/adventure films for the special effects, nonstop action, big-name stars, and "good guys versus bad guys" plots. Action/adventure films offer the audience pure escapism. Dramas are serious and often realistic, and they attract audiences more interested in character development and storyline than special effects. Comedies are another form of escapism, with plots, dialogue, and action all aimed at getting an audience to laugh. Comedies may also contain romantic elements and even special effects.

Horror movies offer a wide variety of special features that certain audiences enjoy. <u>Horror movies often feature aliens.</u> Horror movies may overlap with science fiction and other types of movies. Sometimes they even include comic elements. Horror movies may feature elaborate special effects or the most basic and amateurish camerawork. They may have big-name stars or no-name actors, simple or complex plots, high-tech androids or low-tech monsters. Some people enjoy the thrill of a good scare that a horror movie offers, while others would rather see any other type of movie—or just stay home.

## READ AND RESPOND: A Student Essay

*Alex Boyd is a sophomore at Beloit College in Wisconsin. He is considering a double major in Literary Studies and Sociology and is currently taking a number of English classes. He wrote the following essay in response to a prompt that asked students to write about a personal challenge they had faced and overcome.*

# Decision Time

Title creates interest

For as long as I can remember, I have had difficulty making hard decisions. It is very hard for me to commit to an idea and go with it without constantly questioning myself for it. This has definitely been an issue in pursuing my educational and college goals, but it is by no means an impossible problem to overcome. In fact, I believe that I have overcome my problem of being unable to make serious decisions and have grown from defeating the problem. Some of the decision making problems I have had to overcome are deciding what to study, whether it is better to focus on work or education, prioritization and time management, and being unsure of what I want to do as a career.

Thesis statement

Examples

Topic sentence expands on example in first paragraph

While I was young and going to elementary and middle school, I never had much choice in what I could study. I took math, language arts, history, and social studies. Everybody else took the exact same things too. When I got to high school and had a little choice in what I could study, I panicked. I had no idea what I was doing or what I was really interested in. I couldn't decide what classes to take because I was afraid I might miss something else interesting. However, I ended up talking to some of my teachers and asking what classes they recommended. I was the one who made the final decision about what to study, but it was very helpful to have the opinions of people I respect to think about. I realized that when I have trouble deciding, it helps me to talk to others.

Important realization #1

Topic sentence

Writer continues to expand on and support thesis

Another issue I faced in decision making in education was finding a balance between working and going to school. After graduating from high school, I did not immediately go to college. Instead, I spent a year working and saving up money that I might use for school. While I was doing this, I was thinking about if I was going to college or if I was going to keep working. I had trouble deciding whether I wanted to continue my education or earn money at a job. It was hard for me to figure out how I could do both. I overcame this by taking my time with the decisions. I realized there was no big rush and I could think about it all year. As I worked for more and more time, I decided that going back to school was the right decision for me. Taking my time in decision making helped me realize what I wanted to do.

Important realization #2

Topic sentence

Continuing to expand and support thesis

Like deciding between work and school, I had trouble with deciding what to do with my time while in school. Nearly every night I had homework to do and social or club events to do. I needed to do the homework and study, but I wanted to hang out with friends. I knew what I should decide to do, but I still often had trouble making the right decision. After trying really hard to commit to either academics or my social life, I realized I was struggling in both. I thought about having fun while working and working while having fun, so I was usually stressed. However, I realized that I was trying to make a decision when there really was no decision to make. The two could be balanced easily if I just took the time to do the work and focus to get things done before seeing my friends and being less stressed. I overcame this problem by realizing I was trying to make a decision when I didn't actually have to.

Details are easy to relate to

Important realization #3

Topic sentence

A major reason I am in college is to prepare for a job. One of the largest decisions I have had to make and struggle with is deciding what I would like to do

Important realization #4

Conclusion

Writer emphasizes the importance of being able to make decisions

for a career. While I was in high school, I was convinced I wanted to go to music school and become a professional musician. I had trouble deciding if I should do that or study something that could be better financially. I auditioned for music schools and applied to colleges as well. I overcame my indecision by considering the pros and cons of each side and realizing that if I study something more lucrative, I could afford to still play music. <u>By considering how the two choices might affect my life in the future, I was able to make the decision much easier.</u>

Learning how to make decisions about aspects of my life has been incredibly useful. Although it was hard to overcome the problem, I am glad that I put in the effort to find strategies to help me make difficult decisions. It has helped me in furthering my education, and I know that it will help me in my career and many other aspects of life later on.

## Examining Writing

1. How did Alex organize the essay?
2. Evaluate Alex's topic sentences. Were any too broad, too narrow, or lacking a viewpoint?
3. What additional details could he have provided? How effective were the details he used?
4. Did you recognize any parts of Alex's experience as similar to your own? If this were your essay about decision making, what would your thesis statement be?

# READ AND RESPOND: A Professional Essay

## Thinking Before Reading

The following selection is from a nutrition textbook. In the selection, the author explains what a sustainable food system is and the key elements of such a system.

1. Preview the reading, using the steps discussed in Chapter 1 on page 25.
2. Connect the reading to your own experience by answering the following questions:
    a. How would you define the term *sustainable*? What does it mean to "go green"?
    b. What factors are most important to you when you are grocery shopping?
3. Highlight and annotate as you read.

# What Is a Sustainable Food System?

1270**L**/1014 words

## Joan Salge Blake

1    "Eat Green" or "Eat Sustainably"? If you have seen these phrases in the media lately and are not sure what they mean, you're among friends. According to a recent survey, more than half of American adults are not familiar with the concept of producing food in a sustainable way.

2    To be *sustainable* means being able to be maintained indefinitely. A **sustainable food system**, then, is one that will survive over the long term so that you, and future generations, can be confident that the foods you need for good health will always be available. To maintain a sustainable food system, the natural resources used to produce, transport, and distribute the food are conserved, not destroyed or depleted. That is, minimal natural resources, including soil and water, were depleted to grow the food and minimal energy use and food miles were incurred to transport the food. A **sustainable diet** contains foods that are produced in a way that is ecologically neutral.

3    You may not worry too much about being able to obtain all your favorite foods tomorrow, next week, and in the years to come, but you should. According to research, America's industrialized agriculture system is using topsoil, fossil fuel, and water—all precious natural resources—at unsustainable rates. We are also degrading the environment, reducing biodiversity, and polluting our air and water. Business as usual can't continue as usual if we want the next generation to enjoy the bountiful diet and healthy environment that we have been taking for granted.

**biodiversity**
Having a wide variety of plant and animal species within an environment

4    Abuse of the natural resources required to grow foods can prevent sustainability. Soil, fuel, and water are key natural resources that must be preserved in a sustainable food system.

### The Soil

5    More than 99 percent of the food you eat is produced on land, compared to less than one percent that comes from the sea. All land crops are dependent upon the thin layer of topsoil that sits atop the earth's crust. It's not surprising, then, that numerous experts are concerned about soil degradation.

6    All organisms depend upon the earth's soil. Organisms within the soil, such as bacteria and other microorganisms, feed on the nutrients provided by animal waste products and decaying plant and animal matter. Plants use nutrients in the soil to grow, and to produce fruit, vegetables, nuts, and seeds. Humans and animals later obtain these same nutrients when they eat the plants and plant products.

### The Importance of Biodiversity

7    Achieving and maintaining **biodiversity** is an important part of a sustainable food system, and the extinction of even one member of the system can have dramatic consequences. For example, the 70 percent decline in the honeybee population of more than 20 U.S. states could impact the pollination, and therefore the availability, of certain foods (consider that an estimated 30 percent of the foods that you eat need pollination to flourish). Lack of biodiversity among aquatic systems is also a potential problem. More than 70 percent of commercial fisheries are overharvested, endangering the existence of more than 30 percent of native fish in North America. As biodiversity is reduced, so will be the variety and nutritional quality of your diet.

## Energy

8    Research suggests that almost 16 percent of the total energy consumption in the United States is used in the production, processing, transport, and preparation of our food. As you have read, the use of fossil fuel is costly and the release of carbon dioxide from the burning of it harms the environment. Eating a sustainable diet can both reduce the reliance on fossil fuel and reduce pollution.

9    More energy (as well as land and water) is required to produce a meat-based diet than to produce a plant-based diet. Every pound of animal protein generated from livestock requires approximately 6 pounds of plant protein in the form of feed. Allowing livestock to graze on pasture rather than feeding them a grain diet would cut the amount of fuel needed to produce and transport feed grain in half.

10    Even better, organically and locally grown meat has been shown to use fewer natural resources and be better for the environment than produce (plants) that has to be transported long distances. Does this mean you should avoid eating meat that isn't locally grown? No. Meat is a wonderful, nutritious, and delicious food. However, decreasing the *amount* you eat, the frequency with which you eat it, and/or purchasing grass-fed and locally raised meat when available could help the food system.

11    Producing chemical fertilizers and pesticides for crops also requires large amounts of fossil fuels. Avoiding these chemicals and using natural fertilizers, such as animal manure, not only cuts the use of fossil fuel, but can also can make soil more fertile. Research also shows that crop rotation and other aspects of organic farming result in less soil erosion than nonorganic methods.

Energy-conserving refrigerators, stoves, and other household appliances can reduce energy consumption up to about 60 percent. Visit www.energystar.com for information.

## Water

12    According to the EPA, since the 1950s, the population in America has nearly doubled while our water consumption has more than tripled. Americans, on average, use 100 gallons—about 1,600 full glasses—of water each day. By 2013, it is estimated that more than 35 states will experience water shortages.

13    This heightened demand for water is not only a danger to the environment but also to your health. You need water to survive; therefore, conserving water now makes sense. There are several steps you and/or your family can take to conserve water. Installing water-efficient appliances, including washing machines and dishwashers, helps cut down on water used for daily chores. If all households installed water-efficient appliances, the United States would save more than 3 trillion gallons annually. Low-flow toilets and shower heads can also help save water, as can turning off the tap while washing dishes or brushing your teeth. When it comes to individual water conservation, think of saving water "one gallon at a time."

## Being a More Sustainable Food Consumer

14    If each American set a goal to incorporate three "greener" habits in his/her daily life (see table on p. 324) over the next year, the reduction in the use of natural resources could be dramatic. As you plan, shop for, and prepare your next meal, consider following some of the suggestions in the "Go Green" table, and help promote eating sustainably.

| GO GREEN | |
| --- | --- |
| **What You Can Do** | **How You Can Do It** |
| Purchase locally grown, seasonal foods when possible | Visit the Natural Resources Defense Council Website for an interactive guide to the seasonal foods available in your area. |
| Waste not, want not | Don't buy excessive amounts of food at one time. If you can't eat the food that you purchased before it goes bad, consider donating it to a food pantry and/or shelter. Your excess is someone else's dinner. |
| Eat more plant protein | Go meatless at least one meal a week. For delicious meatless ideas, search online. |
| Plant your own garden | For the ultimate reduction in food miles, plant your produce in your backyard or in containers. To help you develop a green thumb, visit the National Gardening Association's Food Gardening Guide, the ultimate source for information on growing your favorite vegetables, fruits, and herbs, online. |
| Buy from local farm stands, farmers' markets, and community-supported agriculture (CSA) farms | Shop at local farmers' markets and roadside farm stands to find just-picked fruits and veggies (which will be at their peak nutritional value) for minimal food miles. You can also join a CSA to enjoy weekly or monthly boxes of farm-fresh produce delivered to your doorstep or a local pick-up site.<br><br>Find local farmers' markets and community-supported farms in your area online or in your local newspaper. |
| Conserve water in your home | ■ Only run the dishwasher when it is full.<br>■ Recycle cooled cooking water to water your plants and garden.<br>■ Defrost food in your refrigerator rather than under running water.<br>■ Scrape rather than rinse your plates before putting them in the dishwasher.<br><br>Visit the EPA's WaterSense site for more ways to conserve water. |
| Conserve energy in your home | ■ Use pots with lids for a shorter cooking time.<br>■ Turn off an electric stovetop before the food is cooked and let the residual heat finish the dish. |
| Buy foods with less packaging | ■ To reduce the waste you throw in the garbage, buy foods in bulk, with less packaging.<br>■ Use reusable cloth bags to carry your food home from the market or grocery store.<br>■ Recycle food containers.<br><br>For more tips, visit CalRecycle at www.calrecycle.ca.gov/ReduceWaste/Home/#Reuse |

—Blake, *Nutrition and You,* pp. 460–463

# Getting Ready to Write

## Checking Your Comprehension

Answer each of the following questions using complete sentences.

1. What is the definition of a sustainable food system?
2. What are three key natural resources that must be preserved in a sustainable food system?
3. How much of our food is produced on land and how much comes from the sea?
4. Why is the decline in the honeybee population significant?
5. What would be the effect of allowing livestock to graze on pasture rather than feeding them a grain diet?
6. How much water do Americans use on average per day?

## Strengthening Your Vocabulary

Using the word's context, word parts, or a dictionary, write a brief definition of each of the following words as it is used in the reading.

1. depleted (paragraph 2) _____ *seriously decreased* _____
2. degrading (paragraph 3) _____ *damaging* _____
3. bountiful (paragraph 3) _____ *abundant, plentiful* _____
4. aquatic (paragraph 7) _____ *related to water* _____
5. heightened (paragraph 13) _____ *increased* _____
6. incorporate (paragraph 14) _____ *include* _____

## Examining the Reading: Using Idea Maps

Review the reading by completing the missing parts of the following idea map.

**VISUALIZE IT!**

**Title** — **What Is a Sustainable Food System?**

**Thesis** — A sustainable diet contains foods that are produced in a way that is ecologically neutral.

A sustainable food system is one that:

- Will survive over the long term
- Conserves _natural resources_
- Achieves and maintains biodiversity

America's agriculture system uses key resources at unsustainable rates.

Soil

- More than _99 percent_ of our food is produced on land
- _All organisms depend on soil_

_Energy_

- 16 percent of _energy consumption_ is used toward food
- More energy used for _meat_ -based than _plant_ -based diets
- Producing fertilizers and pesticides requires fossil fuels

_Water_

- Water consumption has _tripled_ since the 1950s
- _Demand threatens the environment and health_
- Several steps can be taken to conserve water

**Conclusion** — _If Americans were more sustainable food consumers, the reduction in natural resource use would be dramatic._

## Thinking Critically: Discussion and Journal Writing

React and respond to the reading by discussing the following:

1. How does the author try to convince you of the importance of sustainability? Are the details she includes convincing? Why or why not?

2. Are you concerned about the issues raised in this selection? Which issues are most important to you?

3. What does biodiversity mean? Have you come across this term in any of your classes?

**THINKING VISUALLY**

4. The photograph that accompanies the reading shows an energy efficient appliance. What other photographs or illustrations would be equally or more effective in illustrating energy efficiency?

---

**MySkillsLab®**

Complete
this
Exercise

## Writing About the Reading

### Paragraph Options

1. What is most important to you when you are shopping for food? Is sustainability a priority? Write a paragraph describing the factors you consider as you purchase food.

2. According to the selection, what steps can you take to conserve water? Write a paragraph describing the steps and which ones you might try.

3. Write a paragraph describing the statistic or detail in the selection that you found most surprising, and why.

### Essay Options

4. What do you already do to be "green" in your daily life? Think about what you eat, the vehicle you use for transport, the appliances you have in your home, and how much you recycle, and write an essay discussing what you already do to be "green" and what you could do differently to eat and live more sustainably.

5. What suggestions from the "Go Green" table are you willing to try? Would you consider setting a goal to incorporate three "greener" habits over the next year? Which three habits would you choose? Write an essay answering these questions.

# SELF-TEST SUMMARY

To test yourself, cover the Answer column with a sheet of paper and answer each question in the left column. Evaluate each of your answers as you work by sliding the paper down and comparing your answer with what is printed in the Answer column.

| QUESTION | ANSWER |
|---|---|
| **GOAL 1** Understand general versus specific ideas<br><br>What are general and specific ideas? | A general idea is broad and can apply to many things. A specific idea is detailed and refers to a smaller group or an individual item. |
| **GOAL 2** Identify the topic<br><br>How can you identify the topic of a paragraph? | Look for the one idea the author is discussing throughout the entire paragraph. |
| **GOAL 3** Identify the main idea<br><br>How can you find the main idea of a paragraph? | Find the topic and then locate the one sentence in the paragraph that is the most general. Check to be sure that this one sentence relates to all the details in the paragraph. |
| **GOAL 4** Identify the topic sentence<br><br>What is a topic sentence? | The topic sentence states the main idea of a paragraph. The topic sentence can be located anywhere in the paragraph. The most common positions are first or last, but the topic sentence can also appear in the middle, or first and last. |
| **GOAL 5** Choose a manageable topic<br><br>How does topic breadth affect a paragraph? | In a paragraph with an overly broad topic, the writing will be rambling and unfocused. If the topic is too narrow, you will run out of things to say and have a skimpy paragraph. |
| **GOAL 6** Write effective topic sentences<br><br>What are three tips for writing an effective topic sentence? | ■ The topic sentence must be a complete thought.<br>■ The topic sentence should usually appear first in the paragraph.<br>■ The topic sentence should avoid announcing the topic. |
| **GOAL 7** Revise ineffective topic sentences<br><br>How do you revise an ineffective topic sentence? | If your topic sentence is too broad, revise it so that it focuses on one aspect of your topic. If your topic sentence is too narrow, revise it by making your topic more inclusive. If your topic lacks a viewpoint, generate ideas about your topic to discover a way to approach it. |

# MySkillsLab

For more help with **Main Ideas and Topic Sentences**, go to your learning path in MySkillsLab at http://www.myskillslab.com.

# Details, Implied Main Ideas, and Transitions

## LEARNING GOALS

Learn how to …

■ **GOAL 1**
Identify supporting details in paragraphs

■ **GOAL 2**
Identify implied main ideas

■ **GOAL 3**
Use transitional words and phrases to read paragraphs

■ **GOAL 4**
Choose specific details

■ **GOAL 5**
Develop paragraphs using supporting details

■ **GOAL 6**
Arrange details so they are easy to follow

## THINK About It!

What is happening in the photograph? On the face of it, three teammates seem to be celebrating a victory. But what is the rest of the story? Are they members of an "underdog" team that came from behind to win a championship game? Or did they work together to score the winning run in a particularly tight game with a rival team? Whether you are studying a photograph or reading a paragraph, always look for the details behind the writer's main point. When writing paragraphs, be sure to provide sufficient details to support your topic sentence.

# What Are Supporting Details, Implied Main Ideas, and Transitions?

The details of the athletes jumping in the air, smiling, and throwing their arms around each other in the photograph support the idea that they are celebrating a victory. Similarly, the details of a paragraph enable the writer to provide more complete information about the paragraph's main idea. **Supporting details** are statements that prove or explain the main idea of a paragraph. Supporting details may be reasons, examples, statistics, facts, descriptions, steps, or procedures.

In some paragraphs, as in some photographs, the main point is not stated, but only suggested or implied. The reader has to figure out the writer's main point by analyzing the details and determining what, when taken together, they all mean. In paragraphs, these are called **implied main ideas.**

In photographs, visual clues lead you from one detail to another. Because paragraphs lack the visual clues that photographs offer, writers often use words and phrases, called **transitions**, to lead the reader from one detail to another.

In this chapter you will learn to recognize supporting details, figure out implied main ideas, and use transitions to guide your reading. You will also learn to use supporting details to support your topic sentence and use transitions to guide your reader. Until you become a very skilled writer, it is usually advisable not to write paragraphs with implied main ideas, focusing instead on writing clear and direct topic sentences.

## READING

# Identify Supporting Details in a Paragraph

■ GOAL 1
Identify supporting
details in paragraphs

Here is a sample paragraph. The topic sentence is highlighted in yellow. Notice that the details in this paragraph all concern the ways men and women differ in how they communicate nonverbally.

Men and women communicate differently in their nonverbal messages. You may have observed some or all of these differences in your daily interactions. Women smile more than men. Women stand closer to each other than men do. When they speak, both men and women look at men more than at women. Women both touch and are touched more than men. Men extend their bodies, taking up greater areas of space than women.

—DeVito, *Messages*, p. 150

## Distinguish Between Major and Minor Details

Some details in a paragraph are more important than others. **Major details** are the most important details in a paragraph; they directly explain or prove the main idea. **Minor details** may provide additional information, offer examples, or further explain one or more of the major details. You can visualize a paragraph as shown in Figure 11-1. The less important, minor details appear below the major supporting details that they explain.

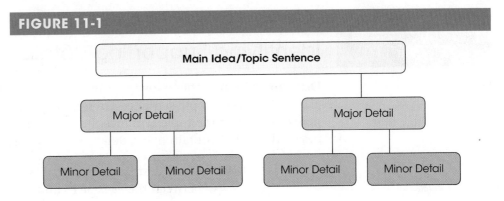

**FIGURE 11-1**

Now study the following paragraph. The major details are highlighted in green.

The skin of the human body has several functions. First, it serves as a protective covering. In doing so, it accounts for 17 percent of the body's weight. Skin also protects the organs within the body from damage or harm. The skin serves as a regulator of body functions. It controls body temperature and water loss. Finally, the skin serves as a receiver. It is sensitive to touch and temperature.

Each of the major details lists one function of human skin. Now study the details that are not highlighted. What function do they serve? Each explains one of the major details by providing more information. You can visualize this paragraph as shown in Figure 11-2.

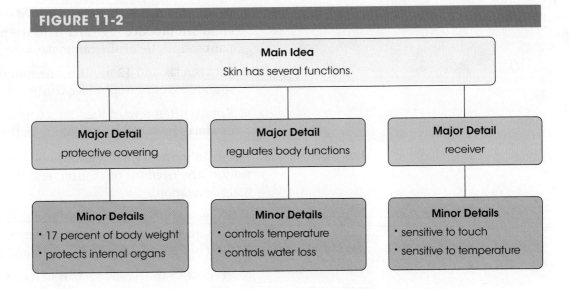

**FIGURE 11-2**

In Figure 11-2 you can see the major details that state the three main functions of the skin. The minor details, such as "controls temperature," provide further information and are less important than the major details.

Look at the paragraph again, and notice how the author has used transitions—words that lead you from one major detail to the next. The words *first* and *finally* are a couple of the transitions that can help you find the major details in a paragraph. Be on the lookout for transitions as you read; they will be discussed more fully later in this chapter.

---

**EXERCISE 11-1**

# Identifying Supporting Details

**Directions:** Each of the following topic sentences states the main idea of a paragraph. After each topic sentence are sentences containing details that may or may not support the topic sentence. Read each sentence and put a check mark beside those that contain major details that support the topic sentence.

1. TOPIC SENTENCE    Many dramatic physical changes occur during adolescence, between the ages of 13 and 15.

   DETAILS    ✓ **a.** Voice changes in boys begin to occur at age 13 or 14.

   ✓ **b.** Facial proportions may change during adolescence.

   ✓ **c.** Adolescents, especially boys, gain several inches in height.

   ___ **d.** Many teenagers do not know how to react to these changes.

   ✓ **e.** Primary sex characteristics begin to develop for both boys and girls.

2. TOPIC SENTENCE    The development of speech in infants follows a definite sequence or pattern of development.

   DETAILS    ✓ **a.** By the time an infant is six months old, he or she can make 12 different speech sounds.

   ___ **b.** Mindy, who is only three months old, is unable to produce any recognizable syllables.

   ✓ **c.** During the first year, the number of vowel sounds a child can produce is greater than the number of consonant sounds he or she can make.

   ✓ **d.** Between six and 12 months, the number of consonant sounds a child can produce continues to increase.

   ___ **e.** Parents often reward the first recognizable word a child produces by smiling or speaking to the child.

3. TOPIC SENTENCE    The main motives for attending a play are the desire for recreation, the need for relaxation, and the desire for intellectual stimulation.

   DETAILS    ✓ **a.** By becoming involved with the actors and their problems, members of the audience temporarily forget about their personal cares and concerns and are able to relax.

   ___ **b.** In America today, the success of a play is judged by its ability to attract a large audience.

    ✓   **c.** Almost everyone who attends a play expects to be entertained.

       **d.** Even theater critics are often able to relax and enjoy a good play.

    ✓   **e.** There is a smaller audience that looks to theater for intellectual stimulation.

**4.** TOPIC SENTENCE  Licorice is used in tobacco products because it has specific characteristics that cannot be found in any other single ingredient.

    DETAILS       **a.** McAdams & Co. is the largest importer and processor of licorice root.

    ✓   **b.** Licorice blends with tobacco and provides added mildness.

    ✓   **c.** Licorice provides a unique flavor and sweetens many types of tobacco.

       **d.** The extract of licorice is present in relatively small amounts in most types of pipe tobacco.

    ✓   **e.** Licorice helps tobacco retain the correct amount of moisture during storage.

**5.** TOPIC SENTENCE  An oligopoly is a market structure in which only a few companies sell a certain product.

    DETAILS    ✓   **a.** The automobile industry is a good example of an oligopoly, even though it gives the appearance of being highly competitive.

    ✓   **b.** The breakfast cereal, soap, and cigarette industries, although basic to our economy, operate as oligopolies.

       **c.** Monopolies refer to market structures in which only one industry produces a particular product.

       **d.** Monopolies are able to exert more control and price fixing than oligopolies.

    ✓   **e.** In the oil industry there are only a few producers, so each producer has a fairly large share of the sales.

## EXERCISE 11-2   Identifying Details

**A. Directions:** Read the following paragraph and complete the diagram that follows. Some of the items have been filled in for you.

    Communication occurs with words and gestures, but did you know it also occurs through the sense of smell? Odor can communicate at least four types of messages. First, odor can signal attraction. Animals give off scents to attract members of the opposite sex. Humans use fragrances to make themselves more appealing or attractive. Smell also communicates information about tastes. The smell of popcorn popping stimulates the appetite. If you smell a chicken roasting, you can anticipate its taste. A third type of smell communication is through memory. A smell can help you recall an event that occurred months or even years ago, especially if the event was an emotional one. Finally, smell can communicate by creating an identity or image for a person or product. For example, a woman may wear only one brand of perfume. Or a brand of shaving cream may have a distinct fragrance, which allows users to recognize it.

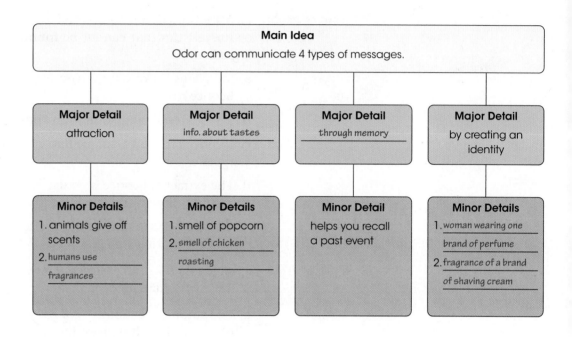

**B. Directions:** Read the paragraph again and list the four transitions the writer uses to help you find the four major details.

**1.** _first_   **2.** _also_   **3.** _third_   **4.** _finally_

The diagram you completed in Exercise 11-2 is a **map**—a visual way of organizing information. By filling in—or drawing—maps you can "see" how ideas in a paragraph or essay are related. Chapter 2 gives you more information about mapping (see p. 38) and about other ways of organizing information.

---

**EXERCISE 11-3**   Understanding Supporting Details

**A. Directions:** Read the following paragraph and complete the map that follows. Some of the items have been filled in for you.

Small group discussions progress through four phases. The first is orientation, when the members become comfortable with each other. Second is the conflict phase. Disagreements and tensions become evident. The amount of conflict varies with each group. The third phase is known as emergence. The members begin to try to reach a decision. The members who created conflict begin to move towards a middle road. The final phase is the reinforcement phase when the decision is reached. The members of the group offer positive reinforcement towards each other and the decision.

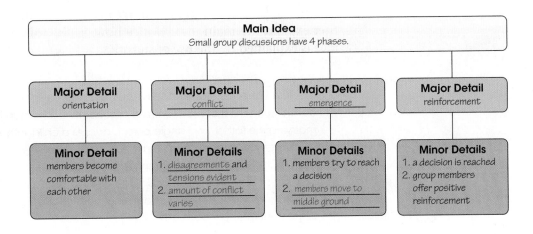

**B. Directions:** Read the paragraph again and list the four transitions the writer uses to help you find the four major details.

**1.**  _first_        **2.**  _second_        **3.**  _third_        **4.**  _final_

## Recognize Types of Details

A writer can use many types of details to explain or support a main idea. As you read, notice the types of details a writer uses and be able to identify the details that are most important. Among the most common types of supporting details are *illustrations and examples*, *facts and statistics*, *reasons*, *descriptions* and *steps* or *procedures*.

### Illustrations and Examples

One way you will find ideas explained is through the use of illustrations or examples. Usually a writer uses **examples** to make a concept, problem, or process understandable by showing its application in a particular situation. In the following paragraph, numerous examples are provided that explain how different languages have different phonemes.

example 1
example 2
example 3

example 4

Every language has its own set of phonemes. English, for example, contains about 21 vowel sounds and 24 consonant sounds; Cantonese, a Chinese dialect, has 8 vowel sounds and 17 consonant sounds; South African Khoisan or "Bushman" has 7 vowel sounds and 41 consonant sounds. Native speakers recognize and produce phonemes from their own language as distinct sounds. For instance, babies in English-speaking communities begin to recognize the sound of the letter *r* as the same sound in *run* and *tear*. Meanwhile, babies in Arabic-speaking communities learn their own set of phonemes, which do not include the same short vowel sounds used in English. Thus, to a native speaker of Arabic, the English words *bet* and *bit* sound the same.

—Uba and Huang, *Psychology*, p. 406

As you read illustrations and examples, be sure to grasp the relationship between the illustration or example and the concept or idea it illustrates.

## Facts and Statistics

Another way a writer supports an idea is by including facts or statistics that further explain the main idea. Notice how, in the following paragraph, the main idea is explained by the use of statistics.

> A single-parent family can be created when a spouse dies and the survivor doesn't remarry, a couple divorces or separates, a woman bears a child without marrying the father, or a single person adopts a child. Although the percentage of children adopted by a single person has soared—rising from approximately *statistic* four percent of adopted children in 1970 to the current rate of approximately *statistic* 33 percent—the overall rate of single-parent families did not change from 1994 *statistic* to 2006, remaining stable at about nine percent of all families. Mothers head *statistic* 87 percent of single-parent families.

—adapted from Kunz, *THINK Marriages and Families*, p. 151

When reading paragraphs developed by the use of facts and statistics, you can expect that these details will answer questions such as *what, when, where,* or *how* about the main idea.

## Reasons

Certain types of main ideas are most easily explained by giving reasons. Especially in argumentative and persuasive writing, you will find that a writer supports an opinion, belief, or action by discussing *why* the thought or action is appropriate. In the following paragraph the writer provides reasons why so few women become involved in quantitative fields.

> What accounts for the scarcity of women in quantitative fields? In early grades, girls show about the same mathematical aptitude as boys, but by high *reason 1* school they score lower than boys on standardized tests. Evidently, mathematical and other quantitative subjects have been labeled "masculine." As a result, girls are not eager to excel in these areas, because such an achievement would *reason 2* make them appear unusual and perhaps unattractive to their peers. Another factor is unconscious bias on the part of teachers and guidance counselors. Despite increased sensitivity to minority and women's issues, counselors still steer women away from college preparatory courses in mathematics and the *reason 3* sciences. Finally, many fields contain so few women that they supply no role models for younger women.

—Curry et al., *Sociology for the Twenty-First Century*, p. 340

You can see that the writers offer several reasons for the scarcity of women in these professions, including peer influences, bias in the schools, and a lack of role models.

### Descriptions

If the purpose of a paragraph is to help the reader understand or visualize the appearance, structure, organization, or composition of an object, then descriptions are often used as a means of paragraph development. **Descriptive details** are facts that help you visualize the person, object, or event being described. The following paragraph describes the eruption of Mount St. Helens, a volcano in Washington state.

descriptive
details

> The slumping north face of the mountain produced the greatest landslide witnessed in recorded history; about 2.75 km³ (0.67 mi³) of rock, ice, and trapped air, all fluidized with steam, surged at speeds approaching 250 kmph (155 mph). Landslide materials traveled for 21 km (13 mi) into the valley, blanketing the forest, covering a lake, filling the rivers below. The eruption continued with intensity for 9 hours, first clearing out old rock from the throat of the volcano and then blasting new material.
>
> —Christopherson, *Geosystems: An Introduction to Physical Geography*, p. 368

Notice how each detail contributes to the impression of a tremendously forceful landslide. Details such as "rock, ice, and trapped air, all fluidized with steam" help you visually re-create a picture of the eruption. In reading descriptive details, you must pay close attention to each detail as you try to form a visual impression of what is being described.

### Steps or Procedures

Paragraphs often explain how to do something or how something works, listing the steps or procedures involved in the process. **Steps** are events that you complete in a specific order. For example, in a paragraph about how to prepare an outline for a speech, the details would list or explain the steps to take in preparing an outline. The following paragraph describes how to follow up after submitting a resume.

> Following up after submitting your resume and application letter is one of the trickiest parts of a job search. First and foremost, keep in mind that employers continue to evaluate your communication skills and professionalism during this phase, so don't say or do anything to leave a negative impression. Second, adhere to whatever instructions the employer has provided. If a job posting says "no calls," for example, don't call. Third, if the job posting lists a close date, don't call or write before then because the company is still collecting applications and will not have made a decision about inviting people for an interview. Wait a week or so after the close date.
>
> —Bovée and Thill, *Business in Action*, pp. xxxiv–xxxv

| EXERCISE 11-4 | Identifying Types of Supporting Details |

WORKING TOGETHER

**Directions:** Working in pairs, read each of the following topic sentences, and discuss what types of supporting details you would expect to be used to develop a paragraph for each one. Be prepared to justify your answers.

1. On Saturday mornings, the farmers' market is a sea of color, with baskets of yellow, green, red, and purple produce lined up neatly on tables presided over by vendors in straw hats and blue aprons.

   Type of detail: _____ description _____

2. The process of becoming a kidney donor begins with a simple blood test.

   Type of detail: _____ steps/procedures _____

3. Laws regulating the sale of certain cold medicines were enacted because chemicals in these medicines were being used to manufacture methamphetamine.

   Type of detail: _____ reason _____

4. Government documents indicate that the total number of Americans living in poverty has decreased, but the definition of the poverty line has also been changed.

   Type of detail: _____ statistics, reasons _____

5. A sudden explosion at 200 decibels can cause massive and permanent hearing loss.

   Type of detail: _____ reasons, facts, statistics _____

| EXERCISE 11-5 | Identifying Types of Details |

**Directions:** Each topic sentence below is followed by a list of details that could be used to support it. Label each detail as *illustration, example, fact, statistic, reason, description, step,* or *procedure.*

1. Individual behaviors significantly influence your risk for chronic disease.

   _statistic_     Physical inactivity and overweight/obesity are each responsible for nearly 1 in 10 deaths in U.S. adults.

   _example_     Dietary risks such as high salt, low omega-3 fatty acids, and high trans fatty acids have a significant effect on mortality.

   _fact/reason_     Excessive alcohol consumption increases risk through cardiovascular disease, other medical conditions, traffic accidents, and violence.

   _step_     The first step in changing an unhealthy behavior is to increase your awareness.

   —adapted from Donatelle, *My Health: An Outcomes Approach*, pp. 6–8

2. Maple trees provide the key ingredient in maple syrup.

_description or step_    The clear sap that drips out of spigots is the starting material for pure maple syrup.

_fact/statistic_    Canada produces about 80 percent of the world's maple syrup.

_reason_    One reason that pure maple syrup is expensive is that harvesting the syrup is a labor-intensive business; each tap must be put in by hand, just as it was hundreds of years ago.

_fact/statistic_    It takes about 40 gallons of sap to make a single gallon of maple syrup.

—Krogh, _Biology: A Guide to the Natural World_, p. 475

3. The family, the media, and the schools all serve as important agents of political socialization.

_reason_    Recent research has demonstrated that one of the reasons for the long-lasting impact of parental influence on political attitudes is simply genetics.

_example_    For example, eight years after researchers first interviewed a sample of high school seniors and their parents, they still found far more agreement than disagreement across the generational divide.

_illustration_    Better-educated citizens are more likely to vote in elections, they exhibit more knowledge about politics and public policy, and they are more tolerant of opposing opinions.

_statistic_    The median age of viewers of CBS, ABC, and NBC news programs in 2008 was 61—19 years older than the audience for a typical prime-time program.

—Edwards et al., _Government in America_, pp. 174–175

4. The number of things plants do for human beings is enormous.

_statistic_    In the world today, up to 90 percent of the calories human beings consume come directly from plants.

_example_    Then there are the products that human beings have learned to derive from plants, among them lumber, medicines, fabrics, fragrances, and dyes.

_reason_    Plants are able to provide us with food because they make their own food through photosynthesis.

_fact_    Plants also produce much of the oxygen that most living things require.

—adapted from Krogh, _Biology: A Guide to the Natural World_, pp. 441–442

5. Adoption is one way that couples can become parents.

*reason*      Adoption benefits children whose birth parents are unable or unwilling to raise them.

*statistic*      Approximately 2 percent of the adult population has adopted children.

*fact*      In *open adoption*, birth parents and adoptive parents know some things about each other and may have a defined ongoing relationship.

*step*      An important step in the adoption process is the home study.

—adapted from Donatelle, *My Health: An Outcomes Approach*, p. 118

# Identify Implied Main Ideas

■ GOAL 2
Identify implied main ideas

In paragraphs, writers sometimes leave their main idea unstated. The paragraph contains only details. It is up to you, the reader, to infer the writer's main point. You can visualize this type of paragraph as follows:

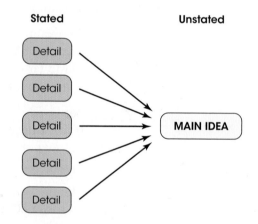

The details, when taken together, all point to a larger, more important idea, an **implied main idea**. Think of the paragraph as a list of facts that you must add up or put together to determine the meaning of the paragraph as a whole. Use the following steps as a guide to find implied main ideas:

1. **Find the topic.** Ask yourself, "What is the one thing the author is discussing throughout the paragraph?"

2. **Decide what the writer wants you to know about that topic.** Look at each detail and decide what larger general idea each explains.

3. **Express this idea in your own words.** Make sure the main idea is a reasonable one. Ask yourself, "Does it apply to all the details in the paragraph?"

Read the following paragraph; then follow the three steps listed above.

Some advertisers rely on star power. Commercials may use celebrities to encourage consumers to purchase a product. Other commercials may use an "everyone's buying it" approach that argues that thousands of consumers could not possibly be wrong in their choice, so the product must be worthwhile. Still other commercials may use visual appeal to catch the consumers' interest and persuade them to make purchases.

The topic of this paragraph is commercials. More specifically it is about devices advertisers use to build commercials. Three details are given: use of star power, an everyone's-buying-it approach, and visual appeal. Each of the three details is a different persuasive device. The main point the writer is trying to make, then, is that commercials use various persuasive devices to appeal to consumers. Notice that no single sentence states this idea clearly.

You can visualize this paragraph as follows:

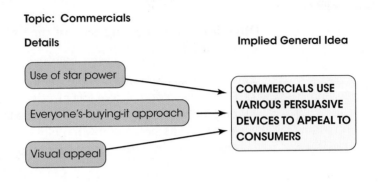

**Topic: Commercials**

**Details** — **Implied General Idea**

- Use of star power
- Everyone's-buying-it approach
- Visual appeal

→ **COMMERCIALS USE VARIOUS PERSUASIVE DEVICES TO APPEAL TO CONSUMERS**

Here is another paragraph. Read it and then fill in the diagram that follows:

Yellow is a bright, cheery color; it is often associated with spring and hopefulness. Green, since it is a color that appears frequently in nature (trees, grass, plants), has come to suggest growth and rebirth. Blue, the color of the sky, may suggest eternity or endless beauty. Red, the color of both blood and fire, is often connected with strong feelings such as courage, lust, and rage.

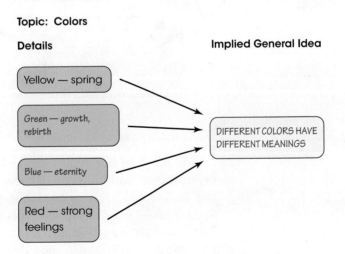

**Topic: Colors**

**Details** — **Implied General Idea**

- Yellow — spring
- Green — growth, rebirth
- Blue — eternity
- Red — strong feelings

→ DIFFERENT COLORS HAVE DIFFERENT MEANINGS

## How to Know if You Have Made a Reasonable Inference

There is a test you can perform to discover if you inferred a reasonable main idea. The idea you infer to be the main idea should be broad enough so that every sentence in the paragraph explains the idea you have chosen. Work through the paragraph, sentence by sentence. Check to see that each sentence explains or gives more information about the idea you have chosen. If some sentences do not explain your chosen idea, your main idea probably is not broad enough. Work on expanding your idea and making it more general.

**EXERCISE 11-6**   Analyzing Implied Main Ideas

**Directions:** After reading each of the following paragraphs, complete the diagram that follows.

1.   In 1920 there was one divorce for every seven marriages in the United States. Fifty years later the rate had climbed to one divorce for every three marriages, and today there is almost one divorce for every two marriages. The divorce rate in the United States is now the highest of any major industrialized nation, while Canada is in a rather distant second place.

—Coleman and Cressey, *Social Problems,* p. 130

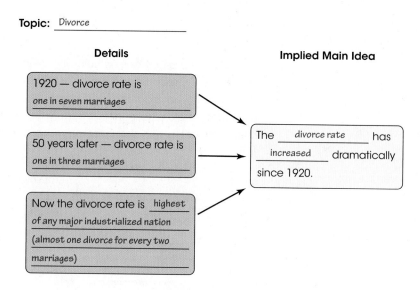

**Topic:** _Divorce_

2.   Immigration has contributed to the dramatic population growth of the United States over the past 150 years. It has also contributed to the country's shift from a rural to an urban economy. Immigrants provided inexpensive labor, which allowed industries to flourish. Native-born children of immigrants, benefiting from education, moved into professional and white collar jobs, creating a new middle class. Immigration also increased the U.S. mortality rate. Due to crowded housing and unhealthy living conditions, disease and fatal illness were common.

**Topic:** Immigration

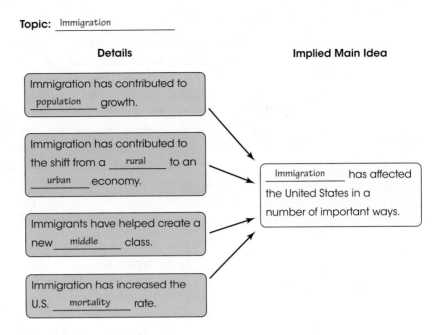

**Details**

Immigration has contributed to __population__ growth.

Immigration has contributed to the shift from a __rural__ to an __urban__ economy.

Immigrants have helped create a new __middle__ class.

Immigration has increased the U.S. __mortality__ rate.

**Implied Main Idea**

__Immigration__ has affected the United States in a number of important ways.

---

## EXERCISE 11-7    Understanding Implied Main Ideas

**Directions:** After reading each of the following paragraphs, select the choice that best answers each of the questions below.

### Paragraph A

A smooth fabric such as silk is equated with luxury, although denim is considered practical and durable. Fabrics that are composed of scarce materials or that require a high degree of processing to achieve their smoothness or fineness tend to be more expensive and thus are seen as being higher class. Similarly, lighter, more delicate textures are assumed to be feminine. Roughness is often positively valued for men, and smoothness is sought by women.

—Solomon, *Consumer Behavior,* pp. 49–50

_a_ 1. What is the topic?
   a. the feel of fabrics
   b. expense in producing fabrics
   c. luxury clothing
   d. roughness in clothing

_d_ 2. What is the writer saying about the topic?
   a. Denim is a practical and durable fabric.
   b. Men and women differ in their perception of quality.
   c. Fabrics made of scarce materials are expensive.
   d. The feel of a fabric influences how consumers regard its quality.

**Paragraph B**

In a classic research study, experimenters told teachers that certain pupils were expected to do exceptionally well—that they were late bloomers. And although the experimenters actually selected the "late bloomers" at random, the students who were labeled "late bloomers" actually did perform at higher levels than their classmates. These students became what their teachers thought they were. The expectations of the teachers may have caused them to pay extra attention to the students and this may have positively affected the students' performance. This same occurrence, called the Pygmalion effect, has been studied in such varied contexts as the courtroom, the clinic, the work cubicle, management and leadership practices, athletic coaching, and stepfamilies.

—adapted from DeVito, *Human Communication*, p. 73

_____d_____ **3.** What is the topic?
    **a.** the struggles of late bloomers
    **b.** how teachers decide on grades
    **c.** the impact of research on situations such as courtrooms
    **d.** how expectations influence results

_____b_____ **4.** From the paragraph it is reasonable to infer that
    **a.** research studies based on classroom performance cause students to get higher grades.
    **b.** students for whom teachers have high expectations usually perform better and meet those expectations.
    **c.** students should be judged based on who they are, not on what teachers think about them.
    **d.** researchers are expanding their work beyond the classroom, into real-life situations.

_____a_____ **5.** Which one of the following details does *not* directly support the paragraph's implied main idea?
    **a.** The Pygmalion effect is being studied in the courtroom.
    **b.** Some students were labeled as late bloomers.
    **c.** The students labeled as late bloomers performed better than other students.
    **d.** Teachers' expectations may have resulted in extra attention to the late bloomer students.

# Use Transitional Words and Phrases to Read Paragraphs

■ GOAL 3
Use transitional words and phrases to read paragraphs

**Transitions** are linking words or phrases that lead the reader from one idea to another. If you get into the habit of recognizing transitions, you will see that they often help you read a paragraph more easily.

In the following paragraph, notice how the underlined transitions lead you from one detail to the next.

> When Su-ling gets ready to study at home, she follows a certain procedure. <u>First of all</u>, she tries to find a quiet place, far away from her kid sisters and brothers. This place might be her bedroom, <u>for example</u>, or it might be the porch or the basement, depending on how much noise the younger children are making. <u>Next</u>, she finds a snack to eat while she is studying, <u>such as</u> chips, an apple, or a candy bar. Sometimes, <u>however</u>, she skips the snack, especially if she is on a diet. <u>Finally</u>, Su-ling takes her books and notes to the quiet spot she has found. She usually does her most difficult homework first <u>because</u> she is more alert at the beginning of her study time.

Not all paragraphs contain such obvious transitions, and not all transitions serve as such clear markers of details. As you can see, transitions may be used for a variety of reasons. They may alert you to what will come next in the paragraph, they may tell you that an example will follow, or they may predict that a different, opposing idea is coming. Table 11-1 lists some of the most common transitions and indicates what they tell you.

| TABLE 11-1  COMMON TRANSITIONS | | |
|---|---|---|
| **Type of Transition** | **Example** | **What They Tell the Reader** |
| **Time sequence** | *first, later, next, finally* | The author is arranging ideas in the order in which they happened. |
| **Example** | *for example, for instance, to illustrate, such as* | An example will follow. |
| **Enumeration** | *first, second, third, last, another, next* | The author is marking or identifying each major point. (Sometimes these may be used to suggest order of importance.) |
| **Continuation** | *also, in addition, and, further, another* | The author is continuing with the same idea and is going to provide additional information. |
| **Contrast** | *on the other hand, in contrast, however* | The author is switching to a different, opposite, or contrasting idea than previously discussed. |
| **Comparison** | *like, likewise, similarly* | The author will show how the previous idea is similar to what follows. |
| **Cause/effect** | *because, thus, therefore, since, consequently* | The author will show a connection between two or more things, how one thing caused another, or how something happened as a result of something else. |

| EXERCISE 11-8 | Using Transitions |

**Directions:** Select the transitional word or phrase from the box below that best completes each of the following sentences. Two of the transitions in the box will be used more than once.

> on the other hand        for example        because        in addition
> similarly                later                next              however

1. As a young poet, e. e. cummings was traditional in his use of punctuation and capitalization. _____Later_____, he began to create his own grammatical rules.

2. Many fruits are high in calories; vegetables, ____on the other hand____, are usually low in calories.

3. In order to sight-read music, you should begin by scanning it. _____Next_____, you should identify the tempo and whether the piece is written in a major or minor key.

4. Many rock stars have met with tragic ends. _____For example_____, John Lennon was gunned down, Buddy Holly and Ritchie Valens were killed in a plane crash, and Janis Joplin died of a drug overdose.

5. Hernando's sister made a delicious birthday cake for him. ____In addition____, she surprised him with a big party.

6. Using your birthdate as your computer password is not advisable _____because_____ hackers may be able to guess your password and access your files.

7. Some scientists believe that intelligence is determined equally by heredity and environment. Other scientists, _____however_____, believe that heredity accounts for about 60 percent of intelligence and environment for the other 40 percent.

8. Tigers tend to grow listless and unhappy in captivity. _____Similarly_____, pandas grow listless and have a difficult time reproducing in captivity.

9. American voters tend to vote according to the state of the economy. _____For example_____, if the economy is good, they tend to vote for the party in power and if the economy is poor, they tend to vote for the party not in power.

10. Lia refused to go to her friend's wedding _____because_____ she knew her ex-husband would be there.

| EXERCISE 11-9 | Understanding Transitions |

**Directions:** Many transitions have similar meanings and can sometimes be used interchangeably. Match each transition in column A with a similar transition in column B. Write your answers in the spaces provided.

| **Column A** | **Column B** |
|---|---|
| _e_ 1. because | a. therefore |
| _g_ 2. in contrast | b. also |

| | | | |
|---|---|---|---|
| _j_ | **3.** for instance | **c.** | likewise |
| _a_ | **4.** thus | **d.** | after that |
| _i_ | **5.** first | **e.** | since |
| _h_ | **6.** one way | **f.** | finally |
| _c_ | **7.** similarly | **g.** | on the other hand |
| _d_ | **8.** next | **h.** | one approach |
| _b_ | **9.** in addition | **i.** | in the beginning |
| _f_ | **10.** to sum up | **j.** | for example |

## EXERCISE 11-10 Identifying Transitions

**Directions:** Read each paragraph below and complete the items that follow.

A.    You can help prevent heat stress by following certain precautions. First, proper acclimatization to hot and/or humid climates is essential. Heat acclimatization increases your body's cooling efficiency; in this process, you increase activity gradually over 10 to 14 days in the hot environment. Second, avoid dehydration by replacing the fluids you lose during and after exercise. Third, wear clothing appropriate for your activity and the environment. And finally, use common sense—for example, on a day when the temperature is 85 degrees and the humidity is 80 percent, postpone your usual lunchtime run until the cool of evening.

—Donatelle, *Health: The Basics*, pp. 290—291

List the transitional words or phrases in this paragraph that suggest enumeration.

**1.** _first_    **2.** _second_    **3.** _third_    **4.** _finally_

B.    One indicator of good advertising is, of course, the impression it makes on consumers. But how can this impact be defined and measured? Two basic measures of impact are *recognition* and *recall*. In the typical recognition test, subjects are shown ads one at a time and asked if they have seen them before. In contrast, free recall tests ask consumers to think of what they have seen without being prompted for this information first. Under some conditions, these two memory measures tend to yield the same results; however, recognition scores tend to be more reliable and do not decay over time the way recall scores do. Recall tends to be more important in situations in which consumers do not have product data at their disposal, so they must rely on memory to generate this information. On the other hand, recognition is more likely to be an important factor in a store, where consumers are confronted with thousands of product options and the task may simply be to recognize a familiar package.

—adapted from Solomon, *Consumer Behavior*, pp. 92–93

List the transitional words or phrases in this paragraph that suggest contrast.

**1.** _in contrast_    **2.** _however_    **3.** _on the other hand_

C.  Tuition vouchers are a set amount of money given by the government to parents that can only be used to pay for public or private school tuition. Supporters of tuition vouchers argue that by giving parents a choice in where they send their children to school, schools will have to pay more attention to the needs of students and their parents or risk losing students to competitive schools with better services. They also argue that schools that are guaranteed students solely because of their location have no incentive to improve. Further, voucher advocates argue that it is unfair that rich families have the ability to choose which school their children attend, but poor families do not.

—adapted from Edwards et al., *Government in America*, pp. 654–655

List the transitional words or phrases in this paragraph that suggest continuation.

1. _____ also _____   2. _____ further _____

D.  The process of making an etching begins with the preparation of a metal plate with a *ground*—a protective coating of acid-resistant material that covers the copper or zinc. The printmaker then draws easily through the ground with a pointed tool, exposing the metal. Finally, the plate is immersed in acid. Acid "bites" into the plate where the drawing has exposed the metal, making a groove that varies in depth according to the strength of the acid and the length of time the plate is in the bath.

—Preble and Preble, *Artforms*, p. 144

List the transitional words or phrases in this paragraph that suggest time sequence.

1. _____ begins _____   2. _____ then _____   3. _____ finally _____

E.  Dangerous and dramatic mass movements, such as rock slides and mudflows, can occur on steep slopes, especially during wet conditions. Steep slopes are prone to rock slides because the force of gravity pushing down on the rocks is likely to exceed the strength of the rocks. Landslides on steep slopes can follow intense rains, because material with a high water content is heavier, weaker, and less able to resist the force of gravity. The sliding material may break down into fluid mud, which flows downhill. Houses built on very steep slopes—along the west coast of North America, for example—risk damage from landslides and mudflows.

—adapted from Bergman and Renwick, *Introduction to Geography*, p. 106

List the transitional words or phrases in this paragraph that suggest the illustration and example pattern.

1. _____ such as _____   2. _____ for example _____

## WRITING

# Choose Specific Details

■ GOAL 4
Choose specific details

**Details**—how things happen and when they happen—are what drive a story. Your writing will improve as you learn to use details and arrange them well. In this section you will learn how to develop details to make your paragraphs clear, lively, and interesting.

Read the following pairs of statements. For each pair, place a check mark on the line before the statement that is more vivid and that contains more information.

1. ____ **a.** Professor Valquez gives a lot of homework.

   ✓ **b.** Professor Valquez assigns 20 problems during each class and requires us to read two chapters per week.

2. ____ **a.** In Korea, people calculate age differently.

   ✓ **b.** In Korea, people are considered to be one year old at birth.

3. ____ **a.** It was really hot Tuesday.

   ✓ **b.** On Tuesday the temperature in New Haven reached 97 degrees.

These pairs of sentences illustrate the difference between vague statements and specific statements. Statement a in each pair conveys little information and also lacks interest and appeal. Statement b offers specific, detailed information and, as a result, is more interesting.

As you generate ideas and draft paragraphs, try to include as many specific details as possible. These details (called **supporting details** because they support your topic sentence) make your writing more interesting and your ideas more convincing.

The paragraph below lacks detail. Compare it with the revised paragraph that follows it. Notice how the revision has produced a much more lively, informative, and convincing paragraph.

---

**Tip for Writers**

*Concrete* is the opposite of *abstract*. Something concrete can be experienced through the senses (by seeing, hearing, tasting, etc.). In contrast, abstractions are ideas, not physical things.

*Specific* is the opposite of *general*. There are many levels of specificity. For example, *beverage* is more specific than *liquid; coffee* is more specific than *beverage; Joe's black coffee* is even more specific.

---

Being a waiter or waitress is a more complicated job than most people think. First of all, you must have a friendly personality. You must be able to maintain a smile no matter what your inner feelings may be. Proper attire and good hygiene are also essential. You have to be good at memorizing what your customers want and make sure each order is made to their specifications. If you are friendly, neat, and attentive to your customers, you will be successful.

## *Revised Paragraph*

Being a waitress is a more complicated job than the average customer thinks. First of all, a friendly, outgoing personality is important. No one wants to be greeted by a waitress who has an angry, indifferent, or "I'm bored with this job" expression on her face. A waitress should try to smile, regardless of the circumstances. When a screaming child hurls a plate of french fries across the table, smile and wipe up the ketchup. Proper attire and good hygiene are important, too. A waitress in a dirty dress and with hair hanging down into the food does not please customers. Finally, attentiveness to customers' orders is important. Be certain that each person gets the correct order and that the food is prepared according to his or her specifications. Pay particular attention when serving salads and steaks, since different dressings and degrees of rareness are easily confused. Following these suggestions will lead to happy customers as well as larger tips.

In this revision, the writer added examples, included more descriptive words, and made all details more *concrete* and *specific*.

Here are a few suggestions for how to include more specific details:

■ **Add names, numbers, times, and places.**

| VAGUE | My uncle bought a used car. |
|---|---|
| MORE SPECIFIC | Yesterday afternoon my uncle bought a red, two-door 1996 Toyota Tercel at the new "Toy-a-Rama" dealership. |

■ **Add more facts and explanation.**

| VAGUE | My iPhone is versatile. |
|---|---|
| MORE SPECIFIC | My iPhone allows me to send and receive email and text messages, surf the Web, listen to music, and take photos. |

■ **Use examples.**

| VAGUE | Dogs learn their owners' habits. |
|---|---|
| MORE SPECIFIC | As soon as I reach for my wire garden basket, my golden retriever knows this means I'm going outside, and he rushes to the back door. |

■ **Draw from your personal experience.**

| VAGUE | People sometimes eat to calm down. |
|---|---|
| MORE SPECIFIC | My sister relaxes every evening with a bowl of popcorn. |

Depending on your topic, you may need to do research to get more specific details. Dictionaries, encyclopedias, and magazine articles are often good sources. Think of research as interesting detective work and a chance to learn. For example, if you are writing a paragraph about the safety of air bags in cars, you may need to locate some current facts and statistics. Your college library and the Internet will be two good sources; a car dealership and a mechanic may be two others.

---

**EXERCISE 11-11**    ## Revising Sentences

**Directions:** Revise each of the following statements to make it more specific.
Answers will vary. Possible answers are shown.

**EXAMPLE**    Biology is a difficult course.

> Biology involves memorizing scientific terms and learning
> some of life's complex processes.

1. I rode the train.

   On Tuesday, I took the Red Line train to Cambridge to visit my cousin.

2. Pizza is easy to prepare.

   Making pizza involves three simple steps: stretching prepared dough,
   adding toppings, and baking.

3. The Fourth of July is a holiday.

   The Fourth of July is fun because my town has a big parade and picnic.

**4.** I bought a lawnmower.

*I bought a used, ten-horsepower John Deere lawnmower from Drake's*

*Garden Shop.*

**5.** The van broke down.

*My brother's 1990 Chevy van blew a gasket.*

---

| EXERCISE 11-12 | Writing a Paragraph Using Specific Details |
|---|---|

**WRITING IN PROGRESS**

**Directions:** Choose three of the following topics and narrow each of them down to a more manageable one. Develop a topic sentence that expresses one main point about each topic. Then brainstorm three specific details you could use to support each topic sentence.

1. Your favorite book or movie

2. How pets help people

3. How to end a relationship

4. A sport (or hobby) you would like to take up

5. A childhood memory

---

# Use Details to Support Your Topic Sentence

■ **GOAL 5**
Develop paragraphs using supporting details

Once you have written a preliminary topic sentence, your next step is to include the details that support your sentence. Just as an advertiser provides facts and information that support the headline, so must you provide details that support your topic sentence.

Let's look at an advertisement for salad dressing. In the ad shown on page 352, the subject is Newman's Own salad dressing. Study the body copy. What kinds of information are provided? Notice that only information that supports the subject is included: all the details describe the salad dressing or encourage readers to try a different variety. These are called *relevant details*. *Relevant* means that the details directly relate to or explain the headline. Notice, too, that a reasonable number of facts are included—enough to make the headline believable and convincing. In other words, a *sufficient* number of *details* are provided to make the headline effective. When you select details to support a topic sentence, they must also be *relevant* and *sufficient*. You must provide a sufficient number of details to make your topic sentence understandable and convincing. However, a detail, no matter how interesting and true, must be left out if it does not support the topic sentence.

### Tip for Writers

*Relevant* information is content about the topic being discussed. The opposite is *irrelevant*. If your teacher marks a sentence *irrelevant*, she means it doesn't belong where you have placed it, so it should be deleted or moved to another paragraph.

## Choose Relevant Details

**Relevant details** directly support the topic sentence. The following paragraph contains two details that do not support the topic sentence, which is shaded. Can you spot them?

(1) Corporations are beginning to recognize the importance of recycling. (2) Our landfills are getting too full, and we are running out of room for our garbage. (3) Many companies are selling products with reusable containers. (4) Tide laundry soap and Jergens hand cream, for example, sell refills. (5) It bothers me that some manufacturers charge the same, or even more, for refills as for the original containers. (6) I believe all cities and towns should have recycling bins to make it easy for individuals to recycle. (7) By recycling tin, glass, plastic, and paper, companies can save valuable natural resources. (8) Some corporations recycle plastic and paper bags to conserve energy and natural resources. (9) Through these methods, corporations are helping to save our environment.

Sentence 5 is not relevant because what companies charge for reusable containers does not relate to the importance of recycling. Sentence 6 is not relevant because it is about towns and individuals, not corporations.

| EXERCISE 11-13 | Selecting Relevant Details |

*WORKING TOGETHER*

**Directions:** Each of the topic sentences listed below is followed by a set of details. Working with a classmate, place check marks on the lines before those statements that are relevant supporting details.

1. TOPIC SENTENCE   People should take safety precautions when outside temperatures reach 95 degrees or above.

   DETAILS   ✓ **a.** It is important to drink plenty of fluids.

   _____ **b.** If you are exposed to extreme cold or dampness, you should take precautions.

   ✓ **c.** To prevent heat exhaustion, reduce physical activity.

   ✓ **d.** Infants and elderly people are particularly at risk for heat exhaustion.

2. TOPIC SENTENCE   Freedom of speech, the first amendment to the U.S. Constitution, does not give everyone the right to say anything at any time.

   DETAILS   _____ **a.** The Constitution also protects freedom of religion.

   _____ **b.** Freedom of speech is a right that citizens of most Western countries take for granted.

   ✓ **c.** Freedom of speech is restricted by slander and libel laws, which prohibit speaking or publishing harmful, deliberate lies about people.

   _____ **d.** Citizens may sue if they feel their freedom of speech has been unfairly restricted.

3 TOPIC SENTENCE   Family violence against women is a growing problem that is difficult to control or prevent.

   DETAILS   ✓ **a.** Abusive partners will often ignore restraining orders.

   ✓ **b.** Violence shown on television may encourage violence at home.

   _____ **c.** New laws make it easier for observers of child abuse to report the violence.

   ✓ **d.** Battered women frequently do not tell anyone that they have been battered because they are ashamed.

   _____ **e.** Violence against the elderly is increasing at a dramatic rate.

## Include Sufficient Details

Including **sufficient details** means including *enough* details to make your topic sentence believable and convincing. Your details should be as exact and specific as possible. The following paragraph lacks sufficient detail:

> Recycling has a lot of positive sides. When you recycle, you receive money if you return used containers. When you recycle, you clean up the earth, and you also save the environment. Less waste and more space are our goals.

Notice that the paragraph is very general. It does not describe any specific benefits of recycling, nor does it explain how recycling saves the environment or creates more space. A revised version is shown below. Notice the addition of numerous details and the more focused topic sentence.

> Recycling offers benefits for consumers and manufacturers as well as for the environment. Consumers benefit from recycling in several ways. Recycling generates revenue, which should, in the long run, reduce costs of products. Soda bottles and cans returned to the store produce immediate cash return. Manufacturers benefit, too, since their costs are reduced. Most important, however, are benefits to the environment. Recycling reduces landfills. It also produces cleaner air by reducing manufacturing. Finally, recycling paper saves trees.

If you have difficulty thinking of enough details to include in a paragraph, try brainstorming, freewriting, or branching. Also, try to draft a more focused topic sentence, as the writer did in the paragraph above. You may then find it easier to develop supporting details. If you are still unable to generate additional details, your topic may be too narrow or you may need to do some additional reading or research on your topic. If you use information from printed sources, be sure to give the author credit by using a citation. Indicate the author, title, place of publication, publisher, and year. Refer to Chapter 18 for more information on documenting sources.

---

| EXERCISE 11-14 | Writing a Paragraph |
| --- | --- |

**WRITING IN PROGRESS**

**Directions:** Write a paragraph developing one of the topic sentences you wrote in Exercise 11-12. Use the specific details you listed, adding more if necessary. Be sure you have included relevant and sufficient details in your paragraph.

---

## Use a Variety of Types of Supporting Details

As you learned earlier in the chapter, there are many types of details that you can use to explain or support a topic sentence. The most common types of supporting details are (1) illustrations or examples, (2) facts or statistics, (3) reasons, (4) descriptions, and (5) steps or procedures.

Using a variety of supporting details to support your topic sentence makes your writing more interesting and engaging for your reader. More important, it also makes your topic sentence more believable, and it is likely that your reader will accept your ideas. For example, if you support a topic sentence asserting that teenage bullying is getting out of control only with examples from your own community, a reader may wonder if your community is the exception rather than the rule. If, however, you offer statistics from a national survey demonstrating that teenage bullying is a common occurrence, then you assure your readers that the problem extends beyond your community.

| EXERCISE 11-15 | ## Writing Supporting Details |

*WORKING TOGETHER*

**Directions:** With a classmate, for each topic sentence, choose at least three different types of details that could be used to support it. Label each detail as *example, fact/statistic, reason, description,* or *steps/procedures.*    Answers will vary.

1. People make inferences about you based on the way you dress.
2. Many retailers with traditional stores have decided also to market their products through Web sites.
3. Many Americans are obsessed with losing weight.
4. Historical and cultural attractions can be found in a variety of shapes, sizes, and locations throughout the world.
5. Using a search engine is an effective, though not perfect, method of searching the Internet.

---

## ! NEED TO KNOW

### Drafting Paragraphs

To draft effective paragraphs, be sure to do the following:

- **Choose a manageable *topic.*** Your topic should be neither too broad nor too narrow.
- **Write a clear *topic sentence.*** Your topic sentence should identify the topic and make a point about that topic.
- **Develop your paragraph by providing *relevant* and *sufficient* details.** Relevant details are those that directly support the topic. Including sufficient details means providing enough details to make your topic sentence believable and convincing.

---

# Arrange Details

■ GOAL 6
Arrange details so they are easy to follow

An important part of writing a paragraph is arranging your details so they are easy to follow, as the example below demonstrates.

Arturio had an assignment to write a paragraph about travel. He drafted the paragraph and then revised it. As you read each version, pay particular attention to the order in which he arranged the details.

### First Draft

This summer I had the opportunity to travel extensively. Over Labor Day weekend I backpacked with a group of friends in the Allegheny Mountains. When spring semester was over, I visited my seven cousins in Florida. My friends and I went to New York City over the Fourth of July to see fireworks and explore the city. During June I worked as a wildlife-preservation volunteer in a Colorado state park. On July 15, I celebrated my twenty-fifth birthday by visiting my parents in Syracuse.

### Revision

This summer I had the opportunity to travel extensively in the United States. When the spring semester ended, I went to my cousins' home in Florida to relax. When I returned, I worked during the month of June as a wildlife-preservation volunteer in a Colorado state park. Then my friends and I went to New York City to see the fireworks and look around the city over the Fourth of July weekend. On July 15th, I celebrated my twenty-fifth birthday by visiting my parents in Syracuse. Finally, over Labor Day weekend, my friends and I backpacked in the Allegheny Mountains.

Did you find Arturio's revision easier to read? In the first draft, he recorded details as he thought of them. There is no logical arrangement to them. In the second version, he arranged the details in the order in which they happened. Arturio chose this arrangement because it fit his details logically.

The three common methods for arranging details are as follows:

- Time sequence
- Spatial arrangement
- Least/most arrangement

## Time-Sequence Arrangement

When you are describing an event or series of events, it is often easiest to arrange them in the order in which they happened. This arrangement is called **time sequence**. The following time-sequence map will help you visualize this arrangement of details.

**VISUALIZE IT!**

**Time-Sequence Map**

Here is how to build a low-fat deli select sandwich.

Start with two slices of whole-grain bread.

Add fat-free smoked chicken breast.

Add low-fat pastrami.

Add one slice of fat-free cheese.

Slather with fat-free mayo.

You can also use time sequence to explain how events happened or to tell a story. For example, you can explain how you ended up living in Cleveland or tell a story about a haunted house. In the following sample paragraph, the student has arranged details in time sequence. Read the paragraph and then fill in the blanks in the time-sequence map that follows it.

### Sample Time-Sequence Paragraph

Driving a standard-shift vehicle is easy if you follow these steps. First, push the clutch pedal down. The clutch is the pedal on the left. Then start the car. Next, move the gearshift into first gear. On most cars this is the straight-up position. Next, give the car some gas, and slowly release the clutch pedal until you start moving. Finally, be ready to shift into higher gears—second, third, and so on. A diagram of where to find each gear usually appears on the gearshift knob. With practice, you will learn to start up smoothly and shift without the car making grinding noises or lurching.

**VISUALIZE IT!**

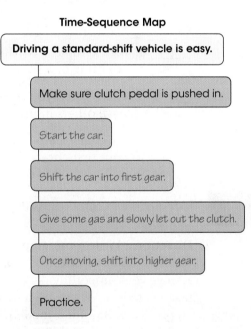

**Time-Sequence Map**

Driving a standard-shift vehicle is easy.

Make sure clutch pedal is pushed in.

Start the car.

Shift the car into first gear.

Give some gas and slowly let out the clutch.

Once moving, shift into higher gear.

Practice.

### Time-Sequence Transitions

Look again at the sample paragraph. Notice that transitions are used to lead you from one step to another. Try to pick them out; underline those that you find. Did you underline *first, then, next,* and *finally*? Using transitions like those listed below will help you to link details in a time-sequence paragraph.

| COMMON TIME-SEQUENCE TRANSITIONS | | |
|---|---|---|
| first | next | before |
| second | during | now |
| third | at the same time | later |
| in the beginning | following | at last |
| then | after | finally |

| EXERCISE 11-16 | Using Time Sequence |

**Directions:** Arrange in time sequence the supporting-detail sentences that follow the topic sentence below. Place a "1" on the line before the detail that should appear first in the paragraph, a "2" before the detail that should appear second, and so on.

**TOPIC SENTENCE** Registration for college classes requires planning and patience.

SUPPORTING-DETAIL SENTENCES

_3_ **a.** Find out which of the courses that you need are being offered that particular semester.

_1_ **b.** Study your degree requirements and figure out which courses you need to take before you can take others.

_4_ **c.** Then start working out a schedule.

_2_ **d.** For example, a math course may have to be taken before an accounting or a science course.

_6_ **e.** Then, when you register, if one course or section is closed, you will have others in mind that will work with your schedule.

_5_ **f.** Select alternative courses that you can take if all sections of one of your first-choice courses are closed.

| EXERCISE 11-17 | Writing a Paragraph Using Time Sequence |

**Directions:** Write a paragraph on one of the following topics. First, write a topic sentence that identifies your topic and expresses your main point about it. Then arrange your supporting-detail sentences in order. Be sure to use transitions to connect your ideas. When you have finished, draw a time-sequence map of your paragraph (see p. 357 for a model). Use your map to check that you have included sufficient details and that you have presented your details in the correct sequence.

1. Going on a disastrous date
2. Closing (or beginning) a chapter of your life
3. Getting more (or less) out of an experience than you expected
4. Having an adventure
5. Having an experience that made you feel like saying, "Look who's talking!"

## Spatial Arrangement

Suppose you are asked to describe a car you have just purchased. You want your reader, who has never seen the car, to visualize it. How would you organize your description? You could describe the car from bottom to top or from top to bottom, or from front to back. This method of presentation is called **spatial arrangement.** For other objects, you might arrange your details from inside to outside, from near to far, or from east to west. Notice how, in the following paragraph, the details are arranged from top to bottom.

### Sample Spatial-Arrangement Paragraph

My dream house will have a three-level outdoor deck that will be ideal for relaxing on after a hard day's work. The top level of the deck will be connected by sliding glass doors to the family room. On this level there will be a hot tub, a large picnic table with benches, and a comfortable padded chaise. On the middle level there will be a suntanning area, a hammock, and two built-in planters for a mini-herb garden. The lowest level, which will meet the lawn, will have a built-in stone barbeque pit for big cookouts and a gas grill for everyday use.

Can you visualize the deck?

### Spatial-Arrangement Transitions

In spatial-arrangement paragraphs, transitions are particularly important since they often reveal placement or position of objects or parts. Using transitions like those listed in the table below will help you to link details in a spatial-arrangement paragraph.

| COMMON SPATIAL-ARRANGEMENT TRANSITIONS | | |
| --- | --- | --- |
| above | next to | nearby |
| below | inside | on the other side |
| beside | outside | beneath |
| in front of | behind | west (or other direction) |

**EXERCISE 11-18**

## Using Spatial Arrangement

**Directions:** Use spatial arrangement to order the supporting-detail sentences that follow the topic sentence below. Write a "1" on the line before the detail that should appear first in the paragraph, a "2" before the detail that should appear second, and so on.

**TOPIC SENTENCE**  My beautiful cousin Audry always looks as if she has dressed quickly and given her appearance little thought.

SUPPORTING-DETAIL SENTENCES

___3___  **a.** She usually wears an oversized, baggy sweater, either black or blue-black, with the sleeves pushed up.

___6___  **b.** Black slip-on sandals complete the look; she wears them in every season.

___5___  **c.** On her feet she wears mismatched socks.

___1___  **d.** Her short, reddish hair is usually wind-blown, hanging every which way from her face.

___2___  **e.** She puts her makeup on unevenly, if at all.

___4___  **f.** The sweater covers most of her casual, rumpled skirt.

| EXERCISE 11-19 | Writing a Paragraph Using Spatial Arrangement |
|---|---|

**Directions:** Write a paragraph on one of the following topics. First, write a topic sentence that identifies your topic and expresses your main point about it. Then use spatial arrangement to develop your supporting details.

1. A secret hiding place
2. The street that leads to your house
3. A photograph or painting that you like
4. Your dream car
5. The inside of an alien spacecraft

## Least/Most Arrangement

Another method of arranging details is to present them in order from least to most or most to least, according to some quality or characteristic. For example, you might choose least to most important, serious, frightening, or humorous. In writing a paragraph explaining your reasons for attending college, you might arrange details from most to least important. In writing about an exciting evening, you might arrange your details from most to least exciting.

As you read the following paragraph, note how the writer has arranged details in a logical way.

### Sample Least/Most Paragraph

This week has been filled with good news. One night when balancing my checkbook, I discovered a $155 error in my checking account—in my favor, for once! I was even happier when I finally found a buyer for my Chevy Blazer that I had been trying to sell all winter. Then my boss told me he was submitting my name for a 50-cent hourly raise; I certainly didn't expect that. Best of all, I learned that I'd been accepted into the Radiology curriculum for next fall.

In this paragraph, the details are arranged from least to most important.

### Least/Most Transitions

In least/most paragraphs, transitions help your reader to follow your train of thought. Using transitions like those listed in the table below will help you link details in a least/most paragraph.

| COMMON LEAST/MOST TRANSITIONS | | |
|---|---|---|
| most important | particularly important | moreover |
| above all | even more | not only . . . but also |
| especially | best of all | |

| EXERCISE 11-20 | Writing a Paragraph Using Least/Most Arrangement |
|---|---|

**Directions:** Write a paragraph on one of the following topics. First, write a topic sentence that identifies your topic and expresses your main point about it. Then use a least/most arrangement to order your details. When you have finished, draw a map of your paragraph. Use your map to check that you have included sufficient details and that you have arranged your details in least/most order.

1. Your reasons for choosing the dorm or apartment you live in
2. Changes in your life since you began college
3. Why people shop online
4. Why you like a certain book or movie
5. Good (or bad) things that have happened to you recently

# Writing Topic Sentences

**Directions:** Working with a classmate, write a topic sentence for each of the following topics. Then indicate what method (time sequence, spatial, or least/most) you would use to arrange supporting details.   Answers will vary. Sample answers provided.

**TOPIC**            relationship with a friend

**TOPIC SENTENCE**   Whenever George and I get together,

he always takes over the conversation.

**METHOD OF ARRANGEMENT**   time sequence

1. **TOPIC**            animals that have humanlike behaviors

   **TOPIC SENTENCE**   My golden retriever and my two-year-old granddaughter

   react in similar ways to household events.

   **METHOD OF ARRANGEMENT**   least/most

2. **TOPIC**            a difficulty that I faced

   **TOPIC SENTENCE**   I was going to drop my math class, but instead I met

   with my teacher and she helped me line up a tutor.

   **METHOD OF ARRANGEMENT**   time sequence

3. **TOPIC**            feeling under pressure

   **TOPIC SENTENCE**   Recently, a number of mishaps have

   increased my level of stress.

   **METHOD OF ARRANGEMENT**   time sequence or least/most

4. **TOPIC**            a favorite dinner menu

   **TOPIC SENTENCE**   For Thanksgiving dinner I served broccoli soup,

   roast turkey with chestnut stuffing, and pecan pie.

   **METHOD OF ARRANGEMENT**   time sequence

5. **TOPIC**            an exciting sporting event

   **TOPIC SENTENCE**   The Super Bowl is an annual event in which two

   championship teams display their talents.

   **METHOD OF ARRANGEMENT**   least/most

| EXERCISE 11-22 | ## Identifying Methods of Arrangement |
|---|---|

*WORKING TOGETHER*

**Directions:** Find several magazine or newspaper ads. Working in a group, identify the method of arrangement of the advertising copy.

| EXERCISE 11-23 | ## Revising Your Paragraph |
|---|---|

**WRITING IN PROGRESS**

**Directions:** Reread the paragraph you wrote for Exercise 11-14 and decide on the best way to arrange the details. Then revise your draft using time-sequence, spatial, or least/most arrangement to arrange your details.

## Use Transitional Words to Connect Details

**Transitional words** allow readers to move easily from one detail to another; they show how details relate to one another. You might think of them as words that guide and signal your reader about how your ideas are organized and signal what is to follow. As you read the following paragraph, notice the transitional words (highlighted in pink) that this student used. The topic sentence is highlighted in yellow.

> We made the most of our day in Denver this summer. First, we strolled around downtown, window shopping and people watching while we sipped our coffee. Then, we headed to the Denver Art Museum to explore new exhibits and the museum's famous American Indian art collection. Next, we made our way to Coors Field for a Colorado Rockies baseball game and spent the afternoon cheering the home team to victory. Afterward, we met our friends in the Five Points neighborhood for some of the best Caribbean food we have ever had.

Table 11-2 shows some commonly used transitional words and phrases for each method of arranging details discussed earlier in this chapter on pages 356–360. To understand how these transitional words and phrases work, review the sample paragraphs for each of these arrangements. Highlight each transitional word or phrase in those paragraphs.

| TABLE 11-2 | FREQUENTLY USED TRANSITIONS |
|---|---|
| **Arrangement** | **Transition** |
| Time Sequence | after, afterward, at last, at the same time, before, currently, during, eventually, finally, first, following, in the beginning, later, meanwhile, next, now, second, soon, suddenly, then, third, until, when |
| Spatial | above, behind, below, beneath, beside, in front of, inside, nearby, next to, on the other side of, outside, to the west (north, etc.) of |
| Least/Most | above all, best of all, especially, even more, moreover, most, most important, particularly important, not only, but also |

You will learn to use additional signal words for other methods of organization in Chapters 12 and 13.

---

**EXERCISE 11-24**  ## Using Transitions

**Directions:** Select the transitional word or phrase from Table 11-2 that best completes each of the following sentences.  *Answers will vary. Possible answers are shown.*

1. We drove slowly because sheets of rain were coming down on the road. _____Suddenly_____, we heard a loud crack and watched in disbelief as a tree fell in front of our car.

2. The campus bookstore is located in a two-story brick building, on the other side of the gym and __to the west (north, etc.)__ of the science building.

3. A child's success in school depends on factors such as regular attendance and cooperation between parents and teachers. _____Above all_____, having a parent's encouragement and support at home helps a child succeed at school.

4. There are several aspects to being an effective listener. _____First_____, be sure to give the speaker your full attention.

5. The first step in marketing research involves defining the problem. _____Next_____, marketers must decide how to collect information about the problem.

---

**EXERCISE 11-25**  ## Revising a Paragraph

**WRITING IN PROGRESS**

**Directions:** Reread the paragraph you revised in Exercise 11-23. As you read, revise your paragraph again by adding transitions to help your reader move from one key detail to the next.

---

## ❗ NEED TO KNOW

### Developing, Arranging, and Connecting Details

Be sure to use interesting and lively **details** to support your topic sentence.

- Choose details that are specific and concrete.
- Within your paragraphs, arrange details in a **logical order.** Three techniques for arranging details are
  - **time-sequence arrangement;** information is presented in the order in which it happened.
  - **spatial arrangement;** descriptive details are arranged according to their position in space.
  - **least/most arrangement;** ideas are arranged from least to most or most to least according to some quality or characteristic.
- Use **transitions** to help your reader move easily from one key detail to the next.

# INTEGRATING READING AND WRITING

## READ AND REVISE

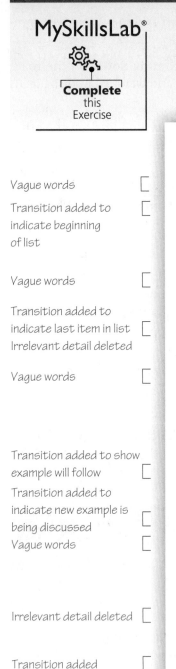

**MySkillsLab®**

**Complete** this Exercise

The following excerpt is from an essay called "You Have 12 Friend Requests and 15 Messages." As you read, underline the topic sentence and transitions in each paragraph. Then revise the essay by adding or deleting transitions, changing vague words to specific words, and deleting any details that are not relevant.

Vague words ☐

Transition added to indicate beginning of list ☐

Vague words ☐

Transition added to indicate last item in list ☐
Irrelevant detail deleted

Vague words ☐

Transition added to show example will follow ☐

Transition added to indicate new example is being discussed ☐

Vague words ☐

Irrelevant detail deleted ☐

Transition added ☐

                              convenient and effective                        interesting

<u>Facebook gives users a ~~very good~~ way to meet new people and make ~~great~~</u>
First, if
<u>new friends.</u> ~~If~~ one doesn't go out much, it's really hard to get to meet new people. Going through Facebook, a user can read about people before taking an interest in them. <u>In addition,</u> if the user is just a shy person and doesn't really like
                    a valuable
to talk a lot but likes to write, this can be ~~an awesome~~ way to meet new people. Making and meeting new friends through Facebook is the biggest thing right
                   Finally, always
now. ~~Twitter is another way to connect with people.~~ ~~Always~~ remember that the user is the one in control of confirming and ignoring a request to be a friend.
             useful function that allows
    <u>Facebook also has this ~~amazing way of letting~~ the user create an event so</u>
<u>that it can be sent out to all those he or she chooses to invite.</u> A Facebook invite saves money, time, and stamps; stamps are expensive now and so are invitations. It's a quick means to make contact with hundreds of people just by creat-
                For example, if
ing one of these events. ~~If~~ someone was trying to get a business started they would send out an event invite explaining their new business venture. Free
                              Furthermore, let's
advertisement on Facebook is a money saver for those just getting started. ~~Let's~~
   a person was planning
say ~~there's going to be~~ a family reunion; his or her invitation will indicate the date, time, place and any other special instructions, but the event will only be sent to close family members and be seen by those he or she chooses to invite.
~~Family reunions can be really hard to organize.~~ <u>Another thing</u> that event invites do is raise money for people who are sick and need help paying their medi-
                             Once again, an
cal bills; these kinds of benefits really help the less fortunate. ~~An~~ event can be created in just minutes and the word can be spread rapidly.

## READ AND RESPOND: A Student Essay

*Bogyeong Son is a student at Bunker Hill Community College where she is studying for an associate's degree. She plans to transfer to a four-year college to obtain a bachelor's degree in business. She submitted this essay to the Writing Rewards Essay Contest sponsored by Pearson Education. The assignment she responded to directed her to write an essay about cultural differences.*

Title gives the subject

Background details

Topic sentence

Topic sentence

Example illustrates language barrier

Example follows, showing her lack of knowledge about American culture

# A Korean Girl in Boston

A common saying is "Do in Rome as the Romans do." There are countries in the world that have their own laws, so we must observe the laws. I am a Korean who lived in Korea for 21 years, but I am living in the United States now. Last year, my older sister and I arrived in Boston after enduring a 16-hour flight. At that time, I did not have any basic knowledge about the United States. The dollar as currency and English as the spoken language were the only things that I knew about. Not knowing English and the U.S. culture was the same as if I went to a field of battle without a gun. My new life started in a place which was alien to me because of a language barrier and culture shock.

The language barrier was the most difficult part of living in another country. Here were the only sentences I could speak: "Hi. My name is Bogyeong Son. I am Korean. Thanks. Sorry. Bye." If I met a real native speaker, my tongue set hard, and my eyes blinked five times a second. The first episode started when my sister and I arrived in Boston's Logan Airport. We finished the long flight and just followed most passengers after we got off the airplane. Because of going through immigration, most people disappeared very quickly, and eventually we lost the way to the exit. If I were in Korea, I would be able to ask someone or read the directory. In order to find the exit, we looked around many times, and one staff member who wore a uniform thought we were strange. So he asked us something, but we could not understand him. We just looked at each other, wondering what to do. We typed the word "exit" by using a dictionary and showed him; finally, we were shown how to go out from the airport.

The next problem was in getting a cab. Fortunately, there were many cabs in front of the airport, so we put the luggage in the trunk, and we could get in the cab easily with a basic "Hi." We did not know how to give the driver our destination, so we just showed him a paper with our hotel address. The problem happened when we got in front of our hotel. After I saw twenty dollars come up on the taxi meter, I opened my wallet and gave the driver twenty dollars, saying, "Thank you." Suddenly his facial emotion changed, and he said something; of course, we did not understand. He repeated "blah blah blah" many times, and eventually I could hear a word: "Tip." He wanted to get a tip. I was unfamiliar with this because in my country, we used to pay exactly what the taxi meter showed us. Because of his scary facial expression, I quickly took ten dollars again and gave it to him. He smiled, and he took our luggage out of the trunk without our help. I paid a ten dollar tip for twenty dollars. It was my first day and I did not have any fundamental knowledge about American culture.

Topic sentence

Because of the language barrier, my life in my new country went on step by step. From the second week, I attended language school and met many friends who were from diverse countries. I realized for the first time how international America was and why America was a melting pot. Of course in class I spoke word-by-word, and now I wonder how I could understand what my teacher said and how I could do my homework. The next week, I got a debit card; I thought banking was very important, so I made sure of all the steps for using the card by using a dictionary when I wrote my information.

Topic sentence

Example of her culture shock

In school, I was faced with culture shock. One day when I was struggling with learning the language, one of my classmates sneezed loudly. Immediately, three people including the teacher said the same thing at the same time, but I just passed that situation by without knowing what it was. A few days later another classmate sneezed, and I was in the same situation. The teacher said it was usual to say "Bless you" to people when they sneezed. From that time, I said "Bless you" automatically when I heard "Ahchoo!" wherever I was. One day my friend told me that "Bless you" was only for sneezes, not coughs. I did not distinguish between a sneeze and a cough, so I said "Bless you" for everyone. The culture shock made me feel confused in my new environment.

Topic sentence

Another example of culture shock was the concept of taxes, which I did not experience in my country. Even when I bought just a chocolate bar, I had to pay tax. In a restaurant I also made a mistake. I ordered some delicious dishes and then ate with my sister, but after we got the check, we found out that tax would be added to the amount. My debit card was at home, so I ran to get it. Now when I look back on that time, I can laugh, but those times when we could not speak English to explain things and when we were very nervous about the situation were horrible to us.

Topic sentence

Descriptive details give more background

My life in my country was completely different. I lived with my lovely parents, and every morning my mom woke me up softly, and then I asked to sleep for five more minutes. There were warm and so delicious meals made by my mom, and my father took me to school comfortably in his car. I was always in their protection. In America, my sister is my only family. We rely on each other, and we cook every meal by ourselves, and then we depend on taking a train instead of my father's car. Every morning I ask to sleep five more minutes as my cell phone goes off clangorously. Especially when I get a cold and feel sick, I pine for my precious family. One by one, the faces of loved ones flash through my mind. After I talk with my family on the phone, I always remind myself that I am going to study harder and be a successful woman.

Conclusion

With these special experiences, now I am leading a fresh second life. I still fight with the language and the culture, but in America, I must make everything by myself and improve my lot by myself. I am ready for any venture.

## Examining Writing

1. What types of supporting details did the writer use in this essay? Which details were most effective?

2. How did the writer arrange her ideas?

3. Underline transitions throughout the essay. What does each transition indicate? Where might additional transitions be useful in guiding the reader?

4. Evaluate the types of words the writer used and underline examples of vague and/or specific language in this essay.

## READ AND RESPOND: A Professional Essay

### Thinking Before Reading

The following selection originally appeared in "Earth Island Journal," an environmental magazine. In the selection, the author discusses the health risks of radiation from cell phone towers and other media technology.

1. Preview the reading, using the steps discussed in Chapter 1 on page 25.

2. Connect the reading to your own experience by answering the following questions:

   a. What health effects have you heard of regarding cell phones, cell phone towers, and other types of technology?

   b. What type of technology do you think carries the most risk?

3. Highlight and annotate as you read.

1270**L**/1212 words

# Wireless Interference: The Health Risks

## Christopher Ketcham

*We now live in a wireless-saturated normality that has never existed in the history of the human race, and the effects of EMFs on human beings are largely untested.*

—Dan McCarthy/DANMCCARTHY.ORG

1    In January 1990, a cell tower goes up 800 feet from Alison Rall's dairy farm in Mansfield, Ohio. By fall, the cattle herd that pastures near the tower is sick, and Rall's three young children begin suffering bizarre skin rashes, raised red "hot spots." The kids are hit with waves of hyperactivity. The girls lose hair. Rall, when she becomes pregnant with a fourth child, can't gain weight.

2      Desperate to understand what is happening to her family and her farm, she contacts an Environmental Protection Agency scientist named Carl Blackman. He's an expert on the biological effects of radiation from electromagnetic fields (EMFs)—the kind of radiofrequency EMFs (RF-EMFs) by which all wireless technology operates, including not just cell towers and cell phones but also wi-fi hubs and wi-fi-capable computers, "smart" utility meters, and even cordless home phones. "With my government cap on, I'm supposed to tell you you're perfectly safe," Blackman tells her. "With my civilian cap on, I have to tell you to consider leaving."

3      When Rall contacts the cell phone company that operates the tower, she is told there is "no possibility whatsoever" that the tower is the source of her ills. But within weeks of abandoning the farm, the children recovered their health, and so did the herd.

4      We all live in range of cell towers now, and we are all wireless operators. As of October 2010 there were 5.2 billion cell phones operating on the planet. "Penetration," in the marketing-speak of the companies, often tops 100 percent in many countries, meaning there is more than one connection per person.

5      I don't have an Internet connection at my home in Brooklyn, and, like a dinosaur, I still keep a landline. Yet even though I have, in a fashion, opted out, I'm bathed in the radiation from cell phone panels on the parking garage next door. The waves are everywhere. We now live in a wireless-saturated normality that has never existed in the history of the human race, and the effects of EMFs on human beings are largely untested.

**carcinogenic**

having the potential to cause cancer

6      In May 2011, the International Agency for Research on Cancer (IARC) issued a statement that the electromagnetic frequencies from cell phones would henceforth be classified as "possibly carcinogenic to humans." The IARC decision followed multiple warnings, mostly from European regulators, about the possible health risks of RF-EMFs. In September 2007, the EU's European Environment Agency suggested that widespread radiofrequency radiation "could lead to a health crisis similar to those caused by asbestos, smoking, and lead in petrol." Double-strand breaks in DNA—one of the undisputed causes of cancer—have been reported in tests with animal cells. Neuroscientists at Swinburne University of Technology in Australia discovered a "power boost" in brain waves when humans were exposed to cell phone radiofrequencies. The brain, one of the lead researchers speculated, was "concentrating to overcome the electrical interference."

7      Yet the major public health watchdogs, in the United States and worldwide, have dismissed concerns. The American Cancer Society reports that "most studies published so far have not found a link between cell phone use and the development of tumors." The cell phone industry's lobbying organization assures the public that cell phone radiation is safe.

8      But according to a survey by Henry Lai of the University of Washington, although only 28 percent of studies funded by the wireless industry showed some type of biological effect from cell phone radiation, 67 percent of independently funded studies showed a bioeffect.

9    Despite the conflicting results, it is clear that some people are getting sick when they are heavily exposed to the new radiofrequencies. And we are not listening to their complaints. Take the story of Michele Hertz. When a local utility company installed a wireless "smart" meter on her house in upstate New York in 2009, Hertz experienced "incredible memory loss," and, at the age of 51, feared she had Alzheimer's. On a hunch, she told Con Edison of New York to remove the wireless meter. Within days, the worst symptoms disappeared. But her exposure to the meters has supersensitized Hertz to all kinds of other EMF sources. "Life," she says, "has dramatically changed."

10    In recent years, I've gotten to know dozens of "electrosensitives" like Hertz. To be sure, they constitute a tortured minority, often misunderstood and isolated. In Santa Fe, New Mexico, I met a woman who had taken to wearing an aluminum foil hat to kill wireless signals. I met a former world record marathoner who had lived at a house ringed by mountains that she said protected the place from cell frequencies. I met people who said they no longer wanted to live because of their condition.

11    The government of Sweden reports that the disorder known as electromagnetic hypersensitivity, or EHS, afflicts an estimated 3 percent of the population. Even the former prime minister of Norway, Gro Harlem Brundtland, has acknowledged that she suffers "strong discomfort" when she is exposed to cell phones. Yet the World Health Organization reports that "there is no scientific basis to link EHS symptoms to EMF exposure." A study conducted in 2006 at the Mobile Phone Research Unit at King's College in London came to a similar conclusion.

12    "The scientific data so far just doesn't help the electrosensitives," says Louis Slesin, editor and publisher of *Microwave News*, a newsletter and website that cover the potential effects of RF-EMFs. "There is electrical signaling going on in your body all the time, and the idea that external electromagnetic fields can't affect us just doesn't make sense."

13    Maria Gonzalez, a nurse who lives in Queens, New York, took me to her daughter's school to see the cell phone masts, which were built in 2005. The operator of the masts, Sprint Nextel, had built a wall of fake brick to hide them from view, but Gonzalez was skeptical. When she read a report published in 2002 about children in Spain who developed leukemia shortly after a cell phone tower was erected next to their school, she went into a quiet panic.

14    Sprint-Nextel was unsympathetic when she telephoned the company to express her concerns. A year later, Gonzalez sued the U.S. government, charging that the Federal Communications Commission had failed to fully evaluate the risks from cell phone frequencies. The suit was thrown out. The judge concluded that if regulators said the radiation was safe, it was safe. The message, as Gonzalez puts it, was that she was "crazy ... and making a big to-do about nothing."

15    I'd venture, rather, that she was applying a commonsense principle in environmental science: the precautionary principle, which states that when something cannot be proven with certainty to be safe, then it should be assumed to be harmful. In a society thrilled with the magic of digital wireless, we have junked this principle. Because of our thoughtlessness, we have not demanded to know the full

consequences of this technology. Perhaps the gadgets are slowly killing us—we do not know. What we do know, without a doubt, is that the electromagnetic fields are all around us, and that to live in modern civilization implies always and everywhere that we cannot escape their touch.

## Getting Ready to Write

### Checking Your Comprehension

Answer each of the following questions using complete sentences.

1. Briefly explain who Alison Rall, Carl Blackman, Michele Hertz, and Maria Gonzalez are, and why they are included in this article.

2. What are six common types of wireless technology operated by electromagnetic fields (EMFs)?

3. According to the selection, how many cell phones were operating in the world as of October 2010?

4. How did the May 2011 statement by the International Agency for Research on Cancer (IARC) classify the electromagnetic frequencies from cell phones?

5. What did the survey by Henry Lai of the University of Washington show about the biological effect from cell phone radiation?

6. What is the "precautionary principle"?

### Strengthening Your Vocabulary

Using the word's context, word parts, or a dictionary, write a brief definition of each of the following words as it is used in the reading.

1. civilian (paragraph 2) _____ a person acting in a nonofficial capacity

2. normality (paragraph 5) _____ the state of being normal or typical

3. undisputed (paragraph 6) _____ without argument

4. speculated (paragraph 6) _____ guessed

5. constitute (paragraph 10) _____ make up, include

6. hypersensitivity (paragraph 11) _____ having increased sensitivity to something

7. afflicts (paragraph 11) _____ badly affects

8. skeptical (paragraph 13) _____ doubtful

## Examining the Reading: Using Idea Maps

Review the reading by completing the missing parts of the following idea map.

**VISUALIZE IT!**

Title → **Wireless Interference: The Health Risks**

Thesis → We live in a world filled with electromagnetic fields (EMFs), and the effects of radiation from EMFs on human beings are unknown.

Examples of people experiencing adverse effects:

Alison Rall's family and farm after installation of _cell phone tower_

Michele Hertz after installation of _wireless utility meter_

Other "electrosensitives" around the world

Facts and statistics about EMFs:

5.2 billion _cell phones_ in use as of October 2010

More than one cell phone per person in many countries

Swedish government reports EHS affects _3 percent of population_

Conflicting reports about EMFs:

IARC classifies cell phone electromagnetic frequencies as _possibly carcinogenic_

European Environment Agency suggests _RF radiation_ could lead to health crisis

Australian neuroscientists discover _power boost in brain waves_ from cell phone RFs

The American Cancer Society finds no link between cell phone use and _the development of tumors_

Cell phone industry lobbyists claim cell phone radiation is _safe_; University of Washington survey shows conflicting results

World Health Organization reports no scientific link between _EHS symptoms_ and EMF exposure

Conclusion → We have become so attached to technology that we have not demanded to know the possibly deadly consequences of the EMFs that surround us.

## Thinking and Writing Critically: Discussion and Journal Writing

Respond and react to the reading by discussing the following:

1. Discuss the types of supporting details the author uses to capture your attention and to inform you about the potential risks of radiation from electromagnetic fields (EMFs). Which types of details are most effective and/or convincing?

2. Are you concerned about the radiation risks described in this selection? Why or why not?

3. What examples of specific and vivid language can you find in the selection? How does the author use language to influence the reader?

4. What details do you notice in the photograph that accompanies the selection? What other type of visual might be appropriate or effective with this subject?

**THINKING VISUALLY**

**MySkillsLab®**

**Complete** this Exercise

## Writing About the Reading

### Paragraph Options

1. This essay identifies EMFs as an environmental risk. Choose another danger in our environment and write a paragraph explaining why it is a problem to be concerned about.

2. Blackman unofficially advised Rall to leave her farm. Write a paragraph explaining whether you think Blackman behaved appropriately or should have done what the Environmental Protection Agency expected him to do. Give reasons for your answer.

3. Write a paragraph discussing your view of the precautionary principle and whether we have "junked" this principle because we are thrilled with wireless technology.

### Essay Options

4. How did this selection affect your opinion about the risks from EMFs? Which supporting details did you find most convincing or compelling? What concerns do you have after reading this selection? Write an essay answering these questions.

5. Will you change your use of technology—or try to limit your exposure—based on what you have learned from this selection? Why or why not? Write an essay explaining your answer.

6. Write an essay in which you summarize the findings of each of the different sources used in the selection and draw your own conclusions about EMFs.

# SELF-TEST SUMMARY

To test yourself, cover the Answer column with a sheet of paper and answer each question in the left column. Evaluate each of your answers as you work by sliding the paper down and comparing your answer with what is printed in the Answer column.

| QUESTION | ANSWER |
|---|---|
| **GOAL 1** Identify supporting details in paragraphs<br><br>What is the difference between major and minor details? What are common types of supporting details? | *Major details* are the most important details in a paragraph; they directly explain or prove the main idea. *Minor details* provide additional information, offer examples, or further explain major details. *Common types of supporting details* include illustrations and examples, facts and statistics, reasons, descriptions, and steps or procedures. |
| **GOAL 2** Identify implied main ideas<br><br>How do you find implied main ideas? | Find the topic, decide what the writer wants you to know about that topic based on the details in the paragraph, and express this idea in your own words. |
| **GOAL 3** Use transitional words and phrases to read paragraphs<br><br>What are transitions? | *Transitions* are linking words or phrases that lead the reader from one idea to another. See Table 11-1 on page 345 for a list of common transitions. |
| **GOAL 4** Choose specific details<br><br>What are four ways you can include more specific details? | Include more specific details by adding names, numbers, times, and places; adding more facts and explanations; using examples; and drawing from your personal experience. |
| **GOAL 5** Develop paragraphs using supporting details<br><br>How do you draft a paragraph and use supporting details to develop it? | Choose a manageable tobic, write a clear topic sentence, and develop the paragraph using relevant and sufficient details, specific language, and transitional words. |
| **GOAL 6** Arrange details so they are easy to follow<br><br>What are three common methods of arranging details? | Three common methods are *time sequence, spatial arrangement,* and *least/most arrangement.* |

# MySkillsLab

For more help with **Details, Implied Main Ideas, and Transitions**, go to your learning path in MySkillsLab at http://www.myskillslab.com.

# Patterns of Organization: Chronological Order, Process, Narration, and Description

## THINK About It!

What do all butterflies have in common? Each has a unique and intricate pattern on its wings. Upon closer inspection, many other common objects also have underlying patterns that help us better understand and classify them. Think of a leaf, or a snowflake, for example. The same way we can look closely and see patterns in nature, we can see specific patterns in how writers organize their ideas. Write a sentence listing at least three other things that have patterns, either in nature, or elsewhere in the world around you.

Organization is important in paragraphs and longer pieces of writing. Good writers follow a clear pattern when they write so that readers can easily find and understand the important points they are making.

## FOCUSING ON READING AND WRITING

# What Are Patterns of Organization?

To learn what patterns of organization are and why they are useful for reading and writing, complete the following activity.

Lists A and B each contain five facts. Which would be easier to learn?

**List A**

1. Cheeseburgers contain more calories than hamburgers.
2. Christmas cactus plants bloom once a year.
3. Many herbs have medicinal uses.
4. Many ethnic groups live in Toronto.
5. Fiction books are arranged alphabetically by author.

**List B**

1. Effective advertising has several characteristics.
2. An ad must be unique.
3. An ad must be believable.
4. An ad must make a lasting impression.
5. An ad must substantiate a claim.

Most likely, you chose list B. There is no connection between the facts in list A; the facts in list B, however, are related. The first sentence makes a general statement, and each remaining sentence gives a particular characteristic of effective advertising. Together they fit into a pattern.

The details of a paragraph, paragraphs within an essay, events within a short story, or sections within a textbook often fit a pattern. If you can recognize the pattern, you will find it easier to understand and remember the content. You will be able to comprehend the work as a unified whole rather than independent pieces of information.

Patterns are useful when you write, as well. They provide a framework within which to organize and develop your ideas and help you present them in a clear, logical manner. Separate sections of this chapter are devoted to reading and writing using each of the patterns of organization shown in the following chart.

| PATTERN OF ORGANIZATION | WHAT IT DOES | AN EXAMPLE OF ITS USE |
|---|---|---|
| **Chronological order** | Explains events in the order in which they occurred | Telling the history of cake making since ancient times |
| **Process** | Explains how something is done or how something works | Explaining how to make a cake |
| **Narration** | Tells a story that makes a point | Telling a story that involves cake |
| **Description** | Uses sensory details to help the reader visualize a topic | Describing the look, taste, texture, or flavor of cake |

Additional patterns are covered in Chapter 13.

# READING AND WRITING TIME SEQUENCE: CHRONOLOGICAL ORDER, PROCESS, AND NARRATION

## What Is Time Sequence?

**GOAL 1**
Understand time sequence

The terms *chronological order* and *process* both refer to the order in which something occurs is done. When writers tell a story, they usually present events in **chronological order**. In other words, they start with the first event, continue with the second, and so on. For example, if you were telling a friend about choosing your college, you would probably start by explaining how you identified schools that offered the program you are interested in, continue by describing your visits to each campus, and end with the result—the college you chose was the best fit for you. You would put events in order according to the *time* they occurred, beginning with the first event. **Process** is a pattern used to explain how something is done or how something works. For example, a writer might explain how to apply for a loan or describe how glass is recycled. **Narration** is another pattern that uses time sequence to tell a story. Whether you are reading or writing, time sequence is used whenever ideas are organized according to the order in which they occurred.

You can visualize and draw the chronological order and process patterns as follows:

**VISUALIZE IT!**

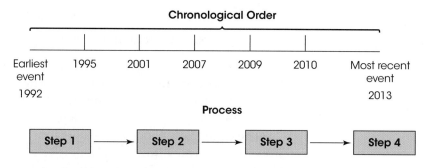

**Chronological Order**

| Earliest event | 1995 | 2001 | 2007 | 2009 | 2010 | Most recent event |

1992                                                                    2013

**Process**

Step 1 → Step 2 → Step 3 → Step 4

## Read Chronological Order and Process

**GOAL 2**
Read chronological order and process

When writers use the chronological order pattern, they often include time transitions (see the "Need to Know" box). They may also use actual dates to help readers keep track of the sequence of events.

> ### ! NEED TO KNOW
>
> ## Common Chronological Order and Process Transitions
>
> | first | before | following |
> |---|---|---|
> | second | after | last |
> | later | then | during |
> | next | in addition | when |
> | another | also | until |
> | as soon as | finally | meanwhile |

In the early 1930s, the newly established Federal Bureau of Narcotics took on a crucial role in the fight against marijuana. Under the directorship of Harry J. Anslinger, a rigorous campaign was waged against the drug and those using it. By 1937 many states had adopted a standard bill making marijuana illegal. In that same year, the federal government stepped in with the Marijuana Tax Act, a bill modeled after the Harrison "Narcotics" Act. Repressive legislation continued, and by the 1950s severe penalties were imposed on those convicted of possessing, buying, selling, or cultivating the drug.

—Barlow, *Criminal Justice in America*, p. 332

Writers also follow a time sequence when they use the process pattern—when they explain how something is done or made. When writers explain how to put together a bookcase, how to knit a sweater, or how bees make honey, they use steps to show the appropriate order. Transitions are used to guide you from one step to the next.

To plant a tulip bulb, follow a few easy steps. First, dig a hole large enough for the bulb and about six inches deep. Next, sprinkle a 1/4 to a 1/2 teaspoon of fertilizer in the hole before placing the bulb in it, pointed end up. Then fill the hole with dirt and press it down firmly. Finally, water the spot where you have planted the tulip.

## EXERCISE 12-1     Using Chronological Order

**Directions:** Using either chronological order or process, put each of the following groups of sentences in the correct order. Write a number from 1 to 4 before each sentence, beginning with the topic sentence.

1. __2__ Vassar College opened its doors in 1865, followed by Smith in 1871, Wellesley in 1877, and Bryn Mawr in 1880.

   __1__ In spite of varied protests, the 1800s saw the admission of women into higher education.

   __4__ Today the great majority of the more than 2,000 institutions of higher learning in the United States are coeducational.

   __3__ Meanwhile, the University of Michigan had admitted women in 1870, and by the turn of the century coed colleges and universities were becoming commonplace.
   —adapted from Kephart and Jedlicka, *The Family, Society, and the Individual*, p. 332

2. __2__ Dissolution begins with physical separation in which you no longer communicate or live with the other person.

   __1__ The breakup, or dissolution, of a romance follows a predictable series of steps.

   __4__ The final goodbye comes when the person becomes an ex-lover, and property is divided and legal matters resolved.

   __3__ Next, comes social, or public, separation in which it is evident to your friends and family that you are no longer involved with the person and you become known as "single."

3. <u>2</u>  The blips meant one thing: high levels of radiation.

   <u>3</u>  The technicians began a frantic search for the problem at their own plant, but they found nothing.

   <u>1</u>  At 9:00 a.m. on Monday, April 28, 1986, technicians at a nuclear plant sixty miles north of Stockholm began to see alarming blips across their computer screens.

   <u>4</u>  They concluded that the problem was not with their own facilities but perhaps with the Soviet Union's nuclear plant to the south, at Chernobyl.
   —adapted from Wallace, *Biology,* p. 572

4. <u>3</u>  He soon had one-third of all Americans over 65 enrolled in his Townsend clubs, demanding that the federal government provide $200 a month for every person over 65—the equivalent of about $2,000 a month today.

   <u>2</u>  The Great Depression made matters even worse, and in 1930 Francis Townsend, a social reformer, started a movement to rally older citizens.

   <u>4</u>  Because the Townsend Plan was so expensive, Congress embraced President Franklin Roosevelt's more modest Social Security plan in June 1934.

   <u>1</u>  In the 1920s, before Social Security provided an income for the aged, two-thirds of all citizens over 65 had no savings and could not support themselves.
   —adapted from Henslin, *Essentials of Sociology,* p. 272

5. <u>4</u>  When you revise, you step back to see whether you have expressed your thoughts adequately; you review your message and rewrite it.

   <u>1</u>  Writing a business message may be organized into three simple stages.

   <u>3</u>  In the writing stage, you decide on the organization and put your message on paper, including details and examples.

   <u>2</u>  During the planning stage, you think about your basic message, your audience, and the best way to convey your thoughts.
   —adapted from Thill and Bovée, *Excellence in Business Communication,* p. 79

## EXERCISE 12-2
## Analyzing Chronological Order/Process Paragraphs

**Directions:** Read each of the following paragraphs. Identify the topic and write a list of the actions, steps, or events described in each paragraph.

1.  Two important traditions are typically performed when new lodging properties are constructed. First, when the final floor is completed, an evergreen tree is placed on the top of the building. This act signifies that the building will rise no higher. It also symbolically ties the building safely to the ground through the "roots of the tree." The second important tradition is performed when the ceremonial ribbon is cut on opening day. At that time, the key to the front door is symbolically thrown onto the roof because it will never be used again. This is a symbol

signifying that the building is more than just a building. It has become a place that will always be open to those who are seeking a home for the night or more appropriately a "home away from home."

—adapted from Cook et al., *Tourism: The Business of Travel*, p. 170

Topic: _____ traditions _____

Steps: _____ place evergreen on top of building, throw front door key on roof _____

2.    In jury selection, the pool of potential jurors usually is selected from voter or automobile registration lists. Potential jurors are asked to fill out a questionnaire. Lawyers for each party and the judge can ask questions of prospective jurors to determine if they would be biased in their decision. Jurors can be "stricken for cause" if the court believes that the potential juror is too biased to render a fair verdict. Lawyers may also exclude a juror from sitting on a particular case without giving any reason for the dismissal. Once the appropriate number of jurors is selected (usually six to twelve jurors), they are impaneled to hear the case and are sworn in. The trial is ready to begin.

—adapted from Goldman and Cheeseman, *The Paralegal Professional*, p. 266

Topic: _____ jury selection _____

Steps: _____ pool is selected, potential jurors fill out questionnaire, bias is evaluated, _____

_____ jurors stricken or excluded, jurors impaneled and sworn in _____

3.    At 12:30 on the afternoon of May 1, 1915, the British steamship *Lusitania* set sail from New York to Liverpool. The passenger list of 1,257 was the largest since the outbreak of war in Europe in 1914. Six days later, the *Lusitania* reached the coast of Ireland. The passengers lounged on the deck. As if it were peacetime, the ship sailed straight ahead, with no zigzag maneuvers to throw off pursuit. But the submarine U-20 was there, and its commander, seeing a large ship, fired a single torpedo. Seconds after it hit, a boiler exploded and blew a hole in the *Lusitania*'s side. The ship listed immediately, hindering the launching of lifeboats, and in eighteen minutes it sank. Nearly 1,200 people died, including 128 Americans. As the ship's bow lifted and went under, the U-20 commander for the first time read the name: *Lusitania*.

—adapted from Divine et al., *America Past and Present*, p. 596

Topic: _____ the Lusitania _____

Steps: _____ ship set sail May 1, 1915; reached Ireland six days later; submarine fired _____

_____ torpedo, boiler exploded, ship listed and sank in 18 minutes _____

# Write Process Paragraphs

■ GOAL 3
Write process
paragraphs

There are two types of process paragraphs—a "how-to" paragraph and a "how-it-works" paragraph.

- **"How-to" paragraphs explain how something is done.** For example, they may explain how to change a flat tire, aid a choking victim, or locate a reference source in the library.

- **"How-it-works" paragraphs explain how something operates or happens.** For example, they may explain the operation of a pump, how the human body regulates temperature, or how children acquire speech.

Here are examples of both types of paragraphs. The first explains how to wash your hands in a medical environment. The second describes how hibernation works. Be sure to study the idea map for each.

### "How-to" Paragraph

Washing your hands may seem a simple task, but in a medical environment it is your first defense against the spread of disease and infection, and must be done properly. Begin by removing all jewelry. Turn on the water using a paper towel, thus avoiding contact with contaminated faucets. Next, wet your hands under running water and squirt a dollop of liquid soap in the palm of your hand. Lather the soap, and work it over your hands for two minutes. Use a circular motion, since it creates friction that removes dirt and organisms. Keep your hands pointed downward, so water will not run onto your arms, creating further contamination. Use a brush to clean under your fingernails. Then rinse your hands, reapply soap, scrub for one minute, and rinse again thoroughly. Dry your hands using a paper towel. Finally, use a new dry paper towel to turn off the faucet, protecting your hands from contamination.

**VISUALIZE IT!**

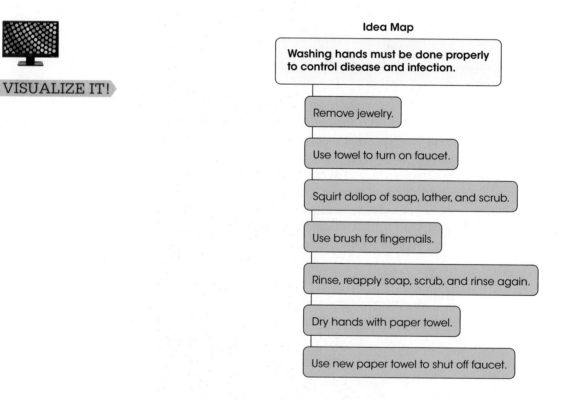

**Idea Map**

Washing hands must be done properly to control disease and infection.

Remove jewelry.

Use towel to turn on faucet.

Squirt dollop of soap, lather, and scrub.

Use brush for fingernails.

Rinse, reapply soap, scrub, and rinse again.

Dry hands with paper towel.

Use new paper towel to shut off faucet.

### "How-It-Works" Paragraph

Hibernation is a biological process that occurs most frequently in small animals. The process enables animals to adjust to a diminishing food supply. When the outdoor temperature drops, the animal's internal thermostat senses the change. Then bodily changes begin to occur. First, the animal's heartbeat slows, and oxygen intake is reduced by slowed breathing. Metabolism is then reduced. Food intake becomes minimal. Finally, the animal falls into a sleeplike state during which it relies on stored body fat to support life functions.

**VISUALIZE IT!**

**Idea Map**

> **Hibernation is a biological process.**

> Outdoor temperatures drop and body senses this.

> Heartbeat and breathing slow.

> Metabolism is reduced.

> Food intake becomes minimal.

> Body falls asleep and relies on stored fat.

## Select a Topic and Generate Ideas

Before you can describe a process, you must be very familiar with it. You should have done it often or have a complete understanding of how it works. Both how-to and how-it-works paragraphs describe steps that occur in a specified order. Begin developing your paragraph by listing these steps in the order in which they must occur. It is helpful to visualize the process.

For how-to paragraphs, imagine yourself actually performing the task. For complicated how-it-works descriptions, draw diagrams and use them as guides in identifying the steps and putting them in the proper order.

---

**EXERCISE 12-3**

**WRITING IN PROGRESS**

## Generating Ideas

**Directions:** Think of a process or procedure you are familiar with, or select one from the following list, and make a list of the steps involved:

1. How to find a worthwhile part-time job

2. How to waste time

3. How to learn to like _____

4. How the NFL football draft works

5. How to win at _____

6. How to make a marriage or relationship work

7. How to protect your right to privacy

8. How to improve your skill at _____

9. How to make your boss want to promote you

## Write Your Topic Sentence

For a process paragraph, your topic sentence should accomplish two things:

■ **It should identify the process or procedure.**

■ **It should explain to your reader why familiarity with the process is useful or important** (*why* **he or she should learn about the process**). Your topic sentence should state a goal, offer a reason, or indicate what can be accomplished by using the process.

Here are a few examples of topic sentences that contain both of these important elements.

> Reading maps, a vital skill if you are orienteering, is a simple process, except for the final refolding.

> Because leisure reading encourages a positive attitude toward reading in general, every parent should know how to select worthwhile children's books.

> To locate books in the library, you must know how to use the computerized catalog.

---

**EXERCISE 12-4**

*WORKING TOGETHER*

## Revising Topic Sentences

**Directions:** Working with a classmate, revise these topic sentences to make clear why the reader should learn the process.

1. Making pizza at home involves five steps.
2. Making a sales presentation requires good listening and speaking skills.
3. Bloodhounds that can locate criminals are remarkable creatures.
4. The dental hygienist shows patients how to use dental floss.
5. Here's how to use a search engine.

---

**EXERCISE 12-5**

**WRITING IN PROGRESS**

## Writing a Topic Sentence

**Directions:** Write a topic sentence for the process you selected in Exercise 12-3.

---

## Develop and Sequence Your Ideas

Because your readers may be unfamiliar with your topic, try to include helpful information that will enable them to understand (for how-it-works paragraphs) and follow or complete the process (for how-to paragraphs). Consider including the following:

■ **Definitions** Explain terms that may be unfamiliar. For example, explain the term *bindings* when writing about skiing.

■ **Needed equipment** For how-to paragraphs, tell your readers what tools or supplies they will need to complete the process. For a how-to paragraph on making chili, list the ingredients, for example.

■ **Pitfalls and problems** Alert your reader about potential problems and places where confusion or error may occur. Warn your chili-making readers to add chili peppers gradually and to taste along the way so the chili doesn't get too spicy.

Use the following tips to develop an effective process paragraph:

1. **Place your topic sentence first.** This position provides your reader with a purpose for reading.

2. **Present the steps in a process in the order in which they happen.**

3. **Include only essential, necessary steps.** Avoid comments, opinions, or unnecessary information because they may confuse your reader.

4. **Assume that your reader is unfamiliar with your topic** (unless you know otherwise). Be sure to define unfamiliar terms and describe clearly any technical or specialized tools, procedures, or objects.

5. **Use a consistent point of view.** Use either the first person ("I") or the second person ("you") throughout. Don't switch between them.

## EXERCISE 12-6    Drafting a Process Paragraph

**WRITING IN PROGRESS**    **Directions:** Draft a paragraph for the process you chose in Exercise 12-3.

## Use Transitions

Transitions are particularly important in process paragraphs because they lead your reader from one step to the next. Specifically, they signal to your reader that the next step is about to begin. In the following paragraph, notice how each of the highlighted transitions signals that a new step is to follow:

Do you want to teach your children something about their background, help develop their language skills, *and* have fun at the same time? Make a family album together! First, gather the necessary supplies: family photos, sheets of colored construction paper, yarn, and glue. Next, fold four sheets of paper in half; this will give you an eight-page album. Unfold the pages and lay them flat, one on top of the other. After you've evened them up, punch holes at the top and bot.tom of the fold, making sure you get through all four sheets. Next, thread the yarn through the holes. Now tie the yarn securely and crease the paper along the fold. Finally, glue a photo to each page. After the glue has dried, have your child write the names of the people in the pictures on each page and decorate the cover. Remember to talk to your children about the people you are including in your album. Not only will they learn about their extended family, they will have great memories of doing this creative project with you.

Refer to the "Need to Know" box on page 376 for a list of commonly used transitional words and phrases that are useful in process paragraphs.

| EXERCISE 12-7 | Revising a Draft |
|---|---|

**WRITING IN PROGRESS**

**Directions:** Revise the draft you wrote for Exercise 12-6. Check transitional words and phrases and add them, as necessary, to make your ideas clearer.

# Write Narrative Paragraphs

■ **GOAL 4**
Write narrative paragraphs

The technique of making a point by telling a story is called **narration**. Narration is *not* simply listing a series of events—"this happened, then that happened." Narration shapes and interprets events to make a point. Notice the difference between the two paragraphs below.

### Paragraph 1: Series of Events

Last Sunday we visited the National Zoo in Washington, D.C. As we entered, we decided to see the panda bear, the elephants, and the giraffes. All were outside enjoying the springlike weather. Then we visited the bat cave. I was amazed at how closely bats pack together in a small space. Finally, we went into the monkey house. There we spent time watching the giant apes watch us.

### Paragraph 2: Narrative

Last Sunday's visit to the National Zoo in Washington, D.C., was a lesson to me about animals in captivity. First, we visited the panda, the elephants, and the giraffes. All seemed slow moving and locked into a dull routine—pacing around their yards. Then we watched the seals. Their trainer had them perform stunts for their food; they would never do these stunts in the wild. Finally, we stopped at the monkey house, where sad, old apes stared at us and watched kids point at them. The animals did not seem happy or content with their lives.

The first paragraph retells events in the order in which they happened, but with no shaping of the story. The second paragraph, a narrative, also presents events in the order in which they happened, but uses these events to make a point: animals kept in captivity are unhappy. Thus, all details and events work together to support that point. You can visualize this narrative paragraph as follows.

**VISUALIZE IT!**

**Idea Map of Paragraph 2**

The visit to the zoo was a lesson to me.

Pandas, elephants, and giraffes followed a dull routine.

Seals performed stunts.

Kids pointed at sad, old apes.

Writing a narrative involves selecting a topic, generating ideas, writing a topic sentence, sequencing and developing your ideas, considering your audience and purpose, and using transitions.

## Select a Topic and Generate Ideas

For shorter pieces of writing, such as paragraphs and short essays, it is usually best to concentrate on a single event or experience. Otherwise, you will have too much information to cover, and you will not be able to include sufficient detail. To generate ideas for a narrative, make a list of events. Don't worry, at this point, about expressing each in sentence form or listing them in the order in which they occurred. Record in the margin any feelings you have about the events. Although you may not include them in the paragraph, they will be helpful in writing your topic sentence.

**EXERCISE 12-8**

WRITING IN PROGRESS

# Generating Ideas

**Directions:** Assume you are taking an introductory psychology class this semester and your instructor has asked you to describe one of the following scenarios. Begin by making a list of the events that occurred.

1. A situation in which you observed or benefited from altruistic behavior (someone helping another person unselfishly, out of concern and compassion)
2. A vivid childhood memory
3. An experience in which you felt stress
4. A time when you were in danger and how you reacted
5. A situation in which you either rejected or gave in to peer pressure

## Write Your Topic Sentence

**A topic sentence** states the main point of your paragraph. Your topic sentence should accomplish two things:

- It should identify your topic—the experience you are writing about.
- It should indicate your view or attitude toward that experience.

For example, suppose you are writing a paragraph about your first day of classes. Your view might be that the campus was confusing and frustrating or that you felt unprepared and did not know what was expected of you in your classes. Here are a few possible topic sentences that indicate a point of view:

Registration was easier than I expected because my advisor was very helpful and explained everything.

Registration was difficult because many of the classes I wanted were closed, and I ended up with a very inconvenient schedule.

Sometimes you may discover your view toward the experience as you are writing about it. For example, a student drafted the following paragraph about registering for her classes:

> Online registration was supposed to be simple, and it was for my friends. My registration was a nightmare. The computer in my advisor's office went down. When she tried to get back online, she learned the main system in the college had failed. We could not find out what classes were available; we could not check prerequisites; we could not even find the times my courses were being offered. We waited a while, and finally she told me to come back tomorrow. I was afraid that all the classes I wanted would be filled before I had a chance to register.

As she was writing, she realized she wished she had known more about the problems of the online registration process before she began. Then she wrote the following topic sentence:

> My first registration day at college might not have been so frustrating if someone had warned me about the possibility of computer system failures at the college and told me to take a hard copy of class listings with me.

## EXERCISE 12-9   Writing a Topic Sentence

**WRITING IN PROGRESS**

**Directions:** For the experience or situation you chose in Exercise 12-8, write a topic sentence that expresses your attitude toward the experience.

## Sequence and Develop Your Ideas

The events in a narrative paragraph are usually arranged in **chronological** order—the order in which they happened. Sometimes, however, you may want to rearrange events to emphasize a point. If you do, make sure the sequence of events is clear enough for the reader to follow.

The following diagram shows you how to visualize a narrative paragraph.

**VISUALIZE IT!**

**Narrative Paragraph Idea Map**

Topic sentence

Event 1

Event 2

Event 3

Event 4

To place the events in the correct sequence, review and number your list of events.

A clear, well-written narrative should provide sufficient detail to allow your readers to understand fully the situation about which you are writing. Try to answer for your readers most of the following questions:

| | |
|---|---|
| **When** did it happen? | **What** events occurred? |
| **Where** did it happen? | **Why** did they happen? |
| **Who** was involved? | **How** did they happen? |

Be sure to include only essential and relevant details. Other details will distract readers from the events you are describing.

| | |
|---|---|
| **EXERCISE 12-10** | # Drafting a Paragraph |
| **WRITING IN PROGRESS** | **Directions:** For the experience or situation you selected for Exercises 12-8 and 12-9, draft a paragraph describing the events in the order in which they occurred. |

## Consider Your Audience and Purpose

When writing a narrative, your audience and your purpose will help determine:

- **How much explanation and which definitions to include about each event.** An audience that is unfamiliar with the event may need more detail than readers who are familiar with it. If you are writing about a baseball game and your audience is made up of baseball fans, then you will not need to explain rules, scoring, and so forth. However, if your audience is not made up of baseball enthusiasts, you may need to explain terms such as *outs*, *home runs*, and *errors*.

- **How much background information to include.** If you are writing about an everyday event, such as a traffic jam, most readers need little explanation about it; however, if you are writing about a holiday such as Cinco de Mayo, you may need to provide your non-Mexican readers with some background about the holiday.

## Use Transitions

As you know from Chapter 11, **transitions** are words that connect ideas to one another. Transitions in narratives lead your readers from one event to another. They make your writing easier to follow and clearly identify important parts of your narrative. In the following paragraph, notice how each of the highlighted transitions signals that the next event is to come.

> I do not usually take risks, especially when it comes to food, but last Saturday I took a bold step and ordered tripe at Tivoli, a local Italian restaurant. When I ordered, the waiter told me there would be a 15-minute delay. I tried to convince myself it would be worth the wait. After waiting 25 minutes, I called the waiter; he apologized and said the kitchen was short-handed and that it would be only another ten minutes. As I waited, I began to ask myself why would I want to eat the stomach of a cow, anyway? Would I hate it? Would I be able to eat it? Finally, my long-awaited tripe arrived. After I tasted it, I realized my fears were silly; it was delicious and well worth the long wait. I wonder what new food I should try next.

Here are some frequently used transitional words and phrases that connect events in a sequence:

> **! NEED TO KNOW**
>
> **Common Narrative Transitions**
>
> | after | finally | later | therefore |
> |---|---|---|---|
> | after that | first | next | third |
> | at last | following | second | while |
> | during | in the beginning | then | |

**EXERCISE 12-11** ## Using Transitions

**Directions:** Complete each sentence by supplying a transitional word or phrase that helps identify the sequence of events, using the "Need to Know" box.

1. ___After___ we left the theater, we stopped for coffee.

2. After a long drive, we ___finally___ reached our destination.

3. ___During___ the movie, an audience member's loudly ringing cell phone distracted everyone.

4. To evaluate the reliability of a Web site, examine its source and ___then/next___ check the date of posting.

5. To preview a textbook chapter, first check the title. Second, read the chapter objectives. ___Third___, read the introduction.

**EXERCISE 12-12**

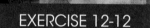 **WRITING IN PROGRESS**

## Revising a Paragraph

**Directions:** Revise the paragraph you wrote for Exercise 12-10. Check it for transitional words and phrases and add them, as necessary, to make your ideas clearer.

# READING AND WRITING DESCRIPTION

# What Is Description?

■ **GOAL 5**
Understand description

**Descriptive** writing creates an impression: It helps the reader visualize the subject. Now suppose summer is over and you just spent a week at a lakeside cottage. You might write the following paragraph describing it:

> The rented cottage was charming because it was old-fashioned and modern at the same time. The bedrooms had colorful green and blue patchwork quilts on the beds and faded antique pictures on the walls, but the mattresses were brand

new and extremely comfortable. The kitchen had the same efficient, shiny new appliances that I have at home, except for the antique wood-burning stove that made the entire room smell pungent with smoke. Every time I entered the living room, my immediate desire was to fling myself onto the huge pillowlike sofa. An old-fashioned radio, hooked rugs, and a handmade checkerboard combined with the wood-burning fireplace to create a rustic atmosphere. From the modern redwood deck I had a peaceful view of the quiet, secluded lake. The cottage took me back in time in the best ways.

## Tip for Writers

Here, the adjective *dominant* means "most important."

VISUALIZE IT!

Your paragraph begins with a topic sentence that identifies your topic (the cottage) and indicates how you feel about it. This feeling or attitude toward the topic is called the **dominant impression**. The remainder of the paragraph offers details that help the reader visualize the cottage and help explain the dominant impression. Each sentence contains vivid and descriptive words and phrases. These details are called **sensory details** because they appeal to the reader's senses—touch, sight, smell, taste, and hearing. You can visualize a descriptive paragraph as follows:

**Descriptive Paragraph Idea Map**

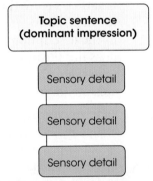

The paragraph on page 389 describing a cottage can be visualized as follows. To save space, sensory details are shown only for the cottage's bedrooms.

**Idea Map**

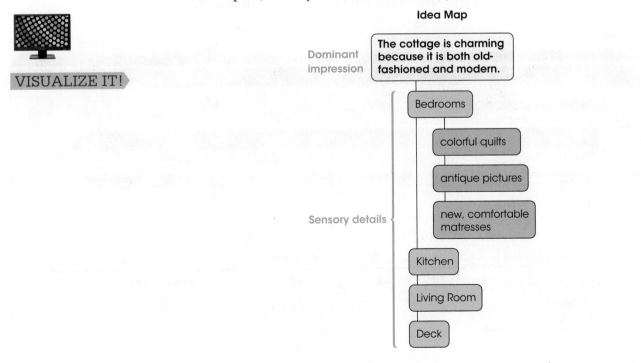

VISUALIZE IT!

| EXERCISE 12-13 | Brainstorming a List |
| --- | --- |

**WORKING TOGETHER**

**Directions:** Working with another student, brainstorm a list of the times in your own life when description played an important role.

# Read Descriptive Paragraphs

■ GOAL 6
Read descriptive paragraphs

A **descriptive paragraph** has three key features—an *overall impression*, *sensory details*, and *descriptive language*. As you read descriptive writing, pay attention to each of these features.

■ **The overall impression.** The **overall impression** is the one central idea the place of writing presents. It is the single, main point that all of the details prove or support. To find the overall impression, ask yourself, "What do all these details and descriptions, taken together, mean or suggest?" Often, this dominant impression is unstated; it is left for you to infer.

■ **Sensory details.** Each detail is important, but the details, when added together, create the overall impression. Be careful not to skip details, and for each, consider what it contributes to the overall meaning. For example, in the description of a man, the detail that his hair was uncombed by itself does not mean much. However, when added together with details that his nails were dirty, his shirt unevenly buttoned, and his shoes untied, it creates the impression of the person as careless and unkempt.

■ **Descriptive language.** **Descriptive language** uses words that create a visual or imaginary picture of the topic. Descriptive language brings the topic to life, so to speak. As you read, be sure to read slowly enough to allow the language to "sink in." Mark and annotate particularly striking or unusual words and phrases. Stop and reflect, too, about why a particularly descriptive phrase was chosen.

When writing a descriptive paragraph, writers use transitions to orient their readers. Some common transitions are shown below.

## ! NEED TO KNOW

### Common Description Transitions

| SPATIAL | | | LEAST/MOST | |
| --- | --- | --- | --- | --- |
| above | inside | over | first | second |
| below | outside | beneath | primarily | secondarily |
| beside | under | | | |
| across | nearby | to the right | also important | particularly |
| facing | next to | to the west (north, etc.) | most important | even more |
| behind | to the left | on the other side | above all | of lesser importance |
| in front of | | | especially | of greater importatnce |

## Reading Descriptive Paragraphs

**Directions:** Underline the topic sentence in each of the following paragraphs and highlight particularly descriptive details.

1.    Earth resembles an egg with a cracked shell. Earth's crust is thin and rigid, averaging 45 kilometers (28 miles) in thickness. Beneath this rigid crust, the rock is like a very thick fluid and is slowly deformed by movements within Earth. While far from the free-flowing substances we know as liquids, the rock just beneath the crust, known as the **mantle**, is fluid enough to move slowly along in convection currents, driven by heat within Earth's core.

—Dahlman et al., *Introduction to Geography*, p. 90

2.    Jackson was one of the most forceful and domineering American presidents. His most striking traits were an indomitable will, an intolerance of opposition, and a prickly pride that would not permit him to forgive or forget an insult or supposed act of betrayal. It is sometimes hard to determine whether principle or personal spite motivated his political actions. As a young man on the frontier, he had learned to fight his own battles. Violent in temper and action, he fought duels and battled the British, Spanish, and Indians with a zeal his critics found excessive. He was tough and resourceful, but he lacked the flexibility successful politicians usually show. Yet he generally got what he wanted.

—Brands, *American Stories, A History of the United States*, p. 254

3.    Sushi preparation is an art that involves careful selection of lovely and delicate ingredients (various seafood or vegetables, or both) to be arranged alongside vinegared rice. Sometimes, sushi is pressed into molds to form long fingers. A familiar style is made by arranging a layer of dried seaweed on a bamboo mat, and then artfully arranging the ingredients on the seaweed before rolling it carefully and tightly to enclose the filling as a long tube. Ultimately, the roll is sliced crosswise for lovely round slices with the seaweed serving as the outer covering.

—McWilliams, *Food Around the World*, p. 357

# Write Descriptive Paragraphs

■ GOAL 7
Write descriptive
paragraphs

Writing an effective descriptive paragraph involves creating a dominant impression, selecting sensory details, using descriptive language, organizing details, and using transitions.

## Create a Dominant Impression with Your Topic Sentence

The dominant impression of a descriptive paragraph is the overall sense you want to convey about your topic or main idea. It is expressed in your topic sentence, usually at the beginning of the paragraph. Suppose you are the music critic for your college newspaper and you are writing about a recent concert. If you felt the audience was appreciative, you might write the following topic sentence:

The audience at the recent Rihanna concert appreciated and responded well to both the old and the new songs that Rihanna and her band performed.

Different dominant impressions of the audience are created, however, by the following topic sentences:

> The antics and immature behavior of the audience at the Rihanna concert ruined the event for me.
>
> Because many in the audience at the recent Rihanna concert were international students, I re.alized that her music has broad appeal.

The dominant impression often reflects your first reaction to a topic. Let's say you are writing about your bedroom. Think of a word or two that sums up how you feel about it. Is it comfortable? Messy? Organized? Your own territory? A place to escape? Any one of these could be developed into a paragraph. For example, your topic sentence might be:

> My bedroom is an orderly place where I am surrounded by things that are of personal value.

The details that follow would then describe objects in which you place personal value. If you have difficulty deciding on or thinking of a dominant impression for a topic, brainstorm a list of words to sum up your observations and reactions. For example, for the topic of your college health office, you might write things such as "friendly," "helpful," "smells like a doctor's office," or "antiseptic and clean." This brainstorming eventually could lead you to write about the health office as a place of impersonal, sterile sights and sounds that houses a warm and caring staff.

## EXERCISE 12-15 Writing Topic Sentences

**Directions:** For two of the following topics, write three topic sentences that each express a different dominant impression.    Answers will vary.

1. **Professional athletes**

   a. The behavior of professional athletes serves as a role model for those who admire them.

   b. Professional athletes who exhibit unprofessional behavior should be heavily fined by the team owners.

   c. Many professional athletes earn high salaries but donate generously to charities and fund-raising events.

2. **A favorite food**

   a. Pizza is both nutritious and easy to prepare.

   b. Pizzas made at home are never as good as ones from a pizzeria.

   c. Pizza can be costly if you don't stick to basic toppings.

3. **A film or television show you have seen recently**

   a. Good Morning America offers both news and human interest stories.

   b. Good Morning America focuses on shocking and tragic events.

   c. Good Morning America aims to amuse and entertain its viewers.

| EXERCISE 12-16 | # Prewriting and Writing a Topic Sentence |

**Directions:** Suppose you are taking a business course and are currently studying advertising. Your instructor has asked you to write a paragraph on one of the following topics. For the topic you select, use prewriting techniques to generate ideas and details. Then write a topic sentence that establishes a dominant impression.

1. Find an ad in a newspaper or magazine that contains a detailed scene. Describe the ad and explain whether or not it is effective. Make note of what props have been placed in the scene, what the models are wearing, and any other details that support your answer.

2. Choose an ad you think is effective. Write a paragraph describing the person you imagine is likely to buy the product. Explain how the ad would appeal to him or her.

3. Suppose you have developed a new product (frozen gourmet pizza or a long-lasting, multicolored highlighter, for example). Write a paragraph describing the product to a company that is interested in distributing it. Be sure to describe your product in a positive, appealing way.

## Develop and Select Sensory Details

All the details in a descriptive paragraph must be relevant to creating your dominant impression. Begin by brainstorming a list of all the details you can think of that describe your topic or support your dominant impression. Try to visualize the person, place, or experience and write down what you see. Your details should enable your reader to paint his or her own mental picture of the topic. Here's a list of details a student produced about working at movie theaters:

| | |
|---|---|
| rude people | crowded concession stands |
| fold-up seats | greasy smell of popcorn |
| big screen | kids running up the aisle |
| headaches | squishy seats you sink into |
| people whispering | people annoying others |
| trash on floor | quieting people down |
| ticket stubs | lines at the box office |
| sticky floors | always crowded |
| dim lights | hurrying, pressure |

If you have not formed a dominant impression, review your list, looking for a pattern to your details. What feeling or impression do many of them suggest? In the preceding list, many of the details convey the feeling of annoyance or dislike.

After you have decided upon an impression, eliminate those details that do not support that impression. For example, the details about the screen, ticket stubs, seats, and lighting in the list above should be eliminated because they do not support the impression of annoyance.

Now read the student's paragraph on the topic of working at movie theaters. Notice how the student developed ideas from the earlier list. The paragraph still contains some details that do not directly support the dominant impression. Watch for them as you read.

Movie theaters are crowded, annoying places to work. I know. I have worked part-time in three different theaters over the past four years. I often leave work with a pounding headache and jangled nerves. There is always time pressure; shows must start on time. Customers are always in a rush. They arrive minutes before a show is about to begin, yet demand to be waited on instantly at the concession stand. One regular and particularly annoying guy wearing baggy sweats and a ball cap once shouted: "Hey, over here! Get me a jumbo popcorn and a large Pepsi, and do it fast before I miss my show!" There was no "please," no "thank you," and no consideration of people standing in line ahead of him. This is just the kind of patron who carelessly spreads handfuls of these yellow kernels all over the theater floor and creates a sticky patch of spilled soda that someone has to clean up at the end of the evening. I do not enjoy assisting pushy people who are rude to others, either. Some customers talk loudly, complain about those in front of them, make obscene gestures, and generally make nuisances of themselves during the show. It is my job to quiet them down. I'd rather throw them out. There would be no "ifs," no "ands," and no "buts," just "You're out of here." Although you do get to see some free movies, working at a movie theater is far from the ideal job.

The detail about wanting to throw annoying people out should be deleted because it does not explain why a theater is a difficult place to work.

---

> ## ❗ NEED TO KNOW
>
> ### Sensory Details
>
> Sensory details appeal to the five senses. Use the following questions to help you uncover sensory details about your subject:
>
> **Touch:** What does it feel like? What is its texture? What is its weight? What is its temperature?
>
> **Smell:** Is it pleasant or unpleasant? Is it mild or strong? Of what other smells does it remind you?
>
> **Taste:** Is it pleasant or unpleasant? Is it sweet, sour, salty, or bitter? Of what favorite flavors does it remind you?
>
> **Sight:** What is the color? Is there a pattern? What size is it? What shape is it?
>
> **Sound:** Is it loud or soft? Is it high or low? Is it pleasant or unpleasant? What other sounds does it remind you of?

---

## EXERCISE 12-17 | Identifying Irrelevant Details

**Directions:** For the following topic sentences, circle the letters of the details that are not relevant to the dominant impression.

1. You don't need a lot of equipment to enjoy fishing.

   a. The only necessary items are a rod and reel.

   b. Fishing rods vary widely in cost.

   c. A net is helpful if you're fishing from a boat.

   d. Take a picnic lunch if you're fishing from a boat.

2. Gambling is addictive and can lead to financial disaster.

   a. Some people are unable to stop because they want to win just one more time.

   (b.) Money is exchanged for gambling chips at casinos.

   (c.) Las Vegas is a place where many people go to gamble.

   d. I know a gambler who often bets his entire paycheck on one horse race.

3. Officials at sporting events must be knowledgeable and skillful and have strong personalities.

   a. Officials must be able to ignore crowd reactions to unpopular calls.

   b. Officials must know the technicalities of the game.

   c. Officials must exert authority and win the respect of the players.

   (d.) The pay that officials receive is not in proportion to their responsibilities.

4. Starting a travel agency is a high-risk venture.

   (a.) The manager must have at least two years' experience.

   b. In most areas, there are many competing agencies.

   c. Profit from each individual client is low, so a great many clients are needed.

   d. Total start-up costs are high, ranging up to $150,000.

---

**EXERCISE 12-18**

**WRITING IN PROGRESS**

## Writing a Descriptive Paragraph

**Directions:** Select one of the topic sentences you wrote for Exercise 12-15 or 12-16, and develop a descriptive paragraph for it, revising it if necessary.

### Use Descriptive Language

Descriptive language is exact, colorful, and appealing. It enables the reader to envision what the writer has seen. Here are two sentences about a day at the beach. The first presents lifeless, factual information; the second describes what the writer saw and felt.

> I went to the beach today, lay on the sand, and read a book.
>
> At Rexham Beach this morning, I spread my soft plaid blanket on the white sand, got out the latest John Grisham novel, and settled down to enjoy the sun's warming rays.

You might think of descriptive language as the way the reader sees the world through the eyes of the writer. One of the best ways to help your reader see is to use specific words, particularly those that draw on your reader's five senses—*sight, hearing, smell, touch,* and *taste.* The student whose paragraph appeared on p. 394 used details like the baggy sweats and ball cap and the sticky patches of spilled soda to help you visualize the situation at the movie theater.

You can also use vivid verbs, adjectives, and adverbs to help your readers see what you are describing. When you can, use exact names of people, places, and objects ("a red Toyota," not "a car").

---

**EXERCISE 12-19**

## Using Descriptive Language

**Directions:** For each of the following items, write a sentence that provides a vivid description. The first one has been done for you.   Answers will vary.

1. An old coat <u>Mr. Busby wore a tattered, faded, stained-around-the-neck, deep burgundy leather coat.</u>

2. A fast-food meal <u>Greasy french fries, an overcooked salty burger, and a watery strawberry milkshake were not worth their price.</u>

3. A bride (or groom) <u>The forty-year-old bride wore a pale pink, tight-fitting gown that seemed more appropriate for a teenager.</u>

4. A sidewalk <u>The cracked and worn sidewalk was split apart, forming dangerous and uneven crevices.</u>

5. The dog behind a sign that warns "Guard Dog on Premises"
<u>The dog bared its teeth, growled menacingly, tucked in his tail, and lowered his ears to warn off the intruder.</u>

---

**EXERCISE 12-20**

WRITING IN PROGRESS

## Revising a Paragraph

**Directions:** Revise the paragraph you wrote for Exercise 12-18, adding descriptive words and phrases.

---

### Organize Details and Use Transitions

The arrangement of details in a description is determined by your topic and by the dominant impression you want to convey. You want to emphasize the most important details, making sure your readers can follow your description.

One of the most common arrangements is spatial organization. If you were describing your college campus, for example, you might start at one end and work toward the other. You might describe a stage set from left to right or a building from bottom to top.

If you were describing a person, you might work from head to toe. But you might prefer to follow another common arrangement: from least to most important. If the dominant impression you want to convey about a person's appearance is messiness, you might start with some characteristics that are only slightly messy (an untied shoe, perhaps) and work toward the most messy (a blue-jean jacket missing one sleeve, stained with paint, and covered with burrs).

Whichever arrangement you choose, transitional words and phrases will help your reader see how details relate to each other and where you are going. For a list of common transitional words and phrases for a spatial arrangement or a least-to-most-important organization, refer to the "Need to Know" box on page 393.

---

**EXERCISE 12-21**

WRITING IN PROGRESS

## Evaluating and Revising a Paragraph

**Directions:** Evaluate the arrangement of details in the paragraph you revised for Exercise 12-20. Does it support your dominant impression? Revise it and add transitional words and phrases, if needed.

# INTEGRATING READING AND WRITING

## READ AND REVISE

**MySkillsLab®**

**Complete** this Exercise

The following excerpt is from an essay called "Salto Waterfall Park." As you read the first two paragraphs, underline sensory details and descriptive language. Then read the last paragraph and revise it by replacing vague words with specific and vivid language and adding more details, based on your own experience of being in a beautiful park.

---

I was ten years old when my grandparents took me to Salto Waterfall Park in Jalisco, Mexico. It was a warm morning. The sky was endlessly blue, stretching for galaxies through the treetops. There was a great smell of flowers in the park. Roses were all across the bridge. The trees made a beautiful view with the mountains. The only sounds were those from lively mockingbirds, wind passing through the treetops, and the river as it flowed over the rocks.

I remember looking out at the water. It was so crystal clear that I could see exotic and tropical fishes of all different colors swim about with no worries. I strolled along the sidewalk, and every once in a while, I stopped to smell the fragrant white flowers of the coffee trees which were scattered throughout the park. People enjoyed hiking in the mountains while children played in the cascades. Older people watched their grandchildren swim in the water. I sat next to rocks covered with moss and read a book.

Although I am older, I still go to Salto Waterfall Park. It is a special place for me. The park still has a lake, the sound of the birds, and a nice landscape. The smell of flowers is the same. I will never forget my moments at the Salto Waterfall Park.

---

## READ AND RESPOND: A Student Essay

*Roan Rodriguez is a student at Temple Junior College. After he completes his basic courses, he plans to obtain an associate's degree in graphic arts and pursue a career as a cartoonist. Rodriguez submitted this essay to the Writing Rewards Essay Contest sponsored by Pearson Education. The assignment he responded to directed him to write an essay describing an unforgettable experience.*

# A Trip to Disney World

1    What is the most magical place in the world? It's Disney World. Ever since I was a little boy, I heard so much about the place, and I finally got the opportunity to go there. To me, Disney represents three qualities: youth, fantasy, and magic. In June 2010, my family and I boarded an airplane to Florida. During the trip, I looked out the window and saw the clouds. As I looked at the clouds, they slowly transformed into the faces of Mickey, Donald, and Goofy. That's when I felt in my heart that this first trip to Disney World would be the most magical one of all time.

2    As soon as we arrived in Florida, there was a sign with huge letters that said, "Walt Disney World Where Dreams Come True," with Mickey on the left and Minnie on the right. That sign gave me a pleasant, warm welcome and made me feel delighted to be at the happiest place on earth.

3    We stayed at the Pop Century Resort Hotel. When we entered the hotel, we felt like we stepped into a time where everything was cool and hip, as music from the 70's, 80's, 90's, and even contemporary music, played. Outside the hotel, the grass was shamrock green and there were giant colorful statues of Mickey and his friends everywhere.

4    After breakfast on our first day, we went to the Magic Kingdom. Throughout the day, my family and I, one by one, took pictures with our favorite Disney characters. Right after the camera flashed, I felt a little magic spell happened that would soon turn all our pictures into lifetime memories. In the background of our photos were magnificent rides. Most of the rides were outdoors and as we tried each one of them, we felt the breeze blowing through our hair and heard the screams of the other riders. An area of the Magic Kingdom that took my breath away was Fantasyland. I was amazed by all the beautiful sights and sounds: the bright and colorful characters; the song "It's a Small World" coming from one of the rides; the laughs of little kids; and the music of other famous Disney songs in the air. Fantasyland made me feel like a child again and this feeling brought tears of joy to my eyes. There were so many attractions in the Magic Kingdom, but one that I fell in love with was "Mickey's PhilharMagic." As the show started, I could see the characters coming out of the screen, smell the pies, feel the water, and for the first time ever, I felt I could fly. After I made my way to the exit door, I was so happy I felt my heart pounding joyfully.

5    The last place we visited in the Magic Kingdom was "Mickey's Toontown Fair." Once we entered the houses of Mickey and his friends, we saw their clean bedrooms, their clothes hanging in the closets, their living rooms all decorated, their kitchen counters covered with luscious food, and their gardens filled with fruits and vegetables. After we came out of Mickey's house, we met Mickey and Minnie for the first time. Mickey was wearing a black tuxedo jacket with a yellow bow tie, red slacks and black shoes. Minnie, on the other hand, was in her red and white polka-dot dress with a red and white polka-dot bow between her ears and yellow shoes. Right after I took a picture with them, I knew in my heart that I would never forget this special moment.

6    That night, I somehow knew another magical event was about to happen. When it got darker, all the lights went off and I heard a voice say, "Ladies and gentlemen!" The audience cheered loudly and excitedly, and when the voice announced, "Disney's Electrical Parade," everyone including myself began to clap with joy. When the parade began, my mouth dropped and my eyes popped with excitement, as all the other spectators did the same. The floats that I saw in the

parade were <u>electrical masterpieces; the lights blinked on and off continuously in many patterns</u>. The characters who were on the floats were <u>colorfully designed</u>. At the end of the parade, it felt like my mind was spinning with <u>tons of bright colors around it</u>. This was a unique and enjoyable experience.

Conclusion     7     Never in my life had I experienced so much excitement and unrestrained childish joy. My impressions of Disney World's youth, fantasy, and magic will last forever.

## Examining Writing

1. Evaluate Rodriguez's use of sensory details and descriptive language in this essay. Which details were most effective? Did you notice any details that were not relevant?

2. How did Rodriguez arrange the details of his narrative? Try to summarize his trip briefly in your own words.

3. What transitions did Rodriguez use to guide the reader?

4. What dominant impressions did Rodriguez create about his trip to Disney World?

## READ AND RESPOND: A Professional Essay

### Thinking Before Reading

The following selection originally appeared in *The Texas Observer* political news magazine. In the selection, the author describes one family's experience with kidnapping in Mexico.

1. Preview the reading, using the steps discussed in Chapter 1 on page 25.

2. Connect the reading to your own experiences by answering the following questions:

    a. What have you heard or read about organized crime in Mexico? How would you describe the typical victims of crime in that country?

    b. What would you do if one of your family members were kidnapped?

3. Highlight and annotate as you read.

1010**L**/2664 words

# Ransom Notes: Serial Kidnapping in Mexico

## Melissa del Bosque

1     "Somebody's taken Carlos." Ana couldn't quite believe what her cousin had just told her over the phone. How could it be true? Ana had been preparing her three young children for bed. The maid was cleaning up in the kitchen. A place was still set for Carlos, her husband, at the dinner table. He hadn't arrived home yet, but that wasn't unusual. He often worked late at his factory. She stared at Carlos' untouched place setting. It couldn't be true.

**maquiladora:**
A Mexican assembly plant that manufactures goods for export to the United States.

2   "They just called," her cousin said with more urgency. "Grab the kids and come to Brownsville." Ana, 41, hung up and tried to remain calm. She didn't want to panic the children. Her cell phone rang again. This time it was Carlos, his voice shaking. "I've been kidnapped, and they want $800,000."

3   "Please tell me you're OK," Ana said.

4   "What money do you have right now?" he asked. Ana and Carlos had done well in Matamoros, but everything they had was invested in his business and the house. They had no more than $1,000 in their bank account. "You know I don't have anything," she said. "What do you want me to do?" Suddenly, a man's gruff voice came on the line. "We're not playing games. We're going to kill him if you don't give us the money." The line went dead.

5   Ana quickly packed their clothes and some valuables, and that night she fled with her children. It was the beginning of the end of her family's once-happy existence in Matamoros, Mexico. Ana and Carlos were both business professionals who had graduated from prestigious universities. They owned a beautiful home and belonged to one of the area's best country clubs. Despite the recession, business wasn't bad—Carlos' maquiladora had recently contracted with a U.S. corporation.

6   That summer night, Ana crossed the international bridge with her children into neighboring Brownsville, Texas. And from there, her life unraveled.

## Violence and Kidnapping in Mexico

7   For generations, poverty-stricken Mexicans have made the same journey across the border, seeking refuge. They've worked in farm fields, in factories, and on construction sites, helping to build the American Dream and feed their families back home. But this time-worn pattern is beginning to change. The number of Mexican immigrants crossing into the United States has dwindled considerably. Last year, it was just one-fifth of what it was a decade ago, when an estimated 500,000 Mexicans crossed every year, according to the Pew Hispanic Center. The economic recession, smaller families, and better educational opportunities, as well as heightened U.S. security, have caused the decline.

8   So it seems paradoxical that an altogether different class of Mexicans is now furtively crossing the border, seeking refuge in the United States. A growing number of wealthy and middle-class Mexicans are fleeing rising violence perpetrated by criminal syndicates that have taken over swaths of Mexico.

9   Mexican drug cartels have long been powerful. But the violence began to spiral out of control after President Felipe Calderon launched a military offensive against the cartels in 2006. Instead of crushing the cartels, as Calderon pledged, the military campaign made them more aggressive. In recent years, the cartels have diversified, branching out from drug smuggling into extortion, human trafficking, car theft, and—most threatening of all for wealthy Mexicans—kidnapping."

10   The cartels began taking over local economies, charging fees for protection, and killing elected officials. They have morphed into organized criminal syndicates, combining ruthless violence with keen business sense. They even have their own lawyers.

11   "They have taken over with brute force many parts of the country," says Alberto Islas, a Mexico City security consultant. Last August a former Mexican security minister told reporters that the government "has lost territorial control, and therefore governability" over at least 50 percent of the country. The increasingly bloody and

intractable violence has resulted in an estimated 40,000 deaths and 10,000 forced disappearances since 2006.

12    Nowhere along the U.S.-Mexico border is the crisis more serious—with the possible exception of Juarez—than in the Mexican state of Tamaulipas, where Ana and her family lived. In 2010 the Gulf and Zeta cartels, former allies, went to war for control of valuable smuggling corridors along the Rio Grande. A gubernatorial candidate, mayors, and other elected officials have been killed or forced into exile. Mass graves dot the countryside. In cities like Reynosa and Matamoros, the police work for the criminals. Armed convoys roam with impunity and collect "taxes." Those who don't pay are kidnapped or killed. Their businesses are torched.

13    But what makes Tamaulipas perhaps even more dangerous than Juarez (often called the most violent city in the world) is that the terror occurs under a cloak of secrecy. The local media were long ago silenced at gunpoint. With little to stop them, kidnappers have become vicious, says Islas. "They ask for a million dollars and if you can't pay it they take your ranch, your business," he says. "It has become common practice." This was the bad luck that befell Ana and Carlos.

14    The day after the kidnapping, Ana woke up in Brownsville to the sound of her cell phone ringing. It was her husband. "Did you get the money?" he asked. She could tell he was close to tears.

15    "Did they hurt you?" she asked. The gruff voice came on the line again. This time he referred to himself as "El Comandante" and said he was the leader of the group. "Where's the money?"

16    "I have gold watches and an SUV," she offered. In the background she could hear muffled screams; it sounded like men were beating her husband. The phone clicked. A few minutes later El Comandante called her back. "Bring the SUV and the watches," he said.

17    Ana drove across the international bridge into Matamoros. She was trembling, but she had no choice. The meeting place was a supermarket parking lot. She had been instructed to leave the SUV running with the gold watches inside. She parked in the designated spot, and right away she spotted them. "I saw a police truck and an SUV. They were dressed all in black," she says. Ana sat frozen in the front seat, unsure of what to do. Her phone rang. "Get out of the car, leave the keys, and go into a shop," a man instructed. She stepped into a McDonald's and watched one of the men in black drive off in her car.

18    When she left the parking lot, Ana went to a relative's nearby home and waited for the next call. It came shortly. "Where's the money?" It was a different man's voice now. Her husband had been moved to another safe house. "Please," she said. "Let him go so we can sell everything. We'll pay you, I swear."

19    But the men didn't let her husband go. Days passed. They called repeatedly, always with the same threat: "Pay or we'll kill your husband." Ana and her children lived in anxious limbo at her cousin's home in Brownsville. After several more days, she received a call from the manager at her husband's factory in Matamoros. An armed convoy was there with trucks to haul away the factory's computers, heavy machinery—everything. The kidnappers had taken their SUV, their gold watches, and now her husband's business. Surely, they would let him go, Ana thought. But she was wrong.

## Immigrating to the U.S.

20      Along the Texas border, signs of the recent exodus of Mexico's business class are everywhere, from the exclusive gated communities inhabited by wealthy Mexicans in Mission to the rented apartments in McAllen and Brownsville where middle-class Mexicans live in fear of both the criminals in Mexico and the U.S. government that wants to send them back. The Internal Displacement Monitoring Centre, based in Geneva, Switzerland, reported that at least 230,000 Mexicans have fled their homes, largely because of cartel violence, since 2007. Half of them came to the United States.

21      For wealthy and middle-class Mexicans, remaining in the United States legally is becoming more difficult. Many Mexicans are applying for an investor visa—known as an EB-5 visa—that requires an investment of $500,000.

22      In McAllen, Marco Ramirez and his partner Efrain Arce opened an EB-5 visa center, called USA Now, where Mexicans with $500,000 or more can invest in the Texas border region. If investors can prove that their businesses have created 10 or more jobs for American citizens, and that their money came from legitimate sources, they and their family members will be granted permanent visas. After five years, they can apply for U.S. citizenship. The company currently has 200 families trying to obtain visas—90 percent of them from Mexico.

23      As Mexico's security crisis deepens, however, the United States seems less willing to open its doors even to wealthy Mexicans. Jaime Diez, a Brownsville immigration attorney, says many of his clients are finding it harder to acquire or keep their investor visas. "There is no more traumatic experience for many of my clients than getting their visas renewed at the U.S. Consulate in Matamoros," Diez says. "People can't sleep the night before because they're so worried their visas will be canceled." As an example, he cites one client who lost his visa because his business went from making $1.5 million in sales to $900,000 during the recession. "They told him his business was no longer productive so they couldn't renew his visa," Diez says.

24      Increasingly, the only avenue left for Mexican citizens is to ask for political asylum, but that too often is denied. In 2010 3,231 Mexicans filed for asylum, but only 1.5 percent of applications were granted, according to the Executive Office for Immigration Review. Most are denied because the U.S. asylum law was created in the 1980s to protect people fleeing authoritarian regimes during the Cold War, not criminal syndicates. For the United States to grant asylum to Mexicans fleeing organized crime is tantamount to admitting that Mexico's government can no longer protect its citizens—a serious blow to an already troubled partnership with Mexico.

25      Three weeks had passed, and still Carlos' captors hadn't released him. Periodically Ana would receive phone calls. Always it was the same question: "Where's our money?" One day she received a call from a man she'd never spoken with before. "We need your husband's accounts receivable invoices," he said. She assumed the cartel planned to collect on the business's outstanding debts.

26      Ana told him she had no idea where her husband kept such things. "We're going to kill him then," he said, and hung up. Ana made some calls to her husband's employees, frantically searching for the invoices. Finally, she found them. She hit redial. A man instructed her to bring the invoices to a shopping mall parking lot in Matamoros that night. When she pulled into the parking lot, she saw a police truck and a convoy of five SUVs, mostly filled with armed teenagers. Shoppers went about their business as a boy not much older than 19 approached her car and demanded the invoices.

27    "When are you going to release my husband?" she pleaded. "When El Comandante gives us the order," the boy said.

28    "Is my husband still alive?"

29    "Do you want to see him?" the boy smirked. He motioned to the SUV at the end of the convoy and it slowly rolled toward them. The window lowered. In the back was her husband, blindfolded and handcuffed. Ana began to sob and begged the boy to release Carlos, but the teenager was unmoved. "Give us the money and we'll let him go," the boy said. The convoy drove away. Ana sat weeping in the parking lot.

30    She had given everything to Carlos' captors but they still wanted $800,000 cash. Ana was losing hope. The next day, she received a phone call from Matamoros. It was a businessman who had been kidnapped by the same men and held in a safe house with Carlos. His family had paid his ransom, and he had been released. He told her several other men were being held with her husband. They'd made a pact with one another—if anyone got out, he would tell the other families that the men were still alive.

31    A few hours later, Carlos called. "Thank you for everything you've done. I love you," he told her. "Take care of the kids. Please tell them I love them." The phone line clicked. Her husband was saying good-bye. Ana was devastated. She didn't hear anything for two more days. When Carlos' captors called again, they wanted the deed to their house as collateral to raise the $800,000 before they released him. Ana wanted proof that he was still alive first. "I need to know that my husband is safe," she said.

32    That night Ana met with another SUV filled with teenagers at a park. The driver lowered the backseat window so she could see her husband. Carlos was blindfolded and handcuffed, but he was alive. Ana felt a momentary sense of relief. She handed over the deed to their home, and the SUV drove away. Later, the kidnappers forced Carlos to sign the documents, and a lawyer notarized the transaction.

33    The next morning, Ana finally received good news. El Comandante had given the order to release Carlos. "Stay awake," the caller advised, ominously. Hours passed but she heard nothing. Finally her cell phone rang, but it was an officer from the military base in Matamoros. Soldiers had encountered an armed convoy, and there was a gun battle. The vehicle carrying Carlos had wrecked, and he'd been found tied up in the car, still alive. Ana rushed to the base to see Carlos. He had some broken ribs and was badly beaten. The soldiers sent them to the local district attorney's office to make a statement about his kidnapping, and Ana pleaded for protection for her family. An official at the DA's office said he could do little. He advised that they leave Matamoros immediately. "Go to the United States," he said.

34    That evening Ana and Carlos crossed the international bridge to Brownsville, where their kids were waiting. They entered the United States legally with visas allowing them to visit for the day, then return to Mexico. For the first time in their lives they didn't go back.

35    That was nearly three years ago. The maid, the house, and the business are all gone. They have only a few cardboard boxes containing documents—what's left of Carlos' factory—and a framed painting of the Virgin of Guadalupe, which reminds Ana of home. Mostly they survive on loans from family and friends. Ana and Carlos both have advanced degrees, but they can't work in the United States because they're not here legally. Sometimes they can't pay their bills, so they move from apartment to apartment in Brownsville. Their former home is just across the Rio Grande, less than 10 miles away. "You can't imagine how horrible it is to be so close and you can't go back," Ana says.

36     Before the kidnapping, Ana and her family might have been able to apply for a coveted investor's visa. But after the kidnapping, they have no money and nowhere to go. Their last chance is to apply for political asylum, but an immigration attorney has already advised them that asylum will be very difficult to win. So they, like thousands of other Mexicans fleeing the violence, face an impossible choice: stay illegally in the United States, or return to Mexico and risk death. Meanwhile, neither government will acknowledge that refugees like them exist.

37     For Ana and Carlos, life in exile is spent hoping and waiting for a miracle. Each morning, they sit at the computer in their small apartment and search for jobs, but in a down economy, few employers are willing to spend the money to secure work visas. Then they read the news coming out of Mexico about the executions, mass graves, and kidnappings, and feel even more discouraged about ever going home.

38     "We were happy in Matamoros," Ana says. "It was a good place to live and then suddenly everything changed."

# Getting Ready to Write

## Checking Your Comprehension

Answer each of the following questions using complete sentences.

1. Who are Ana and Carlos and what happened to them?
2. What four factors caused a decline in the number of Mexicans immigrating to the United States?
3. Why did the violence in Mexico spiral out of control in 2006?
4. What makes the Mexican state of Tamaulipas even more dangerous than Juarez?
5. In addition to investing $500,000, what must investors do to obtain permanent visas through USA Now?
6. Why are most Mexican applications for political asylum denied?
7. What advice did the local district attorney's office give to Ana and Carlos when they asked for protection?

## Strengthening Your Vocabulary

Using the word's context, word parts, or a dictionary, write a brief definition of each of the following words as it is used in the reading.

1. prestigious (paragraph 5) _____ having high status or prestige
2. paradoxical (paragraph 8) _____ contradictory; inconsistent
3. perpetrated (paragraph 8) _____ carried out
4. swaths (paragraph 8) _____ large sections
5. morphed (paragraph 10) _____ changed
6. intractable (paragraph 11) _____ difficult to control or deal with
7. impunity (paragraph 12) _____ freedom from consequences of an action
8. exodus (paragraph 20) _____ a mass departure of people
9. tantamount (paragraph 24) _____ practically the same as
10. coveted (paragraph 36) _____ highly desired

## Examining the Readings Using Idea Maps

Review the reading by filling in the missing parts of the following idea map.

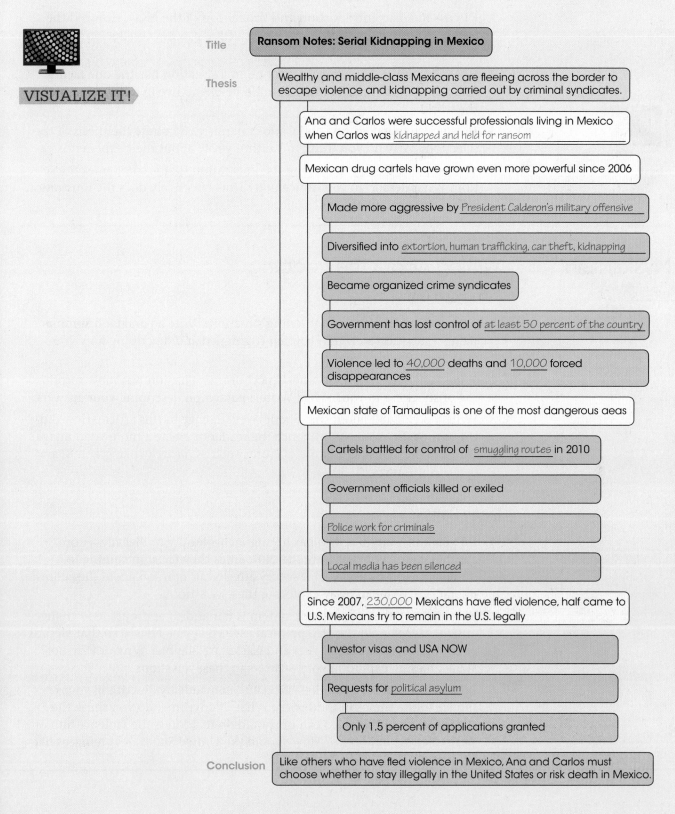

VISUALIZE IT!

**Title** — Ransom Notes: Serial Kidnapping in Mexico

**Thesis** — Wealthy and middle-class Mexicans are fleeing across the border to escape violence and kidnapping carried out by criminal syndicates.

Ana and Carlos were successful professionals living in Mexico when Carlos was *kidnapped and held for ransom*

Mexican drug cartels have grown even more powerful since 2006

Made more aggressive by *President Calderon's military offensive*

Diversified into *extortion, human trafficking, car theft, kidnapping*

Became organized crime syndicates

Government has lost control of *at least 50 percent of the country*

Violence led to *40,000* deaths and *10,000* forced disappearances

Mexican state of Tamaulipas is one of the most dangerous aeas

Cartels battled for control of *smuggling routes* in 2010

Government officials killed or exiled

*Police work for criminals*

*Local media has been silenced*

Since 2007, *230,000* Mexicans have fled violence, half came to U.S. Mexicans try to remain in the U.S. legally

Investor visas and USA NOW

Requests for *political asylum*

Only 1.5 percent of applications granted

**Conclusion** — Like others who have fled violence in Mexico, Ana and Carlos must choose whether to stay illegally in the United States or risk death in Mexico.

### Reacting to Ideas: Discussion and Journal Writing

Get ready to write about the reading by discussing the following:

1. Discuss the title, introduction and conclusion of the essay. How did the author capture your attention? How effective was her conclusion? What does the title mean?

2. How do you think you would respond in a situation like the one facing Ana and Carlos? Discuss what it would be like to live in a lawless part of the world.

3. How effectively does Ana and Carlos's narrative illustrate the thesis of the selection? Why do you think the author wrote about their experience?

4. Write a journal entry describing the illustration that accompanies the selection. What details do you notice in it? How effectively does the illustration reflect the content of the selection?

**THINKING VISUALLY**

**MySkillsLab®**

**Complete** this Exercise

## Writing About the Reading

### Paragraph Options

1. The reading describes a frightening situation. Write a paragraph summarizing a situation in which you felt frightened and describing how you dealt with the experience.

2. What fact, description, or other aspect of this selection was most surprising or shocking to you? Why? Write a paragraph describing your answers.

3. Write a paragraph about the descriptive language in this article. How did the author use words to influence the reader or create a more vivid image? For example, consider her use of words such as *furtively* (paragraph 8) and *ominously* (paragraph 30)

### Essay Options

4. Do you know anyone who has immigrated—legally or illegally—from another country? What were the difficulties they faced in coming to America? Did Ana and Carlos's story affect your opinion about illegal immigration? Write an essay exploring these questions.

5. Do you think the investor visa system is fair and/or appropriate for refugees of violence? Should the U.S. political asylum law be revised so that victims of criminal syndicates like Ana and Carlos are eligible? Why or why not? Write an essay exploring your answers to these questions.

6. Write a brief summary of the article and conclude by describing your response to the situation in Mexico. What, if anything, do you think the United States and Mexico can or should do to address the violence and organized crime in Mexico? How should the United States treat refugees like Ana and Carlos?

# SELF-TEST SUMMARY

To test yourself, cover the Answer column with a sheet of paper and answer each question in the left column. Evaluate each of your answers as you work by sliding the paper down and comparing your answer with what is printed in the Answer column.

| QUESTION | ANSWER |
|---|---|
| ■ GOAL 1 Understand time sequence<br><br>What are time sequence patterns and when are they used? | *Time sequence patterns* include *chronological order, process,* and *narration.* Time sequence is used whenever ideas are organized according to the order in which they occurred. |
| ■ GOAL 2 Read chronological order and process<br><br>What are chronological order and process?<br><br>How do you recognize that an author is using chronological or process patterns? | *Chronological order* is a pattern in which writers present events in order according to the time they occurred, beginning with the first event. *Process* is a pattern used to explain how something is done or how something works.<br><br>Writers usually use time transitions when they write using a chronological or process pattern. |
| ■ GOAL 3 Write process paragraphs<br><br>How do you develop effective process paragraphs? | Place your topic sentence first, present the steps in a process in the order in which they happen, include only essential steps, assume that your reader is unfamiliar with your topic, and use a consistent point of view. |
| ■ GOAL 4 Write narrative paragraphs<br><br>What is narration? What is involved in writing a narrative? | *Narration* is the technique of making a point by telling a story. Writing a narrative involves selecting a topic, generating ideas, writing a topic sentence, sequencing and developing your ideas, considering your audience and purpose, and using transitions. |
| ■ GOAL 5 Understand description<br><br>What is descriptive writing? | *Descriptive writing* creates an impression by helping the reader visualize the subject. |
| ■ GOAL 6 Read descriptive paragraphs<br><br>How do you read descriptive paragraphs? | *As you read descriptive paragraphs,* pay attention to the overall impression, sensory details, and descriptive language. |
| ■ GOAL 7 Write descriptive paragraphs<br><br>What is involved in writing a descriptive paragraph? | *Writing an effective descriptive paragraph* involves creating a dominant impression, selecting sensory details, using descriptive language, organizing details, and using transitions. |

# MySkillsLab

For more help with **Patterns of Organization**, go to your learning path in MySkillsLab at http://www.myskillslab.com.

# 13

# Patterns of Organization: Example, Cause and Effect, and Comparison and Contrast

## THINK About It!

Suppose you had to research and write a paragraph about this disaster. How would you organize your ideas? One option would be to give examples of the devastation it caused. Another would be to explain why the disaster occurred or how it affected those involved. A third option would be to compare or contrast its severity with another similar disaster. Regardless of which option you would choose, your paragraph would follow a logical method of organization. In this chapter you will learn to read and write three methods of organization: *example, cause and effect,* and *comparison and contrast.*

## FOCUSING ON READING AND WRITING

# Why Use Patterns of Organization?

Patterns of organization are useful to both readers and writers. As we discussed in Chapter 12, patterns help readers comprehend and recall what they read, and they help writers organize and present their ideas clearly.

Patterns are useful in a variety of academic situations:

- Professors use patterns to organize their lectures. If you recognize the patterns used to organize a lecture, you will be able to understand and remember it more easily.

- Patterns will help you understand and prepare class assignments, including lab reports, summaries, and case studies.

- Essay exams often contain questions that require you to use one or more patterns. Patterns can also help you present a well-organized, easy-to-read answer.

- Patterns will help you organize your speech, both in formal presentations and in classroom discussions.

## READING AND WRITING EXAMPLE

# What Is an Example?

■ GOAL 1
Understand examples

**Examples** are specific instances or situations that explain a general idea or statement. Peaches and plums are examples of fruit. Presidents' Day and Veterans Day are examples of national holidays. Here are a few sample general statements along with specific examples that illustrate them.

| GENERAL STATEMENT | EXAMPLES |
|---|---|
| I had an exhausting day. | ■ I had two exams. |
| | ■ I worked four hours. |
| | ■ I swam 20 laps in the pool. |
| | ■ I did three loads of laundry. |

| GENERAL STATEMENT | EXAMPLES |
|---|---|
| Research studies demonsrate that reading aloud to children improves their reading skills. | ■ Whitehurst (2007) found that reading picture books to children improved their vocabulary. |
| | ■ Crain-Thompson and Dale (2006) reported that reading aloud to language-delayed children improved their reading ability. |

| GENERAL STATEMENT | EXAMPLES |
|---|---|
| You can improve your efficiency at work by working smarter, not harder. | ■ An efficient day begins the night before: get a good night's sleep.<br><br>■ Every morning, make a list of your priorities for the day and stick to it.<br><br>■ Handle each piece of mail once; either respond to it, forward it to your assistant to handle, or throw it away. |

In each case, the examples make the general statement clear, understandable, and believable by giving specific illustrations or supporting details.

---

**EXERCISE 13-1**

*WORKING TOGETHER*

## Brainstorming Use of Examples

**Directions:** Working with another student, brainstorm a list of examples to illustrate one of the following statements:

1. Effective teaching involves caring about students.
2. Dogs (or cats) make good companions.
3. Volunteerism has many benefits.

---

Example paragraphs consist of examples that support the topic sentence. You can visualize an example paragraph as shown below:

**VISUALIZE IT!**

**Example Paragraph Idea Map**

Topic sentence → Example 1 → Example 2 → Example 3

# Read Examples

■ GOAL 2
Read examples

The **example pattern** uses specific instances or detailed situations to explain an idea or concept. One of the clearest ways to explain something is to give an example. This is especially true when a subject is unfamiliar. Suppose, for instance, that your younger brother asks you to explain what anthropology is. You might give him examples of the topics you study, such as apes and early humans, and the development of modern humans. Through examples, your brother would get a fairly good idea of what anthropology is all about.

When organizing a paragraph, a writer often states the main idea first and then follows it with one or more examples. In a longer piece of writing, a separate paragraph may be used for each example.

Notice how the example pattern is developed in the following paragraph:

> Static electricity is all around us. We see it in lightning. We receive electric shocks when we walk on a nylon rug on a dry day and then touch something (or someone). We can see sparks fly from a cat's fur when we pet it in the dark. We can rub a balloon on a sweater and make the balloon stick to the wall or the ceiling. Our clothes cling together when we take them from the dryer.

—Newell, *Chemistry: An Introduction*, p. 11

In the preceding paragraph, the writer explains static electricity through the use of everyday examples. You could visualize the paragraph as follows:

**VISUALIZE IT!**

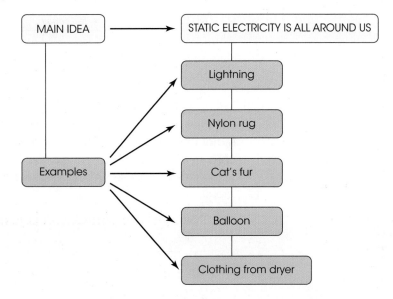

Writers often use transitional words—*for example, for instance,* or *such as*—to signal the reader that an example is to follow.

> Charlie agrees with the old saying that "a dog is a man's best friend." When he comes home from work, for instance, his dog Shadow is always happy to see him. He wags his tail, licks Charlie's hand, and leaps joyously around the room. Shadow is also good company for him. The dog is always there, for example, when Charlie is sick or lonely or just needs a pal to take for a walk. Many pets, such as cats and parakeets, provide companionship for their owners. But Charlie would put his dog Shadow at the top of any "best friend" list.

By using examples and transitions, the writer explains why Shadow is Charlie's best friend.

# Analyzing the Example Pattern

**Directions:** The following paragraphs, all of which are about stress, use the example pattern. Read each of them and answer the questions that follow.

A.   Any single event or situation by itself may not cause stress. But, if you experience several mildly disturbing situations at the same time, you may find yourself under stress. For instance, getting a low grade on a biology lab report by itself may not be stressful, but if it occurred the same week during which your car "died," you argued with a close friend, and you discovered your checking account was overdrawn, then it may contribute to stress.

1. What transition does the writer use to introduce the examples?

   for instance

2. List the four examples the writer provides as possible causes of stress.

   **a.** low grade on biology lab report

   **b.** car "died"

   **c.** argument with a close friend

   **d.** checking account overdrawn

B.   Every time you make a major change in your life, you are susceptible to stress. Major changes include a new job or career, marriage, divorce, the birth of a child, or the death of someone close. Beginning college is a major life change. Try not to create multiple simultaneous life changes, which multiply the potential for stress.

3. Does the topic sentence occur first, second, or last?

   first

4. The writer gives six examples of major changes. List them briefly.

   **a.** new job or career          **d.** birth of a child

   **b.** marriage                    **e.** death of someone close

   **c.** divorce                     **f.** beginning college

C.   Because you probably depend on your job to pay part or all of your college expenses, your job is important to you and you feel pressure to perform well in order to keep it. Some jobs are more stressful than others. Those, for example, in which you work under constant time pressure tend to be stressful. Jobs that must be performed in loud, noisy, crowded, or unpleasant conditions—a hot kitchen, a noisy machine shop, with co-workers who don't do their share—can be stressful. Consider changing jobs if you are working in very stressful conditions.

5. Does the topic sentence occur first, second, or last?

   second

6. What transition does the writer use to introduce the first type of job?

   for example

7. To help you understand "jobs that must be performed in loud, noisy, crowded, or unpleasant conditions," the writer provides three examples. List these examples in the diagram below.

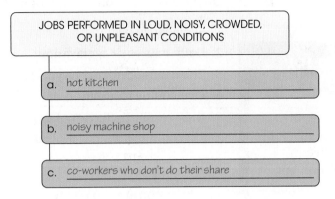

JOBS PERFORMED IN LOUD, NOISY, CROWDED, OR UNPLEASANT CONDITIONS

a. *hot kitchen*

b. *noisy machine shop*

c. *co-workers who don't do their share*

D.      People who respond well to stress focus on doing the best they can, not on how they might fail. It's not that the potential problems have disappeared, it's that successful people believe in the possibility of success. Once success is seen as possible, you can focus on completing the task to the best of your ability. For example, instead of saying "I cannot do this on time," leave out the word *not*. Ask yourself: "How *can* I finish this task on time?" and "How well *can* I do this?"

8. Does the topic sentence occur first, second, or last?

   *first*

9. What transition does the author use to introduce the example?

   *for example*

10. What does the example tell you to do?

    *ask yourself how you can finish a task instead of focusing on how you cannot do it*

# Write Examples

■ GOAL 3
Write examples

Writing paragraphs using examples involves writing a clear topic sentence, selecting appropriate and sufficient examples, arranging your details, and using transitions.

## Write Your Topic Sentence

You must create a topic sentence before you can generate examples to support it. Consider what you want to say about your topic and what your main point or fresh insight is. From this main idea, compose a first draft of a topic sentence. Be sure it states your topic and the point you want to make about it. (See Chapter 10, p. 309, if necessary, for a review of developing your point.) You will probably want to revise your topic sentence once you've written the paragraph, but for now, use it as the basis for gathering examples.

**EXERCISE 13-3**

# Writing a Topic Sentence

**Directions:** Select one of the topics listed below and write a topic sentence for it.

1. Slang language
2. Daily hassles or aggravations
3. The needs of infants or young children
4. Overcommercialization of holidays
5. Irresponsible behavior of crowds or individuals at public events

> **Tip for Writers**
>
> *Slang* is very informal language mostly used in conversation but not in academic writing. Some slang expressions are used only by a particular group (perhaps teenagers or musicians).

## Select Appropriate and Sufficient Examples

Use brainstorming to create a list of as many examples as you can think of to support your topic sentence. Suppose your topic is dog training. Your tentative topic sentence is, "You must be firm and consistent when training dogs; otherwise, they will not respond to your commands." You might produce the following list of examples:

> My sister's dog jumps on people; sometimes she disciplines him and sometimes she doesn't.
>
> Every time I want my dog to heel, I give the same command and use a firm tone of voice.
>
> If my dog does not obey the command to sit, I repeat it, this time saying it firmly while pushing down on his back.
>
> The dog trainer at obedience class used a set of hand signals to give commands to his dogs.

Then you would review your list and select between two and four examples to support your topic sentence. Here is an example of a paragraph you might have written:

> When training dogs, you must be firm and consistent; otherwise, they will not respond to your commands. The dog trainer at my obedience class has a perfectly trained dog. She uses a set of hand signals to give commands to her dog, Belle. The same signal always means the same thing, it is always enforced, and Belle has learned to obey each command. On the other hand, my sister's dog is a good example of what not to do. Her dog Maggie jumps on people; sometimes she disciplines Maggie, and sometimes she doesn't. When she asks Maggie to sit, sometimes she insists Maggie obey; other times she gets discouraged and gives up. Consequently, the dog has not learned to stop jumping on people or to obey the command to sit.

**Idea Map**

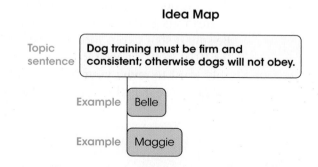

In the example paragraph, you probably noticed that some of the brainstormed examples were used; others were not. New examples were also added. Use the following guidelines in selecting details to include:

■ **Each example should illustrate the idea stated in your topic sentence.** Sometimes you may find that your examples do not clarify your main point or that each example you think of seems to illustrate something slightly different. If your topic is too broad, narrow your topic, using the suggestions in Chapter 10, page 306.

■ **Each example should be as specific and vivid as possible, accurately describing an incident or situation.** Suppose your topic sentence is, "Celebrities are not reliable sources of information about a product because they are getting paid to praise it." For your first example you write: "Many sports stars are paid to appear in TV commercials." "Many sports stars" is too general. To be convincing, your example has to name specific athletes and products or sponsors: "Tom Brady, star quarterback for the Patriots, endorses UGG Boots and Under Armour; LeBron James, basketball superstar, endorses Nike products."

■ **Choose a sufficient number of examples to make your point understandable.** The number you need depends on the complexity of the topic and your reader's familiarity with it. One example is sufficient only if it is well developed. The more difficult and unfamiliar the topic, the more examples you will need. For instance, if you are writing about how poor service at a restaurant can be viewed as an exercise in patience, two examples may be sufficient. Your paragraph could describe your long wait and your rude waiter, and make its point quite powerfully. However, if you are writing about test anxiety as a symptom of poor study habits, you probably would need more than two examples. In this case, you might discuss the need to organize one's time, set realistic goals, practice relaxation techniques, and work on self-esteem.

■ **Draw the connection for your reader between your example and your main point.** The following is a presentation by a social worker during a closed staff meeting at Carroll County Mental Health Services:

> We are continuing to see the aftereffects of last spring's tornado on our clients. In some cases, we have had to make referrals to meet our clients' needs. Several children have suffered PTSD (post traumatic stress disorder). Natoya Johns, for example, has nightmares and panic attacks. Natoya and the other children have been referred to Dr. Browntree at the Children's Clinic. We are also seeing increased occurrences of domestic violence that seem to be due to economic problems caused by the tornado. The worst case was Betsy Coster, who came to her counseling session with broken ribs, a black eye, and bruises. Betsy was referred to Safe Harbor, where she will receive legal and medical assistance while in protected housing. Several cases of substance abuse appeared to be aggravated by the stress of the situation. We put four clients in touch with AA, and Ken Lacoutez was referred to City Hospital for the inpatient program.
>
> (*Note*: Names have been changed to protect client privacy.)

## EXERCISE 13-4    Brainstorming Examples

**WRITING IN PROGRESS**

**Directions:** Brainstorm a list of examples that illustrate the topic sentence you wrote in Exercise 13-3.

---

### ❗ NEED TO KNOW

#### Choosing Appropriate Examples

Use the following guidelines in choosing examples:

- **Make sure your example illustrates your topic sentence clearly.** Do not choose an example that is complicated or has too many parts; your readers may not be able to see the connection to your topic sentence clearly.

- **Choose examples that your readers are familiar with and understand.** If you choose an example that is out of the realm of your readers' experience, the example will not help them understand your main point.

- **Choose interesting, original examples.** Your readers are more likely to pay attention to them.

- **Vary your examples.** If you are giving several examples, choose a wide range from different times, places, people, and so on.

- **Choose typical examples.** Avoid outrageous or exaggerated examples that do not accurately represent the situation.

---

## Arrange Your Details

Once you have selected examples to include, arrange your ideas in a logical sequence. Here are a few possibilities:

- **Arrange the examples chronologically.** If some examples are old and others more recent, you might begin with the older examples and then move to the more current ones.

- **Arrange the examples from most to least familiar.** If some examples are more detailed or technical, and therefore likely to be unfamiliar to your reader, place them after more familiar examples.

- **Arrange the examples from least to most important.** You may want to begin with less convincing examples and finish with the strongest, most convincing example, thereby leaving your reader with a strong final impression.

- **Arrange the examples in the order suggested by the topic sentence.** In the earlier sample paragraph about dog training, being firm and consistent is mentioned first in the topic sentence, so an example of firm and consistent training is given first.

## Use Transitions

Transitional words and phrases are needed in example paragraphs, both to signal to your reader that you are offering an example and to signal that you are moving from one example to another. Notice in the following paragraph how the transitions connect the examples and make them easy to follow:

> Electricity is all around us, often in the form of static electricity. For example, when we walk on a nylon rug and then touch something or someone, we receive a mild electrical shock. This shock occurs because accumulated electrical energy is being discharged. Similarly, when we rub a balloon on a sweater and make the balloon stick to the wall or ceiling, energy is again discharged. Another instance of electrical discharge occurs when clothes cling together after removal from a dryer.

> ## ! NEED TO KNOW
>
> ### Common Example Paragraphs Transitions
>
> | for example | for instance | such as | in particular |
> |---|---|---|---|
> | to illustrate | an example is | also | when |

---

### EXERCISE 13-5

**WRITING IN PROGRESS**

## Writing a Paragraph

**Directions:** Using the list of examples you brainstormed in Exercise 13-3, write a paragraph, arranging your details in a logical sequence and using transitions.

---

## READING AND WRITING CAUSE AND EFFECT

# What Is Cause and Effect?

■ **GOAL 4**
Understand cause
and effect

Writers use the **cause and effect** pattern to explain why an event or action causes another event or action. For example, if you are describing an automobile accident to a friend, you would probably follow a cause and effect pattern. You would tell what caused the accident and what happened as a result.

When a single cause has multiple effects, it can be visualized as shown below:

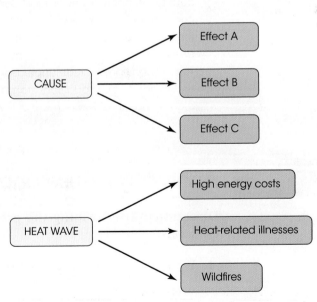

**VISUALIZE IT!**

Sometimes, however, multiple causes result in a single effect. This kind of cause and effect pattern can be visualized this way:

**VISUALIZE IT!**

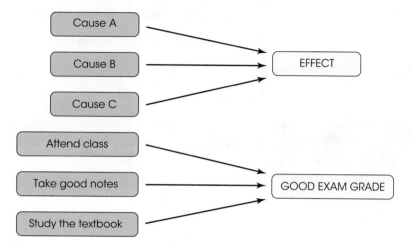

# Read Cause and Effect

■ **GOAL 5**
Read cause and effect

When you read and study ideas involving cause and effect, focus on the connections between or among the events. Sometimes, a single cause produces a single primary effect. If you get your cell phone wet, it may stop working, for instance. Other times, though, there may be multiple effects.

Read the following paragraph, which discusses the multiple causes of a single effect.

> Research has shown that mental illnesses have various causes, but the causes are not fully understood. Some mental disorders are due to physical changes in the brain resulting from illness or injury. Chemical imbalances in the brain may cause other mental illnesses. Still other disorders are mainly due to conditions in the environment that affect a person's mental state. These conditions include unpleasant childhood experiences and severe emotional stress. In addition, many cases of mental illness probably result from a combination of two or more of these causes.

**EXERCISE 13-6**   ## Analyzing Cause and Effect

**Directions:** After reading the preceding paragraph, answer the following questions.

1. What effect is the writer discussing?

   *mental illness*

2. The writer mentions several causes of the effect.

List four of them. (Answers will vary)

a. physical changes

b. chemical imbalances

c. environmental/childhood experiences/stress

d. combination of causes

As you worked on Exercise 13-6, did you notice that the topic sentence tells the reader that the paragraph will be about causes? Topic sentences often provide this important clue in a cause and effect paragraph, so pay close attention to them.

You also may have noticed that the writer uses specific words to show cause and effect. In addition to the word *causes,* he uses the phrases *due to* and *result from.* Writers often use such words to show why one event is caused by another. Look at the following statement:

> Louis forgot to wear his glasses to the restaurant. Consequently, he couldn't read the menu.

The word *consequently* ties the cause—no glasses—to the effect—not being able to read the menu. Here is another example:

> Bill couldn't wait for Nicole because he was already late for work.

In this sentence the word *because* ties the effect—Bill couldn't wait—to the cause—he was already late for work. In both of these examples, the cause and effect words help explain the relationship between two events. As you read, watch for words that show cause and effect; some common ones are listed in the box below.

## ! NEED TO KNOW

### Common Cause and Effect Transitions

| | | | |
|---|---|---|---|
| cause | due to | consequently | resulted in |
| because | reasons | as a result | therefore |
| because of | effect | one result is | thus |
| since | | | |

**EXERCISE 13-7**

## Analyzing Cause and Effect

**A. Directions:** After reading the following paragraph, select the cause and effect word or phrase in the box below that best completes each sentence in the paragraph. Write your answer in the space provided. Not all of the words in the box will be used.

| | | |
|---|---|---|
| consequently | reason | because of |
| result | effects | causes |

The three-car accident on Route 150 had several serious ___effects___. First, and most tragically, two people died when their car overturned. In addition, traffic into the city was delayed for several hours ___because of___ the accident. ___Consequently___, those who were headed to the fairgrounds for the Fourth of July fireworks never got to see the colorful display. Another ___result___, which occurred long afterward, was that the state legislature lowered the speed limit in the area where the accident had occurred. After the legislation passed, several legislators stated that the accident was the main ___reason___ for the change.

**B. Directions:** After reading the preceding paragraph, answer the following questions.

1. What cause is being discussed? _car accident_

2. What four effects does the writer mention?

   a. _two people died_

   b. _traffic was delayed_

   c. _people missed the fireworks_

   d. _speed limit was lowered_

3. Does the topic sentence tell you that this will be a cause and effect paragraph? _yes_

4. Aside from the cause and effect words, list four transitions that the writer uses to lead the reader through the information.

   a. ___first___   b. ___in addition___   c. ___another___   d. ___after___

---

**EXERCISE 13-8** | **Identifying Causes and Effects**

**Directions:** For each of the following paragraphs, list the cause(s) and effect(s) being discussed.

1.  Many regions are experiencing high levels of unemployment. Unfortunately, widespread job loss affects more than household income levels. Household tensions and even domestic violence rise. Indeed, some communities see an increase in all crimes. Loss of self-esteem and hope are some of the more personal ways unemployment hurts.

    Cause(s): _unemployment_

    Effect(s): _household income levels; tensions and even domestic violence rise; increase in all crimes. Loss of self-esteem and hope_

2.  Government leaders need to look harder at the true reasons our violent crime rates have risen. What they will see are people living in poverty, desperately trying to survive. Add to that rampant drug use and you have the perfect conditions for violent gang activity. Furthermore, budget cuts have lessened the police presence and done away with special police programs that were working to keep neighborhoods safe.

    Cause(s): _people living in poverty; rampant drug use; budget cuts have lessened the police presence; done away with special police programs_

    Effect(s): _crime rates have risen_

3.    The Earth is always moving in one way or another. When there is volcanic activity, an earthquake can occur. Also, shifting plates of the Earth's crust along faults will make the ground shake beneath us. Most earthquakes cannot be felt but are measured by sensitive equipment at seismic centers around the globe.

Cause(s): volcanic activity; shifting plates of the Earth's crust along faults

Effect(s): earthquake

4.    Low standardized test scores among minorities caused by biased questions lead teachers to "teach to the test." These same students may improve their performance on the next standardized test but do not receive the well-rounded education needed to succeed in school as a whole and ultimately in life.

Cause(s): low standardized test scores

Effect(s): biased questions; to "teach to the test"

# Write Cause and Effect

**GOAL 6**
Write cause and effect

Writing a cause and effect paragraph involves writing a clear topic sentence that indicates whether you are talking about causes, effects, or both; organizing supporting details; and using transitions.

## Write Your Topic Sentence

To write effective topic sentences for cause and effect paragraphs, do the following:

1.  **Clarify the cause-and-effect relationship.** Before you write, carefully identify the causes and the effects. If you are uncertain, divide a sheet of paper into two columns. Label one column "Causes" and the other "Effects." Brainstorm about your topic, placing your ideas in the appropriate column.

2.  **Decide whether to emphasize causes or effects.** In a single paragraph, it is best to focus on either causes or effects—not both. For example, suppose you are writing about students who drop out of college. You need to decide whether to discuss why they drop out (causes) or what happens to students who drop out (effects). Your topic sentence should indicate whether you are going to emphasize causes or effects. (In essays, you may consider both causes and effects.)

3.  **Determine whether the events are related or independent.** Analyze the causes or effects to discover if they occurred as part of a chain reaction or if they are not related to one another. Your topic sentence should suggest the type of relationship about which you are writing. If you are writing about a chain of events, your topic sentence should reflect this—for example, "A series of events led up to my sister's decision to drop out of college." If the causes or effects are not related to one another, then your sentence should indicate that—for example, "Students drop out of college for a number of different reasons."

Now read the following paragraph that a sales representative wrote to her regional manager to explain why she had failed to meet a monthly quota. Then study the diagram that accompanies it. Notice that the topic sentence makes it clear that she is focusing on the causes (circumstances) that led to her failure to make her sales quota for the month.

> In the past, I have always met or exceeded my monthly sales quota at Thompson's Office Furniture. This January I was $20,000 short, due to a set of unusual and uncontrollable circumstances in my territory. The month began with a severe snowstorm that closed most businesses in the area for most of the first week. Travel continued to be a problem the remainder of the week, and many purchasing agents did not report to work. Once they were back at their desks, they were not eager to meet with sales reps; instead, they wanted to catch up on their backlog of paperwork. Later that month, an ice storm resulted in power losses, again closing most plants for almost two days. Finally, some of our clients took extended weekends over the Martin Luther King holiday. Overall, my client contact days were reduced by more than 25%, yet my sales were only 15% below the quota.

**VISUALIZE IT!**

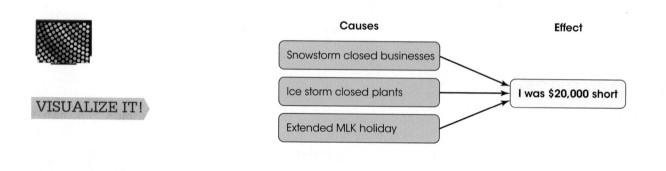

| Causes | | Effect |
| --- | --- | --- |
| Snowstorm closed businesses | → | I was $20,000 short |
| Ice storm closed plants | → | |
| Extended MLK holiday | → | |

---

**EXERCISE 13-9**

**WRITING IN PROGRESS**

## Writing Topic Sentences

**Directions:** Select one of the topics below, and write a topic sentence for a paragraph that will explain either its causes *or* effects.

1. Watching too much TV
2. Children who misbehave
3. The popularity of horror films
4. Rising cost of attending college
5. Eating junk food

---

## Provide Supporting Details

Providing supporting details for cause and effect paragraphs requires careful thought and planning. Details must be relevant, sufficient, and effectively organized.

### Providing Relevant and Sufficient Details

Each cause or effect you describe must be relevant to the situation introduced in your topic sentence. Suppose you are writing a paragraph explaining why you are attending college. Each sentence must explain this topic. You should not include ideas, for example, about how college is different from what you expected.

If, while writing, you discover you have more ideas about how college is different from what you expected than you do about your reasons for attending college, you need to revise your topic sentence in order to refocus your paragraph.

Each cause or reason requires explanation, particularly if it is *not* obvious. For example, it is not sufficient to write, "One reason I decided to attend college was to advance my position in life." This sentence needs further explanation. For example, you could discuss the types of advancement (financial, job security, job satisfaction) you hope to attain.

Jot down a list of the causes or reasons you plan to include. This process may help you think of additional causes and will give you a chance to consider how to explain or support each one. You might decide to eliminate one or to combine several. Here is one student's list of reasons for attending college.

**VISUALIZE IT!**

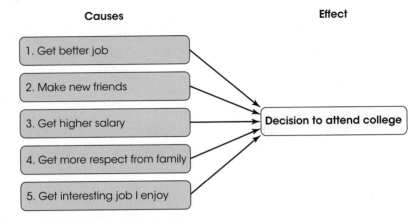

By listing his reasons, this student realized that the first one—to get a better job—was too general and was covered more specifically later in the list, so he eliminated it. He also realized that "get higher salary" and "get interesting job" could be combined. He then wrote the following paragraph:

> There are three main reasons I decided to attend Ambrose Community College. First, and most important to me, I want to get a high-paying, interesting job that I will enjoy. Right now, the only jobs I can get pay minimum wage, and as a result, I'm working in a fast-food restaurant. This kind of job doesn't make me proud of myself, and I get bored with routine tasks. Second, my parents have always wanted me to have a better job than they do, and I know my father will not respect me until I do. A college degree would make them proud of me. A third reason for attending college is to make new friends. It is hard to meet people, and everyone in my neighborhood seems stuck in a rut. I want to meet other people who are interested in improving themselves like I am.

### Organizing Your Details

There are several ways to arrange the details in a cause and effect paragraph. The method you choose depends on your purpose in writing, as well as your topic. Suppose you are writing a paragraph about the effects of a hurricane on a coastal town. Several different arrangements of details are possible:

■ **Chronological** A chronological organization arranges your details in the order in which situations or events happened. The order in which the hurricane damage occurred becomes the order for your details. This arrangement is similar to the narration arrangement, which you learned in Chapter 12. A chronological arrangement works for situations and events that occurred in a specific order.

- **Order of importance** In an order-of-importance organization, the details are arranged from least to most important or from most to least important. In describing the effects of the hurricane, you could discuss the most severe damage first and then describe lesser damage. Alternatively, you could build up from the least to the most important damage for dramatic effect.

- **Spatial** Spatial arrangement of details uses physical or geographical position as a means of organization. In describing the hurricane damage, you could start by describing damage to the beach and work toward the center of town.

- **Categorical** This form of arrangement divides the topic into parts or categories. Using this arrangement to describe hurricane damage, you could recount what the storm did to businesses, roads, city services, and homes.

As the hurricane example shows, there are many ways to organize cause and effect details. Each has a different emphasis and achieves a different purpose. The organization you choose, then, depends on the point you want to make.

Once you decide on a method of organization, return to your preliminary list of effects. Study your list again, make changes, eliminate, or combine. Then rearrange or number the items on your list to indicate the order in which you will include them.

---

**EXERCISE 13-10**    Organizing a Paragraph

**Directions:** Choose one of the following topic sentences and develop a paragraph using it. Organize your paragraph by using one of the methods described above.

1. Exercise has several positive (or negative) effects on the body.

2. Professional athletes deserve (or do not deserve) the high salaries they are paid.

3. There are several reasons why parents should reserve time each day to spend with their children.

4. Many students work two or even three part-time jobs; the results are often disastrous.

---

**EXERCISE 13-11**    Organizing a Paragraph

**WRITING IN PROGRESS**

**Directions:** Write a paragraph developing the topic sentence you wrote for Exercise 13-9. Be sure to include relevant and sufficient details. Organize your paragraph according to one of the methods described above.

## Use Transitions

To blend your details smoothly, use transitional words and phrases. Some common transitions for the cause and effect pattern are listed in the "Need to Know" box on page 419.

The student paragraph on page 423 is a good example of how transitional words and phrases are used. Notice how these transitions function as markers and help you to locate each separate reason.

---

**EXERCISE 13-12**

## Using Transitional Words and Phrases

**Directions:** In each blank, supply a transitional word or phrase that strengthens the connection between the two ideas.   *Answers will vary. Possible answers are shown.*

1. Many companies have day-care centers for children. ___As a result___, employees are able to manage child-care problems easily.

2. Computers provide an easy way to store and process information quickly. ___Consequently___, computers have become an integral part of most businesses.

3. Animal skins are warm and very durable; ___therefore___, almost every culture has made use of them for clothing or shelter.

4. ___Because___ some people refused to accept his views and beliefs, Martin Luther King Jr. was brutally murdered.

---

**EXERCISE 13-13**

## Revising a Paragraph

**WRITING IN PROGRESS**

**Directions:** Reread the paragraphs you wrote for Exercises 13-10 and 13-11. Add transitional words and phrases, if needed, to connect your details.

---

## READING AND WRITING COMPARISON AND CONTRAST

# What Is Comparison and Contrast?

■ GOAL 7
Understand comparison
and contrast

Often a writer will explain an object or idea, especially if it is unfamiliar to the reader, by showing how it is similar to or different from a familiar object or idea. At other times, it may be the writer's purpose to show how two ideas, places, objects, or people are similar or different. In each of these situations a writer commonly uses a pattern called **comparison and contrast**. This pattern emphasizes the similarities or differences between two or more items. There are several variations on this pattern: a paragraph may focus on similarities only, differences only, or both. The comparison pattern can be visualized and mapped as follows:

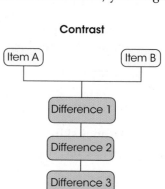

For material that focuses on differences, you might use a map like this:

# Read Comparison and Contrast

■ **GOAL 8**
*Read comparison and contrast*

Often a writer will explain something by using comparison or contrast—that is, by showing how it is similar to or different from a familiar object or idea. Comparison treats similarities, while contrast emphasizes differences. For example, an article comparing two car models might mention these common, overlapping features: radial tires, clock, radio, power steering, and power brakes. The cars may differ in gas mileage, body shape, engine power, braking distance, and so forth. When comparing the two models, the writer would focus on shared features. When contrasting the two cars, the writer would focus on individual differences. Such an article might be diagrammed as follows:

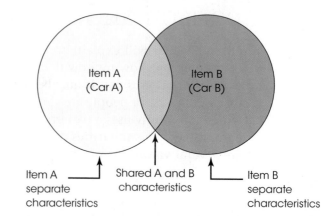

In this diagram, Items A and B are different except where they overlap and share the same characteristics.

In most situations that use the comparison and contrast method, you will find some passages that only compare, some that only contrast, and others that both compare and contrast. To read each type of passage effectively, you must follow the pattern of ideas. Passages that show comparison and/or contrast can be organized in a number of different ways. The organization depends on the author's purpose.

### Comparison

If a writer is concerned only with similarities, he or she may identify the items to be compared and then list the ways in which they are alike. The following paragraph shows how chemistry and physics are similar.

> Although physics and chemistry are considered separate fields of study, they have much in common. First, both are physical sciences and are concerned with studying and explaining physical occurrences. To study and record these occurrences, each field has developed a precise set of signs and symbols. These might be considered a specialized language. Finally, both fields are closely tied to the field of mathematics and use mathematics in predicting and explaining physical occurrences.
>
> —Hewitt, *Conceptual Physics*, pp. 82–84

Such a pattern can be diagrammed as follows:

**VISUALIZE IT!**

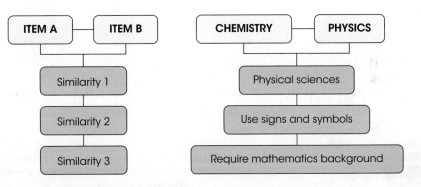

### Contrast

A writer concerned only with the differences between sociology and psychology might write the following paragraph:

> Sociology and psychology, although both social sciences, are very different fields of study. Sociology is concerned with the structure, organization, and behavior of groups. Psychology, on the other hand, focuses on individual behavior. While a sociologist would study characteristics of groups of people, a psychologist would study the individual motivation and behavior of each group member. Psychology and sociology also differ in the manner in which research is conducted. Sociologists obtain data and information through observation and survey. Psychologists obtain data through carefully designed experimentation.

Such a pattern can be diagrammed as follows:

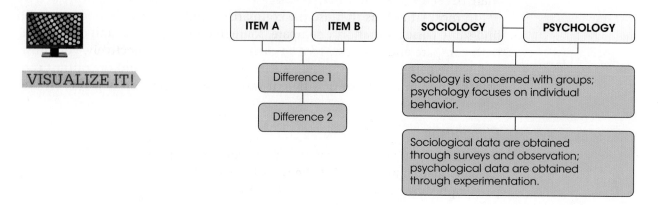

### Comparison and Contrast

In many passages, writers discuss both similarities and differences. Suppose a writer wanted to write a paragraph discussing the similarities and differences between sociology and psychology. She could organize the paragraph in different ways.

■ She could list all the similarities and then all the differences, as shown in this diagram:

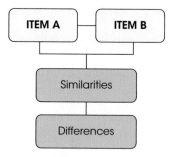

■ She could discuss Item A first, presenting both similarities and differences, and then do the same for Item B. Such a pattern would look like this:

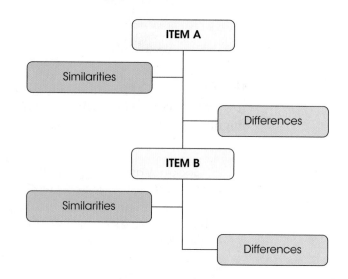

The following paragraph discusses amphibians and reptiles. As you read it, try to visualize its pattern.

<u>Although reptiles evolved from amphibians, several things distinguish the</u> <u>two kinds of animals.</u> Amphibians (such as frogs, salamanders, and newts) must live where it is moist. In contrast, reptiles (which include turtles, lizards and snakes, and crocodiles and alligators) can live away from the water. Amphibians employ external fertilization, as when the female frog lays her eggs on the water and the male spreads his sperm on top of them. By contrast, all reptiles employ internal fertilization—eggs are fertilized inside the female's body. Another difference between amphibians and reptiles is that reptiles have a tough, scaly skin that conserves water, as opposed to the thin amphibian skin that allows water to escape. Reptiles also have a stronger skeleton than amphibians, more efficient lungs, and a better-developed nervous system.

—adapted from Krogh, *Biology: A Guide to the Natural World*, pp. 466–467, 474

VISUALIZE IT!

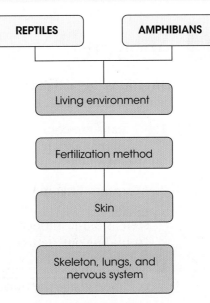

Now read the following passage and decide whether it discusses similarities, differences, or both.

Groups have two types of leaders. The first is easy to recognize. This person, called an **instrumental leader**, tries to keep the group moving toward its goals. These leaders try to keep group members from getting sidetracked, reminding them of what they are trying to accomplish. The **expressive leader**, in contrast, usually is not recognized as a leader, but he or she certainly is one. This person is likely to crack jokes, to offer sympathy or to do other things that help to lift the group's morale. Both types of leadership are essential: the one to keep the group on track, the other to increase harmony and minimize conflicts.

It is difficult for the same person to be both an instrumental and an expressive leader, for these roles tend to contradict one another. Because instrumental leaders are task oriented, they sometimes create friction as they prod the group to get on with the job. Their actions often cost them popularity. Expressive leaders, in contrast, who stimulate personal bonds and reduce friction, are usually more popular.

—adapted from Henslin, *Sociology: A Down-to-Earth Approach*, p. 164

This passage *contrasts* two types of group leaders, focusing on differences between the two types.

Paragraphs and passages that use comparison and contrast often contain transitional words and phrases that guide readers through the material. These include:

---

### ! NEED TO KNOW

## Common Comparison and Contrast Transitions

| COMPARISON | | | CONTRAST | | | |
|---|---|---|---|---|---|---|
| also | likewise | similarly | although | instead | differs from | on the other hand |
| to compare | too | in the same way | in contrast | unlike | on the contrary | |
| both | in comparison | | as opposed to | but | however | |

---

### EXERCISE 13-14   Analyzing Comparison and Contrast

**Directions:** In each of the following sentences, underline the two items that are being compared or contrasted.

1. <u>Humans</u> are complex organisms made up of many sophisticated systems. Yet humans share several characteristics with <u>primates</u> such as gorillas and New World Monkeys.

2. Educators differ in their approaches to teaching reading. One method, <u>whole language</u>, applies a holistic model to literacy. The other main approach, seen as old-fashioned by some, is <u>phonics</u>, where children learn to read by "sounding out" letters and letter combinations.

3. <u>Face-to-face communication</u> and <u>electronic communication</u> share a common goal—the transmission of information.

4. Many actors believe that <u>stage acting</u> requires more overall skill than <u>movie acting</u>. Unlike filmmaking, where actors can make mistake after mistake, knowing that the scene will just be shot again and again until it is right, live theater demands more concentration and preparation since retakes are not possible.

5. <u>Flame retardant</u> and <u>flame resistant</u> fabrics each provide a degree of protection to the person wearing them.

---

### EXERCISE 13-15   Analyzing Comparison and Contrast

**Directions:** Read each of the paragraphs below, and answer the questions that follow.

A.      The term primary group, coined by Charles H. Cooley, refers to small informal groups who interact in a personal, direct, and intimate way. A secondary group, on the other hand, is a group whose members interact in an impersonal manner, have few emotional ties, and come together for a specific purpose. Like primary groups, secondary groups are usually small and involve face-to-face contacts. Although the interactions may be cordial or friendly, they are more formal than primary group interactions. Secondary groups, however, are often just as important as primary groups. Most of our time is spent in secondary groups—committees, professional groups, sales-related groups, classroom groups, or neighborhood groups. The key difference between primary and secondary groups is in the quality of the relationship and the extent of personal intimacy and involvement. Primary groups are person-oriented, whereas secondary groups tend to be goal-oriented.

—Eshleman and Cashion, *Sociology: An Introduction,* p. 88

1. Although the writers are comparing and contrasting primary and secondary groups, what other pattern do they use in the first two sentences?

   definition

2. What words do the writers use to indicate similarities and differences?

   on the other hand     like     difference     whereas

3. The paragraph includes many similarities and differences between primary and secondary groups. List some of the similarities and differences below.

---

**Primary and Secondary Groups**

*Similarities*

1. both small

2. both involve face-to-face contacts/friendly

3. both important

Answers will vary. Possible answers are shown.

*Differences*

1. primary are personal and intimate; secondary are impersonal

2. secondary more formal

3. secondary come together for specific purpose

4. more time spent in secondary groups

5. primary groups are person-oriented; secondary are goal-oriented

---

B.     Small businesses are likely to have less formal purchasing processes. A small retail grocer might, for example, purchase a computer system after visiting a few suppliers to compare prices and features, but a large grocery store chain might collect bids from a specified number of vendors and then evaluate those bids according to detailed corporate guidelines. Usually, fewer individuals are involved in the decision-making process for a small business. The owner of the small business, for example, may make all decisions, and a larger business may operate with a buying committee of several people.

—Kinnear, Bernhardt, and Krentler, *Principles of Marketing,* p. 218

1. What are the writers comparing or contrasting in this paragraph?

   small and large businesses

2. Why are small retail grocers and grocery store chains mentioned?

   as examples to illustrate differences

3. What transitional word or phrase suggests the overall pattern of the paragraph?

but

4. The paragraph includes two major differences between small and large businesses. Fill in these differences below.

| Differences Between Small and Large Businesses | Small Businesses | Large Businesses |
| --- | --- | --- |
| 1. Purchasing processes | Less formal | More formal |
| 2. Decision-making process | Fewer people involved | More people involved |

# Write Comparison and Contrast

■ GOAL 9
Write comparison
and contrast

Writing a comparison and contrast paragraph involves identifying similarities and differences between two items, writing a topic sentence that indicates the item you will be comparing and contrasting and your point, organizing your paragraph, developing your points, and using transitions.

## Identify Similarities and Differences

If you have two items to compare or contrast, the first step is to figure out how they are similar and how they are different. Be sure to select subjects that are neither too similar nor too different. If they are, you will have either too little or too much to say. Follow this effective two-step approach:

1. Brainstorm to produce a two-column list of characteristics.
2. Match up the items and identify points of comparison and contrast.

### Brainstorming to Produce a Two-Column List

Let's say you want to write about two friends—Rhonda and Maria. Here is how to identify their similarities and differences:

1. **Brainstorm and list the characteristics of each person.**

| RHONDA | MARIA |
| --- | --- |
| Reserved, quiet | Age 27 |
| Age 22 | Single parent, two children |
| Private person | Outgoing person |
| Friends since childhood | Loves to be center of attention |
| Married, no children | Loves sports and competition |
| Hates parties | Plays softball and tennis |
| Fun to shop with | |
| Tells me everything about her life | |

2. **When you finish your list, match up items that share the same point of comparison or contrast—age, personality type, marital status—as shown below.**

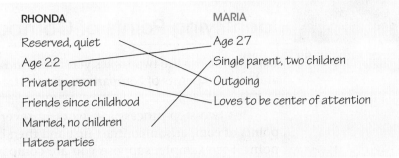

3. **When you have listed an item in a certain category for one person but not for the other, think of a corresponding detail that will balance the lists.** For instance, you listed "friends since childhood" for Rhonda, so you could indicate how long you have known Maria. This will give you additional points of comparison and contrast.

EXERCISE 13-16

## Listing Similarities and Differences

WRITING IN PROGRESS

**Directions:** Make a two-column list of similarities and differences for two of the following topics:

1. Two professional athletes
2. Two political candidates
3. Two restaurants
4. Two neighborhoods you have lived in
5. Two friends
6. Two vampires

### Identifying Points of Comparison and Contrast

The next step is to reorganize the lists so that the items you matched up appear next to each other. Now, in a new column to the left of your lists, write the term that describes or categorizes each set of items in the lists. These are general categories we will call "points of comparison and contrast." **Points of comparison and contrast** are the characteristics you use to examine your two subjects. As you reorganize, you may find it easier to group several items together. For example, you might group some details about Rhonda and Maria together under the category of personality. Study the following list, noticing the points of comparison and contrast in the left-hand column.

| POINTS OF COMPARISON AND CONTRAST | RHONDA | MARIA |
|---|---|---|
| Personality | Quiet, reserved, private person | Outgoing, loves to be center of attention |
| Marital status | Married, no children | Single parent, two children |
| Length of friendship | Friends since childhood | Met at work last year |
| Shared activities | Go shopping | Play softball together, go to parties |

# Identifying Points of Comparison

**Directions:** For the two topics you chose in Exercise 13-16, match up the items and identify points of comparison and contrast.

This two-step process can work in reverse order as well. You can decide points of comparison/contrast first and then brainstorm characteristics for each point. For example, suppose you are comparing and contrasting two restaurants. Points of comparison/contrast might be location, price, speed of service, menu variety, and quality of food. If you are comparing or contrasting Professors Rodriguez and Meyer, you might do so using the following points:

| POINTS OF COMPARISON AND CONTRAST | PROFESSOR MEYER | PROFESSOR RODRIGUEZ |
| --- | --- | --- |
| Amount of homework | | |
| Type of exams | | |
| Class organization | | |
| How easy to talk to | | |
| Grading system | | |
| Style of teaching | | |

You could then fill in columns 2 and 3 with appropriate details, as shown below.

| POINTS OF COMPARISON AND CONTRAST | PROFESSOR MEYER | PROFESSOR RODRIGUEZ |
| --- | --- | --- |
| Amount of homework | Assignment due for every class | Hardly any |
| Type of exams | Essay | Multiple-choice and essay |
| Class organization | Well organized | Free and easy |
| How easy to talk to | Always around, approachable | Approachable but talks a lot |
| Grading system | 50 percent class participation, 50 percent essay exams | 100 percent exams |
| Style of teaching | Lecture | Class discussion, questions |

Once you have completed your three-column list, the next step is to study your list and decide whether to write about similarities or differences, or both. It is usually easier to concentrate on one or the other. If you see similarities as more significant, you might need to omit or de-emphasize differences—and vice versa if you decide to write about differences.

**EXERCISE 13-18**

# Selecting a Topic and Listing Points of Comparison and Contrast

**Directions:** List at least three points of comparison and contrast for each of the following topics. Then choose one topic and make a three-column list on a separate sheet of paper.    Answers will vary.

1. Two films you have seen recently

   Points of comparison and contrast:

   a. type of film (comedy, horror, etc.)

   b. musical score or background

   c. actresses and actors

   d. photography/cinematography

   e. amount of action

2. Two jobs you have held

   Points of comparison and contrast:

   a. hourly wage

   b. type of tasks performed

   c. training required

   d. level of physical activity required

   e. co-workers

3. Baseball and football players

   Points of comparison and contrast:

   a. necessary physical skills

   b. types of training

   c. salary

   d. public opinion

   e. types of fans

## Write Topic Sentence

Your topic sentence should do two things:

- It should identify the two subjects that you will compare or contrast.
- It should state whether you will focus on similarities, differences, or both.

It may also indicate what points you will compare or contrast. Suppose you are comparing two world religions—Judaism and Hinduism. Obviously, you could not cover every aspect of these religions in a single paragraph. Instead, you could limit your comparison to their size, place of worship, or the type of divine being(s) worshipped.

Here are a few sample topic sentences that meet the above requirements:

Judaism is one of the smallest of the world's religions; Hinduism is one of the largest.

Neither Judaism nor Hinduism limits worship to a single location, although both hold services in temples.

Unlike Hinduism, Judaism teaches belief in only one god.

Be sure to avoid topic sentences that announce what you plan to do. Here's an example: "I'll compare network news and local news and show why I prefer local news."

---

**EXERCISE 13-19**

**WRITING IN PROGRESS**

## Writing a Topic Sentence

**Directions:** Write a topic sentence for each of the two topics you worked with in Exercises 13-16 and 13-17.

---

## Organize Your Paragraph

Once you have identified similarities and differences and drafted a topic sentence, you are ready to organize your paragraph. There are two ways you can organize a comparison or contrast paragraph:

- subject by subject
- point by point

### Subject-by-Subject Organization

In the **subject-by-subject method**, you write first about one of your subjects, covering it completely, and then about the other, covering it completely.

Ideally, you cover the same points of comparison and contrast for both, and in the same order. Let's return to the comparison between Professors Meyer and Rodriguez. With subject-by-subject organization, you first discuss Professor Meyer—his class organization, exams, and grading system; you then discuss Professor Rodriguez—her class organization, exams, and grading system. You can visualize the arrangement this way:

**VISUALIZE IT!**

**Subject-by-Subject Organization Map**

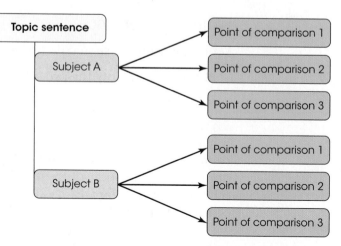

To develop each subject, focus on the same kinds of details and discuss the same points of comparison in the same order. If you are discussing only similarities or only differences, organize your points within each topic, using a most-to-least or least-to-most arrangement. If you are discussing both similarities and differences, you might discuss points of similarity first and then points of difference, or vice versa.

Here is a sample paragraph using the subject-by-subject method and a map showing its organization:

## Tip for Writers

The *most-to-least* arrangement puts the most important point first, then the second most important, and so on in order. *Least-to-most* organization does the reverse and ends with the most important point.

> Two excellent teachers, Professor Meyer and Professor Rodriguez, present a study in contrasting teaching styles. Professor Meyer is extremely organized. He conducts every class the same way. He reviews the assignment, lectures on the new chapter, and explains the next assignment. He gives essay exams and they are always based on important lecture topics. Because the topics are predictable, you know you are not wasting your time when you study. Professor Meyer's grading depends half on class participation and half on the essay exams. Professor Rodriguez, on the other hand, has an easy-going style. Each class is different and emphasizes whatever she thinks will help us better understand the material. Her classes are fun because you never know what to expect. Professor Rodriguez gives both multiple-choice and essay exams. These are difficult to study for because they are unpredictable. Our final grade is based entirely on the exams, so each exam requires a lot of studying beforehand. Although each professor teaches very differently, I am figuring out how to learn from each particular style.

**VISUALIZE IT!**

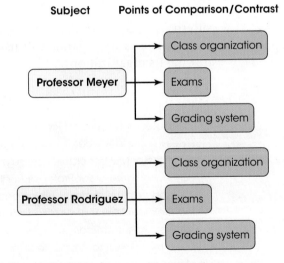

## EXERCISE 13-20   Using Subject-by-Subject Organization

**WRITING IN PROGRESS**

**Directions:** Using the subject-by-subject method of organization, write a comparison or contrast paragraph using one of the topic sentences you wrote for Exercise 13-19.

### Point-by-Point Organization

In the **point-by-point method of organization**, you discuss both of your subjects together for each point of comparison and contrast. You can visualize this organization as follows:

VISUALIZE IT!

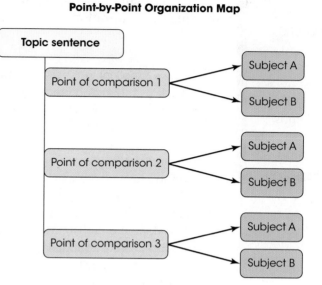

**Point-by-Point Organization Map**

Topic sentence
- Point of comparison 1 → Subject A, Subject B
- Point of comparison 2 → Subject A, Subject B
- Point of comparison 3 → Subject A, Subject B

When using this organization, maintain consistency by discussing the same subject first for each point. (That is, always discuss Professor Meyer first and Professor Rodriguez second.) If your paragraph focuses only on similarities or only on differences, arrange your points in a least-to-most or most-to-least pattern.

Here is a sample paragraph using the point-by-point method and a map showing its organization:

> Professor Meyer and Professor Rodriguez demonstrate very different teaching styles in how they operate their classes, how they give exams, and how they grade us. Professor Meyer's classes are highly organized; we work through the lesson every day in the same order. Professor Rodriguez uses an opposite approach. She creates a lesson to fit the material, which enables us to learn the most. Their exams differ too. Professor Meyer gives standard, predictable essay exams that are based on his lectures. Professor Rodriguez gives both multiple-choice and essay exams, so we never know what to expect. In addition, each professor grades differently. Professor Meyer counts class participation as half of our grade, so if you talk in class and do reasonably well on the exams, you will probably pass the course. Professor Rodriguez, on the other hand, counts the exams 100 percent, so you *have* to do well on them to pass the course. Each professor has a unique, enjoyable teaching style, and I am learning a great deal from both.

**VISUALIZE IT!**

**Points of Comparison/Contrast**      **Subject**

Class organization → Professor Meyer / Professor Rodriguez

Exams → Professor Meyer / Professor Rodriguez

Grading system → Professor Meyer / Professor Rodriguez

---

**EXERCISE 13-21**

**WRITING IN PROGRESS**

## Using Point-by-Point Organization

**Directions:** Using the point-by-point method of organization, write a comparison and contrast paragraph on the topic you chose for Exercise 13-20.

### Develop Your Points of Comparison and Contrast

As you discuss each point, don't feel as if you must compare or contrast in every sentence. Your paragraph should not just list similarities and/or differences. For every point, provide explanation, descriptive details, and examples.

Try to maintain a balance in your treatment of each subject and each point of comparison and contrast. Give equal attention to each point and each subject. If you give an example for one subject, try to do so for the other as well.

### Use Transitions

Transitions are particularly important in comparison and contrast writing. Because you are discussing two subjects and covering similar points for each, your readers can easily become confused. Commonly used transitional words and phrases are listed in the "Need to Know" box on page 430.

Each method of organization uses different transitions in different places. If you choose a subject-by-subject organization, you'll need the strongest transition in the middle of the paragraph, when you switch from one subject to another. You will also need a transition each time you move from one point to another while still on the same subject. In the following paragraph written by a paralegal comparing recent court cases, notice the transitional sentence highlighted in pink:

> *Green v. Lipscomb* and *Walker v. Walker* are the two most recent cases that deal with the custody of siblings. *Green* holds that siblings have a right to live together. It says that when a court decides custody, putting siblings together is the controlling concern. In this case, custody was given to the father because it was in the best interest of the oldest child to live with him. The other children were to live

there as well because it was more important that they live together. *Walker presents a more subjective position.* *Walker* says that while the sibling relationship is an important factor in deciding custody, it alone is not controlling. The best interest of each child must be evaluated. The sibling relationship must be considered in this evaluation.

**Tip for Writers**

For more help writing statements that compare or contrast, review comparative and superlative patterns, in "Reviewing the Basics," C.4 (p. 629).

This paragraph uses a subject-by-subject organization. A strong transition emphasizes the switch from one case to another.

If you choose point-by-point organization, use transitions as you move from one subject to the other. On each point, your reader needs to know quickly whether the two subjects are similar or different. Here is an example:

> Although colds and hay fever are both annoying, their symptoms and causes differ. Hay fever causes my eyes to itch and water. I sneeze excessively, bothering those around me. Colds, on the other hand, make me feel stuffy, with a runny nose and a cough. For me, hay fever arrives in the summer, but colds linger on through late fall, winter, and early spring. Their causes differ, too. Pollens produce hay fever. I am most sensitive to pollen from wildflowers and corn tassels. Unlike hay fever, viruses, which are passed from person to person by air or body contact, cause colds.

Notice that each time the writer switched from hay fever to colds, a transition was used.

---

**EXERCISE 13-22**   ## Using Transitions

**WRITING IN PROGRESS**

**Directions:** Reread the paragraphs you wrote for Exercises 13-20 and 13-21. If necessary, add transitions to make your organization clearer.

---

## ! NEED TO KNOW

### Organizing Your Details

Regardless of the method of organization you choose, it is important to organize the details in each method so that your paragraph or essay is easy to follow. Use the following suggestions:

**For subject-by-subject organization:**

- Be sure to cover the same points of comparison for each subject.
- Cover the points of comparison in the same order in each half of your paragraph or essay.
- Make sure you include a strong transition that signals you are moving from one subject to another.

**For point-by-point organization:**

- As you work back and forth between your subjects, try to mention the subjects in the same order.
- Decide how to organize your points of comparison. You could move from the simplest to the most complex similarity, or from the most obvious to least obvious difference, for example.

# INTEGRATING READING AND WRITING

## READ AND REVISE

MySkillsLab®

**Complete**
this
Exercise

The following paragraph was written to compare two colleges its author attended. This first draft is disorganized because the student focused only on getting his ideas down on paper. You can see that he skips around between the two schools and between various points of comparison. Rewrite this paragraph to make it follow a single method of organization. Add transitions as needed. You may delete or add ideas.   *Sample answer provided in the Instructor's Manual.*

The two colleges I that I have attended are the University of Colorado (UC) in Boulder, Colorado, and Allan Hancock College (AHC) in Santa Maria and both offered me opportunities, but differed greatly in style and focus. AHC offers small classes, and class size is important for getting help when you need it. UC, being a four-year university, offers Bachelor's degrees and preparation for professional schools. AHC is a community college, so most students can affordably live at home. UC offers student clubs that are important in teaching students how to network, communicate, and work together. Classes at UC are taught by a team consisting of a professor, who conducts lectures, a graduate student who conducts recitation classes, and occasionally, a co-seminar class taught by an adjunct professor. At AHC classes are taught by one person, a professor or adjunct. It is nice to be able to feel like your instructor knows you, and that you know him or her. AHC prepares students for careers and transfer to four-year schools. Classes at UC tend to be large. A typical freshman class may have between 150 and 220 students. The environment at UC is competitive; grades are very important. AHC has student clubs, but they don't have the importance that they do at CU. Costs are another factor. Living on campus is expensive at CU.

## READ AND RESPOND: A Student Essay

*Bryan Dube works full-time as a manager of a furniture store. He takes early morning and online courses at Collin College and is two classes away from completing an associate's degree in liberal arts. He plans to continue his education and obtain a bachelor's degree in business administration. Dube submitted this essay to the Writing Rewards Essay Contest sponsored by Pearson Education. The assignment he responded to directed him to write an example essay.*

# Twitter's Appeal

Twitter is arguably one of the fastest growing social media networks in the world. The simple concept of a 140-character status update which asks, "What are you doing?" has gained a lot of popularity with those who saw Facebook as being too complicated or who had privacy concerns with other sites. What started out as a simple way for friends to stay updated with each other in real time has evolved into a medium for brands, news networks, and celebrities to reach out to their fans and followers.

Brands have found many creative ways to utilize Twitter as both an advertising and customer service tool. Companies like Dell and Starbucks have created accounts in which they post updates on new deals or coupons allowing their followers to instantly find out about new savings at those stores. Verizon has utilized Twitter for its viral "DROID" marketing campaign, initiating nationwide scavenger hunts and riddles with free phones as rewards. Companies such as Comcast and JetBlue have found the site to be an effective option for customer service. Comcast users can tweet the customer service account "@comcastcares" with an issue they are having and the employee working with the account at the time can instantly assist them through the site just as they would through e-mail or on the phone.

News organizations such as CNN and Fox News have found the site to be an effective reporting tool as well. Utilizing the site in the same way that the news ticker is used when one watches the news, users receive tweets of news stories in real time, sometimes faster than the reporters on the news can report it. During the recent disaster in Japan, news outlets and general Twitter users alike were reporting on the devastating damage happening around them before it hit the television. The CNN anchor went as far as to ask people watching or following her account to update her on what was happening if they were able to through Twitter. Twitter's mass appeal and ease of use have even allowed news organizations to start up through the site. @BreakingNews aggregates news from all sites around the world and pushes it to users through their account, often much faster than the average large news corporations like CNN will pick it up.

Twitter's appeal extends much farther than just news and advertising, however. Celebrities really fueled the site's popularity in the site's beginnings. Ashton Kutcher famously was in a race with news organization CNN to get one million followers. The movie star posted videos and blogs appealing to his fans to create accounts and follow him, which most did. In response to his eventual winning of the race, Kutcher donated 10,000 mosquito nets to charity. Justin Bieber, Britney Spears, and Diddy all tweet to their followers, sometimes even replying to their followers. Most recently, Charlie Sheen took to Twitter, setting a record for the fastest time gaining one million followers. Users are now set up to get real time updates from him and watch his (what some would call spiraling) life.

Twitter took the simple concept of a status update and built an empire around it. The site may have started out as a social network; however, it can be considered in some aspects as a social media outlet. The constant flow of information provided, from real news to entertainment to updates from friends, makes the site both appealing and useful.

*Title suggests the subject*

*Thesis statement*

*Topic sentence makes first point*

*Examples of companies using Twitter to develop their brands*

*Topic sentence makes second point*

*Specific example of the use of Twitter in news reporting*

*Topic sentence makes third point*

*Examples of celebrities using Twitter*

*Conclusion*

## Examining Writing

1. Evaluate the examples Dube used to support his thesis statement. Did he provide enough examples? What other kinds of evidence could he have used to support his thesis?

2. How did Dube organize his essay? Summarize his main points in your own words.

3. What transitions did Dube use to guide the reader?

4. Evaluate the conclusion. How might it be more effective?

## READ AND RESPOND: A Professional Essay

### Thinking Before Reading

The following selection originally appeared in a music textbook. In the selection, the authors explore the effects of music on the human brain.

1. Preview the reading, using the steps discussed in Chapter 1 on page 25.

2. Connect the reading to your own experience by answering the following questions:

   a. How do you feel when you listen to music?

   b. What types of music do you enjoy? Why?

3. Highlight and annotate as you read.

1140**L**/738 words

# The Benefits of Listening to Music
## Steven Cornelius and Mary Natvig

"Music produces a kind of pleasure which human nature cannot do without."

—Confucius (ca. 551 BCE to 479 BCE)

1 Ninety-three-year-old Veva Campbell slumps wordlessly in her wheelchair. A victim of Alzheimer's disease, she has not spoken, walked, fed herself, or recognized friends and family for over two years. This afternoon, her granddaughter, an out-of-town musician, comes to visit. There is nothing to say or do, so she pulls out her violin and begins to play. Miraculously, Mrs. Campbell sits up and begins singing along to the traditional hymns and old-time songs she recognizes from her youth. When the music stops, Mrs. Campbell retreats back into silence.

2 Our story is not apocryphal. Mrs. Campbell was the coauthor's grandmother. And this demonstration of music's power, remarkable as it may be, is not an isolated example. All over the world music unites and heals, transforms and inspires. This appears to have been the case since the beginning of civilization.

### Music and the Brain

3 The foundation of musical experience resides deep within the mind. Medical science is just beginning to document these complexities. We know, for example, that

severe stutterers, even those unable to get out single spoken words, can sometimes perfectly sing entire sentences. We know that by setting instructions to song, sufferers of autism can learn to execute sequential tasks otherwise far beyond their reach. And we know that when medication fails, those with the neuropsychiatric disorder Tourette syndrome can successfully use drum circles to calm their tics.

4    There is much to learn. Scientists cannot explain the case of Tony Cicoria, a middle-aged physician who, after being struck by lightning, suddenly developed a passion and gift for playing the piano and composing. Nor can they explain the case of Clive Wearing, a British amnesia victim who, despite being able to remember just a few seconds into the past, can still play the piano, read music, and even direct choral rehearsals.

5    The human brain seems to be programmed for song. So fundamental is the human capacity for music that it may have evolved even before speech. Physiologists have shown that a mother's lullaby does double duty by lowering a child's arousal levels while simultaneously increasing the child's ability to focus attention. Music therapists have found that listening to music induces the release of pleasure-producing endorphins that both lower blood pressure and ease the sensation of physical pain. Social scientists believe that music, by bringing people together to perform and listen, may have provided an early model for social cooperation, cohesion, and even reproductive success. If this is correct, then music would seem to be a fundamental building block in the development of culture.

6    Attentive listening is good for the brain. It helps us organize our thinking, give shape to our consciousness, and focus our ideas. These phenomena seem to happen for a variety of reasons and in a number of ways. Our involuntary nervous system—including heart rate, brain waves, and other basic bodily functions—automatically entrains to the sounds we hear. We also respond to music's emotional qualities. Lovely melodies softly played relax us, whereas beating drums and searing trumpets excite us. A favorite song recalls times gone by, whereas the sounds of a national anthem invite us to reflect upon our identity.

7    Music helps structure the analytical mind. Psychological studies suggest that musical training improves one's organizational skills and can even have a positive effect on IQ. Indeed, scientists hypothesize that while performing, musicians are actually engaged in high-powered brain calisthenics. These skills transfer to other areas of life.

## DID YOU KNOW?

### EARS, BRAIN, AND FINGERS

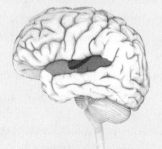

**The human brain, highlighting the auditory cortex.**
The auditory cortex, which grows with musical training, can be up to 130 percent larger in musicians than in nonmusicians. Brains grow when challenged with physical tasks as well. The part of the brain that governs a violinist's left-hand fingers will be larger than the part that governs the right-hand fingers. Presumably, Jimi Hendrix, who played the guitar "backwards," would have shown more brain growth for the right-hand fingers.

8    Clearly, active musical experience affects consciousness in profound ways. But what does this mean for you? What if you do not play music, sing, or dance? Research shows that one need not perform to reap music's benefits. Simply engaging in *active* listening is enough to set the brain in high gear. And the best part of all this is that the effects of listening skills are cumulative. The better you learn to listen today, the more listening techniques you will have available tomorrow.

—Cornelius and Natvig, *Music: A Social Experience*, pp. 2–3

## Getting Ready to Write

### Checking Your Comprehension

Answer each of the following questions using complete sentences.

1. What four conditions or disorders do the authors use to illustrate the benefits of listening to music?
2. Who are Tony Cicoria and Clive Wearing and why are they included in the selection?
3. What are two physiological effects of a mother's lullaby?
4. In what three ways do the authors say attentive listening is good for the brain?
5. What are two psychological effects of musical training?
6. What is the difference between the auditory cortex in musicians and nonmusicians?

### Strengthening Your Vocabulary

Using the word's context, word parts, or a dictionary, write a brief definition of each of the following words as it is used in the reading.

1. apocryphal (paragraph 2) _____ *false* _____
2. sequential (paragraph 3) _____ *in order* _____
3. induces (paragraph 5) _____ *causes* _____
4. cohesion (paragraph 5) _____ *unity* _____
5. entrains (paragraph 6) _____ *adjusts to go along with* _____
6. profound (paragraph 8) _____ *deeply significant* _____

## Examining the Reading: Using Idea Maps

Review the reading by completing the missing parts of the following idea map.

**VISUALIZE IT!**

Title **The Benefits of Listening to Music**

Thesis Music has a powerful impact on the human brain.

Medical effects are not understood

Stuttering, autism, and *Tourette syndrome*

Human brain seems programmed for song

Physiologists showed that mother's lullaby affects child by:

Lowering arousal levels

*Increasing ability to focus attention*

Music therapists found listening to music releases endorphins that:

*Lower blood pressure*

Ease sensation of pain

Social scientists believe music provided early model for *culture*

Attentive listening helps us to:

*Organize our thinking*

*Give shape to our consciousness*

*Focus our ideas*

Musical training may:

Improve *organizational skills*

Have a positive effect on IQ

Conclusion Active musical experience and engaging in active listening both offer benefits.

## Thinking Critically: Discussion and Journal Writing

React and respond to the reading by discussing the following:

1. What is the purpose of the example of Veva Campbell that is used in the first two paragraphs?

2. What type of music do you choose to listen to for different purposes or moods? Write a journal entry describing the types of music you listen to when you are happy, are sad, or need to accomplish a task.

3. Discuss the term "brain calisthenics" (paragraph 7). What other kinds of brain exercises can you think of?

4. Discuss the use of music as a form of therapy. In addition to the examples in the selection, what other applications can you think of for music therapy?

5. What is the purpose of the drawing that accompanies the selection?

**THINKING VISUALLY**

MySkillsLab®

**Complete** this Exercise

## Writing About the Reading

### Paragraph Options

1. Choose a musical performer or group you enjoy and identify several factors that make him, her, or them popular. Give an example illustrating each factor.

2. What makes a song or a particular piece of music appealing to you? Write a paragraph describing three of your favorite songs (or other pieces of music) and explaining why you like them.

3. Write a paragraph comparing listening to recorded music, such as on an iPod, to attending a live concert.

### Essay Options

4. How do you typically listen to music? What is your favorite music for different activities, such as studying, going out, or relaxing at home? Write an essay answering these questions.

5. What would you say are the three most important reasons you listen to music? Write an essay explaining your answer.

6. Choose two songs that you enjoy or two musical artists that you listen to and write a comparison or contrast essay examining their similarities or differences.

# SELF-TEST SUMMARY

To test yourself, cover the Answer column with a sheet of paper and answer each question in the left column. Evaluate each of your answers as you work by sliding the paper down and comparing your answer with what is printed in the Answer column.

| QUESTION | ANSWER |
|---|---|
| ■ GOAL 1  Understand examples<br><br>What are examples? | *Examples* are specific instances or situations that explain a general idea, statement, or concept. |
| ■ GOAL 2  Read examples<br><br>How do writers organize paragraphs when using examples? | Writers often state the main idea first and then follow it with one or more examples. |
| ■ GOAL 3  Write examples<br><br>What are four guidelines for selecting useful and effective examples? | (1) Each example should illustrate the idea stated in your topic sentence; (2) each example should be specific, vivid, and accurate; (3) choose a sufficient number of examples to make your point; and (4) draw the connection for your reader between your example and your main point. |
| ■ GOAL 4  Understand cause and effect<br><br>Why do writers use cause and effect? | Writers use the cause and effect pattern to explain why an event or action causes another event or action. |
| ■ GOAL 5  Read cause and effect<br><br>How do you read cause and effect? | When you read cause and effect paragraphs, focus on the connections between or among the events being described. |
| ■ GOAL 6  Write cause and effect<br><br>How do you write effective topic sentences for cause and effect paragraphs? | Clarify the cause and effect relationship; decide whether to emphasize causes or effects; and determine whether the events are related or independent. |
| ■ GOAL 7  Understand comparison and contrast<br><br>What does the comparison and contrast pattern do? | The comparison and contrast pattern emphasizes the similarities or differences between two or more items. |
| ■ GOAL 8  Read comparison and contrast<br><br>How do you read comparison and contrast effectively? | Passages that show comparison and/or contrast can be organized in different ways. To read comparison and contrast effectively, follow the pattern of ideas and look for transitional words and phrases to guide you through the material. |

*(Continued)*

| QUESTION | ANSWER |
|---|---|
| ■ **GOAL 9** Write comparison and contrast<br><br>What are two ways of organizing a comparison or contrast paragraph? | In the subject-by-subject method, you write first about one of your subjects and then about the other, ideally covering the same points of comparison and contrast for both. In the point-by-point method, you discuss both of your subjects together for each point of comparison and contrast. |

# MySkillsLab

For more help with **Patterns of Organization**, go to your learning path in MySkillsLab at http://www.myskillslab.com.

# 14 Revision and Proofreading

## THINK About It!

Write a sentence describing the garden in the upper left photograph. No doubt you found there was a limited amount of information in it. Now write a sentence describing the garden in the second photograph. How do your descriptions differ?

Many ineffective paragraphs are like the first photograph above. They do not provide enough information and leave the reader frustrated and confused. An effective paragraph contains details that explain and illustrate the topic sentence, like the photo of the summer garden where an abundance of flowers and vegetables illustrate how to grow a successful garden. In this chapter you will learn how to revise paragraphs so they provide your readers with plenty of information. You will also learn to read, examine, and analyze your drafts closely to find problems and errors.

## FOCUSING ON READING AND WRITING

# What Are Revision and Proofreading?

**Revision** is a process of examining and rethinking your ideas as they appear in sentence and paragraph form. It involves finding ways to make your writing clearer, more effective, more complete, and more interesting. When revising you may change, add, delete, or rearrange your ideas and how you have expressed them to improve your writing. Revision also involves careful reading and critical thinking. You have to read closely to determine whether you have said exactly what you meant to say. Then you must be able to step back from what you have written and ask yourself the questions: Will my readers understand what I have written? and Is my message clear? Using the process of peer review, you may also find suggestions from classmates helpful.

**Proofreading** focuses on correctness and involves checking for errors in grammar, spelling, punctuation, and capitalization. It also involves formatting your paragraph to make it easy to read. Proofreading requires close and careful reading, working word by word and sentence by sentence, searching for and correcting errors.

## READING

# Read Carefully and Critically for Revision

■ GOAL 1
Read carefully and
critically for revision

The first step in preparing to revise a draft is to read it critically with the purpose of finding out what works and what doesn't. Use the following suggestions:

- **Create distance.** It is easy to like your own work and see nothing wrong with it. Mentally prepare yourself to look at your writing critically by creating distance between yourself and your work. Try setting it aside for a day or so. Then, when you return, examine it as if someone else wrote it.

- **Plan on and allow enough time to read your draft several times.** It is difficult to check for all aspects of writing at the same time. Each time, read it for a different purpose, using a strategy such as the following:

  **Step 1: Read the draft once, examining your ideas:** Have you said what you want to say? If not, make the necessary changes.

  **Step 2: Read the draft again, evaluating how effectively you have expressed your ideas, again making changes to improve the draft.** Reread to make sure your changes work.

  **Step 3: Read it a third time, checking for correctness.** You might want to read the draft several times, looking for one common error at a time.

- **Print a copy of your draft.** It may be easier to see mistakes or problems if you are reading print copy rather than reading from your computer screen.
- **Read with a pen in hand.** Mark and make notes as you read and reread. If you see something that doesn't sound right or an idea that needs further explanation, mark it so you don't overlook it as you start to rewrite.
- **Read aloud.** When you hear your ideas aloud, you may realize they sound choppy or that a statement seems to stand alone without adequate explanation or support.
- **Check with classmates.** After reading the draft several times, if you are still unsure of what to revise, check with a classmate. Ask him or her to read your draft and offer comments and suggestions. For more on this process, called peer review, see page 468 of this chapter.

# WRITING

# Determine How and When to Revise

■ GOAL 2
Determine how and when to revise

As mentioned above, it is usually best after writing a draft to wait a day before beginning to revise it. You will have a fresh outlook on your topic and will find that it is easier to see what you need to change, add, or delete.

Even after giving yourself some distance from your work, it may be difficult to know how to improve your own writing. Simply rereading may not help you discover flaws, weaknesses, or needed changes. The remainder of this section offers guidelines to follow and questions to ask to help you spot problems. It also shows you how to use a revision map and includes a revision checklist to guide your revision.

# Revise Ineffective Paragraphs

■ GOAL 3
Revise ineffective paragraphs

To revise a paragraph, begin by examining your topic sentence and then, once you are satisfied with it, determine whether you have provided adequate details to support it.

## Revise Ineffective Topic Sentences

Your topic sentence is the sentence around which your paragraph is built, so be sure it is strong and effective. The most common problems with topic sentences include

- The topic sentence lacks a point of view.
- The topic sentence is too broad.
- The topic sentence is too narrow.

Each of these problems is addressed in Chapter 10, page 309. Be sure to review this section.

| EXERCISE 14-1 | Writing a Paragraph |

**Directions:** Write a paragraph on one of the following topics. Evaluate your topic sentence to determine whether it is too broad, is too narrow, or lacks a point of view.

1. A memorable wedding or funeral

2. Your favorite holiday

3. A favorite character in a book or movie

4. A person who is a hero to you

5. An embarrassing experience

## Revise Paragraphs to Add Supporting Details

The details in a paragraph should give your reader sufficient information to make your topic sentence believable. Paragraphs that lack necessary detail are called **underdeveloped paragraphs.** Underdeveloped paragraphs lack supporting sentences to prove or explain the point made in the topic sentence. As you read the following student paragraph, keep the topic sentence in mind and consider whether the rest of the sentences support it.

### Sample Student Paragraph

I am a very impatient person, and my impatience interferes with how easily I can get through a day. If I ask for something, I want it immediately. If I'm going somewhere and I'm ready and somebody else isn't, I get very upset. I hate driving behind someone who drives slowly when I cannot pass. I think that annoys me the most, and it never happens unless I am in a hurry. If I were less impatient, I would probably feel more relaxed and less pressured.

This paragraph begins with a topic sentence that is focused (it is neither too broad nor too narrow) and that includes a point of view. It promises to explain how the writer's impatience makes it difficult for him to get through a day. However, the rest of the paragraph does not fulfill this promise. Instead, the writer gives two very general examples of his impatience: (1) wanting something and (2) waiting for someone. The third example, driving behind a slow driver, is a little more specific, but it is not developed well. The last sentence suggests, but does not explain, that the writer's impatience makes him feel tense and pressured.

Taking into account the need for more supporting detail, the author revised his paragraph as follows:

### Revised Paragraph

I am a very impatient person, and my impatience interferes with how easily I can get through a day. For example, when I decide to buy something, such as a new phone, I *have* to have it right away—that day. I usually drop everything and run to the store. Of course, I shortchange myself on studying, and that hurts my grades. My impatience hurts me, too, when I'm waiting for someone, which I hate to do. If my friend Alex and I agree to meet at noon to work on his car, I get annoyed if he's even five minutes late. Then I usually end up saying something nasty or sarcastic like "What a surprise, you're actually here!" which I regret later. Perhaps I am most impatient when I'm behind the steering wheel. If I get behind a slow driver, I get annoyed and start honking and beeping my horn. I know this might fluster the other driver, and afterwards I feel guilty. I've tried talking to myself to calm down; sometimes it works, so I hope I'm overcoming this bad trait.

Did you notice that the writer became much more specific in the revised version? He gave an example of something he wanted—a phone—and he described his actions and their consequences. The example of waiting for someone was provided by the incident involving his friend Alex. Finally, the writer explained the driving example in more detail and stated its consequences. With the extra details and supporting examples, the paragraph is more interesting and effective.

The following suggestions will help you revise an underdeveloped paragraph:

- **Analyze your paragraph sentence by sentence.** If a sentence does not add new, specific information to your paragraph, delete it or add to it so that it becomes relevant.

- **Think of specific situations, facts, or examples that illustrate or support your topic.** Often you can make a general sentence more specific.

- **Brainstorm, freewrite, or branch.** To come up with additional details or examples to use in your paragraph, try some prewriting techniques. If necessary, start fresh with a new approach and new set of ideas.

- **Reexamine your topic sentence.** If you are having trouble generating details, your topic sentence may be the problem. Consider changing the approach.

> EXAMPLE   Rainy days make me feel depressed.
>
> REVISED   Rainy days, although depressing, give me a chance to catch up on household chores.

- **Consider changing your topic.** If a paragraph remains troublesome, look for a new topic and start over.

| EXERCISE 14-2 | Revising a Paragraph |

**Directions:** The following paragraph is poorly developed. What suggestions would you make to the writer to improve the paragraph? Write them in the space provided. Be specific. Which sentences are weak? How could each be improved? *Answers will vary. Possible answers are shown.*

> I am attending college to improve myself. By attending college, I am getting an education to improve the skills that I'll need for a good career in broadcasting. Then, after a successful career, I'll be able to get the things that I need to be happy in my life. People will also respect me more.

*Make the topic sentence more specific; focus on one or several aspects of self-improvement.*

*Add detail. Name and describe the skills needed for broadcasting. Indicate how a general*

*education or specific courses will provide those skills. Revise and combine the last two sen-*

*tences to draw the paragraph to a close.*

| EXERCISE 14-3 | Evaluating a Paragraph |

**Directions:** Evaluate the following paragraph by answering the questions that follow it. *Answers will vary. Possible answers are shown.*

> One of the best ways to keep people happy and occupied is to entertain them. Every day people are being entertained, whether it is by a friend for a split second or by a Broadway play for several hours. Entertainment is probably one of the nation's biggest businesses. Entertainment has come a long way from the past; it has gone from plays in the park to films in eight-screen movie theaters.

1. Evaluate the topic sentence. What is wrong with it? How could it be revised?

   *The topic sentence is too general. Focus on one kind of entertainment and discuss*

   *its benefits.*

2. Write a more effective topic sentence about entertainment.

   *Television entertainment keeps viewers occupied and happy.*

3. Evaluate the supporting details. What is wrong with them?

   *They need to be more specific.*

   What should the writer do to develop her paragraph?

   *Add descriptive and relevant detail.*

4. Use the topic sentence you wrote in question 2 above to develop a paragraph about entertainment.

| EXERCISE 14-4 | Revising a Paragraph |
| --- | --- |

**Directions:** Draw an idea map of the paragraph you wrote in Exercise 14-1. Revise your paragraph as needed, using the suggestions in this chapter.

---

> ## ❗ NEED TO KNOW
>
> ### Adding Supporting Details
>
> To revise an underdeveloped paragraph,
>
> - analyze your paragraph sentence by sentence.
> - think of specific situations, facts, or examples that illustrate or support your main point.
> - use brainstorming, freewriting, or branching.
> - reexamine your topic sentence.
> - consider changing your topic.

# Use Idea Maps to Spot Revision Problems

■ GOAL 4
Use idea maps to spot revision problems

Some students find revision a troublesome step because it is difficult for them to see what is wrong with their own work. After working hard on a first draft, it is tempting to say to yourself that you've done a great job and to think, "This is fine." Other times, you may think you have explained and supported an idea clearly when actually you have not. In other words, you may be blind to your own paper's weaknesses. Almost all writing, however, needs and benefits from revision. An idea map can help you spot weaknesses and discover what you may not have done as well as you thought.

An idea map will show how each of your ideas fits with and relates to all of the other ideas in a paragraph or essay. When you draw an idea map, you reduce your ideas to a skeleton form that allows you to see and analyze them more easily.

In this section you will learn how to use an idea map to (1) discover problems in a paragraph and (2) guide your revision. This section will discuss five questions to ask that will help you identify weaknesses in your writing, and it will suggest ways to revise your paragraphs to correct each weakness.

- Does the paragraph stray from the topic?
- Does every detail belong?
- Are the details arranged and developed logically?
- Is the paragraph balanced?
- Is the paragraph repetitious?

## Does the Paragraph Stray from the Topic?

When you are writing a first draft of a paragraph, it is easy to drift away from the topic. As you write, one idea triggers another, and that idea another, and eventually you end up with ideas that have little or nothing to do with your original topic, as in the following first-draft student paragraph.

### *Sample Student Paragraph*

#### One Example of Toxic Waste

The disposal of toxic waste has caused serious health hazards. Love Canal is one of the many toxic dump sites that have caused serious health problems. This dump site in particular was used by a large number of nearby industries. The canal was named after a man named Love. Love Canal, in my opinion, was an eye-opener on the subject of toxic dump sites. It took about ten years to clean the dump site up to a livable condition. Many people living near Love Canal developed cancers. There were many miscarriages and birth defects. This dump site might have caused irreversible damage to our environment, so I am glad it has been cleaned up.

The following idea map shows the topic sentence of the paragraph and, underneath it, the supporting details that directly relate to the topic sentence. All the unrelated details are in a list to the right of the map. Note that the concluding sentence is also included in the map, since it is an important part of the paragraph.

**VISUALIZE IT!**

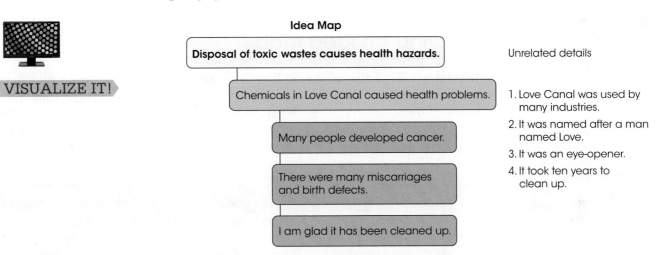

**Idea Map**

| Disposal of toxic wastes causes health hazards. |
| --- |

Chemicals in Love Canal caused health problems.

Many people developed cancer.

There were many miscarriages and birth defects.

I am glad it has been cleaned up.

Unrelated details

1. Love Canal was used by many industries.
2. It was named after a man named Love.
3. It was an eye-opener.
4. It took ten years to clean up.

In this paragraph the author began by supporting her topic sentence with the example of Love Canal. However, she began to drift when she explained how Love Canal was named. To revise this paragraph, the author could include more detailed information about Love Canal health hazards or examples of other disposal sites and their health hazards.

You can use an idea map to spot where you begin to drift away from your topic. To do this, take the last idea in the map and compare it with your topic sentence.

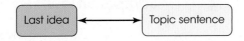

Last idea ⟷ Topic sentence

Does the last idea directly support your topic sentence? If not, you may have drifted from your topic. Check the second-to-last detail, going through the same comparison process. Working backward, you'll see where you started to drift. This is the point at which to begin revising.

### What to Do If You Stray Off Topic

Use the following suggestions to revise your paragraph if it strays from your topic:

- **Locate the last sentence that does relate to your topic, and begin your revision there.** What could you say next that *would* relate to the topic?

- **Consider expanding your existing ideas.** If, after two or three details, you have strayed from your topic, consider expanding the details you have, rather than searching for additional details.

- **Reread your brainstorming, freewriting, or branching to find more details.** Look for additional ideas that support your topic. Do more brainstorming, if necessary.

- **Consider changing your topic.** Drifting from your topic is not always a loss. Sometimes by drifting you discover a more interesting topic than your original one. If you decide to change topics, revise your entire paragraph. Begin by rewriting your topic sentence.

---

**EXERCISE 14-5** ## Drawing an Idea Map

**Directions:** Read the following first-draft paragraph. Then draw an idea map that includes the topic sentence, only those details that support the topic sentence, and the concluding sentence. List the unrelated details to the side of the map, as in the example on page 457. Identify where the writer began to stray from the topic, and make specific suggestions for revising this paragraph.

*Topic sentence*
*The author drifts off topic once she mentions and discusses addiction. She needs to provide reasons why junk food lacks nutrition. She could add examples to support her reasons.*

Junk food lacks nutrition and is high in calories. Junk food can be anything from candy and potato chips to ice cream and desserts. All of these are high in calories. But they are so tasty that they are addictive. Once a person is addicted to junk food, it is very hard to break the addiction. To break the habit, one must give up any form of sugar. And I have not gone back to my old lifestyle in over two weeks. So it is possible to break an addiction, but I still have the craving.

---

## Does Every Detail Belong?

Every detail in a paragraph must directly support the topic sentence or one of the other details. Unrelated information should not be included, a mistake one student made in the following first-draft paragraph.

### Sample Student Paragraph

In a world where stress is an everyday occurrence, many people relieve stress through entertainment. There are many ways to entertain ourselves and relieve stress. Many people watch movies to take their minds off day-to-day problems. However, going to the movies costs a lot of money. Due to the cost, some people rent or stream movies. Playing sports is another stress reliever. Exercise always helps to give people a positive attitude and keeps them in shape.

Racquetball really keeps you in shape because it is such a fast game. A third form of entertainment is going out with friends. With friends, people can talk about their problems and feel better about them. But some friends always talk and never listen, and such conversation creates stress instead of relieving it. So if you are under stress, be sure to reserve some time for entertainment.

The following idea map shows that this writer included four unrelated details:

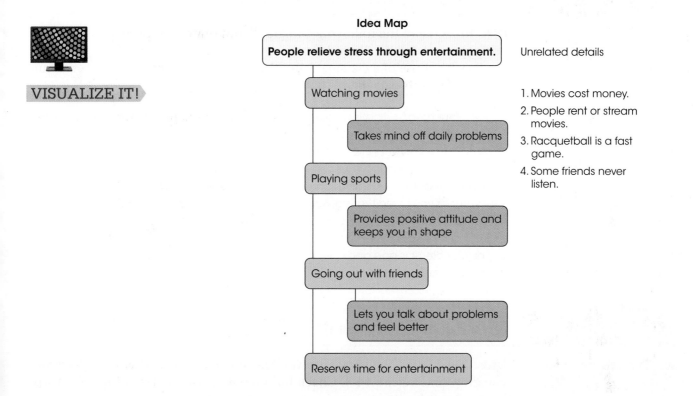

**VISUALIZE IT!**

**Idea Map**

People relieve stress through entertainment.

Unrelated details

Watching movies

Takes mind off daily problems

1. Movies cost money.
2. People rent or stream movies.
3. Racquetball is a fast game.
4. Some friends never listen.

Playing sports

Provides positive attitude and keeps you in shape

Going out with friends

Lets you talk about problems and feel better

Reserve time for entertainment

To spot unrelated details, draw an idea map. To decide whether a detail is unrelated, ask, "Does this detail directly explain the topic sentence or one of the other details?" If you are not sure, ask, "What happens if I take this out?" If meaning is lost or if confusion occurs, the detail is important. Include it in your map. If you can make your point just as well without the detail, mark it "unrelated."

In the sample student paragraph, the high cost of movies and the low-cost alternatives of renting or streaming them do not directly explain how or why movies are entertaining. The racquetball detail does not explain how exercise relieves stress. The detail about friends not listening does not explain how talking to friends is helpful in reducing stress.

### Making Sure Every Detail Belongs

The following suggestions will help you use supporting details more effectively:

■ **Add explanations to make the connections between your ideas clearer.** Often a detail may not seem to relate to the topic because you have not explained *how* it relates. For example, health-care insurance may seem to have little to do with the prevention of breast cancer deaths until you explain that mammograms, which are paid for by some health-care plans, can prevent deaths.

■ **Add transitions.** Transitions make it clearer to your reader how one detail relates to another.

■ **Add new details.** If you've deleted several nonessential details, your paragraph may be too sketchy. Return to the prewriting step to generate more details you can include.

---

**EXERCISE 14-6**

*WORKING TOGETHER*

## Identifying Unrelated Details

**Directions:** Read the following paragraph and draw an idea map of it. Underline any unrelated details and list them to the side of your map. Compare your results with those of a classmate and then decide what steps the writer should take to revise this paragraph.

> Your credit rating is a valuable thing that you should protect and watch over. A credit rating is a record of your loans, credit card charges, and repayment history. If you pay a bill late or miss a payment, that information becomes part of your credit rating. It is, therefore, important to pay bills promptly. Some people just don't keep track of dates; some don't even know what date it is today. Errors can occur in your credit rating. Someone else's mistakes can be put on your record, for example. Why these credit-rating companies can't take more time and become more accurate is beyond my understanding. It is worthwhile to get a copy of your credit report and check it for errors. Time spent caring for your credit rating will be time well spent.

---

**EXERCISE 14-7**

**WRITING IN PROGRESS**

## Identifying Unrelated Details

**Directions:** Study the paragraph you wrote in exercise 14-1 and the idea map you drew for Exercise 14-4. Check for unrelated details. If you find any, revise your paragraph using the suggestions given above.

---

### Are the Details Arranged and Developed Logically?

Details in a paragraph should follow some logical order. As you write a first draft, you are often more concerned with expressing your ideas than with presenting them in the correct order. As you revise, however, you should make sure you have followed a logical arrangement. Chapter 11 discusses various methods of arranging and developing details. The following "Need to Know" box reviews these arrangements:

---

**！ NEED TO KNOW**

#### Methods of Arranging and Developing Details

| METHOD | DESCRIPTION |
|---|---|
| • Time sequence | Arranges details in the order in which they happen |
| • Spatial | Arranges details according to their physical location |
| • Least/most | Arranges details from least to most or from most to least, according to some quality or characteristic |

Chapters 12 and 13 discuss several methods of organizing and presenting material. The "Need to Know" box below reviews these arrangements.

## NEED TO KNOW

### Methods of Organizing and Presenting Material

| METHOD | DESCRIPTION |
| --- | --- |
| • Chronological order | Arranges events in the order in which they occurred |
| • Process | Arranges steps in the order in which they are to be completed |
| • Narration | Makes a point by telling a story |
| • Description | Arranges descriptive details spatially or uses the least/most arrangement |
| • Example | Explains by giving situations that illustrate a general idea or statement |
| • Cause and effect | Explains why something happened or what happened as a result of a particular action |
| • Comparison and contrast | Explains an idea by comparing or contrasting it with another, usually more familiar, idea |

Your ideas need a logical arrangement to make them easy to follow. Poor organization creates misunderstanding and confusion. After drafting the following paragraph, a student drew an idea map that showed her organization was haphazard.

### Sample Student Paragraph

When I was pregnant with my son, I wondered if life would ever be normal again. There were the nights I couldn't sleep because of all the kicking and the baby moving up to my lungs so I couldn't breathe. That was when I really had it! Each month I got bigger and bigger, and after a while I was so big I couldn't bend over or see my feet. Then there was the morning sickness. I don't know why they call it that because you're sick all the time for the first two months. Then there were all those doctor visits during which she told me, "Not for another week or two." Of course, when I realized my clothes didn't fit, I broke down and cried. But all of a sudden everything started up, and I was at the hospital delivering the baby two weeks early, and it's like it happened so fast and it was all over, and I had the most beautiful baby in my arms and I knew it was worth all that pain and suffering.

An idea map lets you see quickly when a paragraph has no organization or when an idea is out of order. This student's map (p. 462), showed that her paragraph did not present the events of her pregnancy in the most logical

VISUALIZE IT!

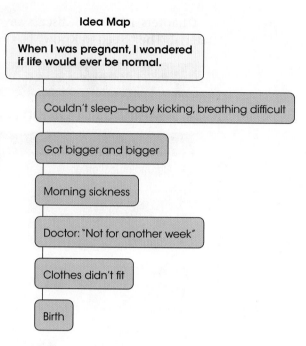

arrangement: time sequence. She therefore reorganized the events in the order in which they happened and revised her paragraph as follows:

## Revised Paragraph

When I was pregnant with my son, I wondered if life would ever be normal again. First there was the morning sickness. I don't know why they call it that because I was sick all the time for the first two months. Of course, when I realized my clothes didn't fit, I broke down and cried. Each month I got bigger and bigger, and finally I was so big I couldn't bend over or see my feet. Then there were the nights I couldn't sleep because of all the kicking and the baby moving up to my lungs so I couldn't breathe. That was when I really had it. Finally, there were all those doctor visits during which she told me, "Not for another week or two." But all of a sudden everything started to happen, and I was at the hospital delivering the baby two weeks early. Everything happened so fast. It was all over, and I had the most beautiful baby in my arms. Then I knew it was worth all that pain and suffering.

### Arranging and Developing Details Logically

The following suggestions will help you revise your paragraph if it lacks organization:

- **Review the methods of arranging and developing details and of organizing and presenting material** (see the "Need to Know" boxes on pp. 460–461). Will one of those arrangements work? If so, number the ideas in your idea map according to the arrangement you choose. Then begin revising your paragraph.

  If you find one or more details out of logical order in your paragraph, do the following:

1. **Number the details in your idea map to indicate the correct order, and revise your paragraph accordingly.**

2.  **Reread your revised paragraph and draw another idea map.**
3.  **Look to see if you've omitted necessary details.** After you have placed your details in a logical order, you are more likely to recognize gaps.

■ **Look at your topic sentence again.** If you are working with a revised arrangement of supporting details, you may need to revise your topic sentence to reflect that arrangement.

■ **Check whether additional details are needed.** Suppose, for example, you are writing about an exciting experience, and you decide to use the time-sequence arrangement. Once you make that decision, you may need to add details to enable your reader to understand exactly how the experience happened.

■ **Add transitions.** Transitions help make your organization obvious and easy to follow.

---

### EXERCISE 14-8 | Evaluating Arrangement of Ideas

**Directions:** Read the following student paragraph, and draw an idea map of it. Evaluate the arrangement of ideas. What revisions would you suggest?

> The minimum wage is not an easily resolved problem; it has both advantages and disadvantages. Its primary advantage is that it does guarantee workers a minimum wage. It prevents the economic abuse of workers. Employers cannot take advantage of workers by paying them less than the minimum. Its primary disadvantage is that the minimum wage is not sufficient for older workers with families to support. For younger workers, such as teenagers, however, this minimum is fine. It provides them with spending money and some economic freedom from their parents. Another disadvantage is that as long as people, such as a teenagers, are willing to work for the minimum, employers don't need to pay a higher wage. Thus, the minimum wage prevents experienced workers from getting more money. But the minimum wage does help our economy by requiring a certain level of income per worker.

---

### EXERCISE 14-9 | Evaluating Arrangement of Ideas

**WRITING IN PROGRESS**

**Directions:** Review the paragraph and idea map you revised for Exercise 14-7. Evaluate the logical arrangement of your points and details, and revise if needed.

---

### Is the Paragraph Balanced?

An effective paragraph achieves a balance among its points. That is, each idea receives an appropriate amount of supporting detail and emphasis. The following student paragraph lacks balance, as the idea map that follows it shows.

## *Sample Student Paragraph*

### Waiting

Waiting is very annoying, exhausting, and time-consuming. Waiting to buy books at the college store is an example of a very long and tiresome task. I need to buy books, and so does everyone else. This causes the lines to be very long. Most of the time I find myself leaning against the wall daydreaming. Sometimes I will even leave the line and hope to come back when the store isn't extremely busy. But that never works because everyone else seems to get the same idea. So I finally realize that I just have to wait. Another experience is waiting for a ride home from school or work. My ride always seems to be the last car to pull up in the parking lot. When I am waiting for my ride, I often wonder what it would be like to own a car or if I will ever make it home. Waiting in line at a fast-food restaurant is also annoying because, if it is fast, I shouldn't have to wait. Waiting for an elevator is also no fun. Waiting just seems to be a part of life, so I might as well accept it.

**VISUALIZE IT!**

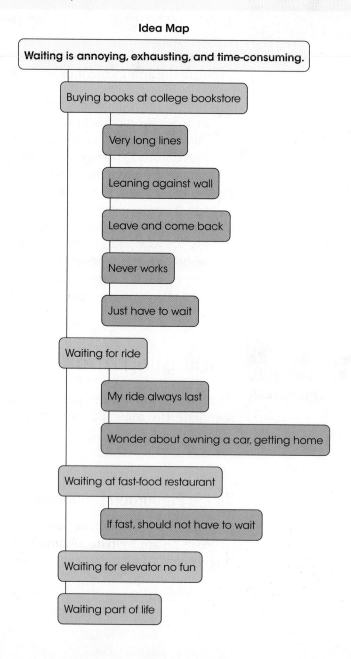

**Idea Map**

**Waiting is annoying, exhausting, and time-consuming.**

Buying books at college bookstore

Very long lines

Leaning against wall

Leave and come back

Never works

Just have to wait

Waiting for ride

My ride always last

Wonder about owning a car, getting home

Waiting at fast-food restaurant

If fast, should not have to wait

Waiting for elevator no fun

Waiting part of life

As the idea map on the previous page shows, a major portion of the paragraph is devoted to waiting in line to buy books. The second example, waiting for a ride, is not as thoroughly explained. The third example, waiting at a fast-food restaurant, is treated in even less detail, and the fourth, waiting for an elevator, has the least detail. To revise, the writer should expand the treatment of waiting for rides, fast food, and elevators, and perhaps decrease the treatment of the bookstore experience. An alternative solution would be for the writer to expand the bookstore experience and eliminate the other examples. In this case, a new topic sentence would be needed.

### Making Sure Your Paragraph is Balanced

The following suggestions will help you revise your paragraph for balance:

- **Not every point or example must have the *same* amount of explanation.** For example, more complicated ideas require more explanation than simpler, more obvious ones. When you are using a least/most arrangement, the more important details may need more coverage than the less important ones.

- **If two ideas are equally important and equally complicated, they should receive similar treatment.** For instance, if you include an example or statistic in support of one idea, you should do so for the other.

---

**EXERCISE 14-10** | Evaluating Balance of Details

**Directions:** Read the following paragraph, and draw an idea map of it. Evaluate the balance of details and indicate where more details are needed.

> I am considering buying a puppy. There are four breeds I am looking at: golden retrievers, beagles, Newfoundlands, and cocker spaniels. Cocker spaniels are cute, but golden retrievers are cute *and* intelligent. Golden retrievers are very gentle with children, and I have two sons. They are also very loyal. But they have a lot of fur, and they shed, unlike beagles, which have short fur. Newfoundlands are very large, and they have dark-colored fur that would show up on my rug. Newfoundlands also drool a lot. My apartment is small, so a Newfoundland is probably just too big, furry, and clumsy.

---

**EXERCISE 14-11** | Evaluating Balance of Details

**WRITING IN PROGRESS**

**Directions:** Review the paragraph and idea map you last revised for Exercise 14-9. Evaluate the balance of details, and revise if necessary.

---

## Is the Paragraph Repetitious?

In a first draft, you may express the same idea more than once, each time in a slightly different way. As you are writing a first draft, repetitive statements may help you stay on track. They keep you writing and help generate new ideas. However, it is important to eliminate repetition at the revision stage. Repetitive statements add nothing to your paragraph. They detract from its clarity. An idea map will bring repetition to your attention quickly because it makes it easy to spot two or more very similar items.

As you read the following first-draft student paragraph, see if you can spot the repetitive statements. Then notice how the idea map below it clearly identifies the repetition.

### Sample Student Paragraph

Chemical waste dumping is an environmental concern that must be dealt with, not ignored. The big companies care nothing about the environment. They would just as soon dump waste in our backyards as not. This has finally become a big issue and is being dealt with by forcing the companies to clean up their own messes. It is incredible that large companies have the nerve to dump just about anywhere. The penalty should be steep. When the companies are caught, they should be forced to clean up their messes.

VISUALIZE IT!

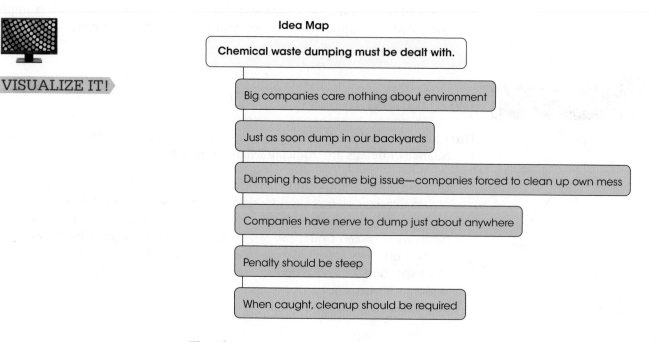

**Idea Map**

Chemical waste dumping must be dealt with.

Big companies care nothing about environment

Just as soon dump in our backyards

Dumping has become big issue—companies forced to clean up own mess

Companies have nerve to dump just about anywhere

Penalty should be steep

When caught, cleanup should be required

The idea map shows that points 1, 2, and 4 say nearly the same thing—that big companies don't care about the environment and dump waste nearly anywhere. Because there is so much repetition, the paragraph lacks development. To revise, the writer first needs to eliminate the repetitious statements. Then she needs to generate more ideas that support her topic sentence and explain why or how chemical waste dumping must be dealt with.

### How to Avoid Repetition

The following suggestions will help you revise a paragraph with repetitive ideas:

- **Try to combine ideas.** Select the best elements and wording of each idea and use them to produce a revised sentence. Add more detail if needed.

- **Review places where you make deletions.** When you delete a repetitious statement, check to see whether the sentence before and the sentence after the deletion connect. Often a transition will be needed to help the paragraph flow easily.

■ **Decide whether additional details are needed.** Often we write repetitious statements when we don't know what else to say. Thus, repetition often signals lack of development. Refer to page 453 for specific suggestions on revising underdeveloped paragraphs.

■ **Watch for statements that are only slightly more general or specific than one another.** For example, although the first sentence below is general and the second is more specific, they repeat the same idea.

> Ringing telephones can be distracting. The telephone that rang constantly throughout the evening distracted me.

To make the second sentence a specific example of the idea in the first sentence, rather than just a repetition of it, the writer would need to add specific details about how the telephone ringing throughout the evening was a distraction.

> The telephone that rang continuously in my neighbor's apartment yesterday woke my baby and made it impossible to get her back to sleep.

## EXERCISE 14-12

## Identifying and Revising Repetitive Statements

**Directions:** Read the following paragraph and delete all repetitive statements. Make suggestions for revision.

*Add several other interesting examples of misbehavior.*

*Add more information on how children are rewarded for poor behavior.*

Children misbehaving is an annoying problem in our society. I used to work as a waiter at Denny's, and I have seen many incidences in which parents allow their children to misbehave. ~~I have seen many situations that you would just not believe.~~ Once I served a table at which the parents allowed their four-year-old to make his toy spider crawl up and down my pants as I tried to serve the food. The parents just laughed. Children have grown up being rewarded for their actions, regardless of whether they are good or bad. ~~Whether the child does something the parents approve of or whether it is something they disapprove of, they react in similar ways. This is why a lot of toddlers and children continue to misbehave.~~ Being rewarded will cause the child to act in the same way to get the same reward.

---

## ! NEED TO KNOW

### Using Idea Maps

An idea map is a visual display of the ideas in your paragraph. It allows you to see how ideas relate to one another and to identify weaknesses in your writing. You can use idea maps to answer the following five questions that will help you revise your paragraphs:

■ Does the paragraph stray from the topic?

■ Does every detail belong?

■ Are the details arranged and developed logically?

■ Is the paragraph balanced?

■ Is the paragraph repetitious?

## Revision Checklist

### Paragraph Development

1. Is the topic manageable (neither too broad nor too narrow)?
2. Is the paragraph written with the reader in mind?
3. Does the topic sentence identify the topic?
4. Does the topic sentence make a point about the topic?
5. Does each sentence support the topic sentence?
6. Is there sufficient detail?
7. Is there a sentence at the end that brings the paragraph to a close?

### Sentence Development

8. Are there any sentence fragments, run-on sentences, or comma splices?
9. Are ideas combined to produce more effective sentences?
10. Are adjectives and adverbs used to make the sentences vivid and interesting?
11. Are relative clauses and prepositional phrases like *-ing* phrases used to add detail?
12. Are pronouns used correctly and consistently?

---

**EXERCISE 14-13**  Identifying and Revising Repetitive Statements

**WRITING IN PROGRESS**

**Directions:** Review the paragraph and idea map you last revised for Exercise 14-11. Identify and revise any repetitive statements.

---

# Use Peer Review

■ GOAL 5
Use peer review

Classmates can often help you realize what is and what is not effective in a piece of writing. They can provide valuable advice and feedback on what you should revise. And you, in turn, can read the writing of others and offer them helpful ideas. This exchange of ideas is often called **peer review.** Use the following suggestions to make this process work for you.

## When You Are the Writer . . .

1. Prepare your draft in readable form. Double-space your work and print it on standard 8.5" × 11" paper.
2. When you receive your peers' comments, weigh them carefully. Keep an open mind, but do not feel that you must accept every suggestion that is made.
3. If you have questions or are uncertain about your peers' advice, talk with your instructor.

## When You Are the Reader . . .

1. Read the draft through at least once before making any suggestions.

2. As you read, keep the writer's intended audience in mind (see Chapter 2). The draft should be appropriate for that audience.

3. Offer positive comments first. Say what the writer did well.

4. Use the Revision Checklists and "Need to Know" boxes in this book to guide your reading and comments. Be specific in your review and offer suggestions for improvement.

5. Be supportive; put yourself in the place of the person whose work you are reviewing. Phrase your feedback in the way you would want to hear it!

---

**EXERCISE 14-14**

## Practicing Peer Review

**WRITING IN PROGRESS**

**Directions:** Exchange the paragraph you wrote for Exercise 14-4 for the one a classmate wrote for the same exercise. Then the two of you should do the following:

1. List two things the writer did well.

   a. _____

   b. _____

2. List two areas for improvement.

   a. _____

   b. _____

---

# Proofread for Correctness

■ GOAL 6
Proofread for correctness

**Proofreading** is a final reading of your paper to check for errors. In this final polishing of your work, the focus is on correctness, so don't proofread until you have done all your rethinking of ideas and revision. When you are ready to proofread your writing, you should check for errors in:

- sentences (run-ons or fragments)
- grammar
- spelling
- punctuation
- capitalization

Part VI, "Reviewing the Basics," gives more detailed information on each topic. The following tips will ensure that you don't miss any errors:

1. **Review your paper once for each type of error.** First, read it for run-on sentences and fragments. Take a short break, and then read it four more times, each time paying attention to one of the following: *spelling, punctuation, grammar,* and *capitalization.*

2. **To find spelling errors, read your paper from last sentence to first sentence and from last word to first word.** Reading in this way, you will not get distracted by the flow of ideas, so you can focus on finding errors. Also use the spell-checker on your computer, but be sure to proofread for the kinds of errors it cannot catch: missing words, errors that are themselves words (such as *of* for *or*), and homonyms (for example, using *it's* for *its*).

3. **Read each sentence aloud, slowly and deliberately.** This technique will help you catch endings that you have left off verbs or missing plurals.

4. **Check for errors one final time after you print your paper.** Don't do this when you are tired; you might introduce new mistakes. Ask a classmate or friend to read your paper to catch any mistakes you missed.

Here is a paragraph that shows the errors that a student corrected during proofreading. Notice that errors in grammar, punctuation, and spelling were corrected.

> Murphy's Law states that if anything can go wrong, it will. The day
> I tried to bake a homemade cake for my friend's birthday was a perfect
> example of Murphy's Law. I had already mixed the flour and sugar when
> I discovered I was out of eggs. On my way to the grocery store to buy
> eggs, I had a flat tire. I was able to change the tire, but when I got to the
> grocery store, I realized that my wallet must have fallen out of my pocket
> When I was changing the tire. I went back to the spot and luckily, my
> wallet was right there by the curb. I bought the eggs and headed to my
> car; then I found that I had locked my keys in it! A police officer helped me
> unlock the car and at that point I gave up. I stopped at a bakery on the
> way to my friend's house and bought her a beautiful cake to go with my
> unbelievable story of Murphy's Law.

The following checklist will remind you to check for spelling, punctuation, and other mechanical errors.

## Proofreading Checklist

1. Does each sentence end with an appropriate punctuation mark (period, question mark, exclamation point, or quotation mark)?

2. Is all punctuation within each sentence correct (commas, colons, semicolons, apostrophes, dashes, and quotation marks)?

3. Is each word spelled correctly?

4. Have you used capital letters where needed?

5. Are numbers and abbreviations used correctly?

6. Are any words left out?

7. Have you corrected all typographical errors?

8. Are your pages in the correct order and numbered?

## EXERCISE 14-15    Proofreading

**WRITING IN PROGRESS**

**Directions:** Prepare and proofread the final version of the paragraph you revised for Exercise 14-13.

# INTEGRATING READING AND WRITING

## READ AND REVISE

**MySkillsLab®**

**Complete** this Exercise

## Revise

The paragraph below strays from its topic and includes details that do not belong. Revise the paragraph by deleting repetitive sentences and sentences that do not directly support the thesis. Add transitions as needed.

Do you have trouble getting out of the house on time in the morning? If you are not a naturally well-organized person, you may need to overcompensate by being super organized in the morning. A detailed checklist can help you accomplish the seemingly impossible goal of leaving home exactly when you are supposed to. ~~It is especially difficult to leave on time if you are tired or feeling lazy.~~ When making such a checklist, most people find it helpful to *For example, do* backtrack to the previous evening. ~~Do~~ you have clean clothes for the next day, or do you need to do a load of laundry? Are your materials for school or work neatly assembled, or is there a landslide of papers covering your desk? *also* Do you need to pack a lunch? You get the picture. In your checklist, include tasks to complete the night before as well as a precise sequence of morning *For instance, if* tasks with realistic estimates of the time required for each task. ~~If~~ you have children, help them make checklists to keep track of homework assignments. ~~Child development experts stress the importance of predictable structure in children's lives. If you live with a friend or spouse, make sure to divide all chores in an equitable way. Often one person tends to be neater than the other, so you may need to make compromises, but having an explicit agreement about household responsibilities can help prevent resentment and conflict at home.~~

# Proofread

The following excerpt contains run-on sentences and fragments, as well as errors in grammar, spelling, punctuation, and capitalization. Proofread the excerpt and correct the errors.

> *It took*     *whole*                            *accident*
> ~~Took~~ me a hole year to get my life back in order from the accedent. Finally,
>
> when I did, I started working I even worked on going back to school to get my
>
>                                          *e*      *c*        *d*
> associate's degree. I wanted to get my degree in ~~E~~arly ~~C~~hildhood ~~D~~evelopment
>                                      *I love*
> because~~;~~ I just love to be around kids. ~~Love~~ how their minds work.
>
>      Now that I am working on my dream nothing is going to keep me from it
>
>                                         *something*
> I work my butt off in all my classes, so I can ~~makes~~ somthing of my life. ~~Even~~
>       *No*
> ~~though no~~ matter how hard I try to forget everything~~:~~ I have scars and pictures
>
> to remind me not to make the same mistake again. I drive a lot more carefully
>
> these days.

*Loretta Scott graduated from high school and went to work first as a nurse's aide and then for ten years as manager of a group home. She was a student at Maysville Community and Technical College, studying for a degree in nursing, when she wrote this essay and submitted it to the Writing Rewards Essay Contest. The assignment she responded to directed her to write an essay about an event that changed her life.*

Title announces subject

# The Event that Changed My Life

Details provide background leading up to thesis

     I worked at a group home in Williamsburg, Ohio, for seventeen years. I started working there at the age of twenty. After working there for seven years, I was offered the position of home manager. It was very hard in the beginning because there was so much to learn and so many people to be responsible for. There were eight males living in the home and each shared a bedroom. The residents ranged in age from fourteen to thirty-six, each having different personalities and levels of disabilities. It was very important to build a bond with each of them and for them to be able to trust that I had their best interest at heart. I enjoyed getting to know each of them, and they became my second family. I never worked a job that took so much out of me, not just physically but mentally. I loved working with the residents, helping them to have the best lives possible and letting them know I would be there for them. I was both shocked and devastated when I was suddenly and unfairly terminated from this job.

I worked hard as a manager because there were a lot of things to do each day. It was very challenging to complete all of the responsibilities. I was on call twenty-four hours a day, seven days a week. I would go to work early and sometimes not leave for several hours after my scheduled shift. I usually didn't mind the constant hustle because I had become used to the fast pace. I always wanted to have my duties complete, so it was hard for me to leave work with things unfinished. There were times when we would be down a manager, and I would have to cover two of the homes. I didn't like that, but it was part of the job. I didn't mind helping out, but I knew there was a price being paid for the lack of a good manager. I could only keep up with the paperwork, schedules, monies, and supplies. I knew that supervision and support was not something I could provide for either home at that time. I was offered other positions during those seventeen years; however, I did not have a degree that was typically required to hold one of those positions, so I declined because I believed that was in the best interest of the residents. I also declined two other manager positions offered from other companies. I didn't feel right about leaving the residents I had worked with for so long.

The last two years of my employment were without a doubt the hardest. The management of the company had changed hands many times. The employees found themselves in a position of what you might call "too many chiefs and not enough Indians." We were expected to work with less staffing and more job duties, which led to much turmoil in the homes. The expectations changed almost daily, as did the paperwork. While supervisors came and went, so did the policies and procedures for completing certain job responsibilities. For example, we changed incident forms at least six times, and on each, a different person was responsible for completing it. I had a supervisor who, for lack of a more definitive word, was very inappropriate, yet somehow she managed to hold onto her job even though she did not complete most of the required work. The employees were being harassed continually from this supervisor. It did not seem to matter that staff were leaving because of her. The director enjoyed spending time with this supervisor, on and off the clock, so a lot was overlooked.

One evening while spending time with my family I received a call that a resident and a staff member had been injured. The staff member was unloading a resident out of a van when the resident and staff member fell out of the back of the van. The staff member had failed to raise the wheelchair lift back up in between transfers of another resident. I immediately left to meet the staff member and resident at the hospital. They were sent to separate hospitals, so I picked up the van at the home and went to stay with the resident and take him home after

*Thesis statement*

*Topic sentence*

*Details explain topic sentence*

*Topic sentence*

*Details explain and support topic sentence*

*Details provide sequence of events leading up to key event*

Topic sentence contains key detail

Conclusion repeats thesis

Details reveal her pain at losing her job

Details show she doesn't know why she was fired

Key point supports her claim of unfair termination

the evaluation. There was an investigation completed later on that week while I was out on a prescheduled vacation. When I was to return to work the following Monday, the director said I was being terminated because it was my fault that the accident occurred because I did not complete a training paper with the staff member. I tried to explain that the staff member was trained and paperwork was completed, but I was dismissed.

I was devastated by losing my job, which was a life changing event. I worked very hard at my job, and I was simply told to leave. I was not permitted to even say goodbye to the residents with whom I had worked for seventeen years. I felt like my whole world had fallen apart. I guess I never really looked at what so many other people had gone through in losing their jobs. I don't know that I will ever completely recover from this. Everybody says it will get easier with time, but it has been eight months, and it doesn't hurt any less now than the day they let me go. Some people have asked me if I know the real reason behind the termination. The week I was on vacation, an investigation was taking place regarding sexual harassment between the director and my supervisor. I guess I should say that with a second investigation and some thought, people thought I may have been the one to call and report them to the company. I did not make that call to the company even though I had been asked to do so twice by the director of nursing. If I had to guess, I would say that the director of nursing made that call. I thought that my termination may have been caused by the fact that I had recently been injured on the job for the second time in less than three months. I had been punched in the nose and then a resident had lost balance and fallen from the second step of a bus onto me. I will probably never know the truth behind the termination; however, the fight for unemployment has gone my way; each of the three attempts the company tried to appeal have been denied. The review board believes, as do I, that it was an unjustified termination.

## Examining Writing

1. How is this essay organized? Summarize the writer's narrative in your own words.

2. Evaluate the details the writer used to support her thesis statement. Use the five questions on page 467 and/or an idea map to discover problems in the essay.

3. If you were a peer reviewer for this writer, what suggestions would you make?

4. Evaluate the title, introduction, and conclusion. How might each be more effective?

# READ AND RESPOND: A Professional Essay

## Thinking Before Reading

The following reading, "Finding a Mate: Not the Same as It Used to Be," is taken from a textbook by James M. Henslin titled *Sociology: A Down-to-Earth Approach, Core Concepts*. As you read this selection, notice how the author uses examples to illustrate his thesis.

1. Preview the reading, using the steps discussed in Chapter 1, page 25.
2. Connect the reading to your own experience by answering the following questions:
   a. How did your parents meet?
   b. What do you think is the best way to find a mate?
3. Highlight and annotate as you read.

1060*L*/617 words

# Finding a Mate: Not the Same as It Used to Be

## James M. Henslin

1   THINGS HAVEN'T CHANGED ENTIRELY. Boys and girls still get interested in each other at their neighborhood schools, and men and women still meet at college. Friends still serve as matchmakers and introduce friends, hoping they might click. People still meet at churches and bars, at the mall and at work. Technology, however, is bringing about some fundamental changes.

2   Among traditional people—Jews, Arabs, and in the villages of China and India—for centuries matchmakers have brought couples together. They carefully match a prospective couple by background—or by the position of the stars, whatever their tradition dictates—arranging marriages to please the families of the bride and groom, and, hopefully, the couple, too.

3   In China, this process is being changed by technology. Matchmakers use computerized records—age, sex, personal interests, and, increasingly significant, education and earnings—to identify compatibility and predict lifelong happiness. But parents aren't leaving the process entirely up to computers. They want their input, too. In one park in Beijing, hundreds of mothers and fathers gather twice a week to try to find spouses for their adult children. They bring photos of their children and share them with one another, talking up their kid's virtues while evaluating the sales pitch they get from the other parents. Some of the parents even sit on the grass, next to handwritten ads they've written about their children.

4    Closer to home, Americans are turning more and more to the Internet. Dating sites advertise that they offer thousands of potential companions, lovers, or spouses. For a low monthly fee, you, too, can meet the person of your dreams.

5    The photos are fascinating in their variety. Some seem to be lovely people, attractive and vivacious, and one wonders why they are posting their photos and personal information online. Do they have some secret flaw that they need to do this? Others seem okay, although perhaps, a bit needy. Then there are the pitiful, and one wonders if they will ever find a mate, or even a hookup, for that matter. Some are desperate, begging for someone—anyone—to make contact with them: women who try for sexy poses, exposing too much flesh, suggesting the promise of at least a good time; and men who try their best to look like hulks, their muscular presence promising the same.

6    Many regular, ordinary people post their profiles. And some do find the person of their dreams—or at least adequate matches. With Internet postings losing their stigma, electronic matchmaking is becoming an acceptable way to find a mate.

7    Matchmaking sites tout "thousands of eligible prospects." Unfortunately, the prospects are spread over the nation, and few people want to invest in a plane ticket only to find that the "prospect" doesn't even resemble the posted photo. You can do a search for your area, but there are likely to be few candidates from it.

8    Do not worry. More technology has come to the rescue. The ease and comfort of "dating on demand" is available. You sit at home, turn on your TV, and use your remote to search for your partner. Your local cable company has done all the hard work—hosting singles events at bars and malls, where they tape singles talking about themselves and what they are looking for in a mate. You can view the videos free. And if you get interested in someone, for just a small fee you can contact the individual.

9    Now all you need to do is to hire a private detective—also available online for another fee—to see if this engaging person is already married, has a dozen kids, has been sued for paternity or child support, or is a child molester or a rapist.

**hookup**
a casual relationship

**Snapshots**

Tall, Dark, and Handsome chats with Buxom Blonde.

www.CartoonStock.com

© Love B022

# Getting Ready to Write

## Checking Your Comprehension

Answer each of the following questions using complete sentences.

1. List six criteria that matchmakers in China use to identify compatibility and predict happiness.

2. According to the author, what is the most inconvenient aspect of Internet dating?

3. Explain how "dating on demand" works.

4. How does the author view electronic dating? Is he enthusiastic or skeptical about how technology has changed the process of finding a mate?

5. What is the purpose of the cartoon included with the selection?

## Strengthening Your Vocabulary

Using the word's context, word parts, or a dictionary, write a brief definition of each of the following words as it is used in the reading.

1. prospective (paragraph 2) ___potential, likely_____

2. compatibility (paragraph 3) ___ability to live together in harmony; like-mindedness___

3. virtues (paragraph 3) ___admirable qualities_____

4. vivacious (paragraph 5) ___lively, outgoing, spirited_____

5. pitiful (paragraph 5) ___pathetic, deserving pity_____

6. stigma (paragraph 6) ___a mark of disgrace or shame_____

## Examining the Reading: Using Idea Maps

Review the reading by completing the missing parts of the following idea map.

VISUALIZE IT!

Title — **Finding a Mate:  Not the Same as It Used to Be**

Thesis — Technology is changing how people go about finding a mate.

Traditional people—Jews, Arabs, those in villages of China and India—have relied for centuries on matchmakers.

In China, technology is changing the matchmaking process.

Computerized records base compatibility on:
- age
- sex
- personal interests
- education
- earnings

In America, people are also turning to technology to find a mate.

Internet dating sites offer:
- Wide variety of people
- Eligible prospects spread over the nation
- Increasingly less stigma

Dating on demand:
- Cable TV company helps singles make tapes of themselves
- Tapes can be viewed for free on TV
- Small fee to make contact
- Online detective service can check background of eligible prospects

Conclusion — Author concludes with comment about the uncertainty of modern electronic dating.

## Thinking Critically: Discussion and Journal Writing

React and respond to the reading by discussing the following:

1. What do you think of the traditional methods of matchmaking described in this selection? How might technology improve upon these methods?

2. Evaluate the criteria that matchmakers use in China to identify compatibility and predict happiness. What traits would you add to the list? Which ones would you remove?

3. Would you trust the description of a person you met online? Why or why not? If you became interested in a person you met online, would you use a detective service to look into his or her background?

4. Why was the cartoon included in the reading? What key point does it emphasize?

**THINKING VISUALLY**

**MySkillsLab®**

Complete
this
Exercise

## Writing About the Reading

### Paragraph Options

1. Write a paragraph describing how you first met a person who is important in your life.

2. If you are single, have you considered using an electronic dating site? Write a paragraph explaining why or why not.

3. Do you agree that Internet dating sites are losing their stigma? Write a paragraph explaining your answer.

### Essay Options

4. Imagine the scene described in paragraph 3, with hundreds of parents trying to make matches for their children in a park in Beijing. If your parents were there, what would they say about you in their "sales pitch" to other parents? Write an essay explaining how you think your parents would describe you. In addition, try writing an ad that your parents might write about you.

5. What can you tell from the reading about the author's attitude toward Internet dating? Write an essay examining the ways the author reveals his feelings toward the subject. Include in your essay specific examples from the selection that show he is sympathetic, suspicious, disapproving, etc. Also, explain how the selection would be different if it were entirely objective. How does the author's tone add to or detract from the reading?

6. What if you were to make a recording for a dating-on-demand video? Write an essay describing what you would want to include about yourself and the person you are hoping to meet.

# SELF-TEST SUMMARY

To test yourself, cover the Answer column with a sheet of paper and answer each question in the left column. Evaluate each of your answers as you work by sliding the paper down and comparing your answer with what is printed in the Answer column.

| QUESTION | ANSWER |
| --- | --- |
| ■ GOAL 1 Read carefully and critically for revision<br><br>What strategies can you use when reading a draft for revision? | Create distance; allow enough time to read your draft several times; print a copy of your draft and read it with a pen in hand; read aloud; and ask a classmate for suggestions. |
| ■ GOAL 2 Determine how and when to revise<br><br>When and how should you revise? | It is usually best to wait a day after writing a draft before beginning to revise. Use idea maps and revision checklists to guide your revision. |
| ■ GOAL 3 Revise ineffective paragraphs<br><br>How do you revise ineffective paragraphs? | Begin revising by examining your topic sentence, and then determine whether you have adequate supporting details. |
| ■ GOAL 4 Use idea maps to spot revision problems<br><br>What revision problems do idea maps help you to identify? | Idea maps can identify where the paragraph strays from the topic, whether supporting details are relevant and logically arranged, and whether the paragraph is balanced or repetitious. |
| ■ GOAL 5 Use peer review<br><br>What is peer review? | Peer review is an exchange of ideas in which you comment on your classmates' writing and they comment on yours, providing feedback to each other on what to revise. |
| ■ GOAL 6 Proofread for correctness<br><br>What are four tips for proofreading for correctness? | Review your paper once for each type of error. Find spelling errors by reading your paper in reverse. Read each sentence aloud. Check for errors one final time after you print your paper. |

# MySkillsLab

For more help with **Revision and Proofreading**, go to your learning path in MySkillsLab at http://www.myskillslab.com.

# Understanding and Organizing Information

## LEARNING GOALS

Learn how to . . .

■ **GOAL 1**
Read to organize and retain information

■ **GOAL 2**
Outline to organize information

■ **GOAL 3**
Map to discover organization

■ **GOAL 4**
Paraphrase to restate ideas of others

■ **GOAL 5**
Summarize to condense information

## THINK About It!

The blueprint above, created by an architect, will be used by the contractor to build the house to certain specifications. Write a sentence explaining how the blueprint helps both the contractor and the owner.

Can you imagine how difficult it would be to keep track of all the details involved in building a house without a blueprint? Much of what you read in college is also filled with details, and you need a system to keep track of them all. This chapter will show you four ways to create a "blueprint" or learning guide for anything you read. It will also explain how these blueprints can help you organize and plan how to express your ideas in writing.

481

# Why Organize Information?

Organizing information is a useful skill for both readers and writers. As a reader, organizing information will help you understand what you read. By writing an outline or drawing a map, for example, you will see how ideas connect and relationships will become clearer. Organizing information also helps you learn it. Numerous studies have shown that information that is connected or grouped together is easier to learn and remember than random, unrelated bits of information. As a writer, organizing information using one or more of the strategies suggested in this chapter will help you see how your ideas fit together and will help you write paragraphs and essays in which the ideas follow logically.

## READING

# Read to Organize and Retain Information

■ GOAL 1
Read to organize and
retain information

Textbooks, articles, and essays contain a wealth of information, but it is impossible for most students to learn and remember it all. The first step in organizing and retaining information, then, is to decide what is important to learn. The next step is to use a system that will help you remember what you have identified as important.

## Decide What to Learn by Analyzing the Task

To know what is important, you have to analyze the assignment. You have to determine why it was given, and what you are expected to learn from it. Use the following tips to analyze the task before you begin reading.

1. **Determine what you must do after you have finished the reading.** Do you have to take a multiple-choice test? Do you need to prepare for a class discussion? Do you have to write an essay exam? Do you have to write a plot summary? Each task requires a different level and type of detail. If you must answer a series of questions at the end of a textbook chapter, read those questions before you begin the assignment. Doing so will provide you with clues regarding what to look for as you read. If you must write a paper or a journal entry in response to a reading, use annotation to help you keep track of ideas as you read.

2. **Study your course syllabus.** Determine how the reading assignment fits into the course and how it connects to other topics and assignments.

3. **Use previewing to assess the difficulty of the assignment.** Technical readings or those that deal with complex ideas may require you to remember a large amount of new terminology and detail, for example.

4. **Assess your background knowledge and familiarity with the topic.** If a topic is difficult or unfamiliar, you will need to learn more detailed information than for familiar topics.

5. **Identify the types of information you need to learn.** Are names, dates, events, definitions, statistics, or research findings important? What is less important? Use your syllabus to help you answer these questions.

| EXERCISE 15-1 | # Deciding What to Learn |

**Directions:** For each of the following reading assignments, discuss with a classmate what types of information are likely to be important.

1. You are reading an article in *Time* magazine about health care reform in preparation for a discussion in your political science class.

2. You are reading the chapter review questions in your marketing text in preparation for an exam that is likely to contain similar questions.

3. You are reading the classified ads to find used furniture for your apartment.

4. You are reading your lab manual in preparation for an environmental science lab.

5. You are reading the course catalog to discover what classes you are interested in taking next semester.

## Use the SQ3R Reading/Study System

**SQ3R** is a system that combines reading and study. Instead of reading a chapter one day and studying it later when a test is announced, you can do both at once using SQ3R. The SQ3R system is a model. Once you see how and why SQ3R works, you can adapt it to suit your own academic needs.

### Steps in the SQ3R System

The SQ3R system involves five basic steps that integrate reading and study techniques. As you read the following steps, some of them will seem similar to the skills you have already learned.

*S—Survey*  Try to become familiar with the organization and general content of the material you are to read. This step is the same as previewing (see Chapter 1, p. 25).

1. **Read the title.**
2. **Read the lead-in or introduction.** (If it is extremely long, read just the first paragraph.)
3. **Read each boldfaced heading and the first sentence that follows it.** If the material lacks headings, read the first sentence of a few paragraphs on each page.
4. **Read the titles of maps, charts, or graphs.**
5. **Read the last paragraph or summary.**
6. **Read the end-of-chapter questions.**

From surveying the material, you should know generally what it is about and how it is organized.

*Q—Question*  Try to form questions that you can answer as you read. The easiest way to do this is to turn each boldfaced heading into a question. Think of these as similar to the guide questions discussed in Chapter 1.

*R—Read*  Read the material section by section. As you read each section, look for the answer to the question you formed from the heading of that section.

*R—Recite*  After you finish each section, stop. Check to see whether you can answer your question for the section. If you can't, look back to find the answer. Then check your recall again. Be sure to complete this step after you read each section.

*R—Review* When you have finished the whole reading assignment, go back to each heading; recall your question and try to answer it. If you can't recall the answer, be sure to look back and find the answer. Then test yourself again.

### Why SQ3R Works

Results of research studies overwhelmingly suggest that students who use the SQ3R system understand and remember what they read much better than students who do not use it.

If you consider for a moment how people learn, it becomes clear why reading/study systems are effective. One major way to learn is through repetition. Consider the way you learned the multiplication tables. Through repeated practice and drills, you learned $2 \times 2 = 4$, $5 \times 6 = 30$, $8 \times 9 = 72$, and so forth. The key was repetition. Reading/study systems provide some of the repetition necessary to ensure learning. SQ3R provides numerous repetitions and increases the amount learned.

SQ3R also has many advantages over ordinary reading:

- Surveying (previewing) gives you a mental organization or structure—you know what to expect.
- You always feel that you are looking for something specific rather than wandering aimlessly through a printed page.
- When you find the information you're looking for, you feel you have accomplished something.
- If you can remember the information in the Recite and Review steps, it is even more rewarding.

---

**EXERCISE 15-2**     ## Using SQ3R

**Directions:** Use the SQ3R method to read and review the professional reading in Chapter 3 titled "The Power of Words" (page 109). Write the questions you create on a separate sheet of paper, leaving space for the answers. Answer your questions after you have read the section.

---

## WRITING

# Outline to Organize Information

■ GOAL 2
Outline to organize
information

**Outlining** is an effective way to organize information and discover relationships between ideas. It forces you to select what is important from each paragraph and determine how it is related to key ideas in other paragraphs. Outlining enables you to learn and remember what you read because the process of selecting what is important and expressing it in your own words requires thought and comprehension and provides for repetition and review. Outlining also prepares you to write. By outlining your ideas before putting them in sentence and paragraph form, you can see how they fit together, rearrange them easily, and see where you need further information.

Outlining involves listing major and minor ideas and showing how they are related. When you make an outline, follow the writer's organization. An outline usually follows a format like the one below:

I. First major topic
   A. First major idea
      1. First key supporting detail
      2. Second key supporting detail
   B. Second major idea
      1. First key supporting detail
         a. Minor detail or example
         b. Minor detail or example
      2. Second key supporting detail
II. Second major topic
   A. First major idea

Suppose you had just read a brief essay about your brother's vacation in Texas. An outline of the essay might begin like this:

I. Favorite cities
   A. San Antonio—beautiful, interesting history
      1. The Alamo
      2. Riverwalk
   B. Houston—friendly people
      1. Seeing Houston Astros play
         a. Excitement of game
         b. Getting lost after leaving Astrodome

Notice that the most important ideas are closer to the left margin. The rule of thumb to follow is this: The less important the idea, the more it should be indented.

Here are a few suggestions for using the outline format:

## ! NEED TO KNOW

### How to Outline

- **Read a section completely before writing.**
- **Don't worry about following the outline format exactly.** As long as your outline shows an organization of ideas, it will work for you.
- **Use words and phrases or complete sentences,** whichever is easier for you.
- **Use your own words, and don't write too much.**
- **Pay attention to headings.** Be sure that all the information you place underneath a heading explains or supports that heading. In the outline above, for instance, the entries "San Antonio" and "Houston" are correctly placed under the major topic "Favorite Cities." Likewise, "The Alamo" and "Riverwalk" are under "San Antonio."

Read the following paragraph on fashions, and then study its outline:

> Why do fashions occur in the first place? One reason is that some cultures, like ours, *value change:* what is new is good, even better. Thus, in many modern societies clothing styles change yearly, while people in traditional societies may wear the same style for generations. A second reason is that many industries promote quick changes in fashion to increase sales. A third reason is that fashions usually trickle down from the top. A new style may occasionally originate from lower-status groups, as blue jeans did. But most fashions come from upper-class people who like to adopt some style or artifact as a badge of their status. But they cannot monopolize most status symbols for long. Their style is adopted by the middle class, maybe copied or modified for use by lower-status groups, offering many people the prestige of possessing a high-status symbol.
>
> —Thio, *Sociology,* p. 534

I. Why fashions occur
  A. Some societies like change.
      1. Modern societies—yearly changes
      2. Traditional societies—may be no change for many years
  B. Industries encourage changes to increase sales.
  C. Changes generally start at top.
      1. Blue jeans an exception—came from lower-class
      2. Usually start as upper-class status symbol, then move to other classes

In this outline, the major topic of the paragraph, "why fashions occur," is listed first. The writer's three main reasons are listed as A, B, and C. Supporting details are then listed under the reasons. When you look at this outline, you can easily see the writer's most important points.

## EXERCISE 15-3   Completing an Outline

**Directions:** After reading the passage below, fill in the missing information in the outline that follows.

### Gossip

There can be no doubt that we spend a great deal of time gossiping. In fact, gossip seems universal among all cultures, and among some groups gossip is a commonly accepted ritual.

**Gossip** involves making social evaluations about a person who is not present during the conversation; it generally occurs when two people talk about a third party.

In the organization, gossip has particularly important consequences and in many instances has been shown to lead to firings, lawsuits, and damaged careers. And because of the speed and ease with which members of an organization can communicate with each other (instant messaging, e-mail, and blogs, for example) gossip can spread quickly and broadly.

People often gossip in order to get some kind of reward; for example, to hear more gossip, gain social status or control, have fun, cement social bonds, or make social comparisons.

Gossiping, however, often leads others to see you more negatively—regardless of whether your gossip is positive or negative or whether you're sharing this gossip with strangers or with friends.

In addition to its negative impact on the gossiper, gossiping often has ethical implications. In many instances gossiping would be considered unethical: for example, when you use it to unfairly hurt another person, when you know it's not true, when no one has the right to such personal information, or when you are breaking a promise of secrecy.

—DeVito, *Human Communication*, p. 154

---

**I.** Gossip
  **A.** Popularity of gossip
    **1.** Occurs in all cultures
    **2.** Commonly accepted ritual in some groups
  **B.** Definition
    **1.** Social evaluations about a person not present
    **2.** Occurs when two people talk about a third
  **C.** Gossip in organizations
    **1.** Consequences include firings, lawsuits, and damaged careers
    **2.** Can spread quickly because of the ease of communication in the organization
  **D.** Reasons for gossip
    **1.** For a reward
    **2.** Examples: to hear more gossip, to gain social status or control, to have fun, to cement social bonds, to make social comparisons
  **E.** Consequences
    **1.** People can see gossiper more negatively
    **2.** Can be unethical
    **3.** Examples: hurting another person, sharing information people have no right to know, breaking promises of secrecy.

---

# Map to Discover Organization

■ GOAL 3
Map to discover
organization

**Mapping** is a visual method of organizing information. It involves drawing diagrams to show how ideas in a paragraph or chapter are related. Some students prefer mapping to outlining because they feel it is freer and less tightly structured.

Maps can take many forms. You can draw them in any way that shows the relationships between ideas. Figures 15-1 and 15-2 (p. 488) show two sample maps of the paragraph about fashions. Look at the maps and then look again at the outline of the fashions paragraph. Notice how the important information is included in each method—it's just presented differently.

As you draw maps, think of them as pictures or diagrams that show how ideas are connected. You can hand draw them or use a word processor. Use the following steps:

> ! **NEED TO KNOW**
>
> ## How to Draw Maps
>
> 1. **Identify the overall topic or subject.** Write it in the center or at the top of the page.
> 2. **Identify major ideas that relate to the topic.** Using a line, connect each piece of information to the central topic.
> 3. **As you discover supporting details that further explain an idea already mapped, connect those details with new lines.**

**FIGURE 15-1 SAMPLE HAND-DRAWN MAP**

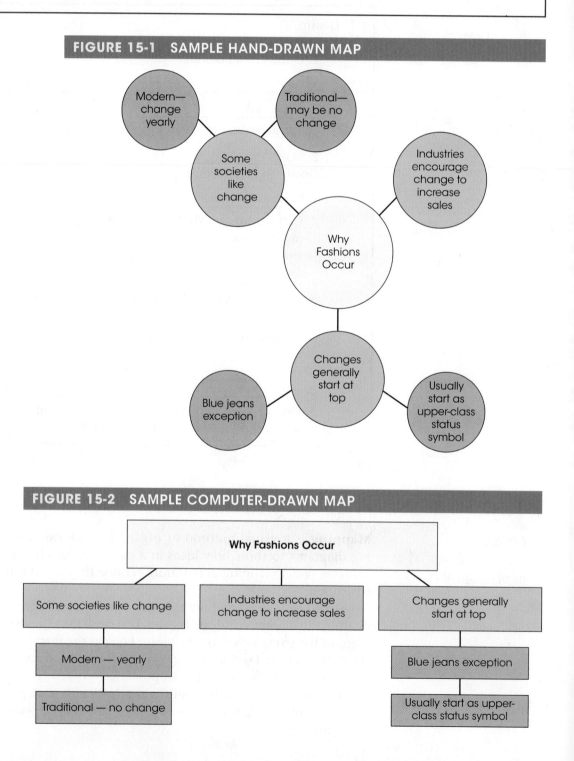

**FIGURE 15-2 SAMPLE COMPUTER-DRAWN MAP**

Once you are skilled at drawing maps, you can become more creative, drawing different types of maps to fit what you are reading. For example, you can draw a *time line* (see Figure 15-3) to show historical events in the order in which they occurred. A time line starts with the earliest event and ends with the most recent.

### FIGURE 15-3  SAMPLE TIME LINE

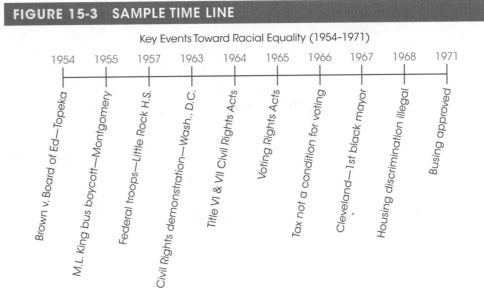

Key Events Toward Racial Equality (1954–1971)

Another type of map is one that shows a process—the steps involved in doing something (see Figure 15-4). This type of map is useful for understanding material written in chronological order or describing a process, as well as for writing using these patterns (see Chapter 12).

### FIGURE 15-4  SAMPLE PROCESS MAP

Process: How to Assemble a Birdhouse

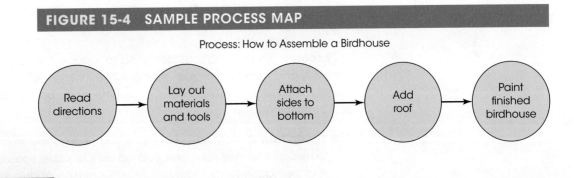

## EXERCISE 15-4  Completing a Map

**Directions:** Read the following paragraph and complete the map on page 490, filling in the writer's main points in the spaces provided. Then answer the question that follows the map.

When your college work load increases, it is tempting to put things off. Here are some suggestions to help you overcome *procrastination*, which is the tendency to postpone tasks that need to be done. First, clear your desk. Move everything except the materials for the task at hand. Once you start working, you will be less likely to be distracted. Second, give yourself five minutes to start. If you are having trouble beginning a task, working on it for just five minutes might spark your motivation. Next, divide the task into manageable parts. Working with just a part of a task is usually less overwhelming. Then, start somewhere, no matter where. It is better to do something rather than sit and stare. Finally, recognize when you need more information. Sometimes you may avoid a task because you're not sure how to do it. Discuss your questions with classmates or with your professor.

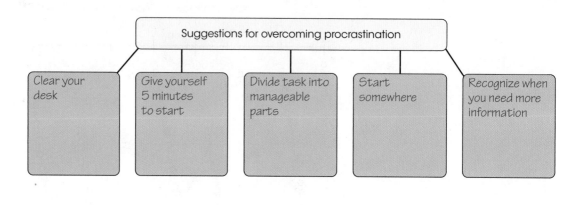

What five transition words does the writer use to introduce the main points?

1. _first_    2. _second_    3. _next_    4. _then_    5. _finally_

EXERCISE 15-5

## Completing a Map

**Directions:** After reading the following paragraphs, complete each section of the map in which a blank line appears. Fill in the writer's main points as well as some supporting details.

**Excuses** are explanations designed to reduce the negative effects of your behavior and help to maintain your positive image. Different researchers have classified excuses into varied categories. One of the best typologies classifies excuses into three main types:

- **I didn't do it:** Here you deny that you have done what you're being accused of. You may then bring up an alibi to prove you couldn't have done it or perhaps you may accuse another person of doing what you're being blamed for ("I never said that" or "I wasn't even near the place when it happened"). These "I didn't do it" types are generally the worst excuses (unless they're true), because they fail to acknowledge responsibility and offer no assurance that this failure will not happen again.

- **It wasn't so bad:** Here you admit to doing it but claim the offense was not really so bad or perhaps there was justification for the behavior ("I only padded the expense account by a few bucks").

- **Yes, but:** Here you claim that extenuating circumstances accounted for the behavior; for example, that you weren't in control of yourself at the time or that you didn't intend to do what you did ("I never intended to hurt him; I was actually trying to help").

—DeVito, *The Interpersonal Communication Book*, p. 220

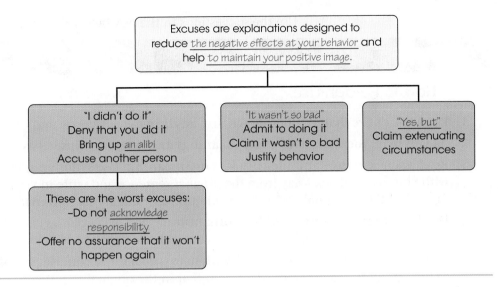

# Paraphrase to Restate Ideas of Others

■ **GOAL 4**
Paraphrase to restate
ideas of others

A **paraphrase** restates the ideas of a passage in your own words. You retain the author's meaning, but you use your own wording. In speech we paraphrase frequently. For example, when you relay a message from one person to another, you convey the meaning but do not use the person's exact words. A paraphrase makes a passage's meaning clearer and often more concise.

Paraphrasing is a useful technique for

- **recording information from reference sources to use in writing a research paper.**
- **understanding difficult material for which exact, detailed comprehension is required.** For instance, you might paraphrase the steps in solving a math problem or the procedures for a lab setup in chemistry.
- **reading material that is stylistically complex, or with an obvious slant, bias, strong tone, or detailed description.**

Study the following example of a paraphrase of the stylistically difficult preamble to the United States Constitution. Notice that it restates in different words the intent of the preamble.

### *Preamble*

We the People of the United States, in Order to form a more perfect Union, establish Justice, insure domestic Tranquillity, provide for the common defence, promote the general Welfare, and secure the Blessings of Liberty to ourselves and our Posterity, do ordain and establish this Constitution of the United States of America.

### *Paraphrase*

The citizens of the United States established the Constitution to create a better country, to provide rightful treatment, peace, protection, and well-being for themselves and future citizens.

Notice first how synonyms were substituted for words in the original—*citizens* for *people*, *country* for *union*, *protection* for *defense*, and so forth. Next, notice that the order of information was rearranged.

Use the suggestions in the box below to paraphrase effectively.

---

## ❗ NEED TO KNOW

### How to Paraphrase

1. **Read the entire material before writing anything.** Read slowly and carefully.

2. **As you read, focus on both exact meanings and relationships between ideas.**

3. **Read each sentence and identify its core meaning.** Use synonyms, replacing the author's words with your words. Look away from the original sentence and write in your own words what it means. Then reread the original and add any additional or qualifying information.

4. **Don't try to paraphrase word by word.** Instead, work with clauses and phrases (idea groups). If you are unsure of the meaning of a word or phrase, check a dictionary to locate a more familiar meaning.

5. **You may combine several original sentences into a more concise paraphrase.** It is also acceptable to present ideas in a different order from that in the original.

6. **Compare your paraphrase with the original for completeness and accuracy.**

7. **Indicate the source of the material you paraphrase in order to avoid plagiarism** (see Chapter 18 for details on citing sources).

---

### EXERCISE 15-6 · Writing Synonyms

*WORKING TOGETHER*

**Directions:** Write synonyms in the margin for the highlighted words or phrases in the following excerpt. Compare and discuss your choices with classmates.

*objective group*

*convince*
*line of thought*
*viewpoint*
*disagreed on/new ideas of*
*right and wrong*

Suppose you and I are debating a moral problem in front of a nonpartisan crowd. You have concluded that a particular course of action is right, while I believe it is wrong. It is only natural for me to ask you, "Why do you think doing such-and-such is right?" If you are unable to give any logical reasons why your position is correct, you are unlikely to persuade anyone. On the other hand, if you can explain the chain of reasoning that led you to your conclusion, you will be more likely to convince the audience that your position is correct. At the very least you will help reveal where there are disputed facts or values. Hence we will reject proposed ethical theories that are not based on reasoning from facts or commonly accepted values.

—Quinn, *Ethics for the Information Age*, p. 60

---

### EXERCISE 15-7 · Writing a Paraphrase

**Directions:** Write a paraphrase of the following paragraph from a nutrition text. *Sample paraphrase provided.*

We tend to think of bones as totally rigid, but if they were, how could we play basketball or even carry an armload of books up a flight of stairs? Bones need to be both strong and flexible, so that they can resist the crunching, stretching, and twisting that occur throughout our daily activities. Fortunately, the composition of bone is ideally suited for its complex job. About 65% of bone tissue is made up of an assortment of minerals (mostly calcium and phosphorus) that provide hardness. These minerals form tiny crystals that cluster around collagen fibers—protein fibers that provide strength, durability, and flexibility. Collagen fibers are phenomenally strong; they are actually stronger than steel fibers of similar size. They enable bones to bear weight while responding to demands for movement.

—Thompson and Manore, *Nutrition for Life*, p. 212

*Bones are not completely inflexible. They must be both sturdy and bendable enough to accommodate our physical activities each day. The hardness in bones comes from minerals such as calcium and phosphorus, which make up about 65% of bone tissue. The minerals make small crystals that collect around collagen fibers. These protein fibers are tough yet flexible, allowing bones to hold up our weight while we move. They are very strong, even more so than steel fibre of equivalent size. This means bones can support weight while allowing a wide range of motion.*

## EXERCISE 15-8

*WORKING TOGETHER*

## Writing a Paraphrase

**Directions:** Write a paraphrase of the bulleted item in Exercise 15-5 on page 490 that begins, "I didn't do it . . . ." When you have finished, compare your paraphrase with that of another student.    *Sample paraphrase provided.*

*One type of excuse is denial that you did what someone thinks you have. You can do this by providing proof that you could not have done it because you were doing something else. Or you can accuse someone else of doing what you are being accused of. These excuses do not work well because you do not accept responsibility for an act or offer reasons why you will not commit it again.*

# Summarize to Condense Information

■ GOAL 5
Summarize to condense information

A **summary** is a compact restatement of the important points of a passage. You might think of it as a shortened version of a longer message. Unlike a paraphrase, a summary does not include all the information presented in the original. Instead, you must select what to include. A summary contains only the gist of the text, with limited background, explanation, or detail. Although summaries vary in length, they are often one-quarter or less of the length of the original.

Summaries are useful in a variety of writing situations in which a condensed overview of material is needed. You might summarize information in preparation for an essay exam, or key points of news articles required in an economics class. Some class assignments also require summarization. Lab reports for science courses include a summary of results. A literature instructor may ask you to summarize the plot of a short story.

To write a good summary, you need to understand the material and identify the writer's major points. Here are some tips to follow:

## ! NEED TO KNOW

### How to Write a Summary

1. **Underline each major idea in the material.**
2. **Write one sentence that states the writer's most important idea.** This sentence will be the topic sentence of your summary.
3. **Be sure to use your own words rather than those of the author.**
4. **Focus on the author's major ideas,** not on supporting details.
5. **Keep the ideas in the summary in the same order as in the original material.**
6. **Indicate the source of the material you summarize to avoid plagiarism** (see Chapter 18 for details on citing sources.)

| EXERCISE 15-9 | Practicing Summarizing |
|---|---|

**A. Directions:** Read the following statements and mark each one true (T) or false (F).

___F___ **1.** Summaries usually contain a lot of detailed information.

___T___ **2.** When writing a summary, it is important to use your own words.

___T___ **3.** The ideas in a summary should be in the same order as in the original material.

**B. Directions:** After reading the following paragraphs, select the choice that best summarizes each one.

___c___ **4.**     When a group is too large for an effective discussion or when its members are not well informed on the topic, a *panel* of individuals may be selected to discuss the topic for the benefit of others, who then become an audience. Members of a panel may be particularly well informed on the subject or may represent divergent views. For example, your group may be interested in UFOs (unidentified flying objects) and hold a discussion for your classmates. Or your group might tackle the problems of tenants and landlords. Whatever your topic, the audience should learn the basic issues from your discussion.

—Gronbeck et al., *Principles of Speech Communication,* p. 302

**a.** Panel members are usually well informed on the subject, even though they may express different views. Members of a panel on UFOs, for example, may disagree about whether they exist.

**b.** Whatever topic a panel discusses, it is important that the audience learns basic information about the topic. For this reason, only well-informed people should participate in panels.

**c.** If a group is very large, or if its members are not familiar with a particular topic, a panel of people is sometimes chosen to talk about the topic. The rest of the group should get essential information from the panel's discussion.

**d.** Panels work effectively in large groups, such as in classrooms. Panels also work well when a group's members don't know very much about a topic. For example, a panel might talk about the problems of tenants and landlords to a group that was not familiar with such problems.

___a___ **5.**     The process of becoming hypnotized begins when the people who will be hypnotized find a comfortable body position and become thoroughly relaxed. Without letting their minds wander to other matters, they focus their attention on a specific object or sound, such as a metronome or the hypnotist's voice. Then, based on both what the hypnotherapist [hypnotist] expects to occur and actually sees occurring, she or he tells the clients how they will feel as the hypnotic process continues. For instance, the hypnotist may say, "You are feeling completely relaxed" or "Your eyelids are becoming heavy." When people being hypnotized recognize that their feelings match the hypnotist's comments, they are likely to believe that some change is taking place. That belief seems to increase their openness to other statements made by the hypnotist.

—Uba and Huang, *Psychology*, p. 148

a. The first step in being hypnotized is for people to feel comfortable and at ease. Then, they pay close attention to a particular item or sound while the hypnotist tells them how they will feel. If they believe their feelings are the same as what the hypnotist is saying, they will be more likely to accept other comments the hypnotist makes.

b. If the hypnotist says, "Your eyelids are becoming heavy," then the person being hypnotized would believe such a statement. The person being hypnotized would also continue to believe other statements the hypnotist makes.

c. The most important part of being hypnotized is to feel comfortable and relaxed. If you are uncomfortable at the beginning, you might not be willing to accept what the hypnotist is saying. To feel relaxed, try to focus on changes that are taking place.

d. If the hypnotist says, "You are feeling completely relaxed," people being hypnotized have to believe that this is true. If such belief does not occur, then it is unlikely that hypnosis will happen. Once the subject feels relaxed, his or her eyelids get heavy.

# INTEGRATING READING AND WRITING

## READ AND RESPOND: A Student Essay

*Elena Pineda is a sophomore at Laredo Community College where she is studying for an associate's degree. She plans to transfer to a university and obtain a bachelor's degree in communication disorders, specializing in either sign language or speech pathology. She submitted this essay to the Writing Rewards Essay Contest sponsored by Pearson Education. The assignment she responded to directed her to write an essay about the influence of Facebook.*

# Facebook's Influence on a Person's Life

Title gives subject

Facebook is a popular way to stay in touch with friends and family, especially among college students. What most students don't realize is that the effects of Facebook on a person's life can be devastating. As you spend more time on Facebook, you may become addicted to it, which can destroy your life in many

Thesis

ways. There are a lot of negative effects of spending too much time on Facebook including physical, social, and economic ones.

Topic sentence

Spending too much time on Facebook has negative physical effects. If you spend too much time in front of the computer, you may gradually gain weight

Details include examples of physical effects

because you may start to eat junk food. Since you don't want to miss any new postings, you may not take the time to prepare a healthy meal. Facebook is addictive to the point you may forget to exercise as you spend hours on the site. Facebook has features such as games, chatting, and the posting of comments that can take away time from physical exercise. The only exercise you may get are your fingers typing on the computer keyboard, and you may even develop carpal tunnel syndrome from typing too much. Logging in to Facebook can damage your body permanently.

Topic sentence

Details explain different ways your social life can be affected

Spending too much time on Facebook affects your social life. Because you want to be logged on to Facebook, you may end up spending less time with your family and friends. You may have less contact with them and may be unable to maintain important relationships. You may not want to go out with your family and friends. You may stop going to the movies, the mall, and clubs. The worst aspect of Facebook is that you may meet very dangerous people and your life could be at risk. Since some prisons allow inmates to use a computer, you don't know if the person you are accepting as a friend is a convicted killer or rapist. There have been cases where young women have met men though Facebook, then gone on dates with these individuals and been hurt, raped, or even killed. Even chatting is dangerous because people do not always tell the truth and can obtain the personal information posted in your profile. Socializing through Facebook, then, can be very dangerous.

Topic sentence

Examples of economic effects

Since Facebook has a lot of different games that you can get addicted to, it may affect you economically. You may want to buy all the items that are advertised. After you spend a certain amount of real money, the games only give you free play coins to use on the site. You need a credit card to buy the pretend money to get the featured items, which are essentially useless.

Topic sentence

On Facebook there are invitations to download updates which may turn out to be computer viruses or allow hackers to access your personal information. Your computer system may be destroyed by viruses, costing you a lot of money in repairs. Another problem to consider is the possibility of identity theft by hackers. This can affect you tremendously as hackers can max out your credit cards, leaving you with a substantial amount of debt for the rest of your life as well as damaging your credit score. Facebook is full of dangers that can impact your economic status if you are not careful.

Conclusion mentions benefits but advises caution

While there are many benefits to Facebook, it pays to be cautious. Be reasonable; stop and think for a moment. The negative effects of Facebook misuse are pretty scary. Since Facebook can affect your life in so many ways, don't let the site take control of your life and the way you live it.

## Examining Writing

1. Paraphrase Pineda's main point about Facebook use.

2. Evaluate the details the writer used to support her thesis statement. What other types of details might have been effective?

3. Summarize either the social, physical, or economic effects described by Pineda in her essay.

4. Evaluate Pineda's conclusion. If you were a peer reviewer, what suggestions might you make to strengthen her conclusion?

## Thinking Before Reading

The following article originally appeared on Greeniacs.com®, a Web site addressing environmental and ecological issues. In the selection, the author discusses important reasons why we should conserve water.

1. Preview the reading, using the steps discussed in Chapter 1 on page 25.
2. Connect the reading to your own experience by answering the following questions:
   a. In what ways do you currently try to conserve water and other resources?
   b. Do you think it is important to conserve water? Why or why not?
3. Highlight and annotate as you read.

1300***L***/1239 words

# Why Conserve Water

## Andrew Parker

1   Living in the United States, where water is plentiful in most areas, it is often easy to forget that a growing portion of the world's population faces significant water shortages and a host of related problems. Water is a global resource, and water shortage is a global issue. Even if your community has enough water right now, it is important to understand the larger issue and take action. Your efforts can help to lessen the global impact of this problem, and they can also spare you from experiencing a severe water shortage in the future.

### Water Shortage—A Global Issue

2   The World Health Organization (WHO) recently reported that on each continent, water shortages impact the lives of one in three people. The WHO also found that over a billion people—more than 20% of the global population—face water scarcities in their own communities.[1] The basic outline of the problem is simple—the amount of water on the earth remains constant, and has not changed for millions of years. If there is a shortage, it must mean that our water habits are to blame. Indeed, that is the case—as our society advanced, we began to use water at rates far beyond a sustainable level. At the end of the 20th century, we were using water at nine times the rate it was used in the early 1900s. During that same period, the global population only increased by a factor of four.[2]

3   The problem would be bad enough if current water usage levels were stable, but unfortunately, our water consumption continues to increase. This means that in just the next couple of decades millions and millions of people will be directly impacted by water scarcity. The proportion of people living in so-called "water

[1]http://www.who.int/features/factfiles/water/en/
[2]http://www.independent.co.uk/environment/climate-change/water-scarcity-now-bigger-threat-than-financial-crisis-1645358.html

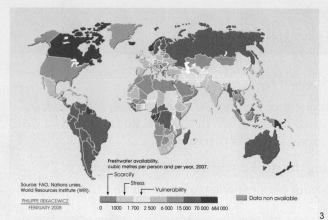

Freshwater availability, cubic metres per person and per year, 2007.

— Scarcity
  — Stress
    — Vulnerability

0   1000  1 700  2 500  6 000  15 000  70 000  684 000    Data non available

Source: FAO, Nations unies,
World Resources Institute (WRI).

PHILIPPE REKACEWICZ
FEBRUARY 2008

SOURCE:  Vital Water Graphics, 2nd. ed., United Nations
              Environment Programme

3

stressed" countries, currently at 1/3, is projected to rise to 2/3 within the next 15 years.[4] This is due to both increased water consumption and projected population growth. If water use per person were held constant, we would still be facing problems due to a rapidly rising global population. Some analysts have predicted increases as high as 45% over the next 30 years![5]

## Effects of Water Shortages

4    Even without factoring in the growing severity of the water crisis, there are already many problems arising from current water shortages. Countries facing water shortages have seen increased rates of waterborne infections, such as cholera and typhoid fever, which result from drinking unsafe water. And because most of the drinkable water (and some that is not) is being consumed, more and more agricultural areas are using waste water to irrigate their crops—a practice that exposes even more people to the risk of disease.[6]

5    Continued agricultural development—and the water necessary to support it—is crucial as the world adapts to support its growing population. About 70% of the water we use is devoted to agriculture, not to individual homes and people.[7,8] Therefore, a shortage of water can result not only in less drinkable water, but less food to eat as well, which puts an even greater strain on the current world hunger crisis.

## AVERAGE WATER USE PER PERSON PER DAY

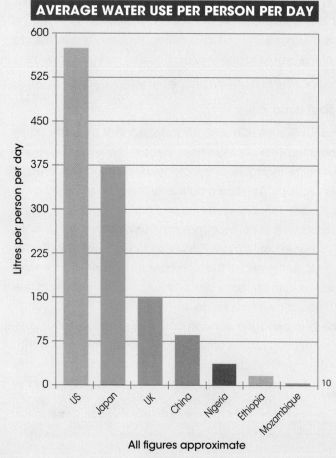

Litres per person per day

600
525
450
375
300
225
150
75
0

US   Japan   UK   China   Nigeria   Ethiopia   Mozambique

All figures approximate

10

## Why Should We Help?

6    Many people in the U.S. and other developed nations are now asking this question. It is, after all, a valid question when you consider that most Americans are able to access and use water freely with no consequences beyond a monthly water bill. Because it is so easy to ignore the problem, education is an important first step—people in developed nations need to know that their overconsumption has, and will continue to have, drastic effects on their local and global environment.

7    Moreover, we use too much water! This point is straightforward—people in the U.S. consume far more water than citizens of any other nation in the world. The average American uses hundreds of gallons per day, much of which—despite being safe to drink—is used for flushing toilets, watering lawns, and other non-vital purposes.[9]

[3]http://www.unep.org/dewa/vitalwater/jpg/0221-waterstress-EN.jpg
[4]http://news.bbc.co.uk/1/hi/sci/tech/3747724.stm
[5]http://www.livestrong.com/article/177896-how-does-saving-water-help/
[6]http://www.who.int/features/factfiles/water/en/
[7]http://news.bbc.co.uk/1/hi/sci/tech/3747724.stm
[8]http://www.worldometers.info/water/
[9]http://www.greeniacs.com/GreeniacsArticles/Water/The-Water-Crisis.html
[10]SOURCE: United Nations Development Programme–Human Development Report 2006. Graph created by Pearson.

We face a global problem of overconsumption, and it makes sense to fix the problem by starting with those who use the most.

8    Many argue that although we Americans consume more than our fair share, we are lucky to have advanced technology and plentiful water sources that have kept us largely immune to the consequences of water scarcity. This argument may have been true in the past, but it is less true today and will cease being a reality in the coming decades. States across the country, including those with large populations such as New York, Florida and California, have experienced severe droughts in recent years. A government report released in 2007 predicted that more than half the states in the U.S. would struggle with significant water shortages in the very near future. [11] Indeed, there are already warning signs, as lakes are shrinking and reservoirs are running low from coast to coast. Jack Hoffbuhr, executive director of the American Water Works Association, summed up the situation with this comment: "Is it a crisis? If we don't do some decent water planning, it could be." [12]

## Water Shortage and Climate Change

9    The growing population and increasing water consumption within the United States contribute not only to a draining of our natural resources, but also accelerate the pace of climate change, otherwise referred to as global warming. Water treatment and processing methods are extremely energy-intensive, and they produce an amount of greenhouse gas equivalent to that of 10 million cars. [13] Many regions of the U.S. are already starting to feel the effects of global warming and the people living there should understand that their water use habits are directly contributing to the problem, both at home and around the world.

## Water Is a Global Resource

10    Despite all the evidence, many individuals still remain unconvinced by the arguments in favor of reducing water usage. For most U.S. residents, the problem has just not grown large enough to warrant a significant change in lifestyle. But our choices about water use don't just affect us—they impact everyone around the world.

11    Tony Allan, a professor at King's College London, recently introduced the idea of **"virtual water."** He defines the term as water that is required to create a product, such as an agricultural crop. [14] The water that goes into these products does not stay in the local community, but instead is often transported to other parts of the world. In this way, regions with plentiful water can share that resource with others who lack it. [15] But this system of sharing virtual water only works as long as there are producers with easy access to water, which is not just a sufficient amount of water for themselves, but enough to invest in products for sale and trade. The parts of the world that meet these criteria are rapidly shrinking, and this means that fewer water-rich products will be available for water-deprived people. [16] It is important to conserve and maintain your local water supply not only for the sake of its future and the future of your community,

[11] http://www.msnbc.msn.com/id/21494919/ns/us_news-environment/t/crisis-feared-us-water-supplies-dry/
[12] Id.
[13] http://www.nrdc.org/water/files/energywater.pdf
[14] http://www.livestrong.com/article/177896-how-does-saving-water-help/
[15] Id.
[16] Id.

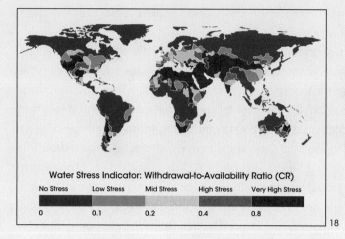

Water Stress Indicator: Withdrawal-to-Availability Ratio (CR)

| No Stress | Low Stress | Mid Stress | High Stress | Very High Stress |
|---|---|---|---|---|
| 0 | 0.1 | 0.2 | 0.4 | 0.8 |

[18]

but because small changes in water availability for you can easily translate into big changes for someone on the other side of the world.

12    Finally, there is a great deal of "water stress" in the U.S., so the "not in my backyard" thought process just can't be sustained for much longer. Water stress is a ratio of water usage and water resources, the higher the ratio, the worse off we are.[17] By starting to change our water consumption habits now, we can prevent a severe crisis at home, and worry less about our children's future as well.

-—Article available at: http://www.greeniacs.com/ GreeniacsArticles/Water/Why-Conserve-Water.html

---

[17]http://www.worldwatercouncil.org/index.php?id=25
[18]Id.

# Getting Ready to Write

## Checking Your Comprehension

Answer each of the following questions using complete sentences.

1. According to the WHO, how many people on each continent are affected by water shortages?
2. How did water usage at the end of the 20th century compare to the usage rate in the early 1900s?
3. What proportion of people are living in "water stressed" countries?
4. What are two examples of water-borne infections which result from drinking unsafe water?
5. What percentage of the water we use is devoted to agriculture?
6. According to the visual "Water Use Around the World," how much water does the average American use per day? Approximately how much does the U.N. recommend as a basic minimum?
7. The amount of greenhouse gas produced by water treatment and processing methods is equivalent to the amount produced by what other source?

## Strengthening Your Vocabulary

Using the word's context, word parts, or a dictionary, write a brief definition of each of the following words as it is used in the reading.

1. host (paragraph 1) _____ multitude
2. impact (paragraph 2) _____ affect
3. scarcities (paragraph 2) _____ shortages
4. stable (paragraph 3) _____ constant, unchanging
5. crucial (paragraph 5) _____ extremely important
6. immune (paragraph 8) _____ not affected, safe
7. accelerate (paragraph 9) _____ speed up

## Examining the Reading: Using Idea Maps

Review the reading by completing the missing parts of the following idea map.

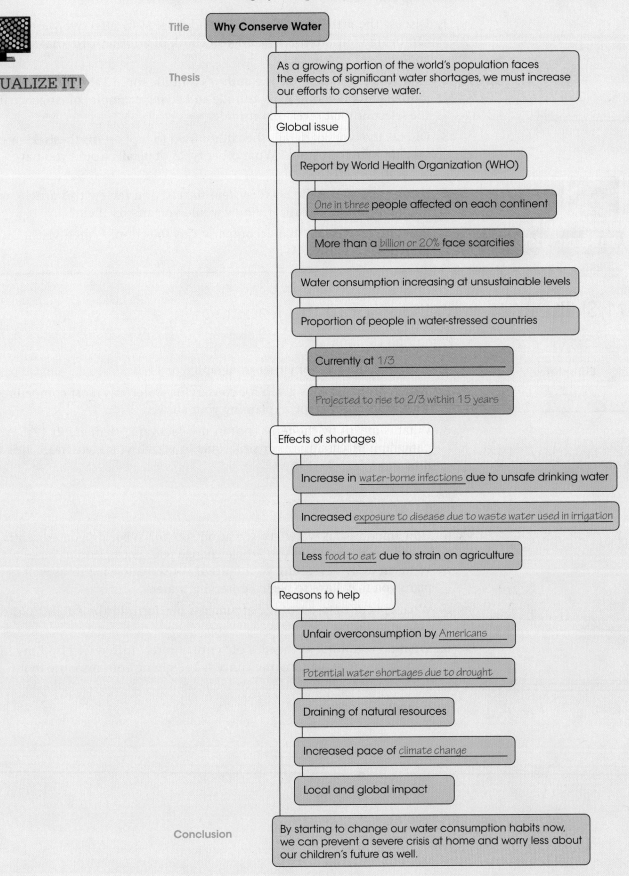

VISUALIZE IT!

Title — **Why Conserve Water**

Thesis — As a growing portion of the world's population faces the effects of significant water shortages, we must increase our efforts to conserve water.

Global issue

Report by World Health Organization (WHO)

_One in three_ people affected on each continent

More than a _billion or 20%_ face scarcities

Water consumption increasing at unsustainable levels

Proportion of people in water-stressed countries

Currently at _1/3_

_Projected to rise to 2/3 within 15 years_

Effects of shortages

Increase in _water-borne infections_ due to unsafe drinking water

Increased _exposure to disease due to waste water used in irrigation_

Less _food to eat_ due to strain on agriculture

Reasons to help

Unfair overconsumption by _Americans_

_Potential water shortages due to drought_

Draining of natural resources

Increased pace of _climate change_

Local and global impact

Conclusion — By starting to change our water consumption habits now, we can prevent a severe crisis at home and worry less about our children's future as well.

## Thinking Critically: Discussion and Journal Writing

Respond and react to the reading by discussing the following:

1. Discuss the article's introduction and title. How effective were each in capturing your attention? Can you think of another title that would be appropriate?

2. How would you describe the author's attitude toward the subject? Write a journal entry describing his attitude and giving examples of language from the selection that reveal his attitude.

3. Discuss the types of details the author used to support his thesis. How convincing were the details? What other types of details would you have liked to see in this article?

4. If you were to use the SQ3R system to read and review this article, what questions would you ask and how would you answer them?

5. Evaluate the visuals that accompany this selection. Which visual did you find most persuasive? Why?

**THINKING VISUALLY**

## MySkillsLab®

**Complete**
this
Exercise

## Writing About the Reading

### Paragraph Options

1. Write a paraphrase for either paragraph 8 or 11.

2. Which of the reasons given for conserving water was most compelling to you? Write a paragraph explaining your answer.

3. What is meant by the term "not in my backyard" (paragraph 12)? Write a paragraph discussing other situations in which you have heard this term used.

### Essay Options

4. How important is water conservation to you? What do you currently do to conserve water? Did this article change your perception of water usage? Write an essay describing your current conservation habits as well as any plans you may have to begin conserving water.

5. What is your opinion of the arguments put forth in the article? Write an essay explaining your ideas.

6. What do you think of the idea of "virtual water" introduced by Tony Allan? Write an essay explaining the concept and giving your response to it.

# SELF-TEST SUMMARY

To test yourself, cover the Answer column with a sheet of paper and answer each question in the left column. Evaluate each of your answers as you work by sliding the paper down and comparing your answer with what is printed in the Answer column.

| QUESTION | ANSWER |
| --- | --- |
| ■ **GOAL 1** Read to organize and retain information<br><br>What are the two steps in organizing and retaining information? How does the SQ3R system help you retain information? | First, decide what is important to learn, then use a system that will help you retain information. The SQ3R system integrates reading and study techniques through five steps: *survey, question, read, recite,* and *review.* |
| ■ **GOAL 2** Outline to organize information<br><br>What is important in creating an outline? | Read a section completely before writing. Place the most important ideas closer to the left margin. Use either words and phrases or complete sentences. Use your own words. Be sure all the information under a heading explains or supports the heading. |
| ■ **GOAL 3** Map to discover organization<br><br>What is mapping? How do you draw a map? | Mapping is a visual method of organizing information. Identify the overall topic and major ideas that relate to the topic. Connect each piece of information to the central topic. As you discover supporting details, connect them with new lines. |
| ■ **GOAL 4** Paraphrase to restate ideas of others<br><br>What is a paraphrase? When is paraphrasing useful? | A paraphrase restates the ideas of a passage in your own words. Paraphrasing is useful for recording information from reference sources and for understanding material that is difficult, detailed, slanted, or stylistically complex. Always cite the source of the material you are paraphrasing to avoid plagiarism. |
| ■ **GOAL 5** Summarize to condense information<br><br>What is a summary? What are the steps in writing a good summary? | A summary is a compact restatement of the important points of a passage. Underline major ideas, write a topic sentence stating the writer's most important idea, use your own words, focus on major ideas, keep ideas in the same order as in the original material, and cite the source of the passage. |

**MySkillsLab** For more help with **Understanding and Organizing Information**, go to your learning path in MySkillsLab at http://www.myskillslab.com.

# 16

# Reading and Thinking Critically About Text

## THINK About It!

What is happening in the photograph on this page? Most likely you said that an athlete has just won a race, but how did you know? No doubt you used clues in the photograph such as the runner's attire, the finish line ribbon, and so forth.

What was the photographer's purpose in taking this photograph? That is, what did he or she want to show or emphasize? The smile on the athlete's face and his gestures are obvious and noticeable in the photograph. The photographer's purpose, then, may be to show the elation of victory. As you read text, you will also need to pick up on clues the author provides, especially when ideas are only suggested instead of directly stated. When you write, you will want to be sure to give your readers the right clues to make clear your purpose and help them understand your ideas. In this chapter you will learn to pick up on clues (called making inferences), evaluate the author's purpose, analyze the author's intended audience, distinguish fact from opinion, and identify bias.

# FOCUSING ON READING AND WRITING

# What Is Critical Reading?

**Reading critically** means questioning, reacting to, and evaluating what you read. Critical reading is an essential skill because most college instructors expect you to understand what you read *and* respond to it critically. When using sources to support or explain your ideas in an essay, be sure to read the sources carefully and critically. Critical reading is also important as you read and evaluate your drafts and look for ways to improve them.

# READING

Reading critically involves asking questions about what you read, rather than just accepting everything you read as true and correct. Many college students who develop their critical thinking skills through their assignments find themselves carrying these skills through to their everyday reading. They may see a headline on a magazine in the supermarket and think, "That doesn't sound possible" or "Do they really expect me to believe this?" They also come to view advertisements and commercials with a more critical eye, wondering if the advertised product really does what it promises to do and whether it is worth the money.

# How to Read Critically

■ GOAL 1
Read critically

To develop the habit of thinking critically as you read, use the following suggestions each time you work with an assignment:

- **Read the selection more than once.** Read it several times, if necessary, to understand the author's message; then read it again to analyze and evaluate the author's ideas.

- **Read with a pen or highlighter in your hand.** Highlight important passages or particularly meaningful or insightful sentences and phrases. Highlighting can be particularly useful for reviewing and summary writing. (For a review of highlighting, see Chapter 1.)

- **Make marginal notes as you read.** Write notes in the margins to record what you are thinking as you read. These notes will be helpful as you write about the reading. (See Chapter 1 for more detailed instructions on annotating.)

- **Ask questions as you read.** Question and challenge the author and the ideas presented. How do the ideas mesh or fit with your own knowledge, experiences, beliefs, and values? If they do not fit, ask why. Do you need to adjust your thinking or do further reading or research on the topic?

## Ask Critical Questions

Asking questions is a way of expanding your thinking, as well as a way of discovering ideas to write about. Here are a few examples of critical questions you might ask about a particular reading.

- **What do you know about the author?** Many readings provide a brief introduction. This *headnote* often provides information about the writer or the context in which the piece was written. Knowing the author's background can help you better understand or appreciate the reading. (In this book, the headnotes are labeled "Thinking Before Reading." For examples, see pp. 528 and 557.)

- **When was the piece written?** Having a sense of the time frame involved can shed light on the issues being discussed. For example, today we take women's rights somewhat for granted. But in the 1800s and early 1900s, women were still struggling for the rights to vote and own property.

- **What emotions does the reading stir in you?** Does it make you thoughtful, cheerful, or angry? Why does the reading have this effect on you?

- **What doesn't sound right or seems impossible or unlikely?** If an idea seems odd or a fact seems not to fit with what you already know, be sure to question it. Check it further through online research or using other sources.

---

**EXERCISE 16-1** | ## Reading Critically

**Directions:** Read the paragraph, and then think critically and analytically to answer the questions that follow. Write a sentence or two answering each question. *Answers will vary. Possible answers are shown.*

> Back in the day, the "typical" marijuana smoker (or at least the stereotype) was a bearded, bell-bottomed hippie who zoned out in front of the TV watching reruns on *Nick at Night* and eating Oreos by the bagful. Today, there's a good chance a user is a senior citizen or a suburban housewife who smokes joints to fight the negative effects of glaucoma or chemotherapy. Pot is going mainstream. The drug is legal with a prescription in 14 states including California, Colorado, and New Jersey, and some feel it's only a matter of time before American voters decide in favor of full-scale legalization.
>
> —Solomon, Marshall, and Stuart,
> *Marketing: Real People, Real Choices*, p. 20

1. Why do the authors begin by describing the stereotype of a marijuana smoker?

   They want to create a dramatic and distinct contrast between the image of marijuana

   users in the past and the type of person who they describe as a marijuana user today.

   The implication is that in the past, marijuana users were less respectable than they are

   today.

2. The authors claim "there's a good chance" that today's users are senior citizens or suburban housewives. Why might this phrase be misleading?

*The phrase is vague and does not provide an actual percentage or figure to back up the claim, nor does it explain the source of this information. The phrase implies that many senior citizens and suburban housewives use marijuana, leaving readers to guess at the actual number; it may actually be a small minority.*

3. What sentence in the passage makes it sound as though marijuana use is becoming common?

*The authors say, "Pot is going mainstream," suggesting that marijuana use is becoming the norm rather than the exception.*

4. What part of the last sentence in the passage provides a fact about the legalization of marijuana? How does the sentence mesh with your own knowledge, experiences, beliefs, and values?

*The drug is legal with a prescription in 14 states including California, Colorado, and New Jersey. Answers will vary about whether it's only a matter of time before American voters decide to legalize marijuana.*

# Make Inferences

■ GOAL 2
Make inferences

Just as you use inference when you study a photograph, you also use it when you try to figure out why a friend is sad or what an author's message is in a particular piece of writing. An **inference** is an educated guess or prediction about something unknown based on available facts and information. It is the logical connection that you draw between what you observe or know and what you do not know.

Here are a few everyday situations. Make an inference for each.

■ You are driving on an expressway and you notice a police car with flashing red lights behind you. You check your speedometer and notice that you are going ten miles per hour over the speed limit.

■ A woman seated alone in a bar nervously glances at everyone who enters. Every few minutes she checks her watch.

In the first situation, a good inference might be that you are going to be stopped for speeding. However, it is possible that the officer only wants to pass you to get to an accident ahead or to stop someone driving faster than you. In the second situation, one inference is that the woman is waiting to meet someone who is late; another is that she is waiting for someone she has never met, maybe a blind date.

When you make inferences about what you read, you go beyond what a writer says and consider what he or she *means*. You have already done this, to some extent, in Chapters 4 and 11 as you inferred the meanings of words from context and figured out implied main ideas. Thus, you know that writers may directly state some ideas but hint at others. It is left to the reader, then, to pick up the clues or suggestions and to figure out the writer's unstated message. This chapter will show you how to do so.

## How to Make Inferences

Making an inference is a thinking process. As you read, you are following the writer's thoughts. You are also alert for ideas that are suggested but not directly stated. Because inference is a logical thought process, there is no simple, step-by-step procedure to follow. Each inference depends on the situation, the facts provided, and the reader's knowledge and experience.

However, here are a few guidelines to keep in mind as you read. These will help you get in the habit of looking beyond the factual level.

1. **Be sure you understand the literal meaning.** Before you can make inferences, you need a clear grasp of the facts, the writer's main ideas, and the supporting details.

2. **Notice details.** Often a particular detail provides a clue that will help you make an inference. When you spot a striking or unusual detail, ask yourself: Why did the writer include this piece of information? Remember that there are many kinds of details, such as descriptions, actions, and conversations.

3. **Add up the facts.** Consider all the facts taken together. Ask yourself: What is the writer trying to suggest from this set of facts? What do all these facts and ideas point toward?

4. **Look at the writer's choice of words.** A writer's word choice often suggests his or her attitude toward the subject. Notice, in particular, descriptive words, emotionally charged words, and words that are very positive or negative.

5. **Understand the writer's purpose.** An author's purpose, which is discussed in the next section, affects many aspects of a piece of writing. Ask yourself: Why did the author write this?

6. **Be sure your inference is supportable.** An inference must be based on fact. Make sure there is sufficient evidence to justify any inference you make.

Keep the preceding guidelines in mind as you read the following passage. Try to infer why Cindy Kane is standing on the corner of Sheridan and Sunnyside.

> An oily midnight mist had settled on the city streets . . . asphalt mirrors from a ten-o'clock rain now past . . . a sleazy street-corner reflection of smog-smudged neon . . . the corner of Sheridan and, incongruously, Sunnyside . . . Chicago.
>
> A lone lady lingers at the curb . . . but no bus will come.
>
> She is Cindy Kane, twenty-eight. Twenty-eight hard years old. Her iridescent dress clings to her slender body. Her face is buried under a Technicolor avalanche of makeup.
>
> She is Cindy Kane.
>
> And she has a date.
>
> With someone she has never met . . . and may never meet again.
>
> Minutes have turned to timelessness . . . and a green Chevy four-door pulls slowly around the corner.
>
> The driver's window rolls down. A voice comes from the shadow . . .
>
> "Are you working?"
>
> Cindy nods . . . regards him with vacant eyes.
>
> He beckons.
>
> She approaches the passenger side. Gets in. And the whole forlorn, unromantic ritual begins all over again. With another stranger.
>
> —Paul Aurandt, *Paul Harvey's The Rest of the Story,* p. 116.

If you made the right inferences, you realized that Cindy Kane is a prostitute and that she is standing on the corner waiting for a customer. Let us look at some of the clues the writer gives that lead to this inference.

- **Descriptive details:** By the way the writer describes Cindy Kane, you begin to suspect that she is a prostitute. She is wearing an iridescent, clinging dress and a lot of makeup, which convey the image of a gaudy, unconventional appearance. As the writer describes the situation, he slips in other clues. He establishes the time as around midnight ("An oily midnight mist"). His reference to a "reflection of smog-smudged neon" suggests an area of bars or nightclubs.

- **Action details:** The actions, although few, also provide clues about what is happening. The woman is lingering on the corner. When the car approaches, she gets in.

- **Conversation details:** The only piece of conversation, the question, "Are you working?" is one of the strongest clues the writer provides.

- **Word choice:** The writer has chosen words that help to convey the image and situation of a prostitute. Cindy is described as "hard," and her makeup is "a Technicolor avalanche." In the last paragraph, the phrase "forlorn, unromantic ritual" provides a final clue.

## EXERCISE 16-2    Analyzing Inferences

**Directions:** Read each of the following passages. Using inference, determine whether the statements following each passage are true (T) or false (F). Write your answer in the space provided before each statement.

A.    Eye-to-eye contact and response are important in real-life relationships. The nature of a person's eye contact patterns, whether he or she looks another squarely in the eye or looks to the side or shifts his gaze from side to side, tells a lot about the person. These patterns also play a significant role in success or failure in human relationships. Despite its importance, eye contact is not involved in television watching. Yet children spend several hours a day in front of the television set. Certain children's programs pretend to speak directly to each individual child. (Mr. Rogers is an example, telling the child "I like you, you're special," etc.) However, this is still one-way communication and no response is required of the child. How might such a distortion of real-life relationships affect a child's development of trust, of openness, of an ability to relate well to other people?

—Weaver, *Understanding Interpersonal Communication*, p. 291

___T___ **1.** To develop a strong relationship with someone, you should look directly at him or her.

___F___ **2.** The writer has a positive attitude toward television.

___F___ **3.** The writer thinks that television helps children relate well to other people.

___T___ **4.** The writer would probably recommend that children spend more time talking to others and playing with other children than watching television.

B.      There is little the police or other governmental agencies can't find out about you these days. For starters, the police can hire an airplane and fly over your backyard filming you sunbathing and whatever else is visible from above. A mail cover allows the post office, at the request of another government or police agency, to keep track of people sending you mail and organizations sending you literature through the mail. Police or other governmental agencies may have access to your canceled checks and deposit records to find out who is writing checks to you and to whom you are writing checks. Even the trash you discard may be examined to see what you are throwing away.

No doubt by now you've realized that all of this information provides a fairly complete and accurate picture about a person, including his or her health, friends, lovers, political and religious activities, and even beliefs. Figure that, if the Gillette razor company knows when it's your eighteenth birthday to send you a sample razor, your government, with its super, interconnecting computers, knows much more about you.

—Lewis Katz, *Know Your Rights*, p. 54

___F___ **5.** The writer seems to trust government agencies.

___T___ **6.** The writer would probably oppose forcing libraries to give the police information about the books you read.

___T___ **7.** The writer is in favor of strengthening citizens' rights to privacy.

C.      George Washington is remembered not for what he was but for what he should have been. It doesn't do any good to point out that he was an "inveterate landgrabber," and that as a young man he illegally had a surveyor stake out some prize territory west of the Alleghenies in an area decreed off limits to settlers. Washington is considered a saint, and nothing one says is likely to make him seem anything less. Though he was a wily businessman and accumulated a fortune speculating in frontier lands, he will always be remembered as a farmer—and a "simple farmer" at that.

Even his personal life is misremembered. While Washington admitted despising his mother and in her dying years saw her infrequently, others maintain that he remembered his mother fondly and considered himself a devoted son. While his own records show he was something of a dandy and paid close attention to the latest clothing designs, ordering "fashionable" hose, the "neatest shoes," and coats with "silver trimmings," practically no one thinks he was vain. Though he loved to drink and dance and encouraged others to join him, the first president is believed to have been something of a prude.

—Shenkman, *Legends, Lies, and Cherished Myths of American History*, pp. 37–38

___T___ **8.** Washington is usually remembered as saintlike because he was one of the founding fathers and our first president.

___T___ **9.** The writer considers Washington dishonest and vain.

___F___ **10.** The writer believes that eventually Americans' attitudes toward Washington will change.

## EXERCISE 16-3    Making Inferences

**Directions:** After reading the following selection, select the choice that best answers each of the questions that follow.

### The Man, The Boy, and The Donkey

A Man and his son were once going with their Donkey to market. As they were walking along by its side a countryman passed them and said: "You fools, what is a Donkey for but to ride upon?" So the Man put the Boy on the Donkey and they went on their way.

But soon they passed a group of men, one of whom said: "See that lazy youngster, he lets his father walk while he rides." So the Man ordered his Boy to get off, and got on himself.

But they hadn't gone far when they passed two women, one of whom said to the other: "Shame on that lazy lout to let his poor little son trudge along." Well, the Man didn't know what to do, but at last he took his Boy up before him on the Donkey.

By this time they had come to the town, and the passers-by began to jeer and point at them. The Man stopped and asked what they were scoffing at. The men said: "Aren't you ashamed of yourself for overloading that poor donkey of yours and your hulking son?" The Man and Boy got off and tried to think what to do. They thought and they thought, till at last they cut down a pole, tied the donkey's feet to it, and raised the pole and the donkey to their shoulders. They went along amid the laughter of all who met them till they came to Market Bridge, when the Donkey, getting one of his feet loose, kicked out and caused the Boy to drop his end of the pole. In the struggle the Donkey fell over the bridge, and his fore-feet being tied together he was drowned.

"That will teach you," said an old man who had followed them: "Please all, and you will please none."

*—Aesop's Fables*

_b_____ 1. Which of the following words or phrases suggests disapproval?
    **a.** teach
    **b.** lout
    **c.** passers-by
    **d.** poor little son

_c_____ 2. Which statement best describes the Man in the fable?
    **a.** The Man is ignorant and uncaring about animal rights.
    **b.** The Man is insensitive to the needs of his son.
    **c.** The Man readily accepts the opinions of others.
    **d.** The Man does not know how to care for a donkey.

_a_____ 3. Why did the Man and Boy tie the donkey to the pole?
    **a.** They attempted to find a solution that met all three criticisms they had received.
    **b.** They were unable to control the donkey by any other means.
    **c.** The Man thought he could save the donkey's life.
    **d.** The son felt threatened by the crowd.

_b_ **4.** The passersby could best be described as
   **a.** angry
   **b.** well-meaning
   **c.** amusing
   **d.** thoughtless

_d_ **5.** The purpose of the story is to explain that
   **a.** animals should be treated with respect.
   **b.** you should ignore the opinions of others.
   **c.** public opinion is usually untrustworthy.
   **d.** you cannot make everyone happy.

# Identify the Author's Purpose

■ **GOAL 3**
Identify the author's purpose

Authors have many different reasons or purposes for writing. Some of the most common purposes are

- ■ **To inform or instruct**. Authors write to present information to their readers.
- ■ **To persuade**. Authors write to convince readers to accept a particular idea or take a particular action.
- ■ **To amuse or entertain**. Authors may write to tell an amusing story, share an entertaining meaningful experience, or make a comment on human behavior.

Read the following statements and try to decide why each was written.

1. About 14,000 ocean-going ships pass through the Panama Canal each year. This averages nearly forty ships per day.
2. New Unsalted Dry Roasted Almonds. Finally, a snack with a natural flavor and without salt. We simply shell the nuts and dry-roast them until they're crispy and crunchy. Try a jar this week.
3. Humans are the only animals that blush or have a need to.

The statements above were written (1) to give information, (2) to persuade you to buy almonds, and (3) to amuse you and make a comment on human behavior.

In each of the examples, the writer's purpose was fairly clear, as it will be in most textbooks, newspaper articles, and reference books. However, in many other types of writing, authors have less obvious purposes. In these cases, an author's purpose must be inferred. Here's how to discover the author's purpose:

## ! NEED TO KNOW

### Identifying the Author's Purpose

1. **Ask yourself, "What is the writer trying to tell me? What does he or she want me to do or think?"** If you've read carefully and the reading is not too long, you will often be able to answer these questions in one or two sentences.

2. **Pay close attention to the title of the piece and the source of the material because these may offer clues.** Suppose an article is titled "Twenty-Six Reasons to Vote in National Elections."

The title suggests that the author's purpose is to urge citizens to vote. If an essay on the lumber industry appears in *Eco-Ideas*, a magazine devoted to environmental preservation, you might predict that the author's purpose is to call for restrictions on the logging industry or for sustainable logging practices.

3. **Look for clues or statements about purpose in the beginning and concluding paragraphs.** Suppose an essay concludes with a statement such as "For all these reasons, it is vitally important to have a job that is rewarding and satisfying." This statement reveals that the author's purpose is to convince readers and win them over to a certain point of view.

---

**EXERCISE 16-4**   Identifying the Author's Purpose

**Directions:** Based on the title of each of the following articles, predict the author's purpose. Answers will vary. Possible answers are shown.

1. Changing Habits: How Online Shopping Can Change Your Life

   to inform

2. I Got Straight A's, but I Wasn't Happy

   to complain

3. Animals Can't Speak: We Must Speak for Them

   to encourage action

4. Guns Don't Kill People: People Kill People

   to argue a position

5. What the Bible Says About the End of the World

   to inform, to interpret

6. Sources of Drug Information

   to inform

7. Holy Week in Spain

   to describe

8. Two Famous Twentieth-Century Composers

   to compare or contrast, to describe

9. Internet Scams: You Could Be Next

   to warn or advise

10. Biofuels: A Look to the Future

   to predict

## EXERCISE 16-5 Writing with Purpose

**Directions:** For each of the following purposes, write a sentence that achieves it.
Answers will vary. Possible answers are shown.

**EXAMPLE** **Purpose:** To make a humorous comment about human behavior

**Sentence:** Mark Twain once said "Never put off until tomorrow what you can do the day after tomorrow."

1. To give advice  To avoid procrastination, divide a project into short, easy-to-accomplish tasks.

2. To persuade a friend to eat healthier foods  Following a healthy diet can help you maintain or lose weight.

3. To provide information about today's weather  Rain and thunderstorms are forecast for later this afternoon in areas south of Buffalo.

4. To give someone directions to your home  To reach my home take Exit 32 and follow the signs for Porter Avenue.

5. To convey what it feels like to be in love  Love is a joyous feeling of happiness and contentment.

# Analyze the Writer's Intended Audience

■ GOAL 4
Analyze the intended audience.

Writers vary their styles to suit their intended audiences. A writer may write for a general-interest audience (anyone who is interested in the subject but is not considered an expert). Most newspapers and periodicals, such as *Time* and *Newsweek*, appeal to a general-interest audience. On the other hand, a writer may have a particular interest group in mind. A writer may write for medical doctors in the *Journal of American Medicine*, for skiing enthusiasts in *Skiing Today*, or for antique collectors in *The World of Antiques*. A writer may also target his or her writing for an audience with particular political, moral, or religious attitudes. Articles in the *New Republic* often appeal to a particular political viewpoint, whereas the *Catholic Digest* appeals to a specific religious group.

Depending on the group of people for whom the author is writing, he or she will change the level of language, choice of words, and method of presentation. One step toward identifying an author's purpose, then, is to ask yourself the question: Who is the intended audience? Your response will be your first clue to determining why the author wrote the article.

## EXERCISE 16-6 Analyzing Intended Audience

**Directions:** After reading each of the following statements, select the choice that best describes the audience for whom each was written.

_c_    **1.** Chances are you're going to be putting money away over the next five years or so. You are hoping for the right things in life. Right now, a smart place to put your money is in mutual funds or bonds.

 a. people who are struggling to pay for basic needs like rent and food
 b. people who are very wealthy and have been investing their money for many years
 c. people with enough income that they can think of investing some for the future
 d. people who are using their extra income to pay off credit-card debt and student loans

_d_    **2.** Think about all the places your drinking water has been before you drink another drop. Most likely it has been chemically treated to remove bacteria and chemical pollutants. Soon you may begin to feel the side effects of these treatments. Consider switching to filtered, distilled water today.

 a. people who have no interest in environmental issues
 b. chemists
 c. employees of the Environmental Protection Agency
 d. people who are concerned about the environment and their health

_b_    **3.** Introducing the new, high-powered Supertuner III, a sound system guaranteed to keep your mother out of your car.

 a. drivers who love music
 b. teenagers who own cars
 c. parents of teenage drivers
 d. specialists in stereo equipment

_a_    **4.** The life cycle of many species of plants involves an alternation of generations in which individuals of the gametophyte generation produce gametes that fuse and develop into individuals of a sporophyte generation.
—adapted from Wallace, _Biology: The World of Life,_ p. 271

 a. biology students
 b. readers of general-interest magazines
 c. gardeners
 d. managers of landscaping companies

_d_    **5.** As a driver, you're ahead of the repair game if you can learn to spot car trouble before it's too late. If you can learn the difference between the drips and squeaks that occur under normal conditions and those that mean big trouble is just down the road, then you'll be ahead of expensive repair bills and won't find yourself stranded on a lonely road.

 a. mechanics
 b. managers of auto-parts stores
 c. car owners who do the repairs and maintenance on their own cars
 d. car owners who are unfamiliar with a car's trouble signs and maintenance

| EXERCISE 16-7 | Analyzing Intended Audience |

**Directions:** Read each of the following statements, and then write a sentence that describes the intended audience. Answers will vary. Possible answers are shown.

1. If you are wondering what you should wear to a job interview, the best advice is to dress as though you already had the job. When in doubt, you will make a better impression by dressing your best rather than wearing casual attire, which might imply that your interest in the job is equally casual.

   *This was written for someone who is planning to interview for a job.*

   _____

2. A recent hacking incident revealed that hundreds of computer users have chosen the word "password" as their password and thousands more use sequential numbers such as "123456." To protect yourself from hacking, create a password that includes a mixture of upper- and lowercase letters, numbers, and symbols, and change your password every month.

   *This was written for people who use computers and want to safeguard the information*

   *they have on their computers.*

3. Bright and White laundry detergent removes dirt and stains faster than any other brand.

   *This was written for people who do laundry.*

   _____

4. One of the perks of being a college student is that you are eligible for a variety of discounts. By showing your student ID card, you can receive discounts at participating restaurants, theaters, and retail stores, and you can also save money on car insurance, travel, cell phone bills, and tickets for sporting events.

   *This was written for college students and possibly their parents/guardians.*

   _____

5. Parking around the concert hall is limited, so ticket holders should plan to carpool or take advantage of the free downtown trolley on the night of the concert.

   *This was written for people planning to attend a concert.*

   _____

# Distinguish Between Fact and Opinion

■ GOAL 5
Distinguish between fact and opinion

The ability to distinguish between fact and opinion is an important part of reading critically. You must be able to evaluate ideas you encounter and determine whether they are objective information from a reliable source or whether they are one person's expression of a personal belief or attitude.

## Facts

**Facts** are statements that can be verified. Statements of fact are objective—they contain information but do not tell what the writer thinks or believes about the topic or issue. The statement "My car payments are $250 per month" is a fact. It can be proven by looking at your car loan statement. Here are a few more statements of fact:

### *Facts*

- The population of the United States in January 2010 was 308,527,759. *(You can check this by looking at Census figures found online and in various fact books and almanacs.)*
- In Washington State, drivers must stop for pedestrians and bicyclists at crosswalks and intersections. *(You can check this in the Washington State Drivers' Guide.)*
- Greenpeace is an organization dedicated to protecting the environment, preserving ancient forests, sustaining the sea and its animals. *(You can check this by reading its mission statement or "About Us" on its Web site.)*

## Opinions

**Opinions** are statements that express a writer's feelings, attitudes, or beliefs. They are neither true nor false. They are one person's view about a topic or issue. The statement "My car payments are too expensive" is an opinion. It expresses your feelings about the cost of your auto payments. Others may disagree with you, especially the company that sold you the car or another person paying twice as much as you are paying. As you evaluate what you read, think of opinions as one person's viewpoint that you are free to accept or reject. Here are a few more examples of opinions:

### *Opinions*

- Bill Clinton was a better president than most people realize. *(Those who dislike Clinton's policies or lifestyle would disagree.)*
- The slaughter of baby seals for their pelts should be outlawed. *(Hunters who make their living selling pelts would disagree.)*
- Population growth should be regulated through mandatory birth control. *(People who do not believe in birth control would disagree.)*

---

**EXERCISE 16-8** | Identifying Fact and Opinion

**Directions:** Read the following statements and mark each one as either fact (F) or opinion (O).

   F    **1.** The Chicago Cubs baseball team has not won the World Series in 103 years.

   O    **2.** Alfred Hitchcock was the greatest director in the history of filmmaking.

   O    **3.** Organic gardening methods produce the biggest, tastiest vegetables.

   F    **4.** Female singers can be classified by pitch as soprano, mezzo-soprano, or contralto.

____F____ **5.** The Galapagos Islands are located on the equator, 600 miles west of mainland Ecuador.

____O____ **6.** Cloud storage for digital data is the wave of the future.

____F____ **7.** A recession is characterized by low prices, high unemployment, and a slowdown in business activity.

____O____ **8.** Bans on texting while driving should apply to all drivers regardless of age.

____F____ **9.** The country that became Iran in 1935 had been known for centuries as Persia.

____O____ **10.** Companies that test their products on animals should be required to disclose their practices to the public.

## Informed Opinion

The opinion of experts is known as **informed opinion.** Such opinions are considered more trustworthy and reliable than those of casual observers or non-professionals. Here are a two examples:

- Regina Benjamin, U.S. Surgeon General: "Because they are sensitive to nicotine, teens can feel dependent on tobacco sooner than adults. There is also evidence that genetics might make it more difficult for some young people to quit smoking once they have started."

- Bill Gates, philanthropist and cofounder of Microsoft: "Improving access to quality education is essential to putting students on a path to compete for good jobs or become entrepreneurs. Worldwide, we must invest more in education. In addition, access to technology and technology skills will be increasingly important elements of economic opportunity—whether you grow up in Africa or Alaska."

Textbook authors, too, often offer informed opinion. As experts in their fields, they may make observations and offer comments that are not strictly factual. Instead, they are based on years of study and research. Here is an example from an American government textbook:

> The United States is a place where the pursuit of private, particular, and narrow interests is honored. In our culture, following the teachings of Adam Smith, the pursuit of self-interest is not only permitted but actually celebrated as the basis of the good and prosperous society.
>
> —Greenberg and Page, *The Struggle for Democracy*, p. 186

The author of this statement has reviewed the available evidence and is providing his expert opinion on what the evidence indicates about American political culture. The reader, then, is free to disagree and offer evidence to support an opposing view.

Some authors are careful to signal the reader when they are presenting an opinion. Watch for words and phrases such as:

| | | | |
|---|---|---|---|
| apparently | this suggests | in my view | one explanation is |
| presumably | possibly | it is likely that | according to |
| In my opinion | it is believed | seemingly | |

| EXERCISE 16-9 | ## Distinguishing Fact and Opinion |

**Directions:** Read each topic sentence. Mark the statements that follow as fact (F), opinion (O), or informed opinion (IO).

1. **Topic sentence:** Cotton farmers use large amounts of fertilizers and pesticides.

   _O_ **a.** Chemical use should be avoided in cotton farming.

   _IO_ **b.** Researchers who have studied chemically sensitive individuals state that organically grown cotton is better for them.

   _F_ **c.** Cotton seeds are treated with fungicide.

   _F_ **d.** In some countries, farmers use DDT on cotton fields.

2. **Topic sentence:** Exercise is an important part of maintaining a healthy lifestyle.

   _O_ **a.** Regular exercise can improve your grades in school.

   _O_ **b.** People who do not exercise are lazy.

   _F_ **c.** Aerobic exercise stimulates blood circulation.

   _IO_ **d.** Doctors suggest stretching and relaxing every time you exercise.

3. **Topic sentence:** Mercury, the planet nearest to the sun, has no atmosphere.

   _O_ **a.** We know all we need to know about the planet Mercury.

   _F_ **b.** Mercury's year equals 88 Earth days.

   _IO_ **c.** Scientists believe that Mercury is uninhabitable.

   _F_ **d.** In 1974, an unmanned spacecraft flew within 460 miles of Mercury.

# Recognize Bias

■ GOAL 6
Recognize bias

When a writer or speaker deliberately presents a one-sided picture of a situation, it is known as bias. **Bias,** then, refers to an author's partiality, inclination toward a particular viewpoint, or prejudice. Now, think of a television commercial you have seen recently. Let's say it is for a particular model of car. The ad tells you its advantages—why you want to buy the car—but does it tell you its disadvantages? Does it describe ways in which the model compares unfavorably with competitors? Certainly not. Do you feel the ad writer is being unfair? Now let's say you know nothing about e-book readers and want to learn about them. You find an article titled "What you need to know about e-book readers." If the author of this article told you all the advantages of e-book readers, but none of their disadvantages, would you consider the article unfair? We expect advertisers to present a one-sided view of their products. In most other forms of writing, however, we expect writers to be honest and forthright. If a writer is explaining instant messaging he or she should explain it fully, revealing both strengths and weaknesses. To do otherwise is to present a biased point of view. You can think of bias as a writer's prejudice.

## How to Detect Bias

To detect bias, ask the following questions:

■ Is the author acting as a reporter—presenting facts—or as salesperson—providing only favorable information?

■ Does the author feel strongly about or favor one side of the issue?

- Does the author seem to be deliberately creating a positive or negative image?
- Does the author seem emotional about the issue?
- Are there other views toward the subject that the writer does not recognize or discuss?

The author's language and selection of facts also provide clues about his or her bias. Specifically, words with strong connotative (emotional) meanings or words that elicit an emotional response on the part of the reader suggest bias.

In the following excerpt from a newspaper article, the author's choice of words (see highlighting) reveals his attitudes toward the police checkpoints.

It started with a tip that checkpoints meant to nab drunken drivers were instead taking away cars, lots of them. The investigation confirmed those fears—and more.

As a report in *The Bee* showed on Sunday, the sobriety stops have become cash cows for California police departments and towing firms—and they're fattening their wallets disproportionately at the expense of Latino motorists.

This hijacking of the checkpoints is an unfair, and likely illegal, corruption of what is an effective tool to keep dangerous drivers off California's highways.

Last year at DUI checkpoints statewide, officers impounded more than 24,000 vehicles from drivers caught without a license but made only 3,200 drunken driving arrests, according to the nonpartisan Investigative Reporting Program at the University of California, Berkeley.

To recover their cars, owners paid an average of $1,805 in towing fees and police fines—a total of more than $13 million statewide. In about 70 percent of seizures, the owners didn't bother to retrieve their vehicles, which then were sold at auction to pay the fees and fines, generating an additional $29 million. Finally, the officers running the checkpoints collected about $30 million in overtime last year.

California law allows police to impound the cars of unlicensed drivers for 30 days if they endanger public safety. But at some checkpoints witnessed by reporters, the seized vehicles appeared just fine. And while getting unlicensed—typically uninsured—motorists off the road is worthwhile, the punishment is out of whack with the crime, especially when DUI suspects typically don't lose their cars.

It's understandable, perhaps, that cash-strapped cities and towns are intoxicated by a revenue generator, especially when federal money often pays for the operations.

It apparently is up to the courts to step in and end this abuse. A case is pending before the 9th U.S. Circuit Court of Appeals that challenges the constitutionality of the California law, arguing that police can't seize vehicles when the only violation is driving without a license.

The appeals court should put this cash cow out to pasture.

—Car Seizure Law Invites Abuses, Views of the editorial board,
*The Sacramento Bee*, February 20, 2010, p. A10

---

**EXERCISE 16-10**  ## Recognizing Bias

**Directions:** Place a check mark in front of each statement that reveals bias.

__✓__ 1. Cities should be designed for the pedestrian, not the automobile.

_____ 2. There are more channels than ever before on cable television.

_✓_    3. The current system of voter registration is a sham.

_✓_    4. Professional sports have become elitist.

_____    5. Space exploration costs millions of dollars each year.

| EXERCISE 16-11 | Identifying Bias |

**Directions:** After reading each passage, select the choice that best answers each of the questions that follow.

The fact that different climate studies reach widely different conclusions is not surprising. Much of the global warming debate centers on the output of highly questionable computer models that conjure figures from scarcely understood variables, dubious raw data and gaping holes filled with assumptions that usually confirm the researchers' biases. No wonder that even as reliable temperature measurements show global temperatures have flatlined or been falling for the past decade, claims of imminent catastrophe have grown more shrill. Garbage in, warming out.

—Editorial, "A Climate of Fraud," *The Washington Times*, November 30, 2011, p. 2

_b_    1. The author seems biased against
    a. all computer models
    b. global warming advocates
    c. global warming measurement
    d. climate study

_c_    2. Which of the following phrases best reveals the author's bias?
    a. "widely different conclusions"
    b. "temperatures have flatlined"
    c. "gaping holes filled with assumptions"
    d. "global warming debate centers on"

Plenty of statistics show a large number of offenders should never go to prison for nonviolent offenses. I, too, believe that the record should be expunged when the sentence is served. It is bad enough to have to pay back fines and court costs and perhaps child support that has accumulated during years in prison. To not be able to rent an apartment or get a job only ensures the person will soon return to prison. Criminologists have known for years that harsh punishments do not prevent crime. The plain fact is prisons are money-makers. Nothing is done for rehabilitation in the prisons, especially the private ones, which are only interested in the money. Frequently, the media, written and broadcast, are responsible for stirring up fear of being "soft on crime." Oklahomans should be thoroughly ashamed to have more women in prison than any other state. Rehabilitation programs work as do monitoring and community service.

—Morrow, "Letter to the Editor: Life After Prison," *Tulsa World*, April 2010, p. A16

___b___  **3.** The author's primary bias concerns the
   **a.** length of criminal sentences in general.
   **b.** imprisonment of nonviolent criminals.
   **c.** media portrayal of crime.
   **d.** cost of imprisonment.

___a___  **4.** Which of the following phrases expresses the author's bias?
   **a.** "offenders should never go to prison for nonviolent offenses"
   **b.** "soft on crime"
   **c.** "Oklahomans should be thoroughly ashamed"
   **d.** "more women in prison"

More than half of all video games are rated as containing violence, including more than 90% of games rated as appropriate for children 10 years or older. These games "provide an ideal environment in which to learn violence and use many of the strategies that are most effective for learning." The player is in the role of the aggressor and is rewarded for successful violent behavior. The games encourage repetitive and long playing to improve scores and advance to higher levels, and in some children and adolescents, promote addiction and an acceptance of violence as an appropriate means of solving problems and achieving goals.

—Masters, "Playing at War" *Women Against Military Madness Newsletter*, March 2010

___b___  **5.** The author is biased concerning
   **a.** the learning strategies children are exposed to.
   **b.** the violence in video games.
   **c.** how much time children spend playing video games.
   **d.** the way video games target young children.

___a___  **6.** Which phrase best suggests the author's bias?
   **a.** "ideal environment in which to learn violence"
   **b.** "encourage repetitive and long playing"
   **c.** "advance to higher levels"
   **d.** "promoting addiction"

## WRITING

# Think Critically When Writing

■ GOAL 7
Think critically when writing

Critical thinking is important for writers as well as readers. Writers need to examine their ideas to be sure they are logical, reasonable, and fairly presented. In this section you will learn to apply the critical reading skills taught earlier in the chapter to your writing skills.

## Use Inferences

It is usually better to state your ideas directly and straightforwardly rather than to leave it up to your reader to infer what you mean. Readers can misunderstand or even make incorrect inferences.

Once in a while, when explaining an idea, you may unintentionally omit information or falsely assume your readers have information or background that they do not, forcing them to make inferences. When writing about your career objectives, for example, you may assume that your readers know that nurses must pass state board exams, but in reality, many people not in health fields may not have that information. When reviewing a draft, reread it once to make sure you have provided your readers with full and complete information.

## Focus Your Purpose

Before beginning to write, identifying your purpose will help you produce a clear and focused draft. Think of purpose as what you hope to accomplish by writing. Once your purpose is clear, you will know the types of information to include, how to organize your ideas, and how to present your ideas clearly. For example, if your purpose is to describe a recent flood in your hometown, you would include descriptive details to help your readers visualize it. Or, if your purpose is to explain the economic impact of the flood on the town's residents, you would include facts and statistics. And, if you were writing to urge rebuilding of your town, you would include reasons and evidence.

---

**EXERCISE 16-12**

*WORKING TOGETHER*

## Analyzing Purpose

**Directions:** For three of the following topics, choose two different purposes and discuss with a classmate how the types of information you would include and how you would organize and present your ideas would differ for each.

1. Diversity in the workplace
2. White-collar crime
3. Organ donation
4. Adoption
5. Performance-enhancing drugs in professional sports

---

## Consider Your Audience

What you write and how you say it is, in part, determined by the audience you are writing for. Try this experiment. Suppose the people below made the following comments to you. How would you respond to each person appropriately? Write what you would say to each person.

| PERSON | COMMENT | YOUR RESPONSE |
|---|---|---|
| **Parent or guardian** | "Don't you think you should take a course in psychology?" | _____ _____ _____ _____ _____ |
| **Employer** | "Have you taken a psychology course yet? If not, you should." | _____ _____ _____ _____ _____ |

*(continued)*

| PERSON | COMMENT | YOUR RESPONSE |
|---|---|---|
| **College instructor** | "I advise you to register for a psychology course." | _____ _____ _____ _____ |
| **Close friend** | "Why don't you take a psych class?" | _____ _____ _____ _____ |

Now analyze your responses. Did you choose different words? Did you express and arrange your ideas differently? Did your tone change? Were some responses casual and others more formal?

Your reaction to each person was different because you took into account who the speaker was as well as what each one said. In writing, your readers are your listeners. They are called your **audience**. As you write, keep your audience in mind. What you write about and how you explain your ideas must match the needs of your audience. Through your language and word choice, as well as through the details you include in your paragraphs, you can communicate effectively with your audience.

Remember, your audience cannot see you when you write. Listeners can understand what you say by seeing your gestures, posture, and facial expressions and hearing your tone of voice and emphasis. When you write, all these nonverbal clues are missing, so you must make up for them. You need to be clear, direct, and specific to be sure you communicate your intended meaning.

## EXERCISE 16-13

*WORKING TOGETHER*

## Considering Your Audience

**Directions:** Select two people from the list below. For each one, write an explanation of why you decided to attend college.

1. Your brother or sister
2. Your favorite teacher
3. Your employer

Do not label which explanation is for which person. In class, exchange papers with a classmate. Ask your classmate to identify the intended audience of each explanation. When you've finished, discuss how the two pieces of writing differ. Then, decide whether each piece of writing is appropriate for its intended audience.

## Use Fact and Opinion

Facts and opinions both have a place in good writing. Facts are essential in supporting and explaining your ideas, so be sure to provide adequate and sufficient facts in the form of statistics, reasons, quotations, descriptions, observations, and so forth. Opinions may be used to express your own ideas on a subject, but be sure to provide evidence to support them. Unsupported opinions are of little use to your readers and may make them feel as if you "haven't done your home-work" in researching and thinking through your topic before writing about it.

## Writing Facts and Opinions

**Directions:** Working with a classmate, write one fact and one opinion for each of the following topics. For each opinion you offer, discuss what types of evidence would be useful in supporting it. *Answers will vary. Possible answers are shown.*

**EXAMPLE**  **TOPIC:**   the environment

**FACT:**   Trash, fertilizers, and auto emissions all pollute the environment.

**OPINION:**   Everyone should get involved in efforts to preserve the environment.

1. Eating

   Fact: A single potato chip contains 10 calories.

   Opinion: Potato chips are best eaten with sour dill pickles.

2. Cars

   Fact: Many people who live in large cities do not own cars.

   Opinion: Owning a car is a big headache.

3. Dogs

   Fact: Dogs are used to locate missing people.

   Opinion: Dogs are great companions.

4. The Internet

   Fact: The Internet allows instant communication.

   Opinion: The Internet is risky and dangerous due to identity theft.

5. Work

   Fact: Full-time work involves a 40-hours-per-week minimum commitment.

   Opinion: Work is a necessary evil.

## Express Bias

Readers appreciate and respect writers who are fair and honest and do not attempt to mislead them. It is acceptable, depending on the assignment and the topic, to express bias, but be sure you acknowledge that you are doing so. You might preface your comments by writing, "In my opinion, . . ." or you could say "I agree with people who believe . . . ."

| EXERCISE 16-15 | Analyzing a Paragraph or Essay |

**Directions:** Choose a paragraph or essay you have written for this class or for another college class. Evaluate your work using each of the following questions, and make any revisions that are needed.

1. Highlight sentences or sections that require your reader to make inferences. Have you supplied sufficient and detailed information to guide your readers in making any inferences you expect them to make?

2. Is your purpose clear? Does your work accomplish your purpose?

3. Who is your intended audience? How did you adjust your writing to suit them?

4. Underline any statements of opinion. Have you provided reasons, examples, or other evidence for any opinions you offer?

5. Do you express bias? If so, have you done so fairly and openly?

# INTEGRATING READING AND WRITING

## READ AND RESPOND: A Student Essay

*Giovanny Guzman is a sophomore at Eastfield College. He plans to transfer to Texas Tech University to obtain a bachelor's degree in history, with the goal of becoming a history professor. He submitted this essay to the Writing Rewards Essay Contest sponsored by Pearson Education. The assignment he responded to directed him to write an essay about mandatory community service.*

Title

# One Year

Some people think it would be a good idea to make 18-years-olds perform one year of national or community service before pursuing college or a paying job. Eighteen-year-olds have too much to worry about as it is. The last thing they need is to be forced into one year of volunteer work where they may either forget whatever they learned in high school (making the transition to college even more difficult), or they may begin to struggle financially due to the fact some 18-year-olds

Thesis statement

already have a family to support. Therefore, 18-year-olds should not be required to perform a year of national or community service because college is more important, some teenagers are only going to become rebels, and teenagers might lose interest in their goals.

Topic sentence

One reason 18-year-olds should not be required to perform a year of national or community service is that college is more important than volunteering. Sure, volunteering is a great way to give back to the community and show how good a person they really are. However, college is by far much more important than doing national or community service. Teenagers need to go to college right after high school because it has been proven that most teenagers who take a year off from schooling will most likely lose whatever they learned in high school, making the transition to college even more difficult. Some teens lose the motivation they had for attending college, so they never enroll in college and end up working dead end jobs, never amounting to anything in their life.

Topic sentence

Another reason 18-year-olds should not be required to perform a year of national or community service is that teenagers who are forced to do something are only going to become rebels. Teenagers are well-known for becoming stubborn and ignoring people when they do not want to do something. Forcing teenagers to do a year of national or community service is only going to cause problems. Teenagers will rebel, most likely causing them to work only whenever they feel like it, and they almost would never really feel like it. Forcing teens to work for free even though they do not want to volunteer is not going to happen without some sort of riots or destruction. Teenagers are at that age when they are starting to become independent adults who are finding out what kind of people they really are. Therefore, they should not forced to do anything, especially volunteering.

Topic sentence

The third reason 18-year-olds should not be required to perform a year of national or community service is that teenagers might lose interest in their goals. Teenagers have a tendency to abandon a goal if it is not met on time, or simply if it is going to take a while to achieve it. For example, if a teenager set a goal to buy a house no later than two years after graduating high school, it is going to be pretty hard having to volunteer for a whole year before he or she can start working to get paid. By having one goal not met, it could have a negative domino effect on every goal the teenager has set. Therefore, teens' lives could completely be destroyed because of being forced to do something the government wanted them to do rather than being free to choose what they want to do.

Conclusion repeats thesis and reasons

Teenagers should not be required to perform a year of national or community service. College is more important than community or national service, and by forcing teenagers to do volunteer work, all kinds of negative effects could happen such as teenagers becoming rebels and losing interest in their long term goals.

## Examining Writing

1. Paraphrase Guzman's thesis in your own words.

2. Evaluate the details in this essay. Which reason given by Guzman was most convincing? Why? What other reasons or details can you suggest that would support his thesis?

3. What was Guzman's purpose in writing this essay? Who was his intended audience?

4. How do the ideas in this essay fit with your own knowledge, experiences, beliefs, and values?

## READ AND RESPOND: A Professional Essay

### Thinking Before Reading

The following selection appeared in *Psychology Today*, a magazine covering aspects of human behavior and mental health. In the selection, the author examines the human tendency to be fascinated by disaster.

1. Preview the reading, using the steps discussed in Chapter 1 on page 25.
2. Connect the reading to your own experiences by answering the following questions:
   a. What is your typical reaction when you see a car accident or other type of disaster?
   b. What do you think of fictional violence in TV shows, movies, or video games?
3. Highlight and annotate as you read.

930***L***/906 words

# The Allure of Disaster
### Eric G. Wilson

1    STOP STARING. I bet you heard this more than once growing up. This command, after all, marks the unbridgeable gap between the impulsiveness of the child, who gawks at whatever seizes his attention, and the adult's social awareness, based on a fear of giving offense.

2    The auto mechanic has a huge mole on his nose. There's a woman crying unaccountably in the supermarket aisle. The little boy looks and looks, while the mother pulls him away, scolding all the while.

3    Most children eventually get the point and quit their gaping. For good reason: Although we're tempted to gaze at the car wreck on the side of the highway, suffering is involved.

4    But let's be honest. We're running late for work We hit a traffic jam. We creep angrily ahead, inch by inch, until we finally see the source of the slowdown: an accident. As we near the scene, we realize that the highway's been cleared. The dented cars are on the shoulder. This is just an onlooker delay, rubberneckers braking to stare.

5    We silently judge all those seekers of sick thrills—or making us late, for exploiting the misfortune of others. Surely we won't look, we tell ourselves as we pull beside the crash. Then it comes: the need to stare, like a tickle in the throat before a cough or the awful urge to sneeze. We hold it back until the last

minute, then gawk for all we're worth, enjoying the experience all the more because it's frowned upon.

6    Why do we do this? Our list of morbid fascinations is longer than we'd like to admit, including disaster footage on the TV news, documentaries featuring animal attacks, sordid reality shows, funny falls on YouTube, celebrity scandals, violent movies and television shows, gruesome video games, mixed martial arts, *TMZ*, *Gawker*, and the lives of serial killers.

7    Everyone loves a good train wreck. We are enamored of ruin. Our secret and ecstatic wish: Let it all fall down. Why? Does this macabre propensity merely reflect humanity's most lurid tendencies? Or might this grimmer side produce unexpected virtues?

8    In *Killing Monsters: Why Children Need Fantasy, Superheroes, and Make-Believe Violence*, Gerard Jones argues that children can benefit from exposure to fictional violence because it makes them feel powerful in a "scary, uncontrollable world." The child's fascination with mayhem has less to do with the fighting and more to do with how the action makes her feel. Children like to feel strong. Those committing violence are strong. By pretending to be these violent figures, children take on their strength and with it negotiate daily dangers.

9    Carl Jung made a similar argument for adults. He maintained that our mental health depends on our shadow, that part of our psyche that harbors our darkest energies, such as murderousness. The more we repress the morbid, the more it foments neuroses or psychoses. To achieve wholeness, we must acknowledge our most demonic inclinations.

10    Yes, I took pleasure in my enemy's tumble from grace. No, I couldn't stop watching 9/11 footage. Once we welcome these unseemly admissions as integral portions of our being, the devils turn into angels. Luke owns the Vader within, offers affection to the actual villain; off comes the scary mask, and there stands a father, loving and in need of love.

11    The gruesome brings out the generous: a strange notion. But think of the empathy that can arise from witnessing death or destruction. This emotion—possibly the grounding of all morals—is rare, but it frequently arises when we are genuinely curious about dreadful occurrences.

12    Renaissance scholars kept skulls on their desks to remind them how precious this life is. John Keats believed that the real rose, because it is dying, exudes more beauty than the porcelain one.

13    In the summer of 2010, I visited the National September 11th Memorial Museum in New York City. Photographs of the tragedy and its aftermath covered the walls. On a portable audio player, I listened to commentaries on each. After an hour of taking in the devastation, raw with sadness and wanting nothing more than to return to my wife and daughter, I stood before a picture of a clergyman praying in an eerie gray haze.

14    The man in the photo was blessing the rescue workers before their day's hellish efforts. They kneeled amidst the fog-covered wreckage, heads bowed. I hit the play button. The commentator spoke. As the search for bodies lengthened and grief and fatigue worsened; as hopes coalesced only to be immediately crushed; as firemen, bonded by their labor, grew close; as those who had lost

their children and their parents, their wives and their husbands, realized the depth of their affection—as all of this was transpiring—this horrific terrain had turned into "holy ground."

15    At that moment, I understood the terrible logic of suffering: When we agonize over what has cruelly been taken from us, we love it more, and know it better, than when we were near it. Affliction can reveal what is most sacred in our lives, essential to our joy. Water, Emily Dickinson writes, is "taught by thirst."

16    Staring at macabre occurrences can lead to mere insensitivity—gawking for a cheap thrill—or it can result in stunned trauma, muteness before the horror. But in between these two extremes, morbid curiosity can sometimes inspire us to imagine ways to transform life's necessary darkness into luminous vision. Go ahead. Stare. Take a picture. It will last longer.

# Getting Ready to Write

## Checking Your Comprehension

Answer each of the following questions using complete sentences.

1. According to the author, what fear keeps adults from staring?
2. What does the author say we do when we come upon a car accident?
3. According to Gerard Jones, what do children gain from exposure to fictional violence?
4. According to Carl Jung, what must we do to achieve wholeness?
5. Why did Renaissance scholars keep skulls on their desks?
6. In the September 11th photograph described by the author, what was the man doing?

## Strengthening Your Vocabulary

Using the word's context, word parts, or a dictionary, write a brief definition of each of the following words as it is used in the reading.

1. unbridgeable (paragraph 1) _____ impossible to cross or span
2. unaccountably (paragraph 2) _____ without explanation
3. morbid (paragraph 6) _____ gruesome
4. sordid (paragraph 6) _____ distasteful
5. macabre (paragraph 7) _____ suggesting death and decay
6. propensity (paragraph 7) _____ tendency, inclination
7. foments (paragraph 9) _____ promotes
8. coalesced (paragraph 14) _____ began to form

## Examining the Readings Using Idea Maps

Review the reading by completing the missing parts of the following idea map.

**VISUALIZE IT!**

Title    **The Allure of Disaster**

Thesis    Our morbid fascination with disaster may serve an important purpose.

Difference between children and adults

Impulsiveness of children, who are told _not to gawk_

Social awareness of adults, who fear _giving offense_

We disapprove of _gawking/rubbernecking_ but we do it anyway

Reasons for our morbid fascination

Gerard Jones: children benefit from exposure to _fictional violence_ because it makes them feel _powerful_

Carl Jung: we must acknowledge our _darker inclinations_ to achieve _wholeness or mental health_

Empathy can arise from witnessing death or destruction

Author's visit to the _National September 11th Memorial Museum_

Sees photo of a clergyman blessing _the rescue workers_

Understands that _suffering/affliction_ reveals what is most sacred

Conclusion    Morbid curiosity can help us understand suffering and transform it into something of value.

## Reacting to Ideas: Discussion and Journal Writing

Get ready to write about the reading by discussing the following:

1. Discuss the title of this selection. Did it capture your interest and provide a clue to the subject of the selection? Can you think of another title that would be effective?

2. Discuss the types of details the author used in this selection. Which details were most effective? Why?

3. Write a journal entry about a time when you witnessed an accident or other disaster, perhaps even the news coverage from September 11, 2001. How did you react?

4. Discuss the author's purpose in writing this article. How would you describe his intended audience?

5. What does the author mean when he says "The gruesome brings out the generous" (paragraph 11)? Do you agree?

6. Can you detect any bias in this selection? Give examples if you can.

7. Discuss the photo on page 528. What does it show? From what point of view is it taken? How does the photo illustrate the author's point?

**THINKING VISUALLY**

---

**MySkillsLab®**

**Complete** this Exercise

## Writing About the Reading

### Paragraph Options

1. How do the ideas in this selection reflect your own experiences or beliefs? On what points do you agree or disagree with the author? Write a paragraph giving your answers.

2. Write a paragraph analyzing the author's choice of words and descriptive or emotional language throughout the selection. How would you describe the author's tone?

3. Choose one of the people quoted in the selection—Gerard Jones, Carl Jung, John Keats, or Emily Dickinson—and write a paragraph describing that person's informed opinion and giving your response to it.

### Essay Options

4. Write an essay responding to the author's claim that "everyone loves a good train wreck." Do you think most people are fascinated by disaster? Are you? What does this fascination reflect about humanity? Do you agree that our morbid fascinations may be beneficial?

5. The author described photographs at the September 11th museum and what they revealed to him about suffering. Write an essay describing an image or photograph—either from your own life or from an event such as September 11—that was especially moving or meaningful to you. Explain how the image or photograph led to a greater understanding of yourself or others.

# SELF-TEST SUMMARY

To test yourself, cover the Answer column with a sheet of paper and answer each question in the left column. Evaluate each of your answers as you work by sliding the paper down and comparing your answer with what is printed in the Answer column.

| QUESTION | ANSWER |
| --- | --- |
| **GOAL 1  Read critically**<br><br>How can you develop the habit of thinking critically when you read?<br><br>What are four questions that will help you read critically? | Read the selection more than once; read with a pen or highlighter in hand; make marginal notes as you read; and ask questions as you read.<br><br>Ask yourself: What do you know about the author? When was the piece written? What emotions does the reading stir in you? What doesn't seem right or seems impossible or unlikely? |
| **GOAL 2  Make inferences**<br><br>What is an inference? How do you make accurate inferences? | An inference is an educated guess or prediction about something unknown based on available facts and information. Understand the writer's literal meaning first, then notice details, add up the facts, consider the writer's word choices and purpose, and be sure your inference is supportable. |
| **GOAL 3  Identify the author's purpose**<br><br>How do you identify the author's purpose? | Ask yourself what the writer is trying to tell you; pay close attention to the title of the piece and source of the material; and look for clues about purpose in the beginning and concluding paragraphs. |
| **GOAL 4  Analyze the intended audience**<br><br>How do writers vary their styles to suit their intended audiences? | Writers will change the level of language, choice of words, and method of presentation, depending on the group of people for whom they are writing. |
| **GOAL 5  Distinguish between fact and opinion**<br><br>What is the difference between fact and opinion? What is informed opinion? | Facts are statements that can be verified; statements of fact are objective. Opinions are statements that express a writer's feelings, attitudes, or beliefs; they are neither true nor false. The opinion of experts is known as informed opinion. |

*(Continued)*

| QUESTION | ANSWER |
|---|---|
| ■ **GOAL 6** Recognize bias<br><br>What is bias? How do you detect bias? | Bias refers to an author's partiality, inclination toward a particular viewpoint, or prejudice. Authors with a bias may favor one side of an issue, deliberately create a positive or negative image, use emotional language, and/or ignore other viewpoints. |
| ■ **GOAL 7** Think critically when writing<br><br>How do you apply critical thinking skills to writing? | Use critical thinking by stating your ideas directly rather than using inferences, identifying your purpose, considering your audience, using fact and opinion, and expressing any bias openly. |

# MySkillsLab

For more help with **Evaluating Sources,** go to your learning path in MySkillsLab at http://www.myskillslab.com.

# Planning, Drafting, and Revising Essays

**17**

## THINK About It!

The photograph above shows a building under construction. Write a sentence explaining how constructing a building is similar to the task of reading or writing.

Your sentence will probably include the idea that writing is a work in progress; it is a series of steps you perform to construct a paragraph or essay. Or you might have said that reading is a process of building meaning from individual words, sentences, and paragraphs in a passage or article. In this chapter you will learn to read and write essays. You will learn how an essay is structured and how to write an effective thesis statement, support your thesis with evidence, and write effective introductions, conclusions, and titles. You will also learn strategies for reading essays.

# FOCUSING ON READING AND WRITING

# What Is an Essay?

If you can read and write a paragraph, you can read and write an essay. The structure is similar, and they have similar parts. A **paragraph** expresses one main idea, called the *topic*, and is made up of several sentences that support that idea. The main idea is expressed in a sentence called the *topic sentence*. An **essay** also expresses one key idea called the *thesis*. This is expressed in a sentence called the *thesis statement*. The chart below shows how the parts of the paragraph are very much like the parts of an essay.

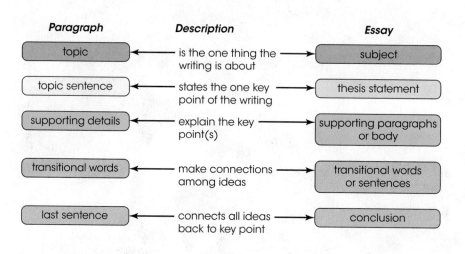

| Paragraph | Description | Essay |
|---|---|---|
| topic | is the one thing the writing is about | subject |
| topic sentence | states the one key point of the writing | thesis statement |
| supporting details | explain the key point(s) | supporting paragraphs or body |
| transitional words | make connections among ideas | transitional words or sentences |
| last sentence | connects all ideas back to key point | conclusion |

Think of the organization of an essay as modeling the organization of a paragraph, with one idea being explained by supporting details. Because an essay is usually at least three paragraphs long, and often more, it needs an opening paragraph, called the *introduction*, that focuses the reader and provides necessary background information before the thesis is presented. The paragraphs that support the thesis are called the *body* of the essay. Due to length and complexity, an essay also needs a final paragraph, called the *conclusion*, to draw the ideas discussed together and bring it to an end. You can visualize the structure of an essay as shown on the following page.

**VISUALIZE IT!**

**The Structure of an Essay**

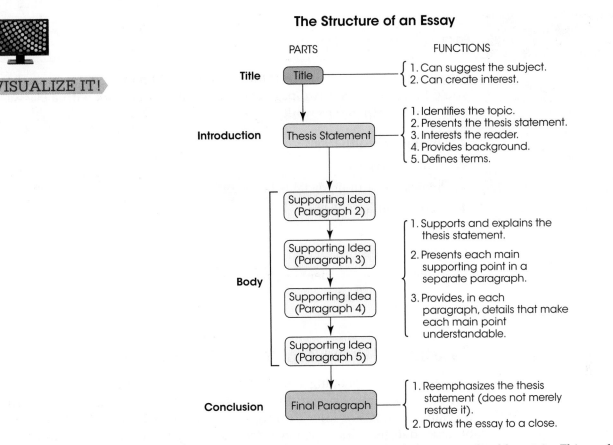

PARTS                    FUNCTIONS

Title — Title
1. Can suggest the subject.
2. Can create interest.

Introduction — Thesis Statement
1. Identifies the topic.
2. Presents the thesis statement.
3. Interests the reader.
4. Provides background.
5. Defines terms.

Body — Supporting Idea (Paragraph 2)
Supporting Idea (Paragraph 3)
Supporting Idea (Paragraph 4)
Supporting Idea (Paragraph 5)
1. Supports and explains the thesis statement.
2. Presents each main supporting point in a separate paragraph.
3. Provides, in each paragraph, details that make each main point understandable.

Conclusion — Final Paragraph
1. Reemphasizes the thesis statement (does not merely restate it).
2. Draws the essay to a close.

*Note:* There is no set number of paragraphs that an essay should contain. This model shows six paragraphs, but in actual essays, the number will vary greatly.

# WRITING

# Plan Your Essay

- **GOAL 1**
  Plan your essay

Planning an essay is similar to planning a paragraph. You begin by selecting a topic and narrowing it to a manageable length. Next, you generate ideas and organize them to support the main point of the essay. Finally, you draft the essay, using adequate supporting information and transitions to connect your ideas.

## Choose a Topic

An essay requires more time spent in planning and organization than does a single paragraph, although the process is the same. It involves selecting an appropriate topic and generating ideas. The topic for an essay should be broader than for a single paragraph. For more information on broadening or narrowing topics, see the section "Revise Your Essay" on page 546. To generate ideas for an essay, use the techniques you learned in Chapter 10 for generating ideas for paragraphs.

| EXERCISE 17-1 | Narrowing a Topic |
|---|---|

*WORKING TOGETHER*

**Directions:** Choose one of the following topics and narrow it down, so that it would be suitable for a two-page essay. Exchange your work with a classmate and evaluate each other's work.

1. Organic or health foods
2. Natural disasters
3. Predictable or unpredictable behaviors
4. Teenage fads or fashions
5. Controlling stress
6. Valued possessions
7. An unfortunate accident or circumstance
8. A technological advance

## Generate and Group Ideas for Your Thesis Statement

The first step in developing a thesis statement is to generate ideas to write about. Use one of the three prewriting methods you have studied: (1) freewriting, (2) brainstorming, and (3) branching. Refer to Chapter 2, pages 62–64, for a review of these strategies. Once you have ideas to work with, the next step is to group or connect your ideas to form a thesis. Let's see how one student, Miriam, produced a thesis following these steps.

The instructor in Miriam's writing course assigned a short (one- to two-page) essay on the effects of technology on modern life. After brainstorming a list of various technologies including cell phones, iPods, and video games, she decided to write about computers and specifically about the Internet. She then did a second brainstorming about uses and effects of the Internet. She came up with the following list:

| | |
|---|---|
| instant messaging | college Web site |
| research for college papers | e-mail—socializing with friends |
| online dating | Facebook |
| Match.com and eHarmony.com | Google to find the answer to anything |
| Mapquest to find directions | online profiles |
| chat rooms | accuracy of online profiles |
| Twitter | |

Miriam's next step in writing her essay was to select usable ideas and try to group or organize them logically. In the preceding brainstorming list, she saw three main groups of ideas: *communicating*, *socializing*, and *online dating*. She sorted her list into categories:

**Communicating:** instant messaging, chat rooms, Twitter

**Socializing:** Facebook, online profiles, friending new people

**Online Dating:** Match.com, eHarmony.com

Once Miriam had grouped her ideas into these categories, she could write a thesis statement:

> The Internet has become an excellent means of communicating, socializing, and meeting potential dates.

This thesis statement identifies her topic—the Internet—and suggests three ways in which it has affected her life. You can see how this thesis statement grew out of her idea groupings. Furthermore, this thesis statement gives her readers clues as to how she will organize the essay. A reader knows from this preview which uses she will discuss and in what order.

## How to Group Ideas

How do you know which ideas to group? Look for connections and relationships among ideas that you generate during prewriting. Here are some suggestions:

- **Look for categories.** Try to discover how you can classify and subdivide your ideas. Think of categories as titles or slots in which you can place ideas. Look for a general term that is broad enough to cover several of your ideas. For example, Miriam broke down the many uses of the Internet into communicating, socializing, and online dating. Suppose you were writing a paper on favoritism. You could break down the topic by a category, such as place.

  SAMPLE THESIS STATEMENT     Whether it's practiced in the workplace, in a classroom, or on Capitol Hill, favoritism is unfair.

- **Try organizing your ideas chronologically.** Group your ideas according to the clock or calendar.

  SAMPLE THESIS STATEMENT     From the ancient Mayans to King Henry VIII's court to present-day Congress, personal relationships have always played a role in professional achievement.

- **Look for similarities and differences.** When working with two or more topics, see if you can approach them by looking at how similar or different they are.

  SAMPLE THESIS STATEMENT     The two great pioneers of psychotherapy, Freud and Jung, agreed on the concept of the libido but completely disagreed on other issues.

- **Separate your ideas into causes and effects or problems and solutions.** You can often analyze events and issues in this way.

  SAMPLE THESIS STATEMENT     The phrase "it takes a village to raise a child" means that birth parents alone do not determine what an individual will grow up to be.

- **Divide your ideas into advantages and disadvantages, or pros and cons.** When you are evaluating a proposal, product, or service, this approach may work.

  SAMPLE THESIS STATEMENT     Deciding on a major before starting college can either help a student stay focused and on track or keep him or her from discovering new interests.

■ **Consider several different ways to approach your topic or organize and develop your ideas.** As you consider what your thesis statement is going to be, push yourself to see your topic from a number of different angles or from a fresh perspective.

For example, Miriam could have examined her brainstorming list and decided to focus only on the Internet as an information source, looking more deeply into search engines and informational Web sites. In other words, within every topic lie many possible thesis statements.

| EXERCISE 17-2 | Generating and Grouping Ideas |
|---|---|
| **WRITING IN PROGRESS** | **Directions:** Generate and group ideas for the topic you narrowed in Exercise 17-1. |

# Draft Your Essay

■ **GOAL 2**
Draft your essay

Drafting your essay involves writing a strong thesis statement, supporting your thesis with substantial evidence, making connections among your ideas clear, and writing your introduction, conclusion, and title.

## Write a Strong Thesis Statement

To develop a sound essay, you must begin with a well-focused thesis statement. A **thesis statement** tells your reader what your essay is about and gives clues to how the essay will unfold. The thesis statement should not only identify your topic but also express the main point about your topic that you will explain or prove in your essay.

Some students think they should be able to just sit down and write a thesis statement. But a thesis statement rarely springs fully formed into a writer's mind: it evolves and, in fact, may change significantly during the process of pre-writing, grouping ideas, drafting, and revising. The next section will show you how to draft a thesis statement and how to polish it into a focused statement.

### *Guidelines for Writing Thesis Statements*

A thesis statement should explain what your essay is about, and it should also give your readers clues to its organization. Think of your thesis statement as a promise; it promises your reader what your paper will deliver. Here are some guidelines to follow for writing an effective thesis statement:

■ **It should state the main point of your essay.** It should not focus on details; it should give an overview of your approach to your topic.

| TOO DETAILED | Because babies don't know anything about the world around them, parents should allow them to touch toys and other objects. |
|---|---|
| REVISED | Because babies don't know anything about the world around them when they are born, they need to spend lots of time touching, holding, and exploring the everyday things we take for granted. |

■ **It should assert an idea about your topic.** Your thesis should express a viewpoint or state an approach to the topic.

| | |
|---|---|
| LACKS AN ASSERTION | Advertisers promote beer during football games. |
| REVISED | One of the reasons you see so many beer ads during ball games is that men buy more beer than women. |

■ **It should be as specific and detailed as possible.** For this reason, it is important to review and rework your thesis *after* you have written and revised drafts.

| | |
|---|---|
| TOO GENERAL | You need to take a lot of clothes with you when you go camping. |
| REVISED | Because the weather can change so quickly in the Adirondacks, it is important to pack clothing that will protect you from both sun and rain. |

■ **It may suggest the organization of your essay.** Mentioning key points that will be discussed in the essay is one way to do this. The order in which you mention them should be the same as the order in which you discuss them in your essay.

| | |
|---|---|
| DOES NOT SUGGEST ORGANIZATION | Learning to read is important for your whole life. |
| REVISED | Literacy is a necessary tool for academic, professional, and personal success. |

■ **It should not be a direct announcement.** Do not begin with phrases such as "In this paper I will . . ." or "My assignment was to discuss . . ."

| | |
|---|---|
| DIRECT ANNOUNCEMENT | What I am going to write about is how working out can make you better at your job. |
| REVISED | Exercise can dramatically improve the performance of everyone, from front office to assembly-line workers. |

■ **It should offer a fresh, interesting, and original perspective on the topic.** A thesis statement can follow the guidelines discussed above, but, if it seems dull or predictable, it needs more work.

| | |
|---|---|
| PREDICTABLE | Complex carbohydrates are good for you. |
| REVISED | Diets that call for cutting out carbohydrates completely are overlooking the tremendous health benefits of whole grains. |

## EXERCISE 17-3 Writing a Thesis Statement

**WRITING IN PROGRESS**

**Directions:** Using the topic you chose in Exercise 17-1 and the ideas you generated about it in Exercise 17-2, develop a thesis statement.

## Support Your Thesis with Substantial Evidence

Every essay you write should offer substantial evidence in support of your thesis statement. This evidence makes up the body of your essay. **Evidence** can consist of personal experience, anecdotes (stories that illustrate a point), examples, reasons, descriptions, facts, statistics, and quotations (taken from sources).

**TABLE 17-1  WAYS TO ADD EVIDENCE**

*Topic: The Internet's Impact*

| Support Your Thesis by | Example |
| --- | --- |
| **Telling a story** (narration) | Relate a story about a couple who met using an online dating service. |
| **Adding descriptive detail** (description) | Give details about one person's Facebook profile. |
| **Giving an example** | Give an example of types of personal likes and dislikes that are included in one person's online profile. |
| **Giving a definition** | Explain the meaning of the term "friendship status." |
| **Making comparisons** | Compare two online dating sites. |
| **Making distinctions** (contrast) | Compare instant messaging with face-to-face conversations. |
| **Explaining how something works** (process) | Explain how to register on Twitter. |
| **Giving reasons** (causes) | Explain what factors contribute to the popularity of chat rooms. |
| **Analyzing effects** | Explain why online profiles can be misleading. |

Many students have trouble locating concrete, specific evidence to support their theses. Though prewriting yields plenty of good ideas and helps you focus your thesis, prewriting ideas may not always provide sufficient evidence. Often you need to brainstorm again for additional ideas. At other times, you may need to consult one or more sources to obtain further information on your topic.

The table above lists ways to support a thesis statement and gives an example of how Miriam could use each one in her essay on different ways to use the Internet. Although it offers a variety of ways Miriam could add evidence to her essay, she would not need to use all of them. Instead, she should choose the one that is the most appropriate for her audience and purpose. Miriam could also use different types of evidence in combination. For example, she could *describe* a particular online dating site and *tell a story* that illustrates its use.

Use the following guidelines in selecting evidence to support your thesis:

- **Be sure your evidence is relevant.** That is, it must directly support or explain your thesis.

- **Make your evidence as specific as possible.** Help your readers see the point you are making by offering detailed, concrete information. For example, if you are explaining the dangers of driving while intoxicated, include details that make that danger seem immediate: victims' names and injuries, types of vehicle damage, statistics on the loss of life, and so on.

- **Be sure your information is accurate.** It may be necessary to check facts, verify stories you have heard, and ask questions of individuals who may have provided information.

- **Locate sources that provide evidence.** Because you may not know enough about your topic and lack personal experience, you may be unable to provide strong evidence. When this happens, locate several sources on your topic.

- **Be sure to document any information that you borrow from other sources.** See Chapter 18, page 569, for more information.

## EXERCISE 17-4

# Writing a First Draft

**Directions:** Write a first draft of an essay for the thesis statement you wrote in Exercise 17-3. Support your thesis statement with at least three types of evidence.

## Make Connections Among Your Ideas Clear

To produce a well-written essay, be sure to make it clear how your ideas relate to one another. There are several ways to do this:

- **Use transitional words and phrases.** The transitional words and phrases that you learned in Chapter 11 for connecting ideas are helpful for making your essay flow smoothly and communicate clearly. Table 17-2 below lists useful transitions for each method of organization.

- **Write a transitional sentence.** This sentence is usually the first sentence in the paragraph. It might come before the topic sentence or it might *be* the topic sentence. Its purpose is to link the paragraph in which it appears with the paragraph before it. Sometimes it comes at the end of the paragraph and links the paragraph to the following one.

- **Repeat key words.** Repeating key words from either the thesis statement or the preceding paragraph helps your reader see connections among ideas.

| TABLE 17-2    USEFUL TRANSITIONAL WORDS AND PHRASES | |
| --- | --- |
| **Method of Development** | **Transitional Words and Phrases** |
| **Least/Most or Most/Least** | most important, above all, especially, particularly important, less important |
| **Spatial** | above, below, behind, beside, next to, inside, outside, to the west (north, etc.), beneath, near, nearby, next to |
| **Time Sequence** | first, next, now, before, during, after, eventually, finally, at last, later, meanwhile, soon, then, suddenly, currently, after, afterward, after a while, as soon as, until |
| **Narration/Process** | first, second, then, later, in the beginning, when, after, following, next, during, again, after that, at last, finally |
| **Description** | see Spatial and Least/Most or Most/Least above |
| **Example** | for example, for instance, to illustrate, in one case |
| **Comparison** | likewise, similarly, in the same way, too, also |
| **Contrast** | however, on the contrary, unlike, on the other hand, although, even though, but, in contrast, yet |
| **Cause and Effect** | because, consequently, since, as a result, for this reason, therefore, thus |

| EXERCISE 17-5 | # Analyzing Your Draft |
|---|---|
| **WRITING IN PROGRESS** | **Directions:** Review the draft you wrote for Exercise 17-4. Analyze how effectively you have connected your ideas. Add key words or transitional words, phrases, or sentences, as needed. |

## Write Your Introduction, Conclusion, and Title

The introduction, conclusion, and title each serve a specific function. Each one strengthens your essay and helps your reader better understand your ideas.

### Writing the Introduction

An introductory paragraph has three main purposes.

1. It presents your thesis statement.
2. It interests your reader in your topic.
3. It provides any necessary background information.

Although your introductory paragraph appears first in your essay, it does *not* need to be written first. In fact, it is sometimes best to write it last, after you have developed your ideas, written your thesis statement, and drafted your essay.

We have already discussed writing thesis statements earlier in the chapter. Table 17-3 provides some suggestions on how to interest your reader in your topic in your introductory paragraph:

| TABLE 17-3 WAYS TO INTEREST YOUR READER | |
|---|---|
| **Technique** | **Example** |
| **Ask a provocative or controversial question** | How would you feel if the job you had counted on suddenly fell through? |
| **State a startling fact or statistic** | Last year, the United States government spent a whopping billion dollars a day on interest on the national debt. |
| **Begin with a story or an anecdote** | The day Liam Blake left his parka on the bus was the first day of what would become the worst snowstorm the city had ever seen. |
| **Use a quotation** | Robert Frost wrote "Two roads diverged in a wood, and I — / I took the one less traveled by, / And that has made all the difference." |
| **State a little-known fact, a myth, or a misconception** | What was Harry S. Truman's middle name? Stephen? Samuel? Simpson? Actually, it's just plain "S." There was a family dispute over whether to name him for his paternal or maternal grandfather, an argument that was settled by simply using the common initial "S." |

A straightforward, dramatic thesis statement can also capture your reader's interest, as in the following example:

The first day I walked into Mr. Albierto's advanced calculus class, I knew I had made a huge mistake.

An introduction should also provide the reader with any necessary background information. Consider what information your reader needs to understand your essay. You may, for example, need to define the term *genetic engineering* for a paper on that topic. At other times, you might need to provide a brief history or give an overview of a controversial issue.

---

| EXERCISE 17-6 | Revising Your Introduction |
|---|---|
| **WRITING IN PROGRESS** | **Directions:** Revise the introduction to the essay you wrote for Exercise 17-4. |

---

### Writing the Conclusion

The final paragraph of your essay has two functions: It should reemphasize your thesis statement and draw the essay to a close. It should not be a direct announcement, such as "This essay has been about . . ." or "In this paper I hoped to show that . . ."

It's usually best to revise your essay at least once *before* working on the conclusion. During your first or second revision, you often make numerous changes in both content and organization, which may, in turn, affect your conclusion.

Here are a few effective ways to write a conclusion. Choose one that will work for your essay.

- **Look ahead.** Project into the future and consider outcomes or effects.
- **Return to your thesis.** If your essay is written to prove a point or convince your reader of the need for action, it may be effective to end with a sentence that recalls your main point or calls for action. If you choose this way to conclude, be sure not to merely repeat your first paragraph. Be sure to reflect on the thoughts you developed in the body of your essay.
- **Summarize key points.** Especially for longer essays, briefly review your key supporting ideas.

If you have trouble writing your conclusion, it's probably a tip-off that you need to work further on your thesis or organization.

---

| EXERCISE 17-7 | Revising Your Conclusion |
|---|---|
| **WRITING IN PROGRESS** | **Directions:** Write or revise a conclusion for the essay you wrote for Exercise 17-4. |

---

### Selecting a Title

Although the title appears first in your essay, it is often the last thing you should write. The title should identify the topic in an interesting way, and it may also suggest the focus. To select a title, reread your final draft, paying particular attention to your thesis statement and your overall method of development. Here are a few examples of effective titles:

> Which Way Is Up? (for an essay on mountain climbing)
>
> A Hare Raising Tale (for an essay on taking care of rabbits)
>
> Topping Your Bottom Line (for an essay on how to increase profitability)

To write accurate and interesting titles, try the following tips:

- **Write a question that your essay answers.** For example: "What Are the Signs That It's Safe to Approach a Strange Dog?"

- **Use key words that appear in your thesis statement.** If your thesis statement is "Diets rich in lean beef can help teenagers maintain higher levels of usable iron," your title could be "Lean Beef Is Good for Teens."

- **Use brainstorming techniques to generate options.** Don't necessarily go with the first title that pops into your mind. If in doubt, try out some options on friends to see which is most effective.

---

### EXERCISE 17-8    Choosing a Title

**WRITING IN PROGRESS**

**Directions:** Come up with a good title for the essay you wrote for Exercise 17-4.

---

# Revise Your Essay

■ **GOAL 3**
Revise your essay

As you revise, look for the following common problems: topics that are too broad or too narrow, ineffective thesis statements, underdeveloped essays, and disorganized essays. Use idea maps to help you spot problems.

## Problem #1: The Topic Is Too Broad

One common mistake in writing an essay is choosing a topic that is *too broad*. No matter how hard you work, if you begin with a topic that is too broad, you will not be able to produce a successful essay. If your topic is too broad, there will be too much information to include, and you will not be able to cover all the important points with the right amount of detail.

Suppose you are taking a sociology class and have been asked to write a two-page paper on your impression of campus life so far. If you just wrote down the title "Campus Life" and started writing, you would find that you had too much to say and probably would not know where to start. Should you write about your classes, meeting new friends, adjusting to differences between high school and college, or managing living arrangements? Here are a few more examples of topics that are too broad:

- Pollution (Choose one type and focus on causes or effects.)
- Vacations (Choose one trip and focus on one aspect of the trip, such as meeting new people.)
- Movies (Choose one movie and concentrate on one feature, such as character development, plot, or humor.)

### *How to Identify the Problem*

Here are the symptoms of a topic that is too broad:

- **You have too much to say.** If it seems as if you could go on and on about the topic, it is probably too broad.

- **You feel overwhelmed.** If you feel the topic is too difficult or the task of writing about it is unmanageable, you may have too much to write about. Another possibility is that you have chosen a topic about which you do not know enough.

- **You are not making progress.** If you feel stuck, your topic may be too broad. It also may be too narrow (see Problem #2).

- **You are writing general statements and not explaining them.** Having too much to cover forces you to make broad, sweeping statements that you cannot explain in sufficient depth.

### *How to Narrow a Broad Topic*

One way to narrow a topic that is too broad is to divide it into subtopics. Then choose one subtopic and use it to develop new ideas for your essay.

Another way to limit a broad topic is to answer questions that will limit it. Here are six questions that are useful in limiting your topic to a particular place, time, kind, or type:

Who?     What?     When?     Where?     Why?     How?

Suppose your topic is job hunting. You realize it is too broad and apply the questions below.

| TOPIC: JOB HUNTING | |
| --- | --- |
| **Questions** | **Examples** |
| **Who?** | Who can help me with job hunting? (This question limits the topic to people and agencies that offer assistance.) |
| **What?** | What type of job am I seeking? (This question limits the topic to a specific occupation.) |
| **When?** | When is the best time to job hunt? (This question limits the topic to a particular time frame, such as right after graduation.) |
| **Where?** | Where is the best place to find job listings? (This question limits the topic to one source of job listings, such as the Internet.) |
| **Why?** | Why is it important to network with friends and family? (This question limits the topic to one way to search for jobs.) |
| **How?** | How should I prepare my résumé? (This question limits the topic to one aspect of job hunting.) |

## Problem #2: The Topic Is Too Narrow

Another common mistake is to choose a topic that is *too narrow*. If you decide to write about the effects of the failure of Canada geese to migrate from western New York during the winter, you will probably run out of ideas, unless you are prepared to do extensive library or Internet research. Instead, broaden your topic to the migration patterns of Canada geese. Here are a few more examples of topics that are too narrow:

- The history of corn mazes in the Ohio River valley
- Shopping on eBay for designer handbags
- The attitude of a nasty receptionist at the veterinarian's office

### How to Identify the Problem

Here are the symptoms of a topic that is too narrow:

- **After a paragraph or two, you have nothing left to say.** If you run out of ideas and keep repeating yourself, your topic is probably too narrow.

- **Your topic does not seem important.** If your topic seems insignificant, it probably is. One reason it may be insignificant is that it focuses on facts rather than ideas.

- **You are making little or no progress.** A lack of progress may signal a lack of information.

- **Your essay is too factual.** If you find you are focusing on small details, your topic may be too narrow.

### How to Broaden a Narrow Topic

To broaden a topic that is too narrow, try to extend it to cover more situations or circumstances. If your topic is the price advantage of shopping for your chemistry textbook on the Internet, broaden it to include various other benefits of Internet shopping for textbooks. Discuss price, but also consider convenience and free shipping. Do not limit yourself to one type of textbook. Specifically, to broaden a topic that is too narrow:

- **Think of other situations, events, or circumstances that illustrate the same idea.**

- **Think of a larger concept that includes your topic.**

---

**EXERCISE 17-9**  Broadening a Topic

**Directions:** Broaden three of the following topics to ones that are manageable in a two-page essay.

1. A groom who wore sneakers to his formal wedding
2. Materials needed for _____ (a craft or hobby)
3. Your parents' attitude toward drugs
4. Your local high school's dress code that prohibits T-shirts with obscenities on them
5. An annoying Internet pop-up
6. A friend's irritating habit
7. A child's first word
8. Missing a deadline for a writing assignment

# Problem #3: The Thesis Statement Needs Revision

The best time to evaluate and, if necessary, revise your thesis statement is after you have written a first draft. At that time you can see if your essay delivers what your thesis promises. If it does not, it needs revision, or you need to refocus your essay.

## How to Identify the Problem

Here are the characteristics of a weak thesis statement:

- The essay does not explain and support the thesis.
- The thesis statement does not cover all the topics included in the essay.
- The thesis statement is vague or unclear.
- The thesis statement makes a direct announcement.

## How to Revise Your Thesis Statement

When evaluating your thesis statement, ask the following questions:

- **Does my essay develop and explain my thesis statement?** As you write an essay, its focus and direction may change. Revise your thesis statement to reflect any changes. If you discover that you drifted away from your original thesis and you want to maintain it, work on revising so that your paper delivers what your thesis statement promises.

- **Is my thesis statement broad enough to cover all the points I made in the essay?** As you develop your first draft, you may find that one idea leads naturally to another. Both must be covered by the thesis statement. For example, suppose your thesis statement is "Because of the number of patients our clinic sees in a day, the need for nurse practitioners has increased dramatically." If, in your essay, you discuss lab technicians and interns as well as nurses, then you need to broaden your thesis statement.

- **Does my thesis statement use vague or unclear words that do not clearly focus the topic?** For example, in the thesis statement "Physical therapy can help bursitis," the word *help* is vague and does not suggest how your essay will approach the topic. Instead, if your paper discusses the effectiveness of physical therapy, this approach should be reflected in your thesis: "When it comes to chronic bursitis, deep tissue massage by a trained physical therapist can be very effective."

- **Does my thesis statement make a direct announcement?** If so, revise to eliminate mention of the essay itself or yourself as the writer. For example, if your thesis statement is "I am going to write about how to reduce cyberbullying," revise it by eliminating mention of yourself and include more about why the issue is important: "Cyberbullying is a growing national problem and there are obvious steps that can be taken to control it."

| EXERCISE 17-10 | Evaluating and Revising Thesis Statements |

**Directions:** Identify what is wrong with each of the following thesis statements and revise each one to make it more effective.

1. Most people like to dance.
2. Call the doctor when you're sick.
3. Everyone should read the newspaper.
4. It's important to keep your receipts.
5. Driving in snow is dangerous.
6. This essay is about sexual harrassment on the job.

## Problem #4: The Essay Is Underdeveloped

An underdeveloped essay is one that lacks sufficient information and evidence to support the thesis.

### How to Identify the Problem

Here are the characteristics of an underdeveloped essay:

■ The essay seems to ramble or is unfocused.

■ The essay repeats information or says the same thing in slightly different ways.

■ The essay makes general statements but does not support them.

■ The essay lacks facts, examples, comparisons, or reasons.

### How to Revise an Underdeveloped Essay

Use the following suggestions to revise an underdeveloped essay:

■ **Delete sentences that are repetitious and add nothing to the essay.** If you find you have little or nothing left, do additional brainstorming, freewriting, or branching to discover new ideas. If this technique does not work, consider changing your topic to one about which you have more to say.

■ **Make sure your topic is not too broad or too narrow.** If it is, use the suggestions for topic revision given earlier in this chapter.

■ **Go through your essay sentence by sentence and highlight any ideas that you could further develop and explain.** Develop these ideas into separate paragraphs.

■ **Make sure each topic sentence is clear and specific.** Then add details to each paragraph that make it sharp and convincing.

| EXERCISE 17-11 | # Writing an Essay |
|---|---|

**Directions:** Evaluate and revise the essay you wrote in Exercise 17-4, using the suggestions given above.

## Problem #5: The Essay Is Disorganized

A **disorganized essay** is one that does not follow a logical method of development. A disorganized essay makes it difficult for your readers to follow your train of thought. If readers must struggle to follow your ideas, they may stop reading or lose their concentration. In fact, as they struggle to follow your thinking, they may miss important information or misinterpret what you are saying.

### How to Identify the Problem

Use the following questions to help you evaluate the organization of your essay:

- Does every paragraph in the essay support or explain your thesis statement?
- Do you avoid straying from your topic?
- Does each detail in each paragraph explain the topic sentence?
- Do you make it clear how one idea relates to another by using transitions?

### How to Revise Disorganized Essays

To improve the organization of your essay, use one of the methods of organization discussed in Chapters 12 and 13. Here is a brief review:

## Tips for Revising

| METHOD OF ORGANIZATION | PURPOSE |
|---|---|
| **Process** | Describes the order in which things are done |
| **Narration** | Presents events in the order in which they happened |
| **Description** | Gives descriptive, sensory details |
| **Example** | Explains a situation or idea by giving circumstances that illustrate it |
| **Cause and Effect** | Explains why things happen or what happens as a result of something else |
| **Comparison and Contrast** | Focuses on similarities and differences |

Once you have chosen and used a method of development, be sure to use appropriate transitions to connect your ideas.

Another way to spot and correct organizational problems is to draw an idea or revision map as discussed on the next page. Using a map will help you visualize the progression of your ideas graphically and see which ideas fit and which do not.

| EXERCISE 17-12 | Evaluating Organization |
| --- | --- |

**Directions:** Evaluate the organization of the essay you wrote in Exercise 17-4. Revise it if needed.

## Use Maps to Guide Your Revision

In Chapter 14, you learned to draw revision maps to evaluate paragraphs. The same strategy works well for essays, too. A **revision map** will help you evaluate the overall flow of your ideas as well as the effectiveness of individual paragraphs.

To draw an essay revision map, begin by listing your title at the top of the page. Write your thesis statement underneath it, and then list the topic of each paragraph. Next, work through each paragraph, recording your ideas in abbreviated form. Then write the key words of your conclusion. If you find details that do not support the topic sentence, record those details to the right of the map. Use the model on p. 553 as a guide.

When you've completed your revision map, conduct the following tests:

1. **Read your thesis statement along with your first topic sentence.** Does the topic sentence clearly support your thesis? If not, revise it to make the relationship clearer. Repeat this step for each topic sentence.

2. **Read your topic sentences, one after the other, without reading the corresponding details.** Is there a logical connection between them? Have you arranged them in the most effective way? If not, revise to make the connection clearer or to improve your organization.

3. **Examine each individual paragraph.** Are there enough relevant, specific details to support the topic sentence?

4. **Read your introduction and then look at your topic sentences.** Does the essay deliver what the introduction promises?

5. **Read your thesis statement and then your conclusion.** Are they compatible and consistent? Does the conclusion agree with and support the thesis statement?

| EXERCISE 17-13 | Drawing a Revision Map |
| --- | --- |

**Directions:** Draw a revision map of the essay you wrote and revised throughout this chapter. Make further revisions as needed.

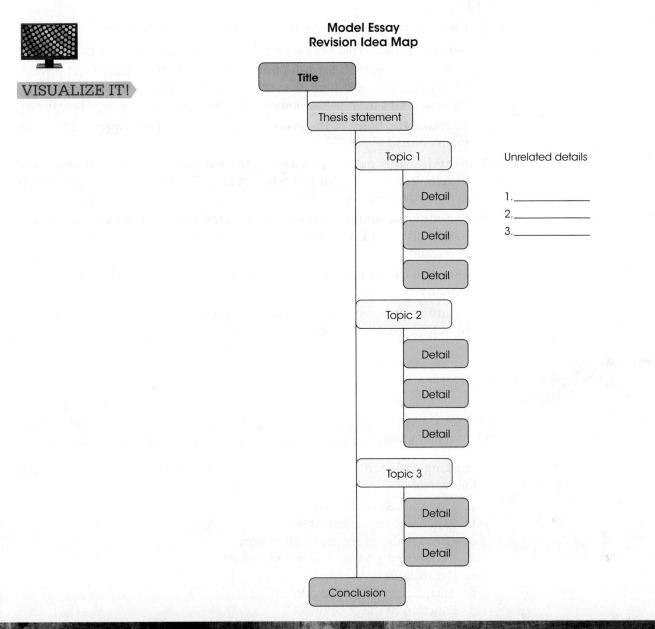

**Model Essay
Revision Idea Map**

VISUALIZE IT!

## READING

# Use Strategies for Reading Essays

■ GOAL 4

Use strategies for reading essays

The professional essays at the end of each chapter are models of good writing. Reading essays provides you with ideas to write about, which can serve as springboards for you to develop your own ideas. By studying the writing of professional writers, you can improve your own writing. You will need to read the essays several times. First, concentrate on understanding them. Then examine the techniques the writers use that you could use in your own writing. Here are a few specific suggestions:

1. **Establish the authority of the writer whenever possible.** In order to trust that the writer is presenting accurate, reliable information, make sure he or she is knowledgeable about or experienced with the subject.

2. **Pay attention to background information the writer provides.** Especially if the subject is one with which you are unfamiliar, you must fill in gaps in your knowledge. If the background supplied is insufficient, consult other sources to get the information you need.

3. **Identify the writer's purpose.** Study how he or she achieves it.

4. **Study the title.** What does it reveal about the essay's content or purpose?

5. **Examine the essay's introduction.** It should do three things: (1) provide needed background information, (2) get you interested in the reading, and (3) state the essay's main point. Observe how the writer accomplishes these things.

6. **Examine the body of the essay.** Study how the writer supports his or her main points.

7. **Examine how paragraphs are organized.** How does the writer state and develop the main point of each paragraph? How are these main points explained or developed?

8. **Examine the sentences the writer creates.** How are the sentences similar to and different from those you write? Are there some sentence patterns you could model?

9. **Examine the writer's use of vocabulary.** What words or phrases seem particularly effective? How could you use them?

10. **Examine the essay's conclusion.** Observe how the writer draws the essay to a close. Could you use this technique?

---

**EXERCISE 17-14**

*WORKING TOGETHER*

## Reading Essays

**Directions:** Use the professional readings "Talking to Koko the Gorilla" (p. 145) and "What Is a Sustainable Food System?" (p. 322) to complete this exercise.

1. Working with another student, compare the two readings in terms of the following:
   a. Effectiveness of the title
   b. Function of the introduction
   c. Effectiveness of the thesis statement
   d. Author's purpose and intended audience
   e. Organization
   f. Adequacy of supporting detail
   g. Function of the conclusion

2. Examine each reading and identify at least two techniques used by one or both of the writers that you could use to improve your own writing.

---

# INTEGRATING READING AND WRITING

## READ AND RESPOND: A Student Essay

*Alphea Bartley works as a home health aide and takes courses at Dutchess Community College, SUNY. She has finished her prerequisite courses and is completing an associate's degree in nursing. She submitted this essay to the Writing Rewards Essay Contest sponsored by Pearson Education. The assignment she responded to directed her to write an essay about working while attending college.*

Title announces subject

## Students Should Not Work Long Hours

It is quite alarming the amount of hours that college students put into work compared to the amount of hours they spend in school and study. Working long hours is exhausting, quickly diminishes the prospect of completing college, and encourages students to skip school and go to work instead. Working long hours leaves students tired and feeling like rag dolls with no energy to go home and do assignments. As a result, students should limit their work to no more than twenty hours per week.

Thesis statement

Topic sentence

Details create mental picture of tired students

Many college students are sleep-deprived from working long hours. They use caffeine to help them stay awake and to attempt to function normally. Try counting the amount of coffee cups that are stuck in the hands of students as they walk through the doors of a campus building each morning; you will be amazed. Coffee is one of the many beverages that students drink just to stay awake for classes each day. "I am so tired, I just want to go to sleep right now," is one of the many cries being echoed from my classmates. Most of them work at least six or seven hours per day, five to six days per week. Being full time students, they spend about six hours in school, three to four days per week. How many hours are left for study and sleep? The answer is, "Not much."

Topic sentence

Limiting work hours is necessary because working too much makes it impossible to have enough time to study. Working more than twenty hours a week adds pressure and stress to an already overwhelming workload of assignments and test preparation. It is not easy for students to function normally in school when they are tired and burned out. Ramona, a classmate, has been working weekends for a while now. She desperately tries to finish her assignments by Thursday night so all she has to do over the weekend is study. However, it has not been working in her favor. She is a home care aide, and most of the time her patient requires so much attention that she is only able to put in a measly six hours of study time for the entire weekend. As a result, she is often not ready for class. By the time she gets to class Monday morning all she can think about is when the class will end so she can go home to sleep. She pays

Example of student whose job interferes with her studying

Another example of overtired/ overworked student

attention to the first ten minutes of what the professor says, and after that she is out of it. My friend Ron, who always comes in ten minutes late with breakfast in hand, takes five minutes to eat it, and that is the only time he is ever awake in class. As soon as he finishes eating, he lays his head on the desk and goes to sleep. When the session is up someone wakes him. The professor got so tired of talking to him about sleeping in class that he offered to bring him a pillow and a blanket. If Ron's parents were to see his grades, I am sure they would ask him to quit his job or reduce the amount of hours that he is working.

Topic sentence

Working too many hours can cause students to lose sight of their goal to finish college. Some students are so eager to save up enough money to buy a newer model phone or game or to keep up with the latest fashion trend that they take any extra hours they can get. And, as their needs for these items increase, they need to put in even more hours. Meanwhile, the prospect of ever finishing college slowly diminishes, and before they realize it, five years have passed and they are still slaving over the same grill flipping burgers or filling soda cups. They complain that they are not paid enough and regret not finishing college. If they had finished college, they would be in a higher paying job and earning enough money to cover their expenses.

Topic sentence acknowledges another viewpoint

In contrast, some people believe that it is fine to work long hours because it creates a balance in their lives and helps them prepare for the real world. They argue that working long hours keeps students occupied after finishing homework. It prevents them from going out with friends and getting caught up in all sorts of trouble such as drugs and illegal activities. When they are at their jobs, they learn discipline, patience, and organization.

Conclusion recognizes that students can work as long as they maintain balance

There is no reason why students cannot work and go to school, as long as they establish a balance so that work does not interfere with study time, school activities, and sleep. If a student wishes to transfer to a four-year college, what would look better on the application: working full-time with poor grades or working part-time with good grades? It does not take a genius to figure out that the line between college and work is a very thin one. That is why schools and other institutions have financial aid and scholarships available to students.

Works Cited

Etzioni, Amitai. "The Fast-Food Factories: McJobs Are Bad for Your Kids."

*The Writer's Response*. Eds. McDonald, Stephen and William Salomone,

4th ed. Boston: Thomson, 2008. 289–293. Print.

## Examining Writing

1. Evaluate the introduction, title, and conclusion of this essay.

2. How effectively did Bartley express her thesis?

3. How did Bartley organize her ideas? What other approach might she have taken toward her topic?

4. Evaluate Bartley's support for her thesis. Was it relevant and specific? What other types of evidence might she have used to strengthen her essay?

5. Overall, how could Bartley improve her essay?

# READ AND RESPOND: A Professional Essay

## Thinking Before Reading

This selection first appeared in a December 2009 issue of *Forbes* magazine. Read the article to find out how and why one man is working to transform the field of artificial limbs. As you read, notice how the author structures the essay by developing a thesis statement and using supporting evidence and detail. Also notice the effective title, introduction, and conclusion.

1. Preview the reading, using the steps discussed in Chapter 1 on page 25.

2. Connect the reading to your own experience by answering the following questions:

    a. What recent medical advances are you aware of that are changing people's lives?

    b. Do you think injuries veterans of recent wars in the Middle East have suffered will put pressure on the U.S. government to increase funding and research in the field of prosthetics?

3. Mark and annotate as you read.

1170**L**/1084 words

# A Step Beyond Human

## Andy Greenberg

1    On his way to a lunch meeting a few years ago Hugh Herr was running late. So he parked his Honda Accord in a handicapped parking spot, sprang out of the car and jogged down the sidewalk. Within seconds a policeman called out, asking

to see his disability permit. When Herr pointed it out on his dashboard, the cop eyed him suspiciously. "What's your affliction?" he asked dryly.

**biomechatronics**
an applied science combining biology, mechanics, and electronics

2    Herr, a slim and unassuming 6-footer with dark, neatly parted hair, took a step toward the officer and responded in an even tone: "I have no [expletive] legs."

3    Blurring the boundaries of disability is a trick that Herr, director of the biomechatronics group at MIT's Media Lab, has spent the last 27 years perfecting. At age 17 both of Herr's legs were amputated 6 inches below the knee after a rock climbing trip ended in severe frostbite. Today he's one of the world's preeminent prosthetics experts. His goal: to build artificial limbs that are superior to natural ones. His favorite test subject: himself. "I like to say that there are no disabled people," says Herr, 45. "Only disabled technology."

4    Herr swaps his feet out to suit his needs. He generally walks on flat carbon-fiber springs inside his shoes but sometimes replaces them with longer carbon bows for jogging. When he goes rock climbing—often scaling cliffs of expert-level difficulty—he switches to one of multiple pairs of climbing legs he's built himself, including small, rubber feet on aluminum poles that stretch his height beyond 7 feet, spiked aluminum claws that replace crampons for ice climbing or tapered polyethylene hatchets that wedge into crevices. "The fact that I'm missing lower limbs is an opportunity," he says. "Between my residual limb and the ground, I can create anything I want. The only limits are physical laws and my imagination."

**crampons**
spikes attached to shoes for ice climbing

5    Over the last several years that imagination has been working overtime. Late next year iWalk, a company Herr founded in 2006, plans to release the PowerFoot One, the world's most advanced robotic ankle and foot. Most prosthetic feet are fixed at a clumsy 90 degrees. The PowerFoot, equipped with three internal microprocessors and 12 sensors that measure force, inertia and position, automatically adjusts its angle, stiffness and damping 500 times a second. Employing the same sort of sensory feedback loops that the human nervous system uses, plus a library of known patterns, the PowerFoot adjusts for slopes, dips its toe naturally when walking down stairs, even hangs casually when the user crosses his or her legs.

**inertia**
the tendency of a body to stay at rest unless acted upon by an outside force

6    The PowerFoot is the only foot and ankle in the world that doesn't depend on its wearer's energy. With a system of passive springs and a half-pound rechargeable lithium iron phosphate battery, the foot—made of aluminum, titanium, plastic and carbon fiber—provides the same 20-joule push off the ground that human muscles and tendons do. It automatically adjusts the power to the walker's speed, but users can also dial that power up or down with a Bluetooth-enabled phone. (And soon, Herr says, with an iPhone application.) One test subject told Herr that his nonamputated leg often tires before his prosthetic-enhanced one. "This is the first time that the prosthesis is driving the human, instead of the other way around," says Herr.

7    Herr frequently wears a pair of his new creations. The next to try the PowerFoot will be the Department of Defense, which is looking for prostheses for the nearly 1,000 soldiers who have lost limbs in Iraq and Afghanistan. The Veterans Administration and the Army are among the investors who funded his MIT research. Veterans, he argues, also make the perfect early adopters, given their athletic, active lifestyles. "These are remarkable people," says Herr. "If the PowerFoot can work for them, it can work for anyone." iWalk hopes to put the PowerFoot on the general market in 2010, priced in the low five figures. The startup has raised $10.2 million from investors, including General Catalyst Partners and WFD Ventures.

*Cyborg evangelist: Herr wears a pair of his disability-defying PowerFoot devices.*

8    Herr's motives extend beyond profit. In 1982 he and a friend climbed Mount Washington in New Hampshire, a place infamous for its unpredictable and nasty weather. They were caught in a snowstorm, losing their way in a near-complete whiteout and subzero temperatures. After three and a half days of crawling along a frozen river, Herr's lower legs were practically destroyed by cold. A member of the rescue team sent after them, 28-year-old Albert Dow, was killed in an avalanche. "I feel a responsibility to use my intellect and resources to do as much as I can to help people. That's Albert Dow's legacy for me," says Herr.

9    Within three months of his amputations Herr was rock climbing with simple prosthetics. Within six months he was in a machine shop, building new feet, using the skills he'd learned at a vocational high school in Lancaster, Pa., where he grew up.

10    While he had previously focused on merely working a trade, Herr became a nearly obsessive student, earning a master's in mechanical engineering at MIT and a Ph.D. in biophysics at Harvard. Once, when his hands suffered from repetitive stress disorder while he was writing his doctoral thesis, he attached a pencil to a pair of sunglass frames and typed with his head. "He's driven to the point of exhaustion, physical degradation," says Rodger Kram, a professor of integrative physiology at the University of Colorado at Boulder, who worked with Herr at Harvard. "Every step he takes, he's forced to think about making prosthetics better."

11    Herr wants to transform how people define disability. Last year he sat on a panel of scientists that confirmed that Oscar Pistorius, a South African sprinter with no legs below the knee, should be allowed to compete in the Olympics. Herr helped discredit arguments that Pistorius got a metabolic advantage from his carbon-fiber legs.

12    Herr has tasted athletic discrimination, too. Because he uses special climbing prosthetics, many dispute his claim to be the second in the world to free-climb a famously challenging pitch near Index Mountain, Wash. "When amputees participate in sports, they call it courageous," he says. "Once you become competitive, they call it cheating." Herr even believes that in the coming decades **Paralympic** athletes will regularly outperform Olympic athletes. We may need special disability laws for humans who decline to have their bodies mechanically enhanced, he says.

**Paralympic**
related to an international competition for athletes with disabilities

13    "Disabled people today are the test pilots for technology that will someday be pervasive," Herr explains. "Eliminating disability and blurring man and machine will be one of the great stories of this century."

## Getting Ready to Write

### Checking Your Comprehension

Answer each of the following questions using complete sentences.

1. Why were Herr's legs amputated?
2. How has Herr turned his disability into an advantage?
3. How does the Department of Defense plan to use Herr's invention?
4. How does Albert Dow motivate Herr?
5. How are prosthetics changing athletics?
6. What does Herr predict will be the future of prosthetics?

## Strengthening Your Vocabulary

Using the word's context, word parts, or a dictionary, write a brief definition of each of the following words as it is used in the reading.

1. affliction (paragraph 1) _____ disability _____

2. preeminent (paragraph 3) _____ top, best _____

3. residual (paragraph 4) _____ remaining _____

4. vocational (paragraph 9) _____ related to an occupation or calling _____

5. degradation (paragraph 10) _____ breakdown _____

6. pitch (paragraph 12) _____ a steep piece of ground _____

7. pervasive (paragraph 13) _____ widespread _____

## Examining the Reading: Using Idea Maps

Review the reading by completing the missing parts of the following idea map.

**VISUALIZE IT!**

Title — **A Step Beyond Human**

Thesis — Hugh Herr had his legs amputated due to frostbite, and now spearheads research and development of artificial limbs.

- He wears artificial limbs of different types for different activities.
- Herr founded iWalk, a prosthetic limb company.
- He plans to release the PowerFoot One, the most advanced robotic foot and ankle.
  - The Department of Defense will use this for veterans who lost limbs.
  - Herr is motivated by Albert Dow, a rescue worker who lost his life trying to save Herr.
- Herr is energetic and driven.
  - Herr was back climbing six months after his amputation.
  - Herr got several degrees to be able to do this type of work.
  - He often pushes himself beyond his physical limits.
- Herr wants to transform how people define disability.
  - He worked to get permission for a sprinter with no legs to be able to compete in the Olympics.
  - His own accomplishments as a climber are disputed because of his use of specialized limbs.

Conclusion — The technology used by disabled people today will someday be used by all people to expand their abilities.

## Thinking and Writing Critically

Get ready to write about the reading by discussing the following:

**THINKING VISUALLY**

1. Write a journal entry about a time you turned a disadvantage into an advantage. How did you do so?

2. Explain how the title of the article relates to the subject. Can you think of another title that would also work for this article?

3. What does the photograph on page 559 reveal about about Herr? What type of person do you think he is based on the photograph?

---

## MySkillsLab®

**Complete** this Exercise

# Writing About the Reading

## Paragraph Options

1. Write a paragraph about how you think most people tend to think about those who have prosthetic limbs. What is a common reaction?

2. Write a paragraph discussing whether a person should take on any responsibility when someone dies trying to help him or her.

3. Herr engaged in risky behavior and suffered the consequences. Write a paragraph explaining either the benefits or drawbacks of a risky situation in which you or someone you know was involved.

## Essay Options

4. There have been advances in robotics that allow humans to exceed their biological limitations. Write an essay discussing the advantages and disadvantages of these technologies.

5. Herr is motivated to do his work because of what happened in his life. Write an essay explaining what in your life has motivated you to pursue an education in your field of study.

6. There are many movies, games, and books that fantasize about what could happen if human/robot combinations got out of control. Write an essay expressing and explaining your point of view about whether these combinations might be useful or dangerous, or both, and whether they should be controlled, and if so, how.

# SELF-TEST SUMMARY

To test yourself, cover the Answer column with a sheet of paper and answer each question in the left column. Evaluate each of your answers as you work by sliding the paper down and comparing your answer with what is printed in the Answer column.

| QUESTION | ANSWER |
|---|---|
| **GOAL 1 Plan your essay** <br> What is involved in planning an essay? | Select a topic and narrow it to a manageable length; then generate ideas and organize them to support your thesis statement. |
| **GOAL 2 Draft your essay** <br> How do you draft your essay? | Write a strong thesis statement, and then support your thesis with substantial evidence. Make connections among your ideas clear. Finally, write your introduction, conclusion, and title. |
| **GOAL 3 Revise your essay** <br> What are common problems in an essay? | Common problems include topics that are too broad or too narrow, ineffective thesis statements, underdevelopment, and disorganization. |
| **GOAL 4 Use strategies for reading essays** <br> What are some strategies for reading essays? | Establish the writer's authority and pay attention to background information. Identify the writer's purpose. Examine the title, the introduction, the body, and the organization of the essay, as well as the writer's use of vocabulary. Finally, examine the essay's conclusion. |

# MySkillsLab

For more help with **Planning, Drafting, and Revising Essays**, go to your learning path in MySkillsLab at http://www.myskillslab.com.

# Using Sources When You Write

## LEARNING GOALS

Learn how to …

■ **GOAL 1**
Locate appropriate sources

■ **GOAL 2**
Accurately record information from sources

■ **GOAL 3**
Use sources to support your ideas

■ **GOAL 4**
Document sources

■ **GOAL 5**
Use MLA style to document sources

## THINK About It!

Write a sentence identifying the issue the photograph confronts. Suppose you were asked to write a paper about this issue. How would you begin? Unless you are very familiar with it, you would need to do research on the topic. You would need to locate print and Internet sources that provide further information, and use that information in your essay. You would need to summarize what you read, being sure to credit the sources you used. In this chapter you will gain an overview of how to find sources and correctly use them as you write an essay.

# What Are Sources?

In completing some of the writing assignments in this book, you may have found yourself wishing you had more detailed facts or information to support your ideas. Suppose, for example, you were writing a paper about various trends in exercise programs, such as Pilates, kick-boxing, and boot camp–style workouts. As you wrote, you realized that it would be helpful to have some statistics about which types of workout programs are drawing the most interest and what kinds of people participate in the different types of programs. By consulting the right books, magazine and newspaper articles, and Web sites, you could find the needed information and use it in your paper (being sure to note where you got it, of course).

Many assignments in college require you to locate and read several sources of information on a topic and then use them to support and "flesh out" your ideas. At other times, you may be asked to examine certain printed sources and come up with a new idea or thesis about them. For example, in a business course you may be asked to read several essays or speeches by a well-known business leader and to develop a thesis about his or her short- and long-term viewpoints on the economy. Or for a journalism course you may be asked to find several different newspaper or magazine accounts of a particular event and write about how coverage varied, depending on where the account was printed.

This chapter will give you an overview of finding appropriate sources and using them correctly as you write papers.

## READING

# Locate Appropriate Sources

■ GOAL 1
Locate appropriate
sources

Libraries are filled with sources—print, electronic, and more. They house thousands of books, journals, videos, DVDs, pamphlets, tapes, and newspapers, as well as computers that enable you to access the World Wide Web. Yet this very abundance of sources means that one of the hardest parts of doing research is locating the sources that will be the most help to you.

Many books have been written on how to do research and how to use and document print and electronic sources. Therefore, this section gives only a brief overview of the research process and offers advice on how to get started.

## Tips for Finding Appropriate Sources

Suppose you are writing an essay about differences in men's and women's communication styles. Although you will find many sources on your topic, not all will be appropriate for your particular assignment.

Some sources may be too technical; others may be too sketchy. Some may be outdated, others too opinionated. Your task is to find sources that will give you good, solid, current information or points of view. Use the following tips:

1. **Keep track of all the sources you use.** There are several good reasons for doing this:

   ■ When you use sources in a paper, you must acknowledge them all at the end of your paper in a <u>bibliography</u> or "Works Cited" list. Providing your reader with information on your sources is called **documentation**.

   ■ You may want to refer to the source again.

   ■ You are more likely to avoid plagiarism if you keep accurate records of your sources. **Plagiarism** is using an author's words or ideas without acknowledging that you have done so. It is a serious ethical error and legal violation. In some colleges, plagiarism is sufficient cause for failing a course or even being dismissed from the college. You can easily avoid plagiarism by properly acknowledging your sources within your paper.

   ■ Record all publication information about each print and electronic source. For print sources, record title, author(s), volume, edition, place and date of publication, publisher, and page number(s). You may want to use index cards or a small bound notebook to record source information, using a separate card or page for each source. Print the home page of Web site sources and bookmark them, in case you need to find them again. You will learn how to document sources you use later in this chapter.

2. **Consult a reference librarian.** If you are unsure of where to begin, ask a reference librarian for advice. It is a reference librarian's job to suggest useful sources. He or she can be very helpful to you.

3. **Use a systematic approach.** Start by using general sources, either print or electronic, such as general reference books and, as needed, move to more specific sources such as periodicals and journals (scholarly magazines written for people focused on a particular area of study).

4. **Use current sources.** For many topics, such as controversial issues or scientific or medical advances, only the most up-to-date sources are useful. For other topics, such as the moral issues involved in abortion or euthanasia, older sources can be used. Before you begin, decide on a cut-off date—a date before which you feel information will be outdated and therefore not useful to you.

5. **Sample a variety of viewpoints.** Try to find sources that present differing viewpoints on the same subject rather than counting on one source to contain everything you need. Various authors take different approaches and have different opinions on the same topic, all of which can increase your understanding of the topic.

6. **Preview articles by reading <u>abstracts</u> or summaries.** Many sources begin with an abstract or end with a summary. Before using the source, check the abstract or summary to determine if the source is going to be helpful.

7. **Read sources selectively.** Many students spend time needlessly reading entire books and articles thoroughly when they should be reading

selectively—skimming to avoid parts that are not on the subject and to locate portions that relate directly to their topic. To read selectively,

■ use indexes and tables of contents to locate the portions of books that are useful and appropriate. In articles, use abstracts or summaries as a guide to the material's organization: the order in which ideas appear in the summary or abstract is the order in which they appear in the source itself.

■ after you have identified useful sections, preview (see p. 25) to get an overview of the material.

■ use headings to select sections to read thoroughly.

8. **Choose reliable, trustworthy sources.** The Internet contains a great deal of valuable information, but it also contains rumor, gossip, hoaxes, and misinformation. Before using a source, evaluate it by checking the author's credentials, considering the sponsor or publisher of the site, checking the date of posting, and verifying links. If you are uncertain about the information presented on a site, verify the information by cross-checking it with another source.

9. **Look for sources that lead to other sources.** Some sources include a bibliography, which provides leads to other works related to your topic. Follow links included in electronic sources.

---

| | |
|---|---|
| **EXERCISE 18-1** | ## Narrowing a Topic and Developing a Thesis Statement |

**WRITING IN PROGRESS**

**Directions:** Choose one of the following broad topics. Use a prewriting strategy to narrow the topic and develop a working thesis statement. Locate at least three reference sources that are useful and appropriate for writing a paper of two to three pages on the topic you have developed. Make a photocopy of the pages you consulted in each source. Print copies of Web sites used. Be sure to record all the bibliographic information for each source.

1. Native American code talkers
2. Urban legends
3. The wedding industry
4. Animal camouflage
5. Freedom of information legislation or "sunshine laws"
6. Test anxiety
7. Homeopathic medicine
8. The early history of your hometown

---

# Record Information from Sources

■ **GOAL 2**
Accurately record information from sources

As you use sources to research a topic, you will need to record usable information that you find. One option is to photocopy the pages from online sources and download and print information from online sources. This is useful if you plan to directly quote the source. Remember, you will need complete source information so you can cite your sources (see p. 570). However, a good essay does not string together a series of quotations. Instead it uses and combines information to come up with new ideas, perspectives, and responses to what is found in the sources. There are several options for keeping track of information—*annotating, paraphrasing,* and *summarizing.* Each of these important skills is covered earlier in this book (see Chapter 1 to review annotating and Chapter 15 to review paraphrasing and summarizing).

# Use Sources to Support Your Ideas

■ GOAL 3
Use sources to support
your ideas

Often when writing an essay you will find that you need additional information to support or explain your ideas. Suppose you are writing an essay on one aspect of crime in America. Your thesis states that mandatory minimum sentencing laws for petty crimes should be replaced with sentencing guidelines. In order to present a convincing paper, you need facts, statistics, and evidence to support your opinions. For example, you might need

- ■ statistics on the numbers of people in prison.
- ■ statistics on the increase in America's incarceration rate.
- ■ statistics on the amount of money spent on prisoners.
- ■ facts on mandatory minimum sentences.
- ■ facts on countries with successful alternatives to prison for lesser offenses.
- ■ evidence that mandatory minimums are ineffective.

To gather this information, you need to consult one or more reference sources. The following guidelines will help you use sources properly:

1. **Write a first draft of your paper.** Before consulting sources to support your ideas, work through the first three steps of the writing process: *prewriting, organizing,* and *drafting.* Get your own ideas down on paper. Once you have drafted your paper, you will be able to see what types of supporting information are necessary. If you research first, you might get flooded with facts and with other writers' voices and viewpoints, and lose your own.

2. **Analyze your draft to identify needed information.** Study your draft and look for statements that require supporting information in order to be believable. For example, suppose you have written

> The prisons in America are bursting with inmates who would be better off in drug treatment programs than locked up with dangerous criminals.

To support this statement, you need statistics on the number of prisoners with drug addictions who have been convicted of minor offenses and incarcerated.

The following types of statements benefit from supporting information:

- ■ **Opinions**

| EXAMPLE | Judges should be allowed to decide on the appropriate level of punishment. |
|---|---|
| NEEDED INFORMATION | What evidence supports that opinion? |

■ **Broad, general ideas**

| EXAMPLE | Incarcerating people for petty crimes is too harsh a punishment. |
|---|---|
| NEEDED INFORMATION | What alternatives are available? What constitutes a petty crime? |

■ **Cause-and-effect statements**

| EXAMPLE | Mandatory minimums are the result of politicians wanting to appear tough on crime. |
|---|---|
| NEEDED INFORMATION | What is the history of mandatory minimum sentencing? Who typically supports or opposes mandatory minimums? |

■ **Statements that assert what should be done**

| EXAMPLE | States should work harder to help minor offenders become contributing members of society. |
|---|---|
| NEEDED INFORMATION | What programs are currently in place? How many offenders are helped? |

3. **Write questions.** Read your draft looking for unsupported statements, underlining them as you find them. Then make a list of needed information, and form questions that need to be answered. Some students find it effective to write each question on a separate index card.

4. **Record information and note sources.** As you locate needed information, make a decision about the best way to record it. Should you photocopy or make a printout of the source and annotate it? Should you paraphrase? Should you write a summary? Your answer will depend on the type of information you are using as well as the requirements of your assignment. Always include complete bibliographic information for each source.

   As you consult sources, you will probably discover new ideas and perhaps even a new approach to your topic. For example, you may learn that some countries rely on a system of restorative justice, in which the criminal must apologize or provide reparation to the victim instead of going to prison for minor crimes. Record each of these new ideas on a separate index card along with its source.

5. **Revise your paper.** Begin by adding or incorporating new supporting information. (The next section of this chapter discusses how to add and document information from other sources.) Then reevaluate your draft, eliminating statements for which you could not locate supporting information, statements that you found to be inaccurate, and statements for which you found contradictory evidence.

---

**EXERCISE 18-2**     Writing a First Draft

**WRITING IN PROGRESS**

**Directions:** Write a first draft of a paper on the topic you chose in Exercise 18-1. To support your ideas, use the three sources you located. If any of these sources are dated or not focused enough for your thesis, you may need to locate additional ones.

# Document Sources

■ GOAL 4
Document sources

Using sources in an essay involves building the information into your paper correctly so as to give credit to the authors from whom you borrowed the ideas. You can incorporate researched information into your paper in one of two ways: (1) summarize or paraphrase the information or (2) quote directly from it. In both cases, you must give credit to the authors from whom you borrowed the information by documenting your sources in a list of references so your reader can locate it easily. Failure to provide documentation of a source is called *plagiarism*.

## What Is Plagiarism and How Can You Avoid It?

**Plagiarism** entails borrowing someone else's ideas or exact words *without giving that person credit*. Plagiarism can be intentional (submitting an essay written by someone else) or unintentional (failing to enclose another writer's words in quotation marks). Either way, it is considered a serious offense. If you plagiarize, you can fail the assignment or even the course.

**Cyberplagiarism** is a specific type of plagiarism. It takes two forms: (1) using information from the Internet without giving credit to the Web site that posted it, or (2) buying prewritten papers from the Internet and submitting them as your own work. For example: If you take information about Frank Lloyd Wright's architecture from a reference source (such as an encyclopedia or Web site) but do not specifically indicate where you found it, you have plagiarized. If you take the six-word phrase "Peterson, the vengeful, despicable drug czar" from a news article on the war on drugs, you have plagiarized.

Here are some guidelines to help you understand exactly what constitutes plagiarism:

### Plagiarism occurs when you . . .

- use another person's words without crediting that person.
- use another person's theory, opinion, or idea without listing the source of that information.
- do not place another person's exact words in quotation marks.
- do not provide a **citation** (reference) to the original source that you are quoting.
- paraphrase (reword) another person's ideas or words without credit.
- use facts, data, graphs, and charts without stating their source(s).

*Using commonly known facts or information is **not** plagiarism*, and you need not provide a source for such information. For example, the fact that Neil Armstrong set foot on the moon in 1969 is widely known and does not require documentation.

### To avoid plagiarism, do the following:

- When you take notes from any published or Internet source, place anything you copy directly in quotation marks.

- As you read and take notes, separate your ideas from ideas taken from the sources you are consulting. You might use different colors of ink or different sections of a notebook page or Word document for each.

- Keep track of all the sources you use, clearly identifying where each idea comes from.

- When paraphrasing someone else's words, change as many words as possible and try to organize them differently. Credit the original source of the information.

- Write paraphrases without looking at the original text so that you rephrase information in your own words. (For more information on writing a paraphrase, see Chapter 15.)

- Use citations to indicate the source of quotations and all information and ideas that are not your own. A **citation** is a notation, set off in parentheses, referring to a complete list of sources provided at the end of the essay. (For more information on citation, see the following page).

As you start researching new areas, you may ask yourself, "How can I possibly write a paper without using someone else's ideas? I don't know enough about the subject!" The good news is that it is *perfectly acceptable* to use other people's ideas in your research and writing. The key things to remember are (1) you must credit all information taken from any published or Internet sources, and (2) you must provide specific information regarding the publication from which the information is taken, as described in the following sections.

---

**EXERCISE 18-3**

WRITING IN PROGRESS

## Identifying Plagiarism

**Directions:** Read the following passage. Place a checkmark next to each statement in the list that follows that is an example of plagiarism.

> **Mexican Americans.** Currently, Mexican Americans are the second-largest racial or ethnic minority group in the United States, but within two decades they will be the largest group. Their numbers will swell as a result of continual immigration from Mexico and the relatively high Mexican birth rate. Mexican Americans are one of the oldest racial-ethnic groups in the United States. Under the terms of the treaty ending the Mexican-American War in 1848, Mexicans living in territories acquired by the United States could remain there and be treated as American citizens. Those who did stay became known as "Californios," "Tejanos," or "Hispanos."
>
> —Curry, Jiobu, and Schwirian, *Sociology for the Twenty-First Century*, p. 207

____X____  1. Mexican Americans are the second-largest minority in the United States. Their number grows as more people immigrate from Mexico.

_____  2. After the Mexican-American War, those Mexicans living in territories owned by the United States became American citizens and were known as Californios, Tejanos, or Hispanos (Curry, Jiobu, and Schwirian, 207).

____X____  3. "Mexican Americans are one of the oldest racial-ethnic groups in the United States."

_____  4. The Mexican-American War ended in 1848.

## Documentation

There are a number of different documentation formats (these are often called *styles*) that are used by scholars and researchers. Members of a particular academic discipline usually use the same format. For example, biologists follow a format described in *Scientific Style and Format: A Manual for Authors, Editors, and Publishers* and writers of psychology and other sociology papers typically use the American Psychological Association (APA) format.

One of the most common methods of documenting and citing sources is that used by the Modern Language Association (MLA). It uses a system of in-text citation: a brief note in the body of the text that refers to a source that is fully described in the "Works Cited" list at the end of the paper, where sources are listed in alphabetical order. The MLA format is typically used in English and humanities papers. Use the following guidelines for providing correct in-text citations using the MLA documentation style.

# Use MLA Style to Document Sources

■ **GOAL 5**
Use MLA style to document sources

For a comprehensive review of MLA style, consult the *MLA Handbook for Writers of Research Papers*, 7th edition, by Joseph Gibaldi.

## MLA In-Text Citations

When you refer to, summarize, paraphrase, quote, or in any other way use another author's words or ideas, you must indicate the source from which you took them by inserting an **in-text citation** that refers your reader to your "Works Cited" list.

Place your citation at the end of the sentence in which you refer to, summarize, paraphrase, or quote a source. It should follow a quotation mark, but come before punctuation that ends the sentence. If a question mark ends the sentence, place the question mark before the citation and a period after the citation.

Here are some guidelines about what to include in your in-text citations and how to incorporate quotations into your paper:

1. **If the source is introduced by a phrase that names the author, the citation need only include the page number.**

   > Miller poses the idea that if a good story is supposed to be a condensed version of life, then life should be lived like a good story in the first place (39).

2. **If the author is not named in the sentence, then include both the author's name and the page number in the citation.**

   > If a good story is supposed to be a condensed version of life, then life should be lived like a good story in the first place (Miller 39).

3. **If there are two or three authors, include the last names of all of them.**

   > Business ethics are important: "Many companies also have codes of ethics that guide buyers and sellers" (Lamb, Hair, and McDaniel 95).

4. **If there are four or more, include only the first author's last name and follow it with "et al.," which means "and others."**

> Therefore, impalas "illustrate the connections between animal behavior, evolution, and ecology" (Campbell et al. 703).

5. **If you have used two or more works by the same author, either include the relevant title in your sentence or include the title, if brief, or an abbreviated version in your citation.**

> In *Stealing MySpace: The Battle to Control the Most Popular Website in America*, Angwin concludes . . . (126).
>
> Or
>
> Angwin concludes  . . . (*MySpace* 120).

6. **When you include a quotation in your paper, you should signal your reader that one is to follow.** For example, use such introductory phrases as the following:

> According to Miller, "[quotation]."
> As Miller notes, "[quotation]."
> In the words of Miller, "[quotation]."

7. **To use a direct quotation, copy the author's words exactly and put them in quotation marks.** You do not always have to quote the full sentences; you can borrow phrases or clauses as long as they fit into your sentence, both logically and grammatically.

> Miller comments that he "wondered whether a person could plan a story for his life and live it intentionally" (39).

8. **If the quotation is lengthy (four sentences or longer), set it apart from the rest of your paper.** Indent the entire quotation one inch from the margin, double-space the lines, and do not use quotation marks. Include an in-text citation after the final punctuation mark at the end of the quotation.

> When discussing adapting a screenplay from his memoir, Miller noted the following:
>
> > It didn't occur to me at the time, but it's obvious now that in creating the fictional Don, I was creating the person I wanted to be, the person worth telling stories about. It never occurred to me that I could re-create my own story, my real life story, but in an evolution. I had moved toward a better me. I was creating someone I could live through, the person I'd be if I redrew the world, a character that was me but flesh and soul other. And flesh and soul better too. (29)

## MLA Works Cited List

Your list of works cited should include all the sources you referred to, summarized, paraphrased, or quoted in your paper. Start the list on a separate page at the end of your paper and title it "Works Cited." Arrange the entries alphabetically by each author's last name. If an author is not named (as in an editorial), then alphabetize the item by title. Double-space between and within entries. Start entries flush left, and if they run more than one line, indent subsequent lines half an inch.

1. **The basic format for a book can be illustrated as follows:**

   | Author | Title | Place of publication | Publisher | Date | Medium of publication |
   |--------|-------|----------------------|-----------|------|------------------------|

   Lin, Marvin. *Kid A*. New York: Continuum, 2011. Print.

   Special cases are handled as follows:

   a. **Two or more authors** If there are two or three authors, include all their names in the order in which they appear in the source. If there are four or more, give the first author's name only and follow it with "et al."

   | Authors | Title |
   |---------|-------|

   Spicer, Mark S., and John R. Covach. *Sounding Out Pop: Analytical Essays in Popular Music*. Ann Arbor: Michigan UP, 2010. Print.

   | | Place of publication | Publisher | Date | Medium of publication |
   |--|----------------------|-----------|------|------------------------|

   b. **Two or more works by the same author** If your list contains two or more works by the same author, list the author's name only once. For additional entries, substitute three hyphens followed by a period in place of the name.

   > Miller, Donald. *A Million Miles in a Thousand Years: What I Learned While Editing My Life*. Nashville: Nelson, 2009. Print.
   >
   > ———. *Searching for God Knows What*. Nashville: Nelson, 2004. Print.

   c. **Editor** If the book has an editor instead of an author, list the editor's name at the beginning of the entry and follow it with "ed."

   > McDannell, Colleen, ed. *Catholics in the Movies*. Oxford: Oxford UP, 2008. Print.

   d. **Edition** If the book has an edition number, include it after the title.

   > DeVito, Joseph A. *Human Communication: The Basic Course*. 11th ed. Boston: Pearson, 2009. Print.

   e. **Publisher** The entire name of the publisher is not used. For example, the Houghton Mifflin Company is listed as "Houghton."

2. **The basic format for a periodical can be illustrated as follows:**

| Author | Article title | Name of periodical volume/issue no. |
| --- | --- | --- |

Wilentz, Sean. "Bob Dylan in America." *The New York Review of Books* 57.18 (2010): 34. Print.

Date Page Medium of
no. publication

Special cases are handled as follows:

a. **Newspaper articles** Include the author, article title, name of the newspaper, date, section letter or number, page(s), and medium of publication. Abbreviate all months except May, June, and July, and place the day before the month.

> Weiner, Jonah. "Shaggy, Yes, but Finessed Just So." *New York Times* 25 Oct. 2009, New York ed.: AR20. Print.

b. **An article in a weekly magazine** List the author, article title, name of the magazine, date, page(s), and medium of publication. Abbreviate months as indicated above.

> Lilla, Mark. "The President and the Passions." *New York Times Magazine* 19 Dec. 2010: MM13. Print.

### Internet Sources

Information on the Internet comes from a wide variety of sources. For example, there are journals that are online versions of print publications, but there are also journals that are published only online. There are online books, articles from online databases, government publications, government Web sites, and more. Therefore, it is not sufficient merely to state that you got something from the Web. Citations for Internet resources must adequately reflect the exact type of document or publication that was used.

Include enough information to allow your readers to locate your sources. For some Internet sources, it may not be possible to locate all the required information; provide the information that is available. For sources that appear only online, include the following information:

- the name(s) of the author, editor, translator, narrator, compiler, performer, or producer of the material
- the title of the work
- the title of the Web site (if different)
- the version or edition used
- the publisher or sponsor of the site (if unknown write n.p.)
- the date of publication (day, month, year), write n.d. if not known
- the medium of publication (Web)
- and the date of access (day, month, year). *Do not* include the URL unless the site cannot be found without using it.

1. **The basic format for an Internet source is as follows:**

> Breihan, Tom. "My Morning Jacket Ready New Album." *Pitchfork*. Pitchfork Media Inc. 3 Mar. 2011. Web. 6 Mar. 2011.

2. **The basic format for an Internet source that originally appeared in print is as follows:** Start your entry with the same information you would for a print source. Then add the title of the Web site or database (in italics) followed by a period, the medium of publication (Web) followed by a period, and the date you accessed the source (day, month, year) followed by a period. DO NOT include the URL unless the site cannot be found without using it.

> Wald, Mathew L. "Study Details How U. S. Could Cut 28% of Greenhouse Gases." *New York Times* 30 Nov. 2007: Business. *nytimes.com*. Web. 12 Aug. 2008.

a.  **Online book**—If you consulted an entire online book, use this format:

> Woolf, Virginia. *Monday or Tuesday*. New York: Harcourt, 1921. *Bartleby.com*. Web. 6 Aug. 2008.

b.  **Online book**—If you consulted part of an online book, use this format:

> Seifert, Kelvin, and David Zinger. "Effective Nonverbal Communication." *Educational Psychology*. Boston: Houghton, 2009. *The Online Books Page*. Web. 6 Feb. 2011.

c.  **Article from an online periodical**—If you accessed the article *directly* from an online journal, magazine, or newspaper, use this format:

> Sommers, Jeffrey. "Historical Arabesques: Patterns of History." *World History Connected* 5.3. University of Illinois at Urbana-Champaign, June 2008. Web. 15 May 2011.

d.  **Article from an online database**—If you accessed an article using an online database, and a Digital Object Locator (DOI) was provided for the article, include it. If not, include the name of the database and the document number, if available.

> Barnard, Neal D., et al. "Vegetarian and Vegan Diets in Type 2 Diabetes Management." *Nutrition Reviews*, 67(5), 255–263. Web. 21 Apr. 2011. doi:10.1111/j.1753-4887.2009.00198.x
>
> Bivins, Corey. "A Soy-free, Nut-free Vegan Meal Plan." *Vegetarian Journal*, 30(1), 14-17. *AltHealth Watch*. Web. 21 Apr. 2011. (2010918153)

e.  **Online government publication**—If you consult a document published by a government entity, use this format:

> United States. Financial Crisis Inquiry Commission. *The Financial Crisis Inquiry Report: Final Report of the National Commission on the Causes of the Financial and Economic Crisis in the United States*. Washington: Financial Crisis Inquiry Commission, 2010. *FDLP Desktop*. Web. 20 Mar. 2011.

### *Other Electronic Sources*

1. **CD-ROM nonperiodical publication**

   > Beck, Mark. F. *Theory & Practice of Therapeutic Massage: Student CD-ROM*. Clifton Park, NY: Milady, 2011. CD-ROM.

2. **Interview from a radio Web site**

   > Merritt, Stephin. Interview. *The Strange Powers of Stephin Merritt & the Magnetic Fields*. KEXP, 10 Dec. 2011. Web. 13 Apr. 2012.

3. **Television documentary viewed on the Internet**

   > Lacy, Susan, prod. "Troubadours." *American Masters*. PBS, 2 Mar. 2011. Web. 16 Apr. 2011.

4. **Photograph viewed on the Internet**

   > Warhol, Andy. *Self-Portrait.*1963–1964. Photograph. *The Warhol.* The Andy Warhol Museum. Web. 17 Aug. 2011.

---

## EXERCISE 18-4    Writing a Works Cited List

**WRITING IN PROGRESS**

**Directions:** Using MLA style, add two quotations to the paper you drafted in Exercise 18-2. Add in-text citations and write a Works Cited list for your paper including entries for all your sources.

---

# INTEGRATING READING AND WRITING

## READ AND RESPOND: A Student Essay

*Alaina Mayer is a community college student who is majoring in nursing. She wrote this essay to complete a sociology assignment that directed her to examine and take a position on a current social issue.*

Alaina Mayer

Professor Thomas

English 101

11 Mar. 2012

Surveillance in America: It's Not Paranoia
If You're Really Being Watched

Have you ever gotten the feeling that your cell phone is communicating with space?

Do you feel like you're constantly being watched? The threat of surveillance

today comes not only from shadowy government agencies but more frequently

from each other. Well-meaning friends who post blurry video of last Friday night

can't be stopped any more than the National Security Agency's (NSA) electronic

dragnet. For better or worse, Americans live in a surveillance state. There are many

sources and tools for surveillance, and each is a violation of privacy.

One means of surveillance is the monitoring of electronic media by the

government. NSA is a little-known federal agency with a secret budget. It breaks

codes and interprets intelligence. The agency is also responsible for "network

warfare"—hacking. Its goal is the same as that of spies throughout history—to gain

an edge by obtaining hard-to-get information and using it as they choose. The

agency doesn't collect information about Americans, "except pursuant to procedures

established by the head of the agency and approved by the Attorney General" (NSA.

gov). In other words, NSA can only collect information about you if it follows the

rules—its rules. Said rules allow an incredible amount of data collection and storage.

According to Wired magazine, NSA collects your Google searches, cellphone

calls, emails, and bookstore purchases. They do so partially with the help of 10–20

data centers placed in telecommunications facilities owned by companies such as

Verizon. NSA also eavesdrops on satellites and conducts what's known as "deep

**Margin notes:**

Title: Introduces the topic

Thesis statement

Topic sentence

Note sources highlighted in purple.

Topic sentence

Mayer 2

packet inspection." In short, it's not just listening to you talk. The agency analyzes everything you do online and sifts it to make sure you're not a danger to the country. Then the information is saved forever to be analyzed by the fastest

*Source*

computers on Earth (Bamford). Electronic surveillance is a powerful intrusion into privacy: your Internet traffic paints an intimate portrait, especially when cross-referenced with Facebook's insight into your social web and cell phone records. The agency can use this to understand you and your relationships in a way that doesn't require questioning or due process. Compiling this data yourself, for your own use, would be almost impossible and a massive intrusion into the privacy of everyone with whom you communicate, yet the federal government is already doing it—to everyone.

*Topic sentence*

The feds are not the only ones keeping an eye on citizens. State governments have taken surveillance a step further, literally watching over their citizens with thousands of surveillance cameras. Nowhere is this more prevalent than in New York City. In Manhattan alone, volunteers counted 4,176 cameras in the 1/6th of the city

*Source*

surveyed (Palmer). Since two horrific murders in 2007, all NYC clubs with a cabaret

*Source*

license are required to have cameras at the entrances and exits (Jones). So you're safe—to the extent that if someone murders you, the police will be able to see grainy footage of the attack if it happened within view of the camera—but you're not free. Whoever's on your shoulder as you stumble will be saved for as long as the camera's owner chooses. You have no way of knowing how long that is or what's going to be done with the footage. It could end up on YouTube or on TV. At least the cameras aren't violating any privacy rights not also held by a random person with a camera—anyone can film you walking out of the bar as long as you remained in public.

*Topic sentence*

Camera usage isn't limited to major metropolitan areas. A Google search for "cameras installed in the downtown area" came up with reports of cameras

Mayer 3

currently installed in cities across America: Meriden, CT; Winooski, Brattleboro and

Richford, VT; Cohoes, NY; Clemson, SC; Columbia and Maplewood, MO; Houma,

LA; Ottumwa, IA; Austin, TX; Colorado Springs, CO; Cheyenne, WY; Klamath Falls,

OR; and Los Angeles and the Bay Area of San Francisco, CA, for example. Even small

towns have cameras that record you walking into a bank, for instance. Most ATMs

have them. International trends show camera surveillance to be on the rise. Great

**Source**

Britain has one camera for every 32 people, according to a recent study (Lewis).

Looking at who owns the cameras reveals who's really watching—

citizens, not the government!

**Topic sentence**

Although cameras may violate privacy, a recent study says they are useful

tools for fighting crime. After analyzing Baltimore, MD, Washington, DC, and

Chicago, IL's police surveillance programs, researchers found watching gets results.

In all three cities the camera systems faced different challenges, but were shown

to be helpful in every step of the criminal justice process, including encouraging

**Source**

witnesses to testify (La Vigne et al.). Slightly more than 95% of the cameras in the

study's sample were owned by private entities. Corporations, apartment buildings

and restaurants have good reasons to install cameras—loss prevention, protection

against liability and overall security concerns make them a reasonable expense for

these and many other employers.

**Topic sentence**

Companies also use national-security style tactics to profile their

customers. The same technologies that predict if you'll make a bomb can tell what

coupons you'll like. Store loyalty cards are one of their surveillance tools. In addition

to delivering perks and discounts, they track everything you buy. (To avoid this, ask

for a store card at the checkout—it usually works for the discounts but not coupons.)

The cards are vital, however, in the case of food recalls. My father recently received a

call about some ham salad he'd purchased. It was prepared with Listeria-tainted

Mayer 4

onions. If he hadn't used the store loyalty card for a discount, the store would have had no way to contact him. Is it worth getting upset about your grocery store knowing you only buy one brand of yogurt if that results in coupons for that brand? However, there are more sophisticated uses for this data. Target's data mining is so precise, a Minneapolis father found out his high-school daughter was pregnant

Source

thanks to a targeted mailing she received (Duhigg). The store—rather, the store's marketing algorithms—knew before he did. Predicting due dates is lucrative—if a woman gets hooked into a specific all-purpose store early in her pregnancy, she'll keep shopping there for baby supplies—and keeping a parent informed was just an unexpected bonus.

Topic sentence

Even if you don't see cameras, look around! You might still be trackable via military satellites, for example. That's thanks to E911, the technology introduced in 2002 that required Global Positioning System (GPS) tracking chips in all new cell

Source

phones (Koerner). Cell phones aren't just holding the GPS that makes you trackable—the rest of their components make plausible deniability nearly impossible. Cell phones are everywhere and many can take photos, record sound and shoot video. Seconds later, that information can be shared, as fast as the phone and the network can send it. Big Brother is watching you, but so can everyone else.

Conclusion reaffirms the thesis and makes a suggestion

If you want to keep your activities to yourself, conduct them in a windowless room without your cell phone, laptop, or anyone else present.

Mayer 5

Works Cited

Bamford, James. "The NSA Is Building the Country's Biggest Spy Center (Watch What

You Say)." *Wired.com. Wired Magazine,* 15 Mar. 2012. Web. 30 July 2012.

Duhigg, Charles M. "How Companies Learn Your Secrets." *Nytimes.com.*

*The New York Times,* 2 Feb. 2012. Web. 30 July 2012.

Jones, Charisse. "Violence Brings Club Crackdown." *USA Today.* Gannett,

4 Apr. 2007. Web. 30 July 2012.

Koerner, Brendan I. "Legal Affairs." *Legal Affairs.* n.p., July 2003. Web. 30 July 2012.

La Vigne, Nancy G., et al. "Evaluating the Use of Public Surveillance Cameras for

Crime Control and Prevention." *Urban.org.* Urban Institute, Sept. 2011.

Web. 30 July 2012.

Lewis, Paul. "You're Being Watched: There's One CCTV Camera for

Every 32 People in UK." *The Guardian.* Guardian News and Media,

02 Mar. 2011. Web. 30 July 2012.

"National Security Agency / Central Security Service." *SIGINT Frequently Asked*

*Questions.* National Security Agency, 15 Jan. 2009. Web. 30 July 2012.

Palmer, Brian. "How Many Surveillance Cameras Are There in Manhattan?" *Slate*

*Magazine.* The Slate Group, 3 May 2010. Web. 30 July 2012.

## Examining Writing

1. How is the essay organized?
2. Examine Mayer's use of sources. What does each reference used contribute to the essay?
3. Other than sources, what other types of support does Mayer use to explain her thesis?
4. Examine the introduction. Does beginning with questions create an effective opener? If so, what other questions might Mayer have included?
5. For what audience does Mayer seem to be writing?
6. What additional information or additional details could have strengthened Mayer's thesis?

# SELF-TEST SUMMARY

To test yourself, cover the Answer column with a sheet of paper and answer each question in the left column. Evaluate each of your answers as you work by sliding the paper down and comparing your answer with what is printed in the Answer column.

| QUESTION | ANSWER |
| --- | --- |
| **GOAL 1** Locate appropriate sources<br><br>How do you find appropriate sources? | Consult a reference librarian for help getting started. Use a systematic approach to find sources that are current, reliable, and trustworthy. Sample a variety of viewpoints and look for sources that lead to other sources. Save time by reading sources selectively and reading abstracts or summaries to preview articles. |
| **GOAL 2** Accurately record information from sources<br><br>What are some ways to record information from sources? | Photocopy pages from print sources and download and print information from online sources. Keep track of information by annotating, paraphrasing, and summarizing. |
| **GOAL 3** Use sources to support your ideas<br><br>How do you use sources to support your ideas? | Before consulting sources, write a first draft and analyze it to identify needed information and form questions that need to be answered. As you locate information, record it and note sources. Then revise your paper by incorporating new information. |
| **GOAL 4** Document sources<br><br>What are two ways to incorporate researched information into your paper?<br><br>What is plagiarism, and what can you do to avoid it? | You can summarize or paraphrase the information or you can quote directly from it.<br>Plagiarism is when you use someone else's words or ideas without crediting him or her. You can avoid plagiarism by placing anything you copy exactly in quotation marks; separating your ideas from those of your sources in your notes; keeping track of the sources you use; paraphrasing accurately, using your own words; and citing and documenting sources. |
| **GOAL 5** Use MLA style to document sources<br><br>What is MLA style? | The Modern Language Association (MLA) style uses in-text citations to refer readers to a list of sources in a "Works Cited" list at the end of an essay. |

# MySkillsLab

For more help with **Using Sources When You Write**, go to your learning path in MySkillsLab at http://www.myskillslab.com.

# Reviewing the Basics: A Brief Grammar Handbook

# OVERVIEW

Most of us know how to communicate in our language. When we talk or write, we put our thoughts into words and, by and large, we make ourselves understood. But many of us do not know the specific terms and rules of grammar. Grammar is a system that describes how language is put together. Grammar must be learned, almost as if it is a foreign language.

Why is it important to study grammar, to understand grammatical terms like *verb*, *participle*, and *gerund* and concepts like *agreement* and *subordination*? There are several good reasons. Knowing grammar will allow you to

- **recognize an error in your writing and correct it.** Your papers will read more smoothly and communicate more effectively when they are error free.

- **understand the comments of your teachers and peers.** People who read and critique your writing may point out a "fragment" or a "dangling modifier." You will be able to revise and correct the problems.

- **write with more impact.** Grammatically correct sentences are signs of clear thinking. Your readers will get your message without distraction or confusion.

As you will see in this part of the text, "Reviewing the Basics," the different areas of grammatical study are highly interconnected. The sections on parts of speech, sentences, punctuation, mechanics, and spelling fit together into a logical whole. To recognize and correct a run-on sentence, for example, you need to know both sentence structure *and* punctuation. To avoid errors in capitalization, you need to know parts of speech *and* mechanics. If grammar is to do you any good, your knowledge of it must be thorough. As you review the following "basics," be alert to the interconnections that make language study so interesting.

Grammatical terms and rules demand your serious attention. Mastering them will pay handsome dividends: error-free papers, clear thinking, and effective writing.

# Understanding the Parts of Speech

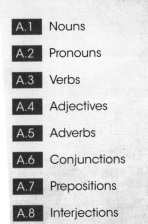

The eight parts of speech are **nouns, pronouns, verbs, adjectives, adverbs, conjunctions, prepositions,** and **interjections**. Each word in a sentence functions as one of these parts of speech. Being able to identify the parts of speech in sentences allows you to analyze and improve your writing and to understand grammatical principles discussed later in this section.

It is important to keep in mind that *how* a word functions in a sentence determines *what* part of speech it is. Thus, the same word can be a noun, a verb, or an adjective, depending on how it is used.

Noun
He needed some blue wallpaper.

Verb
He will wallpaper the hall.

Adjective
He went to a wallpaper store.

| A.1 | Nouns |
| A.2 | Pronouns |
| A.3 | Verbs |
| A.4 | Adjectives |
| A.5 | Adverbs |
| A.6 | Conjunctions |
| A.7 | Prepositions |
| A.8 | Interjections |

## A.1 Nouns

A **noun** names a person, place, thing, or idea.

| People | *woman, winner, Maria Alvarez* |
| Places | *mall, hill, Indiana* |
| Things | *lamp, ship, air* |
| Ideas | *goodness, perfection, harmony* |

The form of many nouns changes to express **number** (**singular** for one, **plural** for more than one): *one bird, two birds; one child, five children*. Most nouns can also be made **possessive** to show ownership by the addition of *-'s*: *city's, Allison's*.

Sometimes a noun is used to modify another noun:

Noun modifying diploma
Her goal had always been to earn a college diploma.

Nouns are classified as proper, common, collective, concrete, abstract, count, and noncount.

1. **Proper nouns** name specific people, places, or things and are always capitalized: *Martin Luther King Jr.; East Lansing; Lexus*. Days of the week and months are considered proper nouns and are capitalized.

Proper noun  Proper noun  Proper noun

In September, Allen will attend Loyola University.

2. **Common nouns** name one or more of a general class or type of person, place, thing, or idea and are not capitalized: *president, city, car, wisdom.*

Common noun  Common noun  Common noun  Common noun

Next fall, the students will enter college to receive an education.

3. **Collective nouns** name a whole group or collection of people, places, or things: *committee, team, jury.* They are usually singular in form.

Collective noun  Collective noun

The flock of mallards flew over the herd of bison.

4. **Concrete nouns** name tangible things that can be tasted, seen, touched, smelled, or heard: *sandwich, radio, pen.*

Concrete noun  Concrete noun

The frozen pizza was stuck in the freezer.

5. **Abstract nouns** name ideas, qualities, beliefs, and conditions: *honesty, goodness, poverty.*

Abstract nouns  Abstract noun

Their marriage was based on love, honor, and trust.

6. **Count nouns** name items that can be counted. Count nouns can be made plural, usually by adding *-s* or *-es: one river, three rivers; one box, ten boxes.* Some count nouns form their plural in an irregular way: *man, men; goose, geese.*

Count noun  Count noun  Count noun

The salespeople put the invoices in their files.

7. **Noncount nouns** name ideas or qualities that cannot be counted. Noncount nouns almost always have no plural form: *air, knowledge, unhappiness.*

Noncount noun  Noncount noun

As the rain pounded on the windows, she tried to find the courage to walk home from work.

# A.2 Pronouns

A **pronoun** is a word that substitutes for or refers to a noun or another pronoun. The noun or pronoun to which a pronoun refers is called the pronoun's **antecedent**. A pronoun must agree with its antecedent in person, number, and gender (these terms are discussed later in this section).

After the campers discovered the cave, they mapped it for the next group, which was arriving next week. [The pronoun *they* refers to its antecedent, *campers*; the pronoun *it* refers to its antecedent, *cave*; the pronoun *which* refers to its antecedent, *group.*]

The eight kinds of pronouns are **personal, demonstrative, reflexive, intensive, interrogative, relative, indefinite,** and **reciprocal.**

1.  **Personal pronouns** take the place of nouns or pronouns that name people or things. A personal pronoun changes form to indicate **person, gender, number,** and **case.**

    **Person** is the grammatical term used to distinguish the speaker (**first person:** *I, we*); the person spoken to (**second person:** *you*); and the person or thing spoken about (**third person:** *he, she, it, they*). **Gender** is the term used to classify pronouns as **masculine** (*he, him*); **feminine** (*she, her*); or **neuter** (*it*). **Number** classifies pronouns as **singular** (one) or **plural** (more than one). Some personal pronouns also function as adjectives modifying nouns (*our house*).

|  | *Singular* | *Plural* |
|---|---|---|
| First person | I, me, my, mine | we, us, our, ours |
| Second person | you, your, yours | you, your, yours |
| Third person | | |
|   Masculine | he, him, his | |
|   Feminine | she, her, hers | they, them, their, theirs |
|   Neuter | it, its | |

First-person singular · First-person singular (pronoun/adjective) · Third-person singular

I called my manager about my new clients. She wanted to know as soon as they placed their first orders. "Your new clients are important to us," she said.

Third-person plural · Third-person plural (pronoun/adjective) · Second-person singular (pronoun/adjective) · First-person plural · Third-person singular

> ### Tip for Writers
>
> *This, that, these,* and *those* all refer to one or more things or people within the speaker's sight, but *that* and *those* refer to things farther away. *This* and *these* refer to what is close to the speaker or writer.
>
> | Distance | Singular | Plural |
> |---|---|---|
> | near | this | these |
> | far | that | those |

A pronoun's **case** is determined by its function as a subject (**subjective** or **nominative case**) or an object (**objective case**) in a sentence. A pronoun that shows ownership is in the **possessive case.** (See p. 626 for a discussion of pronoun case.)

2.  **Demonstrative pronouns** refer to particular people or things. The demonstrative pronouns are *this* and *that* (singular) and *these* and *those* (plural). (*This, that, these,* and *those* can also be demonstrative adjectives when they modify a noun.)

    > This is more thorough than that.
    >
    > The red shuttle buses stop here. These go to the airport every hour.

3. **Reflexive pronouns** indicate that the subject performs actions to, for, or upon itself. Reflexive pronouns end in *-self* or *-selves*.

|  | *Singular* | *Plural* |
|---|---|---|
| First person | myself | ourselves |
| Second person | yourself | yourselves |
| Third person | himself | |
|  | herself | themselves |
|  | itself | |

We excused <u>ourselves</u> from the table and left.

4. An **intensive pronoun** emphasizes the word that comes before it in a sentence. Like reflexive pronouns, intensive pronouns end in *-self* or *-selves*.

The filmmaker <u>herself</u> could not explain the ending.

They <u>themselves</u> repaired the copy machine.

*Note:* A reflexive or intensive pronoun should not be used as a subject of a sentence. An antecedent for the reflexive pronoun must appear in the same sentence.

| INCORRECT | <u>Myself</u> create colorful sculpture. |
|---|---|
| CORRECT | I <u>myself</u> create colorful sculpture. |

5. **Interrogative pronouns** are used to introduce questions: *who, whom, whoever, whomever, what, which, whose.* The correct use of *who* and *whom* depends on the role the interrogative pronoun plays in a sentence or clause. When the pronoun functions as the subject of the sentence or clause, use *who.* When the pronoun functions as an object in the sentence or clause, use *whom* (see p. 627).

<u>What</u> happened?

<u>Which</u> is your street?

<u>Who</u> wrote *Ragtime*? [*Who* is the subject of the sentence.]

<u>Whom</u> should I notify? [*Whom* is the object of the verb *notify*: *I should notify whom?*]

6. **Relative pronouns** relate groups of words to nouns or other pronouns and often introduce adjective clauses or noun clauses (see p. 619). The relative pronouns are *who, whom, whoever, whomever,* and *whose* (referring to people) and *that, what, whatever,* and *which* (referring to things).

In 1836 Charles Dickens met John Forster, <u>who</u> became his friend and biographer.

Jason did not understand <u>what</u> the consultant recommended.

We read some articles <u>that</u> were written by former astronauts.

7. **Indefinite pronouns** are pronouns without specific antecedents. They refer to people, places, or things in general.

<u>Someone</u> has been rearranging my papers.

<u>Many</u> knew the woman, but <u>few</u> could say they knew her well.

## Tip for Writers

Be sure to use a *singular verb* after the *indefinite pronouns* that are grammatically singular: Everybody is here now. Let's eat! (Even though *everybody* means at least three people, it's grammatically singular.)

Here are some frequently used indefinite pronouns:

| SINGULAR | | PLURAL |
|---|---|---|
| another | nobody | all |
| anybody | none | both |
| anyone | no one | few |
| anything | nothing | many |
| each | one | more |
| either | other | most |
| everybody | somebody | others |
| everyone | someone | several |
| everything | something | some |
| neither | | |

8. The **reciprocal pronouns** *each other* and *one another* indicate a mutual relationship between two or more parts of a plural antecedent.

   Armando and Sharon congratulated <u>each other</u> on their high grades.

---

**EXERCISE 1**

## Identifying Nouns and Pronouns

**Directions:** In each of the following sentences, (a) circle each noun and (b) underline each pronoun.

   **EXAMPLE**   (Jamila) parked <u>her</u> (car) in the (lot) <u>that</u> is reserved for (commuters) like <u>her</u>.

1. (Shakespeare) wrote many (plays) <u>that</u> have become famous and important.

2. <u>Everyone</u> <u>who</u> has visited (Disneyland) wishes to return.

3. (Jonathan) <u>himself</u> wrote the (report) <u>that</u> the (president) of the (company) presented to the (press).

4. <u>That</u> (desk) used to belong to <u>my</u> (boss).

5. <u>My</u> (integrity) was never questioned by <u>my</u> (co-workers).

6. The (class) always laughed at (jokes) told by the (professor,) even though <u>they</u> were usually corny.

7. When will (humankind) be able to travel to (Mars?)

8. <u>Whoever</u> wins the (lottery) this (week) will become quite wealthy.

9. As the (plane) landed at the (airport,) many of the (passengers) began to gather <u>their</u> carry-on (luggage.)

10. <u>This</u> (week) <u>we</u> are studying (gravity); next week <u>we</u> will study (heat.)

# A.3 Verbs

Verbs express action or state of being. A grammatically complete sentence has at least one verb in it.

There are three kinds of verbs: **action verbs**, **linking verbs**, and **helping verbs** (also known as **auxiliary verbs**).

1.  **Action verbs** express physical and mental activities.

    > Mr. Royce <u>dashed</u> for the bus.
    >
    > The incinerator <u>burns</u> garbage at high temperatures.
    >
    > I <u>think</u> that seat is taken.
    >
    > The programmer <u>worked</u> until 3:00 a.m.

    Action verbs are either **transitive** or **intransitive**. The action of a **transitive verb** is directed toward someone or something, called the **direct object** of the verb. Direct objects receive the action of the verb. Transitive verbs require direct objects to complete the meaning of the sentence.

    >                Transitive   Direct
    > Subject   verb     object
    > Amalia <u>made</u> clocks.

    An **intransitive verb** does not need a direct object to complete the meaning of the sentence.

    >            Intransitive
    > Subject    verb
    > The traffic <u>stopped</u>.

    Some verbs can be both transitive and intransitive, depending on their meaning and use in a sentence.

    > INTRANSITIVE   The traffic <u>stopped</u>. [No direct object.]
    >
    >                           Direct object
    > TRANSITIVE   The driver <u>stopped</u> the bus at the corner.

2.  A **linking verb** expresses a state of being or a condition. A linking verb connects a noun or pronoun to words that describe the noun or pronoun. Common linking verbs are forms of the verb *be* (*is, are, was, were, being, been*), *become, feel, grow, look, remain, seem, smell, sound, stay,* and *taste.*

    > Their child <u>grew</u> tall.
    >
    > The office <u>looks</u> messy.
    >
    > Mr. Davenport <u>is</u> our accountant.

3.  A **helping (auxiliary) verb** helps another verb, called the **main verb**, to convey when the action occurred (through verb tense) and to form questions. One or more helping verbs and the main verb together

---

**Tip for Writers**

A *direct object* answers the question *Who?* or *What?* about the verb.

---

**Tip for Writers**

Be sure to use an adjective, not an adverb, after a *linking verb*. Use adverbs to describe other verbs: He seems nice. (but) He paints nicely.

form a **verb phrase**. Some helping verbs, called **modals**, are always helping verbs:

| | |
|---|---|
| can, could | shall, should |
| may, might | will, would |
| must, ought to | |

The other helping verbs can sometimes function as main verbs as well:

am, are, be, been, being, did, do, does
had, has, have
is, was, were

The verb *be* is a very irregular verb, with eight forms instead of the usual five: *am, are, be, being, been, is, was, were*.

Helping Main
verb  verb

The store will close early on holidays.

Helping         Main
verb             verb

Will the store close early on New Year's Eve?

## Forms of the Verb

All verbs except *be* have five forms: the **base form** (or dictionary form), the **past tense**, the **past participle**, the **present participle**, and the **-s form**. The first three forms are called the verb's **principal parts**. The infinitive consists of "to" plus a base form: *to go, to study, to talk*. For **regular verbs**, the past tense and past participle are formed by adding *-d* or *-ed* to the base form. **Irregular verbs** follow no set pattern to form their past tense and past participle.

| | *Regular* | *Irregular* |
|---|---|---|
| Infinitive | work | eat |
| Past tense | worked | ate |
| Past participle | worked | eaten |
| Present participle | working | eating |
| *-s* form | works | eats |

Verbs change form to agree with their subjects in person and number (see p. 220); to express the time of their action (**tense**); to express whether the action is a fact, command, or wish (**mood**); and to indicate whether the subject is the doer or the receiver of the action (**voice**).

## Principal Parts of Irregular Verbs

Consult the following list and your dictionary for the principal parts of irregular verbs.

| BASE FORM | PAST TENSE | PAST PARTICIPLE |
|---|---|---|
| be | was | been |
| become | became | become |
| begin | began | begun |

*(Continued)*

| BASE FORM | PAST TENSE | PAST PARTICIPLE |
| --- | --- | --- |
| bite | bit | bitten |
| blow | blew | blown |
| burst | burst | burst |
| catch | caught | caught |
| choose | chose | chosen |
| come | came | come |
| dive | dived, dove | dived |
| do | did | done |
| draw | drew | drawn |
| drive | drove | driven |
| eat | ate | eaten |
| fall | fell | fallen |
| find | found | found |
| fling | flung | flung |
| fly | flew | flown |
| get | got | gotten |
| give | gave | given |
| go | went | gone |
| grow | grew | grown |
| have | had | had |
| know | knew | known |
| lay | laid | laid |
| lead | led | led |
| leave | left | left |
| lie | lay | lain |
| lose | lost | lost |
| ride | rode | ridden |
| ring | rang | rung |
| rise | rose | risen |
| say | said | said |
| set | set | set |
| sit | sat | sat |
| speak | spoke | spoken |
| swear | swore | sworn |
| swim | swam | swum |
| tear | tore | torn |
| tell | told | told |
| throw | threw | thrown |
| wear | wore | worn |
| write | wrote | written |

## Tense

The **tenses** of a verb express time. They convey whether an action, process, or event takes place in the present, past, or future.

The three **simple tenses** are **present, past,** and **future.** The **simple present** tense is the base form of the verb (and the -*s* form of third-person singular subjects; see p. 621); the **simple past** tense is the past-tense form; and the **simple future** tense consists of the helping verb *will* plus the base form.

The **perfect tenses,** which indicate completed action, are **present perfect, past perfect,** and **future perfect.** They are formed by adding the helping verbs *have* (or *has*), *had,* and *will have* to the past participle.

In addition to the simple and perfect tenses, there are six progressive tenses. The **simple progressive tenses** are the **present progressive,** the **past progressive,** and the **future progressive.** The progressive tenses are used for continuing actions or actions in progress. These progressive tenses are formed by adding the present, past, and future forms of the verb *be* to the present participle. The **perfect progressive tenses** are the **present perfect progressive,** the **past perfect progressive,** and the **future perfect progressive.** They are formed by adding the present perfect, past perfect, and future perfect forms of the verb *be* to the present participle.

The following chart shows all the tenses for a regular verb and an irregular verb in the first person. (For more on tenses, see p. 621.)

|  | REGULAR | IRREGULAR |
|---|---|---|
| Simple present | I talk | I go |
| Simple past | I talked | I went |
| Simple future | I will talk | I will go |
| Present perfect | I have talked | I have gone |
| Past perfect | I had talked | I had gone |
| Future perfect | I will have talked | I will have gone |
| Present progressive | I am talking | I am going |
| Past progressive | I was talking | I was going |
| Future progressive | I will be talking | I will be going |
| Present perfect progressive | I have been talking | I have been going |
| Past perfect progressive | I had been talking | I had been going |
| Future perfect progressive | I will have been talking | I will have been going |

## Mood

The **mood** of a verb indicates the writer's attitude toward the action. There are three moods in English: **indicative, imperative,** and **subjunctive.**

1. The **indicative mood** is used for ordinary statements of fact or questions.

> The light flashed on and off all night.
> Did you check the batteries?

2. The **imperative mood** is used for commands, suggestions, or directions. The subject of a verb in the imperative mood is *you*, though it is not always included.

> <u>Stop</u> shouting!
>
> <u>Come</u> to New York for a visit.
>
> <u>Turn</u> right at the next corner.

3. The **subjunctive mood** is used for wishes, requirements, recommendations, and statements contrary to fact. For statements contrary to fact or for wishes, the past tense of the verb is used. For the verb *be*, only the past-tense form *were* is used.

> If I <u>had</u> a million dollars, I'd take a trip around the world.
>
> If my supervisor <u>were</u> promoted, I would be eligible for her job.

To express suggestions, recommendations, or requirements, the infinitive form is used for all verbs.

> I recommend that the houses <u>be</u> sold after the landscaping is done.
>
> The registrar required that Maureen <u>pay</u> her bill before attending class.

## Voice

Transitive verbs (those that take objects) may be in either the active voice or the passive voice. In an **active-voice** sentence, the subject performs the action described by the verb; that is, the subject is the actor. In a **passive-voice** sentence, the subject is the receiver of the action. The passive voice of a verb is formed by using an appropriate form of the helping verb *be* and the past participle of the main verb.

> Subject       Active
> is actor      voice
>
> Dr. Hillel <u>delivered</u> the report on global warming.

> Subject is receiver        Passive voice
>
> The report on global warming <u>was delivered</u> by Dr. Hillel.

---

**EXERCISE 2**     ## Changing Tenses

**Directions:** Revise the following sentences, changing each verb from the present tense to the tense indicated.

> **EXAMPLE**     I <u>know</u> the right answer.
>
> **PAST TENSE**   I knew the right answer.

1. Allison <u>loses</u> the sales to competitors.

   SIMPLE PAST lost

2. Malcolm <u>begins</u> classes at the community college.

   **PAST PERFECT** had begun

3. The microscope <u>enlarges</u> the cell.

   **PRESENT PERFECT** has enlarged

4. Reports <u>follow</u> a standard format.

   **SIMPLE FUTURE** will follow

5. Marissa <u>receives</u> excellent evaluations.

   **FUTURE PERFECT** will have received

6. Juanita <u>writes</u> a computer program.

   **PRESENT PERFECT** has written

7. The movie <u>stars</u> Joseph Gordon-Levitt.

   **SIMPLE FUTURE** will star

8. Dave <u>wins</u> medals at the Special Olympics.

   **SIMPLE PAST** won

9. Many celebrities <u>donate</u> money to AIDS research.

   **PRESENT PERFECT** have donated

10. My nephew <u>travels</u> to Michigan's Upper Peninsula on business.

    **PAST PERFECT** had traveled

# A.4 Adjectives

**Adjectives** modify nouns and pronouns. That is, they describe, identify, qualify, or limit the meaning of nouns and pronouns. An adjective answers the question *Which one? What kind?* or *How many?* about the word it modifies.

| | |
|---|---|
| WHICH ONE? | The <u>twisted</u>, <u>torn</u> umbrella was of no use to its owner. |
| WHAT KIND? | The <u>spotted</u> owl has caused heated arguments in the Northwest. |
| HOW MANY? | <u>Many</u> customers waited for <u>four</u> days for telephone service to be restored. |

In form, adjectives can be **positive** (implying no comparison), **comparative** (comparing two items), or **superlative** (comparing three or more items). (See p. 628 for more on the forms of adjectives.)

Positive

The computer is <u>fast</u>.

Comparative

Your computer is <u>faster</u> than mine.

Superlative

This is the <u>fastest</u> computer I have ever used.

There are two general categories of adjectives. **Descriptive adjectives** name a quality of the person, place, thing, or idea they describe: *mysterious man, green pond, healthy complexion*. **Limiting adjectives** narrow the scope of the person, place, or thing they describe: *my computer, this tool, second try*.

## Descriptive Adjectives

A **regular** (or **attributive**) adjective appears next to (usually before) the word it modifies. Several adjectives can modify the same word.

> The enthusiastic new hair stylist gave short, lopsided haircuts.
> The wealthy dealer bought an immense blue vase.

Sometimes nouns function as adjectives modifying other nouns:

> *tree house, hamburger bun.*

A **predicate adjective** follows a linking verb and modifies or describes the subject of the sentence or clause (see p. 607; see p. 612 on clauses).

> Predicate adjective
>
> The meeting was long. [Modifies the subject, *meeting*.]

## Limiting Adjectives

1. The **definite article**, *the,* and the **indefinite articles**, *a* and *an,* are classified as adjectives. *A* and *an* are used when it is not important to specify a particular noun or when the object named is not known to the reader (*A radish adds color to a salad*). *The* is used when it is important to specify one or more of a particular noun or when the object named is known to the reader or has already been mentioned (*The radishes from the garden are on the table*).

   > A squirrel visited the feeder that I just built. The squirrel tried to eat some bird food.

2. When the possessive pronouns *my, your, his, her, its, our,* and *their* are used as modifiers before nouns, they are considered **possessive adjectives** (see p. 627).

   > Your friend borrowed my laptop for his trip.

3. When the demonstrative pronouns *this, that, these,* and *those* are used as modifiers before nouns, they are called **demonstrative adjectives** (see p. 587). *This* and *these* modify nouns close to the writer; *that* and *those* modify nouns more distant from the writer.

   > Buy these formatted disks, not those unformatted ones.
   > This freshman course is a prerequisite for those advanced courses.

4. **Cardinal adjectives** are words used in counting: *one, two, twenty,* and so on.

   > I read four biographies of Jack Kerouac and seven articles about his work.

5. **Ordinal adjectives** note position in a series.

> The <u>first</u> biography was too sketchy, whereas the <u>second</u> one was too detailed.

6. **Indefinite adjectives** provide nonspecific, general information about the quantities and amounts of the nouns they modify. Some common indefinite adjectives are *another, any, enough, few, less, little, many, more, much, several,* and *some.*

> <u>Several</u> people asked me if I had <u>enough</u> blankets or if I wanted the thermostat turned up a <u>few</u> degrees.

7. The **interrogative adjectives** *what, which,* and *whose* modify nouns and pronouns used in questions.

> <u>Which</u> radio station do you like? <u>Whose</u> music do you prefer?

8. The words *which* and *what,* along with *whichever* and *whatever,* are **relative adjectives** when they modify nouns and introduce subordinate clauses.

> She couldn't decide <u>which</u> job she wanted to take.

9. **Proper adjectives** are adjectives derived from proper nouns: *Spain* (noun), *Spanish* (adjective); *Freud* (noun), *Freudian* (adjective); see p. 585. Most proper adjectives are capitalized.

> Shakespeare lived in <u>Elizabethan</u> England.
> The speaker used many <u>French</u> expressions.

## EXERCISE 3    Adding Adjectives

**Directions:** Revise each of the following sentences by adding at least three adjectives. *Answers will vary. Possible answers are shown.*

> **EXAMPLE**    The cat slept on the pillow.
>
> **REVISED**    *The old yellow cat slept on the expensive pillow.*

1. Before leaving on a trip, the couple packed their suitcases.

   *Before leaving on a weekend skiing trip, the excited couple packed their suitcases.*

   _____

2. The tree dropped leaves all over the lawn.

   *The oak tree dropped multicolored leaves all over the front lawn.*

   _____

3. While riding the train, the passengers read newspapers.

   *While riding the commuter train, the passengers read their morning newspapers.*

   _____

4. The antiques dealer said that the desk was more valuable than the chair.

*The persistent antiques dealer said that the oak desk was worth more than*

*the cherrywood chair.*

5. As the play was ending, the audience clapped their hands and tossed roses onstage.

*As the new Broadway play was ending, the enthusiastic audience clapped their*

*hands and tossed roses onstage.*

6. Stew is served nightly at the shelter.

*Beef stew is served nightly at the local homeless shelter.*

7. The engine roared as the car stubbornly jerked into gear.

*The straining engine roared as the old car stubbornly jerked into second gear.*

8. The tourists tossed pennies into the fountain.

*The tourists tossed their copper pennies into the bubbling fountain.*

9. Folders were stacked on the desk next to the laptop.

*Manila file folders were stacked on the sturdy wooden desk next to the*

*open laptop.*

10. Marina's belt and shoes were made of the same material and complemented her dress.

*Marina's belt and shoes were made of the same navy blue material and complemented her*

*linen dress.*

# **A.5** Adverbs

**Adverbs** modify verbs, adjectives, other adverbs, or entire sentences or clauses (see p. 618 on clauses). Like adjectives, adverbs describe, qualify, or limit the meaning of the words they modify.

An adverb answers the question *How? When? Where? How often?* or *To what extent?* about the word it modifies.

| HOW? | Lian moved <u>awkwardly</u> because of her stiff neck. |
| WHEN? | I arrived <u>yesterday</u>. |
| WHERE? | They searched <u>everywhere</u>. |
| HOW OFTEN? | He telephoned <u>repeatedly</u>. |
| TO WHAT EXTENT? | Simon was <u>rather</u> slow to answer his e-mail. |

Many adverbs end in *-ly* (*lazily, happily*), but some adverbs do not (*fast, here, much, well, rather, everywhere, never, so*), and some words that end in *-ly* are not adverbs (*lively, friendly, lonely*). Like all other parts of speech, an adverb may be best identified by examining its function within a sentence.

> I <u>quickly</u> skimmed the book. [Modifies the verb *skimmed*.]
>
> <u>Very</u> angry customers crowded the service desk. [Modifies the adjective *angry*.]
>
> He was injured <u>quite</u> seriously. [Modifies the adverb *seriously*.]
>
> <u>Apparently</u>, the job was bungled. [Modifies the whole sentence.]

Like adjectives, adverbs have three forms: **positive** (does not suggest any comparison), **comparative** (compares two actions or conditions), and **superlative** (compares three or more actions or conditions; see also p. 628).

Positive                                   Positive
Julian rose <u>early</u> and crept downstairs <u>quietly</u>.

Comparative                                Comparative
Isaiah rose <u>earlier</u> than Julian and crept downstairs <u>more quietly</u>.

Superlative                                Superlative
Cody rose <u>earliest</u> of anyone in the house and crept downstairs <u>most quietly</u>.

Some adverbs, called **conjunctive adverbs** (or **adverbial conjunctions**)—such as *however, therefore,* and *besides*—connect the ideas of one sentence or clause to those of a previous sentence or clause. They can appear anywhere in a sentence. (See p. 189 for how to punctuate sentences containing conjunctive adverbs.)

Conjunctive adverb
James did not want to go to the library on Saturday; <u>however</u>, he knew the books were overdue.

Conjunctive adverb
The sporting goods store was crowded because of the sale. Leila, <u>therefore</u>, was asked to work extra hours.

Some common conjunctive adverbs are listed below, including several phrases that function as conjunctive adverbs.

| COMMON CONJUNCTIVE ADVERBS | | | |
| --- | --- | --- | --- |
| accordingly | for example | meanwhile | otherwise |
| also | further | moreover | similarly |
| anyway | furthermore | namely | still |
| as a result | hence | nevertheless | then |
| at the same time | however | next | thereafter |
| besides | incidentally | nonetheless | therefore |
| certainly | indeed | now | thus |
| consequently | instead | on the contrary | undoubtedly |
| finally | likewise | on the other hand | |

**EXERCISE 4**   ## Using Adverbs

**Directions:** Write a sentence using each of the following comparative or superlative adverbs. Answers will vary. Possible answers are shown.

**EXAMPLE**   better: My car runs better now than even before.

1. farther: Lani lives farther from Portsmouth than I do.

2. most: Anne's paragraph on capital punishment was the most thoughtfully written.

3. more: Three years ago, Washington Street was widened; more recently, lanes for cyclists were added.

4. best: Angelo's makes the best pizza in town.

5. least neatly: My sister's room is the least neatly organized room in our house.

6. louder: When Rihanna came onstage, the crowd's cheering was louder than it had been all evening.

7. worse: In recent polls, the politician fared worse than expected.

8. less angrily: Julio responded less angrily than his brother when the car broke down.

9. later: The bus arrived in Minneapolis 40 minutes later than scheduled.

10. earliest: The earliest I get up is 7:30 a.m.

# A.6 Conjunctions

**Conjunctions** connect words, phrases, and clauses. There are three kinds of conjunctions: **coordinating**, **correlative**, and **subordinating**. **Coordinating** and **correlative conjunctions** connect words, phrases, or clauses of equal grammatical rank. (A **phrase** is a group of related words lacking a subject, a predicate, or both. A **clause** is a group of words containing a subject and a predicate; see pp. 606 and 607.)

1. The **coordinating conjunctions** are *and, but, nor, or, for, so,* and *yet.* These words must connect words or word groups of the same kind. Therefore, two

nouns may be connected by *and,* but a noun and a clause cannot be. *For* and *so* can connect only independent clauses.

Coordinating
Noun    conjunction    Noun

We studied the novels of Toni Morrison and Alice Walker.

Coordinating
conjunction
Verb    Verb

The copilot successfully flew and landed the disabled plane.

Coordinating    Independent
Independent clause    conjunction    clause

The carpentry course sounded interesting, so Meg enrolled.

2. **Correlative conjunctions** are pairs of words that link and relate grammatically equivalent parts of a sentence. Some common correlative conjunctions are *either/or, neither/nor, both/and, not/but, not only/but also,* and *whether/or.* Correlative conjunctions are always used in pairs.

Correlative conjunctions

Either the electricity was off, or the bulb had burned out.

3. **Subordinating conjunctions** connect dependent, or subordinate, clauses to independent clauses (see p. 193). Some common subordinating conjunctions are *although, because, if, since, until, when, where,* and *while.*

Subordinating conjunction

Although the movie got bad reviews, it drew big crowds.

Subordinating conjunction

She received a lot of mail because she was a reliable correspondent.

# A.7 Prepositions

A **preposition** links and relates its **object** (a noun or a pronoun) to the rest of the sentence. Prepositions often show relationships of time, place, direction, and manner.

Preposition    Object of preposition

I walked around the block.

Preposition    Object of preposition

She called during our meeting.

**A. Parts of Speech**

## COMMON PREPOSITIONS

| | | | | |
|---|---|---|---|---|
| along | besides | from | past | up |
| among | between | in | since | upon |
| around | beyond | near | through | with |
| at | by | off | till | within |
| before | despite | on | to | without |
| behind | down | onto | toward | |
| below | during | out | under | |
| beneath | except | outside | underneath | |
| beside | for | over | until | |

Some prepositions consist of more than one word; they are called **phrasal prepositions** or **compound prepositions**.

> Phrasal preposition   Object of preposition
>
> According to our records, you have enough credits to graduate.

> Phrasal preposition   Object of preposition
>
> We decided to make the trip in spite of the snowstorm.

## COMMON COMPOUND PREPOSITIONS

| | | |
|---|---|---|
| according to | in addition to | on account of |
| aside from | in front of | out of |
| as of | in place of | prior to |
| as well as | in regard to | with regard to |
| because of | in spite of | with respect to |
| by means of | instead of | |

The object of the preposition often has modifiers.

> Prep.   Modifier   Obj. of prep.   Prep.   Modifier   Obj. of prep.
>
> Not a sound came from the child's room except a gentle snoring.

Sometimes a preposition has more than one object (a **compound object**).

> Compound object of preposition
> Preposition
>
> The laundromat was between campus and home.

Usually the preposition comes before its object. In interrogative sentences, however, the preposition sometimes follows its object.

> Object of preposition   Preposition
>
> What did your supervisor ask you about?

The preposition, the object or objects of the preposition, and the object's modifiers all form a **prepositional phrase**.

> Prepositional phrase
>
> The scientist conducted her experiment <u>throughout the afternoon and early evening</u>.

There may be many prepositional phrases in a sentence.

> The water <u>from the open hydrant</u> flowed <u>into the street</u>.
>
> The noisy kennel was <u>underneath the beauty salon</u>, <u>despite the complaints of customers</u>.
>
> <u>Alongside the weedy railroad tracks</u>, an old hotel <u>with faded grandeur</u> stood <u>near the abandoned brick station</u> <u>on the edge of town</u>.

Prepositional phrases frequently function as adjectives or adverbs. If a prepositional phrase modifies a noun or pronoun, it functions as an adjective. If it modifies a verb, adjective, or adverb, it functions as an adverb.

> The auditorium <u>inside the conference center</u> has a special sound system. [Adjective modifying the noun *auditorium*.]
>
> The doctor looked cheerfully <u>at the patient</u> and handed the lab results <u>across the desk</u>. [Adverbs modifying the verbs *looked* and *handed*.]

## EXERCISE 5 — Expanding Sentences Using Prepositional Phrases

**Directions:** Expand each of the following sentences by adding a prepositional phrase in the blank.   Answers will vary. Possible answers are shown.

**EXAMPLE**   A cat hid ____under the car____ when the garage door opened.

1. Fish nibbled ____on nearby reeds____ as the fisherman waited.

2. The librarian explained that the books about Africa are located ____in the nonfiction section____ .

3. When the bullet hit the window, shards flew ____in all directions____ .

4. ____In Orlando____ , there is a restaurant that serves alligator meat.

5. Polar bears are able to swim ____long distances____ .

6. Heavy winds blowing ____off the ocean____ caused the waves to hit the house.

7. One student completed her exam ____within an hour____ .

8. A frog jumped ____onto the floating lily pad____ .

9. The bus was parked ____next to the stadium____ .

10. Stacks of books were piled ____on the mantel____ .

# A.8 Interjections

**Interjections** are words that express emotion or surprise. They are followed by an exclamation point, comma, or period, depending on whether they stand alone or serve as part or all of a sentence. Interjections are used in speech more than in writing.

<u>Wow!</u> What an announcement!

<u>So</u>, was that lost letter ever found?

<u>Well</u>, I'd better be going.

# Understanding the Parts of Sentences

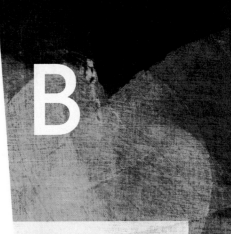

A **sentence** is a group of words that expresses a complete thought about something or someone. A sentence must contain a **subject** and a **predicate**.

| *Subject* | *Predicate* |
|-----------|-------------|
| Telephones | ring. |
| Cecilia | laughed. |
| Time | will tell. |

Depending on their purpose and punctuation, sentences are **declarative**, **interrogative**, **exclamatory**, or **imperative**.

1. A **declarative sentence** makes a statement. It ends with a period.

   Subject  Predicate

   The snow fell steadily.

2. An **interrogative sentence** asks a question. It ends with a question mark (?).

   Subject  Predicate

   Who called?

3. An **exclamatory sentence** conveys strong emotion. It ends with an exclamation point (!).

   Subject  Predicate

   Your photograph is in the company newsletter!

4. An **imperative sentence** gives an order or makes a request. It ends with either a period or an exclamation point, depending on how mild or strong the command or request is. In an imperative sentence, the subject is *you*, but this often is not included.

   Predicate

   Get me a fire extinguisher now! [The subject *you* is understood: (*You*) get me a fire extinguisher now!]

# B.1 Subjects

The **subject** of a sentence is whom or what the sentence is about. It is who or what performs or receives the action expressed in the predicate.

1. The subject is often a **noun**, a word that names a person, place, thing, or idea.

   Adriana worked on her math homework.

   The rose bushes must be watered.

   Honesty is the best policy.

2. The subject of a sentence can also be a **pronoun**, a word that refers to or substitutes for a noun.

   She revised the memo three times.

   I will attend the sales meeting.

   Although the milk spilled, it did not go on my shirt.

3. The subject of a sentence can also be a group of words used as a noun.

   Reading Facebook postings from friends is my idea of a good time.

## Simple Versus Complete Subjects

1. The **simple subject** is the noun or pronoun that names what the sentence is about. It does not include any **modifiers**—that is, words that describe, identify, qualify, or limit the meaning of the noun or pronoun.

   Simple subject
   The bright red concert poster caught everyone's eye.

   Simple subject
   High-speed computers have revolutionized astronomy.

   When the subject of a sentence is a proper noun (the name of a particular person, place, or thing), the entire name is considered the simple subject.

   Simple subject
   John F. Kennedy was a famous leader.

   The simple subject of an imperative sentence is *you*.

   Simple subject
   [You] Remember to bring the sales brochures.

2. The **complete subject** is the simple subject plus its modifiers.

   Complete subject
   Simple subject
   The sleek, black limousine waited outside the church.

   Complete subject
   Fondly remembered as a gifted songwriter, fiddle player, and storyteller, Quintin Lotus Dickey lived in a cabin in Paoli, Indiana.
   Simple subject

## Compound Subjects

Some sentences contain two or more subjects joined with a coordinating conjunction (*and, but, nor, or, for, so, yet*). Those subjects together form a **compound subject**.

Compound subject

Maria and I completed the marathon.

Compound subject

The computer, the printer, and the DVD player were not usable during the blackout.

# B.2 Predicates

The **predicate** indicates what the subject does, what happened to the subject, or what is being said about the subject. The predicate must include a **verb**, a word or group of words that expresses an action or a state of being (for example, *run, invent, build, know, will decide, become*).

Joy swam 60 laps.

The thunderstorm replenished the reservoir.

Sometimes the verb consists of only one word, as in the previous examples. Often, however, the main verb is accompanied by a **helping verb** (see p. 590).

Helping    Main
verb       verb

By the end of the week, I will have worked 25 hours.

Helping Main
verb    verb

The training session had begun.

Helping  Main
verb     verb

The professor did return the journal assignments.

## Simple Versus Complete Predicates

The **simple predicate** is the main verb plus its helping verbs (together known as the **verb phrase**). The simple predicate does not include any modifiers.

Simple predicate

The proctor hastily collected the blue books.

Simple predicate

The moderator had introduced the next speaker.

The **complete predicate** consists of the simple predicate, its modifiers, and any complements (words that complete the meaning of the verb; see p. 609). In general, the complete predicate includes everything in the sentence except the complete subject.

### Tip for Writers

*Did return* is an emphatic past form. This form is often used (instead of the usual past, *returned*) when someone has made a mistake:

Alex said, "The professor didn't return our last essays."

Vera replied, "He did return them. He handed them back the day you were absent."

Complete predicate
Simple predicate

The music <u>sounds</u> better from the back of the room.

Complete predicate
Simple predicate

Bill <u>decided</u> to change the name of his company to something less controversial and confusing.

## Compound Predicates

Some sentences have two or more predicates joined by a coordinating conjunction (*and, but, or,* or *nor*). These predicates together form a **compound predicate**.

Compound predicate

Marcia <u>unlocked</u> her bicycle and <u>rode</u> away.

Compound predicate

The supermarket owner <u>will survey</u> his customers and <u>order</u> the specialized foods they desire.

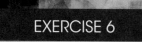

## Identifying Single Subjects and Simple and Compound Predicates

**Directions:** Underline the simple subject(s) and circle the simple or compound predicate(s) in each of the following sentences.

EXAMPLE    Pamela Wong (photographed) a hummingbird.

1. A <u>group</u> of nurses (walked) across the lobby on their way to a staff meeting.

2. The <u>campground</u> for physically challenged children (is funded) and (supported) by the Rotary Club.

3. Forty <u>doctors</u> and <u>lawyers</u> (had attended) the seminar on malpractice insurance.

4. <u>Sullivan Beach</u> (will) not (reopen) because of pollution.

5. The police <u>cadets</u> (attended) classes all day and (studied) late into each evening.

6. <u>Greenpeace</u> (is) an environmental organization.

7. Talented <u>dancers</u> and experienced <u>musicians</u> (performed) and (received) much applause at the open-air show.

8. Some undergraduate <u>students</u> (have been using) empty classrooms for group study.

9. A police <u>officer</u>, with the shoplifter in handcuffs, (entered) the police station.

10. The newly elected <u>senator</u> (walked up) to the podium and (began) her first speech to her constituents.

# **B.3** Complements

A **complement** is a word or group of words used to complete the meaning of a subject or object. There are four kinds of complements: **subject complements**, which follow linking verbs; **direct objects** and **indirect objects**, which follow transitive verbs (verbs that take an object); and **object complements**, which follow direct objects.

## Linking Verbs and Subject Complements

A linking verb (such as *be, become, seem, feel, taste*) links the subject to a **subject complement**, a noun or adjective that renames or describes the subject. (See p. 590 for more about linking verbs.) Nouns that function as complements are called **predicate nominatives** or **predicate nouns**. Adjectives that function as complements are called **predicate adjectives**.

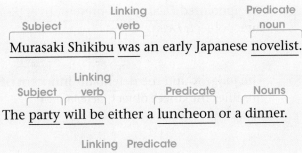

Subject | Linking verb | Predicate noun
Murasaki Shikibu was an early Japanese novelist.

Subject | Linking verb | Predicate | Nouns
The party will be either a luncheon or a dinner.

Subject | Linking verb | Predicate adjective
This cheese tastes moldy.

Subject | Linking verb | Predicate adjectives
The truck was shiny and new.

## Direct Objects

A **direct object** is a noun or pronoun that receives the action of a transitive verb (see p. 590). A direct object answers the question <u>What?</u> or <u>Whom?</u>

Transitive verb | Direct object
The pharmacist helped us. [The pharmacist helped *whom?*]

Transitive verb | Direct objects
Jillian borrowed a bicycle and a visor. [Jillian borrowed *what?*]

## Indirect Objects

An **indirect object** is a noun or pronoun that receives the action of the verb indirectly. Indirect objects name the person or thing <u>*to whom*</u> or <u>*for whom*</u> something is done.

### Tip for Writers

In sentences that tell both *whom* and *what* after the verb, follow the word order shown here:

Amir gave his sister a gift. (Do not use *to*.)

Amir gave a gift to his sister. (Use *to*.)

If you mention the person before the thing, don't use *to*.

Transitive verb / Indirect object / Direct object

The computer technician gave me the bill. [He gave the bill *to whom?*]

Transitive verb / Indirect objects / Direct objects

Eric bought his wife and son some sandwiches and milk. [He bought food *for whom?*]

## Object Complements

An **object complement** is a noun or adjective that modifies (describes) or renames the direct object. Object complements appear with verbs like *name, find, think, elect, appoint, choose,* and *consider.*

Direct object / Noun as object complement

We appointed Dean our representative. [*Representative* renames the direct object, *Dean.*]

Direct object / Adjective as object complement

The judge found the defendant innocent of the charges. [*Innocent* modifies the direct object, *defendant.*]

# B.4 Basic Sentence Patterns

There are five basic sentence patterns in English. They are built with combinations of subjects, predicates, and complements. The order of these elements within a sentence may change, or a sentence may become long and complicated when modifiers, phrases, or clauses are added. Nonetheless, one of five basic patterns stands at the heart of every sentence.

PATTERN 1

| *Subject* | + | *Predicate* |
|-----------|---|-------------|
| I | | shivered. |
| Cynthia | | swam. |

PATTERN 2

| *Subject* | + | *Predicate* | + | *Direct Object* |
|-----------|---|-------------|---|-----------------|
| Anthony | | ordered | | a new desk. |
| We | | wanted | | freedom. |

PATTERN 3

| *Subject* | + | *Predicate* | + | *Subject Complement* |
|-----------|---|-------------|---|----------------------|
| The woman | | was | | a welder. |
| Our course | | is | | interesting. |

**PATTERN 4**

| Subject | + | Predicate | + | Indirect Object | + | Direct Object |
|---------|---|-----------|---|-----------------|---|---------------|
| My friend | | loaned | | me | | a laptop. |
| The company | | sent | | employees | | a questionnaire. |

**PATTERN 5**

| Subject | + | Predicate | + | Direct Object | + | Object Complement |
|---------|---|-----------|---|---------------|---|-------------------|
| I | | consider | | her singing | | exceptional. |
| Lampwick | | called | | Jiminy Cricket | | a beetle. |

---

**EXERCISE 7**    # Adding Complements

**Directions:** Complete each sentence with a word or words that will function as the type of complement indicated.    Answers will vary. Possible answers are shown.

**EXAMPLE**    The scientist acted _____ proud _____ as he announced his latest invention.    *predicate adjective*

1. The delivery person handed _____ Luls _____ the large brown package.    *indirect object*

2. Ronald Reagan was an American _____ president _____ .    *predicate noun*

3. The chairperson appointed Yesenia our _____ director of public relations _____ .    *object complement*

4. Protesters stood on the corner and handed out _____ flyers _____ .    *direct object*

5. The secretary gave _____ Alex _____ the messages.    *indirect object*

6. Before the storm, many clouds were _____ visible _____ .    *predicate adjective*

7. The beer advertisement targeted _____ young adults _____ .    *direct object*

8. The Super Bowl players were _____ skilled athletes _____ .    *predicate noun*

9. The diplomat declared the Olympics _____ a success _____ .    *object complement*

10. Shopping malls are _____ busy _____ before Christmas.    *predicate adjective*

B. Parts of Sentences

# B.5 Expanding the Sentence with Adjectives and Adverbs

A sentence may consist of just a subject and a verb.

> Linda studied.
>
> Rumors circulated.

Most sentences, however, contain additional information about the subject and the verb. Information is commonly added in three ways:

- by using adjectives and adverbs;
- by using phrases (groups of words that lack either a subject or a predicate or both);
- by using clauses (groups of words that contain both a subject and a predicate).

## Using Adjectives and Adverbs to Expand Your Sentences

**Adjectives** are words used to modify or describe nouns and pronouns (see p. 595). Adjectives answer questions about nouns and pronouns such as *Which one? What kind? How many?* Using adjectives is one way to add detail and information to sentences.

| | |
|---|---|
| WITHOUT ADJECTIVES | Dogs barked at cats. |
| WITH ADJECTIVES | Our three large, brown dogs barked at the two terrified, spotted cats. |

*Note:* Sometimes nouns and participles are used as adjectives (see p. 591 on participles).

Noun used as adjective

People are rediscovering the milk bottle.

Present participle used as adjective    Past participle used as adjective

Mrs. Simon had a swimming pool with a broken drain.

**Adverbs** add information to sentences by modifying or describing verbs, adjectives, or other adverbs (see p. 598). An adverb usually answers the question *How? When? Where? How often?* or *To what extent?*

| | |
|---|---|
| WITHOUT ADVERBS | I will clean. |
| | The audience applauded. |
| WITH ADVERBS | I will clean very thoroughly tomorrow. |
| | The audience applauded loudly and enthusiastically. |

# B.6 Expanding the Sentence with Phrases

A **phrase** is a group of related words that lacks a subject, a predicate, or both. A phrase cannot stand alone as a sentence. Phrases can appear at the beginning, middle, or end of a sentence.

| | |
|---|---|
| WITHOUT PHRASES | I noticed the stain. |
| | Sal researched the topic. |
| | Manuela arose. |
| WITH PHRASES | Upon entering the room, I noticed the stain on the expensive carpet. |
| | At the local aquarium, Sal researched the topic of shark attacks. |
| | An amateur astronomer, Manuela arose in the middle of the night to observe the lunar eclipse but, after waiting ten minutes in the cold, gave up. |

There are six kinds of phrases: **noun; verb; prepositional; verbal (participial, gerund,** and **infinitive); appositive;** and **absolute.**

## Noun and Verb Phrases

A noun plus its modifiers is a **noun phrase** (*red shoes, the quiet house*). A main verb plus its helping verb is a **verb phrase** (*had been exploring, is sleeping;* see p. 590 on helping verbs.)

## Prepositional Phrases

A **prepositional phrase** consists of a preposition (for example, *in, above, with, at, behind*), an object of the preposition (a noun or pronoun), and any modifiers of the object. (See p. 602 for a list of common prepositions.) A prepositional phrase functions like an adjective (modifying a noun or pronoun) or an adverb (modifying a verb, adjective, or adverb). You can use prepositional phrases to tell more about people, places, objects, or actions. A prepositional phrase usually adds information about time, place, direction, manner, or degree.

### As Adjectives

The woman with the briefcase is giving a presentation on meditation techniques.

Both of the telephones behind the partition were ringing.

### As Adverbs

The fire drill occurred in the morning.

I was curious about the new human resources director.

The conference speaker came from Australia.

With horror, the crowd watched the rhinoceros's tether stretch to the breaking point.

A prepositional phrase can function as part of the complete subject or as part of the complete predicate, but should not be confused with the simple subject or simple predicate.

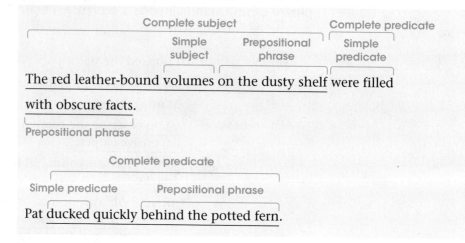

## Verbal Phrases

A **verbal** is a verb form that cannot function as the main verb of a sentence. The three kinds of verbals are **participles**, **gerunds**, and **infinitives**. A **verbal phrase** consists of a verbal and its modifiers.

### Participles and Participial Phrases

All verbs have two participles: present and past. The **present participle** is formed by adding *-ing* to the infinitive form (*walking, riding, being*). The **past participle** of regular verbs is formed by adding *-d* or *-ed* to the infinitive form (*walked, baked*). The past participle of irregular verbs has no set pattern (*ridden, been*). (See p. 591 for a list of common irregular verbs and their past participles.) Both the present participle and the past participle can function as adjectives modifying nouns and pronouns.

Past participle
as adjective        Present participle
                    as adjective

Irritated, Martha circled the confusing traffic rotary once again.

A **participial phrase** consists of a participle and any of its modifiers.

Participial phrase

Participle

We listened for Isabella climbing the rickety stairs.

Participial phrase

Participle

Disillusioned with the whole system, Kay sat down to think.

Participial phrase

Participle

The singer, having caught a bad cold, canceled his performance.

## Gerunds and Gerund Phrases

A **gerund** is the present participle (the *-ing* form) of the verb used as a noun.

> <u>Shoveling</u> is good exercise.
>
> Rex enjoyed <u>gardening</u>.

A **gerund phrase** consists of a gerund and its modifiers. A gerund phrase, like a gerund, is used as a noun and can therefore function in a sentence as a subject, a direct or indirect object, an object of a preposition, a subject complement, or an appositive.

Gerund phrase

<u>Photocopying</u> the report took longer than La Tisha anticipated. [Subject]

Gerund phrase

The director considered <u>making</u> another monster movie. [Direct object]

Gerund phrase

She gave <u>running</u> three miles daily credit for her health. [Indirect object]

Gerund phrase

Before <u>learning</u> Greek, Omar spoke only English. [Object of the preposition]

Gerund phrase

Her business is <u>designing</u> collapsible furniture. [Subject complement]

Gerund phrase

Hana's trick, <u>memorizing</u> license plates, has come in handy. [Appositive]

## Infinitives and Infinitive Phrases

The **infinitive** is the base form of the verb as it appears in the dictionary preceded by the word *to*. An **infinitive phrase** consists of the word *to* plus the infinitive and any modifiers. An infinitive phrase can function as a noun, an adjective, or an adverb. When it is used as a noun, an infinitive phrase can be a subject, object, complement, or appositive.

Infinitive phrase

<u>To love</u> one's enemies is a noble goal. [Noun used as subject.]

Infinitive phrase

The season <u>to sell</u> bulbs is the fall. [Adjective modifying *season*.]

Infinitive phrase

The chess club met <u>to practice</u> for the state championship. [Adverb modifying *met*.]

Sometimes the *to* in an infinitive phrase is not written.

> Jacob helped us <u>learn</u> the new accounting procedure. [The *to* before *learn* is understood.]

*Note:* Do not confuse infinitive phrases with prepositional phrases beginning with the preposition *to*. In an infinitive phrase, *to* is followed by a verb; in a prepositional phrase, *to* is followed by a noun or pronoun.

## Appositive Phrases

An **appositive** is a noun that explains, restates, or adds new information about another noun. An **appositive phrase** consists of an appositive and its modifiers. (See p. 644 for punctuation of appositive phrases.)

> Appositive
>
> Claude Monet completed the painting <u>*Water Lilies*</u> around 1903. [Adds information about the noun *painting*]

> Appositive phrase
>
> Appositive
>
> Francis, <u>my neighbor</u> with a large workshop, lent me a wrench. [Adds information about the noun *Francis*]

## Absolute Phrases

An **absolute phrase** consists of a noun or pronoun and any modifiers followed by a participle or a participial phrase (see p. 614). An absolute phrase modifies an entire sentence, not any particular word within the sentence. It can appear anywhere in a sentence and is set off from the rest of the sentence with a comma or commas. There may be more than one absolute phrase in a sentence.

> Absolute phrase
>
> The winter being over, the geese returned.

> Absolute phrase
>
> Senator Arden began his speech, his voice rising to be heard over the loud applause.

> Absolute phrase
>
> A vacancy having occurred, the hotel manager called the first name on the reservations waiting list.

**EXERCISE 8**

# Expanding Sentences with Adjectives, Adverbs, and Phrases

**Directions:** Expand each of the following sentences by adding adjectives, adverbs, and/or phrases (prepositional, verbal, appositive, or absolute). Answers will vary. Possible answers are shown.

**EXAMPLE**    The professor lectured.

**EXPANDED**    Being an expert on animal behavior, the professor lectured about animal-intelligence studies.

1. Randall will graduate. Randall, my friend from grade school, will graduate from Camden County College this May.

2. The race began. After a false start, the athletes lined up at the starting blocks and the race began.

3. Walmart is remodeling. Aiming for a new look, Walmart is remodeling its stores.

4. Hillary walked alone. Needing time to think, Hillary walked alone.

5. Manuel repairs appliances. Manuel repairs appliances at his shop in Charlestown.

6. The motorcycle was loud. The motorcycle was loud enough to attract the attention of pedestrians along the sidewalk.

7. My term paper is due Tuesday. Now that I have an extension, my term paper is due Tuesday.

8. I opened my umbrella. Hoping to stay dry, I opened my umbrella when it started to drizzle.

9. Austin built a garage. Being skilled in construction, Austin built a garage at the side of his parents' house.

10. Lucas climbs mountains. Lucas climbs mountains with the Appalachian Hiking Club.

# B.7 Expanding the Sentence with Clauses

A **clause** is a group of words that contains a subject and a predicate. A clause is either **independent** (also called **main**) or **dependent** (also called **subordinate**).

## Independent Clauses

An **independent clause** can stand alone as a grammatically complete sentence.

| Independent clause | Independent clause |
|---|---|
| Subject Predicate | Subject Predicate |

The alarm sounded, and I awoke.

| Independent clause | Independent clause |
|---|---|
| Subject Predicate | Subject Predicate |

The scientist worried. The experiment might fail.

| Independent clause | Independent clause |
|---|---|
| Subject Predicate | Subject Predicate |

He bandaged his ankle. It had been sprained.

## Dependent Clauses

A **dependent clause** has a subject and a predicate, but it cannot stand alone as a grammatically complete sentence because it does not express a complete thought. Most dependent clauses begin with either a **subordinating conjunction** or a **relative pronoun**. These words connect the dependent clause to an independent clause.

| COMMON SUBORDINATING CONJUNCTIONS | | |
|---|---|---|
| after | in as much as | that |
| although | in case | though |
| as | in order that | unless |
| as far as | in so far as | until |
| as if | in that | when |
| as soon as | now that | whenever |
| as though | once | where |
| because | provided that | wherever |
| before | rather than | whether |
| even if | since | while |
| even though | so that | why |
| how | supposing that | |
| if | than | |

### Tip for Writers

Remember that some of these words have two meanings. For example, *once* can mean "one time" or "after." *While* can mean "at the same time" or "but."

| RELATIVE PRONOUNS | |
|---|---|
| that | which |
| | who (whose, whom) |
| whatever | whoever (whomever) |

These clauses do not express complete thoughts and therefore cannot stand alone as sentences. When joined to independent clauses, however, dependent clauses function as adjectives, adverbs, and nouns and are known as **adjective (or relative) clauses, adverb clauses**, and **noun clauses**. Noun clauses can function as subjects, objects, or complements.

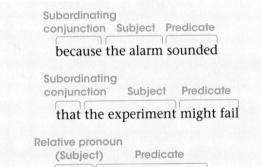

### Adjective Clause

Dependent clause

He bandaged his ankle, which had been sprained. [Modifies *ankle*]

### Adverb Clause

Dependent clause

Because the alarm sounded, I awoke. [Modifies *awoke*]

### Noun Clause

Dependent clause

The scientist worried that the experiment might fail. [Direct object of *worried*]

### Elliptical Clause

Sometimes the relative pronoun or subordinating conjunction is implied or understood rather than stated. Also, a dependent clause may contain an implied predicate. When a dependent clause is missing an element that can clearly be supplied from the context of the sentence, it is called an **elliptical clause**.

> Elliptical clause
>
> The circus is more entertaining than television [is]. [*Is* is the understood predicate in the elliptical dependent clause.]
>
> Elliptical clause
>
> Canadian history is among the subjects [that] the book discusses. [*That* is the understood relative pronoun in the elliptical dependent clause.]

Relative pronouns are generally the subject or object in their clauses. *Who* and *whoever* change to *whom* and *whomever* when they function as objects (see p. 627).

# Writing Correct Sentences

## C.1 Uses of Verb Tenses

The **tense** of a verb expresses time. It conveys whether an action, process, or occurrence takes place in the present, past, or future. There are 12 tenses in English, and each is used to express a particular time. (See p. 591 for information about how to form each tense.)

The **simple present tense** expresses actions that are occurring at the time of the writing or that occur regularly. The **simple past tense** is used for actions that have already occurred. The **simple future tense** is used for actions that will occur in the future.

| | |
|---|---|
| SIMPLE PRESENT | The chef <u>cooks</u> a huge meal. |
| SIMPLE PAST | The chef <u>cooked</u> a huge meal. |
| SIMPLE FUTURE | The chef <u>will cook</u> a huge meal. |

The **present perfect tense** is used for actions that began in the past and are still occurring in the present or are finished by the time of the writing. The **past perfect tense** expresses actions that were completed before other past actions. The **future perfect tense** is used for actions that will be completed in the future.

| | |
|---|---|
| PRESENT PERFECT | The chef <u>has cooked</u> a huge meal every night this week. |
| PAST PERFECT | The chef <u>had cooked</u> a huge meal before the guests canceled their reservation. |
| FUTURE PERFECT | The chef <u>will have cooked</u> a huge meal by the time we arrive. |

The six progressive tenses are used for continuing actions or actions in progress. The **present progressive tense** is used for actions that are in progress in the present. The **past progressive tense** expresses past continuing actions. The **future progressive tense** is used for continuing actions that will occur in the future. The **present perfect progressive, past perfect progressive,** and **future perfect progressive tenses** are used for continuing actions that are, were, or will be completed by a certain time.

| | |
|---|---|
| PRESENT PROGRESSIVE | The chef <u>is cooking</u> a huge meal this evening. |
| PAST PROGRESSIVE | The chef <u>was cooking</u> a huge meal when she ran out of butter. |
| FUTURE PROGRESSIVE | The chef <u>will be cooking</u> a huge meal all day tomorrow. |
| PRESENT PERFECT PROGRESSIVE | The chef <u>has been cooking</u> a huge meal since this morning. |

| PAST PERFECT PROGRESSIVE | The chef <u>had been cooking</u> a huge meal before the electricity went out. |
| FUTURE PERFECT PROGRESSIVE | The chef <u>will have been cooking</u> a huge meal for eight hours when the guests arrive. |

Writing all forms of a verb for all tenses and all persons (first, second, and third, singular and plural) is called **conjugating** the verb. Irregular verbs have an irregularly formed past tense and past participle (used in the past tense and the perfect tenses). (See p. 591 for a list of the forms of common irregular verbs.) Here is the complete conjugation for the regular verb *walk*.

## CONJUGATION OF THE REGULAR VERB *WALK*

|  | Singular | Plural |
|---|---|---|
| Simple present tense | I walk<br>you walk<br>he/she/it walks | we walk<br>you walk<br>they walk |
| Simple past tense | I walked<br>you walked<br>he/she/it walked | we walked<br>you walked<br>they walked |
| Simple future tense | I will (shall) walk<br>you will walk<br>he/she/it will walk | we will (shall) walk<br>you will walk<br>they will walk |
| Present perfect tense | I have walked<br>you have walked<br>he/she/it has walked | we have walked<br>you have walked<br>they have walked |
| Past perfect tense | I had walked<br>you had walked<br>he/she/it had walked | we had walked<br>you had walked<br>they had walked |
| Future perfect tense | I will (shall) have walked<br>you will have walked<br>he/she/it will have walked | we will (shall) have walked<br>you will have walked<br>they will have walked |
| Present progressive tense | I am walking<br>you are walking<br>he/she/it is walking | we are walking<br>you are walking<br>they are walking |
| Past progressive tense | I was walking<br>you were walking<br>he/she/it was walking | we were walking<br>you were walking<br>they were walking |
| Future progressive tense | I will be walking<br>you will be walking<br>he/she/it will be walking | we will be walking<br>you will be walking<br>they will be walking |
| Present perfect progressive tense | I have been walking<br>you have been walking<br>he/she/it has been walking | we have been walking<br>you have been walking<br>they have been walking |
| Past perfect progressive tense | I had been walking<br>you had been walking<br>he/she/it had been walking | we had been walking<br>you had been walking<br>they had been walking |
| Future perfect progressive tense | I will have been walking<br>you will have been walking<br>he/she/it will have been walking | we will have been walking<br>you will have been walking<br>they will have been walking |

Following are the simple present and simple past tenses for the irregular verbs *have*, *be*, and *do*, which are commonly used as helping verbs (see p. 590).

## IRREGULAR VERBS *HAVE, BE,* AND *DO*

| | Have | Be | Do |
|---|---|---|---|
| Simple present tense | I have<br>you have<br>he/she/it has<br>we/you/they have | I am<br>you are<br>he/she/it is<br>we/you/they are | I do<br>you do<br>he/she/it does<br>we/you/they do |
| Simple past tense | I had<br>you had<br>he/she/it had<br>we/you/they had | I was<br>you were<br>he/she/it was<br>we/you/they were | I did<br>you did<br>he/she/it did<br>we/you/they did |

## Special Uses of the Simple Present Tense

Besides expressing actions that are occurring at the time of the writing, the simple present tense has several special uses.

| | |
|---|---|
| HABITUAL OR RECURRING ACTION | She works at the store every day. |
| GENERAL TRUTH | The sun rises in the east. |
| DISCUSSION OF LITERATURE | Gatsby stands on the dock and gazes in Daisy's direction. |
| THE FUTURE | He leaves for Rome on the 7:30 plane. |

## Emphasis, Negatives, and Questions

The simple present and the simple past tenses of the verb *do* are used with main verbs to provide emphasis, to form negative constructions with the adverb *not*, and to ask questions.

| | |
|---|---|
| SIMPLE PRESENT | Malcolm does want to work on Saturday. |
| SIMPLE PRESENT | He does not want to stay home alone. |
| SIMPLE PRESENT | Do you want to go with him? |
| SIMPLE PAST | Judy did write the proposal herself. |
| SIMPLE PAST | She did not have the money to pay professionals. |
| SIMPLE PAST | Did she do a good job? |

The modal verbs *can, could, may, might, must, shall, should, will,* and *would* are also used to add emphasis and shades of meaning to verbs. Modals are used only as helping verbs, never alone, and do not change form to indicate tense. Added to a main verb, they are used in the following situations, among others:

| | |
|---|---|
| CONDITION | We can play tennis if she gets here on time. |
| PERMISSION | You may have only one e-mail address. |
| POSSIBILITY | They might call us from the airport. |
| OBLIGATION | I must visit my mother tomorrow. |

## Tips for Writers

The usual simple present tense form is this: Malcolm wants to work on Saturday. The *emphatic form* is sometimes used to correct a mistake:

Ivan says, "Malcolm does not want to work on Saturday."

Maria replies, "He does want to work on Saturday." (or) "Yes, he does."

C. Writing Correct Sentences

## Common Mistakes to Avoid with Verb Tense

Check your writing carefully to make sure you have avoided these common mistakes with verb tenses.

1. **Make sure the endings *-d* and *-ed* (for past tenses) and *-s* and *-es* (for third-person singular, simple present tense) are on all verbs that require them.**

   | INCORRECT | I have walk three miles since I left home. |
   | CORRECT | I have walked three miles since I left home. |

2. **Use irregular verbs correctly** (see p. 591).

   | INCORRECT | I will lay down for a nap. |
   | CORRECT | I will lie down for a nap. |

3. **Use helping verbs where they are necessary to express the correct time.**

   | INCORRECT | I go to class tomorrow. |
   | CORRECT | I will go to class tomorrow. |

4. **Avoid colloquial language or dialect in writing.** Colloquial language is casual, everyday language often used in conversation. Dialect is the language pattern of a region or an ethnic group.

   | INCORRECT | I didn't get the point of that poem. |
   | CORRECT | I didn't understand the point of that poem. |
   | INCORRECT | The train be gone. |
   | CORRECT | The train has gone. |

Other common mistakes with verbs are failing to make the verb agree with the subject (see p. 220) and using inconsistent or shifting tenses.

---

| EXERCISE 9 | ## Correcting Verb Form and Tense Errors |

**Directions:** Correct any of the following sentences with an error in verb form or verb tense. If a sentence contains no errors, write "C" for correct beside it.

   **EXAMPLE**   You ~~is~~ next in line.
                       *are*

_____ 1. Mercedes called and ask Jen if she wanted a ride to the basketball
            game.
                       *ed*

_____ 2. Eric went to a party last week and ~~meets~~ a girl he knew in high
            school.
                       *met*

___C___ 3. I cook spaghetti every Wednesday, and my family always enjoys it.

_____ 4. A package come in yesterday's mail for my office mate.
                       *a*

_____ 5. Louisa ~~wears~~ <sup>wore</sup> a beautiful red dress to her sister's wedding last week.

_____ 6. Marni answered a letter she receive<sup>d</sup> from her former employer.

_____ 7. Rob waited until he was introduced, and then he r<sup>a</sup>un on stage.

_____ 8. The audience laughed loudly at the comedian's jokes and applauds<sup>ed</sup> spontaneously at the funniest ones.

___c___ 9. The group had ordered buffalo-style chicken wings, and it was not disappointed when the meal arrived.

_____10. Julie spen<sup>t</sup>ds the afternoon answering correspondence when sales were slow.

---

# C.2 Subjunctive Mood

The **mood** of a verb conveys the writer's attitude toward the expressed thought. There are three moods in English. The **indicative mood** is used to make ordinary statements of fact and to ask questions. The **imperative mood** is used to give commands or make suggestions. The **subjunctive mood** is used to express wishes, requirements, recommendations, and statements contrary to fact (see p. 593).

| INDICATIVE | Laurel lies in the sun every afternoon. |
| IMPERATIVE | Lie down and rest! |
| SUBJUNCTIVE | It is urgent that she lie down and rest. |

The subjunctive mood requires some special attention because it uses verb tenses in unusual ways. Verbs in the subjunctive mood can be in the present, past, or perfect tense.

| PRESENT | His mother recommended that he apply for the job. |
| | If truth be told, Jacob is luckier than he knows. |
| PAST | If she walked faster, she could get there on time. She ran as if she were five years old again. |
| PERFECT | If I had known his name, I would have said hello. |

Here are several rules for using the subjunctive correctly:

1. **For requirements and recommendations, use the present subjunctive (the infinitive) for all verbs, including** *be***.**

   Mr. Kenefick requires that his students be drilled in safety procedures.

   The dentist recommended that she brush her teeth three times a day.

2. **For present conditions contrary to fact and for present wishes, use the past subjunctive (the simple past tense) for all verbs; use** *were* **for the verb** *be* **for all subjects.**

   I wish that the workday began later.

   If Andrew were not so stubborn, he would admit that Adele is right.

---

**Tip for Writers**

In *subjunctive* (contrary-to-fact) present-tense statements, use a past tense verb in the *if* clause and a modal auxiliary plus an infinitive verb in the main clause:

If I lived in Minnesota, I would need a good pair of winter boots.

---

**Tip for Writers**

Note that in *contrary-to-fact statements*, the verb in the main clause usually begins with a modal auxiliary or *wish*.

3. **For past conditions contrary to fact and for past wishes, use the perfect subjunctive (*had* plus the past participle) for all verbs, including *be*.**

> If Roman had been at home, he would have answered the phone when you called.
>
> When Peter told me what an exciting internship he had abroad last summer, I wished I had gone with him.

# C.3 Pronoun Case

A pronoun changes **case** depending on its grammatical function in a sentence. Pronouns may be in the **subjective case**, the **objective case**, or the **possessive case**.

| PERSONAL PRONOUNS | | | |
|---|---|---|---|
| **SINGULAR** | **SUBJECTIVE** | **OBJECTIVE** | **POSSESSIVE** |
| First person | I | me | my, mine |
| Second person | you | you | your, yours |
| Third person | he, she, it | him, her, it | his, her, hers, its |
| **PLURAL** | **SUBJECTIVE** | **OBJECTIVE** | **POSSESSIVE** |
| First person | we | us | our, ours |
| Second person | you | you | your, yours |
| Third person | they | them | their, theirs |
| **RELATIVE OR INTERROGATIVE PRONOUNS** | | | |
| | **SUBJECTIVE** | **OBJECTIVE** | **POSSESSIVE** |
| Singular and plural | who | whom | whose |
| | whoever | whomever | |

## Pronouns in the Subjective Case

Use the **subjective case** (also known as the **nominative case**) when the pronoun functions as the subject of a sentence or clause (see p. 587) or as a subject complement (also known as a predicate nominative; see p. 609). A predicate nominative is a noun or pronoun that follows a linking verb and identifies or renames the subject of the sentence.

> Subject
>
> She has won recognition as a landscape architect.

> Subject complement
>
> Cathie volunteers at the local hospital. The most faithful volunteer is she.

The subjective case is also used when a pronoun functions as an appositive to a subject or subject complement.

The only two seniors, <u>she</u> and her best friend, won the top awards.

## Pronouns in the Objective Case

Use the objective case when a pronoun functions as a direct object, indirect object, or object of a preposition (see pp. 609 and 610).

Direct object
Gabriel helped <u>her</u> with the assignment.

Indirect object
Gabriel gave <u>her</u> a book.

Objects of the preposition
Gabriel gave the book to <u>him</u> and <u>her</u>.

The objective case is also used when the pronoun functions as the subject of an infinitive phrase or an appositive to an object.

Subject of infinitive   Infinitive phrase
I wanted <u>him</u> to go straight home.

Direct object    Appositive to object
The district manager chose two <u>representatives</u>, Lauren and <u>me</u>.

*Note:* When a sentence has a compound subject or compound objects, you may have trouble determining the correct pronoun case. To determine how the pronoun functions, mentally recast the sentence without the other noun or other pronoun in the compound construction. Determine how the pronoun functions by itself and then decide which case is correct.

Subjective case

<u>They</u> and Teresa brought the beverages. [Think: "*They* brought the beverages." *They* is the subject of the sentence, so the subjective case is correct.]

Objective case

Behind you and <u>me</u>, the curtains rustled. [Think: "Behind *me*." *Me* is the object of the preposition *behind,* so the objective case is correct.]

## Pronouns in the Possessive Case

Possessive pronouns indicate to whom or to what something belongs. The possessive pronouns *mine, yours, his, hers, its, ours,* and *theirs* function just as nouns do.

Subject

Hers is the letterhead with the bright blue lettering.

Direct object

I liked hers the best.

The possessive pronouns *my, your, his, her, its, our,* and *their* are used as adjectives to modify nouns and gerunds (see p. 596).

Our high-school reunion surprised everyone by its size.

Your attending that reunion will depend on your travel schedule.

### *Who* and *Whom* as Interrogative Pronouns

When *who, whoever, whom,* and *whomever* introduce questions, they are interrogative pronouns. How an interrogative pronoun functions in a clause determines its case. Use *who* or *whoever* (the subjective case) when the interrogative pronoun functions as a subject or subject complement (see p. 609). Use *whom* or *whomever* (the objective case) when the interrogative pronoun functions as a direct object or an object of a preposition.

Subject

SUBJECTIVE CASE     Who is there?

Object of preposition

OBJECTIVE CASE     To whom did you give the letter?

### *Who* and *Whom* as Relative Pronouns

When *who, whoever, whom,* and *whomever* introduce subordinate clauses, they are relative pronouns. How a relative pronoun functions in a clause determines its case. Use *who* or *whoever* (subjective case) when a relative pronoun functions as the subject of the subordinate clause. Use *whom* or *whomever* (objective case) when a relative pronoun functions as an object in the subordinate clause.

| | |
|---|---|
| SUBJECTIVE CASE | The lecturer, who is a journalist from New York, speaks with great insight and wit. [*Who* is the subject of the subordinate clause.] |
| OBJECTIVE CASE | The journalist, whom I know from college days, came to give a lecture. [*Whom* is the direct object of the verb *know* in the subordinate clause.] |

## C.4 Correct Adjective and Adverb Use

Adjectives and adverbs modify, describe, explain, qualify, or restrict the words they modify (see pp. 595 and 598). **Adjectives** modify nouns and pronouns. **Adverbs** modify verbs, adjectives, and other adverbs; adverbs can also modify phrases, clauses, or whole sentences.

| ADJECTIVES | red car; the <u>quiet</u> one |
|---|---|
| ADVERBS | <u>quickly</u> finish; <u>only</u> four reasons; <u>very</u> angrily |

## Comparison of Adjectives and Adverbs

**Positive** adjectives and adverbs modify but do not involve any comparison: *green, bright, lively.*

**Comparative** adjectives and adverbs compare two persons, things, actions, or ideas.

| COMPARATIVE ADJECTIVE | Michel is <u>taller</u> than Latoya. |
|---|---|
| COMPARATIVE ADVERB | Antonio reacted <u>more calmly</u> than Robert. |

Here is how to form comparative adjectives and adverbs. (Consult your dictionary if you are unsure of the form of a particular word.)

1. **If the adjective or adverb has one syllable, add *-er*. For certain two-syllable words, also add *-er*.**

   cold → colder      slow → slower      narrow → narrower

2. **For most words of two or more syllables, place the word *more* in front of the word.**

   reasonable → more reasonable      interestingly → more interestingly

3. **For two-syllable adjectives ending in *y*, change the *y* to *i* and add *-er*.**

   drowsy → drowsier      lazy → lazier

   **Superlative** adjectives and adverbs compare more than two persons, things, actions, or ideas.

| SUPERLATIVE ADJECTIVE | Michael is the <u>tallest</u> member of the team. |
|---|---|
| SUPERLATIVE ADVERB | She studied <u>most diligently</u> for the test. |

Here is how to form superlative adjectives and adverbs:

1. **Add *-est* to one-syllable adjectives and adverbs and to certain two-syllable words.**

   cold → coldest      fast → fastest      narrow → narrowest

2. **For most words of two or more syllables, place the word *most* in front of the word.**

   reasonable → most reasonable      interestingly → most interestingly

3. **For two-syllable adjectives ending in *y*, change the *y* to *i* and add *-est*.**

   drowsy → drowsiest      lazy → laziest

---

**C. Writing Correct Sentences**

---

## Tip for Writers

When writing *superlative statements*, always use *the*. Use *much* only in questions and negatives. In affirmative statements, use *a lot of* or *some*.

Do you have <u>much</u> time for painting now that you're going to school?

Yes, I still have <u>a lot of</u> time for painting. (or) No, I don't have <u>much</u> time.

## Irregular Adjectives and Adverbs

Some adjectives and adverbs form their comparative and superlative forms in irregular ways.

### Tip for Writers

Use *littler* and *littlest* for size; use *less* and *least* for amount (quantity). Use *little/less/least* before noncount nouns; use *few/fewer/fewest* before plural nouns:

The littlest of Lana's eight children is only two years old; Lana has less time to spend with her friends now that she has a big family. She has *fewer* friends now.

| POSITIVE | COMPARATIVE | SUPERLATIVE |
|---|---|---|
| **Adjectives** | | |
| good | better | best |
| bad | worse | worst |
| little | littler, less | littlest, least |
| **Adverbs** | | |
| well | better | best |
| badly | worse | worst |
| **Adjectives and Adverbs** | | |
| many | more | most |
| some | more | most |
| much | more | most |

## Common Mistakes to Avoid

1. **Do not use adjectives to modify verbs, other adjectives, or adverbs.**

   INCORRECT   Peter and Mary take each other serious.

   CORRECT   Peter and Mary take each other seriously. [Modifies the verb *take*]

2. **Do not use the adjectives *good* and *bad* when you should use the adverbs *well* and *badly*.**

   INCORRECT   Juan did good on the exam.

   CORRECT   Juan did well on the exam. [Modifies the verb *did*]

3. **Do not use the adjectives *real* and *sure* when you should use the adverbs *really* and *surely*.**

   INCORRECT   Jan scored real well on the exam.

   CORRECT   Jan scored really well on the exam. [Modifies the adverb *well*]

   INCORRECT   I sure was surprised to win the lottery.

   CORRECT   I surely was surprised to win the lottery. [Modifies the verb *was surprised*]

4. **Do not use *more* or *most* with the *-er* or *-est* form of an adjective or adverb.** Use one form or the other, according to the rules above.

   INCORRECT   That was the most tastiest dinner I've ever eaten.

   CORRECT   That was the tastiest dinner I've ever eaten.

5. **Avoid double negatives—that is, two negatives in the same clause.**

| INCORRECT | He did <u>not</u> want <u>nothing</u> in the refrigerator. |
| CORRECT | He did <u>not</u> want <u>anything</u> in the refrigerator. |

6. **When using the comparative and superlative forms of adverbs, do not create an incomplete comparison.**

| INCORRECT | The heater works <u>more efficiently</u>. [More efficiently than what?] |
| CORRECT | The heater works <u>more efficiently than it did before we had it repaired.</u> |

7. **Do not use the comparative form for adjectives and adverbs that have no degree.** It is incorrect to write, for example, *more square, most perfect, more equally,* or *most straight.* Do not use a comparative or superlative form for any of the following adjectives and adverbs:

| ADJECTIVES | | | | |
|---|---|---|---|---|
| complete | equal | infinite | pregnant | unique |
| dead | eternal | invisible | square | universal |
| empty | favorite | matchless | supreme | vertical |
| endless | impossible | parallel | unanimous | whole |
| **ADVERBS** | | | | |
| endlessly | infinitely | uniquely | | |
| equally | Invisibly | universally | | |
| eternally | perpendicularly | | | |
| impossibly | Straight | | | |

## EXERCISE 10    Using Adjectives and Adverbs Correctly

**Directions:** Revise each of the following sentences so that all adjectives and adverbs are used correctly. If the sentence is correct, write "C" for correct beside it.    *Corrected sentences will vary.*

     **EXAMPLE**    I answered the question polite<sub>∧</sub>.ˡʸ

_____ 1. Michael's apartment was more expensive.

_____ 2. When I heard the man and woman sing the duet, I decided that the woman sang best.

__C__ 3. Our local movie reviewer said that the film's theme song sounded badly.

_____ 4. The roller coaster was excitinger than the merry-go-round.

_____ 5. *The Casual Vacancy* is more good than *The Hive.*

_____ 6. Susan sure gave a rousing speech.

_____ 7. Last week's storm seemed worst than a tornado.

_____ 8. Some women thought that the Equal Rights Amendment would guarantee that women are treated more equally.

_____ 9. Taking the interstate is the most fast route to the outlet mall.

_____10. Professor Reed had the better lecture style of all my instructors.

# C.5 Sentence Variety

Good writers use a variety of sentence structures to avoid wordiness and monotony and to show relationships among thoughts. To achieve **sentence variety**, do not use all simple sentences or all complex or compound sentences, and do not begin or end all sentences in the same way. Instead, vary the length, the amount of detail, and the structure of your sentences.

1. **Use sentences of varying lengths**.

2. **Avoid stringing simple sentences together with coordinating conjunctions (*and, but, or,* and so on)**. Instead, use some introductory participial phrases (see p. 614).

> SIMPLE    There was a long line at the deli, so Chris decided to leave.
>
> VARIED    Seeing the long line at the deli, Chris decided to leave.

3. **Begin some sentences with a prepositional phrase**. A preposition shows relationships between things (*during, over, toward, before, across, within, inside, over, above*). Many prepositions suggest chronology, direction, or location (see p. 601).

> During the concert, the fire alarm rang.
>
> Inside the theater, the crowd waited expectantly.

4. **Begin some sentences with a present or past participle (*cooking, broken;* see p. 210)**.

> Barking and jumping, the dogs greeted their master.
>
> Still laughing, two girls left the movie.
>
> Tired and exhausted, the mountain climbers fell asleep quickly.

5. **Begin some sentences with adverbs** (see p. 598).

> Angrily, the student left the room.
>
> Patiently, the math instructor explained the assignment again.

6. **Begin some sentences with infinitive phrases (*to* plus the infinitive form: *to make, to go;* see p. 161)**.

> To get breakfast ready on time, I set my alarm for 7 a.m.

7. **Begin some sentences with a dependent clause introduced by a subordinating conjunction** (see p. 618).

   <u>Because</u> I ate shellfish, I developed hives.

8. **Begin some sentences with a conjunctive adverb.**

   <u>Consequently</u>, we decided to have steak for dinner.

(see p. 618)

---

**EXERCISE 11**  ## Practicing Sentence Construction Techniques

**Directions:** Combine each of the following pairs of simple sentences into one sentence, using the technique suggested in brackets. *Answers will vary. Possible answers are shown.*

**EXAMPLE**    **a.** The dog barked and howled.

**b.** The dog warned a stranger away.
[Use present participle (-*ing* form).]

**COMBINED**   *Barking and howling, the dog warned a stranger away.*

1. **a.** Professor Clark has a Civil War battlefield model.

   **b.** He has it in his office.
   [Use prepositional phrase.]

   *Professor Clark has a Civil War battlefield model on the shelf in his office.*

2. **a.** Toby went to Disneyland for the first time.

   **b.** He was very excited.
   [Use past participle (-*ed* form).]

   *Excited, Toby went to Disneyland for the first time.*

3. **a.** Teresa received a full scholarship.

   **b.** She does not need to worry about paying her tuition.
   [Use subordinating conjunction.]

   *Because Teresa received a full scholarship, she does not need to worry about paying her tuition.*

4. **a.** Lance answered the phone.

   **b.** He spoke with a gruff voice.
   [Use adverb.]

   *Gruffly, Lance answered the phone.*

**5. a.** The truck choked and sputtered.

  **b.** The truck pulled into the garage.
   [Use present participle (-*ing* form).]

Choking and sputtering, the truck pulled into the garage.

**6. a.** Rich programmed his DVR.

  **b.** He recorded his favorite sitcom.
   [Use infinitive (*to*) phrase.]

To record his favorite sitcom, Rich programmed his DVR.

**7. a.** The postal carrier placed a package outside my door.

  **b.** The package had a foreign stamp on it.
   [Use prepositional phrase.]

The postal carrier placed a package with a foreign stamp on it outside my door.

**8. a.** The instructor asked the students to take their seats.

  **b.** She was annoyed.
   [Use past participle (-*ed* form).]

Annoyed, the instructor asked the students to take their seats.

**9. a.** Shyla stood outside the student union.

  **b.** She waited for her boyfriend.
   [Use present participle (-*ing* form).]

Waiting for her boyfriend, Shyla stood outside the student union.

**10. a.** Bo walked to the bookstore.

  **b.** He was going to buy some new highlighters.
   [Use infinitive (*to*) phrase.]

To buy some new highlighters, Bo walked to the bookstore.

# C.6 Redundancy and Wordiness

Redundancy results when a writer says the same thing twice. Wordiness results when a writer uses more words than necessary to convey a meaning. Both redundancy and wordiness detract from clear, effective sentences by distracting and confusing the reader.

## Eliminating Redundancy

A common mistake is to repeat the same idea in slightly different words.

> The remaining chocolate-chip cookie is the only one left, so I saved it for you. [*Remaining* and *only one left* mean the same thing.]
>
> The vase was oval in shape. [Oval is a shape, so *in shape* is redundant.]

To revise a redundant sentence, eliminate one of the redundant elements.

## Eliminating Wordiness

1. **Eliminate wordiness by cutting out words that do not add to the meaning of your sentence.**

   | | |
   |---|---|
   | WORDY | In the final analysis, choosing the field of biology as my major resulted in my realizing that college is hard work. |
   | REVISED | Choosing biology as my major made me realize that college is hard work. |
   | WORDY | The type of imitative behavior that I notice among teenagers is a very important, helpful aspect of their learning to function in groups. |
   | REVISED | The imitative behavior of teenagers helps them learn to function in groups. |

   Watch out in particular for empty words and phrases.

   | Phrase | Substitute |
   |---|---|
   | until such time as | until |
   | due to the fact that | because |
   | at this point in time | now |
   | in order to | to |

2. **Express your ideas simply and directly, using as few words as possible.**
   Often by rearranging your wording, you can eliminate two or three words.

   > the fleas that my dog has → my dog's fleas
   >
   > workers with jobs that are low in pay → workers with low-paying jobs

3. **Use strong, active verbs that convey movement and give additional information.**

> WORDY    I was in charge of two other employees and needed to watch over their work and performance.
>
> REVISED   I supervised two employees, monitored their performance, and checked their work.

4. **Avoid sentences that begin with "*There is*" and "*There are.*"** These empty phrases add no meaning, energy, or life to sentences.

> WORDY    There are many children who suffer from malnutrition.
>
> REVISED   Many children suffer from malnutrition.

| EXERCISE 12 | Eliminating Redundancy and Wordiness |
| --- | --- |

**Directions:** Revise each of the following sentences to eliminate redundancy and wordiness.   *Revisions will vary.*

> EXAMPLE   Janice, who is impatient, usually cannot wait for class to end and packs up all of her books and notebooks in her backpack before the class is over.
>
> REVISED   *Janice is impatient and usually packs everything in her backpack before class ends.*

1. My co-workers are friendly, nice, and cooperative and always willing to help me.

2. Eva and Joe are returning again to the branch office where they met.

3. Lynn changed from her regular clothes into her shorts and T-shirt in order that she could play basketball.

4. Due to the fact that Professor Reis assigned 100 pages of reading for tomorrow, I will be unable to join the group of my friends at the restaurant tonight.

5. In my mythology class, we discussed and talked about the presence of a Noah's ark–type story in most cultures.

6. Darryl offered many ideas and theories as to the reason why humans exist.

7. There are many children who have not been immunized against dangerous childhood diseases.

8. Scientists have been studying the disease AIDS for many years, but they have been unable to find a cure for the disease.

9. The brown-colored chair was my father's favorite chair.

10. The briefcase that Julio has carried belonged to his brother.

# **C.7** Diction

**Diction** is the use and choice of words. Words that you choose should be appropriate for your audience and express your meaning clearly. The following suggestions will help you improve your diction:

1. **Avoid slang expressions.** Slang refers to the informal, special expressions created and used by groups of people who want to give themselves a unique identity. Slang is an appropriate and useful way to communicate in some social situations and in some forms of creative writing. However, it is not appropriate for academic or career writing.

| | |
|---|---|
| SLANG | My sister seems permanently out to lunch. |
| REVISED | My sister seems out of touch with the world. |
| SLANG | We pigged out at the ice cream shop. |
| REVISED | We consumed enormous quantities of ice cream at the ice cream shop. |

2. **Avoid colloquial language.** Colloquial language refers to casual, everyday spoken language. It should be avoided in formal situations. Words that fall into this category are labeled *informal* or *colloquial* in your dictionary.

| | |
|---|---|
| COLLOQUIAL | I almost flunked bio last sem. |
| REVISED | I almost failed biology last semester. |
| COLLOQUIAL | What are you all doing later? |
| REVISED | What are you doing later? |

3. **Avoid nonstandard language.** Nonstandard language consists of words and grammatical forms that are used in conversation but are neither correct nor acceptable standard written English.

| *Nonstandard* | *Standard* |
|---|---|
| hisself | himself |
| knowed | known, knew |
| hadn't ought to | should not |
| she want | she wants |
| he go | he goes |

4. **Avoid trite expressions.** Trite expressions are old, worn-out words and phrases that have become stale and do not convey meaning as effectively as possible. These expressions are also called *clichés*.

| *Trite Expressions* | | |
|---|---|---|
| needle in a haystack | sadder but wiser | as old as the hills |
| hard as a rock | white as snow | pretty as a picture |
| face the music | gentle as a lamb | |

### EXERCISE 13   Practicing Correct Diction

**Directions:** Revise each of the following sentences by using correct diction.   Answers will vary.

**EXAMPLE**   This here building is Clemens Hall.

**REVISED**   This building is Clemens Hall.

1. Jean ~~freaked out~~ <sup>was thrilled</sup> when I told her she won the lottery.

2. He ~~go~~ <sup>went</sup> to the library.

3. The campus is ~~wider than an ocean~~. <sup>very large</sup>

4. Marty sits next to me in ~~chem~~. <sup>chemistry class</sup>

5. Sandy's new stereo ~~is totally cool and has an awesome sound.~~ <sup>has incredible sound.</sup>

6. We ~~went nuts~~ when our team won the game. <sup>cheered and ran onto the field</sup>

7. ~~Them~~ <sup>H</sup>home theater systems ~~sure~~ are <sub>very</sub> expensive.

8. I think Nathan is ~~as sharp as a tack~~ <sup>very intelligent</sup> because he got every question on the exam right.

9. Nino ~~blew~~ <sup>skipped</sup> class ~~off~~ today to go rock climbing with his ~~pals~~. <sup>friends</sup>

10. Dr. Maring's pager beeped in the middle of the meeting and she had to ~~hightail it~~ <sub>get</sub> to a phone <sub>quickly</sub>.

# Using Punctuation Correctly

## D.1 End Punctuation

### When to Use Periods

Use a period in the following situations:

1. **To end a sentence unless it is a question or an exclamation.**

   We washed the car, even though we knew a thunderstorm was due later in the day.

   *Note:* Use a period to end a sentence that states an indirect question or indirectly quotes someone's words or thoughts.

   INCORRECT   Samantha wondered if she would be on time?

   CORRECT   Samantha wondered if she would be on time.

2. **To punctuate many abbreviations.**

   M.D.   B.A.   p.m.   B.C.   Mr.   Ms.

   Do not use periods in acronyms, such as *NATO* and *AIDS,* or in abbreviations for most organizations, such as *NBC* and *NAACP.*

   *Note:* If a sentence ends with an abbreviation, the sentence has only one period, not two.

   The train was due to arrive at 7:00 p.m.

### When to Use Question Marks

Use question marks after direct questions. Place the question mark within the closing quotation marks.

She asked the deli assistant, "How old is this cheese?"

*Note:* Use a period, not a question mark, after an indirect question.

She asked the deli assistant how old the cheese was.

## Tip for Writers

**Punctuation**

Using punctuation incorrectly can sometimes change the meaning of your sentences. Here are two examples:

1. The children who stayed outside got wet. (Only some of the children got wet.)
The children, who stayed outside, got wet. (All of the children got wet.)
2. Did she finally marry Roger?
Did she finally marry, Roger?

## When to Use Exclamation Points

Use an exclamation point at the end of a sentence that expresses particular emphasis, excitement, or urgency. Use exclamation points sparingly, however, especially in academic writing.

What a beautiful day it is!          Dial 911 right now!

# D.2 Commas

The comma is used to separate parts of a sentence from one another. If you omit a comma when it is needed, you risk making a clear and direct sentence confusing.

## When to Use Commas

Use a comma in the following situations:

1. **Before a coordinating conjunction that joins two independent clauses** (see p. 189).

   Terry had planned to leave work early, but he was delayed.

2. **To separate a dependent (subordinate) clause from an independent clause when the dependent clause comes first in the sentence** (see p. 191).

   After I left the library, I went to the computer lab.

3. **To separate introductory words and phrases from the rest of the sentence.**

   Unfortunately, I forgot my umbrella.

   To pass the baton, I will need to locate my teammate.

   Exuberant over their victory, the football team members carried the quarterback on their shoulders.

4. **To separate a nonrestrictive phrase or clause from the rest of a sentence. A nonrestrictive** phrase or clause is added to a sentence but does not change the sentence's basic meaning.

   To determine whether an element is nonrestrictive, read the sentence without the element. If the meaning of the sentence does not essentially change, then the commas are *necessary*.

   My sister, who is a mail carrier, is afraid of dogs. [The essential meaning of this sentence does not change if we read the sentence without the subordinate clause: *My sister is afraid of dogs.* Therefore, commas are needed.]

   Mail carriers who have been bitten by dogs are afraid of them. [If we read this sentence without the subordinate clause, its meaning changes considerably: *Mail carriers are afraid of (dogs).* It seems to say that *all* mail carriers are afraid of dogs. In this case, adding commas is not correct.]

**5. To separate three or more items in a series.**

*Note:* A comma is *not* used *after* the last item in the series.

I plan to take math, psychology, and writing next semester.

**6. To separate coordinate adjectives: two or more adjectives that are not joined by a coordinating conjunction and that equally modify the same noun or pronoun.**

The thirsty, hungry children returned from a day at the beach.

To determine if a comma is needed between two adjectives, use the following test. Insert the word *and* between the two adjectives. Also try reversing the order of the two adjectives. If the phrase makes sense in either case, a comma is needed. If the phrase does not make sense, do not use a comma.

The tired, angry child fell asleep. [*The tired and angry child* makes sense; so does *The angry, tired child.* Consequently, the comma is needed.]

Sarah is an excellent psychology student. [*Sarah is an excellent and psychology student* does not make sense, nor does *Sarah is a psychology, excellent student.* A comma is therefore not needed.]

**7. To separate parenthetical expressions from the clauses they modify.** Parenthetical expressions are added pieces of information that are not essential to the meaning of the sentence.

Most students, I imagine, can get jobs on campus.

**8. To separate a transition from the clause it modifies.**

In addition, I will revise the bylaws.

**9. To separate a quotation from the words that introduce or explain it.**

*Note:* The comma goes *inside* the closed quotation marks.

"Shopping," Julia explained, "is a form of relaxation for me."

Julia explained, "Shopping is a form of relaxation for me."

**10. To separate dates, place names, and long numbers.**

October 10, 1989, is my birthday.

Dayton, Ohio, was the first stop on the tour.

Participants numbered 1,777,716.

**11. To separate phrases expressing contrast.**

Jorge's good nature, not his wealth, explains his popularity.

| EXERCISE 14 | Adding Commas |

**Directions:** Revise each of the following sentences by adding commas where needed.

>    **EXAMPLE**    Until the judge entered, the courtroom was noisy.

1. "Hello," said the group of friends when Joan entered the room.

2. Christian Bale,the actor in the film,was very handsome.

3. My parents frequently vacation in Miami,Florida.

4. Drunk drivers,I suppose,may not realize they are not competent to drive.

5. Jeff purchased a television,couch,and dresser for his new apartment.

6. Luckily,the windstorm did not do any damage to our town.

7. Frieda has an early class,and she has to go to work afterward.

8. After taking a trip to the Galápagos Islands,Mark Twain wrote about them.

9. The old,dilapidated stadium was opened to the public on September 15, 1931.

10. Afterward,we will go out for ice cream.

# D.3 Unnecessary Commas

It is as important to know where *not* to place commas as it is to know where to place them. The following rules explain where it is incorrect to place them:

1. **Do not place a comma between a subject and its verb, between a verb and its complement, or between an adjective and the word it modifies.**

> INCORRECT The stunning, imaginative, and intriguing, painting, became the hit of the show.
>
> *(Adjective — intriguing, Subject — painting, Verb — became)*
>
> CORRECT The stunning, imaginative, and intriguing painting became the hit of the show.

2. **Do not place a comma between two verbs, subjects, or complements used as compounds.**

> *Compound verb — called ... asked*
>
> INCORRECT Marisol called, and asked me to come by her office.
>
> CORRECT Marisol called and asked me to come by her office.

3. **Do not place a comma before a coordinating conjunction joining two dependent clauses** (see p. 618).

> Dependent clause
>
> INCORRECT    The city planner examined blueprints that the park designer had submitted, and that the budget officer had approved.
>
> Dependent clause
>
> CORRECT    The city planner examined blueprints that the park designer had submitted and that the budget officer had approved.

4. **Do not place commas around restrictive clauses, phrases, or appositives.** Restrictive clauses, phrases, and appositives are modifiers that are essential to the meaning of the sentence.

> INCORRECT    The girl, who grew up down the block, became my lifelong friend.
>
> CORRECT    The girl who grew up down the block became my lifelong friend.

5. **Do not place a comma before the word *than* in a comparison or after the words *like* and *such as* in an introduction to a list.**

> INCORRECT    Some snails, such as, the Oahu tree snail, have more colorful shells, than other snails.
>
> CORRECT    Some snails, such as the Oahu tree snail, have more colorful shells than other snails.

6. **Do not place a comma next to a period, a question mark, an exclamation point, a dash, or an opening parenthesis.**

> INCORRECT    "When will you come back?," Dillon's son asked him.
>
> CORRECT    "When will you come back?" Dillon's son asked him.
>
> INCORRECT    The bachelor button, (also known as the cornflower) grows well in ordinary garden soil.
>
> CORRECT    The bachelor button (also known as the cornflower) grows well in ordinary garden soil.

7. **Do not place a comma between cumulative adjectives.** Cumulative adjectives, unlike coordinate adjectives (see p. 641), cannot be joined by *and* or rearranged.

> INCORRECT    The light, yellow, roses were a lovely birthday surprise.
> [*The light and yellow and rose blossom* does not make sense, so the commas are incorrect.]
>
> CORRECT    The light yellow roses were a lovely birthday surprise.

# **D.4** Colons and Semicolons

## When to Use a Colon

A **colon** follows an independent clause and usually signals that the clause is to be explained or elaborated on. Use a colon in the following situations:

1. **To introduce items in a series after an independent clause.** The series can consist of words, phrases, or clauses.

   > I am wearing three popular colors: magenta, black, and white.

2. **To signal a list or a statement introduced by an independent clause ending with *the following* or *as follows*.**

   > The directions are as follows: take Main Street to Oak Avenue and then turn left.

3. **To introduce a quotation that follows an introductory independent clause.**

   > My brother made his point quite clear: "Never borrow my car without asking me first!"

4. **To introduce an explanation.**

   > Mathematics is enjoyable: it requires a high degree of accuracy and peak concentration.

5. **To separate titles and subtitles of books.**

   > *Biology: A Study of Life*

   *Note:* A colon must always follow an independent clause. It should not be used in the middle of a clause.

   | INCORRECT | My favorite colors are: red, pink, and green. |
   | CORRECT | My favorite colors are red, pink, and green. |

## When to Use a Semicolon

A **semicolon** separates equal and balanced sentence parts. Use a semicolon in the following situations:

1. **To separate two closely related independent clauses not connected by a coordinating conjunction** (see p. 199).

   > Sam had a 99 average in math; he earned an A in the course.

2. **To separate two independent clauses joined by a conjunctive adverb** (see p. 618).

> Margaret earned an A on her term paper; consequently, she was exempt from the final exam.

3. **To separate independent clauses joined with a coordinating conjunction if the clauses are very long or if they contain numerous commas.**

> By late afternoon, having tried on every pair of black jeans in the mall, Marsha was tired and cranky; but she still had not found what she needed to complete her outfit for the play.

4. **To separate items in a series if the items are lengthy or contain commas.**

> The soap opera characters include Marianne Loundsberry, the heroine; Ellen and Sarah, her children; Barry, her ex-husband; and Louise, her best friend.

5. **To correct a comma splice or run-on sentence** (see p. 199).

## Correcting Sentences Using Colons and Semicolons

**EXERCISE 15**

**Directions:** Correct each of the following sentences by placing colons and semicolons where necessary. Delete any incorrect punctuation.

**EXAMPLE**    Samuel Clemens disliked his name; therefore, he used Mark

Twain as his pen name.

1. The large, modern, and airy, gallery houses works of art by important artists, however, it has not yet earned national recognition as an important gallery.

   The large, modern, and airy gallery houses works of art by important artists;

   however, it has not yet earned national recognition as an important gallery.

2. Rita suggested several herbs to add to my spaghetti sauce, oregano, basil, and thyme.

   Rita suggested several herbs to add to my spaghetti sauce: oregano, basil, and thyme.

3. Vic carefully proofread the paper, it was due the next day.

   Vic carefully proofread the paper; it was due the next day.

4. Furniture refinishing is a great hobby, it is satisfying to be able to make a piece of furniture look new again.

   Furniture refinishing is a great hobby; it is satisfying to be able to make a piece of furniture

   look new again.

5. The bridesmaids in my sister's wedding are as follows, Judy, her best friend Kim, our sister, Franny, our cousin, and Sue, a family friend.

   *The bridesmaids in my sister's wedding are as follows: Judy, her best friend; Kim, our sister;*

   *Franny, our cousin; and Sue, a family friend.*

6. Mac got a speeding ticket, he has to go to court next Tuesday.

   *Mac got a speeding ticket; he has to go to court next Tuesday.*

7. I will go for a swim when the sun comes out, it will not be so chilly then.

   *I will go for a swim when the sun comes out: it will not be so chilly then.*

8. Carlos was hungry after his hockey game, consequently, he ordered four hamburgers.

   *Carlos was hungry after his hockey game; consequently, he ordered four hamburgers.*

9. Sid went to the bookstore to purchase *Physical Anthropology Man and His Makings*, it is required for one of his courses.

   *Sid went to the bookstore to purchase Physical Anthropology: Man and His Makings; it is*

   *required for one of his courses.*

10. Here is an old expression, "The way to a man's heart is through his stomach."

    *Here is an old expression: "The way to a man's heart is through his stomach."*

# D.5 Dashes, Parentheses, Hyphens, Apostrophes, Quotation Marks

## Dashes (—)

The dash is used to (1) separate nonessential elements from the main part of the sentence, (2) create a stronger separation, or interruption, than commas or parentheses, and (3) emphasize an idea, create a dramatic effect, or indicate a sudden change in thought.

> My sister—the friendliest person I know—will visit me this weekend.
>
> My brother's most striking quality is his ability to make money—or so I thought until I heard of his bankruptcy.

Do not leave spaces between the dash and the words it separates.

## Parentheses ( )

Parentheses are used in pairs to separate extra or nonessential information that often amplifies, clarifies, or acts as an aside to the main point. Unlike dashes, parentheses de-emphasize information.

Some large breeds of dogs (golden retrievers and Newfoundlands) are susceptible to hip deformities.

The prize was dinner for two (maximum value, $50) at a restaurant of one's choice.

## Hyphens (-)

Hyphens have the following primary uses:

1. **To split a word when dividing it between two lines of writing or typing** (see p. 653).

2. **To join two or more words that function as a unit, either as a noun or as a noun modifier.**

   | | |
   |---|---|
   | mother-in-law | single-parent families |
   | 20-year-old | school-age children |
   | state-of-the-art sound system | |

## Apostrophes (')

Use apostrophes in the following situations:

1. **To show ownership or possession.** When the person, place, or thing doing the possessing is a singular noun, add -'s to the end of it, regardless of what its final letter is.

   | | |
   |---|---|
   | The man's DVD player | John Keats's poetry |
   | Aretha's best friend | |

   With plural nouns that end in -s, add only an apostrophe to the end of the word.

   | | |
   |---|---|
   | the twins' bedroom | postal workers' hours |
   | teachers' salaries | |

   With plural nouns that do not end in -s, add -'s.

   | | |
   |---|---|
   | children's books | men's slacks |

   Do not use an apostrophe with the possessive adjective *its*.

   | | |
   |---|---|
   | INCORRECT | It's frame is damaged. |
   | CORRECT | Its frame is damaged. |

2. **To indicate omission of one or more letters in a word or number.** Contractions are used in informal writing, but usually not in formal academic writing.

   | | |
   |---|---|
   | it's [it is] | hasn't [has not] |
   | doesn't [does not] | '57 Ford [1957 Ford] |
   | you're [you are] | class of '99 [class of 1999] |

### Tip for Writers

*Its*, *your*, *his*, and *their* are *possessive* forms that go before nouns. Their meanings are possessive, so don't use an apostrophe in these words. On the other hand, *it's*, *you're*, *he's*, and *they're* are all contractions of pronouns with *is* or *are*, so an apostrophe is needed in each of these words.

# Quotation Marks (" ")

Quotation marks separate a direct quotation from the sentence that contains it. Here are some rules to follow in using quotation marks.

1. **Quotation marks are always used in pairs.**

   *Note:* A comma or period goes at the end of the quotation, inside the quotation marks.

   > Jasmina declared, "I never expected Nathan to give me a gift for Christmas."
   >
   > "I never expected Nathan to give me a gift for Christmas," Jasmina declared.

2. **Use single quotation marks for a quotation within a quotation.**

   > My literature professor said, "Byron's line 'She walks in beauty like the night' is one of his most sensual."

   *Note:* When quoting long prose passages of more than four typed lines, do not use quotation marks. Instead, set off the quotation from the rest of the text by indenting each line ten spaces from the left margin. This format is called a **block quotation.**

   > The opening lines of the Declaration of Independence establish the purpose of the document:
   >
   > > When in the Course of human events it becomes necessary for one people to dissolve the political bonds which have connected them with another, and to assume among the powers of the earth, the separate and equal station to which the Laws of Nature and of Nature's God entitle them, a decent respect to the opinions of mankind requires that they should declare the causes which impel them to the separation.

3. **Use quotation marks to indicate titles of songs, short stories, poems, reports, articles, and essays.** Books, movies, plays, operas, paintings, statues, and the names of television series are italicized (or underlined to indicate italics).

   > "A Case of Fever" (short story)
   > *The Daily Show* [or The Daily Show] (television series)
   > "The Road Not Taken" (poem)

4. **Colons, semicolons, exclamation points, and question marks, when not part of the quoted material, go outside of the quotation marks.**

   > What did Ethan mean when he said, "People in glass houses shouldn't throw stones"?

**EXERCISE 16**

# Adding Appropriate Punctuation Marks

**Directions:** To the following sentences, add dashes, apostrophes, parentheses, hyphens, and quotation marks where necessary.

**EXAMPLE**    "You are not going out dressed that way!" said Frank's roommate.

1. My daughter in law recently entered medical school.

   My daughter-in-law recently entered medical school.

2. At the bar I worked at last summer, the waitresses tips were always pooled and equally divided.

   At the bar I worked at last summer, the waitresses' tips were always pooled and equally divided.

3. Youre going to Chicago next summer, aren't you?

   You're going to Chicago next summer, aren't you?

4. The career counselor said, The computer field is not as open as it used to be.

   The career counselor said, "The computer field is not as open as it used to be."

5. My English professor read aloud Frost's poem Two Look at Two.

   My English professor read aloud Frost's poem "Two Look at Two."

6. Martin asked me if I planned to buy a plasma television for our Super Bowl party.

   Frank asked me if I planned to buy a plasma television for our Super Bowl party.

7. Rachel the teaching assistant for my Chinese class spent last year in China.

   Rachel—the teaching assistant for my Chinese class—spent last year in China.

8. Macy's is having a sale on womens boots next week.

   Macy's is having a sale on women's boots next week.

9. Trina said, My one year old's newest word is Bzz, which she says whenever she sees a fly.

   Trina said, "My one-year-old's newest word is 'Bzz.' which she says whenever she sees a fly."

10. Some animals horses and donkeys can interbreed, but they produce infertile offspring.

    Some animals (horses and donkeys) can interbreed, but they produce infertile offspring.

# E Managing Mechanics and Spelling

## E.1 Capitalization

In general, **capital letters** are used to mark the beginning of a sentence, to mark the beginning of a quotation, and to identify proper nouns. Here are some guidelines on capitalization:

| *What to Capitalize* | *Example* |
|---|---|
| 1. First word in every sentence | Prewriting is useful. |
| 2. First word in a direct quotation | Sarah commented, "That exam was difficult!" |
| 3. Names of people and animals, including the pronoun *I* | Batman<br>Maya Angelou<br>Spot |
| 4. Names of specific places, cities, states, nations, geographic areas or regions | New Orleans<br>the Southwest<br>Lake Erie |
| 5. Government and public offices, departments, buildings | Williamsville Library<br>House of Representatives |
| 6. Names of social, political, business, sporting, cultural organizations | Boy Scouts<br>Buffalo Bills |
| 7. Names of months, days of the week, holidays | August<br>Tuesday<br>Halloween |
| 8. In titles of works: the first word following a colon, the first and last words, and all other words except articles, prepositions, and conjunctions | *Biology: A Study of Life*<br>"Once More to the Lake" |
| 9. Races, nationalities, languages | African American, Italian, English |
| 10. Religions, religious figures, sacred books | Hindu, Hinduism, God, Allah, the Bible |
| 11. Names of products | Bounty, Acura |
| 12. Personal titles when they come right before a name | Professor Rodriguez<br>Senator Hatch |
| 13. Major historic events | World War I |
| 14. Specific course titles | History 201,<br>Introduction to Psychology |

| EXERCISE 17 | Practicing Capitalization |

**Directions:** Capitalize words as necessary in the following sentences.    Circled letters need capitalization.

**EXAMPLE**    Farmers in the m̲idwest were devastated by floods last summer.

1. My mother is preparing some special foods for our (h)anukkah meal; (r)abbi (e)pstein will join us.

2. My (a)merican (p)olitics professor used to be a judge in the town of (e)vans.

3. A restaurant in the (g)alleria (m)all serves (k)orean food.

4. A graduate student I know is writing a book about (b)uddha titled *(t)he (g)reat (o)ne: (w)ays to (e)nlightenment.*

5. (a)t the concert last night, (l)ady (g)aga changed into many different outfits.

6. An (e)mployee announced over the loudspeaker, "(a)ttention, customers! (w)e have (p)epsi on sale in (a)isle (t)en!"

7. Karen's father was stationed at (f)ort (b)radley during the (i)raq (w)ar.

8. Last (t)uesday the (s)tate (a)ssembly passed (g)overnor (a)llen's budget.

9. Boston is an exciting city; be sure to visit the (m)useum of (f)ine (a)rts.

10. Marcos asked if (i) wanted to go see the (c)irque du (s)oleil at (s)hea's (t)heatre in (n)ovember.

# E.2 Abbreviations

An **abbreviation** is a shortened form of a word or phrase that is used to represent the whole word or phrase. The following is a list of common acceptable abbreviations:

| What to Abbreviate | Example |
|---|---|
| 1. Some titles before or after people's names | Mr. Ling<br>Samuel Rosen, M.D.<br>*but* Professor Ashe |
| 2. Names of familiar organizations, corporations, countries | CIA, IBM, VISTA, USA |
| 3. Time references preceded or followed by a number | 7:00 a.m.<br>3:00 p.m.<br>A.D. 1973 |
| 4. Latin terms when used in footnotes, references, or parentheses | i.e. [*id est,* "that is"]<br>et al. [*et alii,* "and others"] |

Here is a list of things that are usually *not* abbreviated:

| | | *Example* | |
| --- | --- | --- | --- |
| *What Not to Abbreviate* | | *Incorrect* | *Correct* |
| 1. Units of measurement | | thirty in. | thirty inches |
| 2. Geographic or other place names when used in sentences | | N.Y. Elm St. | New York Elm Street |
| 3. Parts of written works when used in sentences | | Ch. 3 | Chapter 3 |
| 4. Names of days, months, holidays | | Tues. | Tuesday |
| 5. Names of subject areas | | psych. | psychology |

EXERCISE 18 | Correcting Inappropriate Use of Abbreviations

**Directions:** Correct the inappropriate use of abbreviations in the following sentences. If a sentence contains no errors, write "C" for correct beside it.

   *miles*   *New York City*
**EXAMPLE**   We live 30 ~~mi.~~ outside ~~NYC~~.

_____

                                                        *Street*
_____ 1. Frank enjoys going to swim at the YMCA on Oak ~~St.~~

_____

     *Professor*                                *page*
_____ 2. ~~Prof.~~ Jorge asked the class to turn to ~~pg.~~ 8.

_____

                          *feet*
_____ 3. Because he is seven ~~ft.~~ tall, my brother was recruited for the high
        *basketball*
     school ~~b-ball~~ team.

_____

_C_ 4. When I asked Ron why he hadn't called me, he said it was Verizon's
     fault (i.e., his phone hadn't been working).

_____

                    *Kansas City*                *Wednesday*
_____ 5. Tara is flying TWA to ~~KC~~ to visit her parents next ~~Wed.~~

_____

_C_ 6. At 11:30 p.m., we settled in to watch an episode of *Dr. Who,* which
     had just been shown on the BBC.

_____

       *week*      *chemistry laboratory*
_____ 7. Last ~~wk.~~ I missed my ~~chem. lab.~~

_____

                                    *question*         *question number*
_____ 8. The exam wasn't too difficult; only ~~ques.~~ number 15 and ~~ques. no.~~
     31 were extremely difficult.

_____

_____ 9. Dr. Luc removed the mole from my ~~rt.~~ hand using a laser.  
                                 *right*

_____ 10. Mark drove out to ~~L.A.~~ to audition for a role in Speilberg's new movie.  
                            *Los Angeles*

# E.3 Hyphenation and Word Division

On occasion you must divide and hyphenate a word on one line and continue it on the next. Here are some guidelines for dividing words.

1. **Divide words only when necessary.** Frequent word divisions make a paper difficult to read.

2. **Divide words between syllables.** Consult a dictionary if you are unsure how to break a word into syllables.

> di-vi-sion        pro-tect

3. **Do not divide one-syllable words.**

4. **Do not divide a word so that a single letter is left at the end of a line.**

> INCORRECT    a-typical  
> CORRECT      atyp-ical

5. **Do not divide a word so that fewer than three letters begin the new line.**

> INCORRECT    visu-al  
> CORRECT      vi-sual  
> INCORRECT    caus-al [This word cannot be divided at all.]

6. **Divide compound words only between the words.**

> some-thing        any-one

7. **Divide words that are already hyphenated only at the hyphen.**

> ex-policeman

### Tip for Writers

A *syllable* is a group of letters with one vowel sound, such as *tall* or *straight*. In a dictionary, the first, bold-faced listing of a word has dots to show where the word can be divided with a hyphen and continued on the next line:

trans•por•ta•tion

## EXERCISE 19   Practicing Division

**Directions:** Insert a diagonal (/) mark where each word should be divided. Mark "N" in the space provided if the word should not be divided.

**EXAMPLE**    every/where

| | | | | |
|---|---|---|---|---|
| _____ | **1.** en/close | | _____ | **6.** disgusted |
| N | **2.** house | | _____ | **7.** chan/delier |
| _____ | **3.** sax/ophone | | _____ | **8.** head/phones |
| N | **4.** hardly | | N | **9.** swings |
| _____ | **5.** well-known | | N | **10.** abyss |

# E.4 Numbers

Numbers can be written as numerals (600) or words (six hundred). Here are some guidelines for when to use numerals and when to use words:

| When to Use Numerals | Example |
|---|---|
| 1. Numbers that are spelled with more than two words | 375 students |
| 2. Days and years | August 10, 2010 |
| 3. Decimals, percentages, fractions | 56.7<br>59 percent<br>1¾ cups |
| 4. Exact times | 9:27 a.m. |
| 5. Pages, chapters, volumes; acts and lines from plays | chapter 12<br>volume 4 |
| 6. Addresses | 122 Peach Street |
| 7. Exact amounts of money | $5.60 |
| 8. Scores and statistics | 23–6    5 of every 12 |

| When to Use Words | Example |
|---|---|
| 1. Numbers that begin sentences | Two hundred ten students attended the lecture. |
| 2. Numbers of one or two words | sixty students,<br>two hundred women |

## EXERCISE 20    Practicing Correct Number Usage

**Directions:** Correct the misuse of numbers in the following sentences. If a sentence contains no errors, write "C" for correct beside it.

                                                     *five hundred*

**EXAMPLE**    The reception hall was filled with ~~500~~ guests.

_____

  C   **1.** At 6:52 a.m. my roommate's alarm clock went off.

_____

               *three*                                     *$9.99*

 _____ **2.** I purchased ~~3~~ turtlenecks for ~~nine dollars and ninety-nine cents~~ each.

_____

_____ 3. 35 floats were entered in the parade, but only 4 received prizes.

_____

_____ 4. Act ~~three~~ of *Othello* is very exciting.

_____

_____ 5. Almost ~~fifty~~ percent of all marriages end in divorce.

_____

__C__ 6. The Broncos won the game 21–7.

_____

_____ 7. We were assigned volume ~~two~~ of *Don Quixote,* beginning on page 351.

_____

_____ 8. The hardware store is located at ~~three forty-four~~ Elm Street, ~~2~~ doors down from my grandmother's house.

_____

_____ 9. Maryanne's new car is a ~~2~~-door V-8.

_____

_____10. Our anniversary is June ~~ninth, nineteen eighty-nine~~.

_____

# E.5 Suggestions for Improving Spelling

Correct spelling is important to a well-written paragraph or essay. The following suggestions will help you submit papers without misspellings:

1. **Do not worry about spelling as you write your first draft.** Checking a word in a dictionary at this point will interrupt your flow of ideas. If you do not know how a word is spelled, spell it the way it sounds. Circle or underline the word so you remember to check it later.

2. **Keep a list of words you commonly misspell.** This list can be part of your error log.

3. **Every time you catch an error or find a misspelled word on a paper returned by your instructor, add it to your list.**

4. **Study your list.** Ask a friend to quiz you on the words. Eliminate words from the list after you have passed several quizzes on them.

5. **Develop a spelling awareness.** You'll find that your spelling will improve just by your being aware that spelling is important. When you encounter a new word, notice how it is spelled and practice writing it.

6. **Pronounce words you are having difficulty spelling.** Pronounce each syllable distinctly.

7. **Review basic spelling rules.** Your college library or learning lab may have manuals, workbooks, or computer programs that cover basic rules and provide guided practice.

8. **Be sure to have a dictionary readily available when you write.**

9. **Read your final draft through once, checking only for spelling errors.** Look at each word carefully, and check the spelling of those words of which you are uncertain.

# E.6 Six Useful Spelling Rules

The following six rules focus on common spelling trouble spots:

1. **Is it *ei* or *ie*?**

   *Rule:* Use *i* before *e*, except after *c* or when the syllable is pronounced *ay* as in the word *weigh.*

   > *i* before *e:* believe, niece
   >
   > except after *c:* receive, conceive
   >
   > or when pronounced *ay:* neighbor, sleigh

   | *Exceptions:* | either | neither | foreign | forfeit |
   |---|---|---|---|---|
   | | height | leisure | weird | seize |

2. **When adding an ending, do you keep or drop the final *e*?**

   *Rules:* **a.** Keep the final *e* when adding an ending that begins with a consonant. (Vowels are *a, e, i, o, u,* and sometimes *y;* all other letters are consonants.)

   > hope → hopeful    aware → awareness
   >
   > live → lively    force → forceful

   **b.** Drop the final *e* when adding an ending that begins with a vowel.

   > hope → hoping    file → filing
   >
   > note → notable    write → writing

   | *Exceptions*: | argument | truly | changeable |
   |---|---|---|---|
   | | awful | manageable | courageous |
   | | judgment | noticeable | outrageous |
   | | acknowledgment | | |

   > **Tip for Writers**
   >
   > The final *e* must remain on a word (before adding an ending) if the *e* is needed to keep a "soft" *c* sound (like *s*) or a "soft *g*" sound (like *j*) on the preceding letter. Two examples are *noticeable* and *manageable.*

3. **When adding an ending, do you keep the final *y*, change it to *i*, or drop it?**

   *Rules:* **a.** Keep the *y* if the letter before the *y* is a vowel.

   > delay → delaying    buy → buying    prey → preyed

**b.** Change the *y* to *i* if the letter before the *y* is a consonant, but keep the *y* for the *-ing* ending.

> defy → defiance     marry → married
> → defying     → marrying

4. **When adding an ending to a one-syllable word, when do you double the final letter if it is a consonant?**

   *Rules:*  **a.** In one-syllable words, double the final consonant when a single vowel comes before it.

   > drop → dropped     shop → shopped     pit → pitted

   **b.** In one-syllable words, *don't* double the final consonant when two vowels or a consonant comes before it.

   > repair → repairable     sound → sounded
   > real → realize

5. **When adding an ending to a word with more than one syllable, when do you double the final letter if it is a consonant?**

   *Rules:*  **a.** In multisyllable words, double the final consonant when a single vowel comes before it *and* the stress falls on the last syllable. (Vowels are *a, e, i, o, u,* and sometimes *y.* All other letters are consonants.)

   > be•'gin → beginning     trans•'mit → transmitted
   > re•'pel → repelling

   **b.** In multisyllable words, do *not* double the final consonant (a) when two vowels or a vowel and another consonant come before it *or* (b) when the stress is not on the last syllable.

   > despair → despairing     'ben•e•fit → benefited
   > conceal → concealing

6. **To form a plural, do you add -*s* or -*es*?**

   *Rules:*  **a.** For most nouns, add -*s.*

   > cat → cats     house → houses

   **b.** Add -*es* to words that end in *o* if the *o* is preceded by a consonant.

   > hero → heroes     potato → potatoes

   *Exceptions:* *zoos, radios, ratios,* and other words ending with two vowels.

   **c.** Add -*es* to words ending in *ch, sh, ss, x,* or *z.*

   > church → churches     fox → foxes     dish → dishes

# Error Correction Exercises

Revise each of the following paragraphs. Look for errors in sentence structure, grammar, punctuation, mechanics, and spelling. Rewrite these paragraphs with corrections.

## EXERCISE 21

Jazz is a type of music, originating in new orleans in the early Twenties, and contained a mixture of African and European musical elements. There are a wide variety of types of jazz including: the blues, swing, bop and modern. Jazz includes both hard and soft music. Unlike rock music, jazz does not goes to extremes. Rock bands play so loud you can't understand half of the words. As a result, jazz is more relacking and enjoyable.

*Jazz is a type of music, originating in New Orleans in the early 1920s, and contains a mixture of African and European musical elements. There is a wide variety of types of jazz including the blues, swing, bop, and modern. Jazz includes both hard and soft music. Unlike rock music, jazz does not go to extremes. Rock bands play so loudly it is difficult to understand the words. As a result, jazz is more relaxing and enjoyable.*

## EXERCISE 22

every one thinks vacations are great fun but that isnt allways so. Some people are to hyper to relax when their on vaccation. My sister Sally is like that. She has to be on the move at alltimes. She can never slow down and take it easy. She goes from activity to activity at a wild pace. When Sally does have a spare moment between activities, she spends her freetime thinking about work problems and her family and their problems and what she should do about them when she gets back. Consequently, when Sally gets back from a vacation she is exhausted and more tense and upset then when she left home.

*Everyone thinks vacations are great fun, but that is not always the case. Some people are too stressed to relax on their vacation. My sister Sally is a good example. She has to be on the move at all times. She goes from activity to activity at a wild pace. When Sally does have a spare moment between activities, she spends her free time thinking about work, family problems, and what she should do about them when she gets home. Consequently, when Sally gets back from a vacation, she is exhausted and more tense and upset than when she left home.*

## EXERCISE 23

Soap operas are usually serious eposodes of different people in the world of today. There about fictuous people whom are supposed to look real. But each character has their unique prblems, crazzy relationships and nonrealistical quirks and habits.In real live, it would never happen.The actors are always getting themself into wiered and unusall situation that are so of the wall that they could never be real. Its just to unreal to have 20 looney people all good frinds.

*Soap operas are usually serious episodes about different people in the world of today. They are about fictitious people who are supposed to appear real; however, these characters have their unique problems, crazy relationships, and unrealistic quirks and habits that in real life would never happen. It is not possible for so many odd people to be good friends.*

## EXERCISE 24

Here are two forms of music, we have rock music and we have country music. First, these two sound differen. Rock music is very loud and with a high base sound, sometimes you can't even understand the words that the singer is singing. On the other hand, country music is a bit softer with a mellow but up beat sound. Although country music sometimes sounds boring, at least you can understand the lyrics when listening to it. Country singers usually have a country western accent also unlike rock singers.

*Rock and country are two kinds of music that sound very different. Rock music is very loud with a high bass sound, and sometimes you cannot even understand the words. On the other hand, country music is softer, with a mellow but upbeat sound. Although country music sometimes sounds boring, at least you can understand the lyrics.*

## EXERCISE 25

### What A Good Friend Is

I have this friend Margaret who is really not too intelligent. It took awhile before I could accept her limitations. But, I had to get to know Margaret and her feelings. We are like two hands that wash each other. I help her, she helps me. when I need her to babysit for me while I'm at work it's done. If she needs a ride to the dentist she's got it. All I need is to be given time to do them. We help each other and that is why we are friends.

Good friends; Friends that do for one another. To tell the friend the truth about something that is asked of them. And for the other to respect your views as you would theirs. A friend is there to listen if you have a problem and to suggest something to help solve the problem but, yet not telling you just what to do. Or just to be the shoulder to cry on. Good friends go places and do things together. Good Friends are always there when you need them.

*A Good Friend*

*I have a friend, Margaret, who is really not too intelligent. Once I got to know Margaret and her feelings, I could accept her limitations. I help her and she helps me. If I need her to baby-sit for me while I'm at work, it is done. If she needs a ride to the dentist, I take her. We help each other and that is why we are friends.*

*Good friends are people who help each other and respect each other's views. A friend is there to listen if you have a problem and to help solve the problem, rather than just telling you what to do. A friend will also give you a shoulder to cry on. Good friends go places and do things together and are always there when you need them.*

## EXERCISE 26

### Putting Labels on People

People tend to label someone as stupid if they are slower and takes more time in figuring out an assignment or just trying to understand directions. My friend Georgette is a good example. People make fun of her. When a person has to deal with this type of ridicule by her fellow students or friend she start to feel insecure in speaking up. She start to think she is slower mentally, she gets extremely paranoid when asked to give answer in class. She feels any answer out of her mouth will be wrong. Her self-image shoots down drastically, like a bottom less pit. that She will avoyd in answering all answers even when she's almost positive she's right. It's the possibility of being wrong that will keep her from speaking. Then when some one else gives the answer she seess she was right, she would become extremely anoid at herself for not answering the question. As a result, she start to run away from all challenges, even the slightest challenge will frighten her away. Do from the teasing of her friends, Georgette will lock herself away from trying to understand and her famous words when facing to a challenge will be I can't do it!

Therefore, when a person makes a mistake, you should think of what you say before you say it and be sure it's not going to hurt the person. You comments may help destroy that person self confidence.

*Putting Labels on People*

*People tend to label others as "stupid" if they are slower and take more time in figuring out assignments or in understanding directions. My friend Georgette is a good example. People make fun of her, and it makes her feel insecure about speaking up. She starts to doubt herself, and she gets extremely paranoid when asked to give answers in class. She is afraid to be wrong. She will avoid answering all questions even if she is almost positive that she is right. When someone else gives the answer, and she sees that she was right, she is annoyed at herself for not answering the question. As a result, she starts to run away from all challenges. Due to her friends' teasing, Georgette locks herself away; her famous words when facing a challenge are, "I can't do it!"*

*Therefore, when someone makes a mistake, it is important to think before saying something that will hurt that person. Your comments may help to destroy that person's self-confidence.*

# ELL Guide for Nonnative Speakers of English

## PART SEVEN

# TO THE STUDENT

A cartoon once showed two apprehensive cats walking into a classroom. The sign on the door read, "Barking 101." Perhaps you felt a little like one of those nervous cats when you first entered a classroom to study English. Perhaps you wondered whether you were trying to do the impossible. But you were determined. After all, English is the most widely spoken language in the world, and it is the language of international business, technology, travel, sports, and entertainment. In short, it's an extremely useful language for work and for fun.

By now, you've reached a certain comfort level with English, a significant achievement. But now, the bar is higher. Your goal is to write correct, coherent, college-level English. This textbook and ELL Guide are designed to help you reach that goal. However, the book can do the job only in combination with your time and effort.

"How does one eat an elephant?" an old joke asks. The answer is "One bite at a time." You cannot master a language in a month or even in a year, but you can speed up the ongoing process of improving your English skills by these methods:

1. **Use and study English daily, as many hours a day as you can.** Read it and speak it with friends. Study vocabulary. (Perhaps set a goal of learning four new words a day.) Seek out opportunities to hear and use English by going to museums, libraries, and English-language movies. Use the Internet to do practice exercises and communicate with other ELL students around the world. (See the list of Web sites at the end of this guide.)

2. **Trust your ear—but not always.** You've been using English a long time, so sometimes what sounds right to you *is* right, even if you don't understand why. However, also realize that, if you have been speaking English mostly with people who are also nonnative speakers, you may have "fossilized" errors. In other words, what sounds right to you, because you've heard it so much, may actually be wrong. Ask your friends who are native English speakers to correct your errors in grammar and word usage.

3. **Keep in mind that writing isn't speaking.** When you speak, you often use incomplete sentences, and that's fine, but in writing, you should use complete sentences. When you speak, intonation helps to convey your meaning; in writing, punctuation is needed to do that. Writing (especially academic writing) is more formal; it is not the place for slang.

4. **Learn to self-correct.** Listen to your own speech, and try to catch errors. Reread the writing you do for school (and not just for your English class). Reread it several times, each time looking for a different type of error or weakness. Writing is a *process*. A good piece of writing rarely comes from one draft.

5. **Remember that all four language skills—speaking, listening, reading, and writing—are interrelated.** If you work hard on one of these skills, that is likely to improve your skills in the other three areas as well. In particular, if you read a lot of published writing in English, you will see how people who know the language well construct sentences, paragraphs, and entire pieces of writing. This will improve your writing.

6. **English has the largest vocabulary of any language, and it is also a highly idiomatic language; don't depend upon your bilingual dictionary to answer all your questions about it.** You should also have an ELL dictionary. It defines words in the simplest vocabulary possible, shows you how to use words in sentences, provides definitions of idioms, explains the differences between similar words that are often confused, and does much more.

You are one of about 1.5 billion speakers of English, a truly global language. Your efforts to improve your English skills will surely enrich your life.

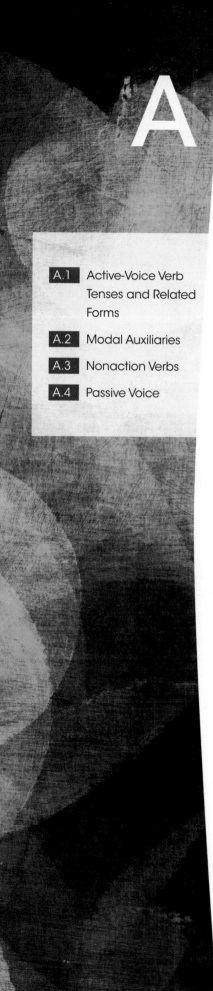

# A Verbs

## A.1 Active-Voice Verb Tenses and Related Forms

### Ways to Write About the Present

1. **Simple present tense.** Use the simple present tense for (1) actions that happen repeatedly and (2) continuing actions expressed with nonaction verbs. (See section A.3 in this Guide for a list of these verbs.) The affirmative form of the simple present is only one word. It uses the infinitive except when the subject is third-person singular. Then the verb must end in -s.

   How can a third-person singular subject be recognized? Remember that first person means the speaker or writer: *I* or *we*. Second person means the listener or reader: *you*. Third person includes everyone and everything else. *Singular* means "one."

   Use the third-person singular verb form with the following subjects:

   | | |
   |---|---|
   | AN UNCOUNTABLE NOUN | That <u>music sounds</u> beautiful. |
   | | My <u>homework is</u> difficult. |
   | SOME ABSTRACT NOUNS | Is <u>happiness</u> an achievable goal? |
   | | Is this <u>transportation</u> safe? |
   | A GERUND | <u>Being</u> late for work <u>isn't</u> a good idea. |
   | | <u>Having</u> a good job <u>is</u> important. |
   | A COLLECTIVE NOUN | My <u>family enjoys</u> picnics. |

   Singular collective nouns usually take a singular verb. For exceptions, see "Reviewing the Basics" on page 223.

   To make a third-person singular verb, add -s or -es to the infinitive. Add -es if the verb ends in *ch, sh, s, x,* or *z* (*I wash, she washes*). If the verb ends in a consonant + *y*, change the *y* to *i* and add -es (*I try/he tries*).

   | | |
   |---|---|
   | AFFIRMATIVE | <u>I want</u> a used car. |
   | | <u>Carlos fixes</u> cars. |
   | | <u>Carlos has</u> his own repair shop. |

   (*Note:* The verb *have* has an irregular third-person singular form: *has*.)

For most questions, use *do* except for third-person singular, which uses *does*:

> Why <u>do you need</u> a car?
>
> Why <u>does a car need</u> gas?

For questions with a question word or phrase as the subject, don't use a helping verb.

> <u>Who needs</u> a car?
>
> <u>How many Americans own</u> cars?

For negative sentences, use *don't* (or *do not*) for all subjects except third-person singular. Use *doesn't* (or *does not*) for third-person singular. Don't put an *-s* or *-es* on the main verb.

> NEGATIVE    <u>Horses don't have</u> toes.
>
> <u>My dog doesn't have</u> long ears.

When *have* is the main verb, Americans use a helping verb. They don't say, "My dog hasn't long ears."

When using the verb *be*, use *am*, *is*, or *are* for affirmative. Use *am not*, *isn't*, or *aren't* for negative. For questions with *be*, put the correct form of *be* before the subject.

> <u>Are you</u> a new student here? <u>Am I</u> in this class? <u>Is this book</u> yours?

2. **Present continuous tense.** Use *am, is,* or *are* + _____*ing*. Use this tense for actions happening at this moment or during a time period not yet ended. It can also be used for future when a future time expression is stated or implied.

> AFFIRMATIVE    <u>I am painting</u> my living room this week.
>
> <u>We're sitting</u> in class right now.
>
> QUESTIONS    <u>Are you enjoying</u> this flight?
>
> <u>How many people are flying</u> on this plane?
>
> NEGATIVE    <u>I'm not writing</u> my essay tonight.
>
> <u>Joe and I aren't playing</u> tennis tomorrow.

## When an Action or Condition Continues from Past to Present

1. **Present perfect tense.** Use *has* for third-person singular, *have* for all other subjects. Then add the past participle of the main verb. The past participle may be irregular.

2. **Present perfect continuous tense.** Use *has been* for third-person singular, *have been* for all other subjects. Then add the *-ing* form (the present participle) of the main verb.

Use these two tenses for actions or conditions that started in the past and continue into the present. For nonaction verbs, such as *like* and *want*, which cannot be used in a continuous tense, use present perfect. For many sentences, you can use either tense.

| | |
|---|---|
| AFFIRMATIVE | I have <u>spoken</u> English for many years. |
| | I have <u>been speaking</u> English since I <u>was</u> a child. |
| QUESTIONS | How long <u>have you been speaking</u> English? |
| | Who <u>has been teaching</u> you? |
| | <u>Have you ever been</u> to England? (meaning "at any time in your life") |
| NEGATIVE | My brother <u>hasn't learned</u> any English yet. |
| | My sisters <u>haven't</u> either. |

*Note:* For indefinite past uses of the present perfect, see the following section on past tenses.

## Ways to Write About the Past

1. **Simple past tense.** Regular verbs end in *-ed*; irregular verbs have other forms. Use this tense to write about past actions, especially those that occurred only once. Use *did* in most questions and negatives. Use the infinitive of the main verb with *did* or *didn't*.

| | |
|---|---|
| AFFIRMATIVE | I <u>went</u> to a movie last Saturday. |
| | I <u>walked</u> all the way there. |
| QUESTIONS | <u>Did</u> you <u>like</u> the movie? |
| | Who <u>went</u> with you? |
| NEGATIVE | I <u>didn't like</u> the movie. |
| | I <u>didn't go</u> with anyone. |

When using the verb *be*, use *was* for singular and *were* for plural. The verb after *you* is always plural.

Why <u>were you</u> late? (This might be asked of one person or more than one.)

The trains <u>weren't</u> on time this morning.

2. **Past continuous tense.** Use *was* or *were* + _____*ing*. Use this tense to write about actions that continued for a period of time.

I <u>was doing</u> homework all evening, so I missed a good TV show.

Use this tense when a longer, earlier action is interrupted by a shorter action:

They <u>were driving</u> too fast when the accident <u>happened</u>.

Use the past continuous after *while*; use the simple past after *when*.

| AFFIRMATIVE | While I <u>was driving</u> on the highway, another car hit mine. |
|---|---|
| QUESTIONS | <u>Were</u> you <u>listening</u> to the radio when the accident happened? |
| | <u>Who was driving</u> when the accident happened? |
| NEGATIVE | I was driving, but I <u>wasn't driving</u> fast at all. |

3. **Present perfect tense.** Use *have* or *has* + the past participle. This tense (or the simple past) can be used to write about a past action if the sentence doesn't tell *when* it happened. Don't use it with *ago* phrases or *when* clauses, because these tell a definite past time. Present perfect is often used to tell about repeated past actions. Use *has* with third-person singular subjects.

| AFFIRMATIVE | <u>I've visited</u> your country many times. |
|---|---|
| | My brother <u>has been</u> there, too. |
| QUESTIONS | What countries <u>have you visited</u>? |
| | <u>Who has traveled</u> with you? |
| NEGATIVE | I <u>haven't visited</u> any South American countries yet. |

4. **Past perfect tense.** Use *had* + the past participle. Use this tense when there are two past actions in the same sentence. Put the earlier action in past perfect and the later one in simple past. (*Note:* If there is a word such as *before* or *after* that clarifies which action occurred first, you can use the simple past tense for both verbs.)

| AFFIRMATIVE | I <u>had already studied</u> English before I <u>came</u> to the United States. |
|---|---|
| QUESTION | <u>Had</u> you <u>thought</u> about leaving home for a long time before you <u>left</u>? |
| NEGATIVE | I <u>hadn't spoken</u> a word of English before I <u>arrived</u> here. |

5. **Past perfect continuous tense.** Use *had been* + _____*ing*. Use this tense when a sentence has two past actions, and the earlier one continued for a while.

| AFFIRMATIVE | I <u>had been living</u> in Paris for many years before I <u>came</u> here. |
|---|---|
| QUESTIONS | <u>Whom had you been living with</u> before you got your own apartment? |
| NEGATIVE | I <u>hadn't been sharing</u> an apartment with anybody until I <u>came</u> to the United States. |

6. **The form *used to* is followed by an infinitive (base form) verb with no ending.** Use this verb form to write about something that was true in the past but isn't anymore. *Used to* tells about actions that happened many times or conditions that lasted a long time.

| AFFIRMATIVE | I <u>used to live</u> in South America, but now I live in North America. |
|---|---|

## Ways to Write About the Future

1. **Simple future tense.** Use *will* or *shall* + the infinitive verb form. Use the simple future for something that will happen very soon, for promises, and for formal speech or writing.

> Salesman to customer: "I'll get those shoes for you right away."
>
> I'm sorry my essay is late. I'll turn it in by Monday.
>
> Our economy will be in trouble if inflation continues.

*Note:* When the verb in the main clause is in the future, the verb in a subordinating time clause is in the present tense. If it's a third-person-singular verb, it must end in -*s*.

| | |
|---|---|
| AFFIRMATIVE | When Boris comes to visit Chicago, we'll go sightseeing. |
| QUESTIONS | Who will come with him? Where will he stay? |
| NEGATIVE | He won't stay in my apartment. It's too small. (*will not = won't*) |

2. **Use the present tense of *be* + *going to* + the infinitive of the main verb to talk about general plans**, especially in casual conversation. Contractions are usually used.

| | |
|---|---|
| AFFIRMATIVE | I'm going to be at work until 10 o'clock tonight. |
| QUESTIONS | When are you going to quit that terrible job? |
| NEGATIVE | I'm not going to leave my current job until I find another one. |

3. **Future continuous tense.** Use *will be* + the present participle (the -*ing* form) of the main verb. Use this tense to write about continuing actions in the future.

| | |
|---|---|
| AFFIRMATIVE | The plane will be arriving late, but my uncle will be waiting for me. |
| QUESTIONS | Will you be staying with your uncle? Will you be paying him rent? |
| NEGATIVE | I won't be paying him any rent until I find a job. |

4. **Present tenses for future actions.** You can use either of the present tenses to talk about the future if there is a time expression or some other indication of future meaning.

> John is coming to Los Angeles soon.
>
> His plane arrives next Monday at noon.

5. **Future perfect.** Use *will have* + the past participle. Use this tense to write about an action that is now in the future but will be in the past when a stated future time comes.

> By next summer, I will have finished two years of college.

6. **Future perfect continuous.** Use *will have been* + the present participle. This tense is also used for future actions that will, at some later time, be past.

> I will have been attending this school for four years by the time I graduate.

# A.2 Modal Auxiliaries

"Modals are really strange and confusing," one ELL student remarked. It's true. These ten little words are used to convey a great many different meanings such as ability, possibility, permission, opportunity, advice, obligation, necessity, a promise, a request, an offer, an inference—or the negative of any of these. The following chart lists uses and examples.

| MODALS | USES | SAMPLE SENTENCES |
|---|---|---|
| **will/would/shall** | future | I'll go with you to the movie. |
| | a promise | We'll help you tomorrow. |
| | subjunctive | I would help you if I had time. |
| | wants | I'd like some coffee, please. |
| | future, first person | We shall win this election! |
| **can/could** | present ability | Miguel can swim very well. |
| | suggestion | We could go to a movie or watch TV. |
| | past (in)ability | I couldn't swim when I was a child. |
| | past opportunity not taken | We could have gone swimming, but we played tennis instead. |
| **may/might** | possibility | He may (might) be in New York City. |
| | past possibility | He may (might) have gone to New York City. |
| **should/ought to** | advice | You should quit smoking. |
| | obligation | I should visit my sick aunt. |
| | past mistake | I shouldn't have eaten six hot dogs. |
| **must** | necessity | You must pay taxes. |
| | inference | Lin isn't home. She must be at the library. |
| | inference about the past | She must have gone to the library. (She probably went to the library.) |

*Note:* When writing about the past, don't use *must* for the meaning of necessity. Use *had to*:

I had to go to the doctor yesterday because I felt very sick.

## Modals and Contractions

1. The only modals that have contractions are

    *would* = 'd (the same contraction as is used for *had*): *I'd, he'd, they'd*, etc.
    *will* = 'll: *I'll, she'll, we'll*, etc.

2. The irregular contraction for *will not* is *won't*.

3. Most modals can be contracted with *not* (*can't, couldn't, shouldn't*, etc.), but Americans rarely contract *may, ought,* or *shall* with *not*.

4. When speaking, people may say, "Darren'll be here soon." However, in a piece of writing, don't contract a noun and a verb. Write "Darren will be here soon." or "He'll be here soon."

## A Few Rules for Using Modals

1. **Never put an ending on a modal verb.** Unlike most other auxiliary (helping) verbs, modal verbs do not have endings that tell person or tense.

2. **Never put an ending on the verb immediately after a modal.** Use the infinitive.

3. **Note that the modal verb phrase is the same for both present and future.**

   I can help you now. (or) I can help you tomorrow.

4. **Don't use *to* after a modal except for *ought to*.**

   She ought to get a dog.
   She should get a dog.

5. **Use *shall* only with *I* or *we*.** *Shall* is usually used for more serious matters and/or in more formal situations. Americans don't use it much except for offers such as "Shall I get you some coffee?" or suggestions such as "Shall we go now?"

## Why Are Modals Confusing?

The main reason modals are confusing is that most of them have more than one meaning.

1. ***Could* + an infinitive verb has two meanings.**

   | FUTURE | We could buy a car next month. |
   |--------|--------------------------------|
   | PAST | I couldn't speak English last year. |

2. ***Could have* + a past participle has two meanings.**

   | PAST OPPORTUNITY NOT TAKEN | We could have bought a big house, but we liked this one. |
   |----------------------------|----------------------------------------------------------|
   | A PAST POSSIBILITY | "Why wasn't Brian at his sister's birthday party last Saturday?"<br>"We're not sure. He could have been out of town that day." |

   *Could* is the only modal that has both a two-word and a three-word form for talking about the past. The negative uses of these forms also have different meanings.

   | LACK OF ABILITY | I couldn't go to my friend's house last night because I had to study. |
   |-----------------|----------------------------------------------------------------------|
   | IMPOSSIBILITY | You couldn't have seen me at Lisa's party. I wasn't there. |

3. ***Should have* plus a past participle refers to a past mistake.** It has a negative meaning. It means the subject didn't do something and regrets not doing it. On the other hand, *shouldn't have* plus a past participle means the subject did something and regrets that.

   I shouldn't have bought a motorcycle last year.

   I should have gotten a car instead.

4. *May* can mean permission or possibility (or the negatives of these).

PERMISSION    You <u>may not bring</u> your nail clippers on the airplane.

POSSIBILITY    You <u>may get</u> into trouble if you try.

5. **Many other expressions have the same meanings as modal phrases:**

| | |
|---|---|
| You <u>may not smoke</u> on the airplane. | You're <u>not allowed to smoke</u> on the airplane. |
| I <u>must go</u> home soon. | I <u>have to go</u> home soon. |
| You <u>shouldn't drink</u> any more beer. | You'd <u>better not drink</u> any more beer. |
| You <u>can't drive</u> without a license. | You're <u>not supposed to drive</u> without a license. |
| I <u>would rather have</u> tea than coffee. | I'd <u>prefer</u> tea to coffee. |

# A.3 Nonaction Verbs

Some verbs listed in the following chart are never, or usually not, used in continuous tenses.

| VERBS NOT USUALLY USED IN CONTINUOUS TENSES |
|---|
| **Sensory perception**: *see, hear, taste, smell* |
| I <u>see</u> our teacher, Dr. Franklin, over there. |
| **Mental activity:** *believe, forget, mean, know, think, recognize, remember, understand* |
| I <u>believe</u> he saw me, too. |
| **Ownership/possession:** *belong, have, own, possess* |
| She <u>owns</u> a boat, but she <u>doesn't have</u> a car. |
| **Feelings/opinions/attitudes:** *appreciate, dislike, hate, love, need, prefer, seem, want* |
| Dr. Franklin <u>loves</u> her five dogs, but she <u>dislikes</u> all other animals. |
| **Other:** *cost* |
| Textbooks <u>cost</u> a lot of money these days. |

# A.4 Passive Voice

## How to Make Passive Voice Tenses

1. **In active voice sentences,** the subject performs the action of the verb.

   <u>People speak</u> English all over the world.

   <u>No one has seen</u> him for a week.

   **In passive voice sentences,** the subject does not do the action; something happens to the subject.

   <u>English is spoken</u> all over the world.

   <u>He hasn't been seen</u> for a week.

2. **Of the 12 active voice tenses, eight are used in passive.** To make a passive verb, put the verb *be* in the tense you want, and then add the past participle (see chart).

| EIGHT PASSIVE VOICE TENSES | |
|---|---|
| **Tense** | **Example** |
| Simple present | Every four years, a president is elected in the United States. |
| Present continuous | Is a president being elected this year? |
| Present perfect | Sometimes the same candidate has been elected to serve two terms. |
| Simple past | Franklin Roosevelt was elected president four times from 1932 to 1944. |
| Past continuous | Was your family living in the United States when those elections were being held? |
| Past perfect | President Roosevelt had recently been elected for his fourth term when he died in April 1945. |
| Simple future | The next presidential election won't be held until 2016. |
| Future perfect | By December 2016, another presidential election will have been held. |

3. **Passive sentences can also be made with modals.**

   For the present or future, use a modal + *be* + the past participle.

   > The dog should be fed. (This is advice. The poor dog is hungry.)

   For the past, use a modal + *have been* + the past participle:

   > The dog should have been fed. (He wasn't fed. That was a mistake.)

4. **There are only two continuous tenses used in passive: present and past.**

   To make these tenses, use *being*. Use *am/is/are being* for present and *was/were being* for past.

   > The injured player was being carried from the field when the ambulance came.

5. **Make a passive tense negative by making the first verb negative.**

   > My dog won't be fed again until seven o'clock.
   > He hasn't been fed since breakfast.

6. **Make questions with the passive voice the usual way: put the first helping verb before the subject.**

   > Why won't your dog be fed sooner?
   > Is your cat being fed right now?

## When to Use Passive Voice

Most writing should be in the active voice, but there are times when the passive voice is the better choice. Here are the main reasons for using the passive voice.

1.  **The doer of the action is unknown.**

    This house was built 50 years ago.

2.  **The doer of the action isn't important.**

    Q: Is this bread fresh?

    A: It was baked this morning. (It doesn't matter who baked it.)

3.  **The person or people who did the action are obvious.**

    I was born in April.

    *You don't need to say, "My mother bore me in April." or "My mother gave birth to me in April." Everyone knows that your mother did it.*

4.  **The speaker does not want to mention the source of certain information.**

    I was told that Julio and Louise are getting divorced.

5.  **Passive is often used to talk or write about the creation of a work of art.**

    *War and Peace* was written by Tolstoy.

    Use *by* before the doer of the action in passive.

6.  **Passive is often used to avoid a vague *you, they*, or *someone*.**

    The store will be remodeled next month.

    *Not*   They will remodel the store next month.

    Papers can be typed in the computer lab.

    *Not*   You can type a paper in the computer lab.

7.  **Passive is often used in scientific and other scholarly writing.**

    Five explosive chemicals were put into the test tube before the lab blew up.

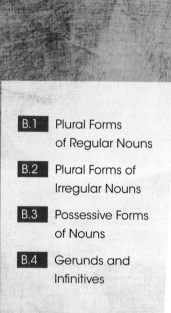

# B Nouns

## B.1 Plural Forms of Regular Nouns

Two sections of "Reviewing the Basics" give you a comprehensive review of noun usage. Section A.1 (p. 585) covers the seven categories of nouns. Section E.1 (p. 650) reviews which nouns need to be capitalized. The section on avoiding subject–verb agreement errors on page 220 provides explanation and practice with subject–verb agreement. Here is a chart of spelling rules for plural nouns.

| SPELLING RULES FOR PLURAL NOUNS | |
| --- | --- |
| **1.** Make most nouns plural by adding *-s.* | *school/schools   desk/desks* |
| **2.** When the singular form ends in *ch, sh, s, x,* or *z,* add *-es.* | *tax/taxes   watch/watches* |
| **3.** When the singular ends in *f* or *fe,* change it to *-ves.* | *knife/knives   shelf/shelves* <br> exceptions: *chiefs, roofs* |
| **4.** When the singular ends in a consonant + *y,* change *y* to *i,* then add *-es.* If it ends in a vowel + *y,* just add *-s.* | *city/cities   toy/toys* |
| **5.** When the singular ends in a consonant + *o,* add *-es.* When it ends in a vowel + *o,* just add *-s.* | *tomato/tomatoes   hero/heroes* <br> *studio/studios   ratio/ratios   radio/radios* <br> **musical exceptions:** *solos, pianos, cellos,* <br> *sopranos* |

## B.2 Plural Forms of Irregular Nouns

Nouns that do not form their plurals by adding *-s* or *-es* are called **irregular nouns.** Here are some examples.

1. **Some common irregular plurals:**

   *foot/feet   tooth/teeth   child/children   woman/women   man/men*

2. **Some academic irregular plurals:**

   *alumnus/alumni   analysis/analyses   crisis/crises   datum/data*

   *hypothesis/hypotheses   parenthesis/parentheses   thesis/theses*

3. **Some words with both a regular and an irregular plural:**

   *person/people* or *persons*

   *appendix/appendices* or *appendixes   medium/media* or *mediums*

   *memorandum/memoranda* or *memorandums   syllabus/syllabi* or *syllabuses*

4. Some words with only one form for singular and plural:

   *deer, fish, sheep*

5. Some words with a plural form only:

   *pants, glasses* (for eyes), *clothes, groceries*

6. Some words that look plural but can be singular:

   *news* (always singular), *series, means*

# B.3 Possessive Forms of Nouns

To make a noun possessive, do the following:

1. **Add an apostrophe + -*s* to all singular nouns and to plural irregular nouns.**

   *Columbus's ships    the library's book collection    the children's home*

2. **Add just an apostrophe to nouns that are plural and regular (end in -*s*).**

   *the students' desks    the professors' office    two cities' museums*

For more explanation and examples, see "Reviewing the Basics," D.5, "Apostrophes" (p. 646).

# B.4 Gerunds and Infinitives

Gerunds and infinitives are called *verbals* because they are words made from verbs. However, they function as nouns in a sentence. A *gerund* is the same form as a present participle, the verb used to make continuous tenses; it is the infinitive + *-ing* (*waiting, running,* etc.). An *infinitive* is the base form of a verb, usually preceded by *to* (*to wait, to run,* etc.).

| COMMON USES OF GERUNDS AND INFINITIVES | |
|---|---|
| **1.** As subjects of clauses, either a gerund or an infinitive can be used. The gerund is used more often. | Studying is hard work.<br>To study is hard work.<br>Raising children is difficult.<br>(*Raising* is the subject, not *children,* so the verb is singular.) |
| **2.** As objects of prepositions, only gerunds (not infinitives) can be used. Use a gerund even after the preposition *to.* | Maria is interested in starting her own business.<br>She's looking forward to being her own boss. |
| **3.** When using a verbal as the object of a verb, sometimes you need a gerund, sometimes an infinitive; sometimes either one is okay. | Maria wants to start her own business. She will enjoy being her own boss. She likes being (or to be) the boss. |

Try to learn the common verbs that take only gerunds as direct objects if the direct object is a verbal. (The list includes *admit, avoid, consider, delay, deny, dislike, enjoy, miss, practice, suggest,* and many more.) Once you know these, you can safely use the full infinitive (with *to*) for most others. For a longer list of verbs followed by gerunds and other information about gerund and infinitive constructions, go online to the first Web site listed in section G of this ESL Guide.

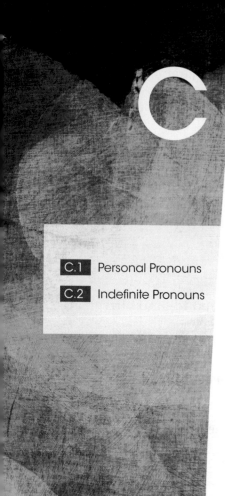

# C

# Pronouns

Two sections of this book provide explanations and practice with pronoun usage. To review pronouns, read Chapter 9 (pp. 262–273) and the following section in "Reviewing the Basics": A.2 (pp. 586–587).

# C.1 Personal Pronouns

The following chart shows the uses of personal pronouns:

| PERSONAL PRONOUNS | | | | |
|---|---|---|---|---|
| Subject Pronouns | Object Pronouns | Possessive Pronouns (As Adjectives) | Possessive Pronouns | Reflexive Pronouns |
| I | me | my | mine | myself |
| you | you | your | yours | yourself (-ves) |
| he | him | his | his | himself |
| she | her | her | hers | herself |
| it | it | its | — | itself |
| we | us | our | ours | ourselves |
| they | them | their | theirs | themselves |

## Subject Pronouns

1. **Use a subject pronoun (*I, we,* etc.) as the subject of a clause and after a linking verb.**

   They (*not* Them) are nice.

   It is he. (*not* him)

2. **When using a compound subject, use subject pronouns.**

   Sandi and I (*not* me) are working on this project together.

3. **When using pronouns in compound subjects, it's polite for the speaker or writer to refer to himself or herself last and to the listener or reader first.**

   You and they (*not* They and you) can meet with Santiago and me on Friday.

4. **Remember that *you* takes a plural verb even when referring to only one person.**

### Object Pronouns

1. **Use object pronouns after a verb.**

   Please help <u>them</u> do this research.

2. **Use object pronouns after a preposition.**

   The professor gave our graded papers to <u>us</u>.

### Pronouns Used as Possessive Adjectives

1. **Use the possessive adjective pronouns before a noun.** For example, use *our* and *my*, not *us* and *mine*.

   Dr. Nguyen called <u>our</u> pharmacy to give <u>my</u> prescription to the pharmacist.

2. **Be careful about spelling!** Don't confuse *his* with *he's* (*he is*), *your* with *you're* (*you are*), or *their* with *they're* (*they are*) or *there*.

### Possessive Pronouns Used as Pronouns

1. **These forms are not used before a noun. They replace the noun.**

   These books aren't Juanita's. They're <u>mine</u>. (*not* <u>mine books</u>)

2. **Compare these forms with the ones used as possessive adjectives.** Note that, except for *mine*, the forms used as pronouns all end in -*s*. Only *his* is the same in both forms.

### Reflexive Pronouns

Reflexive pronouns have two main uses.

1. **They are used when the subject did, does, or will do something to himself or herself.**

   I hurt <u>myself</u>.   *but*   My dog hurt <u>me</u>.

2. **They are used for emphasis.**

   The chancellor <u>herself</u> visited our class. (She didn't send someone else.)

*Note*: Reflexive pronouns have a singular and a plural form for the second person. To one person say, "Did you hurt <u>yourself</u>?" To more than one, say "Did you hurt <u>yourselves</u>?"

# C.2 Indefinite Pronouns

Study the list of indefinite pronouns in "Reviewing the Basics," A.2., "Pronouns" (p. 589). Use a singular verb with all pronouns listed in the singular columns, even if they refer to several people or things.

<u>Everything</u> <u>is</u> ready, and <u>everyone</u> <u>is</u> here.

# D Adjectives and Adverbs

To read about types of adjectives, see "Reviewing the Basics," A.4, "Adjectives" (p. 595). To review comparative and superlative patterns and irregular adjectives and adverbs, see "Reviewing the Basics," C.4, "Correct Adjective and Adverb Use" (p. 628). For samples of comparisons of equality using *as . . . as,* look in the ELL Guide E.2, "Transitional Words and Phrases: Transitions for Equality, Addition, and Similarity" (p. 692).

## D.1 Some Grammatical Reminders

1. *Well* is usually an adverb, but it is also used as an adjective to mean "healthy."

2. *Much* is used in questions and negative statements but not in affirmative statements.

    > Does he have <u>much</u> money?
    >
    > Yes, he has <u>a lot of</u> (<u>a great deal of</u>) money.

3. **Which form should you use—an adjective or an adverb?** If the word describes a noun or pronoun, use an adjective. If it describes a verb, adjective, or another adverb, use an adverb. If it tells *how* something is, was, or will be done, use an adverb.

    > She is a <u>quick</u> runner.   *but*   She runs <u>quickly</u>.

4. **Most adjectives can be made into adverbs by adding *-ly*.** However, some words can be adjectives or adverbs; for example, *hard* and *fast.*

    | ADJECTIVE | Carlos is a hard worker. |
    |---|---|
    | ADVERB | He works <u>hard</u>. |

    Don't use *hardly* as an adverb for *hard. Hardly* means "almost not at all."

    > He has <u>hardly</u> any money. (He has almost no money.)

5. **Note these spelling changes when making comparative and superlative forms:**

    | Y TO I | healthy, healthier, healthiest |
    |---|---|
    | DOUBLING | big, bigger, biggest |

    To review doubling rules, see "Reviewing the Basics," E.6, "Six Useful Spelling Rules," #4 and #5 (p. 657).

# D.2 Relative (Adjective) Clauses

1. **A relative (adjective) clause, like all clauses, has a subject and verb.** However, a relative clause isn't a complete sentence; it's a dependent clause, so it must be attached to a main idea.

   > The huge statue <u>that stands in New York Harbor</u> is called the Statue of Liberty.

2. **A relative clause can be introduced by one of these words:** *who, whom, that, which, whose, whoever, whomever, when,* or *where.*

3. **With restrictive clauses, which identify or limit the subject, no commas are used.**

4. **With nonrestrictive clauses, which do not identify or limit the meaning of the subject, commas are used before the clause begins and also at the end—unless the clause comes at the end of a sentence.** See examples of restrictive and nonrestrictive clauses in the following chart.

   | WHEN TO USE *WHO, THAT,* AND *WHICH* | |
   |---|---|
   | Use *who* . . . | to talk about a person or people (singular or plural):<br><br>I know the name of the man *who* designed the Statue of Liberty. |
   | Use *that* . . . | to talk about a person, animal, or thing (singular or plural) for restrictive clauses only (the ones without commas):<br><br>The day *that* the statue was unveiled there was a big celebration. |
   | Use *which* . . . | to talk about things and animals only; generally, for nonrestrictive clauses:<br><br>Liberty's right arm, *which* is high in the air, holds a torch. |

5. **An adjective clause describes a noun or, occasionally, a pronoun.** It must be placed immediately after the word it describes. Otherwise, the sentence might be confusing.

   | INCORRECT | The Statue of Liberty is in New York Harbor, <u>which was built by Frederic Bartholdi.</u> |
   |---|---|
   | CORRECT | The Statue of Liberty, <u>which was built by Frederic Bartholdi,</u> is in New York Harbor. |

   (The statue, not the harbor, was built by Bartholdi.)

6. ***Whose* is the possessive form of *who*.** It is used to indicate a relationship or ownership. The usual pattern is a noun, *whose*, another noun.

   > The woman <u>whose poem</u> is written on Liberty's pedestal is Emma Lazarus.

7. **Warning! Don't use *what* to begin an adjective clause.** *What* is used to introduce noun clauses. Noun clauses answer the question *who* or *what* about the verb.

   | NOUN CLAUSE | Lydia asked <u>what material the statue was made of.</u> "Copper," a <u>guide said.</u> |
   |---|---|

8. **What's the difference between *who* and *whom*?** *Who* is a subject pronoun, like *I* and *they*; *whom* is an object pronoun, like *me* and *them*. Americans seldom use *whom* in informal speaking or writing, but it is appropriate in serious speeches and academic writing. Use *whom* as the object of a verb or a preposition.

| | |
|---|---|
| *WHO* AS A SUBJECT | Bartholdi is the man <u>who</u> designed the Statue of Liberty. |
| *WHOM* AS THE OBJECT OF THE VERB USED | The woman <u>whom</u> Bartholdi used as the model for the face was probably his mother. |
| *WHOM* AS THE OBJECT OF A PREPOSITION | The guide <u>whom</u> Lydia spoke to was very polite. <br> or <br> The guide to <u>whom</u> Lydia spoke was very polite. |

# Transitional Words and Phrases

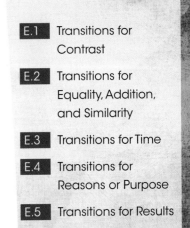

Transitions are words and phrases used within sentences, between sentences, or between paragraphs to help readers understand how one idea relates to the next.

# E.1 Transitions for Contrast

There are several ways to express an idea that ends with a surprising result or condition.

## Coordinating Conjunctions (*but* and *yet*)

1. ***Yet*, which often means "up to now," is also a synonym for *but*.** When using *but* or *yet* as a coordinating conjunction (connecting two complete ideas that could be separate sentences), place a comma before the transition.

   > I like coffee, <u>but</u> I never drink it. (or) I like coffee, <u>yet</u> I never drink it.

2. **Do not use a comma after a coordinating conjunction if the idea that follows is not a complete thought.** To be a complete thought, the clause must have a subject, verb, and complete idea.

   | NO COMMAS | I like <u>dogs but</u> not cats. |
   |---|---|
   | | We saw <u>tigers but</u> didn't see elephants at the zoo. |

   There is no subject after *but* in the examples above.

   | COMMAS | I like <u>dogs, but I</u> don't like cats. |
   |---|---|
   | | We saw the <u>tigers, but we</u> didn't see elephants. |

   *I* is the subject after *but* in the first example. *We* is the subject after *but* in the second example.

## Subordinating Conjunctions (*although, even though, though, and while*)

1. ***Although, even though*, and *though* all mean the same and are grammatically the same.** Note that *although* is one word, but *even though* is two words. *While*, which is often used to connect two actions happening at the same time, is also a contrast word meaning *but*. Never write clauses that begin with subordinating conjunctions as complete sentences.

   | INCORRECT | <u>Even though Joe is in debt.</u> He bought his wife a diamond necklace. |
   |---|---|
   | CORRECT | Even though Joe is in debt, he bought his wife a diamond necklace. |

2. **Also, put the more important idea in the main (independent) clause and the less important idea in the subordinate (dependent) clause.**

| INCORRECT | Even though Joe bought his wife a diamond necklace, he is in debt. |
| --- | --- |
| CORRECT | Even though Joe is in debt, he bought his wife a diamond necklace. |

3. **Sentences with subordinating conjunctions are reversible.** Either clause can come first.

| CORRECT | Even though Joe is in debt, he bought his wife a diamond necklace. |
| --- | --- |
| CORRECT | Joe bought his wife a diamond necklace even though he's in debt. |

## Conjunctive Adverbs (*however, nevertheless, still,* and *nonetheless*)

When using one of these contrast words, place a semicolon before the transitional word and a comma after it, or use a period before the conjunctive adverb and a comma after it.

| INCORRECT | She loved the necklace, however, she returned it. |
| --- | --- |
| CORRECT | She loved the necklace; however, she returned it. |

**Warning:** The other contrast conjunctive adverbs have a more limited meaning than *however.* Use *nevertheless, still,* or *nonetheless* when the first clause states a truth and the second clause (which usually has the same subject) states a surprising fact about that truth.

Marcia is very smart; nevertheless, (*or* however) she doesn't get good grades.

Jose is a good student; however, (*not* nevertheless) his brother isn't.

## Phrases that Indicate Contrast

Write a subject and verb after *in spite of the fact that.*

In spite of the fact that it's raining, I want to take a walk.

Don't use a subject and verb after *despite.*

Despite the rain, I want to take a walk.

# E.2 Transitions for Equality, Addition, and Similarity

## Some Patterns for Discussing Things, Places, or People that Are the Same or Similar

1. **Use helping verbs to complete comparisons with short forms.**

New York City has a lot of skyscrapers, and *so does* Chicago.

New York City has a lot of skyscrapers, and Chicago *does, too.*

2. **Use a noun (not an adjective) after *the same*.**

    He is the same height as his father. (*not* the same tall).
    New York's skyscrapers are not the same style as Chicago's.

3. **Use *similarly* or *likewise* between two complete ideas.**

    Chicago has a lot of skyscrapers; similarly (*or* likewise), New York City is famous for its skyscrapers. (You can use a period or a semicolon between the clauses.)

4. **Use *like* before a noun (or an adjective and a noun). Use *alike* after a verb.**

    Chicago, like New York City, has a lot of skyscrapers.
    Chicago and New York City are alike (*or* the same) in this way: both have skyscrapers.

## Word Pairs to Discuss Similarities

Both Orville Wright and his brother Wilbur worked on the invention of the airplane.

Neither Orville nor Wilbur is alive today. (Note the singular verb with *neither*.)

Not only did Stephanie Kwolek develop new polymer fibers, but she also invented Kevlar, which is used to make bulletproof vests.

## Words to Use to Add Similar Things, Places, or People

1. **Use the coordinating conjunction *and*. Use a comma when *and* connects two complete ideas.**

    Edison was a famous inventor, and so was Alexander Graham Bell.

2. **Use the conjunctive adverbs *besides, moreover, furthermore,* and *also*.** (Don't confuse *besides* with *beside*, which means "next to.")

    Tourists can visit Edison's home in New Jersey; besides, his home in Florida is open to the public.

3. **Use the phrases *in addition* and *in addition to*.**

    In addition to my home phone, I also have an office phone, a cell phone, an e-mail account, and a Facebook page. Why couldn't you get in touch with me?

    I have three phone numbers; in addition, I have three e-mail accounts.

# E.3 Transitions for Time

1. **One action happened, happens, or will happen after another action.**

   Any of these—*when, as soon as, once,* or *after*—can be inserted into the blank below:

   > I'll get a full-time job _____ I finish school.
   >
   > *As soon as* means "immediately after."

   *Then* or *next* can be inserted after a semicolon or a period but not after a comma.

   | | |
   |---|---|
   | INCORRECT | I'll finish school, then I'll get a full-time job. |
   | CORRECT | I'll finish school; then, I'll get a full-time job. (OR) I'll finish school, and then I'll get a full-time job. |

2. **Two actions happened, happen, or will happen at the same time.**

   > While I was watching TV, my roommate was studying. (complex sentence)
   >
   > I was watching TV; meanwhile, my roommate was studying. (compound sentence)

3. **An action continued, continues, or will continue up to a stated time. Then the first action ends.**

   > I'll wait here until Linette arrives.

4. **An action continued from a stated time in the past up to the present.**

   > I've been waiting for Linette since noon.

5. **An action will happen if something else doesn't happen (or vice versa).**

   > I'll eat lunch alone unless Linette arrives.
   >
   > I won't eat lunch alone unless Linette never arrives.

# E.4 Transitions for Reasons or Purpose

1. **Use a subject and verb after *because* but not after *because of*.**

   > I took a Canadian Rockies tour because I wanted to see the beautiful scenery.
   >
   > My brother couldn't go with me because of his job (or) because he had to work.

2. **Either *so* or *so that* can be used before a reason or a purpose.**

   > We went to the International Peace Park so that we could see the mountains and glaciers.

3. **Before a purpose or reason, an infinitive or *in order* + an infinitive can also be used.**

> We took a cruise on Waterton Lake <u>to look</u> for mountain goats and other wild animals.
>
> We went to Banff <u>in order to see</u> this picturesque town beloved by skiers.

# E.5 Transitions for Results

1. **Use the coordinating conjunction *so* preceded by a comma to express a result.**

> We didn't have much rain during the trip<u>, so</u> our trip was very nice.

2. **In the following sentence, you can put any of these in the blank: *therefore, consequently*, or *as a result*.**

> I enjoyed my Canadian trip; _____, I'm taking another one next summer.

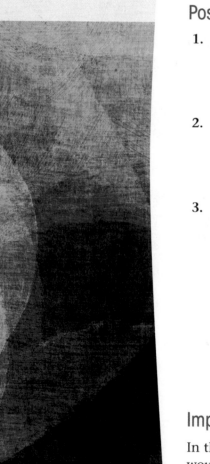

# F Conditional Statements and Subjunctive Verb Forms

## F.1 Statements with *If* Clauses

*If* statements are of two main types: (1) those about a possibility and (2) those about something that cannot possibly happen (or have happened), at least not within the stated time period. Both types are reversible; the *if* clause can come first or second.

### Possibility: Past, Present, and Future

1.  **Some statements express uncertainty about the past.**

    > Julia's children probably cried all morning if their trip was cancelled.
    > (The speaker doesn't know if their trip was cancelled or not.)

2.  **Some statements express uncertainty about what's happening in the present.**

    > If it's raining in L.A. now, Julia and the children may be at home.

3.  **Some statements express uncertainty about the future.** These are about what might happen under certain circumstances.

    > If it stops raining soon, Julia and the children will go to Disney World.

    Other ways to express uncertainty about the future are the following:

    > If my car starts, I'll go out. If not, I'll stay home.
    > I'll go out unless my car doesn't start. I won't go out unless my car starts.
    > If my car starts, I'll go out; otherwise, I'll stay home.

### Impossibility: Subjunctive Statements

In these subjunctive sentences, the speaker or writer is imagining that things would be different if something impossible could (or did) happen.

1.  **Present unreal, active voice.**

    > If cars had wings, they could fly. (They don't have wings, so they can't fly.)

    The verb in the *if* clause is past; the main clause verb is a modal + an infinitive.

2. **Present unreal with the verb** *be*.

> If I <u>were</u> taller, I <u>might be</u> a basketball player. (I'm not tall enough for basketball.)

The verb in the *if* clause is *were* with all subjects; the main clause verb begins with a modal.

3. **Past unreal, active voice.**

> If no one <u>had invented</u> cars or airplanes, the air <u>would have</u> <u>remained</u> unpolluted.
>
> (We have cars and airplanes, so we have polluted air.)

The *if* clause verb is past perfect; the main clause verb is a modal + *have* + a past participle.

# **F.2** Additional Uses of the Subjunctive

1. **Statements with *wish* are usually about something impossible.** Clauses beginning *I wish* use a past tense verb to tell about the present and past perfect to tell about the past:

> PRESENT  I wish I <u>could go</u> to Disneyland this year, but I don't have enough money.
>
> PAST  I wish I <u>hadn't bought</u> a car; then, I <u>would have had</u> enough money for a vacation.

2. **Subjunctive forms are used in some statements about recommendations and requirements.** See "Reviewing the Basics," C.2, "Subjunctive Mood" (p. 625) and A.3, "Verbs" (under "Mood") p. 593.

# Web Sites for ESL Students

The Internet offers a wealth of free Web sites for practicing all four English skills—listening, reading, speaking, and writing. Listed below are just a few of the sites that offer grammar explanations and quizzes (with answers), games, reading materials, sites for communicating with ESL and EFL students from around the world, and much more. Some of the sites listed below are linking sites; they direct users to other ESL sites for activities.

**The Owl at Purdue:** http://owl.english.purdue.edu/owl/resource/627/04

**the ESL Loop:** http://tesol.net/esloop/

**ESL Independent Study Lab:** http://legacy.lclark.edu/~krauss/

**TTESL/TEFL/TESOL/ESL/EFL/ESOL Links:** http://iteslj.org/links

**Guide to Grammar and Writing:** http://grammar.ccc.commnet.edu/grammar

*Note:* Sometimes online addresses change. If a site is unreachable via the URL, type its name into Google to get a link to it.

There are also ESL dictionaries online. The *Longman Dictionary of Contemporary English Online* (http://www.ldoceonline.com) has an 88,000-word vocabulary and gives sample sentences to show how words are used. It's an excellent reference tool.

# Credits

## Photo Credits

**Cover:** Exactostock/SuperStock; **background design:** Qweek/iStockphoto; **Need to Know icon:** Roman Sotola/Shutterstock; **Visualize It icon (monitor):** Goory/Shutterstock; **Visualize It icon (screen):** Adistock/Shutterstock; **Thinking Visually icon:** Kak2s/Shutterstock; **p. 1 (top):** Steven Georges/ZUMA Press/Newscom; **(bottom):** David Grossman/Alamy; **p. 3:** Bogyeong Son; **p. 4 (top):** Jack Sullivan/Alamy; **(middle, left to right):** Orange Line Media/Shutterstock; Lasse Kristensen/Shutterstock; Wavebreakmedia Ltd/Shutterstock; Yuri Arcurs/Shutterstock; Yuri Arcurs/Shutterstock; **p. 5:** Andrii Muzyka/Shutterstock; **p. 7:** Ammentorp/Fotolia; **p. 8:** Eric Audras/PhotoAlto SAS/Alamy; **p. 9 (paper):** Aron Hsiao/Fotolia; **(letter grade):** Deepspacedave/Shutterstock; **p. 12:** Vege/Fotolia; **p. 13:** AberCPC/Alamy; **p. 15:** Uwimages/Fotolia; **p. 17:** Gemenacom/Fotolia; **p. 18:** AntonioDiaz/Fotolia; **p. 19:** Moodboard/Alamy; **p. 20:** RelaxFotode/iStockphoto; **p. 22:** Kate Davison/ZUMA Press/Newscom; **p. 27:** *Bizarro* copyright © 1999 Dan Piraro. Distributed by King Features Syndicate; **p. 42:** Felipe Rodriguez/VW Pics/Superstock; **p. 47 (left to right):** Orange Line Media/Shutterstock; Lasse Kristensen/Shutterstock; Wavebreakmedia Ltd/Shutterstock; Yuri Arcurs/Shutterstock; Yuri Arcurs/Shutterstock; **p. 51:** Bettmann/Corbis; **p. 57:** Flirt/SuperStock; **p. 77:** Santiago Quintana Garcia; **p. 80:** A.F. Archive/Alamy; **p. 88:** Sergio Azenha/Alamy; **p. 115:** Krista Kennell/Sipa Press/AP Images; **p. 145:** Dr. Ronald H. Cohn/Gorilla Foundation/koko.org; **p. 148:** Dr. Ronald H. Cohn/Gorilla Foundation/koko.org; **p. 152:** World Wildlife Fund; **p. 179:** SunnyPhotography/Alamy; **p. 183:** Jeff Greenberg/Alamy; **p. 203:** Ben Lewis/Alamy; **p. 208:** Peter Atkins/Fotolia; **p. 231:** Courtesy Canine Companions for Independence; **p. 236:** Danita Delimont/Alamy; **p. 254:** Yuliya Seitkulova; **p. 257:** AGE Fotostock/SuperStock; **p. 262:** Tony Lilley/Alamy; **p. 285:** Dave Myers; **p. 286:** Dave Myers; **p. 287:** Dave Myers; **p. 289:** RayArt Graphics/Alamy; **p. 294:** Bob Daemmrich/Alamy; **p. 296 (left):** Dorling Kindersley/Getty Images; **(right):** Africa Studio/Shutterstock; **p. 319:** Alex Boyd; **p. 323:** ZUMA Wire Service/Alamy; **p. 329:** Kazuhiro Nogi/AFP/Getty Images/Newscom; **p. 352:** Courtesy of Newman's Own and Gotham Advertising; **p. 365:** Bogyeong Son; **p. 367:** Jack Sullivan/Alamy; **p. 374:** Olga Nayashkova/Alamy; **p. 397:** Roan Rodriguez; **p. 400:** Matt Rota; **p. 408:** Kazuhiro Nogi/AFP/Getty Images/Newscom; **p. 441:** Brian Dube; **p. 444:** DK Images; **p. 450 (top):** Andrea Jones/Garden Exposures Photo Library; **(bottom):** Andrea Jones/Garden Exposures Photo Library; **p. 472:** Loretta M. Scott; **p. 476:** www.CartoonStock.com; **p. 481:** Valerijs Kostreckis/Alamy; **p. 495:** Elena Pineda; **p. 504:** Emmanuel Dunand/AFP/Getty Images; **p. 526:** Giovanny Guzman; **p. 528:** Simon Weller/Photonica World/Getty Images; **p. 535:** Roman Milert/Fotolia; **p. 559:** Simon Bruty/Sports Illustrated/Getty Images; **p. 563:** David Grossman/Alamy.

## Text Credits

### Chapter 1

**p. 26:** Carole Wade and Carol Tavris, *Invitation to Psychology*, 5th ed., p. 461, © 2012. Reprinted and electronically reproduced by permission of Pearson Education, Inc., Upper Saddle River, New Jersey.

**p. 32:** Curtis O. Byer and Louis W. Shainberg, *Living Well: Health in Your Hands*, 2nd ed. New York: HarperCollins College Publishers, 1995, pp. 78–79.

**p. 34:** James M. Henslin, *Sociology: A Down-to-Earth Approach*, 10th ed., p. 272, © 2010. Reprinted and electronically reproduced by permission of Pearson Education, Inc., Upper Saddle River, New Jersey.

**p. 35:** Janice Thompson and Melinda Manore, *Nutrition for Life*, 3rd ed., p. 233, © 2013. Reprinted and electronically reproduced by permission of Pearson Education, Inc., Upper Saddle River, New Jersey.

**p. 41:** James M. Henslin, *Sociology: A Down-to-Earth Approach*, 10th ed., Figure 11–7, p. 317, © 2010. Reprinted and electronically reproduced by permission of Pearson Education, Inc., Upper Saddle River, New Jersey.

**p. 42:** James M. Henslin, *Sociology: A Down-to-Earth Approach*, 10th ed., p. 39, © 2010. Reprinted and electronically reproduced by permission of Pearson Education, Inc., Upper Saddle River, New Jersey.

**p. 44:** Ronald J. Ebert and Ricky W. Griffin, *Business Essentials*, 8th ed., p. 38, © 2011. Reprinted and electronically reproduced by permission of Pearson Education, Inc., Upper Saddle River, New Jersey.

**p. 44:** George C. Edwards III, Martin P. Wattenberg, and Robert L. Lineberry, *Government in America: People, Politics, and Policy*, 14th ed., p. 201, © 2009. Reprinted and electronically reproduced by permission of Pearson Education, Inc., Upper Saddle River, New Jersey.

**p. 45:** Rebecca J. Donatelle, *Health: The Basics, Green Edition*, 9th ed., p. 104, © 2011. Reprinted and electronically reproduced by permission of Pearson Education, Inc., Upper Saddle River, New Jersey.

**p: 46:** Saundra K. Ciccarelli and J. Noland White, *Psychology*, 3rd. ed., Figure 2-6 and excerpt from p. 56, © 2012. Reprinted and electronically reproduced by permission of Pearson Education, Inc., Upper Saddle River, New Jersey.

**p. 47:** John D. Carl, *THINK Sociology*, 1st ed., p. 197, © 2010. Reprinted and electronically reproduced by permission of Pearson Education, Inc., Upper Saddle River, New Jersey.

**p. 50:** Saundra K. Ciccarelli and J. Noland White, *Psychology: An Exploration*, 1st. ed., pp. 365–367, © 2010. Reprinted and electronically reproduced by permission of Pearson Education, Inc., Upper Saddle River, New Jersey.

**p. 52:** Robert J. Sternberg, "A Triangular Theory of Love," *Psychological Review*, vol. 93, no. 2 (1986), pp. 119–135. Published by the American Psychological Association. Adapted with permission.

## Chapter 2

**p. 66:** James M. Henslin, *Sociology: A Down-to-Earth Approach*, 6th ed. Boston: Pearson Allyn & Bacon, 2003, pp. 380–381.

**pp. 70, 72, 78:** First draft, revision, and final draft of student essay "The Space In-Between" by Santiago Quintana Garcia. Reprinted by permission of the author.

**p. 80:** Dorothy Hoffman, "What Makes a Scary Movie Scary," October 28, 2010. Reprinted by permission of Dorothy Hoffman. http://www.helium.com/items/1996372-what-makes-a-scary-movie-scary

## Chapter 3

**p. 100:** W. B. Yeats, "Sailing to Byzantium" from *The Tower*. New York: The Macmillan Company, 1928.

**p. 105:** John Randolph Fuller, *Criminal Justice: Mainstream and Crosscurrents*, 2nd ed. Upper Saddle River, NJ: Pearson Prentice Hall, 2010, p. 135.

**p. 105:** John Randolph Fuller, *Criminal Justice: Mainstream and Crosscurrents*, 2nd ed. Upper Saddle River, NJ: Pearson Prentice Hall, 2010, p. 280.

**p. 106:** John Randolph Fuller, *Criminal Justice: Mainstream and Crosscurrents*, 2nd ed. Upper Saddle River, NJ: Pearson Prentice Hall, 2010, p. 120.

**p. 106:** Frederick K. Lutgens, Edward J. Tarbuck, and Dennis Tasa, *Essentials of Geology*, 10th ed. Upper Saddle River, NJ: Pearson Prentice Hall, 2009, p. 160.

**p. 107:** Frederick K. Lutgens, Edward J. Tarbuck, and Dennis Tasa, *Essentials of Geology*, 10th ed. Upper Saddle River, NJ: Pearson Prentice Hall, 2009, p. 484.

**p. 109:** Steven A. Beebe, Susan J. Beebe, and Mark V. Redmond, *Interpersonal Communication: Relating to Others*, 6th ed., pp. 157–161, © 2011. Reprinted and electronically reproduced by permission of Pearson Education, Inc., Upper Saddle River, New Jersey.

## Chapter 4

**p. 127:** James M. Henslin, *Sociology: A Down-to-Earth Approach*, 10th ed., p. 99, © 2010. Reprinted and electronically reproduced by permission of Pearson Education, Inc., Upper Saddle River, New Jersey.

**p. 132:** James M. Henslin, *Social Problems*, 6th ed. Upper Saddle River, NJ: Pearson Prentice Hall, 2003, p. 118.

**p. 132:** James M. Henslin, *Social Problems*, 6th ed. Upper Saddle River, NJ: Pearson Prentice Hall, 2003, p. 72.

**p. 133:** Michael D. Johnson, *Human Biology: Concepts and Current Issues*, 2nd ed. San Francisco: Pearson Benjamin Cummings, 2003, p. 27.

**p. 135:** Edward F. Bergman and William H. Renwick, *Introduction to Geography: People, Places, and Environment*, 2nd ed. Upper Saddle River, NJ: Pearson Prentice Hall, 2002, p. 323.

**p. 136:** Edward F. Bergman and William H. Renwick, *Introduction to Geography: People, Places, and Environment*, 2nd ed. Upper Saddle River, NJ: Pearson Prentice Hall, 2002, p. 332.

**p. 136:** Edward F. Bergman and William H. Renwick, *Introduction to Geography: People, Places, and Environment*, 2nd ed. Upper Saddle River, NJ: Pearson Prentice Hall, 2002, p. 329.

**p. 141:** James M. Henslin, *Social Problems*, 6th ed. Upper Saddle River, NJ: Pearson Prentice Hall, 2003, p. 187.

**p. 141:** James M. Henslin, *Social Problems*, 6th ed. Upper Saddle River, NJ: Pearson Prentice Hall, 2003, p. 192.

**p. 141:** James M. Henslin, *Social Problems*, 6th ed. Upper Saddle River, NJ: Pearson Prentice Hall, 2003, p. 205.

**p. 145:** Alex Hannaford, "Talking to Koko the Gorilla," as appeared in *The Week*, October 14, 2011. A longer version appeared originally in the *London Telegraph*, September 17, 2011. © Telegraph Media Group Ltd. 2011.

## Chapter 5

**p. 178:** Steven Doloff, "Norteño en Manhattan," *The Epoch Times*, January 9, 2009. Steven Doloff is a professor of Humanities and Media Studies at the Pratt Institute. His essays have appeared in *The New York Times*, *The Washington Post*, *The Boston Globe*, and *The Philadelphia Inquirer*. Reprinted with permission of the author.

## Chapter 6

**p. 202:** John J. Macionis, *Sociology*, 14th ed., pp. 17–18, © 2012. Reprinted and electronically reproduced by permission of Pearson Education, Inc., Upper Saddle River, New Jersey.

## Chapter 7

**p. 228:** Lekisha Roberson, "My Kids' Father." Pearson Writing Rewards Student Essay Contest. Copyright © Pearson Education, Inc.

**p. 229:** Randy Brown, "Scenes from a Service-Dog Graduation," http://www.redbullrising.com/2012/04/scenes-from-service-dog-graduation.html (April 4, 2012). Reprinted by permission of the author.

## Chapter 8

**p. 254:** Yuliya Seitkulova, "Freedom to Buy Candy." Pearson Writing Rewards Student Essay Contest. Copyright © Pearson Education, Inc.

**p. 256:** Leticia Salais, "Saying 'Adios' to Spanglish." From *Newsweek*, December 8, 2007. © 2007 The Newsweek/Daily Beast Company, LLC. All rights reserved. Used by permission and protected by the Copyright Laws of the United States. The printing, copying, redistribution, or retransmission of the Material without express written permission is prohibited. www.thedailybeast.com/newsweek.html

## Chapter 9

**p. 284:** Mark A. Krause, *Psychological Science: Modeling Scientific Literacy*, 1st ed. Boston: Pearson, 2012, p. 614.

**p. 284:** Robin Bade and Michael Parkin, *Essential Foundations of Economics*, 6th ed. Upper Saddle River, NJ: Pearson Prentice Hall, 2013, p. 306.

**p. 284:** Audrey Berman, Shirlee J. Snyder, and Debra S. McKinney, *Nursing Basics for Clinical Practice*, 1st ed. Upper Saddle River, NJ: Pearson Prentice Hall, 2011, p. 418.

**p. 284:** Les Rowntree, et al., *Diversity Amid Globalization: World Regions, Environment, Development*, 5th ed. Upper Saddle River, NJ: Pearson Prentice Hall, 2012, p. 348.

**p. 284:** Walter E. Volkomer, *American Government*, 14th ed. Boston: Pearson, 2013, p. 248.

**p. 286:** Dave Myers, "When Someday Finally Came." Pearson Writing Rewards Student Essay Contest. Copyright © Pearson Education, Inc.

**p. 288:** John J. Macionis, *Society: The Basics*, 12th ed., p. 123, © 2013. Reprinted and electronically reproduced by permission of Pearson Education, Inc., Upper Saddle River, New Jersey.

## Chapter 10

**p. 299:** Rebecca J. Donatelle, *Health: The Basics, Green Edition*, 9th ed., p. 424, © 2011. Reprinted and electronically reproduced by permission of Pearson Education, Inc., Upper Saddle River, New Jersey.

**p. 300:** Frederick K. Lutgens, Edward J. Tarbuck, and Dennis Tasa, *Essentials of Geology*, 10th ed. Upper Saddle River, NJ: Pearson Prentice Hall, 2009, p. 62.

**p. 300:** Michael R. Solomon, *Consumer Behavior: Buying, Having, and Being*, 8th ed. Upper Saddle River, NJ: Pearson Prentice Hall, 2009, p. 35.

**p. 300:** Colleen Belk and Virginia Borden Maier, *Biology: Science for Life with Physiology*, 3rd ed. San Francisco: Pearson Benjamin Cummings, 2010, p. 438.

**p. 300:** James M. Henslin, *Sociology: A Down-to-Earth Approach*, 10th ed., p. 149, © 2010. Reprinted and electronically reproduced by permission of Pearson Education, Inc., Upper Saddle River, New Jersey.

**p. 301:** Michael R. Solomon, *Consumer Behavior: Buying, Having, and Being*, 8th ed. Upper Saddle River, NJ: Pearson Prentice Hall, 2009, pp. 392–393.

**p. 301:** Rebecca J. Donatelle, *Health: The Basics, Green Edition*, 9th ed., p. 282, © 2011. Reprinted and electronically reproduced by permission of Pearson Education, Inc., Upper Saddle River, New Jersey.

**p. 301:** Ronald J. Ebert and Ricky W. Griffin, *Business Essentials*, 7th ed. Upper Saddle River, NJ: Pearson Prentice Hall, 2009, p. 12.

**p. 302:** John D. Carl, *THINK Sociology*, 1st ed., p. 51, © 2010. Reprinted and electronically reproduced by permission of Pearson Education, Inc., Upper Saddle River, New Jersey.

**p. 302:** Roy A. Cook, Laura J. Yale, and Joseph J. Marqua, *Tourism: The Business of Travel*, 4th ed. Upper Saddle River, NJ: Pearson Prentice Hall, 2010, p. 347.

**p. 302:** Peter A. Facione, *THINK Critically*. Upper Saddle River, NJ: Pearson Prentice Hall, 2011, p. 90.

**p. 304:** Curtis O. Byer and Louis W. Shainberg, *Living Well: Health in Your Hands*, 2nd ed. New York: HarperCollins College Publishers, 1995, p. 289.

**p. 304:** Alex Thio, *Sociology: A Brief Introduction*, 7th ed. Boston: Pearson Allyn & Bacon, 2008, p. 141.

**p. 305:** Joseph A. DeVito, *Human Communication: The Basic Course*, 7th ed. New York: Longman, 1997, p. 78.

**p. 305:** Ronald J. Ebert and Ricky W. Griffin, *Business Essentials*, 7th ed. Upper Saddle River, NJ: Pearson Prentice Hall, 2009, p. 161.

**p. 305:** George C. Edwards III, Martin P. Wattenberg, and Robert L. Lineberry, *Government in America: People, Politics, and Policy*, 14th ed., p. 306, © 2009. Reprinted and electronically reproduced by permission of Pearson Education, Inc., Upper Saddle River, New Jersey.

**p. 306:** Colleen Belk and Virginia Borden Maier, *Biology: Science for Life with Physiology*, 3rd ed. San Francisco: Pearson Benjamin Cummings, 2010, p. 305.

**p. 306:** Michael R. Solomon, *Consumer Behavior: Buying, Having, and Being*, 8th ed. Upper Saddle River, NJ: Pearson Prentice Hall, 2009, p. 21.

**p. 306:** James M. Henslin, *Sociology: A Down-to-Earth Approach*, 10th ed., p. 85, © 2010. Reprinted and electronically reproduced by permission of Pearson Education, Inc., Upper Saddle River, New Jersey.

**p. 320:** Alex Boyd, "Decision Time." Pearson Writing Rewards Student Essay Contest. Copyright © Pearson Education, Inc.

**p. 322:** Joan Salge Blake, *Nutrition and You*, 2nd ed., pp. 460–463, © 2012. Reprinted and electronically reproduced by permission of Pearson Education, Inc., Upper Saddle River, New Jersey.

## Chapter 11

**p. 330:** Joseph A. DeVito, *Messages: Building Interpersonal Communication Skills*, 4th ed. New York: Longman, 1999, p. 150.

**p. 335:** Laura Uba and Karen Huang, *Psychology*. New York: Longman, 1999, p. 406.

**p. 336:** Jenifer Kunz, *THINK Marriages and Families*, 1st ed. Boston: Pearson Education, 2011, p. 151.

**p. 336:** Tim Curry, Robert Jiobu, and Kent Schwirian, *Sociology for the Twenty-First Century*, 2nd ed. Upper Saddle River, NJ: Prentice Hall, 1999, p. 340.

**p. 337:** Robert W. Christopherson, *Geosystems: An Introduction to Physical Geography*, 4th ed. Upper Saddle River, NJ: Prentice Hall, 2000, p. 368.

**p. 337:** Courtland L. Bovée and John V. Thill, *Business in Action*, 6th ed. Upper Saddle River, NJ: Pearson Prentice Hall, 2013, pp xxxiv–xxxv.

**p. 338:** Rebecca J. Donatelle, *My Health: An Outcomes Approach*. San Francisco: Pearson Benjamin Cummings, 2013, pp. 6–8.

**p. 339:** David Krogh, *Biology: A Guide to the Natural World*, 5th ed. San Francisco: Pearson Benjamin Cummings, 2011, p. 475.

**p. 339:** George C. Edwards III, Martin P. Wattenberg, and Robert L. Lineberry, *Government in America: People, Politics, and Policy*, 15th ed. New York: Pearson Longman, 2011, pp. 174–175.

**p. 339:** David Krogh, *Biology: A Guide to the Natural World*, 5th ed. San Francisco: Pearson Benjamin Cummings, 2011, pp. 441–442.

**p. 340:** Rebecca J. Donatelle, *My Health: An Outcomes Approach*. San Francisco: Pearson Benjamin Cummings, 2013, p. 118.

**p. 342:** James Coleman and Donald R. Cressey, *Social Problems*, 6th ed. New York: HarperCollins College Publishers, 1996, p. 130.

**p. 343:** Michael R. Solomon, *Consumer Behavior: Buying, Having, and Being*, 4th ed. Upper Saddle River, NJ: Prentice Hall, 1999, pp. 49–50.

**p. 344:** Joseph A. DeVito, *Human Communication: The Basic Course*, 11th ed. Boston: Pearson Allyn & Bacon, 2009, p. 73.

**p. 347:** Rebecca J. Donatelle, *Health: The Basics*, 5th ed. San Francisco: Pearson Benjamin Cummings, 2003, pp. 290–291.

**p. 347:** Michael R. Solomon, *Consumer Behavior: Buying, Having, and Being*, 5th ed. Upper Saddle River, NJ: Prentice Hall, 2002, pp. 92–93.

**p. 348:** George C. Edwards III, Martin P. Wattenberg, and Robert L. Lineberry, *Government in America: People, Politics, and Policy*, 10th ed. New York: Pearson Longman, 2002, pp. 654–655.

**p. 348:** Duane Preble and Sarah Preble, *Artforms: An Introduction to the Visual Arts*, 7th ed. Upper Saddle River, NJ: Pearson Prentice Hall, 2002, p. 144.

**p. 348:** Edward F. Bergman and William H. Renwick, *Introduction to Geography: People, Places, and Environment*, updated 2nd ed. Upper Saddle River, NJ: Prentice Hall, 2003, p. 106.

**p. 365:** Bogyeong Son, "A Korean Girl in Boston." Pearson Writing Rewards Student Essay Contest. Copyright © Pearson Education, Inc.

**p. 367:** Christopher Ketcham, "Warning: High Frequency," *Earth Island Journal*, Winter 2012. As appeared in *Utne Reader*, May/June 2012, titled "Wireless Interference: The Health Risks of RF-EMFs." Reprinted by permission of Earth Island Journal.

## Chapter 12

**p. 377:** Hugh D. Barlow, *Criminal Justice in America*. Upper Saddle River, NJ: Pearson Prentice Hall, 2000, p. 332.

**p. 377:** William M. Kephart and Davor Jedlicka, *The Family, Society, and the Individual*, 7th ed. New York: HarperCollins College Publishers, 1991, p. 332.

**p. 378:** Robert A. Wallace, *Biology: The World of Life*, 7th ed. Menlo Park, CA: Benjamin Cummings, 1997, p. 572.

**p. 378:** James M. Henslin, *Essentials of Sociology*, 2nd ed. Boston: Allyn and Bacon, 1998, p. 272.

**p. 378:** John V. Thill and Courtland L. Bovée, *Excellence in Business Communication*, 4th ed. Upper Saddle River, NJ: Pearson Prentice Hall, 1999, p. 79.

**p. 378:** Roy A. Cook, Laura J. Yale, and Joseph J. Marqua, *Tourism: The Business of Travel*, 4th ed. Upper Saddle River, NJ: Pearson Prentice Hall, 2010, p. 170.

**p. 379:** Thomas F. Goldman and Henry R. Cheeseman, *The Paralegal Professional*, 3rd ed. Upper Saddle River, NJ: Pearson Prentice Hall, 2011, p. 266.

**p. 379:** Robert A. Divine, et al., *America Past and Present*, Combined Volume, 9th ed. New York: Pearson Longman, 2011, p. 596.

**p. 391:** Carl T. Dahlman, Edward F. Bergman, and William H. Renwick, *Introduction to Geography: People, Places, and Environment*, 5th ed. Upper Saddle River, NJ: Pearson Prentice Hall, 2011, p. 90.

**p. 391:** H. W. Brands, et al., *American Stories: A History of the United States*, 2nd ed. Boston: Pearson, 2012, p. 254.

**p. 391:** Margaret McWilliams, *Food Around the World: A Cultural Perspective*, 3rd ed. Upper Saddle River, NJ: Pearson Prentice Hall, 2011, p. 357.

**p. 398:** Roan Rodriguez, "A Trip to Disney World." Pearson Writing Rewards Student Essay Contest. Copyright © Pearson Education, Inc.

**p. 399:** Melissa del Bosque, "Ransom Notes: Serial Kidnapping in Mexico," as appeared in *Utne Reader*, March/April 2012. Originally published in *The Texas Observer*, © November 1, 2011, pp. 44–45 titled "No Safe Place." Reprinted with permission of The Texas Observer.

## Chapter 13

**p. 411:** Sydney B. Newell, *Chemistry: An Introduction*. Boston: Little, Brown, 1980, p. 11.

**p. 427:** Paul G. Hewitt, *Conceptual Physics*, 5th ed. Boston: Little, Brown, 1985, pp. 82–84.

**p. 429:** David Krogh, *Biology: A Guide to the Natural World*, 4th ed. San Francisco: Pearson Benjamin Cummings, 2009, pp. 466–467, 474.

**p. 429:** James M. Henslin, *Sociology: A Down-to-Earth Approach*, 10th ed., p. 164, © 2010. Reprinted and electronically reproduced by permission of Pearson Education, Inc., Upper Saddle River, New Jersey.

**p. 430:** J. Ross Eshleman and Barbara Cashion, *Sociology: An Introduction*, 2nd ed. Boston: Little, Brown, 1985, p. 88.

**p. 431:** Thomas C. Kinnear, Kenneth L. Bernhardt, and Kathleen A. Krentler, *Principles of Marketing*, 4th ed. New York: HarperCollins College Publishers, 1995, p. 218.

**p. 442:** Bryan Dube, "Twitter's Appeal." Pearson Writing Rewards Student Essay Contest. Copyright © Pearson Education, Inc.

**p. 443:** Steven Cornelius and Mary Natvig, *Music: A Social Experience*, 1st ed., pp. 2–3, © 2012. Reprinted and electronically reproduced by permission of Pearson Education, Inc., Upper Saddle River, New Jersey.

### Chapter 14

**p. 472:** Loretta Scott, "The Event that Changed My Life." Pearson Writing Rewards Student Essay Contest. Copyright © Pearson Education, Inc.

**p. 475:** James M. Henslin, *Sociology: A Down-to-Earth Approach, Core Concepts*, 3rd ed., p. 303, © 2009. Reprinted and electronically reproduced by permission of Pearson Education, Inc., Upper Saddle River, New Jersey.

### Chapter 15

**p. 486:** Alex Thio, *Sociology*, 5th ed. New York: Longman, 1998, p. 534.

**p. 486:** Joseph A. DeVito, *Human Communication: The Basic Course*, 11th ed. Boston: Pearson Allyn & Bacon, 2009, p. 154.

**p. 490:** Joseph A. DeVito, *The Interpersonal Communication Book*, 13th ed. Boston: Pearson, 2013, p. 220.

**p. 492:** Michael J. Quinn, *Ethics for the Information Age*, 2nd ed. Boston: Pearson Addison Wesley, 2006, p. 60.

**p. 492:** Janice Thompson and Melinda Manore, *Nutrition for Life*, 3rd ed., p. 212, © 2013. Reprinted and electronically reproduced by permission of Pearson Education, Inc., Upper Saddle River, New Jersey.

**p. 494:** Bruce E. Gronbeck et al., *Principles of Speech Communication*, 12th brief ed. New York: HarperCollins College Publishers, 1995, p. 302.

**p. 494:** Laura Uba and Karen Huang, *Psychology*. New York: Longman, 1999, p. 148.

**p. 495:** Elena Pineda, "Facebook's Influence on a Person's Life." Pearson Writing Rewards Student Essay Contest. Copyright © Pearson Education, Inc.

**p. 497:** Andrew Parker, "Why Conserve Water," July 26, 2011. Available at www.greeniacs.com. Reprinted by permission of greeniacs.com

**p. 498:** Freshwater Availability map by Philippe Rakecewicz, from *Vital Water Graphics: An Overview of the State of the World's Fresh and Marine Waters*, 2nd ed. Copyright © 2008, United Nations Environment Programme (UNEP). Reprinted by permission of United Nations Environment Programme.

**p. 500:** Water Stress Indicator: Withdrawal-to-Availability Ratio (CR) map. Reprinted by permission of WaterGAP, University of Frankfurt, Germany.

### Chapter 16

**p. 506:** Michael R. Solomon, Greg W. Marshall, Elnora W. Stuart, *Marketing: Real People, Real Choices*, 7th ed. Upper Saddle River, NJ: Pearson Prentice Hall, 2012, p. 20.

**p. 508:** Paul Aurandt, *Paul Harvey's The Rest of the Story*, edited and compiled by Lynne Harvey. Garden City: NY: Doubleday, 1977, p. 116.

**p. 509:** Richard L. Weaver II, *Understanding Interpersonal Communication*, 4th ed. Glenview, IL: Scott, Foresman, 1987, p. 291.

**p. 510:** Lewis Katz, *Know Your Rights*. Cleveland, OH: Banks-Baldwin Law Publishing Co., 1993, p. 54.

**p. 510:** Richard Shenkman, *Legends, Lies, and Cherished Myths of American History*. New York: Morrow, 1988, pp. 37–38.

**p. 515:** Robert A. Wallace, *Biology: The World of Life*, 4th ed. Glenview, IL: Scott, Foresman, 1987, p. 271.

**p. 518:** Edward S. Greenberg and Benjamin I. Page, *The Struggle for Democracy*, 2nd ed. New York: HarperCollins College Publishers, 1995, p. 186.

**p. 520:** Editorial Board, "Car Seizure Law Invites Abuses." From *The Sacramento Bee*, February 20, 2010. © 2010 The McClatchy Company. All rights reserved. Used by permission and protected by the Copyright Laws of the United States. The printing, copying, redistribution, or retransmission of this Content without express written permission is prohibited. www.sacbee.com

**p. 521:** Editorial, "A Climate of Fraud," *The Washington Times*, November 30, 2011, p. 2.

**p. 521:** Betty P. Morrow, excerpt from Letter to the Editor: "Life after Prison," *Tulsa World*, April 8, 2010, p. A16. Reprinted by permission of World Publishing Company.

**p. 522:** Carol Masters, from "Playing at War" from *WAMM Newsletter* (Women Against Military Madness), Vol. 28, No. 2, March 2010. Reprinted by permission of Carol Masters.

**p. 526:** Giovanny Guzman, "One Year." Pearson Writing Rewards Student Essay Contest. Copyright © Pearson Education, Inc.

**p. 528:** Eric G. Wilson, "The Allure of Disaster," *Psychology Today* blog, March 13, 2012. Reprinted by permission of the author. Eric G. Wilson is Thomas H. Pritchard Professor of English at Wake Forest University. He is author of many books, including *Everyone Loves a Good Train Wreck*, from which this essay is adapted.

### Chapter 17

**p. 555:** Alphea Bartley, "Students Should Not Work Long Hours." Pearson Writing Rewards Student Essay Contest. Copyright © Pearson Education, Inc.

**p. 557:** Andy Greenberg, "A Step Beyond Human." From *Forbes*, November 25, 2009. © 2009 Forbes. All rights reserved. Used by permission and protected by the Copyright Laws of the United States. The printing, copying, or retransmission of this Content without express written permission is prohibited. www.Forbes.com

### Chapter 18

**p. 570:** Tim Curry, Robert Jiobu, and Kent Schwirian, *Sociology for the Twenty-First Century*, 3rd ed. Upper Saddle River, NJ : Prentice Hall, 2002, p. 207.

# Index